# An Introduction to Information Science

*Additional Volumes in Preparation*

# An Introduction to Information Science

Roger R. Flynn
Department of Information Science
University of Pittsburgh
Pittsburgh, Pennsylvania

CRC Press
Taylor & Francis Group
Boca Raton  London  New York

CRC Press is an imprint of the
Taylor & Francis Group, an **informa** business

First published 1987 by MARCEL DEKKER, INC.

Published 2019 by CRC Press
Taylor & Francis Group
6000 Broken Sound Parkway NW, Suite 300
Boca Raton, FL 33487-2742

First issued in paperback 2019

ISBN 13: 978-0-367-45154-7 (pbk)
ISBN 13: 978-0-8247-7508-7 (hbk)

**Visit the Taylor & Francis Web site at
http://www.taylorandfrancis.com**

**and the CRC Press Web site at
http://www.crcpress.com**

Library of Congress Cataloging in Publication Data

Flynn, Roger R., [date]
    An introduction to information science.

    (Books in library and information science ; vol. 49)
    Includes index.
    1. Information science. 2. Library science. I. Title.
II. Series: Books in library and information science ;
v. 49.
Z665.F62 1987    020    86-24369
ISBN 0-8247-7508-2

This book is dedicated to

*Allen Kent*
*Distinguished Service Professor*
*University of Pittsburgh*

**and**

*Anthony, Christopher, and Ida*

# Preface

Information science is a relatively new field and has its origins in various branches of study. Mathematical communication theory (Shannon, Claude F. and Weaver, Warren, *The Mathematical Theory of Communication*. Urbana: University of Illinois Press, 1980) gave impetus to the notion of information as a measurable quantity, one related to uncertainty. Hence, information was looked upon as data that reduces one's uncertainty. The development of automated bibliographic retrieval systems (Kent, Allen, *Information Analysis and Retrieval*. New York: John Wiley and Sons, 1971) focused on the storage and retrieval aspects of information, and introduced methods of data organization and "labeling" (indexing) as well as methods of querying data bases. The study of business information systems (Davis, Gordon B., *Management Information Systems: Conceptual Foundations, Structure, and Development*. New York: McGraw-Hill, 1974), both operational—e.g., payroll program—and managerial—e.g., management information systems (MIS) and, more recently, decision support systems (DSS)—introduced notions of data processing and the use of data in decision-making. These disciplines are primarily concerned with information as an external commodity, data in a data base that can be manipulated, retrieved, transmitted, and "used." This text addresses questions of interest to all three themes. The emphasis is on external information systems, in contrast to human information processing, i.e., cognitive psychology. It is anticipated that as both fields progress the meld between external information systems (usually automated) and the internal human information processing system will increase, with each posing problems and solutions for the other.

The text presents information as data that enables efficient action. It assumes the use of a model relevant to a given situation. The model specifies what data is relevant. As the introduction to Section I indicates, the need for data arises from blocked actions. This need is formalized in a question, and the search for data is the search for an answer to that question.

The text is designed for use in an introductory level undergraduate course. Most of the material has been used in teaching such a course at the University of Pittsburgh. Over a thousand students from various disciplines and with various intentions have taken the course. Some are poten-

tial majors, others are students seeking an elective that gives them an
overview of the field, and others are decided majors. The text addresses
all three groups by attempting to give an overview that is skill-oriented.
The overview is sufficient for the undecided to have a basis of decision,
the electives to get a feel for the field of study, and the major to set the
stage for future study. The skill orientation provides the major with the
necessary cognitive equipment for future study. It also gives the non-
majors and undecided students a picture that reflects the day-to-day practice of a professional in the areas of information system design, implementation, and operation.

Although the text is aimed at the introductory undergraduate level, it
is anticipated that anyone new to the field can benefit from a reading of
at least parts of the text and from a consideration of the structure of the
material. Information science is a relatively new field with at best a sketchy
definition at the current time. In addition it requires a knowledge of concepts and skills from various disciplines. This text is one attempt at giving
a structure to the field.

All chapters are treated at an introductory level. Hence, readers coming to the book from other disciplinary backgrounds will find certain material already familiar. The reader is encouraged to pick and choose from
the text. The introduction to each section should serve to indicate how
each topic interfaces with the rest of the material.

Developing the course material has been a lengthy process of selection,
trial, and revision. The outline of the text reflects a combination of pedagogical and consistency considerations. The intent was to find an intuitively appealing structure that could also integrate the various disciplinary
strains with the phenomenon of information as the central focus. The process of question-answering served both purposes: the search for information begins with blocked action (blocked through lack of knowledge, not
because of physical incapabilities); the blocked action is a problem, a
"knowledge problem"; the problem is voiced in the form of a question,
the information need; the surfacing of the need stimulates the information-
seeking behavior, i.e., the collection of data (or the identification of an
appropriate model followed by the search for data); the data, suitably manipulated, provides the answer to the question, and, assuming the answer
to be appropriate, the initial blocked action is resumed. If such situations
are expected to arise in the future the relevant data and model may be
stored in order to replace future processing by retrieval.

Several topics have been omitted: the development and use of models,
hypothesis testing in data analysis, research design and experimental design, questions of knowledge representation, the three great data base
models, the use of natural language in human/computer dialogue, the
measure of information, and control systems involving feedback. It is anticipated that these and other topics will be treated in a second course.
To include all the topics in a single text would have been unwieldy and
economically unfeasible for a single course.

With the exception of the first section, which has a single introductory
chapter, and the second section, which has three chapters, each section
consists of two chapters relevant to that topic. Each section is introduced
by an overview of the topic, as is each chapter within the section. Each
chapter also has a list of objectives that highlight the topics to be mastered.
These can serve as a checklist upon finishing the chapter.

## Acknowledgments

The production of this book has been made possible through the efforts of several people: Professor Allen Kent; Linda Romantino, Pearl Berger, and Hoa Phung; my family, Anthony, Christopher, and Ida; friends; and the students who took the course IS10, Introduction to Information Science. I thank them for their support.

*Roger R. Flynn*

# Contents

x · Contents

# *I*
# Introduction

This section provides an overview for the course. It includes a rather simple but fairly thorough example of information science as question-answering. The purpose of the example is to illustrate the generation of an information need by an action that is blocked due to lack of knowledge, the eventual resolution of the need by an appropriate "data response," and the use of this answer in completing the original goal-directed action. Hence, information is viewed as data that enables effective action, i.e., knowledge relevant to a given situation. Data is taken in the broad sense of (1) a model of the situation, and (2) values for the variables appropriate to the model.

As indicated above, a need for information arises as a result of an action that is blocked due to lack of knowledge—an "information problem." The information need is expressed in the form of a question. The genesis of the need and its representation in a question leads to information-seeking behavior, the result being an answer to the question posed. This answer takes the form of a list of actions deemed sufficient to obtain the goal initially sought and blocked. If more than one answer is identified as sufficient for obtaining the goal, the agent is required to make a choice; that is, to enter into the act of decision-making. Finally, having made a decision, the chosen action is implemented.

Hence, the cycle from information need to information use is:

- Goal-directed activity blocked by lack of knowledge (information problem).
- Formulation of lack of knowledge in the form of a question (information need).
- Response to the need by seeking data (information-seeking behavior).
- Generation of zero or more answers. If list of answers:
    is empty, than a solution is impossible at this time.
    contains only one item, it is possible to move to the implementation stage.
    contains more than one item, it is possible to choose among actions (decision-making) then move to implementation.

The occurrence of the first result, a null answer, may be due to the lack of a proper model for the situation at hand or to an inability to estimate

the values of the relevant variables in that model. There is no choice here
but to develop (or find) either such a model or a suitable estimation procedure. The action will remain blocked until either can be done.

The cycle of information generation/utilization does not require the external storage and retrieval of information. However, assuming that the situation in which the blockage occurred has a high probability of recurring or
that the situation is important enough to require preparation for its reoccurrence even if that reoccurrence is of low probability, we will record the
data for future use. This leads to the question of physical coding of data,
its logical organization in representing entities and events, and its physical
organization in file structures that will enable efficient storage or fast retrieval. The storage decision is an expected utility decision, balancing the
expected value of the situation, that is, the probability of reoccurrence
times the value of correct action against the costs of (1) storage and retrieval, or (2) regeneration of the data on demand.

Finally, since the information system is often automated, we enter into
the realm of human/machine communication and data displays. One use of
displays is to present output data. Another is to present options that the
user has (menus) or to guide data entry (data forms). The study of displays is "1-way" communication. The topic of human/machine communication
extends the discussion to include 2-way communication, i.e., conversation.
The user puts commands, questions, and data to the machine, and the
machine returns "results" by searching data bases and by performing
operations on the input or stored data.

Notably absent from the scenario as so far presented (until the last
sentence of the previous paragraph) is data manipulation, traditionally considered one of the mainstays of information science. In the model presented
here, data manipulation is an auxiliary activity, but necessary in order to
bring the data into a form in which it can be used. The form is dictated by
the model the agent is using in coping with the relevant situation. For textual data, the manipulation may be as simple as a sort, presenting the more
salient items of the model "before" the less salient features. For numerical
data the manipulations are arithmetic or logical transformations dictated by
equations used in the mathematical model. In this light the activities of
data processing are necessitated by the fact that data are often collected in
a form that is not directly usable, but are "fed into" a transformation processor that "massages" them into the desired form. One of the models so
used is a model of the generation of knowledge, which involves statistical
manipulation of data in order to make statements about the world. Other
models are more application oriented, e.g., the use of market research
in order to estimate demand for a product or services.

While the example presented in the first chapter is relatively "light" in
nature, it is purposely so. The example is meant to serve as an advance
organizer for the topics presented throughout the text. The text itself is
skill oriented, establishing a minimal set of skills that enable one to interact
with the scientists and professionals involved in studying and using information, both as an end in itself and as a means to effective action.

# 1
# Information Science as Question-Answering

## Objectives

The purpose of this chapter is to set the stage for the rest of the text. Various topics that reoccur in the study of information and information systems are here presented through an example instead of formally. The example, obtaining lunch in a strange town, is a simple one. However, it involves most of the concepts that are treated more formally in later chapters. It is meant to be a painless introduction, and has been useful as the introductory lecture in the first course in information science taught at the University of Pittsburgh, where it has been shown to be an introduction to which the students can intuitively relate.

In contrast to the remaining chapters of the text, the emphasis in the first chapter is on an overall understanding of concepts rather than of particular skills, terms, and procedures. However, the reader should obtain some sense of the following:

1. The relationship of questions and answers to problem-solving and decision-making
2. The components of an information system: acquisition, transmission, processing, storage and retrieval, and display
3. The process by which one makes decisions, e.g., the calculation of an expected value
4. Sources of error and failure in an information system, e.g., coding errors, lack of accuracy in the data, lack of timeliness in providing the data, or the provision of irrelevant data

## Introduction

The approach to information science taken in this text is one of question-answering. The reason for this approach is that it is readily comprehensible. We have all experienced information booths, say in the lobby of a large building or hospital, and we recognize them as places to go up to have our questions answered. We also have used the information services of telephone companies, which respond to our needs by answering very specific questions, such as "What is the phone number of my friend, Anthony Michaels?" with such data as "422-7543." Because of this common bond of experience, it is relatively easy to expand the process of question-answering into the concepts, techniques, and procedures that information professionals encounter during their everyday activities. A more general approach would be to take information science as the study of the generation, preservation, and communication of information. We will use both models as convenient.

## An Example

An overview of the activities involved in generating and using information can be given through the use of a simple example. We have just arrived in a strange town, by bus, at noon, and we are hungry. One of our problems is to find a place to eat.

## Collecting the Data

One of the first steps we must take is to collect data on the restaurants in the area. We may do this by consulting a document, such as the phone book, wherein we would look up "restaurants" in the yellow pages. In terms of the generic data collection methods, we would call this the use of archives, which are records (documents, data) already collected and organized by someone else. In this case, the someone else is the phone company. An alternate method of data collection would be to ask someone who seems to be a native, say the person selling newspapers. This would be the method of data collection called report-by-others.

Whatever the method by which we collect the data, the result of our efforts will be a list of names of restaurants, in this case:

Joe's Diner
Swank-U-Pay
Mary's Place

## Choosing a Technology

This list now exists in the phone book or in the mind of the newspaper vendor, as well as in the mind of the person seeking the information. If we do not trust our memory, we might wish to store this information on a sheet of paper that we can carry in our pocket—an external storage medium. In order to do this, we need some minimal technology, e.g., a writing device such as a pencil, and a storage medium such as a piece of paper or a notebook. Using this technology, we would copy certain portions of the information from the phone book (or newspaper vendor's verbal comments) to the sheet of paper. If we restrict our attention to the case of the phone book, one or two more points may be made in regard to storing the data.

## Choosing the Relevant Data

The data in the phone book may include information for which we have no need. For example, if the listing is a paid advertisement, it might look like

Joe's Diner

Hamburgers

Pizza

We do the best for you

Open 10AM till Midnite

7 Days a Week

247 North Avenue

Call 422-7513

FIGURE 1.1

Figure 1.1. We would obviously not record every piece of data. In fact, it is likely that only the name of the diner, the address, and the phone number would be of use to us. We would record only those items and omit the rest. We know that the menu (hamburgers, pizza) will be available later, at Joe's, and the judgment "We do the best for you" is a "self-report" (another method of data collection) that is no doubt biased to some degree. We might or might not record the hours that the restaurant is open (10 A.M. to midnight) and the days (7 days a week). The decision to record or not to record this information would depend on our purposes. For example, if we wish to use the information this one time only, we would most likely not record the information. This would be the case if we were on a stopover, planning to leave town again shortly, and not to return. In this case, we would simply note the hours open, compare them to the current hour (noon), observe that the restaurant is now open, then discard the information.

On the other hand, if we were coming to town to take a new job, and thus planning to stay, we might well expect to return to the restaurant more than once. In this case, we would record the hours and days that the restaurant is open.

The point to be made here is that the information that we "store" ("record," "save") depends on the probability of our needing to retrieve the information in the future. If we intend to use the information again, we save it. In this example, we will need the name of the restaurant (its label) in order to identify it when we arrive at its location. We also need its location (address) in order to find the restaurant, and we might record the phone number in case we get lost en route. If we were confident of not getting lost, we might not record the phone number. In any case, the information we gather is only that which is relevant to our purposes.

## Coding the Data

In recording the information, we will no doubt take shortcuts, recording "Joe's" as a shortened version of "Joe's Diner," and "Ave." as a shortened version of "Avenue." This process of recording the information in short form is known as coding. Coding is one aspect of the more general problem of data representation. In this sense the code is a representation of meaning, a physical means of recording statements about ourselves and our environment.

Besides representing meaning, the choice of a proper code is dependent on the medium used to store and transmit data, as well as the devices used to process it. If we expect to process the data by computer, it will be stored in the form of a computer code, such as ASCII, EBCDIC, or binary. The transformation from one code to another is also dictated by the circumstances of processing, storing, and transmitting the information. These activities often involve the translation of the data from one medium to another. In the case of collecting the data from the phone book, the data is already stored in the medium of the printed page; we transform the code to a mental image by reading the data (device: eyes; medium of storage: the neural system and the brain), then transform this mental image to another written code, our notations on a sheet of paper (device: pencil; medium: paper). In the case of asking the newspaper vendor, his or her mental code is transformed into a verbal code (speech or natural language) at our request, transformed again from the person's speech to our mental code, and transformed again to the written notation on the notepad.

### Manipulating the Data

In addition to coding the data, we may manipulate it in some way. The manipulation might be noncomputational, e.g., putting the list of restaurants in alphabetical order, or it may be computational, e.g., comparing the distances to each restaurant. For example, let us suppose that the following are the restaurants we have found in the vicinity:

| | |
|---|---|
| Mary's Place | 1312 East End |
| Joe's Diner | 247 North Avenue |
| Swank-U-Pay | 49 Upper Avenue |

One method of manipulating this list would be to put it in alphabetical order by restaurant name:

| | |
|---|---|
| Joe's Diner | 247 North Avenue |
| Mary's Place | 1312 East End |
| Swank-U-Pay | 49 Upper Avenue |

An alphabetical listing would be useful if we expected to create a fairly large file over an extended period of time, since the ordering of the list by name would facilitate retrieval. Other types of organization might be by type of restaurant or by price range. The alphabetical listing is typical of files organized by "key" (or identification field). The organization by type of restaurant is characteristic of files organized on secondary fields (called inverted files). The type of file organization chosen depends on the size of the file and the access patterns to the data: how often we access the file (frequency of access), how many items we access (activity), how fast we need a response (response time), and the type of access (to insert data, delete data, update the data elements, or simply search for and display a particular data record). A short list, such as our list of restaurants, can be stored in almost any fashion, since it can be scanned quickly. Longer lists will need an organization suited to the purposes for which the data is retained. The purposes are determined by the "user" of the information.

In this particular example the distance to the restaurant might be of interest to us. If we are on a stopover with limited time, the distance can outweigh considerations of taste or cost of food, decor, and the like. If distance were a factor, we would embark on another effort at data collection, consulting a map (another form of existing records or archived information), the newspaper vendor, etc. In the case of the map, we would be involved in the transformation of information stored as a series of lines and spaces between the lines into a numerical representation, such as "2 blocks away." The list would then be ordered by distance:

| | |
|---|---|
| 1 block | Swank-U-Pay |
| 2 blocks | Joe's Diner |
| 3 blocks | Mary's Place |

at least mentally, if not on the physical medium.

## Using the Data

If distance were the only factor of interest to us, we could now choose the nearest, Swank-U-Pay, and begin walking in that direction. Of course, factors other than distance could be involved: e.g., the cost of the food, its taste, the atmosphere of the restaurant, and the friendliness of the people who work there. If this is the case, we become involved in the process of decision-making, evaluating each restaurant on each criterion.

## Problem-Solving and Decision-Making

The original situation, finding a place to eat, is a type of problem situation. One definition of a problem is a discrepancy between the current state of affairs (being hungry and not knowing where to eat) and some desired state (the goal). The essence of the solution to the problem is to find a sequence of actions through which we can pass from the current state to the goal state. In our case this involves the identification of the restaurants and the directions to each restaurant.

If the list of alternative actions contains more than a single alternative, the "user" of the information passes from the stage of problem-solving to the stage of decision-making. The task is to select one alternative from the many. This may be done haphazardly, by simply choosing "at random" or in a more systematic manner. The systematic approach to decision-making would involve the identification of the relevant criterion with respect to our goals, the evaluation of each alternative on each criterion, the formulation of some measure by which to summarize the individual evaluations, and the comparison of the alternatives according to their rating on the summary measure.

## A Decision Matrix

In order to evaluate the alternatives, we might create a decision matrix (Figure 1.2). The criterion or parameters of choice are those set by the decisionmaker. These will reflect the characteristics of the situation (what criteria are relevant to achieving the goal) as well as personal preferences, e.g., if taste is a more important concern than cost.

| Restaurants | Parameters of choice | | |
|---|---|---|---|
| | Good taste? | Low cost? | Nearby? |
| 1. Joes' Diner | ——— | ——— | ——— |
| 2. Mary's Place | ——— | ——— | ——— |
| 3. Eat-A-Burger | ——— | ——— | ——— |
| 4. Swank-U-Pay | ——— | ——— | ——— |
| 5. Plain Home Cooking | ——— | ——— | ——— |

FIGURE 1.2

## Establishing the Values

The creation of the decision matrix introduces the notion of "subinformation goals": the evaluation of each alternative on each criterion. We must establish some measure that will allow us to fill in values for each blank line.

The criteria have been transformed into questions that can be answered "yes" or "no," and these questions have been phrased in such a way that "yes" is always good and "no" is always bad (e.g., good taste?, low cost?).

As a first attempt at making a decision, we simply fill in the matrix with these "yes" or "no" answers (Figure 1.3a). The yes/no ratings categorize the restaurants on each alternative. The restaurants Joe's Diner, Mary's Place, and Plain Home Cooking belong to the category of restaurants serving good food (or, stating it another way, they have the property of serving good food). The restaurants Eat-A-Burger and Swank-U-Pay lack this property. The classification is both exhaustive and mutually exclusive, with all restaurants being classified and none falling into two different sets on the same category, Figure 1.3b.

| Restaurant | Criteria | | |
|---|---|---|---|
| | Good taste? | Low cost? | Nearby? |
| 1. Joe's Diner | Yes | Yes | No |
| 2. Mary's Place* | Yes | Yes | Yes |
| 3. Eat-A-Burger | No | Yes | Yes |
| 4. Swank-U-Pay | No | No | No |
| 5. Plain Home Cooking | Yes | No | Yes |

FIGURE 1.3a  *Indicates our choice

| Dimension: Taste | |
|---|---|
| Good Restaurants | Bad Restaurants |
| 1, 2, 5 | 3, 4 |

FIGURE 1.3b

The categorization is independent for each dimension, so that we need a summary measure to evaluate the restaurants across all three dimensions. In the case of the yes and no responses, a simple count of the yes classifications will do, resulting in the choice of Mary's Place as the preferred means to our goal. In counting the yes responses, the assumption is that each criterion is equally important. If this is not the case, the dimensions would be "weighted" according to their relative importance.

### Quantitative Scales

A more refined method of measuring would grade each restaurant on a three-part scale (good, fair, and poor), or even a five-part scale (very good, good, fair, poor, and very poor).

A matrix for a three-part scale of good, fair, and poor might look like Figure 1.4. The matrix is consistent with the previous scale if the ratings of fair and good are replaced by "yes," the rating of poor replaced by "no." Yet the refinement of the scale brings with it problems of summarization. Are two fairs equal to one good? Is a good and a poor equal to one fair?

The decision to count two goods and a poor as "better" than one good and a fair results in number 5, Plain Home Cooking being the choice over number 2, Mary's Place, which was the "winner" on the yes and no scale.

The yes and no scale obliterated any difference between fair and good. This "smoothing" or "smearing" of the difference, coupled with the decision

| | Criteria | | |
|---|---|---|---|
| Restaurant | Good taste? | Low cost? | Nearby? |
| 1. Joe's Diner | Fair | Good | Poor |
| 2. Mary's Place | Fair | Good | Fair |
| 3. Eat-A-Burger | Poor | Good | Good |
| 4. Swank-U-Pay | Poor | Poor | Poor |
| 5. Plain Home Cooking* | Good | Poor | Good |

FIGURE 1.4   *Indicates our choice

|  | Criteria | | |
| Restaurant | Good taste? | Low cost? | Nearby? |
|---|---|---|---|
| 1. Joe's Diner | Fair | Good | Poor |
| 2. Mary's Place | Fair | Good | Fair |
| 3. Eat-A-Burger | Poor | Good | Good |
| 4. Swank-U-Pay | Fair | Poor | Fair |
| 5. Plain Home Cooking* | Good | Fair | Good |

FIGURE 1.5  *Indicates our choice

rule on weighting goods, fairs, and poors is responsible for the change in the decision. Both the rating scales and the summarization procedures are different in the two examples.

The matrix in Figure 1.5 was constructed with "fair" representing a middle area that was originally evaluated as "yes" in some instances, as "no" in others. Again, the example indicates that the choice of the scale and measurement technique can substantially influence the decision.

As the scale becomes more refined it is useful to move from a categorical classification scheme to a numerical scale, say 1 to 10, with 10 being the best. The summary measure now becomes a matter of addition of ratings, if we assume the criteria are equally weighted (Figure 1.6). The matrix is consistent with the previous matrices if ratings 8 through 10 are taken as having produced unequivocal "yes" responses on the previous ratings, ratings of 1 through 3 having produced judgments of "no;" and ratings of 4 through 7 having produced the ambiguous "fair," which may have received some "yes" judgments and some "no" judgments in the first matrix presented.

|  | Criteria | | | |
| Restaurant | Good taste? | Low cost? | Nearby? | Total |
|---|---|---|---|---|
| 1. Joe's Diner | 6 | 9 | 2 | 17 |
| 2. Mary's Place | 6 | 8 | 7 | 21 |
| 3. Eat-A-Burger | 3 | 10 | 9 | 22 |
| 4. Swank-U-Pay | 4 | 1 | 4 | 9 |
| 5. Plain Home Cooking* | 10 | 4 | 9 | 23 |

FIGURE 1.6  *Indicates our choice

## Weighting the Criteria

The above examples treated all criteria as equally important, but this is not always the case. A fairly rich person might consider taste to be very important, cost inconsequential. Someone less financially blessed, perhaps a student, might have a different set of priorities. The priorities may be a result of objective factors in the situation, such as the lack of money, or of subjective factors, such as a preference for nice decor over a preference for a particular type of food. The objective factors would be the constraints within which the decision has to be made (and the problem solved). The subjective factors would be constraints inherent in the particular decisionmaker (agent of the action), and would differ across decisionmakers.

One method of assigning weights is to assign values from 0 to 1 so that all portions add to 1 (exactly as probabilities are assigned). A taste-conscious decisionmaker might assign the values:

| | Criteria | | |
|---|---|---|---|
| Restaurants | Good taste? .5 | Low cost? .3 | Nearby? .2 |
| 1. Joe's Diner | 6 | 9 | 2 |
| 2. Mary's Place | 6 | 8 | 7 |
| 3. Eat-A-Burger | 3 | 10 | 9 |
| 4. Swank-U-Pay | 4 | 1 | 4 |
| 5. Plain Home Cooking | 10 | 4 | 9 |

(a)

| | Criteria | | | |
|---|---|---|---|---|
| Restaurants | Good taste? .5 | Low cost? .3 | Nearby? .2 | Total |
| 1. Joe's Diner | 3 | 2.7 | .4 | 6.1 |
| 2. Mary's Place | 3 | 2.4 | 1.4 | 6.8 |
| 3. Eat-A-Burger | 1.5 | 3.0 | 1.8 | 6.3 |
| 4. Swank-U-Pay | 2 | .3 | 0.8 | 3.1 |
| 5. Plain Home Cooking* | 5 | 1.2 | 1.8 | 8.0 |

(b)

FIGURE 1.7   *Indicates our choice

|  | Criteria | | | |
| Restaurants | Good taste? .1 | Low cost? .8 | Nearby? .1 | Total |
|---|---|---|---|---|
| 1. Joe's Diner | .6 | 7.2 | .2 | 8.0 |
| 2. Mary's Place | .6 | 6.4 | .7 | 7.7 |
| 3. Eat-A-Burger* | .3 | 8.0 | .9 | 9.2 |
| 4. Swank-U-Pay | .4 | .8 | .4 | 1.6 |
| 5. Plain Home Cooking | 1.0 | 3.2 | .9 | 5.1 |

FIGURE 1.8  *Indicates our choice

Taste       .5
Cost        .3
Distance    .2

A person who considers distance to be an important criterion might choose the following weights:

Taste       .1
Cost        .1
Distance    .8

These weights would be used to adjust the points awarded to each criterion. One method of computation is to multiply each rating by the weight, then sum the results to obtain an "average" rating (or expected value). For the matrix in Figure 1.7a, the weighted ratings would be those shown in Figure 1.7b. This decisionmaker, adhering to the use of the expected value calculation, would choose restaurant 5. The decisionmaker weighting cost most heavily arrives at a different choice given the same restaurants and the same ratings (Figure 1.8).

## Other Criteria

Of course, the three criteria of taste, cost, and proximity are not the only criteria that might apply. "Prestige" might be an important factor to some restaurant goers, and, assuming that Swank-U-Pay has a large prestige factor, it could rise rapidly in the rankings.

The actual decision that is made is not as important to the information specialist as the ability to fill in the necessary information to make that decision:

1. The list of restaurants
2. The list of criteria
3. The relative weight to be assigned to each criterion by the decisionmaker
4. The ratings of each restaurant on each of the criteria
5. The computation of the total score for each restaurant
6. The comparison of the summary tools, yielding a ranked list of choices or a single "overall best" choice

Cost conscious

1.  Eat-A-Burger           9.2
2.  Joe's Diner            8.0
3.  Mary's Place           7.7
4.  Plain Home Cooking     5.1
5.  Swank-U-Pay            1.6

Taste conscious

1.  Plain Home Cooking     8.0
2.  Mary's Place           6.8
3.  Eat-A-Burger           6.3
4.  Joe's Diner            6.1
5.  Swank-U-Pay            3.1

FIGURE 1.9

Data Display

Step 6 addresses the output of the data results. One suitable display for the data on restaurants would be a ranked list. For the decisionmakers in question, the two lists would exhibit a different order, reflecting the per-

| | Criteria | | | |
|---|---|---|---|---|
| Restaurants | Good taste? .5 | Low cost? .3 | Nearby? .2 | Total |
| 1. Joe's Diner | 3 | 2.7 | 4 | 6.1 |
| 2. Mary's Place | 3 | 2.4 | 1.4 | 6.8 |
| 3. Eat-A-Burger | 1.5 | 3.0 | 1.8 | 6.3 |
| 4. Swank-U-Pay | 2 | .3 | 0.8 | 3.1 |
| 5. Plain Home Cooking | 5 | 1.2 | 1.8 | 8.0 |

(a)   Display 1

| | Restaurants | Total score |
|---|---|---|
| Choose | 1. Plain Home Cooking | 8.0 |
| | 2. Mary's Place | 6.8 |
| | 3. Eat-A-Burger | 6.3 |
| | 4. Joe's Diner | 6.1 |
| | 5. Swank-U-Pay | 3.1 |

(b)   Display 2

FIGURE 1.10

sonal preferences of the decisionmakers, although the principle behind each listing is the same (Figure 1.9).

The summary data are often more readily comprehensible than a complete listing. The complete listing is shown in Figure 1.10a. The data of interest are hidden in the full display, but highlighted in the summary display, Figure 1.10b. The price for this highlighting is the loss of detail. Given only the summary display one cannot tell whether Plain Home Cooking was judged superior because of the taste of its food, its economic pricing structure, or its proximity. In fact, one cannot even tell that these were the three criteria involved. The trade-off between economy of information transmitted or stored versus its completeness is a recurring issue. Similar trade-offs will be encountered between using up storage space to save processing time and vice versa, as well as between the time spent organizing input data at the time of storage versus the time spent searching for it at the time of retrieval.

## Implementation of the Chosen Alternative

Once a decision has been made, the chosen alternative must be implemented. In our case, we must proceed from the bus station to the restaurant of choice, order the food, eat it, pay for it, and return to the bus station. The successful implementation of the chosen course of action will not always depend solely on our own efforts. It may also involve certain "states of nature" or the actions of other agents. If we are walking to the restaurant, our progress involves monitoring traffic patterns and traffic signals. If a car is in our path or if the traffic light is red, we must temporarily suspend our progress. Our "course of action" involves a subset of actions, some of which are conditional in nature:

If traffic is heavy, wait before crossing.
If road is clear, cross.

To tell if the conditional portion of the statement is fulfilled, we must monitor the environment for ongoing indications of its "status" (the state of the world) and adjust our actions accordingly.

To judge the effectiveness of our actions we also become involved in "feedback" loops, i.e., monitoring the effects of our actions. In walking to the restaurant, we may watch the addresses of the buildings we pass. If the bus station is at 355 West Main and the restaurant is at 632 West Main, the addresses should continually increase until we arrive at the intended location. Indications of error in our execution of the action would be decreasing addresses or addresses larger than 632 West Main. In either case the solution of the problem is to turn around, i.e., to adjust our action by walking in the opposite direction. The adjustment of our input action (walking in a particular direction) by the analysis of the effects of our action (the output, here the sequence of addresses) is what is meant by feedback. We feed back the results of our actions to the input control mechanism.

## Evaluating the Information

One means of evaluating the information we generate and use is to examine it in relationship to the success of the chosen action in achieving the goal.

Lack of achievement can be due to physical factors (a bridge is out on the road from the bus station to the restaurant) or deficiency in the knowledge base (the restaurant is no longer at the location named in the phone book). Achievement of the goal indicates that neither difficulty occurred. The information used is a conjunction of the correct list, correct evaluation of the alternatives, and correct information about the respective states of the environment and ourselves in the implementation stage. Some portions of the data might have been incorrect, e.g., the rating of a restaurant not chosen might have been too high; since the data was not used it would not be uncovered. Since the error is on the high side, and we still did not choose that alternative, the error had no bearing on our final choice. An error on the low side, rating taste as a 6 instead of a 10, could have substantially altered the decision and may have caused our decision to be less than optimal, although the subjective judgment of a successful outcome indicates that the action was at least satisfactory. In many situations the number and complexity of factors influencing the outcome, along with constraints on time and funds, force the decisionmaker to "satisfice" rather than optimize.

The assessment of the outcome is an indirect measure of the quality of the information. Direct measures are its accuracy, relevance, and timeliness. The accuracy of the data is its "truth value." Do the data statements represent the real state of affairs? The relevance of the data concerns its applicability to this particular situation. Examples failing the test of accuracy are innumerable: inclusion in the list of a restaurant that has gone out of business, wrong recording of the address, wrong ratings, etc. The error "restaurant out of business" indicates the time dependency of data statements, requiring continual update to maintain the quality of the data. Such errors as an incorrect address are often due to the transposition of digits (recording 49 as 94), simple transcription errors (recording N. and S.), or incorrect spelling. Techniques of error detection and correction, such as limit checks, digit checks, and "spell" dictionaries, are used to uncover such as errors. Errors of omission can occur, such as the absence of street signs, as well as errors of data communication, such as poorly designed displays.

Examples of irrelevant data would be a list of movie theaters rather than restaurants, ratings on irrelevant criteria, and signals from the environment that are not applicable, say the signaling of a train on tracks that are not in our path. I was going to say the sounding of a foghorn to signal the lunch hour at a local factory, but this would be relevant, if unanticipated, information to a restaurant seeker.

Nonrelevant data is problematic because of its "noise" effect. It distracts the consumer of the information from the relevant data, as a skillful propagandist well knows. Examples are often found in responses to essay tests.

The timeliness of the data addresses the question of its being generated or retrieved in the time frame necessary to take action. Taken in this sense it is a factor of efficacy, taking efficacy as the ability to achieve the given goal. The efficacy is in terms of influencing the action rather than producing it. The influence consists of an indication of the correct action (accuracy) in the context of the situation (given goal and state of the environment) in the time frame necessary to act. The contextual constraints may involve other resources, such as the funds and technology available, and social and legal constraints, but the concern voiced most often is with regard to time, since failure on this point will make the other concerns inconsequential.

It may seem that relevance is a measure of the efficiency of the information system rather than a measure of the efficacy of the information itself, and the term is so used in the evaluation of bibliographic retrieval systems. However, the relevance of the data is also a necessary condition of continued, controlled efficacious action (haphazard success may occur sporadically but in a manner outside out repeated control).

## Evaluating the Information System

Various definitions of systems are offered in almost every discipline. They usually have the flavor of a set of entities interacting (e.g., physical systems) or a set of entities and the relationships among them (abstract or physical systems). Information systems are taken to be a set of people, procedures, and technology used to provide information. In evaluating such a system we would first look at the accuracy, relevance, and timeliness of the data, and the efficacy of the information produced. Given that two or more systems are efficacious, they would then be evaluated along the lines of efficiency, the cost in terms of resources necessary to produce the information. Costs are often reckoned in terms of money, time, and human effort. Time appears in a different role here: in terms of efficacy, the time constraint is an upper limit on the length of search. Having satisfied this upper limit, differences may still exist between two systems. The human effort expended may be physical (fatigue at a terminal) or mental (effort expended in sorting through nonrelevant data, which is why this is used as a measure of efficiency as well as efficacy). The design of an efficient and effective information system requires the analysis of user needs (what questions will be asked, under what constraints) and the matching of technology (computer processing versus manual) and procedures (organization of data, direction of data flow, methods of preserving the integrity of the data) to fit those needs.

A major question in the design of such a system is the anticipatory nature of the information need. Predictable questions can be handled quite efficiently (or not at all if we preclude the question with a periodic report), as exemplified in the telephone information system. The predictability may be due to the repetitiveness of certain situations (e.g., it is always unbearable in Chicago in the winter) or to dicta (e.g., we will accept questions about phone numbers in our city, but not about recipes for baked goods). "Generalized" information systems, such as the general purpose library, are inherently less efficient. They inevitably collect data that have potential use, but the potential is not always actualized. Yet the collection of only data that are relevant to expected situations can hinder the efficacy of the information system. When unanticipated needs arise, the data at hand are not usually sufficient. The trade-off is between efficacy across all situations, even the unanticipated, and efficiency for a particular anticipated situation.

## The Components of an Information System

While various models of an information system are given, they usually include the following components:

1. Data acquisition
2. Data processing
3. Data storage and retrieval
4. Data transmission
5. Data communications

One or more components may receive emphasis in a particular system. Data entry systems and real time monitoring systems will emphasize the efficiency of the acquisition system; query systems that concentrate on the interface with the user (query language or command language) will emphasize communication; modeling systems such as those used in aircraft simulation and traditional data processing systems (bank transactions, statistical packages, scientific computing) will emphasize processing; and systems in which the user(s) and the data base are physically dispersed will emphasize transmission. Most components will be present in varying degrees in each of these system types.

## Sources of Failure

While it may seem natural or trivial that a phone book or map does its job, the opportunities for failure in the information system are myriad. As mentioned above, one common source of error is in transposition. While the error may have limited consequences in an address (49 Harlan Drive may be close to 94 Harlan Drive), it could be more difficult to correct in the case of a phone number recorded incorrectly or a date (e.g., expecting to greet a visitor at the airport on the 12th, when the arrival date is really the 21st, because of operator error in the transmission of the message). One of the prime concerns in the design of an information system is recovery from failures. These failures may be physical (e.g., traffic light out, computer system down) or of content (e.g., transposition errors, obsolete data). As indicated earlier, various means of data verification, error detection, and error correction are used to combat content errors. Physical failures are handled by diagnosis and repair, as well as by backup systems and the development of more reliable technologies. The measures relevant here are mean (average) time between failures (MTBF) and mean time to repair (MTTR). A system averaging 85 hr between failures (synonomous with time "up") is "better" than one averaging 70 hr between failures. A system averaging 5 hr to repair (once "down") is better than one averaging 2 days to repair. Backup systems, especially those fully duplicated, reduce the MTBF and MTTR indirectly. The backup system does not prevent the failure of the primary system, nor does it hasten its repair; however, the effect of having two systems is that the entire operation "appears" not to have failed and the repair time is less crucial as long as it is well within the MTBF. A fully duplicated system is usually too expensive to maintain except for the most critical or profitable situations. An analysis of the relative importance of the system components can guide the allocation of resources to enhance reliability.

Reliability is one measure of the availability of the system, hence of the information produced (or coproduced) by the system. Another is the accessibility in terms of hours "open." This is especially a concern for systems that transmit data across distances that span different time zones. Having access to a data base in California during the working hours of 9 to 5 (California time) is equivalent to having access from noon to 8 P.M. for a user on the East Coast.

The ideal system would be perfectly reliable, always accessible, error free, instantaneous in processing and retrieval, as well as economical, esthetic, and pleasant to use. The dictates of reality cause us to be satisfied with somewhat less.

## Summary

In this chapter we have given a general overview of the activities involved in seeking, processing, and using information. The remainder of the text will be concerned with the concepts and skills required in each of the various stages, and in building information systems.

The text is divided into the following sections:

II. Data Collection and Analysis
III. Data Organization and Use
IV. Coding the Data
V. File Structures
VI. Data Retrieval
VII. Data Display
VIII. Human/Machine Communication
IX. Data Manipulation
X. Decision-Making and Problem-Solving

## Recommended Reading

At the close of each chapter, other readings will be recommended. These will usually be secondary sources, e.g., other texts, since the reader is expected to be a novice in the area. These sources will lead to more advanced articles for the reader wishing to explore a given area in more depth.

The recommendations are particularly difficult for this first chapter, since there is little material on the treatment of information science as a discipline, and even less so on the paradigm of question-answering. Some work has been done in the areas of logic and artificial intelligence, of which the following may be of interest to the reader. There are also some compendia of articles on information and information science. These are not, however, introductory in nature.

Belnap, Nuel D. Jr., and Steel, Thomas B. Jr., *The Logic of Questions and Answers*, New Haven, CT: Yale University Press, 1976.

Debons, Anthony, Fitzgerald, Inez, and Kukich, Karen, *Readings in the Information Sciences*, Lexington, Mass.: Xerox Individualized Publishing, 1975.

Lehnert, Wendy G., *The Process of Question Answering*, N.J.: Lawrence Erlbaum Associates, Inc., 1978.

Minsky, Marvin, ed., *Semantic Information Processing*, Cambridge, Mass.: Massachusetts Institute of Technology, 1968.

Saracevic, Tefko, ed., *Introduction to Information Science*, New York: R. R. Bowker Company, 1970.

Books on the design of information systems, usually automated, are more plentiful. Some representative works are:

Burch, John G. Jr., Strater, Felix R., and Grudnitski, Gary, *Information Systems: Theory and Practice*, 3rd ed., New York: John Wiley and Sons, 1983.

Kent, Allen, *Information Analysis and Retrieval*, New York: John Wiley and Sons, 1971.

Senn, James A., *Analysis and Design of Information Systems*, New York: McGraw-Hill, 1984.

Works on human information processing are:

Lindsay, Peter H. and Norman, Donald, A., *Human Information Processing: An Introduction to Psychology*, 2nd ed., New York: Academic Press, 1977.

Solso, Robert L., *Cognitive Psychology*, New York: Harcourt Brace Jovanovich, 1979.

# *II*
# Data Collection and Analysis

We begin the discussion of the search for information with a discussion of the methods and tools available for collecting data. The general methodologies of observation, self-report, report-by-others, and the use of archives are examined. The former are used in "original research," i.e., in collecting new data. The last method, using archives, uses data already collected, either in its current form of after some manipulation. The data may be found in either private or public data banks, e.g., libraries or on-line data bases.

   The second chapter in this section, Chapter 3, introduces the notion that the data collected are an answer to the question posed, although the derivation of "the answer" requires some interpretation of the data. The notion of conditional probability is introduced to illustrate the transfer of information across data items. This analysis is independent of such statistical techniques as the computation of significance tests, correlations, or regression equations. However, these techniques are introduced as natural consequences. We then examine whether or not data dependence is noteworthy (using the chi-square test of significance); the direction and strength of the association (correlation); and the form of the association (regression). This treatment is spread over Chapters 3 and 4, "Data Analysis" and "Making Predictions." The ultimate purpose of finding associations and their forms is to be able to predict values on variables or the occurrence of events. Prediction of such values can serve as the basis of controlling outcomes (if we can manipulate the input variables of a relationship) or in the adjustment of our actions to take into account predicted, but uncontrollable data (e.g., taking an umbrella along on cloudy days).

   The treatment of data collection should also include the notion of what data to collect (sampling) and the organization of data into tables and summary measures (i.e., the mean, the standard deviation), as well as the use of theoretical distributions, e.g., the normal distribution. Discussion of these matters is deferred to Section III. If the discussion appears to be too statistical for one reading or series of lectures, one can defer the reading of some sections, e.g., until after the treatment of coding and data storage and retrieval. The topics are grouped to reflect their logical placement in the structure of the text, which does not necessarily reflect the interest level of the reader or student.

# 2
# Data Collection Methods

## Objectives

Upon completion of this chapter, the reader should be able to:

1. List and explain the four major categories of data collection
2. Give at least two examples of each of the four major categories, with an advantage and a disadvantage of each
3. Define an indicator and explain its purpose
4. Define and explain the concepts of reliability and validity
5. Distinguish between content validity and criterion validity
6. Distinguish between demographic data and sensitive data
7. Explain the concept of reactivity in research
8. Distinguish between the cognitive and the affective states
9. Determine appropriate instruments for ascertaining a particular type of data
10. Discuss the strengths and weaknesses of a given instrument for a given task
11. List and explain the sources of error in doing research
12. Distinguish between systematic and random error

## Introduction

The search for knowledge begins with the collection of data. In this chapter, we study four general categories of data collection techniques:

1. Observation
2. Self-report
3. Report-by-others
4. Archives

The first three methods are generally used to do "original data collection," i.e., to arrive at answers for which we have no previous data. The last method, the use of archives or existing records, is "nonoriginal" in the sense that we use data that has already been collected by someone else, although we may manipulate it in new ways in order to provide information that is new (original). A brief explanation of each method is given here, followed by a more detailed examination of each.

In observation, we "watch" the person or event in order to discover the information we need. We "see for ourselves." The terms *watch* and *see* are meant to represent any of the modes of sensing the environment. Counting smiles and laughs in order to ascertain a person's level of happiness would be one example. Another might be counting cars passing a particular corner in order to ascertain the level of traffic. In regard to our restaurant example, walking down the street looking for restaurant signs would be an example of observation.

In self-report, we simple ask the person about his or her feelings, knowledge, etc., on a certain topic. For example, if I wished to get a rating on the quality of restaurants, asking the owner of the restaurant (or the chef) would be self-report. In terms of the happiness example, the investigator would simply ask you if you were happy, rather than counting smiles. The thing to note about self-report is that the person is asked about him- or herself. If we ask for an opinion about somebody else, the method is report-by-others. An example that might clarify this distinction is the consideration of a job applicant. If we ask the applicant whether or not he or she is an enthusiastic and hard worker, the response made by the applicant is considered self-report. If we ask a former employer for a letter of recommendation about the applicant, the method of data collection is report-by-others.

As can be gleaned from the above examples, report-by-others involves asking a "third party" for an evaluation of a person or asking a "second party" about an event. The polling of sports writers to name the nation's best football team is another example. Self-report means asking a "second party" about him- or herself.

The use of archives involves data collected by someone else, as in a census, which we use subsequently, e.g., in looking up the population of Pittsburgh. It is the use of already existent records.

At times, the methods will seem to blend. For example, if we use the Michelin guide to get a rating of restaurants, we are using already existing records, or archives. However, these records also represent a report-by-others, since the ratings are the opinions of the Michelin people. The blending of archives with other types of data collection methods is a necessary concomitant of the fact that archival records represent the result of former original data collection methods. Thus, each set of records can be studied in order to ascertain what method was used to collect the data in the first place, and this method will likely be observation, self-report, report-by-others, or a blend of the three. In the case of the Michelin guide, the makers of the guide presumably visited the restaurants in question, sampling their respective fares. This would be observation. They then published their judgment, which we read "in archival form" as a "judgment by others." Hence, the distinction between data collection methods is not always as clear-cut as will be presented here.

## Observation: A Definition

Observation is the method of collecting data in which the data collector (researcher) senses the events in question, either directly or through some intermediary device. The sensation of events without an intermediary device is illustrated by a librarian physically observing and noting the number of patrons entering the library. An example of observation done through an intermediary device would be to count the same patrons by installing an electric eye at the door. There are several ways to subdivide observation methods, each of which illustrates a separate issue.

## Laboratory Versus Natural Setting

One of the ways to distinguish the various categories of observation is to differentiate between:

1.  Laboratory (or controlled) observation and
2.  Observation done in a natural setting

In the laboratory setting, we take people out of their natural habitat and watch them. For example, an investigator might select three people to interact in a group, present them with a topic, then watch the group interact. The main danger here is that the people may act differently in the laboratory from the way they would in a real situation. For example, it is probably easier to say "I would rather die than steal" in a contrived setting than it would be if one were actually faced with the prospect of stealing to prevent starvation.

The main advantage of the laboratory setting is in the control we can exercise over the variables we wish to study, and the greater ability we have to exclude extraneous variables. Thus, if an investigator is studying the effects of a certain diet on a person's health, he or she can be more sure that the person being observed (the subject) is not "nibbling" on forbidden fruits if the subject is kept in a laboratory and fed at regular intervals (as in a hospital) than if the subject is allowed to go about his or her daily activities.

The advantages and disadvantages of the natural setting, or "field study," are the inverse of the laboratory setting. Assuming that subjects do not "see us watching," they will act as they always act in a natural setting. Our study should thus be more valid. However, we will have less control over the events that we wish to study, which may be costly in time and money spent "waiting for the desired events to occur"; in addition, the influence of extraneous factors (such as stress inducing more eating) will be harder to control.

## Obtrusive Versus Unobtrusive Observation

The problem of whether or not the observer is "seen" leads to the categorization:

1.  Obtrusive data collection methods vs.
2.  Unobtrusive data collection methods

Measures in which the subject knows he or she is being observed are termed *obtrusive*. Obtrusive measures may lead to differences in performance from that which would ordinarily occur. Thus, if an investigator is trying to assess the number of keyboarding errors made by a beginning student at the teletype, pulling up a chair and peeking over his or her shoulder is not a very good method. It probably will serve only to make the subject perform more slowly, make more errors, get more nervous, and hate the experimenter. In fact, the only valid conclusion that could come from this experiment is that "watching a person to count his or her errors is likely to lead to an increase in the number of errors committed."

An unobtrusive means of collecting the same data would be to have a computer program count the number of times the delete or backspace key is hit, or the number of times an error message is given. Note, however, that even the use of a computer program to count the errors can become obtrusive and affect performance if the processing time significantly affects the normal response time at the teletype. Methods of observation that cause the subject to change his or her behavior are called "reactive"; they themselves cause the subject to react. The goal in all research is to introduce measures that are "nonreactive"—measures that do not interfere at all. Complete noninterference is an ideal. It can probably never be fully attained, but the interference should be reduced as much as possible under the given circumstances.

## Direct Versus Indirect

Another division of observation methods is:

1. Direct
2. Indirect

In direct observation, we "watch" the subject. Again, the term *watch* is used to represent all forms of direct sensation (e.g., touching an apple to see if it is smooth, or listening to a person's speech habits to determine the presence or absence of an accent). An indirect measure is one in which we watch the subject's traces. An example is the trace left by a person on the electric eye counter at the library. Other examples might be the observation that children must reside in a particular home from evidence of toys in the yard, or the judgment that a person has just taken a shower from the observation of wet hair.

Indirect measures are less likely to be reactive than direct observation; however, they have a drawback in that we must "infer" what really happened from the traces, and, as might be expected, the inferences can be wrong. (For example, in the case of wet hair, it may be raining outside.)

## Participatory Versus Nonparticipatory Observation

The final division we make is between:

1. Participatory vs.
2. Nonparticipatory

methods of observation.

In participatory observation, we become one of the group. Thus, if an investigator wanted to observe factory workers on the job, he would apply for a job in that factory, and not let any of the workers know he was doing research. Nonparticipatory observation is what occurs when researchers who are an "outside team" come in to "look around." Participatory observation should be less reactive, but it will normally be more time consuming, and may even require putting in a day's work!

## Advantages and Disadvantages of Observation

The primary advantage of simple observation is that we "see for ourselves," i.e., an attempt is made to eliminate bias. No matter how often someone tells an investigator that castor oil is "good," the proof of the pudding is in how many times he or she actually drinks it; actions do speak louder than words.

Of course, one of the major drawbacks to observation is that it is often time consuming and expensive. If we want to get a sample of someone's eating habits over the course of a year, we have to take the time and effort to be at her dinner table or at the restaurants she frequents on several different days at several different mealtimes.

Observation is not always expensive in time and money. For example, observing the speed of our car by using a speedometer takes almost no time (a single glance), and the cost only involves the price of the speedometer, which is spread over the lifetime of the car. In general, methods that use indirect observation will tend to be as costly as the device used, and will usually require less time on the part of the observer, unless the device must be monitored continuously (e.g., the monitors watched by air controllers). Direct observation will be costly in time, unless the observation takes place during an activity we must normally perform (e.g., observing people's clothing or physical expressions on the bus while we ride to work). If the observers are paid a salary, these methods of observation will also entail a substantial cost.

Another major drawback of direct observation is that not all of a person's actions are accessible to direct observation. For example, if I want to determine someone's patterns of recreation at home, and I do not have a constant invitation to be in his or her living room, my observations will be somewhat hindered, unless I am willing to risk being arrested as a Peeping Tom.

Finally, one of the biggest drawbacks to direct observation is that persons being observed may change their behavior if they know they are being observed. Thus, there is a much lower proportion of shoplifting when people know that the store detective is watching than when they know that he is out to lunch.

The effect of the observer on the one observed is termed *reactivity*. One of the most famous examples of the effect of the observers on the behavior of the observed is the case of the Hawthorne experiments conducted at the Western Electric Company near Chicago (summary from Chapanis, 1959, pp. 74-75). The essence of the experiment was that over a 2-year period, a group of five workers was subjected to variations in the number, duration, and time of rest periods, as well as in the quitting time at the end of the day. The investigators found that *no matter what they did, production increased*. Various explanations have been offered for this phenomenon, but the main point as far as we are concerned here is that the knowledge that they were being observed affected their performance. The results were not indicative of the true unobserved behavior.

Problems such as the "influence of the observer" lead researchers to look for "unobtrusive" measures, ones in which the observed person does not know that he or she is being observed (see Webb, Campbell, Schwartz, and Sechrest, 1966). One example of such unobtrusive measures listed by the authors is the procedure used to estimate the effect of television on reading habits: library withdrawals were examined; fiction titles had dropped; nonfiction remained the same (p. 2). The conclusion was that television had replaced some recreational reading. Another example might be assessing the relative popularity of a painting in a museum by comparing the "wornness" of the rug in front of that painting with that in front of other paintings. Of course, these methods have their drawbacks as well; besides subtle sampling biases identified by the authors, consider the problem of determining whether more women or men like the painting. It is somewhat difficult to ascertain the sex of the museum patron from a consideration of rug wear and tear. In fact, the relative merits and drawbacks of the many different methods lead the authors to suggest a multipronged approach to research, using several methods in order to ascertain the true behavior and/or beliefs of an individual or group (pp. 29, 34).

## Observation: What to Watch, and When

In order to remember the events we observe, we usually have to make some sort of external record of them. We cannot record everything (although we could make a movie, as when psychiatric therapy sessions are videotaped). Even if we could record everything, we usually would not wish to, since not all events are pertinent or "relevant" to our inquiry. Thus, we wish to record only relevant events, but this brings up the question "What is a relevant event?" The investigator must operationalize the definition of the behavior he or she is attempting to observe. For example, if one is studying aggressiveness, does a light punch on the shoulder indicate an "aggressive act," or does it indicate a "playful show of affection"? The categorization of the actions into meaningful, observable, and *definable* groups is probably as serious a problem as the reactivity of the method. In fact, these problems of categorization apply not only to the methods of observation, but to all the methods of collecting data.

The problem of categorization involves two separate levels. One is the definition of the categories at an "intellectual" level. For example, we might decide that we are comparing religious people with nonreligious people. At the superficial level, this distinction seems clear: religious people believe in God, go to church, etc.; nonreligious people do not. The problem comes when we attempt to "operationalize" our definition, the level at which we must translate an abstract idea into concrete observable actions. Are religious people those who simply say they are religious, e.g., by marking a box in a form they fill out? Must they attend church a certain number of times per year? Must they pray a certain number of times a day? A familiar form of operationalizing a definition is in the use of IQ tests. What the administrator of the test wishes to measure is intelligence; what is actually measured is the set of "correct" responses to a set of questions or tasks, which may or may not represent "general intelligence."

Finally, we come to the question of "How long is an action?" Again, if we are studying aggressive behavior, does a fistfight in which nineteen blows are struck constitute one action or nineteen? Or, if you return for "seconds" at dinner, is that one order or two? We must agree on some "natural duration" of an "act." This is the problem of categorization in a broader context.

Self-Report: General Description

The use of self-report is based on the dictum that "nobody knows a person like the person knows himself"—his or her inner feelings, secret thoughts, and desires, the things he or she never tells to anybody else. The deep probing into the inner self is one of the primary advantages of the self-report. Another advantage is that it is relatively quick and easy compared to observation techniques. We do not have to stand around and watch for hours; we simply ask the person for a quick summary.

The primary disadvantage to self-report lies in the phrase "the things he or she never tells to anybody else." If people do not reveal them to anybody else, why should we expect them to tell us? How can we assure ourselves that the self-report is true? The self-report of a burglar that "I didn't do it" may not inspire great confidence on our part. The tendency to withhold information or to distort the facts, especially when the topic is threatening, can be somewhat overcome by the assurance of anonymity: "No names will be used." But, even in the case of "guaranteed" anonymity, the person must believe and trust the person doing the research. In some forms of self-report, e.g., the interview, the subject is *not* anonymous to the interviewer. Thus, the method of self-report may be subject to bias in the responses of the person being queried.

Another more subtle problem is that the person may really not know himself better than others know him. The practical joker who sees himself as happy-go-lucky and popular may have a view clearly different from the victims who consider him a pain in the neck. Thus, while self-report offers the chance for greater depth of study with possibly more valid results in a more economical time and cost frame, it also poses the risk of having untrue or distorted reports. The distortion can be counteracted by an application of the method of "seeing for ourselves" through observation. It is a good practice to handle bias by using more than one method of measurement: e.g., if we wish to study food preferences, we can ask the person whether or not she likes fish, and then observe what she orders for lunch; or watch the person order, then ask if she prefers what we think she prefers. If two or more methods corroborate the same data, we can place more confidence in that data.

Measurement Tools

When doing direct observation, say, watching people on the bus to see how often they smile, the measuring instrument is our sensory facilities, in this case our eyes. In doing indirect observation, an auxiliary tool is used as the measuring instrument. For example, in measuring the speed at which one's car is traveling, we use the speedometer, a display that is "driven" by a mechanism connected to the rotation of the wheels.

The general methods of data collection refer to the person doing the measurement—the observer. If the researcher is doing the measurement himself or herself, it is "observation." If he or she asks someone else, it is either self-report or report-by-others. The distinction between self-report and report-by-others lies in who is being "reported about." If you report about yourself ("I feel good"), it is self-report. If you report about someone else ("The boss is grumpy") it is report-by-others.

Typical measuring instruments used in both self-report and report-by-others are the questionnaire and the interview. We discuss these next.

## The Interview

The interview technique probably offers the opportunity for the greatest amount of data-gathering about individuals. If an open-ended technique is used, where the respondent can talk freely, and the person interviewing can follow up various "leads," an interview can lead to results not even anticipated. Thus, in interviewing a weatherperson about the effects of the winter weather on Pittsburgh transportation systems, he or she may slip into the topic of the impact of the cold weather on the Florida citrus crop, and how a group of weatherpersons took advantage of their predictions of an unexpected freeze to make a windfall killing in the futures market by buying frozen orange juice before the freeze and then selling it at inflated prices after the freeze. A whole new topic of economic impact and social ethnics thus enters the horizon.

However, in an unstructured interview, there is a little control over what is discussed, and if we are interviewing several people, the results of interviewing one person may not be comparable to the results of interviewing another person, because the interviews differed in content and manner. This problem can be overcome by restricting the questions to a certain list, and by restricting the nature of the responses, but in so doing we lose some of the power of "probing." If we restrict the responses to a given list, the interview actually becomes similar to a questionnaire.

An example of the structured interview question is the following, used by Sears, Maccoby, and Levin, in their study *Patterns of Child Rearing* (pp. 491-493) as reported in Kerlinger, 1973 (p. 484):

> All babies cry, of course (Note that the interviewer puts the parent at ease about her child's crying.) Some mothers feel that if you pick up a baby every time it cries, you will spoil it. Others think that you should never let a baby cry for very long. (The frame of reference has been clearly given. The mother is also put at ease no matter how she handles her baby's crying.) How do you feel about this?
> (a) What did you do about this with X?
> (b) How about in the middle of the night?

The questions

How did you do about this with X?
How about in the middle of the night?

are set out ahead of time. Even the form of the interview (e.g., "all babies cry") is structured.

The problem of categorization becomes particularly difficult in the unstructured interview. For example, Labov (1972) lists the following excerpt from an interview he conducted while studying the speech patterns on Martha's Vineyard (p. 31):

> I think actually it's a very hard thing to make that decision...It comes to you later, that you should have made it before. I have an-

other son—Richard—is an aeronautical engineer. He really loves the island. And when he decided to be an aeronautical engineer we discussed it—at length—and I told him that at that time: you just can't live on Martha's Vineyard...He works at Grumman, but he comes home every chance he gets and stays as long as he can.

We could classify the respondent's words in a number of fashions:

1. The difficulty of deciding on college ("it's a very hard thing")
2. The process of problem-solving ("it comes to you later")
3. The economics of Martha's Vineyard ("you just can't live on Martha's Vineyard")
4. Family ties ("he comes home every chance he gets")

Actually, what Labov was studying was the "love of the island" ("he really loves the island"), not so much of Richard, but of his mother. Labov's thesis was that people who chose to stay on the island developed distinctly different speech patterns from those who chose to leave, and thus categorized the people interviewed according to this variable. The problem of categorizing the results is one that should be tackled before we begin doing the interviews, so that we are clear in "what we are looking for." Of course, compromises can be made between the open-ended and the closed forms of interviewing; starting with a set list of questions and responses, but allowing either the interviewer of the interviewee to use these as "jumping off" points to other topics, or as instigations to further investigate the motives and reasons behind the response.

Another major problem with the interview technique is the amount of training necessary to become proficient at interviewing. An unexperienced interviewer can easily bias the interviewee's responses (e.g., if the person being interviewed wishes to please—or displease—the interviewer); or he or she can arouse fear or suspicion in the interviewee, thus restricting the freedom of response. In addition to the training required for the interviewer, the process of interviewing is costly in both time and money. In fact, it is this cost factor that often leads to the use of the questionnaire.

## The Questionnaire

The questionnaire attacks the problem of getting a lot of data fast. While an interview with a single person may take anywhere from half an hour to several hours, a short questionnaire can be administered to a group of people at one time. Because it can be distributed to many people fairly easily, it is economical in terms of both time and money, and hence has been one of the most widely used forms of data-gathering.

On the negative side, a good questionnaire takes quite a lot of time to construct and test; it usually allows only a closed range of responses, and the responses may not be entirely true, especially if the questions involve a topic that is personally threatening. A questionnaire administered by the teacher as to "the value of this course" is likely to get higher responses than the same question put to a student in informal conversation with the other students at the student union.

Of course, the problem of veracity is common to all types of self-report. This disadvantage can be somewhat combated in the questionnaire by administering the form to a group, and having all respondents omit their names, in order to insure "anonymity." However, even such an "assurance" of anonymity may not be effective. For example, the question "Do you now have veneral disease?" may not get a 100% truthful response from someone who should say "yes," but is afraid you might start a guessing game as to who it could be. The next criticism of the questionnaire is actually the reason why researchers often turn to the interview technique. While it is possible to construct an "open-ended" questionnaire, most questionnaires tend to be of the "closed type," i.e., the questions admit only a selected range of responses. Thus, a question might be:

Do you watch TV at night?

_____Yes _____No _____Sometimes

While the question will give us some idea of the viewing habits of our audience, it does not admit such qualifications as "Yes, on Sunday evening, but never on a worknight." The respondent is "locked into" the available responses. The question could also be incomplete. For example, the question

I choose to eat:

a. Fish    b. Beef    c. Cheese

does not allow for a response of "peanut butter and jelly." We could amend the question to read:

I choose to eat:

a. Fish    b. Beef    c. Cheese    d. Other

but then we have no way of ascertaining what "other" consists of. To combat this problem, questionnaires are often constructed with one set of structured responses, followed by a line labeled "Any comments?" which allows the person to expand on the response. Of course, these questionnaires take more time to interpret.

The subject of "good" and "bad" questions brings us to our final problem; the task of constructing a good questionnaire can require quite a bit of time and effort in "pretesting" and rewriting the questions. The ease of sliding into ambiguity can be seen from the following "seemingly innocuous" question

Do you like sports?

_____Yes _____No

which can mean "do you like to play sports" or "do you like to watch sports being played" or "do you think they are a good thing for people to do," etc. The designer of the questionnaire must exert some effort to choose questions that measure what he or she wishes to measure (validity), then state them clearly to assure consistency of response (reliability). In order to achieve these goals, the questionnaire is often "tried out" on a pilot population in order to discover problems that lead to modification by rephrasing, or adding or deleting items.

## Demographic Data

Some questions are particularly suited to the questionnaire. These are the so-called demographic items. Demographic data are the statistics about a person's life (vital statistics), including birthdate, age, city of residence, and social standing, e.g., middle class, upper class, marital status, and level of education. These questions are used to group or "type" people, so that we can make such statements as "more married people prefer Blisto soap; single people prefer Risto." These questions are particularly suited to the "closed response," since they are normally about "factual" data. Thus, it is rather difficult to misinterpret a question such as

Place of birth_____

although it can be done!

Very often, a questionnaire will be used to collect background data about a person or group, even though we are going to use some other technique to probe the person's "personality." By personality, we mean the "less physical" characteristics that we later summarize as "cognitive" (knowledge) and "affective" (attitudes), and that include measures of achievement, aptitude, attitudes, belief, and intent. Both types of information, the demographic and the more personal traits, are important for research on users. In fact, very often a demographic characteristic can be used to predict a personality characteristic, as when we say "most people in southern Illinois are conservative and vote Republican." Of course, the determination of personal characteristics is often more difficult than the determination of demographic ones. Besides the questionnaire, archival records, such as the birth and marriage records of a municipality or the census statistics of the country can be used to provide demographic information on an individual or group.

## The Mailed Questionnaire

The mailed questionnaire is an attempt to widen the audience to which we administer our questionnaire. Instead of administering it to twenty-five or fifty people physically present, we can contact a few hundred people not physically present. It is a particularly good device to use when the people we want to reach are scattered far and wide (e.g., deans of various universities or police chiefs in various cities) thus making the cost and time of either assembling all the subjects or traveling to each subject prohibitive.

The major problem with the mailed questionnaire is that there is usually a very low rate of return, often as low as 10%, before follow-up letters. In order to increase the rate of return, the researcher can combine three tactics:

1. Write a "good" cover letter, explaining the purposes of the research and its importance, so that the respondent feels positively about filling out the questionnaire.
2. Keep the questionnaire itself simple and short, so that filling it out is not a burden.

3. Establish a deadline for returns, after which polite "follow-up" letters can be sent to the nonrespondents, asking them if they have "accidentally overlooked" the deadline.

Even with the above techniques, some of the potential respondents will fail to return the completed questionnaire. Some follow-up of these people must be done to see if they are significantly different from the respondents in the variable(s) we want to measure. If there is not a significant difference in their standing on the variables we are studying, these respondents can be ignored. However, if there is a significant difference, we must adjust our results accordingly. For example, if we mail out a questionnaire to ascertain "happiness in my job," the responders may contain a proportionately larger percentage of "happy workers," the nonrespondents being mainly "unhappy workers"; if we were to conclude that 90% of the population was "happy in their job," we might be misled by this difference in the types of people who actually did fill out and return the questionnaire.

The major advantage of the mailed questionnaire is its economy. Its disadvantages are the disadvantages of all questionnaires (e.g., the respondent is "locked into" a given response) in addition to the added difficulty of getting a good number of returns, which may be quite expensive in terms of the time spent on follow-up letters and in getting fairly complete results.

## Report-by-Others

If we can't "see for ourselves" (observation) and don't want to ask the person being observed (self-report), an alternative approach is to ask someone else (report-by-others). This is the method used in requesting letters of recommendation. Thus, if we were attempting to ascertain the scholastic achievement of a group of students, we might ask their teacher to "rank them" in order of competence. In essence, evaluation by others is "observation by someone else." The primary advantage of report-by-others is that it saves us the time, money, and effort of observing for ourselves, or of interviewing the subject. The main problem with a report by someone else is in "judging the judge." As every student knows, some teachers are "tough" markers, while others are "easy"; thus, one person's *C* might be another's *A*. There are differences in the underlying scales the judges use to rate the students. Some attempt to compensate for the difference in judges and their respective scales is made when we say "that's a good school," or "that school's easy," when assessing the "worth" of school grades. We will treat three methods of obtaining report-by-others:

1. Rating scales
2. Ranking
3. Sociograms

## Rating Scales

In a rating scale, we present the judge with a set of categories to choose from, and he or she marks the one that best describes the respondent. In appearance, they are very much like questionnaires. Thus, we might ask:

Is the subject honest?

1. Very        2. A little        3. Not at all

As can readily be seen, the responses might be quite different if we were asking a burglar to do the rating as opposed to a policeman. This is the problem of "respondent bias." Is the judge an "overrater" or an "underrater"? Another problem in using a rating scale is the so-called halo effect. The halo effect means that the rating on one trait tends to influence the rating on another trait. For example, a teacher rates a particular student high on intelligence, after observing the student doing very well in classroom exercises. She also rates the student high on courage and leadership, although she has never seen the student in a situation calling for either! Of course, this halo tendency also works in reverse; low marks on one trait cause low marks on other traits. The tendency can be combated by making sure we restrict the categories in which we ask for judgments only to those in which we can be reasonably sure the judge has competence.

## Rankings

If one judge knows several of the subjects, we may ask him or her to rank them on some trait. A "ranking" is simply a listing of the subjects from "best to worst" or "most to least." Thus, in assessing the achievement of a high school class in biology, the teacher may rank Mary first, Harry second, and George third. The fact that the same person is ranking all three subjects somewhat alleviates the problem of response bias, in that the judge supposedly applies the same bias to all students. However, a problem arises when comparing the rankings of several judges. Would another biology teacher also rank Mary first? The extent of this problem can be seen by comparing the rankings of judges at a boxing match or beauty contest; they are seldom in complete agreement.

Another problem arises when we try to compare rankings applied to individuals in different groups. How does being the "third-best" hitter in the major leagues compare with being the best in AAA minor leagues? Finally, the size of the group makes a difference. Placing third in a three-person contest is not the greatest compliment in the world. Likewise, placing tenth in a class of 50 is not quite the same thing as placing tenth in a class of 2,000.

## Sociograms

While ratings and rankings are most often applied to assessments of achievement, attitudes, and traits, the sociogram is very often applied to assess such things as "popularity" or "communication patterns." The essence of the technique is to ask each individual in a group to write down the names of the three, five, or whatever number of people they would "most like to work with," or with whom they have "the most contact," etc., and then to process the results to get a picture of the group's "interaction pattern." Thus, if we have a group of five people:

1. Joe
2. John
3. Jim
4. Jane
5. Janet

and each fills out a form with the "most liked" two people, we might find that Janet is named on four forms, while Jim is not named on any. Presumably, Janet is popular, and Jim is not. The name socio*gram* comes from the fact that we can actually draw the relationships. For example, if Joe picked John and Janet, we would draw the graph shown in Figure 2.1, where the circles or nodes represent people, and the arrows represent "choices." A complete graph might look like Figure 2.2, where the fact that three arrows point to Janet indicates her "centrality" to the group, while the lack of any arrows pointing to Jim indicate his "isolation." The mutual arrows among John, Joe, and Janet indicate a "clique."

We can apply sociometric techniques to the assessment of achievement or attitudes by choosing suitable questions:

Name the two best mathematicians in the class.
    or
Name the two most conservative members of the committee.

Finally, we can get some idea of communication channels by asking something like:

I most often get my information from (name two members of your organization).

A good treatment of the various sociometric methods is found in Kerlinger, 1973 (pp. 356ff).

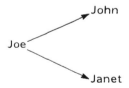

FIGURE 2.1

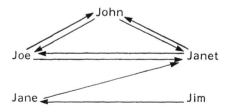

FIGURE 2.2

## Archival Records

The final general method of collecting data is the use of archival records. Archival records are data that have been collected by someone else, and which we exploit. For example, we might use the sales records of a grocery store to ascertain the "tastes" of the community in regard to fish and beef.

Archival records are normally divided into two types:

1. Public
2. Private

Public records are things like the census, and marriage, birth, and death records, which are accessible to all who desire to peruse them. Private records include the sales records of a privately owned store, e.g., Sears, or someone's private diary. The use of archival records is brilliantly treated in Webb et al., 1966 (pp. 53ff). One of their more ingenious examples is the following account of S. Winston's work, originally published in the *American Journal of Sociology* (1932, 38, pp. 225-231):

> Take Winston's (1932) research. He wanted to examine the preference for male offspring in upper-class families. He could have interviewed prospective mothers in affluent homes, or fathers in waiting rooms. Indeed, one could pay obstetricians to ask, 'What would you like me to order?'...

> But Winston went to the enormous bank of birth records and manipulated them adroitly. He simply noted the sex of each child in each birth order. A preference for males was indicated, he hypothesized, if the male-female ratio of the last child born in families estimated to be complete was greater than that ratio for all children in the same families...

That is, hypothesizing that couples were more likely to "quit when they got what they wanted," he looked to see if more people quit after a boy or after a girl (p. 57).

Of course, there are many problems inherent in the use of archival records, e.g., was the recordkeeper complete? Accurate? Biased? And, more important, are there alternative explanations for the data? For example, did the people involved in the above example stop having babies for religious or economic reasons, rather than because "they got what they wanted"? (Winston overcame the economic objection by choosing upper-class families who could presumably afford as many children as they wanted.)

An example of the use of sales records is the ranking of famous figures in popularity by a consideration of the value placed on their autograph. The same authors (Webb et al.) list the data shown in Table 2.1 as an example of the worth of the autograph of various public figures in 1964. Again, there are various explanations for the variance in worth, e.g., the rarity of the autograph. However, it is interesting to note that a modern figure, Winston Churchill, who was still alive at the time, had already outstripped Napolean in the marketplace.

TABLE 2.1

| John Hancock | $250.00 |
|---|---|
| Winston Churchill | 225.00 |
| Napoleon I | 185.00 |
| Charles Dickens | 125.00 |
| Ralph Waldo Emerson | 110.00 |
| Cesar Franck | 75.00 |
| Daniel Webster | 65.00 |
| Calvin Coolidge | 55.00 |
| John Quincy Adams | 37.50 |
| Aldous Huxley | 22.50 |

The main advantage of archival records is the massive amount of "ready-made" data. Of course, one of the primary disadvantages is that the researcher cannot ask all the questions he or she would like to ask. For example, if the researcher would like to know the exact time of day that an item was purchased, and this is not recorded, he or she is out of luck. However, by using several files, certain "gaps" in the data can be overcome. For example, a school record of a student may or may not contain the student's sex, but a correlation of the student's school record with the birth record for that same student would certainly yield that bit of data.

The more serious fault of records is the difficulty of ascertaining their completeness and freedom from bias. Normally, this will demand the use of several methods of analyzing the data from several sources, looking for confirmation of the data at hand.

## Using More Than One Method

As indicated above, more than one method of data collection can be used in order to answer a particular question. Thus, if I wish to collect data on the number of accidents that occur at a particular intersection, I can watch (observe), interview the neighbors (report-by-others), or check the police accident reports (archives). About the only method that cannot be used easily with nonhuman data is the self-report, since very few nonhumans talk about themselves. However, the methods of the interview, questionnaire, etc., can be applied to report-by-others in a fashion similar to that used for self-report. Thus we might ask people to rate a particular intersection for "safety." It is usually desirable to combine two or more methods in order to insure that we are indeed getting the "true picture."

## Ascertaining the State of a Person's Mind

One of the more difficult things to measure is the state of a person's mind. Things like automobile accidents are clearly visible, but the amount of knowledge a person has on a particular subject, say mathematics, or a person's attitude toward a product we are selling, is not readily visible.

The major problem in describing the state of a person's mind is that we cannot see it. As indicated above, one method of attacking this problem is to use a person's actions as an indicator of the organization in his mind. Thus, if we see a person order fish fourteen times and beef only once, we might say "He prefers fish to beef," or, we could simply ask the person point blank, "What type of food do you prefer: beef or fish?" If he answers "fish," we have some estimate of his mental state. If we prod him further, asking "how much more do you like fish than beef?" and he answers "ten times as much," we have a clearer estimate. In fact, if he answers "ten times as much," we can begin to quantify our data. The first method, watching the person order food, is the method of observation. The second method, asking the person, is an interview. Both methods are "indicators."

## Indicator: A Definition

An indicator can be defined as "something observable that we measure in order to estimate the measure of something that is not observable, but which we hypothesize (suppose) exists." For example, the trait "happy" is not really observable; but smiles and laughs are. We note the number of smiles and laughs a person "has" or "does" in a day, and use these to indicate the amount of "happiness" he or she has. If there are a lot of smiles and laughs, we say he or she is a "happy person," if there are very few smiles and laughs, he or she might be said to be "sad" or "dour."

One indicator that all students are familiar with is the test. We hypothesize that a student gleans some knowledge from a course in information science, that all the classes, readings, etc., have increased his or her knowledge of the field. How do we test our hypothesis? We make the student place some marks on a sheet of paper and compare her marks to our marks. If they compare favorably, we conclude that the student learned something. If they don't match, we conclude that she didn't learn anything.

For example, the examination might be a true-false exam. The student is instructed to mark a $T$ next to the items that she thinks are true, and an F next to the items she judges to be false. If the test is properly constructed, with no obvious "tip-offs," the student has a 50-50 chance of getting each question correct, or, from the pessimistic point of view, a 50-50 chance of getting each question wrong. Her chances of getting the entire set of questions right (let us arbitrarily set the total at ten questions) is much less than 50%. In fact, using statistical methods (the binomial distribution), we can calculate the student's chances of getting all ten questions right "by chance" as less than one-tenth of 1%. Her chance of getting at least a 70 by guessing is about 17%.

The test seems to combine the methods of self-report and observation. In one sense the test is like a complex questionnaire. Yet, in another sense, we are watching the reactions of the person as she places marks on a sheet of paper in response to the test items. We have a set of "answers" to the questions:

    T  T  F  T  F  F  F  T  F  F

and we compare the student's set of "marks on a sheet of paper" with our marks on the sheet of paper. Wherever the marks agree, the student is correct; where they disagree, she is "wrong." If the two distributions of T's and F's are the same, the student gets 100%, and we presume that she has learned the material. If only seven of the ten marks agree, we still presume that she learned the material, but we are somewhat less sure. In fact, in the case of the 100% score, we have less than "one in a thousand" as our doubt, but the second case could happen in "one out of six" cases.

Note, however, that the pencil marks are not knowledge. The pencil marks are simply pencil marks. Yet, we presume that the pencil marks tell us about the student's knowledge. The pencil marks are visible; we can compare them, count them, etc. We can actually evaluate them in relation to our own pencil marks, so we do. We then make the giant leap; we assume that these visible pencil marks are an accurate representation of the invisible knowledge we really wish to measure, but cannot measure directly. The pencil marks are an indirect measure of the knowledge.

The fact that we are using an indirect measure should not scare us off. Scientists in the so-called hard sciences use such measures often. For example, very few scientists have ever walked from earth to a distant star, yet, they feel that they have accurate measures of the distances to the stars, distances that have been calculated from separate sittings or photographs and the laws of trigonometry. However, the very fact that the indirect measures are indirect, and that we merely assume that they tell us about the "invisible" phenomenon, e.g., "mental state," should alert us to the possibility that *we can be wrong*.

## Reliability and Validity: Testing the Test

The "room for error" means that we must "test the test." Two measures are often applied to tests in order to determine if they are "worthwhile": reliability and validity. Reliability means that "when we administer the same or an equivalent test to the same person or persons at two different times, we get substantially the same results." Thus, if I administer an IQ test to you, and you score 100, a second administration of the same or an equivalent test at another time should also result in your scoring "around" 100. We include the term "around" to indicate that the results of two separate administrations of a test are seldom "exactly the same," but that they should be "in the ballpark." Barring some intervening circumstances, such as having a splitting headache, you should not score 100 on one day, 140 the next, and 72 on the third.

A ruler is "reliable" if it accurately measures your height as 6 ft. 1 in. on Tuesday morning, then gives the same result on Wednesday afternoon. If the ruler indicates that you are 6 ft. 1 in. on Tuesday, but indicates 5 ft. 3 in. on Wednesday, we would say the ruler was "unreliable," and return it to the hardware store for a better model. The same is true of tests used to ascertain the mental states of individuals.

Validity is the quality we refer to when we say that the test "measures what it is supposed to measure." For example, if I give a course on ancient history, then administer a test from Modern Physics in order to assess your knowledge of ancient history, the test would not be valid. While it may seem that validity is an easy quality to assess, it is not so in reality. For example, what do IQ tests measure? Do they really measure intelligence, or do they measure proficiency in taking exams or other cultural properties? These are questions that are hotly debated, and they are questions of validity. This point is illustrated by the following hypothetical example.

The Air Force runs into a problem of testing the validity of an exam designed to separate the "good" pilots from the "bad" ones. The problem arises as follows:

1. All potential pilots take the exam.
2. A score is set at which we would separate those likely to succeed as pilots from those unlikely to succeed.
3. If the test were known to be valid, we would refuse pilot training to those below the cutoff score.
4. However, to prove the validity of the test, we should see if the scores for good pilots correlate with actual performance *and* the score for bad pilots *also correlates* with performance.
5. To correlate the bad scores on the test with flying performance, we cannot refuse pilot training to the "bad scores," at least in the first batch of trainees.

The point is that if the Air Force had refused training to the low scorers in the first batch of trainees, one could never tell if these pilots would have done a bad job; we could not test the test. The Air Force should therefore administer the test to everybody, score the tests, make predictions about success or nonsuccess based on the test results, then put the tests in a place for safekeeping and *not* refer to them for the duration of the pilots' careers. (This "not referring to them" is done to avoid prejudicial treatment based on the test scores.) Then, after the careers are over, the judgments can be made about pilots being "good" and "bad" in their flying skills, the test scores could be compared with actual performance in order to see if the test was a "good predictor" or a "bad predictor." Of course, if a test turns out to be a bad predictor, we must start all over again. Validity is not an easy thing to establish.

Although we have developed the concepts of reliability and validity in relationship to examinations and tests, both concepts are much broader in scope. In fact, measures of reliability and validity are pertinent to every method of collecting data. Thus, in our example of choosing a food, if we observed the person choosing fish fourteen out of fifteen times in one period, but then observed him choosing beef thirteen out of fifteen times in another period, we would have to conclude that our observations were not reliable. In the example of the happy man, if we later found out that the number of smiles and laughs didn't really indicate happiness very well, we would conclude that our observations were not valid.

Types of Validity

We wish to distinguish between two types of validity: content validity and criterion validity. Content validity is most often applicable to school-type examinations. It asks the question "Do these questions pertain to the material covered in the currciulum?" The example of using physics questions to test a class on history is an example of "no content validity." Whether or not the questions used on a testing or measuring instrument possess content validity is a question usually settled by a judge or panel of judges.

In the typical classroom test, the teacher is the judge (maybe not always a perfect judge?). In instruments designed for a wider audience, we might get a panel of judges, e.g., high school mathematics teachers from across the country, in order to judge the content validity of a mathematics test to be given nationally to high school seniors.

Content validity is primarily *descriptive*. It says "these items are representative of the field they are supposed to represent." Criterion validity is *predictive*. It seeks to use this measuring instrument in order to predict success on the job, in school, etc. The success in the thing predicted *is the criterion*. Thus, if I use a driver's examination to predict "good" and "bad" drivers, and 99% of the good drivers never have an accident, the test has "criterion validity"; the criterion of safe driving has validated the test. However, if 95% of those passing the driving test turn out to be "bad" drivers (as indicated by number of accidents, number of tickets, etc.), the test lacks criterion validity, and it's "back to the drawing boards." Of course, assuming that we do not issue licenses to those failing the tests, we have no way of checking on their performance (unless a few drive illegally, and we know it); thus, we cannot say how many "bad" drivers were really good, and should have been issued a license. This was the problem with the Air Force test for pilots. Without studying the "failures" on our test, we have not really established criterion validity in its fullest sense: the fully valid test should always "pass those who will succeed," and always "fail those who will not succeed"; if we don't let the "failures" play the game, we have no way of ascertaining whether the latter statement is verified.

A third type of validity exists, called "construct" validity, which is related to the verification of psychological and sociological theories. We will not treat it in this text.

## Research in the Physical and Behavioral Sciences

Research in the natural sciences, such as physics and chemistry, is often performed on inanimate objects. We measure the weights of things (e.g., the atomic weight of oxygen), and record their color or smell (e.g., copper sulfate yields a blue-colored solution, or the sulphides often have an unpleasant odor). The measurement techniques may become quite complex, as in the efforts of Michelson and other scientists in measuring the speed of light. However, the characteristics being measured are often clearly delineated, i.e., the characteristics of mass, density, velocity, and the like have agreed-upon definitions.

This is not always the case in studying human beings. Some of the characteristics of humans, such as age and sex, are very well defined. Others, such as achievement in math, are fairly well defined. Still others, such as "personality type" or "managerial style" are quite difficult to define. We next examine some of the questions involved in measuring things like achievement, aptitude, and attitude.

## Achievement, Aptitude, and Attitude

Tests can be used to measure various characteristics. Some of the most popular are knowledge about a subject, as in a classroom test, or attitudes toward a topic, such as the public polls in which people indicate their preferences for a certain political candidate. Some of the types of things we would like to measure are:

1. Achievement
2. Aptitude
3. Personality traits
4. Attitudes
5. Ideas

Achievement normally refers to the knowledge we have already gleaned. It refers to our ability to recognize, recall, and use certain facts and principles, for example, our ability to respond "1492" to the question "When did Columbus arrive in America?" Most school exams measure achievement.

Aptitudes refer to what we are capable of doing, e.g., when we say "he can be a great quarterback" or "she can be a good computer programmer." Aptitudes are closely bound up with achievement, because what we can do is often predicated on what we already have done, e.g., when we counsel someone on a career in mathematics because he or she has gotten straight A's in algebra, geometry, trigonometry, and calculus. Aptitudes are also tied up with a personality traits, as when we say that a person has the aptitude to be a good student because he or she has a high IQ.

Personality traits refer to some enduring characteristic of the person, as when we say that a person has a high IQ, or that a person is "conservative" or "happy."

Attitudes refer to a person's "feelings" or values toward an object, action, or institution, e.g., when we say that "she likes math" or "murder is bad."

Finally, by "ideas," we mean the mental concept or "connotation" that a given word has for a person—the "meaning" he or she attributes to the object, action, or institution denoted by that word. The meaning can be a set of features, e.g., when we say thus, that "school" connotes a "warm, friendly" thing to Johnny, but a "dull, boring" thing to Mary.

## The Objective Test

We have already given an example of the objective test in discussing the true-false test as an indicator. Objective tests are primarily used as achievement and/or aptitude tests. The close affinity between these two uses is seen in a test such as the College Entrance Examination Board (CEEB) exams, which are administered toward the end of high school. They are measuring "aptitude for success in college," but they certainly do so by measuring "achievement in high school." The distinction is one of "to what use the results will be put," i.e., a distinction of purpose, than it is a distinction in content. If I use the results to give you a grade on your high school work, I have given an "achievement" exam; if I use the results to say whether or not you should attend the local university, I am using the exam to measure "aptitude." The achievement tests are primarily "descriptive," while the aptitude tests are "predictive."

The primary advantage of objective tests is their "objectivity." No matter who does the scoring, or when, the results should be the same. This is not true of the "less objective" type of test, e.g., the essay. Objective tests also tend to be higher in reliability than the less objective method. Their main problem is with validity. Of the two types of validity that are involved, achievement tests are primarily concerned with content validity, i.e., "is the content of the test the same as the content of the curriculum?" This can usually be established by an "expert judge," or panel of judges. The aptitude test is more concerned with criterion or predictive validity: "Do the results of the test really predict success or nonsuccess on the variable we wish to predict?" Thus, if we use the CEEB to predict academic success in college, we would first have to select a criterion of academic success, for example, the QPA (quality point average) in college, then see if those who scored high on the CEEB exam also achieved a high QPA. If the exam turns out to be a good predictor, we say that it has criterion validity; if the exam turns out to be a bad predictor, it lacks criterion validity.

A final type of objective test that is of special interest in both the information and educational fields is the "diagnostic test." Instead of giving a single "pass-fail" score, such as 72%, an "aggregated" score, the diagnostic test attempts to distinguish among the various items on a test, so that we can make such statements as "the subject is doing well in math, but poorly in reading." This allows one to diagnose "areas of need," as well as to rank people in various categories. This diagnosis of a person's relative strength and weaknesses can then give direction to any attempts to "inform" the person in the areas needed.

## Attitude Scales

While objective tests are primarily geared to testing "cognitive" achievement and aptitude—what one "knows"—attitude scales attempt to assess "feelings" and "values"—a person's "affective" side.

## Cognitive Versus Affective Dimensions

While we may tend to associate information activities with the cognitive domain, there are equally important applications in the affective domain. As a first step in distinguishing these types of activities, we consider the definitions of the cognitive and affective domains as found in Bloom et al. (1974):

'cognitive' is used to include activities such as remembering and recalling knowledge, thinking, problem solving, creating... [p. 2]

the affective domain...includes objectives which describe changes in interest, attitudes, and values...the development of appreciations and adequate adjustment. [p. 7]

A typical cognitive task is the addition of two numbers. Success or failure on this type of task is most often assessed by achievement exams. The subject is administered a test including questions like:

Add:   5
      +3

If the subject responds "8," we assume that he can add two numbers; if he responds with any other number, we assume that he does not "know how to add two numbers."

An affective measurement would be a person's attitude toward smoking. Attitudes are normally assessed by observation (have we seen the subject smoke a cigarette, or buy a pack of cigarettes?), interview (we simply ask the subject if he or she smokes), or questionnaire (we have the subject answer yes or no to the question: do you smoke?). However, more specialized examples of "attitude scaling" exist, e.g., the Likert scale.

### The Likert Scale

In a Likert-type scale, the subject is presented with a statement:

> Smoking is unhealthy

and a "scale for responding":

Disagree ___ ___ ___ ___ ___ ___ ___ Agree
        1    2    3    4    5    6    7

She then places a mark in the blank that most closely describes her attitude about the statement. For example, a respondent who marks blank 1:

> Smoking is unhealthy

Disagree  X   ___ ___ ___ ___ ___ ___ Agree
        1    2    3    4    5    6    7

indicates that she strongly disagrees with the statement; she does *not* believe that smoking is unhealthy. Someone who strongly agrees with the statement would mark blank number 7. Someone who was undecided would mark blank 4. Someone who agrees that smoking is unhealthy, but not strongly, might mark blank 5 or 6. The number of blanks in the scale may be varied, although 3, 5, and 7 blanks are commonly used.

One of the major advantages of a Likert-type scale is that it gives us a quantitative assessment of a person's attitudes. Thus, someone who marks blank 7 on the above scale is more "antismoking" than someone who marks the blank 5. By administering the scale at two different times, we can measure how much a person's attitudes have changed; e.g., by administering the scale before and after a "nonsmoking" campaign, we can assess the impact of the campaign.

However, the use of a scale to measure attitudes introduces some serious problems. One of the problems is that people tend to have a "set way" of filling in scales. Thus, some people tend to "always agree" with statements, while others might tend to be "neutral." Some prefer to always mark the extremes, the 1 and 7 positions, while still others tend to mark the more central or "conservative" positions. These tendencies to respond in a "set way" might be called the respondent's "personal equation," and some attempt should be made to ascertain the equation for each respondent, so that their scores may be adjusted.

An even more serious problem is the individual's interpretation of the scale. What may constitute a neutral response for one person, may be an "extreme disagree" for another. Wyer (1974) gives a good example of how different interpretations of the "range" of a scale can give rise to widely disparate results (pp. 37ff). The simplest way to explain the problem is with regard to a physical example, judging weights. We ask two people to judge the weight of objects. One of these judges is very strong, and considers 20 lb. to be "medium." The other is somewhat weaker and judges 10 lb. to be "medium." In judging a 15-lb. weight, the strong judge will call the weight "light," while the weaker judge will call it "heavy," which tells a lot more about the judges than it does about the weight! The reader is encouraged to see Wyer for a more complete treatment of the problems of response categories and what effect they have on what we really learn from the administration of an attitude scale.

## The Semantic Differential

A scale that is similar in appearance to the Likert scale, but which is used to measure the meaning of concepts or ideas, is the semantic differential. Developed by Osgood, Suci, and Tannenbaum (1975) the semantic differential consists of one "concept," e.g., cigarette-smoking, followed by a series of adjectives that are arranged as antonyms or "opposite poles" (Figure 2.3). The subject marks the blanks that most describe his or her "feelings toward" or "ideas about" cigarette-smoking. Thus, somebody who marked the scale as shown in Figure 2.4a considers smoking to be slightly good, very beautiful, but also very weak, very sociable, somewhat graceful, dirty, neutral on masculine-feminine, active, hot, and neutral on wise-foolish. The responses are mixed. He or she might smoke, or at least be favorably disposed toward the activity, but with "reservations." Someone who marks the scale as shown in Figure 2.4b considers smoking to be very bad, very ugly, very weak, somewhat sociable, very graceful, very dirty, very feminine, passive, hot, and foolish. Whether or not the person

---

Cigarette smoking

| | | | | | | | | |
|---|---|---|---|---|---|---|---|---|
| good | —— | —— | —— | —— | —— | —— | —— | bad |
| ugly | —— | —— | —— | —— | —— | —— | —— | beautiful |
| weak | —— | —— | —— | —— | —— | —— | —— | strong |
| sociable | —— | —— | —— | —— | —— | —— | —— | unsociable |
| graceful | —— | —— | —— | —— | —— | —— | —— | awkward |
| clean | —— | —— | —— | —— | —— | —— | —— | dirty |
| masculine | —— | —— | —— | —— | —— | —— | —— | feminine |
| active | —— | —— | —— | —— | —— | —— | —— | passive |
| hot | —— | —— | —— | —— | —— | —— | —— | cold |
| wise | —— | —— | —— | —— | —— | —— | —— | foolish |

---

FIGURE 2.3

### Cigarette smoking

| good | | | X | | | | | bad |
|---|---|---|---|---|---|---|---|---|
| ugly | | | | | | | X | beautiful |
| weak | X | | | | | | | strong |
| sociable | X | | | | | | | unsociable |
| graceful | | X | | | | | | awkward |
| clean | | | | | | | X | dirty |
| masculine | | | | X | | | | feminine |
| active | | X | | | | | | passive |
| hot | X | | | | | | | cold |
| wise | | | | X | | | | foolish |

### Cigarette smoking

| good | | | | | | | X | bad |
|---|---|---|---|---|---|---|---|---|
| ugly | X | | | | | | | beautiful |
| weak | X | | | | | | | strong |
| sociable | | X | | | | | | unsociable |
| graceful | X | | | | | | | awkward |
| clean | | | | | | | X | dirty |
| masculine | | | | | | | X | feminine |
| active | | | | | X | | | passive |
| hot | X | | | | | | | cold |
| wise | | | | | | X | | foolish |

**FIGURE 2.4**

smokes, he or she does not seem to like it very much; we say "whether or not the person smokes," because the responses of "somewhat sociable, very graceful" and "very feminine" indicate that the respondent might be a woman who smokes because of social pressures while considering it a "very dirty" habit; or, the responses could indicate someone who does not smoke because of health and character reasons, "even though it looks nice."

The response of "very feminine" indicates that this person associates smoking with Virginia Slim-type ads, while a response of "very masculine" might indicate the Marlboro cowboy is uppermost in his or her mind.

The semantic differential is constructed with polar adjectives drawn from three general categories:

| | 1 | 2 | 3 | 4 | 5 | 6 | 7 | |
|---|---|---|---|---|---|---|---|---|
| Easy | __ | __ | X | 0 | __ | __ | __ | Difficult |
| Fast | __ | __ | X | 0 | __ | __ | __ | Slow |
| Happy | __ | X | 0 | __ | __ | __ | __ | Sad |
| Full | __ | X | 0 | __ | __ | __ | __ | Empty |
| Go | __ | __ | X | 0 | __ | __ | __ | Stop |
| Fun | __ | X | 0 | __ | __ | __ | __ | Work |
| Open | __ | X | 0 | __ | __ | __ | __ | Closed |
| Rich | __ | __ | X 0 | __ | __ | __ | __ | Poor |
| Interesting | __ | __ | X0 | __ | __ | __ | __ | Boring |
| Clear | __ | X | 0 | __ | __ | __ | __ | Confusing |

FIGURE 2.5 X = achievers; 0 = Non-achievers.

1. Evaluative (good-bad)
2. Potency (strong-weak)
3. Activity (fast-slow)

An abbreviated list, compiled from Osgood by Isaac and Michael (1975; p. 104), can be found in the appendix. Isaac and Michael (1976) also give a good example of how the semantic differential might be used to compare the conceptions of groups as well as individuals. The data represent the responses of eighth grade achievers and eighth grade nonachievers to the concept "school." The profile patterns are shown in Figure 2.5, with the achievers shown as $X$'s and the nonachievers as $O$'s. The more positive responses of the achievers are indicated visually in that all their answers lie to the left of those of the nonachievers. Whether the "dullness" of school causes the nonachievement, or whether the nonachievement causes the bad conception is another question.

## Projective Techniques

The final type of test that we consider is that which uses projective techniques. Probably the most well known of the projective techniques tests is the Rorschach inkblot test, in which the subject tells what he sees (his projection of himself into the inkblots) in the relatively unstructured figures. However, more conventional projective techniques are available, e.g., word association, wherein I say a word, and you respond with the first word that comes to mind; or "role-playing," wherein the experimenter assigns such roles as "boss" and "person applying for a job" to the subjects, then lets them "play them out." The supposed advantage of projective techniques is that they allow the "true inner person" to come out; their main disadvantage lies in the need to interpret just what the actions of this true inner person really indicate. Because of this difficulty in interpreting what usually amounts to a mass of unstructured data, projective techniques often show a lower reliability than other techniques. However, Webb et al. (1966) cite two interesting studies (Solley and Haigh, 1957, and Craddick,

1961) in which children were asked to draw Santa Claus, once before Christmas, and once after Christmas. The size of Santa in the pre-Christmas drawings was consistently larger than the size of Santa in the post-Christmas drawings. Thus, the children unconsciously projected their anticipations very clearly and concisely.

## Error in Measuring

No measure of a person's mind is going to be completely accurate. In fact, no measurement of anything is "perfect." Of course, some measurements will be better than others, but the point is that there will usually be some error in any measurement. Having examined the methods of collecting data, we will now look at some of the sources of error and some of the ways of estimating the amount of error in doing such data collection.

## Sources of Error

One of the most valuable pieces of information we can ever have about our efforts to collect data is a knowledge of the places we can go wrong and the ways in which our results can be misleading. There are three primary places that error or "variation" can creep into the process of collecting the data:

1. In the observer
2. In the observed
3. In the instrument used

We will examine these in turn.

## Variation in the Observer

An example of variation in results caused by variation in the observer can be seen most easily in the interview technique. A good interviewer can elicit responses—honest responses—to items that a more inept interviewer might not ascertain. Even with the same person conducting an interview at two different times, he or she might feel "chipper" while conducting the first interview, doing a fine job, but "tired" during the second interview, with less than spectacular results.

Another example of variation in the observer is given by Singer in his work *Experience and Reflection* (1959). It is the account of Bessel's discovery of the "personal equation" in taking measurements:

...In 1922, Bessel had before him a record of time observations made by different observers, each observation giving the time at which each of these observers noted the occurrence of one and the same event (the transit of a heavenly body across the crosshairs of his telescope)...

of a certain three observers, A, B, C,...A's times were systematically later than B's, and systematically earlier than C's. The result was only to be interpreted in one of two ways: either one observer was

right, the other two wrong; or the observations of at least two were
subject to a systematic error, varying with the observer in magnitude
or direction... The former had been the accepted interpretation before
Bessel's time, subject to the obvious embarrassment of deciding which
observer was right and wrong. The latter interpretation was proposed
by Bessell...Bessell...recognized every observer to be affected by
what he called a personal equation.

As we have noted, the personal equation is something every student is
aware of when he or she elects either to take a course because the professor is an "easy marker," or to skip a course because the professor is a
"tough marker."

### Variation in the Observed

Even machines don't perform with exactly the same efficiency every day.
But they are probably more stable than human beings. We have all experienced "off days," and, one hopes, even more often, we've experienced
days on which we "got up on the right side of the bed." A test administered to someone on a "good" day may give results quite different from the
same test administered to the same person on an "off" day.

More subtle than the variations in performance of a single individual
are the variations between individuals, called "individual differences."
While some of these differences are precisely what we want to measure,
e.g., differences in voting patterns between liberals and conservatives,
other differences can be confounding to our results. For example, in administering a questionnaire consisting of Likert scale-type questions, some
individuals may prefer strong statements, marking the 1 and 7 positions
more than the middle positions, while others may prefer to be more conservative, marking the middle positions more than the extremes. These
are the "personal equations" of the respondent. The respondent's interpretation of the scale is also a crucial factor, as in the case of the strong man
and the weak man judging the weight of the objects.

Another subtle problem can arise in research that calls for volunteers
to cooperate in an experiment. The type of person who responds to the call
for volunteers may be a member of a "select" group; e.g., some people
may be more curious, more exhibitionistic, more introspective, more "something" than the general population, and thus bias our results. This is
actually a problem in sampling and in the generalizability of results, and
can be overcome either by "adjusting" the results of the research, or by
eliminating the voluntary participation in favor of a random sample of
"conscripted" subjects when possible.

The learning of an individual can also have an effect when more than
one administration of a test is involved. For example, one method of testing
whether or not a particular lecture or class has had an effect on a student
is to give the student a test before the lecture (pretest) and a test after
the lecture (posttest) and compare the results. A better performance on
the posttest than on the pretest indicates that the lecture did have a
positive effect. However, it can be that the better performance on the
posttest was due to learning on the part of the individual *caused by the
pretest,* and that the lecture itself had little or no effect.

This type of change induced by the administration of the measurement instrument is particularly noticeable on tests administered to assess attitude change. Items answered "neutral" or "don't know" on the pretest may be answered more positively or negatively on the posttest, simply because the individual has thought about the issue as a result of his or her encounter with it on the pretest. Any treatments given to induce attitude change, e.g., propaganda letters, may have had no effect whatsoever.

Finally, as we indicated in our treatment of questionnaires and interviews, the respondent may deliberately falsify or withhold information, especially where such information is socially "loaded." Thus, someone who advocates war as a way to help the economy may not indicate his or her true feelings on a questionnaire; or a rapist may not indicate his true sexual behavior to even such investigators as Kinsey or Masters and Johnson.

## Variation in the Instrument

The problem of variation in the instrument is the problem of reliability: "If I give the same or a similar type test to the same person or group next week, will I get the same results?" One method of ascertaining reliability is the "test-retest" method. We make up what we feel to be "equivalent" forms of the same test, and administer both forms to the same group at two different times. If those who scored high on the first exam also score high on the second one, and those who scored low again score low, we consider the test to be "reliable." We say that the scores from the first test "correlate" with those from the second test. Of course, if we do give "equivalent forms" on two separate days, we must attempt to determine whether any variation in the results is due to unreliability in the test, or to learning (or forgetting) in the individual. The problem of reliability, like the problem of validity, is a complex one.

Another technique is to divide one test into two subparts, usually designating the odd-numbered questions as one part, and the even-numbered questions as the other part. If the person's performance on both "parts" is similar, we feel that the test is reliable. This method is called the "split-half" technique. It escapes the problem of learning and forgetting between tests, but introduces other problems, such as "balancing" the content and difficulty of the two halves.

## Systematic Versus Nonsystematic Error

Systematic error is error that occurs "in the same direction" all the time. An example would be the case of an "easy grader," a teacher who systematically gives higher grades than the average teacher. Another example is the variation in the response times of Bessell's observers; one observer was always fastest, another always slowest, the third always in the middle.

Systematic errors can be handled by simply adjusting the scores. Thus, if I know that an *A* was given by a particularly "easy" teacher, I could consider that *A* to be a *B*; I simply deflate the grade. In the case of the speedy Bessell observer, I add some figure to his responses in order to bring them into line with the middle or slow observer. (Or, I subtract some time from the slower respondent to bring him in line with the "speedy" one.)

Of course, adjustment brings in some problems of its own. For example, what if one of the "easy" teacher's students really did deserve an A? How do I distinguish between the "real" A's and the "inflated" A's? Tricky situations like these lead us to look for "corroborative" methods of data collection. For example, we might check all of the A students in the easy teacher's class with these students' performance in other classes; if they got A's in the other classes, maybe they deserved the A in this class. (Note that we say "maybe"; adjusting ratings is never easy.)

Nonsystematic errors are errors that occur by chance. They do not occur in the same direction for each individual every time. For example, one day I may wake up on the right side of the bed, and do abnormally well on an exam; another day, I wake up with a head cold, and do abnormally badly. The chance errors tend to cancel each other out, i.e., the good days are balanced by the bad days, so that we wind up with an "average performance" over the long run. These nonsystematic errors are handled by statistical techniques, e.g., by assigning people randomly to different groups, hoping that the randomness of the assignment will tend to "balance out" the people having good, bad, and in-between days.

## Summary

In this chapter we have given a cursory overview of the various methods and instruments used in doing research on individuals, groups, and events. The major categories of data collection treated have been:

1. Observation
2. Self-report
3. Report-by-others
4. Archival records

We have indicated the need for attaining reliability and validity in our measuring techniques, and have cautioned against the problem of reactivity, i.e., the researcher's efforts causing a person to act differently from the way he or she normally acts.

Reliability has been defined as "getting the same measurement" if the instrument is administered to the same person on two different occasions. Of course, the "same person" presents a problem, since people change over time. Validity was divided into two types: content validity, in which the items on the instrument are apropos to the topic or trait being measured; and criterion validity, which demands the instrument correctly predict success or failure on some related act, e.g., on the job or in school. We have distinguished between measurements of

1. Demographic data, such as birth date
2. Cognitive characteristics, such as knowledge of mathematics
3. Affective characteristics, such as liking or disliking mathematics

and indicated where certain measures are especially appropriate for measuring a given type of data: questionnaires or archival records for demographic data; achievement tests for cognitive data; and rating scales, like the Likert scale, for attitudinal data.

We have indicated some of the advantages and disadvantages of each instrument. For example, in observation we "see for ourselves," thus avoiding the truthfulness problem of self-report. But it takes time, money, and effort to personally observe, much of which can be eliminated by asking the person we are observing (self-report) or someone who knows the person (report-by-others) or even investigating records already assembled by someone else (archives). We have indicated the places where research can go wrong, e.g., with variation in the observer, variation in the observed, or variation in the instrument itself. We have also distinguished between systematic error and random error, with some hint as to how to handle these errors. Finally, we have emphasized that the instruments treated are "indicators," attempts to externalize the nonobservable inner state of a person's mind, since information is intimately tied to this mental organization.

## Related Readings

Bloom, Benjamin et al., eds. *Taxonomy of Educational Objectives: The Classification of Educational Goals: Handbook I: Cognitive Domain*, New York: David McKay Company, Inc., 1974.

Chapanis, Alphonse, *Research Techniques in Human Engineering*, Baltimore: Johns Hopkins Press, 1959.

Isaac, Stephen and Michael, William B., *Handbook in Research and Evaluation*, 1st ed., San Diego: EdITS Publishers, 1976.

Kerlinger, Fred N., *Equations of Behavioral Research*, 2nd ed., New York: Holt, Rinehart and Winston, Inc., 1973.

Krathwohl, David R., Bloom, Benjamin S., and Masia, Bertram B., *Taxonomy of Educational Objectives: The Classification of Educational Goals: Handbook II: Affective Domain*, New York: David McKay Company, Inc., 1974.

Labov, William, *Sociolinguistic Patterns*, Philadelphia: University of Pennsylvania Press, 1972.

Lindvall, C. M. and Nitko, Anthony J., *Measuring Pupil Achievement and Aptitude*, 2nd ed., New York: Harcourt Brace Jovanovich, Inc., 1975.

Osgood, Charles R., Suci, George J., and Tannenbaum, Percy H., *The Measurement of Meaning*, 1st ed., Urbana: University of Illinois Press, 1975.

Siegel, Sidney, *Nonparametric Statistics for the Behavioral Sciences*, New York: McGraw-Hill, 1956.

Singer, Edgar Arthur, in *Experience and Reflection*, C. West Churchman, ed. Philadelphia: University of Pennsylvania Press, 1959.

Webb, Eugene J., Campbell, Donald T., Schwartz, Richard D., and Sechrest, Lee, *Unobtrusive Measures: Nonreactive Research in the Social Sciences*, Chicago: Rand McNally, 1966.

Wyer, Robert S., Jr., *Cognitive Organization and Change: An Information Processing Approach*, New York: John Wiley, 1974.

# 3
# Data Analysis

## Objectives

Upon completion of this chapter, the student should be able to:

1. Calculate conditional and unconditional probabilities
2. Recognize dependent and independent data items
3. Distinguish between expected frequencies and observed frequencies
4. Calculate a chi-square value
5. Use a table of critical values to determine the significance of the chi-square value
6. Give an informal explanation of degrees of freedom

## Introduction

In some cases the result of the data collection stage is a direct answer to the question. Examples are questions about the attributes of some entity

> Q: What is the color of John's hair?
>
> A: Brown
>
> Q: What is the population of Pittsburgh?
>
> A: 423,938
>
> Q: When did Columbus sail to America?
>
> A: 1492

and of questions that are "inverted" in the sense that they list attributes or characteristics of the entity and seek the name of someone or something having these attributes:

> Q: Which of our employees has both typing ability and data processing background?
>
> A: John

TABLE 3.1

|  | F: was able to fly | $\overline{F}$: was not able to fly | Totals |
|---|---|---|---|
| P: passed test | 50 | 0 | 50 |
| $\overline{P}$: did not pass test | 0 | 50 | 50 |
| Totals | 50 | 50 | 100 |

Q:   Who are the students majoring in physics?

A:   _____ Mary   _____ Ruth   _____ Bill

Very often, however, the response to our question is data that is not a direct answer to our question, and that must be analyzed in order to produce the desired response. An example is the previously mentioned use of a paper and pencil test to discriminate among potential pilots by an air force or airline. The idea is that it is too expensive to let a "job applicant" test-fly a plane in order to judge his or her adequacy. Instead, we use other tests, cheaper and easier to implement, in order to collect data that "transfers" to the situation of piloting the plane. Among these is the paper and pencil test.

In order to validate the test, we administer it to all potential pilots, and judge them as passing or failing the written test. We then hire this entire batch of pilots and examine their flying ability. The results of the data collection phase are given in Table 3.1. The data shown are hypothetical, but the analysis would be the same on empirically obtained data.

The interpretation of the table is as follows:

- The rightmost row values are totals for the categories "passing the test" and "not passing the test." Thus, 50 people passed the test, 50 did not.
- The column totals give similar figures for the columnar variable, "ability to fly," which has two values "can fly" and "cannot." Again, 50 people can fly, 50 cannot.
- The total in the lower right-hand corner represents the "grand" total, all people involved in the study. The same 100 people both took the test and did the flying, hence, they are represented both in the row totals and in the column totals; the total "population" is 100, not 200.
- The "cell" numbers (50,0,0,50) represent the conjunction (intersection or "anding") of the data values on both variables. Thus, there are 50 people who passed the test and also could fly, and none who passed and were not able to fly. There is one cell for each possible combination of values (a cross-product of the values from variable A to those of variable B). Some of these potential combinations will be realized in the data (50 people passing and flying), but others may be empty, indicating that no one had this particular combination of values.

TABLE 3.2

|     | F   | $\bar{F}$ | T   |
|-----|-----|-----|-----|
| P   | 40  | 20  | 60  |
| $\bar{P}$ | 25  | 15  | 40  |
| T   | 65  | 35  | 100 |

The data shown here were chosen arbitrarily to allow visual interpretation, an "ideal" or extreme case. Other possible data configurations are more common. See Table 3.2, e.g., where 60 people passed the test and 40 did not; 65 people could fly and 35 could not. All four intersections have values: passed and could fly, 40; passed yet could not fly, 20; etc.) In a real application these data values would be determined empirically. Note that we indicate "passing" with a single letter P, "not passing" with a bar (negation) over the $P$: $\bar{P}$. Similarly, we use an $F$ for flying, and $\bar{F}$ for not flying.

Is the Test Any Good?

The question that interests us is: Is the test any good? Can we use it to make predictions about someone's flying ability? The answer in this set of data is that it is "perfect." If we look at the data in Table 3.1, we see that all the people who passed the test were able to fly, and those who failed it could not. The results of the test are a perfect predictor of flying ability.

Conditional and Unconditional Probability

In examining the test results, we can talk about two types of probability: the unconditional or absolute probability of a person having a given trait, and the conditional probability, meaning that a person is likely to have a particular trait because he or she is known to possess some other trait. In terms of the example, there are four unconditional probabilities:

p (passing the test)
p (not passing)
p (having the ability to fly)
p (not being able to fly)

These probabilities are calculated from the row and column totals. For the data given in Table 3.1, they are:

$$p(P) = \frac{50}{100} = \frac{1}{2}$$

$$p(\bar{P}) = \frac{50}{100} = \frac{1}{2}$$

$$p(F) = \frac{50}{100} = \frac{1}{2}$$

## TABLE 3.3

|  | Variable X | |  |
|---|---|---|---|
| Variable Y | Value A | Value B |  |
| Value C | 40 | 20 | 60 |
| Value D | 25 | 15 | 40 |
|  | 65 | 35 | 100 |

$$p(\overline{F}) = \frac{50}{100} = \frac{1}{2}$$

For the data in Table 3.3, the unconditional probabilities would be:

Variable Y

$$p(C) = \frac{60}{100} = .6$$

$$p(D) = \frac{40}{100} = .4$$

Variable X

$$p(A) = \frac{65}{100} = .65$$

$$p(B) = \frac{35}{100} = .35$$

The reader should note that within a variable the probabilities sum to 1:

$p(P) = \frac{1}{2}$

$p(\overline{P}) = \frac{1}{2}$    sum = 1

$p(C) = .6$

$p(D) = .4$    sum = 1

For two-valued variables, the probability of one value on a given variable can be deduced from the other value on that same variable:

$p(P) = \frac{1}{2}$

$p(\overline{P}) = 1 - p(P) = 1 - \frac{1}{2} = \frac{1}{2}$

$p(C) = .6$

$p(D) = 1 - .6 = .4$

The meaning of the transfer of information becomes clear in considering the conditional probabilities and their relationships to the unconditional probabilities. We now turn to that topic.

## A Notation for Conditional Probabilities

A conditional probability is the likelihood of an entity having a given trait knowing that it possesses another trait. In terms of our example, we wish to know the probability of a person's being able to fly given that we know he or she passed the pencil and paper test. The notation for this probability is:

$p(F \mid P)$

where the vertical bar represents the phrase "given that." The probability of a person's not being able to fly given that he or she passed the test is:

$p(\overline{F} \mid P)$

Similarly, the notations:

$p(P \mid F)$

$p(\overline{P} \mid F)$

represent the questions:

What is the probability that a person passed the test given that we know that he or she can fly (pilot a plane)?

and

What is the probability that a person did not pass the test given that he or she can fly?

Each value of one variable can be combined with each value of the other variable in stating conditional probabilities. Hence, for our data we could ask:

$p(P \mid F)$ $p(\overline{P} \mid F)$ $p(P \mid \overline{F})$ $p(\overline{P} \mid \overline{F})$

$p(F \mid P)$ $p(\overline{F} \mid P)$ $p(F \mid \overline{P})$ $p(\overline{F} \mid \overline{P})$

or 2*2 combinations in each direction (given passed, given can fly). A 3-by-2 table (Table 3.4) would have six possible equations in each direction. Given variable X with values D and E, we have the conditional probabilities:

$p(A \mid D)$, $p(B \mid D)$, $p(C \mid D)$, $p(A \mid E)$, $p(B \mid E)$, $p(C \mid E)$

Given variable Y with values A, B, and C, we have:

$p(D \mid A)$, $p(E \mid A)$, $p(D \mid B)$, $p(E \mid B)$, $p(D \mid C)$, $p(E \mid C)$

TABLE 3.4

| | Variable X | | |
|---|---|---|---|
| Variable X | A | B | C |
| D | | | |
| E | | | |

Not all of the questions will be of interest. We will perform calculations only on those items that are of interest. In our example, this is primarily $p(F|P)$, the probability that a person has the ability to fly given that he or she has passed the written test. As the example indicates, the "given" portion of the conditional probabilities is usually dictated by the situation. We will have data on the written results before we allow (or don't allow) someone to fly a plane, hence we wish to predict from the test results (the known) to the flying ability (the unknown).

### Calculating the Conditional Probabilities

To calculate the probability of flying given that we know someone passed the test, we restrict our attention to the row involved with passing the test (Figure 3.1). We ignore the data for the total population and concentrate on this subject.

There are 50 people in the subset of people passing the test (row total). Of these 50 people, all 50 were able to fly:

$$p(F|P) = \frac{50}{50} = 1.00$$

Similarly, none of the 50 were unable to fly:

$$p(\overline{F}|P) = \frac{0}{50} = 0.00$$

To calculate the conditional probabilities we use the cell values of the given subset, placing these values over the row (or column) total for that subset.

For the second set of hypothetical data (Table 3.3), the conditional probabilities of A and B, knowing that a person (or object) possesses trait C on variable X are:

$$p(A|C) = \frac{40}{60} = .67$$

$$p(B|C) = \frac{20}{60} = .33$$

If the prediction were from the trait A on variable Y to the variable X, we would have:

$$p(C|A) = \frac{40}{65}$$

$$p(D|A) = \frac{25}{65}$$

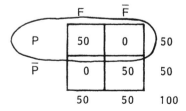

FIGURE 3.1

The reader should compute $p(P|F)$, $p(\overline{P}|F)$, $p(C|B)$, $p(D|B)$ and $p(A|D)$, $p(B|D)$ as an exercise.

Note that the conditional probabilities within a subset also sum to 1:

$p(F|P) = 1.00$  
$\quad\quad\quad\quad\quad\quad$ sum $= 1$  
$p(\overline{F}|P) = 0.00$

$p(A|C) = .67$  
$\quad\quad\quad\quad\quad\quad$ sum $= 1$  
$p(B|C) = .33$

This is because we are treating the subsets as if they were the entire population. It is the population of those who have the trait of interest.

## Interpretation of the Conditional Probabilities

As the above discussion indicates, the unconditional probability of a person being able to fly a plane in our population of 100 was 1/2 (50 of the 100 subjects possessed the ability to fly). This is the probability of "a person taken at random" being able to fly, with no other knowledge about that person.

However, given the information that the person did indeed pass the written test, the probability of that person being able to fly became 1.00 or certitude.

$$p(F|P) = \frac{50}{50} = 1.00$$

The knowledge about passing the test increases our knowledge about the ability to fly. This is what we mean by the transfer of information. Knowing that a person failed the test also tells us about the ability to fly.

$$p(F|\overline{P}) = \frac{0}{50} = 0.00$$

That is, we are certain that he or she cannot fly.

## Independence and Dependence

The transfer of information from one data value to another is based on the dependence of the data items. When data items are independent, knowledge of one item has no effect on the knowledge about the other item. An example would be the data of Table 3.5. In this case, the probability "in the general population" of a person being able to fly is 1/2:

$$p(F) = \frac{50}{100} = .50$$

Restricting our attention to the subset of people passing the written test, the conditional probability $p(F|P)$ is still 1/2.

$$p(F|P) = \frac{25}{50} = \frac{1}{2}$$

$$p(\overline{F}|P) = \frac{25}{50} = \frac{1}{2}$$

TABLE 3.5

|  | F | $\overline{F}$ | Total |
|---|---|---|---|
| P | 25 | 25 | 50 |
| $\overline{P}$ | 25 | 25 | 50 |
| Total | 50 | 50 | 100 |

Given the information about passing the test, we know nothing further about the ability to fly. The data on passing the test has told us nothing.

## Independent Data: No Prediction

Data items that are independent (such as the 25-25-25-25 table) offer no ability to predict from the occurrence of one data item to the occurrence of the other data item. That is, the probability of occurrence of the second item (here flying ability) is the same whether or not we have ascertained the data value for a person on the other data item. No "better prediction" can be made. In terms of statistics, the data are not correlated. In terms of the transfer of information, we say that the first item is not a predictor of the second.

## The Test for Independence

The test for independence is the comparison between the unconditional probability and the conditional probability of an event happening or an object possessing a certain trait. In the case in which they are equal

$$p(F) \quad = \frac{1}{2}$$

$$p(F \mid P) = \frac{1}{2}$$

the data elements (variables) are independent and no prediction can be made from one to the other. If the conditional probability is unequal to the unconditional probability

$$p(F) \quad = \frac{1}{2}$$

$$p(F \mid P) = 1.00$$

the data elements are dependent and a prediction can be made from one to the other. Here the knowledge of the person's passing the test "enhances" our estimate of the likelihood that he or she can pilot a plane. In fact, the enhancement is perfect, raising our "equiprobable guess" (1/2, 1/2 for F vs $\overline{F}$) to certitude (1.00 for F, 0.0 for $\overline{F}$).

The transfer can also diminish the likelihood of the second data value's occurrence:

$$p(F) \quad = \frac{1}{2}$$

$$p(F \mid \overline{P}) = 0.00$$

This still enables a prediction. It is just that the prediction is that the second attribute is less likely to occur given the known value on the first attribute. In fact, with the conditional probability of zero, the assertion is that the second attribute (flying ability) cannot be possessed by the person given the knowledge that he or she failed the written test. Because the data on the written test predicts flying ability or the lack thereof with certitude, we called the test a perfect predictor. Usually the predictors will be imperfect, raising or diminishing our probability estimates, but not to the extent of certitude. An example are the data in Table 3.3. The probability of C occurring is 6/10

$$p(C) = \frac{60}{100} = .6$$

but the probability of C occurring given that A has occurred is:

$$p(C \mid A) = \frac{40}{60} = .67$$

Since the two probabilities are not equal, the data elements are dependent, and the occurrence of A slightly increases our estimate that the object or person will also possess trait C (.60 to .67). Similarly, the possession of trait B diminishes the likelihood of the entity possessing trait C

$$p(C) \quad = .60$$

$$p(C \mid B) = \frac{20}{60} = .33$$

quite a considerable drop. Whether or not the change in likelihood is "practical," i.e., can be applied with significant changes in the probabilities, depends on the magnitude of the dependence. (The word *significant* has been used here solely in its sense of an English word meaning "of note.") Statistical tests can be applied to measure the degree of dependence, and its "statistical significance."

### Independent Data

Another example of independent data, a little more realistic than the 25-25 table is Table 3.6.

TABLE 3.6

|  | M | N | Totals |
|---|---|---|---|
| S | 28 | 12 | 40 |
| T | 42 | 18 | 60 |
| Total | 70 | 30 | 100 |

The probability of M occurring is

$$p(M) = \frac{70}{100} = .7$$

and the probability of M occurring given that S or T occurred is still .7

$$p(M \mid S) = \frac{28}{40} = \frac{7}{10} = .7$$

$$p(M \mid T) = \frac{42}{60} = \frac{7}{10} = .7$$

so that the occurrence of M is independent of the values obtained on the S/T variable. Similarly,

$$p(S) = \frac{40}{100} = .4$$

$$p(S \mid M) = \frac{28}{70} = \frac{4}{10} = .4$$

$$p(S \mid N) = \frac{12}{30} = \frac{4}{10} = .4$$

so that the occurrence of S is independent of the values obtained for the M/N variable.

## Relationship Between the Margin Totals and Cell Frequencies

If we examine the independent data in Table 3.5, we see that the cell frequencies are obtained from the product of the row total and the column total for that cell, divided by the grand total. For example, for cell (1,1), we have:

$$\frac{RT * CT}{GT} = \frac{40 * 70}{100} = \frac{2800}{100} = 28$$

Similarly, for cell (1,2), we have:

$$\frac{RT * CT}{GT} = \frac{40 * 30}{100} = 12$$

The reader should obtain the values for cells (2,1) and (2,2).

The reason that the frequencies reflect the row and column marginal total values is related to probability theory and the independence of the events. The row and column totals can be used to compute a probability for the individual data values:

$$p(S) = \frac{40}{100}$$

$$p(T) = \frac{60}{100}$$

$$p(M) = \frac{70}{100}$$

$$p(N) = \frac{30}{100}$$

The cell values represent the joint occurrence of both data values. For independent events, the probability of this joint occurrence is the product of the individual probabilities.

$$p(S \text{ and } M) = \frac{40}{100} * \frac{70}{100}$$

$$p(S \text{ and } N) = \frac{40}{100} * \frac{30}{100}$$

$$p(T \text{ and } M) = \frac{60}{100} * \frac{70}{100}$$

$$p(T \text{ and } N) = \frac{60}{100} * \frac{30}{100}$$

Thus, the probability of S and M occurring is .4 * .7 or .28. The cell values, however, are not probabilities, but frequencies or counts. The count can be taken by multiplying the total population figure (100) by the probability of the joint occurrence:

$$\text{Cell frequency, SM} = \frac{40}{100} * \frac{70}{100} * 100$$

which simplifies to:

$$\frac{40 * 70}{100}$$

Thus, the shorthand calculation is:

$$\frac{\text{Row total} * \text{column total}}{\text{Total population}}$$

With independent data, the totals in the cells will always be equal to the number obtained by this calculation. With dependent data, the cell frequencies will be "other than" the value of this calculation.

## Expected Values

We have looked at cell frequencies and probabilities, conditional and unconditional, to determine whether data are dependent or independent. Dependent data is a source of transfer of information from one variable to the other. Independent data does not allow such a transfer of information; one variable tells us nothing new or extra about the other.

Statisticians attack the same set of data from a slightly different point of view. They are interested, as are we, in determining whether two variables show a measure of association (dependency). The method of determining the presence of dependency is to compare data that has been empirically collected with a "theoretical" distribution. In terms of our data tables, the theoretical distribution is the distribution that would result from independent data items, the cell frequencies that we have just examined. Given the row and column totals (Figure 3.2a), the statistician computes the "expected" frequencies, or "independent" cell values (Figure 3.2b), where the symbol $f_e$ stands for expected frequency. The statistici-

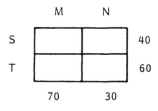

(a)

| | M | N | |
|---|---|---|---|
| S | $f_e=28$ | $f_e=12$ | 40 |
| T | $f_e=42$ | $f_e=18$ | 60 |
| | 70 | 30 | 100 |

(b)

| | M | N | |
|---|---|---|---|
| S | $f_o=10$ | $f_o=30$ | 40 |
| T | $f_o=60$ | $f_o=0$ | 60 |
| | 70 | 30 | |

(c)

FIGURE 3.2

an then takes the observed frequencies and sees if they deviate from the independent values. For example, with the data of Figure 3.2c, the "observed" frequencies ($f_o$) are quite different from the "expected" frequencies. We can even compute how far off the observed frequencies are from the expected (Table 3.7a). As the reader can see, the deviations from the expected values "cancel out" if summed.

$$- 18 + 18 + 18 - 18 = 0$$

This can be avoided if we take the absolute value of the deviations.

$$18 + 18 + 18 + 18 = 72$$

Observed data that are the same as the expected values (Table 3.6) will have "zero deviation" (Table 3.7b) so that the sum of the absolute value of the deviations gives us an idea of how far the observed frequencies (empirically collected data) deviate from the independent case. This is another way of saying how closely the data items are dependent on each other or how closely they are associated.

TABLE 3.7

(a)

| Cell | $f_o$ | $f_e$ | Difference $f_o - f_e$ |
|------|-------|-------|------------------------|
| SM | 10 | 28 | −18 |
| SN | 30 | 12 | +18 |
| TM | 60 | 42 | +18 |
| TN | 0 | 18 | −18 |

(b)

| Cell | $f_o$ | $f_e$ | Difference $f_o - f_e$ |
|------|-------|-------|------------------------|
| SM | 28 | 28 | 0 |
| SN | 12 | 12 | 0 |
| TM | 42 | 42 | 0 |
| TN | 18 | 18 | 0 |
| | | | 0 |

## Chi-Square

One calculation performed to test the difference between an observed distribution and a theoretical distribution is called chi-square. The difference between the observed value and the theoretical value is squared

$$(o-e)^2$$

and this value is divided by the expected frequency

$$\frac{(o-e)^2}{e}$$

The squaring of the difference performs two functions:

1. It provides a positive value, so that the deviations do not sum to zero.
2. It causes greater weight to be given to large deviations than to small ones.

A deviation of 4 would result in the square 16. A deviation of 8, only twice as large, would result in a square of 64, four times the value of $4^2$. Deviations three times as large (12) or four times as large (16) would result in equations that are nine times as large (144 to 16) and sixteen times as large (256 to 16).

The use of the expected frequencies in the denominator allows for "normalization" of the deviations. A deviation of 4 with respect to an expected value of 4

$$\frac{(8 - 4)^2}{4} = \frac{4^2}{4} = \frac{16}{4} = 4$$

is relatively larger than a deviation of 4 with an expected value of 1000.

$$\frac{(1004 - 1000)^2}{1000} = \frac{4^2}{1000} = \frac{16}{1000} = .016$$

The idea is that the "relative size" or importance of the deviation depends on the size of the number we expected to obtain. It is a better indication of the strength of deviation than the absolute size.

The same calculation

$$\frac{(o - e)^2}{e}$$

is performed for each cell, the results being summed. A simple notation for summation is the Greek letter sigma ($\Sigma$) so that the formula is some-times written

$$\chi^2 = \sum_{i=1}^{\eta} \frac{(o_i - e_i)^2}{e_i}$$

where the subscript i is used to "count off" as many cells as we have (for us n = 4). The symbol $\chi$ is the Greek letter chi, so the expression $\chi^2$ is "chi-square."

For the data of Figure 3.2c, the calculation would be:

$$\frac{(10 - 28)^2}{28} + \frac{(30 - 12)^2}{12} + \frac{(60 - 42)^2}{42} + \frac{(0 - 18)^2}{18}$$

$$= \frac{18^2}{28} + \frac{18^2}{12} + \frac{18^2}{42} + \frac{18^2}{18} = 64.3$$

The final result of the calculation is called the chi-square statistic. Tables have been developed to aid in the interpretation of the $\chi^2$ value, indicating the values at which the deviation can be considered "statistically signifi-cant." The tables are based on the likelihood of obtaining certain values of chi-square.


## Determining the Significance of the Deviation

The tables used to interpret the $\chi^2$ value are derived from a theoretical distribution, called the $\chi^2$-square distribution. What this distribution gives is the relative distribution of deviation values. The $\chi^2$-square distribution is really a series of distributions, each varying in the number of degrees of freedom in the data. The essence of the theory is that data with fewer degrees of freedom will experience less chance deviation than data that allow many degrees of freedom. For our data there is only one degree of freedom:

(R − 1) * (C − 1) =

(2 − 1) * (2 − 1)  = 1 * 1 = 1

where

R = rows, C = columns

so that we will examine our obtained $\chi^2$ value against the $\chi^2$ distribution for df = 1. In a table of $\chi^2$ values for df = 1, we will find such entries as:

$\chi^2{}_{0.05}$      $\chi^2{}_{0.01}$

3.841        6.635

This indicates that a value as great as 3.841 would occur only 5% of the time by chance. A value of 6.635 would occur only 1% of the time by chance. Our value, 64.3, far exceeds these values, so it is "significant" at these levels. The smaller number (.01) indicates greater significance, a rarer event. We would say that the value of 64.3 is significant at the 0.01 level. This implies that it is also significant at the 0.05 level. It may be that it is also significant at the 0.001 level (i.e., happens once in 1,000 times by chance), but the tables consulted by the author (Freund, 1981) did not have data available for this level.

The purpose of the significance level is to indicate the rarity of the event in data that are truly independent. Due to the vagaries of drawing a sample, it is possible that the observed frequencies may deviate from the expected frequencies by as much as 6.635 by chance alone, but *not very often*.

The "not very often" is more definitely delineated by a probability: once in 100 trials (or samples). This is called the "alpha" ($\alpha$) level of the significance value. Since we would expect $\chi^2$ value giving an alpha value of .01 to occur in only one out of 100 samples "by chance," we could conclude that the value is probably "not due to chance." This is the same as saying that the data are very likely dependent, or that the assumption of independent data items should be "rejected" as too improbable with a $\chi^2$ value of 64.3.

It could be that the value obtained was a chance occurrence and that our assertion that the data are related is incorrect. However, the chance of our being wrong in this manner is slight. We thus "infer" that there is some mechanism associating the data values, and indicate the probability of our being wrong by the alpha level.

## The Degrees of Freedom

The reason the degrees of freedom for the row with two cells = 1 can be seen from an examination of the row totals and the cell values. For the 2 * 2 table of Figure 3.2c, shown again in Figure 3.3, the entry of the value 10 in the top left cell (Figure 3.3) fixes the value for the top right cell at 30; otherwise, the row will not sum to 40. In fact, fixing the one cell at 10 determines the values of all three remaining cells.

For TM, the sum of 10 and N(TM) must equal 70. (N = "number of" or "frequency of")
Therefore, N(TM) = 60.

For SN, the sum of 10 and N(SN) = 40.
Therefore, N(SN) = 30.

|   | M | N |   |
|---|---|---|---|
| S | 10 |   | 40 |
| T |   |   | 60 |
|   | 70 | 30 |   |

FIGURE 3.3

```
_____
                          60
_____
```
(a)

```
_____
   10                     60
_____
```
(b)

```
_____
   10      20             60
_____
```
(c)

FIGURE 3.4

For TN, the sum of N(SN) or 30 and N(TN) must equal 30. Therefore, N(TN) = 0.

A row of three cells would have (C-1) or two degrees of freedom. For example, given the row total 60 in Figure 3.4a, the first cell may be anything up to 60, say 10 (Figure 3.4b), and, given the 10, the second cell may be anything between 0 and 50, say 20 (Figure 3.4c). The value of the third cell is now fixed at 30 (no freedom), so that there were two "free values," or two degrees of freedom.

Of course, the cell values are not arrived at arbitrarily, but by the results of data collection. It is only in the estimation of the degrees of freedom that we consider what (how many) values "might be free." The considerations for a column of values are similar to those of the row values, a given column having (r-1) degrees of freedom.

The degrees of freedom for the entire matrix is the product of these two values. Hence, the 5 * 4 table of Figure 3.5 would have (5-1) * (4-1) = 4 * 3 = 12 degrees of freedom.

The interpretation of the degrees of freedom is that a larger df allows more variability in the data due to chance factors alone. Hence, the chi-square values for larger df are also larger in order to attain a given level of significance, as the following discussion indicates.

FIGURE 3.5

TABLE 3.8 (Values obtained from Freund)

| D.f. | $\chi^2 0.5$ | $\chi^2 0.1$ |
|------|------|------|
| 1 | 3.841 | 6.635 |
| 2 | 5.991 | 9.210 |
| 3 | 7.815 | 11.345 |
| 4 | 9.488 | 13.277 |
| 5 | 11.070 | 15.086 |
| . | . |
| . | . |
| . | . |

## Behavior of the $\chi^2$ Distribution

If we look at the values in a table of "significant" $\chi^2$-square values (Table 3.8) we see that the values for an alpha level of .01 are always greater than the values for an alpha level of .05 at the same degrees of freedom. This reflects the fact that large deviations are less likely "due to chance alone." The larger the deviation, the more significant it is.

Also, the values increase in a given column, i.e., for a given alpha level, higher degrees of freedom require larger deviations to be considered significant. The greater number of degrees of freedom indicates more cells in the table, more sources for variation from the expected values. With more sources of chance variation, the size of a significant deviation, a deviation not construed as occurring "by chance" must be larger.

## Using $\chi^2$

The ways in which the $\chi^2$ distribution is used are numerous enough to defy any listing.

One type of problem familiar to any consumer is the following, adapted from Freund. Samples of various automobile tires (or TVs, microcomputers, etc.) are taken. Out of three samples of 200 products taken from three different manufacturers, the following number of defective items are found:

A: 10
B: 25
C: 5

The question is "Do the proportions of defective products vary in a way that indicates that one manufacturer is better than another?" or, alternatively, "Could the proportions have occurred by chance?" In terms of a "crossbreaks" table, the data would be displayed as shown in Table 3.9. The "row by column" table is called a crossbreak because it "breaks out" the data by "crossing" the values of one variable, quality of merchandise (values defective, not defective), with the values of the other variable, manufacturer (values A, B, and C).

The tables are also called contingency tables. This reflects their relationship to the analysis of dependency between the variables by means of

TABLE 3.9

| Quality of Merchandise | Manufacturer | | | |
|---|---|---|---|---|
| | A | B | C | |
| Defective | 10 | 25 | 5 | 40 |
| Not defective | 190 | 175 | 195 | 560 |
| | 200 | 200 | 200 | 600 |

conditional probabilities. The count for the value defective for the variable quality is 10 *given* that the manufacturer is A (variable manufacturer has value A). The "given" part can be rephrased in English as "contingent upon the manufacturer being A, we can expect the number of defectives to be 10 in this set of data." Or, more simply "if we are talking about A, they had 10 defectives in this lot." The label "contingency tables" is derived from this use of the word *contingency* in English.

### The Analysis

Since the sample sizes of all companies are the same (200 tires each), the calculation of the expected number of defective items is straightforward. We multiply the absolute probability of being defective (40/600) times the sample size

$$\frac{40 * 200}{600} = 13 \frac{1}{3}$$

so that data indicating "equal quality" of the tires (in terms of proportion of defectives) for each company would be that shown in Table 3.10. The calculation of $\chi^2$ for our obtained data would be

$$\frac{(10 - 13\ 1/3)^2}{13\ 1/3} + \frac{(25 - 13\ 1/3)^2}{13\ 1/3} + \frac{(5 - 13\ 1/3)^2}{13\ 1/3}$$

$$+ \frac{(190 - 186\ 2/3)^2}{186\ 2/3} + \frac{(175 - 186\ 2/3)^2}{186\ 2/3} + \frac{(195 - 186\ 2/3)^2}{186\ 2/3}$$

$$= \frac{(-3\ 1/3)^2}{13\ 1/3} + \frac{(11\ 2/3)^2}{13\ 1/3} + \frac{(-8\ 1/3)^2}{13\ 1/3}$$

$$+ \frac{(3\ 1/3)^2}{186\ 2/3} + \frac{(-11\ 2/3)^2}{186\ 2/3} + \frac{(8\ 1/3)^2}{186\ 2/3} \approx 17.4$$

TABLE 3.10

| | A | B | C |
|---|---|---|---|
| Defective | 13 1/3 | 13 1/3 | 13 1/3 |
| Not defective | 186 2/3 | 186 2/3 | 185 2/3 |

For two degrees of freedom

$$(R - 1) * (C - 1) = (2 - 1) * (3 - 1) = 1 * 2 = 2$$

The value of 17.4 is significant at the .01 level; hence, the hypothesis that there is no difference between the companies should be rejected. There seems to be "some connection" or association between the company and the number of defective tires.

## Just Arithmetic

The reader who is sometimes taken aback by formulas and lengthy calculations—as the author often is despite having studied and taught mathematics —should be assured that the above calculation involves nothing more than arithmetic. The mathematically inclined may skip this section.

It is probably simpler to do the arithmetic by converting all the values to fractions. Also, since the squaring of a number eliminates any negative signs, we omit them. The result of converting to fractions is:

$$\frac{(10/3)^2}{40/3} + \frac{(35/3)^2}{40/3} + \frac{(25/3)^2}{40/3}$$

$$+ \frac{(10/3)^2}{560/3} + \frac{(35/3)^2}{560/3} + \frac{(25/3)^2}{560/3}$$

The fact that the numerator repeats for each cell in the "vertical" direction and that the denominators are the same for each "row" will cause us to perform fewer calculations. We need square only three numbers. The results are:

$$\frac{(100/9)}{40/3} + \frac{(1225/9)}{40/3} + \frac{(625/9)}{40/3}$$

$$+ \frac{(100/9)}{560/3} + \frac{(1225/9)}{560/3} + \frac{(625/9)}{560/3}$$

Since we now have "two sets" of common denominators, we can add the numerators of these groups together, arriving at

$$\frac{1950/9}{40/3} + \frac{1950/9}{560/3}$$

or

$$\frac{1950}{9} * \frac{3}{40} + \frac{1950}{9} * \frac{3}{560}$$

cancellation yields

$$\frac{65}{4} + \frac{65}{56} = 16.25 + 1.16$$

$$= 17.41 \approx 17.4$$

The reader should note the form of the partial result.

$$\frac{65}{4} + \frac{65}{56}$$

The first term comes from row 1 of the original data, the second term from row 2. This observation will come in handy shortly.

## Proportions Versus Numbers

We indicated that we were testing the proportion of defective products here. Hence, the total number of items in the sample is relevant. An alternative calculation could have been applied if the data had been reported in proportions

| A | B | C |
|---|---|---|
| $\frac{10}{200} = .05$ | $\frac{25}{200} = .125$ | $\frac{5}{200} = .025$ |

by comparing this obtained distribution of proportions with the theoretical "expected proportion" under the assumption (hypothesis) of "no difference." The assumption of "no difference" is often called the null hypothesis, from the use of the phrase "no difference," although not all null hypotheses assume no difference. The more generic term might be the "tested hypothesis." The theoretical expectation is taken from the proportion of defective items in the entire population, here

$$\frac{40}{600} = \frac{1}{15} = .067$$

Hence, we would compare the obtained proportions

| A | B | C |
|---|---|---|
| .05 | .125 | .025 |

with the expected proportions

| A | B | C |
|---|---|---|
| .067 | .067 | .067 |

"under the assumption of no difference in proportions." The results would be equivalent to those found here with the use of the frequency counts. In fact, for more than two proportions one test is to convert the proportions to counts (by using the sample size) and use chi-square! (See Runyon and Haber, 1982.)

## Other Questions

One might be tempted, however, to compare just the number of defective items

| A | B | C | Total |
|---|---|---|-------|
| 10 | 25 | 5 | 40 |

not considering the number of nondefective parts. This analysis is valid, but it answers a different question than the above analysis. That this is so can be seen from the form of the chi-square calculation when reduced to its two "row parts." The expression is:

TABLE 3.11

| Obtained | 190 | 165 | 175 | 560 |
|---|---|---|---|---|
| Expected | 183 1/3 | 183 1/3 | 183 1/3 | 560 |

$$\frac{65}{4} + \frac{65}{56}$$

When restricting our attention to the number of defective items alone, we would calculate only the first term of this expression. The degrees of freedom would be the same (3 − 1 = 2), so the derivation of a different value with the same df cannot possibly be answering the same question.

When restricting attention to the defective products alone, the obtained data are:

|  | A | B | C | Total |
|---|---|---|---|---|
| Defectives | 10 | 25 | 5 | 40 |

If the number of defectives were equally distributed, the expected distribution of defective items would be:

|  | A | B | C |
|---|---|---|---|
| Defectives | $13\frac{1}{3}$ | $13\frac{1}{3}$ | $13\frac{1}{3}$ |

The calculation of the chi-square statistic would be

$$\frac{(10 - 13\ 1/3)^2}{13\ 1/3} + \frac{(25 - 13\ 1/3)^2}{13\ 1/3} + \frac{(5 - 13\ 1/3)^2}{13\ 1/3}$$

$$= \frac{100/9}{40/3} + \frac{1225/9}{40/3} + \frac{625/9}{40/3}$$

$$= \frac{1950/9}{40/3} = \frac{65}{4}$$

The initial question asked whether the *proportions* varied in a "significant way." The proportions are:

$$\frac{10}{200}, \quad \frac{25}{200}, \quad \frac{5}{200}$$

The second analysis restricts attention only to defective products. It considers the defective items as the total relevant entities, and looks for a difference in these frequencies, but does not consider the number of non-defective items, i.e., it ignores the sample size.

In considering only the defective products, the value of the chi-square statistic will be significant, since 65/4, or 16.25, is still quite large. However, if we had concentrated on the number of nondefective products (Table 3.11), the result would be the second term of the equation, 65/56 or 1.16. This would *not* be significant. Indeed, the question we ask and the analysis we perform in order to answer the question do make a difference.

TABLE 3.12

| Person | Attitude before campaign | Attitude after campaign |
|--------|--------------------------|-------------------------|
| 1 | M | M |
| 2 | M | L |
| 3 | M | M |
| 4 | L | L |
| 5 | M | M |
| 6 | M | M |
| 7 | L | M |
| 8 | M | M |

## McNemar's Test

One might conclude that one should always consider the proportions, and not consider the counts. Yet, one example of the use of chi-square that is often given in considering "related samples" is the McNemar test (see McNemar, 1962; Siegel, 1956).

The essence of the situation being studied is that some "treatment" has been applied to a group of people. For example, we may have polled people as to their attitudes on some issue (I prefer more movies in the Student Union on weekdays vs. I prefer fewer movies...); we then show a film, have an advertising campaign, or some other "treatment," then "ask again." The test looks for a difference in the number of people who change from "more to less" versus those who change from "less to more."

Say the data is similar to that shown in Table 3.12. The data would be arranged in a table as shown in Figure 3.6a. We had five persons "remain" in the opinion "more" (subjects 1, 3, 5, 6, 8); one switch from more to less (subject 2); one switch from less to more (subject 7); and one remain in the opinion less (subject 4). If we concentrate on the number of

|       | More | Less |
|-------|------|------|
| More  | 5    | 1    |
| Less  | 1    | 1    |

Figure 3.6(a)

| to More → Less | to Less → More | |
|----------------|----------------|---|
| 1              | 1              | 2 |

FIGURE 3.6

"switchers," we see the same number go from "more to less" as from "less to more" (Figure 3.6b). Without computation this should show "no difference." The McNemar test performs this calculation. It takes the total number (count) of people changing their views, here two, then takes half this as the expected value of the number changing in either direction, here one-half of two (or one), and looks for a significant deviation from this expected value in one direction or another. It considers only the two cells that indicate "switching one's opinion," hence, it would calculate the statistic (value derived from the data)

$$\frac{1 - 1}{1} + \frac{1 - 1}{1} = \frac{0}{1} + \frac{0}{1} = 0$$

The value of zero cannot indicate a statistically significant difference between the two groups (switch from for to against, switch from against to for), since it indicates "no difference." We do not need to look for the "critical value" (value at which one declares an obtained value statistically significant) in a table. The McNemar test computes the difference in number of changes. However, one can look at the data another way.

If we are interested in the proportion of the original opinion holders who switched, we have:

| More to less | Less to more |
|:---:|:---:|
| $\frac{1}{6}$ | $\frac{1}{2}$ |

There is a difference. Half the "less people" have switched, when only one-sixth of the "more people" have switched. In terms of proportions, the advertising campaign seems to have had "more effect" on the people previously "voting less."

If the proportions are "true" and current campus opinion is reflected in the count taken in a census of the campus

| More films | Fewer films |
|:---:|:---:|
| 60 | 140 |

and we want more films, an advertising campaign that results in a switch of one-sixth of the mores to less, will result in a "loss" of 10 more voters. However, converting half the current less voters to more will result in a net gain of 70 voters. We should be 60 votes better off

| Total Population After Ad | |
|:---:|:---:|
| More | Less |
| 120 | 80 |

and we have achieved our purposes.

## An Aid to Inference

The purpose of performing statistical tests is to aid us in the process of inference. One can "see" that data such as those depicted in Figure 3.7a are "striking" (significant) and that the results depicted in Figure 3.7b are not. But what about the cases in between, Figures 3.7c and 3.7d? When do these become significant? The statistical tests compute the proba-

|   | F | F̄ |
|---|---|---|
| P | 50 | 0 |
| P̄ | 0 | 50 |

(a)

|   | F | F̄ |
|---|---|---|
| P | 25 | 25 |
| P̄ | 25 | 25 |

(b)

| 26 | 24 |
|----|----|
| 24 | 26 |

(c)

| 30 | 20 |
|----|----|
| 20 | 30 |

(d)

FIGURE 3.7

bility of getting certain distributions under "assumed conditions" such as "equal proportions." If the likelihood of an extreme result that has been obtained is "very slight" under the assumptions, then we reject the assumptions. If the likelihood is "less rare," we say the slight variation in the data may be due to chance (factors not considered, but that must have had a differentiating effect on the data values).

The computation of the alpha level is really an aid to the judgment of "rarity" (very rare = .001, rare = .01, pretty rare = .05, not so rare = .10, chance = .40 or .50). However, the appropriate analytic tool depends on the nature of the data collected, the amount of data, and the questions being asked. In fact, the question being asked must precede both the research design (how to collect the data, how to analyze it) and its implementation. Most researchers will require the aid of experts in the field of research design and statistical analysis at this point.

## Interpreting the Result

The $\chi^2$ simply indicates that an association exists; it does not identify which company is better or worse. However, we can scan the data to see that company B, with 25 defective items, seems to be performing more poorly than companies A and C, with 10 and 5 defective items, respectively.

We could be wrong in our evaluations. It could be that company B really produces a higher proportion of good tires than companies A or C "in the long run," and that our sample of 200 was a quirk; however, the statistical test indicates that this conclusion is less likely than the conclusion that B is "different from" A and C.

## Other Distributions and Tests

A variety of theoretical distributions can be used to analyze data. One distribution that is popular in operations research is the binomial distribution. This is often used in determining whether a batch of products is "acceptable" or whether it contains "too many defectives" in a fashion similar to our examination of the tire problem. The binomial distribution is used in two outcome situations, i.e., defective/not defective or pass/fail, when one hypothesizes a certain proportion of items falls into one category or another. For example, one may hypothesize that the proportion of defective products in one's manufacturing process is .05 (then the proportion of nondefective items is .95). One draws a sample and compares the closeness of the proportion of defective items in it with the hypothesized value for the "population" (all items manufactured).

A similar use is made of the hypergeometric distribution. The binomial distribution is used when sampling is done "with replacement," the hypergeometric if sampling is done "without replacement." The term *replacement* refers to the question of whether or not the item sampled is "put back" before drawing the next sample. The significance (English word) of the replacement is that sampling without replacement reduces the size of the population with each object drawn (e.g., drawing an ace from a deck of cards reduces the size of the deck from 52 to 51), while sampling with replacement does not reduce the population size (if we put the ace back before the next draw, the deck again numbers 52). The difference in the size of the deck affects the probability calculations in estimating the likelihood of getting certain results based on chance alone.

In some circumstances (e.g., burning light bulbs till they fail in order to determine their average life span) one cannot put the items back. Another example is to test teaching methods. Once a student has learned a topic under a given teaching method he or she cannot be put back into the general population of the unlearned and tested again. These would be instances in which one should use the hypergeometric distribution and tables of significance based on that distribution. The use of the binomial distribution is more popular because tables of significant values are more readily available (and the formula describing the distribution less foreboding). One can use the binomial distribution to approximate the hypergeometric if the population is large relative to the sample (e.g., taking a sample of 20 light bulbs from a batch of 1,000), since the effect of nonreplacement on the population size is negligible. However, one should be aware of the assumptions behind the use of the statistical tests one employs in aiding the process of making inferences. The use of tests that do not match one's situation is worse than useless since it can give misleading results. In practice, the binomial distribution is often used in both cases if the "lot" being sampled is large, since the replacement or lack thereof has less effect in these cases.

The word *distribution* simply means a set of probability values. These values can be discrete, as in the probability of rolling a given value with a die (Table 3.13a), or they can be continuous, as in the picture of a "bell curve" or normal distribution. The distributions have a characteristic shape (the bell) even when they are discrete. For example, the distribution of the probability values for throwing various values of a die is uniform (all probabilities the same) or flat.

One uses the theoretical distributions (the ones one thinks are applicable to the situation) to test observed distributions to see if one's hypotheses about a situation are correct. For example, in rolling a die, one may hypothesize that the die is fair. However, if one sees the "observed distribution" of Table 3.13b, one may begin to question the validity of one's assumption (hypothesis). One may begin to suspect that someone is cheating.

TABLE 3.13

| Value | Probability |
| --- | --- |
| 1 | 1/6 |
| 2 | 1/6 |
| 3 | 1/6 |
| 4 | 1/6 |
| 5 | 1/6 |
| 6 | 1/6 |

(a)

| Value | Observed Probability |
| --- | --- |
| 1 | 1/2 |
| 2 | 0 |
| 3 | 0 |
| 4 | 1/2 |
| 5 | 0 |
| 6 | 0 |

(b)

One is comparing the expected distribution of values (here we expect a uniform or chi-square-type distribution) with the observed (obtained) distribution to see if they match. If they match, one's expectations (assumptions) are probably correct. If not, one's assumptions (hypotheses) may have to be revised.

A distribution relied on heavily by educators, social scientists, and statisticians is the "normal distribution" or bell-shaped curve. Poisson distributions of arrival rates and exponential distributions of service times are used in the study of queues (lines), e.g., at the bank, the grocery store, or in the line of jobs waiting for the central processor's attention in a computer. Our purpose is not to examine all the distributions, but to alert the reader to their existence and use. They are used to aid one in drawing inferences from samples of data. These inferences may refer to a description of the population (the average height of the American adult male is 5 ft., 10 in.) or to a hypothesis one has (the die is fair). The first type of inference is called an estimation study: we estimate population values from sample values. The latter is called a testing of hypotheses.

The process of inference leaves room for doubt. There could be sampling errors, inaccuracies in the measurement of a trait, etc.; however, assuming a properly selected sample (e.g., a random sample) and adequate measurement tools, the use of statistical tests based on theoretical distributions allows us to place some level of confidence in the statements we make.

## Continuous and Discrete Distributions

The normal distribution is continuous. The binomial and hypergeometric distributions are discrete. By continuous we mean that all values, e.g., 1.5 or 1.523 can be taken on; discrete distributions take on only specific values, usually integral values. As the discrete distributions take on a large n, i.e., a large number of objects are measured, their shape approaches that of continuous distributions, so that the distribution of values expected under the assumption of the dsicrete distribution, say the binomial, may be approximated by those expected under the assumption of a continuous distribution, e.g., the normal. That is, the values calculated with the corresponding formulas become "quite close."

## Related Readings

Alder, Henry. L. and Roessler, Edward B., *Introduction to Probability and Statistics*, 4th ed. San Francisco: W. H. Freeman and Co., 1968.

Churchill, Jr., Gilbert A., *Marketing Research: Methodological Foundations*, 2nd ed. Hinsdale, IL: The Dryden Press, 1979.

Cooke, D., Craven, A. H., and Clarker, G. M., *Basic Statistical Computing*, London: Edward Arnold Ltd., 1982.

Freund, John E., *Statistics: A First Course*, 3rd ed. Englewood Cliffs, NJ: Prentice-Hall, 1981.

Harnett, Donald L. and Murphy, James L., *Introductory Statistical Analysis*, 2nd ed. Reading, MA: Addison-Wesley, 1980.

Knuth, Donald E., *The Art of Computer Programming: Seminumerical Algorithms*, Vol. 2. Reading, MA: Addison-Wesley, 1969.

McNemar, Quinn, *Psychological Statistics*, 3rd ed. New York: John Wiley & Sons, 1962.

Runyon, Richard P. and Haber, Audrey, *Business Statistics*, Homewood, IL: Richard D. Irwin, Inc., 1982.

Siegel, Sidney, *Nonparametric Statistics for the Behavioral Sciences*, New York: McGraw-Hill, 1956.

# 4
# Making Predictions

## Objectives

At the end of this chapter the reader should be able:

1. To explain the concepts of positive, negative, and no correlation
2. To calculate the Spearman rank order coefficient
3. To indicate the difference between causality and correlation
4. To explain the testing of the significance of a statistic
5. To explain the use of a regression line to make predictions
6. To distinguish between linear correlation and nonlinear correlation

## Introduction

One use of the data that we collect is to make predictions of values. The predictions will often allow us to control the outcome of events that we cannot control directly. For example, we usually cannot control the occurrence or nonoccurrence of rain. However, if we can use data on cloud formations, wind velocities, and the like, we can control the effect of a predicted rain by carrying an umbrella.

Making predictions usually involves projecting results based on data that are readily attainable (the current cloud formations and wind velocities) to data that are not readily attainable (the state of the weather 2 hr from now). Hence, we are involved in the "association" of variables, the way values on one variable "covary" with those of the other variable. In Chapter 3 we saw that the data values on passing a written test covaried in a positive direction with flying ability, i.e., those who passed the test could fly. This is the sign of a good test. However, we could have used the results even if the outcome of the test was that the people who passed it could not fly.

## Predicting with a Bad Test

We now return to the example of the written test used to predict flying ability. Suppose that the data had turned out to be that shown in Table

TABLE 4.1

|   | F | $\bar{F}$ |
|---|---|---|
| P | 0 | 50 |
| $\bar{P}$ | 50 | 0 |

4.1. The test would certainly seem to be "bad" in the sense that its avowed purpose of indicating who has the ability to fly by who passes the test is not fulfilled. The data are quite the opposite. All who pass the test lack the ability to fly; all who fail possess the ability.

Despite the seeming incongruity of the test we can use it as a perfect predictor as easily as the test in which those who passed could fly. Performance on the test is "negatively" related to flying ability. Those who pass are sent home, those who fail are hired.

### Positive, Negative, and No Correlation

Data that is dependent will exhibit some sort of correlation. The meaning of the term *correlation* is indicated by writing it as *co-relation*. The data values on one variable are related to the data values in the other variable. They "co-vary" in the sense that the changes in value in one data item are reflected in changes in value in the other item. Three items are of interest in examining correlation: *positive correlation, negative correlation,* and *no correlation*. In explaining the concept of correlation we assume that we have data that is more finely distinguished than the categorical data examined so far. The data may either be discrete (e.g., comparing the number of dollars earned with the number of times a family eats out), or it may be continuous (e.g., comparing the way height varies with variations in weight for a group of individuals). However, initially we will not consider the actual values on the two variables.

### Positive Correlation

A positive correlation indicates that the values of one variable "go in the same direction" as the values of the other variable. For example, height is positively correlated with weight; taller people tend to be heavier than shorter people. If we were to graph height against weight (Figure 4.1a), where we use the terms *high* and *low* in place of actual values, people of "lesser" height would tend to have lesser weights, (Figure 4.1b), and people with "larger" heights would tend to have larger weights (Figure 4.1c). If we now fill in the intermediate values, the diagram would approximate a straight line in the upward or "positive slope" direction (Figure 4.1d). The line would not be perfectly straight, since the data do not correlate perfectly (positive correlation of 1.0). This is indicated by the "scatter" of the data around the hypothetical line connecting the bottom left portion of the plot to the upper right portion. If the data correlated perfectly, the plot would be a straight line (or a line of some sort—it might be a curved line). This would be the case with a mathematical func-

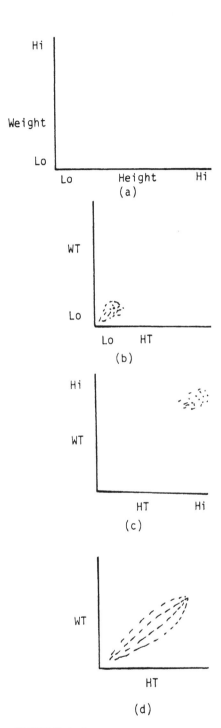

FIGURE 4.1

| X | Y=2X + 1 |
|---|----------|
| 1 | 3 |
| 2 | 5 |
| 3 | 7 |
| 4 | 9 |
| . | |
| . | |
| . | |

(a)

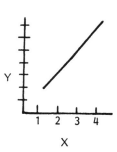

(b)

FIGURE 4.2

tion, such as Y = 2X + 1. The data values for Y covary exactly with those of X (Figure 4.2a). A graph of the values is a straight line (Figure 4.2b).

Many empirical relationships will approximate a straight line, but most will not produce a perfectly straight one. There will be scatter due to people or objects that don't exactly fit the pattern, e.g., tall people who are quite slight, or shorter people who are stockier.

If the data are not "linearly" related, the correlation might be indicated by a curved line. For example, the data of Figure 4.3a graphs as the curve of Figure 4.3b. For purposes of our discussion, the data will be assumed to be linearly related, producing a straight line rather than a curved one. We will leave the intricacies of discovering nonlinear relationships to more advanced texts.

Negative Correlation

The pattern for a negative correlation is similar to that of a positive one; the data values "go in opposite directions." Increasing values on one variable produce decreasing values on the other variable. An example would be age and running speed in adults. As we get older, we tend to get slower; younger people are faster. The diagram would be similar to that of Figure 4.4, where the negative shape of the approximately straight line gives the correlation its name.

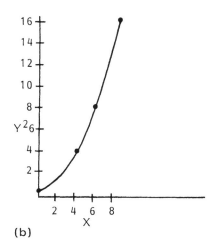

| X | $Y = X^2$ |
|---|---|
| 1 | 1 |
| 2 | 4 |
| 3 | 9 |
| 4 | 16 |

(a)

(b)

FIGURE 4.3

## No Correlation

Data that are not correlated will not exhibit a pattern; or, more precisely, they exhibit a pattern in which low values on one variable are tied to both high and low values on the other variable, and vice versa. An example might be height and intelligence, measured by an IQ score (hypothetical example). If the two variables are not correlated we will find tall people

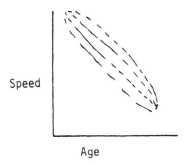

Speed

Age

FIGURE 4.4

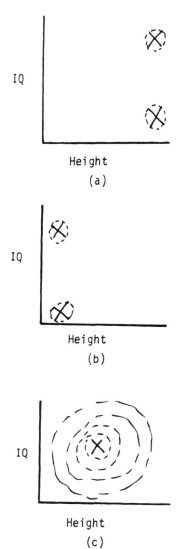

FIGURE 4.5

who have low scores as well as high scores on an IQ test (Figure 4.5a), as well as short people who have high IQs and short people who have low IQs (Figure 4.5b), and virtually all combinations in between, so that the full diagram will resemble a cloud (Figure 4.5c).

In the case of noncorrelated data, we cannot predict from one data value to another. Given that a person's height is 6 ft. 2 in., I have little idea whether his or her IQ is 102 or 147. On the other hand, we can predict from one data value to another with data that are correlated, whether the correlation be positive or negative. Hence, knowing that a person is 6 ft. tall, I am more likely to guess a weight of 180 lb. than one of 95 lb.

Knowing that a person is 18 yr old, I can predict with some measure of confidence that he or she is a faster runner than a person aged 79. In terms of weather forecasts, temperatures in the 90s lead to the expectation of "no snow" (negative correlation); the presence of clouds of certain types may indicate the imminence of rain (positive correlation). A good weatherperson's predictions should correlate well with the actual weather, and a weatherperson whose predictions show no correlation with the actual weather had better be very entertaining.

The case of noncorrelated data is equivalent to the statement that the two variables are independent. This was the case of the test results that showed all values of 25 in the written test of the previous discussion. Independent data are not correlated; dependent data are. In practice, we usually attempt to see if data values are correlated by comparing data on samples of the two populations (sets of data) in question. In that case we will need a statistical test to "test the significance" of the value of an obtained correlation, i.e., to ascertain if the correlation value could have turned up by chance even though the variables we measured are really independent (not correlated, not related).

## Calculating a Correlation Value

In order to illustrate the process of estimating the strength of correlation between data items, we present the "nonparametric" statistic, Spearman's rank order correlation coefficient. Other measures, such as the Pearson product moment correlation exist and are probably used as or more often than the Spearman statistic. Which one uses depends on the type of data one has. The term *nonparametric* refers to a class of statistics that can be used on data that make few assumptions about the population from which the sample data have been drawn. Parametric statistics make assumptions about the underlying distributions of the data (e.g., that the populations sampled have relatively the same variance (variability) or that the underlying distribution is normal). Because there are fewer assumptions, the nonparametric statistics are more general in their applicability. They are usually "weaker" in uncovering statistical differences, which is why statisticians prefer the parametric tests when applicable. However, that will not concern us here.

## Spearman's Rank Order Coefficient

To illustrate the calculation of the rank order coefficient of correlation we will examine the covariance of the data on hours studied for an exam with performance on that exam. Hypothetical data for the example are shown in Table 4.2.

We have purposely chosen the hypothetical data so that there are no ties either in hours studied or in raw scores on the exam. Real data would rarely be so tractable. If ties exist, the calculation can still be performed, with the tied scores being assigned the average of the applicable ranks. If no ties exist, the results of the Spearman calculation and the results obtained from the parametric calculation on the ranks are identical. In any case, the investigator will have to do with what he or she has as data. to do with what he or she has as data.

TABLE 4.2

| Student | Hours studied | Raw exam scores |
|---|---|---|
| Joe | 3 | 70 |
| Mary | 4 | 85 |
| William | 5 | 80 |
| Harry | 7 | 90 |
| Larry | 6 | 87 |
| Bob | 8 | 95 |

The calculation of the Spearman statistic is based on the formula

$$r_s = 1 - \frac{6\Sigma d^2}{n(n^2 - 1)}$$

where d represents differences between the ranks of "data pairs" and n is the number of pairs we have.

The first step in calculating Spearman's r rho* is to translate the raw data into ranked data (Table 4.3). We then compare the ranks to compute the difference between them for each student, and square the differences to avoid summing to zero (Table 4.4). The difference column indicates that the rank is the same in both the number of hours studied and the test scores received for four of the students, with two having their ranks "out of order." This is a visual indication of highly correlated data. The sum of $d^2$ is 2; the number of pairs is 6. We now plug these values into the formula:

$$r_s = 1 - \frac{6(2)}{6(6^2 - 1)}$$

$$= 1 - \frac{12}{210} = .943$$

*Roman letters, r, indicate values obtained from a sample; Greek letters, rho, indicate the population value being estimated by the sample.

TABLE 4.3

| Student | Hours studied | Exam scores | Rank Hours | Rank Scores |
|---|---|---|---|---|
| Joe | 3 | 70 | 6 | 6 |
| Mary | 4 | 85 | 5 | 4 |
| William | 5 | 80 | 4 | 5 |
| Harry | 7 | 90 | 2 | 2 |
| Larry | 6 | 87 | 3 | 3 |
| Bob | 8 | 95 | 1 | 1 |

TABLE 4.4

| Student | Rank Hours | Rank Scores | d | $d^2$ |
|---|---|---|---|---|
| Joe | 6 | 6 | 0 | 0 |
| Mary | 5 | 4 | +1 | 1 |
| William | 4 | 5 | −1 | 1 |
| Harry | 2 | 2 | 0 | 0 |
| Larry | 3 | 3 | 0 | 0 |
| Bob | 1 | 1 | 0 | 0 |

A perfect positive correlation is indicated by a value of 1.00, indicating that our value of .94 is quite high. The student should note that the 6 in the formula and the 6 for the value of n are two different numbers. The number of pairs could just as easily have been 10, 7, or 20, but the 6 in the formula is a constant, a result of the derivation of the formula.

A perfect correlation would be found for the data in Table 4.5, in which we switched the number of hours studied by Mary and William. There are no deviations in rank for a given student, so that the sum of $d^2$ is zero and the formula yields

$$1 - \frac{6(0)}{6(35)} = 1 - 0 = 1$$

a perfect correlation of the ranks in the two sets of data.

### Interpreting the Result

We might hazard the inference that studying more produces higher scores on the test. However, this is a large leap from what the data warrant. The data say the totals in hours studied and scores obtained on a test "go together." They do not say that one event caused the other. For example, the data in Table 4.6 correlate. However, we would hardly conclude

TABLE 4.5

| Student | Hours studied | Raw exam scores | Rank Hours | Rank Scores | d | $d^2$ |
|---|---|---|---|---|---|---|
| Joe | 3 | 70 | 6 | 6 | 0 | 0 |
| Mary | 5 | 85 | 4 | 4 | 0 | 0 |
| William | 4 | 80 | 5 | 5 | 0 | 0 |
| Harry | 7 | 90 | 2 | 2 | 0 | 0 |
| Larry | 6 | 87 | 3 | 3 | 0 | 0 |
| Bob | 8 | 95 | 1 | 1 | 0 | 0 |

TABLE 4.6

| Student | Hours spent per week | | Rank hours spent | |
|---|---|---|---|---|
| | Studying | Cleaning | Studying | Cleaning |
| Michael | 20 | 5 | 3 | 3 |
| Bill | 30 | 8 | 1 | 1 |
| Ann | 25 | 7 | 2 | 2 |

that the hours spent studying caused the hours spent cleaning. A more likely interpretation is that both totals are caused by some other factor, say the relative industriousness of each student.

If one event causes another, e.g., the sun shining causing the temperature to rise, the data will be correlated. However, the fact that data are correlated does not necessitate causality. Correlated data between variables X and Y can arise for various reasons (Figure 4.6).

The type of relationship between X and Y posed by the investigator is a "theory" or "model" and must be supported by data and arguments other than correlation. For example, if X occurs before Y in time, it is more likely that X causes Y than that Y causes X. If we can additionally show theoretical reasons for positing the role of causality to X, e.g.,

Hypothesis 1: Studying more produces more knowledge of the subject.
Hypothesis 2: The possession of more knowledge of the subject yields better results on an exam.
Conclusion: Studying more produces better results on an exam.

$$\text{Deduction from } A \longrightarrow B$$
$$\text{and } \underline{B \longrightarrow C}$$
$$A \longrightarrow C$$

and we can support the hypotheses, we have a stronger argument than the simple examination of correlated data.

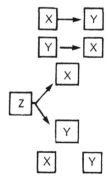

1. X produces Y (X causes Y)

2. Y produces X (Y causes X)

3. A third factor, Z, produces both X and Y (X and Y are both effects of a common cause)

4. Accidentally, there is no true relationship between X and Y, but sample data shows a correlation by chance

FIGURE 4.6

That the hypotheses must be supported is evident from the fact that empirical studies that might dispute hypothesis 1 (that more hours spent studying provide more knowledge of the subject) are possible. An efficient student may study less and learn more than a less efficient student. Only if both hypotheses are true will the conclusion be true (the conclusion is valid given the hypotheses, but its truth value depends on the truth value of the premises).

Very few people would dispute the second hypothesis, "all things being equal," i.e., discounting such factors as test anxiety or having attended a party the night before. However, the fact that nobody disputes a hypothesis is hardly evidence of its truth value, as assumptions about the flatness of the earth, or the theory of the earth as center of the universe, popular a few hundred years ago, attest. More recent popular assumptions also have had to undergo revision: that matter is continuous (atomic theory), that light moves through an ether (it could not be found), and that presidents are always honest men (various scandals).

### Negative Correlations

The data shown in Table 4.7 exhibit a negative correlation. The differences in rank are given in Table 4.8, and the formula yields

$$r_s = 1 - \frac{6(6)}{3(9 - 1)}$$

$$= 1 - \frac{36}{24}$$

$$= 1 - 1.5 = -.5$$

TABLE 4.7

| Student | Hours studied | Exam scores | Rank | |
|---|---|---|---|---|
| | | | Hours | Score |
| Joe | 4 | 82 | 2 | 3 |
| Mary | 8 | 90 | 1 | 2 |
| Chris | 2 | 95 | 3 | 1 |

TABLE 4.8

| Student | Rank | | d | $d^2$ |
|---|---|---|---|---|
| | Hours | Scores | | |
| Joe | 2 | 3 | −1 | 1 |
| Mary | 1 | 2 | −1 | 1 |
| Chris | 3 | 1 | +2 | 4 |
| | | | | 6 |

TABLE 4.9

| | Rank | | | |
| Student | Hours | Scores | d | $d^2$ |
| --- | --- | --- | --- | --- |
| Joe | 1 | 3 | −2 | 4 |
| Mary | 2 | 2 | 0 | 0 |
| Chris | 3 | 1 | +2 | 4 |
| | | | | 8 |

which seems to be only a moderate negative correlation. The smallness of the value obtained is due to the size of the sample.

A perfectly negative correlation would be obtained from the data of Table 4.9. The reader should perform the calculation.

Sample Size

The sample size of three pairs restricts the values we can obtain on the correlation coefficient. The six possible cases are shown in Table 4.10, which indicates one of the reasons small samples are not desirable: the calculation of the statistics based on the sample are restricted in their

TABLE 4.10

| | | | |
| --- | --- | --- | --- |
| | 1 | 1 | |
| | 2 | 2 | |
| (a) | 3 | 3 | corr = +1 |
| | 1 | 1 | |
| | 2 | 3 | |
| (b) | 3 | 2 | corr = +.5 |
| | 1 | 2 | |
| | 2 | 1 | |
| (c) | 3 | 3 | corr = +.5 |
| | 1 | 2 | |
| | 2 | 3 | |
| (d) | 3 | 1 | corr = −.5 |
| | 1 | 3 | |
| | 2 | 1 | |
| (e) | 3 | 2 | corr = −.5 |
| | 1 | 3 | |
| | 2 | 2 | |
| (f) | 3 | 1 | corr = −1.0 |

TABLE 4.11

| Student | Hours studied | Exam score | Rank Hours | Rank Scores |
|---------|---------------|------------|------------|-------------|
| Joe | 3 | 70 | 6 | 7 |
| Mary | 5 | 85 | 4 | 5 |
| William | 4 | 80 | 5 | 6 |
| Harry | 7 | 90 | 2 | 3 |
| Larry | 6 | 87 | 3 | 4 |
| Bob | 8 | 95 | 1 | 2 |
| Millie | 1 | 100 | 7 | 1 |

range of values. For example, with three pairs it is impossible to have "no correlation" regardless of the data. Another reason that small samples are not desirable is that they are more subject to "sampling error," the inclusion of an extreme case in the sample that will not be balanced out by the other data. An example would be the data on students shown in Table 4.11. The differences in ranks for the data are shown in Table 4.12. The calculation of Spearman's r yields

$$1 - \frac{6(42)}{7(48)} = 1 - \frac{3}{4} = +\frac{1}{4}$$

a relatively low positive correlation value.

The first six data items are perfectly correlated (1.0, Table 4.11) so that the addition of the unique case, Millie, who hardly studies, but gets all $A$'s, has thrown everybody off one (d = -1 for all but Millie), and her own difference in ranks (+6) swells the sum of $d^2$ by 36, creating the illusion of data that is less highly correlated than we know it to be by the previous example.

TABLE 4.12

| Student | d | $d^2$ |
|---------|-----|-----|
| Joe | −1 | 1 |
| Mary | −1 | 1 |
| William | −1 | 1 |
| Harry | −1 | 1 |
| Larry | −1 | 1 |
| Bob | −1 | 1 |
| Millie | +6 | 36 |
| | | 42 |

TABLE 4.13

| Student | Rank Hours | Rank Scores | d | $d^2$ |
|---|---|---|---|---|
| A | 1 | 2 | -1 | 1 |
| B | 2 | 4 | -2 | 4 |
| C | 3 | 1 | +2 | 4 |
| D | 4 | 3 | +1 | 1 |
| | | | | 10 |

## A Larger Sample

With as few as four students we can illustrate a case of zero correlation (Table 4.13). The calculation of the Spearman statistic is:

$$r_s = 1 - \frac{6(10)}{4(15)}$$

$$= 1 - \frac{60}{60} = 1 - 1 = 0$$

The data indicate that sometimes someone who ranks relatively high on one score ranks relatively high on the other score (A is 1 and 2, respectively), but that is not always the case (B is ranked second on the first score, but last on the second score). The fact that sometimes someone is high on both scores, but not always, illustrates the nonpredictability from data with no correlation.

## Visualizing Patterns

The case of perfect negative correlation with four students is illustrated in Table 4.14, where the ranks of each person are the reverse of each other on the two variables. The calculation is:

TABLE 4.14

| Student | Rank Hours | Rank Scores | d | $d^2$ |
|---|---|---|---|---|
| A | 1 | 4 | -3 | 9 |
| B | 2 | 3 | -1 | 1 |
| C | 3 | 2 | +1 | 1 |
| D | 4 | 1 | +3 | 9 |
| | | | | 20 |

TABLE 4.15   $r_s = 1 - 0 = 1$

| Student | Rank | | d | $d^2$ |
| | Hours | Scores | | |
| --- | --- | --- | --- | --- |
| A | 4 | 4 | 0 | 0 |
| B | 3 | 3 | 0 | 0 |
| C | 2 | 2 | 0 | 0 |
| D | 1 | 1 | 0 | 0 |

$$r_s = 1 - \frac{6(20)}{4(15)}$$

$$= 1 - 2 = -1$$

Perfect positive correlation is shown in Table 4.15, where the ranks are identical. Often a visual examination of the data, if suitably or "luckily" arranged, will reveal patterns that suggest relationships.

### The Significance of the Correlation

As indicated above, the significance of the obtained correlation coefficient will depend not only on its value but on the size of the sample data. The essence of the test is to compare the value of the correlation coefficient obtained with the sample to values that might be obtained by chance for all possible samples of the same size. This requires knowledge of the "sampling distribution" of the statistic. In many cases the distribution of possible samples is "normal," i.e., it follows the normal curve. The test examines "how far out" on the curve an obtained sample value is. The likelihood of being this far out on the curve is stated as a probability, .05 or .01, under the hypothesis that it was a chance event. If this likelihood is too low, the "chance explanation" is rejected.

In cases in which the normal curve is not applicable, another theoretical distribution; say chi-square or the t-distribution, is often applicable. The use of each is similar in method, although the probabilities associated with certain "areas under the curve" change.

### The Strength of the Prediction

As indicated earlier, one of the reasons we look for correlations in the data is to facilitate making predictions from one data value (the one that is accessible) to data values on other variables that are "less accessible." One can also determine "how much" the data helps. For example, in the data on the diagnostic test and flying ability, the proportion of good flyers in the nation was .50

Proportions

| Fly | $\overline{\text{Fly}}$ |
|-----|------|
| .50 | .50 |

If we hired individuals "at random," i.e., without a diagnostic test, we would be right half the time, wrong half the time. With the data on the tests, we are right all the time. The reduction in our error rate is 50%. Alternatively, the increase in our being correct is 50%.

The strength of a correlation value r is found by squaring that value. Hence, if one obtains an r-value of .8, one squares it and obtains the value .64. This latter value is interpreted as the amount of variation in the one variable that can be explained by the variation in the other variable. In the case of the correlation value of .8, the amount of variation in Y (the one variable, e.g., performance on the test) explained by the variation in the other variable (X, e.g., the hours studied) would be 64%.

The strength of the association does not indicate causality (as discussed above), but it does indicate whether or not one variable is a good or strong predictor of the other variable. For example, an obtained correlation value of .2 has a strength of association of .04, and is a relatively poor predictor of the other variable even if the measure of association, the correlation value of .2, were shown to be statistically significant (as could happen if it was obtained with very large samples).

## Regression Lines

The predictions about flying ability made on the basis of the evidence of the written test were gross measurements. They simply placed people into the categories of having or not having the ability to fly. Measures of flying ability could be developed that are quantitative in the sense that they assign a numerical score from 1 through 10, designating either discrete scores (1 or 2 but not 1.5) or "continuous" measurements (allowing any values, such as 1.5, to some degree of precision). With data that is "quantitative," such as that usually obtained for such variables as height and weight, we can develop a more refined predictor. The predictor is called a "regression equation." We will examine linear equations only, but the concept is more general.

A regression equation is a straight line that represents the relationship between values obtained on one variable (X) and values obtained on another variable (Y). One example is the hypothetical relationship between scores on the Graduate Record Exam (GRE) and quality point average (QPA) in graduate school shown in Figure 4.7. Knowing one's GRE score, we can predict one's QPA.

GRE of 400 = *prediction* QPA 2.5
GRE of 450 = *prediction* QPA 2.75
GRE of 500 = *prediction* QPA 3.00
.
.
.

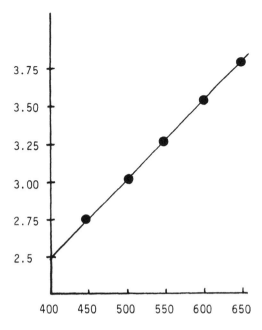

FIGURE 4.7

We emphasize that the score estimated for the QPA is a prediction. It may or may not be actualized, i.e., a student who scores 400 on the GREs may obtain a QPA of 2.5, or he or she might attain a QPA higher or lower than 2.5. The value of 2.5 is our "most likely estimate" or "expected value" of the QPA for a student with a GRE score of 400.

The GRE score is not a prediction, but a value already obtained by the student. It is the data that is available (on past performance) that is being used to predict the data that is unavailable (future performance). The graph of the straight line enhances visual comprehension of the relationship, here a positive correlation between GRE and QPA. However, for calculations, it is usually more useful to have the equation of the line. For the data on GRE scores and QPA shown in Table 4.16, one form of the equation would be

$$Y = 2.5 + \frac{1}{200} (X - 400)$$

TABLE 4.16

| GRE(X) | QPA(Y) |
|---|---|
| 400 | 2.5 |
| 450 | 2.75 |
| 500 | 3.0 |
| 550 | 3.25 |
| 600 | 3.50 |
| 650 | 3.75 |

or

$$QPA = 2.5 + \frac{1}{200} (GRE - 400)$$

The method used to obtain the equation in this example was to visually obtain the values of two points, then use these to create the slope-intercept form of a linear equation:

1. Obtain slope from two points.

$$\frac{2.75 - 2.5}{450 - 400} = \frac{.25}{50} = \frac{1}{200}$$

2. Intercept is taken as Y = 2.5, X = 400. Adjust for X not being zero by subtracting 400 from value of X.

$$Y = 2.5 + \frac{1}{200} (X - 400)$$

This is not the method usually used to obtain the equation; it is a consequence of my having started with a known hypothetical straight line instead of starting with obtained data. However, the interpretation of the equation is the same: the slope indicates the direction of the relationship, the Y-intercept indicates the value of Y when X is the value zero (or here 400). In empirical studies (studies in which one has collected data on the real world) we would use a statistical formula to create the equation or feed the data into a computer-based statistical package that would do the calculations for us (taking care to select the formula of calculation suited to our data).

The regression equation is an "ideal" relationship. The data obtained from empirical observations do not usually fall exactly on a straight line. They are scattered as shown in Figure 4.8a. A straight line is "forced" on the data (Figure 4.8b) to show a close fit.

The most common method of "forcing" a straight line on the data is the "least squares" method. The method chooses the line that minimizes the squared deviations of the data values from the line. The deviations of the data represent errors in predicting. They are obtained data points not lying exactly on the predictor line that is selected (Figure 4.9).

The error or deviation is squared for the same reason that deviations from the expected values in the calculation of chi-square, or deviations from the mean in computing the variance and standard deviation of a distribution are squared: the squared values avoid the sum of zero, and they emphasize the larger deviations. Since the deviations represent "error" in the prediction, a line is chosen that minimizes this error.

The method of calculation uses two formulas

$$a = \frac{(\Sigma y)(\Sigma x^2) - (\Sigma x)(\Sigma xy)}{n(\Sigma x^2) - (\Sigma x)^2}$$

$$b = \frac{n(\Sigma xy) - (\Sigma x)(\Sigma y)}{n(\Sigma x^2) - (\Sigma x)^2}$$

where a and b represent the y-intercept and the slope in the equation

$$y = a + bx$$

(a)

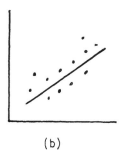

(b)

FIGURE 4.8

The symbols involving the sigmas may seem foreboding, but they represent simple additions or multiplications. For example, the symbol $\Sigma x$ means "add up the x-values"; $\Sigma y$ means "add up the y-values"; the symbol $\Sigma xy$ means "multiply each x value by each y value, then add these products." The one distinction that might cause difficulty is the distinction between

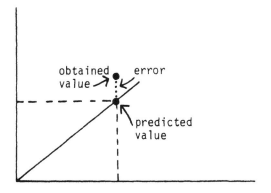

FIGURE 4.9

TABLE 4.17

| Student | Hours studied(x) | $x^2$ | Exam scores(y) | x*y |
|---------|------------------|-------|----------------|-----|
| Joe | 3 | 9 | 70 | 210 |
| Mary | 4 | 16 | 85 | 340 |
| William | 5 | 25 | 80 | 400 |
| Harry | 7 | 49 | 90 | 630 |
| Larry | 6 | 36 | 87 | 522 |
| Bob | 8 | 64 | 95 | 760 |
| Total | 33 | 199 | 507 | 2862 |

$$(\Sigma x^2)$$

and

$$(\Sigma x)^2$$

The first notation means square all the x values, then add the squares. The second means add the $x$'s, then square the result. While the equations may seem foreboding, they can be used in a cookbook fashion. If we take the data on hours studied (x) and grade in the exam (y) to be "truly quantitative," we can compute the data of Table 4.17. The sum of the x-values ($\Sigma x$) is 33; the sum of the x-values squared ($\Sigma x^2$) is 199; the sum of the y-values ($\Sigma y$) is 507; the sum of the x-values multiplied by the y-values ($\Sigma xy$) is 2862; and the sum of the x-values (33) squared [i.e., $(\Sigma x)^2$] is 1089; n, the number of score pairs is 6. The reader should note that the sum of the squared x-values ($\Sigma x^2$) is different from the sum of the x-values squared [$(\Sigma x)^2$]. Plugging these values into formulas, we get

$$a = \frac{(\Sigma y)(\Sigma x^2) - (\Sigma x)(\Sigma xy)}{n(\Sigma x^2) - (\Sigma x)^2}$$

$$= \frac{507 * 199 - 33 * 2862}{6 * 199 - 1089}$$

$$= \frac{100,893 - 94,446}{1194 - 1089}$$

$$= \frac{6,447}{105} = 61.4$$

$$b = \frac{n(\Sigma xy) - (\Sigma x)(\Sigma y)}{n(\Sigma x^2) - (\Sigma x)^2}$$

$$= \frac{6 * 2862 - 33 * 507}{105} \qquad \text{(Denominator is the same)}$$

$$= \frac{17172 - 16731}{105}$$

$$= \frac{441}{105} = 4.2$$

so that the equation

y = a + bx

becomes

y = 61.4 + 4.2x

or

Score on test = 61.4 + 4.2 * (hours studied)

If someone studied 3 hr we expect the score on the test to be

61.4 + 4.2(3) = 61.4 + 12.6 = 74

As the data on Joe indicate, he studied 3 hr, but obtained a test score of 70. His performance was slightly below what we expected, although the discrepancy between the observed score (70) and the predicted score (74) is not great. We distinguish between the observed score (y) and the predicted score (y') by the prime notation:

y          = 70 (observed)

y'         = 74 (predicted)

Deviation = -4 (error)

For someone studying for 4 hr we expect

y' = 61.4 + 4.2(4)

   = 61.4 + 16.8

   = 78.2

The observed score for Mary, who did study for 4 hr, is 85; she did better than expected.

y'         = 78.2

y          = 85

Deviation = +6.8

The score predicted by the equation (y') and the observed score (y) will coincide relatively infrequently. However, if the regression equation is fairly good (or, more accurately, if the data allow a regression equation

TABLE 4.18

| Student | Hours studied | Predicted exam scores |
|---------|---------------|------------------------|
| Joe     | 3             | 85                     |
| Mary    | 4             | 85                     |
| William | 5             | 85                     |
| Harry   | 7             | 85                     |
| Larry   | 6             | 85                     |
| Bob     | 8             | 85                     |

TABLE 4.19

| Student | Hours studied | Predicted exam scores |
|---------|---------------|------------------------|
| Joe | 3 | 74 |
| Mary | 4 | 78.2 |
| . | | |
| . | | |
| . | | |
| . | | |

to be "closely fitted," i.e., if the data are highly correlated) the predictions will be in the ballpark.

Without the regression equation, we would predict a value of 84.5 or 85 for each student on the test score. Eighty-five is the class mean on the test (507/6), and in the absence of other information, it is the "expected value." Hence, without the regression equation our predictions would be "invariant" (Table 4.18). The regression equation provides variability in our guesses, the variability being based on our knowledge of the hours studied. That is, knowing Joe studied 3 hr, we predict that he will score 74, and knowing Mary studied 4 hr, we predict a test score of 78.2 (Table 4.19), and so on.

## Why Predict When We Have the Scores?

The reader may be wondering why we predict a value on the test score when we already have the actual scores. The response is that the equation has been developed on this set of data, but will be used on other students (or these students) in the future. To develop the equation, we need both sets of scores. Once the equation has been developed, we use it to predict the outcomes of other events (scores on other tests), given only the hours studied. The "relationship" between hours studied and test scores may be employed in a pragmatic sense

To do well, study long.

or in a theoretical sense

One of the major factors in achieving success in college is the length of time studied.

Other researchers might then study other factors, such as the "quality" or "intensity" of the study, leading to maxims such as "study well, not long." The quality of "intensity" is more difficult to measure than the "length of time" one studies, which is one of the reasons studies involving lengths of time are attractive and may be more numerous than studies involving "quality of time spent studying."

TABLE 4.20

| Person | Score |
|--------|-------|
| 1 | P |
| 2 | P |
| 3 | F |
| 4 | F |
| 5 | P |
| 6 | F |
| 7 | P |
| 8 | F |

## Prediction and Control

We can use the relationship between data items to achieve control of relevant outcomes. For example, in the data on the diagnostic test and flying ability, we use the variation in the test scores (Table 4.20) to develop a hiring policy ("hire only those who pass") to remove variation in the quality of pilots (Table 4.21). The initial variegated population has now become homogeneous.

## Types of Data

In this chapter we have been remiss in not distinguishing between various types of data. At this point it would be useful to point out that there are different "levels" of data and that different statistical tests are appropriate with each. Data such as eye color or sex is called categorical data. The data elements are "put into categories" or "classified." There is no numerical significance to data that are purely categorical. There is not even any "natural order" to the data. Hence, we may identify men as 0, women as

TABLE 4.21

| Person | Test results | Hiring results | Judgment of flying ability |
|--------|--------------|----------------|----------------------------|
| 1 | P | H | good |
| 2 | P | H | good |
| 3 | F | | |
| 4 | F | | |
| 5 | P | H | good |
| 6 | F | | |
| 7 | P | H | good |
| 8 | F | | |

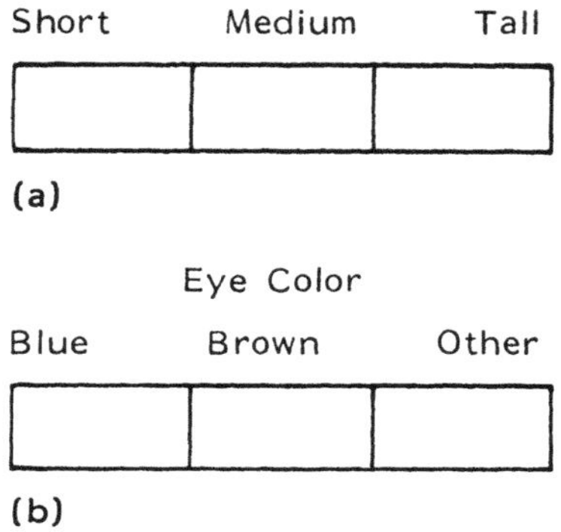

Short        Medium        Tall

```
┌──────────┬──────────┬──────────┐
│          │          │          │
└──────────┴──────────┴──────────┘
```

(a)

Eye Color

Blue         Brown         Other

```
┌──────────┬──────────┬──────────┐
│          │          │          │
└──────────┴──────────┴──────────┘
```

(b)

FIGURE 4.10

1, in a code, but the use of the 0/1 code does not imply that women are better than men, or "higher" (although some might think that interpretation is justified). Such data uses numbers as "labels" to identify items, much as the numerals on football jerseys or lockers.

Some data can be ordered in that we can tell one entity has "more of an attribute" than another. Hence, saying someone is tall, another short, does order the people according to height, although it does not say "how much taller." Thus, the categories in Figure 4.10a do have a natural ordering, with more of the quantity being illustrated in the categories to the right. The categories in Figure 4.10b have no natural order, so that we could put "other" in the middle. To put tall in the middle of short and medium (short, tall, medium) would cause an uneasiness.

Analysis using conditional and unconditional probabilities is appropriate with data that is "only" categorical. For certain problems, so is the use of a chi-square calculation. The calculation of the Spearman rank order correlation coefficient, as the name implies, requires data that is at least ordered.

The use of such calculations as the Pearson correlation coefficient and the development of a regression equation require data that is quantitative. There are two commonly discussed types of quantitative data, the interval scale and the ratio scale. Without going into the distinction between these scales here, we illustrate a quantitative scale with height or weight, both ratio scales. The recording of heights at 6 ft. or 3 ft. does imply an ordering, but it also implies "stronger data," data that can be manipulated arithmetically. Hence, someone who is 6 ft. tall is "twice as tall" as someone who is 3 ft. tall (the meaningful ratio of the individual scores are where the scale gets its name). Differences or intervals are also meaningful: the "distance" from a height of 4 ft. to a height of 6 ft. is 2 ft., and is equal to the distance from 6 ft. to 8 ft.

## Linear and Nonlinear Correlation

As indicated earlier, data can be correlated in ways that are depicted by curves rather than by a straight line. These relationships are "curvilinear" and use regression techniques that are "nonlinear." However, the principle is the same; one is attempting to fit a mathematical relationship to the data. The use of the mathematical relationship facilitates the prediction of data values on one variable from data values on the other in an "automatic fashion." Hence, if the relationship seems to be

$$Y = X^2 + 3$$

we can take a value for X (that we know), say 5, plug it in, and get a predicted value for Y, here 28 ($5^2$ plus 3), with Y being the variable in which we are "really interested."

The crucial point is to find a model that is valid for the situation we are attempting to describe. The development of such models and their validation are topics studied under the rubrics of model-building and theory development. They are epitomized by the empirical models of physics and other natural sciences, in which many variables are related by formulas that give exact predictions (point estimates, since they predict the value of a single "data point" as a "point," not as a range of values). For example, knowing the value of a body's specific gravity (density) and comparing it to the density of water, one can tell whether the body will float or sink, and, if it floats, how far above water the surface of the body will be, all predictions that are of use to shipbuilders.

Empirical models are those about the real world, i.e., they are models that make assertions about objects "outside the model." This is in contrast to nonempirical systems, including such deductive systems as algebra or logic, which are self-contained, assuming a given set of objects and axioms. One goal of the empirical scientist is to analyze data in such a way that he or she can develop a body of knowledge that can be fit to a mathematical model. The mathematical model then can be manipulated to make predictions (statements) about the real world objects. The development of a regression equation is an attempt to do this for a narrow range of data (a few variables). It does so without a theory of causality, using correlation of data values as the sole source of predictability. However, a researcher will often be interested in finding a theory to explain the predictability in the data. The regularity is assumed to be due to some underlying cause and if the cause can be identified, one understands or explains the relationships one finds rather than simply using them. This, of course, is not an easy task, and has kept scientists in various disciplines (subject areas) busy for millenia. Even when our model seems to be generally accepted, e.g., in Newtonian dynamics (theory of motion), subsequent knowledge may find instances to which the model does not apply and revise it, e.g., in the dynamics (laws of motion) developed by Einstein.

## Seeking Help

In using statistical techniques to analyze data, one must be aware of both the type of data and the techniques available for analyzing each type. In addition, one must worry about the way a sample of data is selected, what measuring instruments are used to record the observations, and the types of questions that various statistical tools are suitable to "help answer" (the answer is not definitive). One is usually well advised to seek help from professionals in the areas of research design and statistical analysis whenever planning a research venture, as well as in the consumption of data generated by others, say research reports or advertising claims.

## Related Readings

Freund, John E., *Statistics: A First Course*, 3rd ed. Englewood Cliffs, NJ: Prentice-Hall, 1981.

Hamburg, Morris, *Statistical Analysis for Decision Making*, 2nd ed. New York: Harcourt Brace Jovanovich, 1970.

Li, Jerome C. R., *Statistical Inference I*, Ann Arbor, MI: Edwards Brothers, Inc., 1964.

Minium, Edward W., *Statistical Reasoning in Psychology and Education*, 2nd ed. New York: John Wiley & Sons, 1978.

Runyan, Richard P. and Haber, Audrey, *Business Statistics*, Homewood, IL: Richard D. Irwin, Inc., 1982.

Siegel, Sidney, *Nonparametric Statistics for the Behavioral Sciences*, New York: McGraw-Hill, 1956.

# *III*
# Data Organization and Use

The first chapter in this section addresses the issue of summarizing data, with an emphasis on its descriptive use. The concepts of frequency, relative frequency, and cumulative frequency are briefly treated. The primary emphasis here is on the use of summarization to achieve an understanding of the data when excessive detail obscures patterns.

Measures of central tendency, such as the mode, median, and mean are introduced, with some discussion of data types and the calculations appropriate to each. A discussion of the use (or misuse) of statistics to give varying impressions (interpretations) of the same data follows.

A study of measures of variability (the "spread" of the data) follows a discussion of the measures of central tendency (the "position" of the data). The primary focus is on the standard deviation with the eventual goal being the development of the normal distribution.

The chapter closes with a statement of the relationship between uncertainty and variability in the data: more variability in a set of data yields more uncertainty about the value of a particular occurrence (individual) on the trait in question; and more uncertainty about the occurrence yields a greater need for information. The relationship is not further developed in the chapter, but is one of the referring background themes of the text, and will be treated explicitly in Chapter 19. Other treatments may be found in Bierman, Bonini, and Hausman (1973).

Chapter 6 follows up on the development of the normal curve to show how one can use such distributions to design equipment or other things, in this case a doorway. A similar use of data to control situations, in this case the level of service in a bank, is also illustrated. The problems presented are estimation problems, hence, the notion of sampling is introduced in regard to measuring populations. The notion of hypothesis-testing is not introduced. The reasons for this were pedagogical. The text is not a text in statistics; hence, too lengthy a discussion of statistical techniques might prove distracting from the remaining notions, e.g., data storage and retrieval, data display, human/machine communications, data manipulation, and data use in decision-making. Furthermore, the use of hypothesis-testing emphasizes the development of models, while the use of estimation is necessary even when a model already exists for a given situation (e.g.,

when it rains, take an umbrella; estimation problem: likelihood of rain).
Hence, one needs some knowledge of estimation even with a model in hand.

Finally, the notion of estimation seemed simpler to grasp in an introductory text than the notion of hypothesis-testing, and the notions of sampling and sampling distributions introduced in the study of estimation procedures are prerequisite to understanding hypothesis-testing and model-building. Hence, these were viewed as more fundamental and suitable for the introductory text. It is anticipated that future courses would treat the problems of generating and testing hypotheses, as well as embedding particular hypotheses in a more general model or theory.

# 5
# Understanding the Data

## Objectives

Upon completion of this chapter the reader should be able to:

1.  Explain the trade-off between easier comprehension of summarized data and loss of information
2.  Arrange data in a distribution of frequencies, relative frequencies, and cumulative frequencies
3.  Calculate the mean, variance, and standard deviation for a set of data
4.  Explain the difference between the mean, median, and mode
5.  Explain the data types: categorical, ordered, interval, and ratio, and indicate the measures of central tendency appropriate to each
6.  Explain the concepts of measures of central tendency and measures of spread
7.  Indicate how the use of different statistics, say median and mode, or median and mean, can give a different impression when reporting on the same data
8.  Explain the normal distribution (in terms of percentages in various intervals of the curve and the position of the mean)
9.  Explain how the position of a score in terms of standard deviations can give an idea of its "normalness" or rarity
10. Calculate the interval points for a given set of data, either starting with raw scores, or having been given the mean and the standard deviation
11. Explain the relationship between variability and uncertainty
12. Interpret curves of
    a.  Same mean, different variances
    b.  Different means, same variance
    c.  Different means, different variances

## Introduction

The treatment of data analysis was premature in the sense that we gave only slight indication of where the data in the tables originated. Of course, it initially arises from the "observations" made with one or more of the data collection methods mentioned earlier: a survey has been taken of people's preferences in regard to the current political candidates; a test has been administered to a group of job applicants; people's performance on the job has been monitored (observed); sales receipts have been examined. We enclose the word *observations* in quotes here, because it is applied to data obtained by any of the methods in discussions of data analysis. The data are also frequently described as "measurements," a term that more aptly indicates how the numbers (or scores) arise.

However, the "raw" data is also manipulated in order to create more compact descriptions. This manipulation is often as simple as creating counts or tallies, as in the data in the "crossbreak" or "contingency" tables. Other manipulations are more involved, as in the calculation of the standard deviation. The reason for the anticipatory treatment was to give the reader a sense of the payoff involved in collecting and analyzing data. The analysis provides answers to our questions, and the answers allow us to control the environment directly or to predict certain outcomes and prepare to cope with them. We now step back to examine some of the statistical measures that aid us in describing, summarizing, and understanding a set of data values.

## Understanding the Data

The primary problem when faced with a set of data is the comprehension of its "meaning." What is the data telling us? An example can clarify the difficulty involved in analyzing and summarizing data. Suppose we have administered a test to 100 students and have obtained the raw scores shown in Table 5.1. The raw scores contain the "entire" information about the

TABLE 5.1

| Student code | Score |
|---|---|
| AA | 70 |
| AB | 68 |
| AC | 75 |
| AD | 87 |
| AE | 91 |
| AF | 82 |
| AG | 83 |
| AH | 68 |
| AI | 95 |
| AJ | 93 |
| AK | 61 |
| . | . |
| . | . |
| . | . |
| DT | 52 |
| DU | 87 |
| DV | 91 |

TABLE 5.2

| Student code | Test item | Score | Cumulative total | Total score |
|---|---|---|---|---|
| AA | 01 | 0 | 0 | |
| | 02 | 1 | 1 | |
| | 03 | 1 | 2 | |
| | 04 | 0 | 2 | |
| | . | . | . | |
| | . | . | . | |
| | . | . | . | |
| | 199 | 1 | 139 | |
| | 200 | 1 | 140 | 140/200 = .70 |
| AB | 01 | 0 | 0 | |
| | 02 | 1 | 1 | |
| | 03 | 1 | 2 | |
| | 04 | 1 | 3 | |
| | 05 | 1 | 4 | |
| | . | . | . | |
| | . | . | . | |
| | . | . | . | |
| | 199 | 0 | 136 | |
| | 200 | 0 | 136 | 136/200 = .68 |
| DV | 01 | 1 | 1 | |
| | 02 | 1 | 1 | |
| | . | . | . | |
| | . | . | . | |
| | . | . | . | |
| | 200 | 1 | 182 | 182/200 = .91 |

performance of the students, at least in terms of the "overall performance" of each student. As shown here, they do not include a breakdown of the individual test items. Say the test had 200 items. A more complete report would be that shown in Table 5.2. The values 0 and 1 in the "score" column indicate right (1) or wrong (0). The point is that a complete listing of all the data, the total information, is often not informative at all. We need some method of summarizing the data in order to make it comprehensible.

## Summarizing the Individual's Performance

The first method used to summarize the data of Table 5.2 was to compute a total score for each student to describe his or her performance on the test, leading to Table 5.1. This was done by creating the ratio

Total points student scored
Total possible points

| Number Answered Correctly | Number Answered Incorrectly | Total Items |
|---|---|---|
| 140 | 60 | 200 |

(a)

| Correct | Incorrect |
|---|---|
| .70 | .30 |

(b)

FIGURE 5.1

For the first student, AA, the calculation was

$$\frac{140}{200} = .70$$

This type of summary of individual performance led to the distribution of scores originally shown in Table 5.1.

The calculation of the student score is based on a count of the items answered correctly. This count is then expressed as a proportion of the highest possible count. In a tabular display, the count data would be shown as in Figure 5.1a. In terms of proportions, the table would be that of Figure 5.1b.

The reader will note that by expressing the number in the form of a proportion we get a "normalized" score that can be compared with performance on other tests, either of the same student over time

Student AA

| Test 1 | .70 |
|---|---|
| Test 2 | .65 |
| Test 3 | .82 |

or across students

| Student AA | .70 |
|---|---|
| Student BB | .68 |

In using the proportions we have also lost data, the information about the total number of items in the test. The summarization of data usually results in the production of a new value that is desirable for one goal (e.g., to compare scores) at the cost of a loss of some other information. In the case of the test scores, the loss can be prevented by keeping a table of tests and their lengths

| Test | Length (# of items) |
|------|---------------------|
| 1 | 200 |
| 2 | 150 |
| 3 | 250 |

so that we can later "weight" performances by the number of test items answered, giving greater credence to the scores on longer tests, less to those on short quizzes. For the data

| Tests for student AA | Scores | Length |
|----------------------|--------|--------|
| Test 1 | .70 | 140 |
| Test 4 | .52 | 10 |

we would most likely take the value of .70, obtained on a long test, as a "more true" estimate of student AA's ability than test 4, which was based on only 10 items. We could also compute an average by multiplying .70 by 140/150 and .52 by 10/150 and summing the results. However, we will not always be able to store all the relevant data. We will face a trade-off between the completeness of the information and the economy of storage. In addition, the comparison through summary totals is preferrable to a comparison of students' performance on each item in terms of understanding overall performance. The detailed data, Figure 5.2, is too specific to get the "big picture." We "throw some data away," or, what amounts to the same thing stated positively, we "abstract" certain data.

## Summarizing Class Performance

Besides questions about individual students such as "Did AA do better or worse or equal to student BB?", we would like to ask certain questions

|  | Student AA | Student AB |
|--------|------------|------------|
| Item 01 | 0 | 0 |
| Item 02 | 1 | 1 |
| Item 03 | 1 | 1 |
| Item 04 | 0 | 1 |

FIGURE 5.2

TABLE 5.3

| Score | Frequency |
|-------|-----------|
| 1.00 | 0 |
| .99 | 1 |
| .98 | 2 |
| .97 | 1 |
| . | . |
| . | . |
| . | . |
| .85 | 12 |
| .84 | 11 |
| . | . |
| . | . |
| . | . |
| .71 | 4 |
| .70 | 0 |
| .69 | 2 |
| .68 | 2 |
| .67 | 0 |
| No one below .68 | |

about class performance: Did the class do well? poorly? How does this class compare with previous classes? In order to summarize the data on the entire class, we could create a "frequency distribution" of the raw scores. A frequency distribution lists the number of students obtaining a particular score. For example, we might have the data of Table 5.3.

The frequency distribution has the same data as the original raw scores, simply organized in a different way, at least in terms of the scores themselves. (We have lost the data on which student had which score.) The frequency distribution allows for more ready comprehension of the data in that we can ascertain certain factors at a glance. The "range" of the scores was from .68 to .99; nobody got 100 and nobody got below 60 (an F in our class). Furthermore, some of the more "popular" scores were .85 and .84, as opposed to the less frequent scores of .98 or .68. It is the ability to make these statements about the data that motivates our efforts at reorganization.

## An Example

In order to give a complete example, we consider a fewer number of scores (Table 5.4). The frequency distribution would be that of Table 5.5, where we see that the range of scores is from .50 through .90, and that the most popular score (called the "mode" from the French word for "fashionable") is .70, with four people obtaining the score.

TABLE 5.4

| | |
|---|---|
| AA | .70 |
| AB | .80 |
| AC | .70 |
| AD | .90 |
| AE | .70 |
| AF | .60 |
| AG | .50 |
| AH | .90 |
| AI | .70 |
| AJ | .80 |
| AK | .60 |
| AL | .80 |

TABLE 5.5

| Score | Number of people obtaining score |
|---|---|
| .90 | 2 |
| .80 | 3 |
| .70 | 4 |
| .60 | 2 |
| .50 | 1 |

Relative Frequencies

The frequency distribution of raw scores can be transformed into a "relative frequency" distribution by dividing each category total by the total number of students (Table 5.6). The relative frequencies should sum to one, although they sometimes do not due to rounding error.

TABLE 5.6

| Score | # in Category | Relative frequency |
|---|---|---|
| .90 | 2 | 2/12 = .167 |
| .80 | 3 | 3/12 = .250 |
| .70 | 4 | 4/12 = .333 |
| .60 | 2 | 2/12 = .167 |
| .50 | 1 | 1/12 = .083 |

TABLE 5.7

| Score | Frequency | Cumulative frequency |
|-------|-----------|----------------------|
| 90 | 2 | 2 |
| 80 | 3 | 5 |
| 70 | 4 | 9 |
| 60 | 2 | 11 |
| 50 | 1 | 12 |
|  | $\overline{12}$ |  |

## Cumulative Frequency Distribution

In creating a cumulative distribution, we simply add the frequencies or the relative frequencies. The term *cumulative frequency* (no word *relative*) refers to the cumulation of the frequencies (no word *relative*) or count data (Table 5.7), while *cumulative proportions* (or *cumulative percentages*, if the distribution is in percents) refer to the cumulation of the relative frequencies (Table 5.8).

The direction in which the data is accumulated will depend on the type of questions one wishes to answer. For example, the data of Table 5.9 allows such statements as

40% of the class obtained scores of .80 or .90, say *A* or *B* in our grading scheme.

to be made easily. It is not readily apparent from the cumulative frequencies that only one student "failed" the exam, although this is evident from the frequencies or counts.

The proportion of students "failing" could be obtained from the cumulative frequencies by subtraction

$$1.000 - .917$$

since the proportion of .917 represents all the students obtaining "60 or above," or else from the relative frequencies.

If we sum the relative frequencies from the bottom up, we obtain Table 5.10. This type of cumulative frequency facilitates such statements as:

TABLE 5.8

| Score | Cumulative frequency | Cumulative relative frequency |
|-------|----------------------|-------------------------------|
| 90 | 2 | .167 |
| 80 | 5 | .417 |
| 70 | 9 | .750 |
| 60 | 11 | .917 |
| 50 | 12 | 1.000 |

TABLE 5.9

| Raw score | Frequency | Relative frequency | Cumulative frequency |
|---|---|---|---|
| .90 | 2 | .167 | .167 |
| .80 | 3 | .250 | .417 |
| .70 | 4 | .333 | .750 |
| .60 | 2 | .167 | .917 |
| .50 | 1 | .083 | 1.000 |

TABLE 5.10

| Scores | Frequency | Relative frequency | Cumulative frequency |
|---|---|---|---|
| .90 | 2 | .167 | 1.000 |
| .80 | 3 | .250 | .833 |
| .70 | 4 | .333 | .583 |
| .60 | 2 | .167 | .250 |
| .50 | 1 | .083 | .083 |

One-quarter of the class scored .60 or less,
i.e., *D* or *F*.

The two distributions are equivalent in that one can be derived from the other through mathematical manipulation:

% of class scoring .80 or above =
1 - percent scoring .70 or below =
1 - .583 = .417

A slightly different cumulation from the bottom up is used to calculate the "proportion of people scoring below a given score value." We cumulate the values at an offset of one interval (Table 5.11).

TABLE 5.11

| Raw score | Frequency | Relative frequency | Cumulative frequency |
|---|---|---|---|
| — | — | — | 1.000 |
| .90 | 2 | .167 | .833 |
| .80 | 3 | .250 | .583 |
| .70 | 4 | .333 | .250 |
| .60 | 2 | .167 | .083 |
| .50 | 1 | .083 | .000 |

The value of the cumulative frequency for an interval indicates the proportion of the population "exceeded" by a person in that interval. The student with a score of .50 exceeded no one; a student with a score of .60 exceeded .083 of the population, namely, the person with the score of .50; and the people scoring .70 surpassed .250 of the population. If the proportions are transformed into percentages

    .250       25%

we have the percentile ranking of each interval. Someone who ranks in the 99th percentile exceeds the majority of the population on that attribute (this may be good or bad, depending on the attribute). Someone in the fifth percentile ranks relatively low on the trait.

## Grouping Data

Our original frequency distribution of raw scores (Table 5.1) listed too many scores to be meaningful at a glance. When faced with such a lengthy frequency distribution we group the scores in order to see some general trends. Rules of thumb are sometimes given to guide the grouping. One such rule is that the intervals of the frequency distribution should all be equal, or that there should be a relatively small number of intervals, say between 6 and 15 or 12 and 20 (Freund, 1981). Grouping the original data into intervals of .90 and above, or .80 and above, does not yield equal intervals. The top interval, .90 through 1.00 includes eleven scores, the middle intervals (.60-.69, .70-.79, .80-.89) have 10 scores each, and the final interval, though labeled .50, is really "under .60," so that it includes the range from 0 through .59. However, this arrangement suits the purpose of our collecting the data: assigning grades.

## Terminology

The terms *frequency, relative frequency,* and *cumulative frequency* have specified meanings in the statistics literature, although they are used with various meanings by nonstatiticians. The term *frequency* refers to the original counts (Table 5.12a). The frequencies should always sum to the total number of subjects, objects, or "data elements." The term *relative*

TABLE 5.12a

| Score | Frequency count |
|-------|:-:|
| .90 | 2 |
| .80 | 3 |
| .70 | 4 |
| .60 | 2 |
| .50 | 1 |
| | 12 |

TABLE 5.12b

| Score | Relative frequency (proportion) |
|-------|-------------------------------|
| 90 | .167 |
| 80 | .250 |
| 70 | .333 |
| 60 | .167 |
| 50 | .083 |
| | 1.000 |

*frequency* is used to describe the data with the counts converted into proportions of the total population (Table 5.12b). These should always sum to one.

## Proportions and Percentages

Two other terms that are used interchangeably in common parlance but have specific meanings in the jargon of statisics are *proportion* and *percentage*. The term *proportion* refers to the decimal representations

.70 or .167

Here the test scores are the proportion of questions answered correctly, and the relative frequencies are the proportion of data elements in a given interval of scores.

Percentages are proportions converted by multiplying by 100:

.70 * 100 = 70%
.167 * 100 = 16.7%

## Single Measures of Description

The use of frequency distributions gives an overall picture of the data. They describe the distribution of the data across the scale of measurement. They indicate the relative position of the scores (ours were nearer to 100 than to 0) and their spread (ours ranged from 68 to 99). However, it is sometimes desirable to have single measures of description. Two of the most common are the mean and the standard deviation.

## The Mean: A Measure of Central Tendency

As we indicated earlier, a set of "raw" data is not always readily comprehensible. If I tell a student that he or she has achieved test scores of

42, 75, 31, 87, 92, 83, 75, 83

the student is likely to reply, "but what is my grade?" A more useful measure for this purpose is the average or "arithmetic" mean of the scores

Mean = 71

a "summary score" that can be used to assign a grade, say $C$, to the student.

The mean is referred to as a measure of central tendency. It tells us where the scores "clustered." It gives a single number that is representative of all scores in our set of data. Because we use one score to describe all the scores, it is a summary measure of the data. While most readers are probably familiar with the method of calculating the mean, we give a brief description here.

## Calculating the Mean

The mean (or average) is calculated by adding all the scores then dividing this sum by the number of scores. For example, if you have taken five tests in a course and have scored 90, 80, 70, 85, and 95 on these five exams; your average or mean score is calculated by adding the five scores

$$90 + 80 + 70 + 85 + 95 = 420$$

then dividing this total by 5

$$\frac{420}{5} = 84$$

so that your average is 84.

The process is sometimes summarized in the notation:

$$\frac{\Sigma x}{N}$$

where the symbol sigma ($\Sigma$) means "to sum," the symbol x refers to the raw score values, and the symbol N indicates the number of raw scores. To indicate more explicitly that there are usually several raw scores, the notation

$$\frac{\sum_{i=1}^{N} x_i}{N}$$

is used. The subscript i

$$x_i$$

is ranged over the values 1 through N

$$\sum_{i=1}^{N}$$

so that we add all the x's from $x_i$ through $x_N$. For our data, this would be

$$x_1 + x_2 + x_3 + x_4 + x_5$$

or

$$90 + 80 + 70 + 85 + 95 = 420$$

The summation gives the numerator. The denominator N then causes the division

$$\frac{420}{5} = 84$$

We introduce the formal notation to familiarize the reader with the methodology of expressing thoughts common to mathematics and statistics data. While the somewhat complex notation often expresses a relatively easy concept, the benefit of the notation, once one is familiar with it, is a succinct and unambiguous representation of certain ideas.

Note that while the mean of the scores was 84, not one score is actually that number. The number 84 represents the point around which the actual scores "seemed to gather," the point they "centered on." It may or may not represent a real score.

## Calculating the Mean from the Frequency Listing

To calculate the mean from a frequency distribution such as that shown in Table 5.13 we use multiplication and addition. The scores within each category are multiplied by the frequency of the score (Figure 5.3a). This has the same effect as independently adding the individual scores (Figure 5.3b). These products are then summed, and the total divided by the number of scores (Figure 5.3c). The process is equivalent to, but computationally faster than adding the individual scores. If the categories allow scores of several values, e.g., 80–89, with scores obtained for 80, 81, etc., the "midpoint" of the interval is used in place of the single values 90 and 80. Then the computation is the same.

If the scores are expressed in terms of relative frequencies instead of "raw" frequencies, we compute the product of the score and the relative frequency (Figure 5.4). The mean is the sum of the column S*Rf. There is no need to divide by the total number of scores, since this division by 25 has already been performed in computing the relative frequencies. The result of this latter calculation, multiplying a relative frequency (or a probability) times a "value" (here the scores), then summing the products to obtain the mean is called "the expected value." This terminology reflects the fact that the mean is considered the expected value in cases in which we have "no other information" about an individual or other entity. If we had to predict a test score about an arbitrary student, we would predict the value of the mean, here 74.4. In this particular case, raw scores rounded to the nearest whole number, we would not get a value of 74.4,

## TABLE 5.13

| Score | Frequency |
| --- | --- |
| 90 | 4 |
| 80 | 8 |
| 70 | 9 |
| 60 | 3 |
| 50 | 1 |

| Score(S) | Frequency(F) | S*F |
|----------|--------------|-----|
| 90 | 4 | 360 |
| 80 | 8 | |
| 70 | 9 | |
| 60 | 3 | |
| 50 | 1 | |

FIGURE 5.3a

| |
|---|
| 90 |
| 90 |
| 90 |
| 90 |
| 360 |

FIGURE 5.3b

| Score | Frequency | S*F |
|-------|-----------|-----|
| 90 | 4 | 360 |
| 80 | 8 | 640 |
| 70 | 9 | 630 |
| 60 | 3 | 180 |
| 50 | 1 | 50 |
| | 25 | 1860 |

1860 ÷ 25 = 74.4, mean

FIGURE 5.3c

so we might predict a value of 74 or 70. We could also use one of the other measures of central tendency, e.g., the median or mode, to make a prediction. The arithmetic mean (or simply the mean) is only one type of "expected value." However, the calculation of the particular value called "the expected value" results in the calculation of the arithmetic mean. The notation for the expected value is

$$EV = p_1 V_1 + p_2 V_2 + p_3 V_3 + \ldots + p_N V_N$$

| Scores | Relative frequency (RF) (f ÷ 25) | S*RF |
|--------|-----------------------------------|------|
| 90 | .16 | 14.40 |
| 80 | .32 | 25.60 |
| 70 | .36 | 25.20 |
| 60 | .12 | 7.20 |
| 50 | .04 | 2.00 |
| | 1.00 | 74.40 |

FIGURE 5.4

where p stands for the probability of a score's occurrence, here its relative frequency; and V stands for the value of the item in question, here the score itself. Thus, we multiply p*V for each probability-value pair. Here we had five such pairs, so that n is 5.

$$EV = p_1V_1 + p_2V_2 + p_3V_3 + p_4V_4 + p_5V_5$$

$$= .16(90) + .32(80) + .36(70) + .12(60) + .04(50)$$

$$= 74.40$$

The repeated summation is indicated by a sigma, using the i-subscript notation

$$EV = \sum_{i=1}^{n} p_iV_i$$

## The Median

The median is another measure of central tendency. It is the "middle score" in a distribution in terms of value. For the scores

80, 90, 70, 85, 95

we would obtain the median by first sorting the scores in ascending or descending order

70, 80, 85, 90, 95

then find the middle score by "inspection" (or counting).

70, 80, 85, 90, 95

If there are an odd number of scores, the median will be an actual score, here 85. If there are an even number of scores, the median will be the average of the two middle scores.

65, 70, 80, 85, 90, 95

median = 82.5

In this case, the score will not be a real score unless the two middle values are equal.

70, 80, 85, 85, 90, 95

median = 85

The median is considered a good measure of the central tendency in cases in which a single data value (or a set of data values) is extreme and distorts the mean.

TABLE 5.14

| Income | Frequency | I*F | |
|---|---|---|---|
| $1,000,000 | 12 | 12,000,000 | Mean = 14,500,000/262 |
| $10,000 | 250 | 2,500,000 | Median = average of 131st |
| | | 14,500,000 | and 132nd score |

### Effect of Extreme Scores on Mean and Median

Given the data

20, 89, 90, 95, 96

the mean would be 78. The median would be 90. The value of the mean has been "pulled down" by the score of 20. The value of the median, 90, would remain unchanged whether the value of the lowest score were 20, 15, or 88. It is the middle score regardless of the values of the scores beneath or above it. (Only the number of such scores, not their actual value, makes a difference.)

In one sense the mean gives a better picture of the data in that it takes into account the value of all scores. The median does not take the value into account except for ordering of the scores and (in some cases) in the calculation of a mean score for two middle scores

65, 70, 80, 85, 90, 95
↑    ↑

82.5

and in this case it takes into account only the value of the two scores. The median is thus a descriptive measure based on less information. However, in the case of relatively few extreme scores, the "weakness" in the calculation of the median becomes its strength; its value is unaffected by extreme scores.

A typical example of a situation in which the median is useful is in statements about "average" income. Given the frequencies of Table 5.14, the mean would be $55,343.51 or $55,000 to the nearest thousand dollars. A more accurate picture of the state of the "general" population would be the mean of $10,000 (the 131st and 132nd scores will both be $10,000).

### The Mode

The mode is another measure of central tendency. It indicates the "most popular" or most frequently occurring score. In the data of Table 5.15, the score 82, which occurred three times, would be the modal score. The mode is easily identified on a bar graph of frequencies or relative frequencies (Figure 5.5a) since it is the highest bar or "peak" of the distribution. Some distributions are "bimodal" in that they have two peaks (Figure 5.5b). This is often indicative of two different populations. If the results of a test are as shown in Table 5.16, the graphic display (Figure 5.5c) indicates that we have two different groups of students: those

TABLE 5.15

| Student | Test Score |
|---------|------------|
| A | 70 |
| B | 82 |
| C | 71 |
| D | 85 |
| E | 82 |
| F | 90 |
| G | 73 |
| H | 71 |
| I | 82 |
| J | 87 |

getting the material and those not. Whether or not these differences reflect differences in background, motivation, abilities, study habits, or other characteristics would require further study and further data collection and analysis.

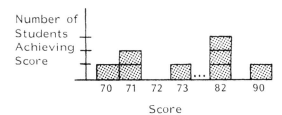

(a)

(b)

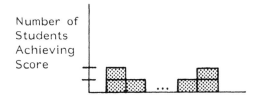

(c)

FIGURE 5.5

TABLE 5.16

| Student | Score |
| --- | --- |
| A | 62 |
| B | 91 |
| C | 92 |
| D | 63 |
| E | 92 |
| F | 62 |

### The Word Average

The three measures of central tendency—mean, median, and mode—are all called "averages." There are also other measures of central tendency referred to as averages. The term *average* is ambiguous. In common parlance it is usually considered synonymous with the arithmetic mean. However, in discussing data it is usually best to use the terms *mean, median,* or *mode* rather than the term *average.*

### Types of Data

The question of data type or "level of measurement" applies to the measures of central tendency. The calculation of the mean is not appropriate to all data. For example, if we have data on the number of students of each sex

Males       52
Females     48

these might be coded with a zero for male, a one for female (Figure 5.6). The numerical appearance of the 0 and 1 suggests that they might be used in a calculation, such as

$$0 * 52 = 0$$
$$1 * 48 = \underline{48}$$
$$48 \div 100 = .48, \text{ mean}$$

However, the statement that the average student is a .48 is difficult to interpret, being neither male nor female.

As indicated earlier, data such as that on sex, eye color, or religion is categorical data. The objects or events are placed in categories, but the categories are not "quantitative" in the sense of height or weight. For such data only the mode is appropriate. The mean is inappropriate because

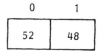

FIGURE 5.6

of the lack of a quantitative scale. The median is also inappropriate because there is no natural ordering of the scores. Boxes on eye color could just as well be listed in the order blue, brown, green, and grey as in the order grey, green, blue, and brown. There is no "middle" category or score.

If data can be ordered, such as the temperature of a cup of coffee, IQ scores, or the quality point average (QPA) of students, both the median and the mode can be computed. The data is referred to as "ordered" or "ranked" data. Thus, in the set of temperatures

15°, 20°, 45°, 80°, 92°

the median temperature would be 45°. The mode is not very meaningful here, since each score occurs only once. They are all the mode. In the data

15°, 20°, 20°, 20°, 45°, 60°, 80°, 92°, 98°

the median would be 45°, the mode 20°. As the reader can glean from the example, the choice of statistic can give a varying picture of the data.

The mean is appropriate only with data that is quantitative (in the sense of an "interval" or a "ratio" scale). A ratio scale is one with an absolute zero and equal intervals between the units of the scale. Height and weight are such scales. Presumably IQ is not, and certainly the Fahrenheit and centigrade scores are not. On the Fahrenheit scale the zero point is less than the freezing point of water (32°F), while on the centigrade scale the zero point is at the freezing point of water (0°C). The zero point on these scales is a convention and does not represent a "true zero point." It does not mean "zero of some quantity," say heat. Similar comments apply to the IQ scale in that its zero point probably does not indicate the lack of any intelligence whatsoever. However, the primary reason why some claim that a given IQ scale is not "quantitative" is that it often lacks equal intervals. The distance from an IQ of 100 to an IQ of 130 may not be the same as the distance from an IQ of 120 to an IQ of 150. The scores can be ordered: an IQ of 150 is greater than an IQ of 100; but we can't say exactly how much greater. (Some claim equal intervals for some IQ scales, but this is disputed.)

The temperature scale is an "equal interval" scale in that the unit of measurement, the degree, is the same throughout the scale. Hence, differences between temperatures, such as 73°-70°, are comparable to differences at other points of the scale, say 43°-40°. The hierarchy of scales is:

1. Categorical
2. Ordered
3. Equal interval
4. Ratio

The mode is appropriate to all four; the median is appropriate to ordered and quantitative; and the mean to interval and ratio scales.

The name *ratio* indicates that ratios of individual numbers, which are necessary to the arithmetic calculation of division, are meaningful. A person 6 ft. tall is twice the size of a person three ft. tall. This is not the case with nonratio scales. The intelligence of a person with an IQ of 100 is not necessarily twice that of a person with an IQ of 50. The number one football team in the nation (rank order) is not necessarily twice as good as the number two team, and blue eyes are not twice as anything as brown eyes (wavelengths of light not being considered).

## The Hot and Cold Coffee

One of the more interesting examples of the use and misuse of such statistical measures as the mean and median is given by Skyrms (1966). He uses the data of Table 5.17a. The data do not allow for a mean calculation, at least as listed here, but they do allow for the calculation of the mode, the median, or both. The mode, or most popular data value, is cold (four occurrences). With nine scores, the median or middle score is tepid (with four scores being more warm, four being colder).

If we ask about the "typical" or "average" cup of coffee in the establishment, someone using the mode would reply

It is cold.

while someone using the median would reply

It is tepid.

Since neither of these replies is particularly appetizing, the difference would have no pragmatic effect; we will not patronize the restaurant in either case. The point, however, is that the description of "reality" changed with the statistic used, even though the reality (the data values) were static. Such a "moving" account of the state of the world is not always desirable.

## Use or Misuse?

One might ask whether the use of either the median or the mode is a misuse of statistics. The question is not an easy one. Given the data on coffee temperature, which is ordered along the dimension of heat, both the mode and the median are legitimate statistics. That each gives a "different picture" is a result of the interaction between the statistic and the data. The mode says that the most commonly occurring event is the reception of a cold cup of coffee. The median says that half the time you get a cup of coffee better than tepid, half the time one worse than tepid. In fact, in this instance the median is probably the statistic least damaging to the restaurant.

TABLE 5.17a

| Category | Frequency |
| --- | --- |
| Boiling Hot | 2 |
| Comfortably Hot | 2 |
| Tepid | 1 |
| Cold | 4 |

TABLE 5.17b

| | |
|---|---|
| Boiling Hot | 2 |
| Comfortably Hot | 3 |
| Tepid | 2 |
| Cold | 2 |
| Very Cold | 2 |

The reason the question of misuse comes up is shown in the data of Table 5.17b. The median is still tepid, but the mode is comfortably hot. Any restaurant operating in the rational manner of the "economic man" would report the mode and discard the median. A competitor would report the median and a presumably impartial food critic might report both. (For an interesting discussion of ways to "lie with statistics," see Huff [1954]).

## Measures of Spread

Distributions of data can exhibit the same mean (or median or mode) yet not represent the same "picture." For example, the test scores for students A, B, and C

    A;   70, 70, 70
    B:   60, 70, 80
    C:   40, 70, 100

all have a mean score of 70, but they certainly do not exhibit the same performance characteristics over time. Student A, Steady Eddie, shows no variation in his scores; student B, Mild Mary, shows some variance; and student C seems to be manic-depressive!

In order to summarize the variability of scores, we need a measure of "range" or "spread." Just as there are several measures of central tendency, there are several measures of variability.

## The Range

The range of scores is a measure of variability that is analogous to the median. It considers the values of only two scores, the highest and the lowest

    Range = high score − low score

The respective ranges of students in the previous illustration are

| Student | High | Low | Range |
|---|---|---|---|
| A | 70 | 70 | 0 |
| B | 60 | 80 | 20 |
| C | 40 | 100 | 60 |

We sometimes state the range in English by stating the high and low scores

Student B's scores ranged from 60 through 80.

instead of performing the subtraction, but the idea is the same.

## The Standard Deviation

The measure of variability analogous to the mean is the standard deviation. In calculating the standard deviation, we examine the distance of each score from the mean—its "deviation" from the mean—then attempt to summarize the deviations of all scores in the distribution.

## Calculating the Standard Deviation

To calculate the standard deviation we first compare each score to the mean in order to obtain its deviation value. Using the data from the earlier example of calculating the mean we have the deviations shown in Table 5.18a. The individual deviations exhibit both a magnitude and a direction. They are "vectors." (A vector is simply a value that possesses both magnitude and direction, e.g., the description of the hands of a clock, where the minute hand could be described by its relationship to the position 12 and the size of its distance from 12: 2 min before, 3 min after; or the velocity of a car: 30 mph due west.)

The student's performance on test 1 was "below average" (direction −) but just by a little (magnitude 4); the student's performance on the fifth test was above average (direction +) by quite a bit (magnitude 11).

In order to describe the deviations of all scores we might attempt to take a total of the individual deviations. If we do so we see that the sum is zero. The positive deviations (+6 + 1 + 11 = +18) balance the negative deviations (−4 + −14 = −18). One method of handling this cancellation of values is to take the absolute value of the deviations. However, in calculating the standard deviation, the method used is to square each deviation (Table 5.18b).

As in the calculation of chi-square, the squared value has two desirable properties

1. It makes the numbers positive
2. It weights large deviations more heavily than small deviations:

## TABLE 5.18a

| Score | Mean | Deviation |
| --- | --- | --- |
| 80 | 84 | −4 |
| 90 | 84 | +6 |
| 70 | 84 | −14 |
| 85 | 84 | +1 |
| 95 | 84 | +11 |

TABLE 5.18b

| d | $d^2$ |
|---|---|
| -4 | 16 |
| +6 | 36 |
| -14 | 196 |
| +1 | 1 |
| +11 | 121 |

$$d = 2 \qquad d^2 = 4$$
$$d = 10 \qquad d^2 = 100$$

where the deviations differ by only 8 points, but the squares differ by 96 points

After squaring the deviations we sum these squared values ($\Sigma d^2$; Table 5.19) then take the "average" or mean of this sum

$$\frac{\Sigma d^2}{N} = \frac{370}{5} = 74$$

This value, the "mean squared deviation" is called the "variance." It is also referred to as a "mean square" because it is the mean of the squared deviations. The sum of the squared deviations ($d^2$) is referred to as the "sum of squares." Hence, we could write

$$\text{Mean square} = \frac{\text{sum of squares}}{\text{number of scores}}$$

or

$$\text{Variance} = \frac{\Sigma d^2}{N}$$

The variance is a useful measure in many statistical calculations. The final step in the calculation of the standard deviation is to "undo" the squaring of the deviations by taking the square root of the variance

$$\text{S.D.} = \text{SQRT (variance)}$$

For our data this is

TABLE 5.19

| d | $d^2$ |
|---|---|
| -4 | 16 |
| +6 | 36 |
| -14 | 196 |
| +1 | 1 |
| +11 | 121 |
| | 370 |

TABLE 5.20

| Raw score | Mean | d | $d^2$ |
|---|---|---|---|
| 80 | 84 | −4 | 16 |
| 90 | 84 | +6 | 36 |
| 70 | 84 | −14 | 196 |
| 85 | 84 | +1 | 1 |
| 95 | 84 | +11 | 121 |
| | | | 370 |

$370/5 = 74$, variance

$\sqrt{74} \approx 8.6$, standard deviation

$$SQRT(74) = > 8.6$$

We use the notation d for the deviations. An alternative notation is

$$(x - \mu)$$

where we explicitly indicate the method by which the deviations are obtained: subtracting the value of the mean from each score. The sum of squares is then

$$SS = \Sigma(x - \mu)^2$$

the variance is

$$var = \frac{\Sigma(x - \mu)^2}{N}$$

and the standard deviation is

$$\sigma = \frac{\Sigma(x - \mu)^2}{N}$$

In summary, the process is:

1. Calculate the mean of the raw scores.
2. Calculate deviation of each score from the mean.
3. Square the deviations.
4. Sum the squared deviations [yielding sum of squares $\Sigma d^2$ or $\Sigma(x - \mu)^2$].
5. Divide by the number of scores (yielding variance).
6. Take the square root of the variance (yielding standard deviation).

A summary of the process is shown in Table 5.20.

## Sample Values and Population Values

We are currently treating the mean and the standard deviation as descriptive measures of a population. They are used to summarize the data on the class, and the class is considered to be the "entire population." When talking about the population values (parameters) it is customary to use the Greek letters mu and sigma

μ ≡ mean of the population

σ ≡ standard deviation of the population

When talking of sample data (i.e., statistics computed on sample data) the notation "x-bar" (or y-bar) and "s" is used

$\bar{x}$ ≡ mean of a sample (also $\bar{y}$)

s ≡ standard deviation of a sample

The individual scores are indicated by an uppercase $X$ in the population (and an uppercase $Y$), a lowercase $x$ in the sample data, but usage varies. The number of scores is indicated by an uppercase $N$ in the population, a lowercase $n$ in the sample.

These notations are common usage in statistics, not mathematics, generally speaking, where a lowercase $x$ and a lowercase $n$ might be more common. One can usually determine the meaning of the notation from the context of the discussion.

When working with sample data the calculations of the standard deviation are sometimes slightly different from those used for calculating population values. For example, if the population standard deviation is being estimated from the sample standard deviation, the calculation of the standard deviation is made with n − 1 in the denominator

$$s = \frac{\Sigma d^2}{n - 1}$$

This adjustment makes the denominator smaller, and the entire fraction larger. The reason for "inflating" the value of the standard deviation is that the variability of a sample is systematically smaller than the population value. We adjust for this "bias" by inflating the sample value a bit. (Note: the variance of a single sample could be greater than that in the population variance; however, the "usual" state of affairs is for the sample to have less variability.)

The mean of a sample is considered to be an "unbiased" estimate of the population mean, hence its value is not adjusted in the calculations. This is not to say that the sample mean is always accurate, an exact replica of the population mean. It is usually incorrect by some amount. However, when the mean is inaccurate, the inaccuracies are just as likely to be on the side "too large" as the side "too small." It is not biased in a single direction. If we took many samples the deviations of the sample means above the value of the true mean would be balanced by deviations below the true mean, canceling each other in a manner similar to balancing deviations in the raw scores. The average of all sample means for a sample of a given size will be the "true" mean of the population. This averaging of all values to the true population value is what is meant by an unbiased estimation. This is not true of the average value of sample standard deviations, if calculated with n in the denominator. The average of the sample values will be biased in the "low" direction so that we should inflate the value obtained in a sample to get a more accurate estimate of the population value. The average of the estimates made with n − 1 in the denominator will be equal to the true population value; i.e., the calculation with n − 1 in the denominator is an unbiased estimator.

FIGURE 5.7

## Distributions of Data

Very often we find that our "observed" data fit certain theoretical distributions of data. One of the most familiar of these distributions is the "normal curve." The form of the normal curve is the familiar bell shape that is often used to "balance the A's with the F's" on an exam (Figure 5.7). The "normal curve" is really a family of curves, each of which exhibits a given mathematical relationship between the mean and standard deviation of the data. We will be interested not in the formula itself, but in the interpretation of normally distributed data. That the data are normally distributed should be established by the researcher or by prior theory (e.g., it is often assumed that such naturally occurring attributes as the physical characteristics of height and weight, or the mental characteristic of intelligence are normally distributed). Statistical tests, such as chi-square, can be used to empirically determine if a set of data approximates the normal distribution.

## An Example of Normally Distributed Data

Probably the simplest way to understand the normal curve is to see one "in action." Suppose that we toss a coin 30 times, noting the result of each toss. At the end of 30 tosses, we would "expect" to have 15 outcomes of

TABLE 5.21 Number of Heads in 30 Tosses of a Coin

| | | | | | | | | | |
|---|---|---|---|---|---|---|---|---|---|
| 11 | 16 | 17 | 15 | 17 | 16 | 19 | 18 | 15 | 13 |
| 11 | 17 | 17 | 12 | 20 | 23 | 11 | 16 | 17 | 14 |
| 16 | 12 | 15 | 10 | 18 | 17 | 13 | 15 | 14 | 15 |
| 16 | 12 | 11 | 22 | 12 | 20 | 12 | 15 | 16 | 12 |
| 16 | 10 | 15 | 13 | 14 | 16 | 15 | 16 | 13 | 18 |
| 14 | 14 | 13 | 16 | 15 | 19 | 21 | 14 | 12 | 15 |
| 16 | 11 | 16 | 14 | 17 | 14 | 11 | 16 | 17 | 16 |
| 19 | 15 | 14 | 12 | 18 | 15 | 14 | 21 | 11 | 16 |
| 17 | 17 | 12 | 15 | 14 | 17 | 9 | 13 | 16 | 13 |
| 12 | 14 | 17 | 18 | 12 | 14 | 17 | 19 | 17 | 19 |

heads and 15 outcomes of tails (since the two outcomes are equally probable). This might be the case; then it might not be the case. We might actually have gotten 16 heads and 14 tails, or 17 heads and 13 tails. The actual numbers would be "around" 15, but they might "deviate" by a little bit. In an experiment carried out by Feynman (1963), the results of 100 tosses of 30 pennies were as follows (numbers indicate the number of heads; Table 5.21). We can see that not all 100 instances (samples) of 30 tossed coins came out exactly 15 heads and 15 tails. In fact, only 13 of the samples came out exactly 15 and 15. Eighty-seven trials came out with some other figures. However, the "some other figures" are "not usually" too far from 15. In fact, the fewest number of heads was 9, which occurred only once; the largest number was 23, which occurred only once. While these values are "pretty extreme," it is noteworthy that there were never any values as small as 8, nor any as large as 24. Furthermore, the most popular deviations from "15 and 15 heads" were "14 heads," "16 heads," and "17 heads," all of which hover around the "expected value" of 15.

## The Frequency Table

We can get a better picture of the distribution of the results by creating a frequency table showing the number of heads and the number of times that number for heads occurred (Table 5.22). Such a table shows that the majority of trials tended to cluster around the middle values of 14, 15, 16, and 17, with very few values out at the "tail" ends of 9 and 23.

TABLE 5.22

| Number of heads | Frequency |
| --- | --- |
| 9 | 1 |
| 10 | 2 |
| 11 | 7 |
| 12 | 11 |
| 13 | 7 |
| 14 | 13 |
| 15 | 13 |
| 16 | 16 |
| 17 | 14 |
| 18 | 5 |
| 19 | 5 |
| 20 | 2 |
| 21 | 2 |
| 22 | 1 |
| 23 | 1 |

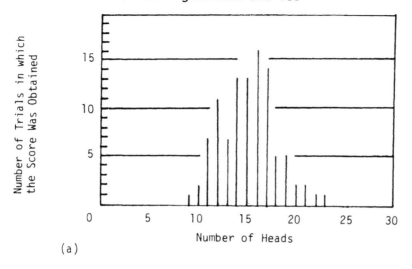

(a)

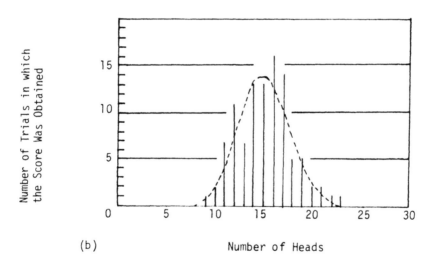

(b)

FIGURE 5.8

## A Graphic Display

We can get an even better "picture" if we draw a line graph, bar chart, or histogram of the data. The line graph for these data is shown in Figure 5.8a. The height of the bars indicate the number of times we got that many heads, i.e., the "counts."

Finally, if we impose a "normal curve" onto our graph, we can see that the 100 trials of 30 tosses do indeed "approximate" the normal curve (Figure 5.8b).

## Idealizations

As Professor Feynman points out in his text (a text in physics, not statistics), physical laws are approximations of reality (p. 12-2). The laws summarize things in an ideal way, telling us what would occur under idealized conditions. Mathematical descriptions of data, which is what the normal curve really gives, are also idealizations; seldom do we have a set of data that perfectly fits the normal curve. However, if the data does approximate the normal curve, we can make some useful calculations and predictions based on the nature of the normal curve.

## The Intervals of Interest

The primary intervals of interest on the normal curve are those between 1, 2, and 3 standard deviations above and below the mean. If we know the mean of a set of data, we have certain expectations about individual scores. For example, if the mean height of the adult male is 5 ft. 10 in. (hypothetical) we expect the heights of most men to be close to 5'10", 5'11", 6'0", 5'9", and 5'8". We expect very few heights to be 7'0 in. or 4'6 in. For normally distributed data the standard deviation formalizes this expectation of the magnitude and frequency of the deviations of individual scores from the group mean. We can expect

- 68% of the population to have data values on the attribute in question that fall within the interval from one standard deviation above the mean to one standard deviation below the mean
- 95% of the population to have data values within the interval of two standard deviations above the mean through two standard deviations below the mean
- 99% of the population to have data values in the interval of three standard deviations above the mean through three standard deviations below the mean
- Very few people to have data values exceeding three standard deviations in either direction
- The mean itself to have a deviation value of zero

These values can be illustrated by considering various areas under the normal curve.

## The Mean

The highest point of the curve is the mean (also mode and median; Figure 5.9a). The area above the mean (scores higher than the mean) is equal to the area beneath the mean, with 50% of the scores falling above the mean, and 50% below (Figure 5.9b). This distribution is only roughly approximated in the first example, the test scores, since there are three scores above the mean of 84 (90, 85, 95), and only two scores below (80, 70). We say that the data is approximated by the normal curve; the fit is not exact. A larger number of scores would give a better fit (if the data truly is normally distributed).

If we now divide the area under the curve into "standard deviations above and below the mean," indicating one standard deviation above the

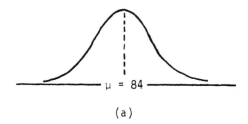

(a)

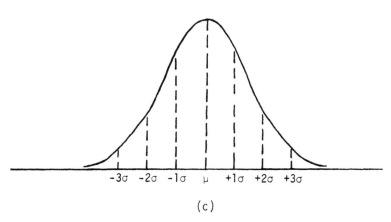

(b)

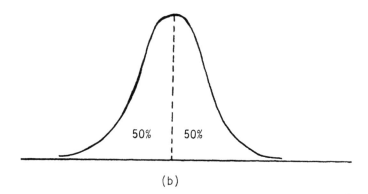

(c)

FIGURE 5.9

mean by $+\sigma$, and one standard deviation below the mean by $-\sigma$, the curve looks like Figure 5.9c. It is in this representation of the normal curve that we can place percentages on the number of scores falling within the intervals.

1. 68% of the scores fall between one standard deviation above and below the mean (Figure 5.10a).
2. 95% of the scores fall between two standard deviations above and below the mean (Figure 5.10b).

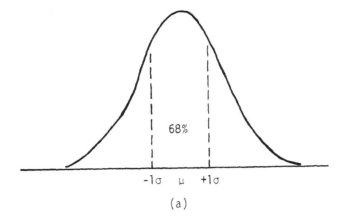

(a)

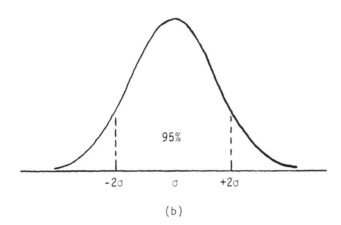

(b)

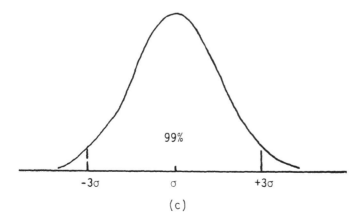

(c)

FIGURE 5.10

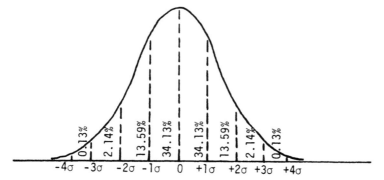

FIGURE 5.11

3. 99% of the scores fall between three standard deviations above and below the mean (Figure 5.10c).

Actually, these numbers are approximations. A more accurate picture of the percentages is shown in Figure 5.11, where we see that 34.13% of the actual scores will be 1σ above the mean, and 34.13% will be 1σ below the mean, giving a total of 68.26% in the interval bracketed by one standard deviation above and below the mean. However, we will use the approximations of 68%, 95%, and 99% for our three intervals, since these numbers are close enough for our purposes, and easier to use than the more accurate values.

## Calculating the Intervals

A frequently recurring task in the use of normally distributed data is the creation of the interval values in terms of the raw scores. The computations are quite straightforward. Using the data on test scores

$$\mu = 84$$

$$\sigma = 8.6$$

we compute the 68% interval by adding and subtracting the value 8.6 to (or from) the mean

Low value  : 84 − 8.6 = 75.4

High value : 84 + 8.6 = 92.6

   or 75.4 through 92.6

Checking the original data, 3 of the 5 scores (60% rather than 68%) are found in this interval (the scores of 80, 90, and 85 being between 75.5 and 92.6).

The 95% interval will be calculated as

Low value  : 84 − 2(8.6) = 84 − 17.2 = 66.8

High value : 84 + 2(8.6) = 84 + 17.2 = 101.2

The value of 101.2 is outside the range of test scores (100% being high) so that we would state the 95% interval as

66.8 to 100.0

This would prevent the data from being exactly normally distributed, but it is an occurrence that creeps into real situations.

The 99% interval would be

Low value  : $84 - 3(8.6) = 84 - 25.8 = 58.2$

High value : $84 + 3(8.6) = 84 + 25.8 = 109.8$

(artificially cut off at 100%)

so that 99% of the scores would be expected in the interval 58.2 through 100.0.

In terms of Professor Feynman's example, the theoretical mean of the set of tosses is 15. If the reader will accept the fact that the theoretical standard deviation of the obtained means (obtained on each toss of 30 coins) is approximately 2.8, we would expect

68% of the trials to result in means in the interval $15 \pm 2.8$ or from 12.2 to 17.8
95% in the interval $15 \pm 2(2.8)$
$= 15 \pm 5.6$ or 9.4 to 20.6
97% to be in the interval $15 \pm 3(2.8)$
$= 15 \pm 8.4$ or 6.6 to 23.4

Since the obtained means can only be integers, we convert these intervals to whole numbers*

12.2 − 17.8 ⟶ 13 to 17 (68%)

9.4 − 20.6 ⟶ 10 to 20 (95%)

6.6 − 23.4 ⟶ 7 to 23 (99%)

The obtained frequencies were

| Interval | Frequency |
|---|---|
| 13 - 17 | 63% |
| 10 - 20 | 95% |
| 7 - 23 | 100% |

so that the theory and the empirical results are quite close.

## Different Distributions

The theoretical distribution most applicable to the data in this example is the binomial distribution, which is a distribution of "counts" that is applicable in "two-outcome" events. Tossing a coin is such a two-outcome event

---

*The numbers were not "rounded" but artificially chosen for purposes of the example. This is not standard practice; it is probably equivalent to searching around for "better data."

(heads or tails). Other two-outcome events are "potential customer comes into store, potential customer does not come into store"; "purchase, don't purchase"; "light bulb works, light bulb doesn't work"; "person stays alive today, person doesn't." Such events are often of interest to business organizations, e.g., in the study of sales, or in quality control, and, as in the case of staying alive, in the study of data relevant to insurance rates.

Not all studies of two-event processes would use the binomial distribution. There are other assumptions that should be verified before its use in a given situation. For example, the events should be "independent" and their probability of occurrence "static" or "the same" over all trials. These assumptions are fulfilled in coin-tossing experiments in which the outcome of the toss of one coin presumably has no effect on the outcome of the toss of another coin, and the probability of heads remains at one-half (as does the probability of tails). It is not necessary that the probabilities of the two events be equal. For example, one event may occur with the probability .2 (say the probability of a potential customer actually making a purchase), the other with the probability .8.

In using the binomial distribution one needs to know the number of "trials," as well as the probability of each event. If a coin is tossed three times, there are three "trials." The possible outcomes are stated as the number of occurrences of a given event (the event of interest is called a success, even if it is "not successful," e.g., a defective light bulb). For the toss of a coin, with heads being called a success, the possible outcomes are:

0 Heads
1 Heads
2 Heads
3 Heads

The probability of each event can be calculated directly for a small number of trials. For zero heads, this can occur only if we have the three individual outcomes

T   T   T

Each of these outcomes T occurs with probability of one-half. To calculate the probability of all three events occurring, we multiply the individual probabilities

$$\frac{1}{2} \cdot \frac{1}{2} \cdot \frac{1}{2} = \frac{1}{8}$$

so the probability of obtaining zero heads (or, what is the same, three tails) is

| Outcome | Probability of Outcome |
| --- | --- |
| 0 Heads | 1/8 |

Similar reasoning applies to the event of three heads. The only way this can occur is

H   H   H

and the multiplication of individual probabilities yields

$$\frac{1}{2} \cdot \frac{1}{2} \cdot \frac{1}{2} = \frac{1}{8}$$

so we have

| Outcome of 3 Trials | Probability of Outcome |
|---|---|
| 0 H | 1/8 |
| 3 H | 1/8 |

and we still need to calculate the probabilities of the outcomes 1H and 2H.

## Independent Events

Multiplying the individual probabilities to get the value for "both" events (event 1 = H *and* event 2 = H) or "all" events, here

(toss 1 = H) *and* (toss 2 = H) *and* (toss 3 = H)

only applies if the events are independent, hence the assumption of "independence" of events before using the binomial distribution to a two-event process (also called Beroulli processes after the mathematician who developed the theory). In the case of dependent events, a different formula for the conjunction of events is applicable. The cooccurrence of two individual events is also called a "joint event."

## The Probabilities of 1H and 2H

The calculation of the event 1H is a little more complex than that of 0H and 3H. The event 1H can occur in three different ways

H   T   T

T   H   T

T   T   H

*Each* of these ways has a probability of 1/8. This is from the multiplication rule for independent events (tosses)

p(HTT)  = p(H) * p(T) * p(T)

$$= \frac{1}{2} * \frac{1}{2} * \frac{1}{2} = \frac{1}{8}$$

FIGURE 5.12a

so that we have the probability of 1/8 for *each* outcome

$$p(HTT) = \frac{1}{8}$$

$$p(THT) = \frac{1}{8}$$

$$p(TTH) = \frac{1}{8}$$

However, in describing the "overall outcome" as "one head," we are saying that the individual outcomes of (HTT) or (THT) or (TTH) will be taken
to be "equivalent." We will say "one head occurred" if (HTT) *or* (THT)
*or* (TTH) occurred. When combining "mutually exclusive" events in the
"or" condition, we add the individual probabilities, hence, for (HTT),
(THT), or (TTH) we compute

$$\frac{1}{8} + \frac{1}{8} + \frac{1}{8} = \frac{3}{8}$$

The probability of obtaining one head in three tosses is 3/8.

We say "mutually exclusive" events because the simple addition formula
does not apply if the events are not mutually exclusive. The description
"mutually exclusive" means two of the events cannot occur "together."
For this data, the interpretation is that the events (HTT) and (THT)
cannot both occur in the same set of three tosses. An example of outcomes
that are not mutually exclusive would be:

The next person who comes through the door will be a woman.
The next person who comes through the door will be an electrician.

Both outcomes, female and electrician, could occur together (Figure 5.12a).
They can "intersect" in one person, a female electrician. Mutually exclusive
events have no "common" intersection, no "overlap" of diagrammed outcomes (Figure 5.12b).

The reader should verify that the probability of the outcome "two
heads" is also 3/8. This can be done by direct calculation as above. It
also follows from the fact that the events 0H, 1H, and 3H have one "or"
probability of 5/8, leaving the value of 3/8 as the only possible value
for the remaining event "two heads."

The distribution of possible outcomes is

| T | T | |
|---|---|-----|
| T | T | etc. |
| T | H | |

FIGURE 5.12b

0H  1/8

1H  3/8

2H  3/8

3H  1/8

Total  8/8 = 1 ("Something happens" always)

This is the "theoretical" distribution for all possible "experiments" of tossing three coins. In any particular toss of the coins (either all three together or "one after the other") only *one* of the above possibilities will occur. For example, in one toss performed on a Saturday morning in the Oakland section of Pittsburgh, the author "obtained" the result

HTH

This event occurred with "hindsight" probability of 1.0; i.e., it did occur. Its *a priori* probability was 1/8 if taken as *exactly the sequence* HTH. If interpreted as the outcome "two heads," its a priori theoretical probability was 3/8.

By comparing the outcome actually observed (observed distribution) with the theoretical distribution, one can tell how "rare" the outcome is in the total picture. With three tosses the rarity is not striking for any outcome, since such an event as "all heads" occurs with a probability of 1/8. However, if more tosses were involved—say 10—the a priori probability of obtaining all 10 heads

HHHHHHHHHH

is

$$\frac{1}{2} * \frac{1}{2} * \frac{1}{2} * \frac{1}{2} * \frac{1}{2} * \frac{1}{2} * \frac{1}{2} * \frac{1}{2} * \frac{1}{2} * \frac{1}{2}$$

or

$$(\frac{1}{2})^{10}$$

which is

$$\frac{1}{1024}$$

or "one in a thousand." We might begin to examine the coin for "fairness," at least if it is someone else's coin and we happen to be gambling for money.

### Why the Normal Distribution?

One might ask at this point about the intrusion of the normal distribution in the above discussion. How did it get into the picture if the binomial distribution is the applicable distribution?

Good question. One answer is that it was a nice example. Another is that under certain circumstances the normal distribution can be used to describe a binomial (Bernoulli) process.

Under certain conditions the results of the binomial distribution can be described by (approximated by) the normal distribution. The case of coin-tossing is one of these instances. If a coin is tossed a sufficient number of times, say 30 as in our example, it can be shown (by mathematical derivation) that the binomial distribution will be approximated by a normal distribution with

Mean = np (p = probability of a success)

Standard deviation = $\sqrt{npq}$
                    (q = probability of a failure)

In our case, p equals q, both having the value 1/2

$$p = q = \frac{1}{2}$$

and n is the number of trials (30). The mean is then

$$\text{Mean} = 30 * \frac{1}{2} = 15$$

That is, we would expect 15 of the 30 tosses to show "heads." This is what we indicate informally above.

The standard deviation of the "distribution of all samples of size 30" would be

$$\sigma = \sqrt{npq}$$

$$= \sqrt{30 * 1/2 * 1/2}$$

$$= \sqrt{7.5}$$

$$\approx 2.8$$

which is what we asked the reader to take on faith above.


## The Distribution of Samples

A single toss of 30 coins (or 30 tosses of a single coin) can be taken to be a sample from the "theoretical population" of all tosses of 30 coins. It is this theoretical population that has the parameters

Mean = np (here 15)

$$\sigma = \sqrt{npq} \text{ (here 2.8)}$$

The data shown here, 100 experiments of 30 tosses each, can be taken as 100 samples drawn from this population of "30 toss experiments." (The word *experiment* can be taken to mean "happening" in this context, or better, "type of happening," with each experiment being one instance of the happening "toss 30 coins.")

The mean of each "toss of 30" is a "sample mean." This sample mean can be used to estimate the population mean. Here we know the theoretical population mean (15), so we don't *have to* estimate it, but the analysis is the same in cases in which the population mean is unknown. In any event, the analysis can be useful to make judgements about the coin if not about the population mean.

TABLE 5.23

| Sample mean value | Frequency |
|---|---|
| 9 | 1 |
| 10 | 2 |
| 11 | 7 |
| 12 | 11 |
| 13 | 7 |
| 14 | 13 |
| 15 | 13 |
| 16 | 16 |
| 17 | 14 |
| 18 | 5 |
| 19 | 5 |
| 20 | 2 |
| 21 | 2 |
| 22 | 1 |
| 23 | 1 |

There are, then, 100 sample means, distributed as shown earlier and reported here in Table 5.23. The "bulge" in the middle of the distribution (around 14, 15, 16) is one tipoff that the data might be normally distributed, although that is an aside in the current discussion.

Since the sample means (means of each 30-toss) are not exactly the same each time, i.e., not 15 each time, they have a "distribution." In this distribution, some of the sample means are "wrong" when used as estimates of the population mean. In fact, 87 of the estimates are wrong! (All values that are not 15.) However, as we indicated earlier, most are not "far wrong." In fact, 63% of the observed values are within 2 units (counts) on either side of the theoretical mean (the interval from 13 to 17). And 95% are within the interval 10 thorugh 20 (5 units on either side of the theoretical mean). We begin to see the picture emerge: the data presented by the binomial process can be analyzed by the same analysis that we apply to normally distributed data. The sample means are normally distributed! This is true not only in this case of binomial distribution but in most cases that have sample sizes of 30 or more, *regardless* of the population's "shape," i.e., regardless of the population distribution.

Making Inferences

We can now show how data is used to make inferences. Suppose that we are gambling and we "assume" that the coin, which was supplied by the house, is "fair," i.e., the chances of getting heads are 1/2, likewise tails. This assumption would be called the "null" or working hypothesis. The assumption is that "nothing is wrong." (The word "null" is used to indicate the idea of the "expected outcome" if there is no difference between this coin and a theoretically fair one.)

*If* nothing is awry we'd expect the overall outcome of 30 tosses to be in the vicinity of 14, 15, or 16 heads, maybe even 20 or 10. But, if on the first 30 tosses we "see" 29 heads (observe in the sense used in discussing observation as a data collection method), we might question the "null hypothesis" in favor of an "alternative hypothesis," i.e., that something is fishy!

In terms of standard deviation, the "score" of 28 heads is about five standard deviations above the "hypothesized" mean if the coin is fair

| | |
|---|---|
| Score: | 29 |
| Hypothetical mean: | 15 |
| Deviation: | 14 |
| Theoretical deviation of sample values: | 2.8 |
| Ratio of 14 to 2.8 = | 5 |

This extreme of a value seems a little bit "too extreme." It is unlikely that it would occur by chance *if* the coin were fair (probability of occurrence certainly less than .001; in fact, less than 1 in a million.) so we "reject" our initial hypothesis of "no difference from other fair coins" (reject the null hypothesis) in favor of the alternative hypothesis (coin is biased) and search for a weapon or a lawyer. We draw the conclusion (infer) that the coin is biased from the sample data )observing 29 heads in a 30-toss sample).

When to Use Which

One can always use the binomial distribution with data that fulfills the assumptions, e.g., the coin toss. Hence, there is no need for using the normal distribution. However, the tables for the binomial distribution have differing values for different n and p values. Hence, if n = 3; p = 1/2, the tables have

| Number of Successes | Probability of Obtaining That Number of Successes |
|---|---|
| 0 H | 1/8 |
| 1 H | 3/8 |
| 2 H | 3/8 |
| 3 H | 1/8 |

For n = 2, p = 1/2, the table would have*

| | |
|---|---|
| 0 H | 1/4 |
| 1 H | 1/2 |
| 2 H | 1/4 |

*The reader should verify these values by direct calculations.

If there is a wide range of n values (say 2 through 5,000), coupled with a wide range of p values (say .01 to .99), the size of the table data becomes unwieldy.

Tables are thus usually provided for "smallish" values of n, where the normal distribution might not apply. For extremely large values, the normal distribution can usually be applied. And, as we will see later, the "various" normal distributions can be translated into one "standard form" that results in a single table regardless of the sample size.

In our earlier discussion, we used the binomial distribution to predict that 10 heads would be observed in 10 tosses less than once in 1,000 "samples." If the "house" produces such a result we would draw almost the same inference from the calculations made with the probabilities calculated "directly" with the binomial distribution as we would with those calculated using the normal distribution

Score:                                  10 heads
Theoretical mean:                        5
Observed standard deviation:             10 − 5 = 5
Theoretical standard deviation:          1.6

$\sqrt{npq} = \sqrt{10 * 1/2 * 1/2} = \sqrt{2.5} \approx 1.6$

Ratio of 5 (observed S.D.)
to 1.6 (theoretical S.D.):
greater than 3

We said "almost" because the exact probabilities with smaller samples and differing values of p would not necessarily be the same when calculated by the binomial calculation and calculated in terms of standard deviations. But, in larger samples (30 or more) and values of p near 1/2, the "fit" of the binomial results to the normal results will be snug enough.


Interpreting the Standard Deviation

While the use of the standard deviation involves several computations in finding (1) the value of the mean, (2) the value of the standard deviation, and (3) the determination of the three intervals, its use in understanding data and evaluating individuals on a particular attribute is quite straight-forward.

For example, many standardized tests exist in which the mean and standard deviation are reported for the population on which the test was developed. Assuming that the person or group to which we plan to administer this test is comparable to the population for which the test was intended, we can use the results of our administration of the test to make such evaluations as "good," "bad"; "fast," "slow"; "smart," "not so smart"; or simply "average" in regard to that individual or entity. We did this with the coin. Other examples are presented here.

Say an IQ test is known to have a mean of 100 and a standard deviation of 15. (Despite cautions of noninterval or nonratio scales when considering IQ results, some tests are treated as if they produce quantitative data. In any case, the analysis of similar data on less controversial measures would be the same.) In administering the test to Mary Collins, we find that she has achieved a score of 148. Assuming that she did not previously know the contents of the test, and that the test is indeed valid, i.e., it does measure intellectual ability, we can fairly safely infer that Mary is quite intelligent. She has scored over three standard deviations above the mean. Similarly, John Sloan, with a score of 102, is "fairly average," and Jack Buckingham, with a score of 83 is "below average."

Similar comments apply to aptitude or achievement tests. A given test (e.g., SAT or GRE) might have a mean score of 500, a standard deviation of 100. A student scoring 800 on such a test shows "strong aptitude" and would be a good candidate for admission to a given school. A student scoring 200 will have a lesser chance of admission.

Football coaches often employ empirical standards to evaluate potential players for their team. For example, the "standard" (derived from timing past players) for running the 40-yd. dash might be 4.6 sec., with a standard deviation of .1 sec. (for football players, not for the general population). A player with a time of 4.3 is quite fast, and a player with a time of 5.1 will have difficulty not only in making the team, but in beating the rest of the team to the training table.

## The Curve Never Ends

Note that in the diagrams of the normal curve, the curve never touches the baseline, or zero value (Figure 5.13a). Theoretically, the curve never ends. While about 99% of the scores are contained in the part of the curve drawn, there is no section we can draw that can be said to contain 100% of the scores. This is the theory. In interpreting the theory in terms of empirically collected data, we can say that it is very unlikely, a "rare occasion," but it is possible for some scores to lie to the extreme left or extreme right of the mean, "way out" on the curve (Figure 5.13b).

In fact, this particular data point might bear more attention than the other 99% of the data points that do lie within the three standard deviations above and below the mean. We would first like to ascertain if it were a "mistake," and, of course, if it were a mistake—possibly a wrong calculation or an incorrect measurement—we would discard the data point. However, if we determine that the point is not a mistake, but a valid data point, then we would begin to investigate this strange phenomenon with great care.

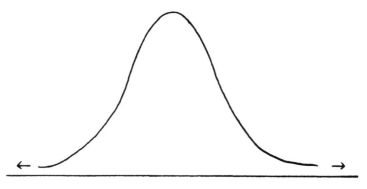

FIGURE 5.13a

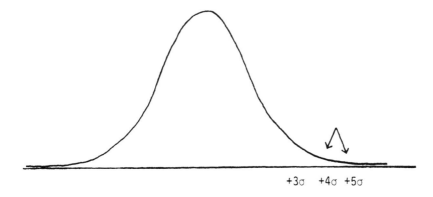

$+3\sigma$   $+4\sigma$   $+5\sigma$

FIGURE 5.13b

## Discrete and Continuous Distributions

The binomial distribution is a discrete distribution. The values whose probabilities it estimates are whole numbers or counts: 1 head or 2 heads, not 1.236 heads. The normal distribution is a continuous distribution. It can be used to estimate the probabilities of values that are "fractional," e.g., the probability of getting a score that is 1.2 or 2.8 standard deviations beyond the mean. However, as the discussion has indicated, if the number of discrete values is large enough (say 30 or 50), the discrete data can be interpreted with a theoretically continuous distribution.

## Comparing Different Distributions

When comparing data on different groups, say algebra scores obtained on a standard test by two different high school classes, or comparing the data on different traits of a single group, say height and weight, the data may differ in the mean, the standard deviation, or both.

The situation of two groups with different means and the same standard deviation can be drawn as shown in Figure 5.14a, where the spread of the two curves is equal, but their placement or "position" on the number line is different. This might be the case in a comparison of heights between a group of males and a group of females. The two groups would have different average heights, say 5 ft. 4 in. and 5 ft. 10 in., but similar variability within each group, say a standard deviation of 4 in. in each group.

If groups have the same mean but different standard deviations, say

Mean = 36

$SD_1$ = 4

$SD_2$ = 2

their position on the number line would be the same, but the spread of the curves would be different (Figure 5.14b), with the taller, thinner

(a)

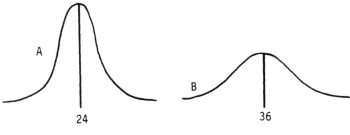

(b)

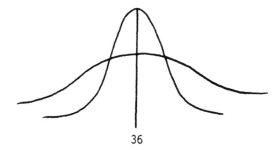

(c)

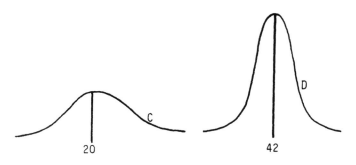

(d)

FIGURE 5.14

curve having the lesser spread (smaller standard deviation); and the flat-
ter, wider curve the greater spread (larger standard deviation).

Of course, groups can differ in both mean and standard deviation
(Figure 5.14c), where group A has a lower mean, but more homogeneous
scores, while B has a higher mean and more spread; or where C has lower
a mean and large standard deviation, while D has a higher mean and smaller deviation (Figure 5.14d).

## A Family

The normal distribution is not a single curve, but a family of curves.
The members of the family are distinguished by their mean and standard
deviations. Hence, as indicated above, two populations that have different
means but the same standard deviations

    Mean height male: 6 ft.
    Mean height female: 5 ft. 4 in.
    Standard deviation, both groups: 2 in.

would have normal curves of the "same spread" at different locations on
the number line (Figure 5.15). Curves of the same mean and different
standard deviations are at the same "location," but have different spreads.

The existence of a family of curves would mean that we would have
to create tables for each curve, i.e., each "pairing" of a mean and a
standard deviation. This would result in just as unwieldy a tome as the
"relatively complete" binomial tables. However, the values of the mean
and standard deviations can be expressed in a way that results in a single
table, called the table of "z-values," and the associated probabilities of
these z-values.

## Variability and Uncertainty

The relationship between the variability in a set of data and our uncertainty in predicting the performance on a particular trial of a given individual
is of special interest to the information scientist. The general rule is the
greater the variability, the greater the uncertainty. Or, in terms of the
standard deviation, the greater the standard deviation, the greater our
uncertainty in predicting. Uncertainty and variability are positively correlated.

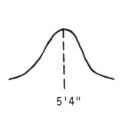 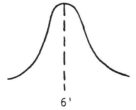

FIGURE 5.15

The example of student test performance is a good illustration of this point. Our uncertainty about student A's performance on the next test is virtually nil (70, 70, 70...). Our uncertainty about student B's performance on the next test is "moderate" (somewhere between 60 and 80), and we have no idea what student C will do!

A dollar figure can be placed on the value of a prediction and this value is related in part to the uncertainty of the situation as described by the variability. This is why a weatherperson is more valuable in an area with variable weather (say Chicago: windy, rainy, sunny; temperatures 89, 31, 40, 70) than in a relatively unchanging clime (Paradise Island: sun, sun, sun; temperatures 89, 89, 89, 88, 89).

The value of information is directly related to the value of a decision we have to make based on that information. We would be more careful about gathering data on the value of a house or car we wish to purchase (from appraisers, consumer reports, etc.) than we would about a magazine we wished to purchase, even if the variability in quality of magazines were greater than the variability in the quality of houses or cars. And the weatherperson on Paradise Island might be needed to predict the occurrence of hurricanes rather than of temperatures.

## Related Readings

Alder, Henry L. and Roessler, Edward B., *Introduction to Probability and Statistics*, 4th ed. San Francisco: W. H. Freeman and Co., 1968.

Bierman, Jr., Harold, Bonini, Charles P. and Hausman, Warren H., *Quantitative analysis for business decisions*, 4th ed., Homewood IL: Richard D. Irwin, Inc., 1973.

Churchill, Gilbert A. Jr., *Marketing Research: Methodological Foundations*, 2nd ed. Hinsdale, IL: The Dryden Press, 1979.

Feynman, Richard P., Leighton, Robert B., and Sanos, Matthew, *The Feynman Lectures on Physics*, Vol. I. Reading, MA: Addison-Wesley, 1963.

Freund, John E., *Statistics: A First Course*, 3rd ed. Englewood Cliffs, NJ: Prentice-Hall, 1981.

Harnett, Donald L. and Murphy, James L., *Introductory Statistical Analysis*, 2nd ed. Reading, MA: Addison-Wesley, 1980.

Huff, Darrell, *How to Lie with Statistics*, New York: W. W. Norton & Company, 1954.

Knuth, Donald E., *Seminumerical Algorithms: The Art of Computer Programming*, Vol. 2. Reading, MA: Addison-Wesley, 1969.

Li, Jerome C. R., *Statistical Inference I*, Ann Arbor, MI: Edward Brothers, Inc., 1964.

Minium, Edward W., *Statistical Reasoning in Psychology and Education*, 2nd ed. New York: John Wiley & Sons, 1978.

Siegel, Sidney, *Nonparametric Statistics: For the Behavioral Sciences*, New York: McGraw-Hill, 1956.

Skyrms, Brian, *Choice and Chance: An Introduction to Inductive Logic*, Belmont, CA: Dickenson Publishing Co., 1966.

# 6
# Estimating and Using Data Values

## Objectives

Upon completion of this chapter the reader should be able to

1. Define or explain an estimation problem
2. Describe and execute a procedure for creating a random sample
3. Distinguish between samples of convenience and random sampling
4. Distinguish between stratified samples and cluster samples
5. Indicate why a biased sample may be of benefit in some problems
6. Distinguish between sampling with and without replacement
7. Explain the concept of the sampling distribution of sample means
8. Explain the difference between the distribution of raw scores in a population and the distribution of sample means
9. State and explain the relationship between the variance of sample means and the variance of population raw scores
10. Create confidence intervals for the mean
11. Use estimated values for the mean and standard deviation of a population to design an artifact
12. Indicate how the use of data tables can alleviate the need to sample

In Chapter 5 we used data to describe a population (with "complete" data, i.e., a "census" of all people in the population). In this chapter we extend the discussion to the problem of estimating "population values" from a sample. The example used will be an engineering problem: the construction of a doorway that will allow "most people" to pass through.

## Action Under Certainty

The situation envisioned is one in which the agent has complete (or virtually complete) control over the outcome of his or her actions. He or she can act with assurance that the outcome will be achieved if the relevant data values are known and the appropriate action implemented. In constructing a doorway, the appropriate action will be to create an opening that is the correct size. The relevant data is "the correct or right size."

## Using a Model

The assumption in actions under certainty is that a valid model exists for taking action. This assumption fits many situations, e.g., ordering food in a restaurant, where we have models or scripts of customer/serviceperson behavior; or launching planes and space ships, where the required velocity (hence, energy or fuel requirements, length of runway, and the like) can be calculated for a given vehicle. (We treat the use of models in Chapter 17.) When using a model there are usually some values that must be estimated, and that is the purpose of this chapter: the illustration of the estimation of values. A more complex problem would be the development of the model itself. The model for the construction of a doorway is quite simple. This is not the case for more complex models, e.g., queuing theory or a model of how the economy works.

## Estimating Height

In order to find the proper size doorway one could measure all adults in the population of interest. This would be a "census." Even in taking a census one must define the population of interest. Who are we measuring? The people of Chicago? All my friends? The people of the United States? The population of interest is called the "target" population. If this population is of manageable size, say "our friends," we may choose to take a "census" (measure everybody). However, if this population is less manageable, we might take a sample of the population. A sample is a subset of the population. The measurement of the people in the sample should be less costly and less time consuming than the measurement of the population. The result of our study can also be more accurate with sample data if it is difficult to control the implementation of the measurement technique, e.g., hiring and managing a cadre of interviewers (see Williams, 1978 or Churchill, 1979).

## Kinds of Samples

Various types of sampling methods exist. One of the simplest is the "convenience" sample: we simply measure the people "at hand." This type of sample is often used when research is carried out in the classroom or work environment, taking "these students" or "these workers" as representative of some larger group, say all students of that grade level in school or even of "all people." An example of a convenience sample with regard to our problem would be taking the average height of the students in a given class as the estimate of the average height of the American adult. Whether such a convenience group will give a value that is representative of the target population or not is something the researcher has to establish. If the question one is trying to answer is "attitude of people toward pep rallies," student data may be representative of "all students of that age group" but not necessarily of "all Americans" (including their parents, their younger brothers and sisters, and neighbors of the university). Of course, whether or not any study ever needs to include such a wide population as "all Americans," ranging from, say, 2 year olds to retirees, is another question. Some studies, such as the testing of a vaccine, have a very large population as their target. Other studies, e.g., the preferences for different brands of infantwear, have a small target population: parents (or the infants themselves).

One of the difficulties with convenience samples is that they may introduce sampled bias. For example, if I am trying to measure the mean height of the adult American male and I choose to measure the basketball team (I am the coach so they are convenient), my estimate may be a bit off. It might be a good estimate of the mean height of the American collegiate basketball player (but it may not be), or it might by chance even be a good estimate of the average height of the adult American, if my team is not particularly tall. The point is that it might be either of these and we will not know which. This is actually true of all sampling methods: the sample actually drawn might be a good one or a bad one in terms of the results obtained. However, a method more "objective" than one's own convenience is often sought in drawing a sample. One that is popular with researchers is the simple random sample. The popularity of the random sample is due in part to the fact that it allows for the use of statistical calculations based on probability theory. It is not so easy to calculate the likelihood of drawing various samples from a population using convenience samples, since the amount of bias introduced by one's own convenience differs from situation to situation and from person to person. With random samples, however, one can talk about the likelihood of drawing certain samples.

The simple random sample can be roughly described as one in which each person included in the sample is included "by chance" (as opposed to our deliberate choice, i.e., convenience, or their choice, e.g., volunteers). More technical explanations can be found in standard texts on statistics, especially in texts on sampling (see Churchill, 1979 or Williams, 1978).

## Drawing a Random Sample

We illustrate drawing a "simple" random sample with an example. The reason for using the adjective "simple" is to distinguish this method from more complex methods of sampling (e.g., a stratified sample, which also uses randomness in the selection process but has a more complex design).

If one can obtain a list of all the people (or objects or things) in the target population, one could "label" each one with a number, write these numbers on individual sheets of paper (or bingo balls), place them in a hat (a big one), shake thoroughly, and draw out a fixed number of names (the number of names "drawn" being the sample size). Alternatively, one could label the entities, then use a random number table as a substitute for the pieces of paper. A random number table is one in which the digits appear with equal probability and "by chance." Equal probability is not enough. For example, the sequences

1  2  3  4  5  6  7  8  9  0

and

2  4  6  8  0  1  3  5  7  9

have equally occurring digits but are not "random." The random element could be introduced by using bingo balls and a mechanism for shaking and dispersing the balls, or a "pseudorandom number generator" on a computer.

TABLE 6.1

| | |
|---|---|
| 1 | John |
| 2 | Mary |
| 3 | Bill |
| 4 | Jack |
| 5 | Harriet |
| 6 | Geraldine |
| 7 | Max |
| 8 | Tony |
| 9 | Phil |
| 10 | Anne |

Also, tables of random numbers have been prepared by various organizations (e.g., the Rand Corporation).

In practice it may not be so easy to obtain the list of people, but we assume that one exists. Say we have 10 individuals in the target population, labeled as shown in Table 6.1. Say also that the random numbers in a portion of a random number table are

6   5   1   9   2   9   3

and we want a sample size of three. If we started reading the table at the leftmost point and went horizontally, we would find 6, 5, and 1 as the first three digits. We would include the persons labeled 6, 5, and 1

Geraldine, Harriet, John

in the sample.

If there were more people in the sample, say 50, we would take more digits; in the case of 50 we would take two digits at a time. The people could be labeled 1 through 50. With the digits shown above, the first pair, 65, would be disregarded. The second pair, 19, would cause somebody to be selected, and so on. With 50 people, a scheme that would allow us to avoid discarding digits would be to label the people 00 through 49, and 50 through 99, Table 6.2) so that either the value 01 or the value 51 would mean that Mary was selected.

TABLE 6.2

| | |
|---|---|
| 00, 50 | John |
| 01, 51 | Mary |
| . | |
| . | |
| . | |
| 49, 99 | Quincy |

## Quota Samples

A quota sample is used when one wants to include a certain proportion of the population in each category of a classification scheme. For example, if one were interested in breaking down the population by sex, one would set a quota, such as 50% females and 50% males (or there about). Presumably the quotas represent the proportions of these groups in the population. Hence, on income we might set quotas of 20% rich, 60% middle class, and 20% poor, having defined these adjectives according to some criterion, say "annual income over $100 thousand equals rich." A quota sample may also be a convenience sample, e.g., we may just approach people for an interview as we see them on the street or as they enter the local fast food restaurant; or it may be achieved through random sampling. The primary characteristic of the quota sample is setting the quota, which ensures that all relevant categories of the population are included in the sample. It also helps ensure representativeness of the sample in the categories of people or things included. If the quota sample is drawn by convenience, it is usually referred to simply as a quota sample. If it is drawn by random sampling from the categories, it is referred to as a stratified sample.

## Stratified Samples

Stratified samples are similar to quota samples in that they divide the population into categories and "fill" the categories according to the proportion of people in each category in the parent population. However, the people within the categories are selected randomly, not by convenience. We will not use a stratified sample in our study of height, but we wish to make one point about the accuracy of the results achieved with a stratified sample. A stratified sample can result in a more accurate result if the variable on which we stratify the population is truly related to the variable we wish to measure. (The accuracy is not in the point estimate of the mean, but in the lack of variability among the samples taken).

In measuring height we could use "visual shortness or tallness" as a means of stratification. This is, of course, directly related to the variable we wish to measure—actual height. In order to see the effect of stratification we will consider a population in which there are nine people, three in each of three categories: visually short, visually medium, and visually tall. We list the people and their actual heights here

| | |
|---|---|
| Short people: | John, 2 ft |
| | Mary K., 2 ft |
| | Bill, 2 ft |
| Medium people: | Jack, 4 ft |
| | Anne, 4 ft |
| | Mary L., 4 ft |
| Tall people: | Anthony, 6 ft |
| | Chris, 6 ft |
| | Anne Marie, 6 ft |

The numbers are rigged but the point is the same. If the entire group is taken as one clump, we could conceivably draw such samples as

```
John, 2 ft
Mark K., 2 ft      Sample mean = 2 ft
Bill, 2 ft

John, 2 ft
Mary K., 2 ft      Sample mean = 2.67 ft
Anne, 4 ft
```

However, if we visually classify people into the relative categories of tall, medium, and small, or if we use some correlated measure, say weight, to group them, the resulting "strata" should be similar to the grouping shown above and repeated here

| Small | Medium | Tall |
|---|---|---|
| John | Jack | Anthony |
| Mary K. | Anne | Chris |
| Bill | Mary L. | Anne Marie |

Although other methods of apportioning people are possible, we will apportion them according to the relative size of the strata in the population. Since the three groups are equal in size, i.e., occur with equal probability in the population, we select the same number from each group. For a total sample size of three, we will select one person from each group. One possible sample is

Sample

```
John, 2 ft
Anne, 4 ft      Sample mean = 4 ft
Chris, 6 ft
```

This sample mean, 4 ft, is equal to the population mean, also 4 ft.
As a little reflection on the nature of the strata indicates

| Strata | Heights |
|---|---|
| Stratum 1 | 2, 2, 2 |
| Stratum 2 | 4, 4, 4 |
| Stratum 3 | 6, 6, 6 |

all sample sizes of three chosen so that one person comes from each stratum, will result in a sample with one person with a height of 2 ft, one with a height of 4 ft, and one 6-footer, hence a sample mean of 4 ft, an estimate of the "true population value" that is exactly accurate. The reason for this is that the use of stratification has reduced the variability within each group (here to zero). And the differences in strata accurately re-

flect ("account for") the differences in the target population. By stratifying, we have eliminated the possibility of greatly distorted samples.

## The Number of Possible Stratified Samples

There are 27 different stratified samples of size three that can be drawn
from this population. This results from the fact that we have three possible choices for each stratum, and there are three strata. We multiply the
number of choices in each stratum

    3 * 3 * 3 = 27

If the strata were

    1:  2,2,2,2,2
    2:  4,4,4
    3:  6,6,6,6

there would be

    5 * 3 * 4 = 60

possible stratified samples.
    Yet, if we ignore the identity of the individuals selected, and concen-
trate only on their heights, they are all the "same sample"

    (2,4,6)

We will not obtain distorted samples, such as all people in the sample being
6 ft, if the stratification variable, visual height, has indeed stratified the
population correctly with respect to the variable we wish to measure, actual
height. It is the elimination of the extreme samples that allows stratified
sampling to be a better tool than simple random sampling when one knows
the values for the subjects on a variable that is correlated with the variable one wants to measure. To see the point more clearly we illustrate the
number and composition of simple random samples. There are "more" simple
random samples and the samples themselves can be "distorted" in composition.

## Number of Samples in a Simple Random Sample

If we drew a simple random sample size of three from the same population
size of nine, "with replacement," there would be 729 possible samples
(Figure 6.1). These samples would include the extreme cases such as
three people being 2 ft tall in a single sample. The stratification has eliminated these extreme possibilities.
    In practice we probably could not sample with replacement in measuring
or interviewing people, since they might become annoyed. In quality control situations, say in testing light bulbs, we would also not sample with
replacement, since after a bulb burns out it cannot be tested again. If
we sample without replacement, the number of possible samples would be

    9 * 8 * 7 = 504

with "one less person to choose from" at each selection point. Some of
these would also be extremes, such as (2,2,2), (2,2,4), or (6,6,6).

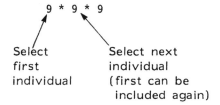

FIGURE 6.1

Stratification removes some of the variability in the samples that can be drawn by removing the possibility of drawing the extreme samples. We will not be able to go into all of the sampling methods in detail, and some, such as the use of stratification, usually require the expertise of specialists. Our main interest has been to show that methods exist that can be superior (but need not be) to simple random sampling.

### Choosing Wrong

If the variable by which we stratify is "bad" in that it is not related to the variable of interest, the benefit of stratification will be lost. The result of stratifying on an irrelevant variable can be indicated by a research design in which we choose eye color as the relevant variable to stratify with, erroneously thinking it to be correlated with height. Let us suppose that the people "collect" as follows:

| Eye Color | Individual | Height |
|-----------|------------|--------|
| Blue | John | 2 ft |
| | Anne | 4 ft |
| | Anthony | 6 ft |
| Green | Bill | 2 ft |
| | Jack | 4 ft |
| | Anne Marie | 6 ft |
| Brown | Mary K. | 2 ft |
| | Mary L. | 4 ft |
| | Chris | 6 ft |

The strata are no longer homogeneous. In fact the variability within each stratum reflects the variability in the population as a whole. The samples drawn after stratification would not be different from those drawn from the population as a whole (although there would be fewer possible samples, still 27).

## Cluster Sampling

Cluster sampling is similar to stratification sampling except that the strata occur in a naturally occurring group, e.g., a family. We use an example from Williams (1978) to illustrate the notion of cluster sampling. Suppose that the heights of the members of three different families are as follows:

| Family 1 | Family 2 | Family 3 |
| --- | --- | --- |
| Mom, 4 ft | Mom, 6 ft | Mom, 6 ft |
| Dad, 6 ft | Dad, 4 ft | Dad, 4 ft |
| Child, 2 ft | Child, 2 ft | Child, 2 ft |

If we choose not to sample from the entire population of nine people, but, for reasons of convenience, cost, and time, we decide to choose one family randomly then measure all people in that family, we again glean the benefit of what Williams refers to as "the clever use of groups." Each family (cluster) exhibits "in miniature" the pattern of the population, and we again obtain samples of mean 4, the accurate reflection of the population mean, and we do so from each sample drawn. Like stratification, cluster sampling reduces the variability in the samples that can be drawn.

The difference between stratified sampling and cluster sampling can be seen by considering these contrasts

1.  In strata, the groups are homogeneous "within"; members of one group are closer in value to each other (2,2,2) than to outsiders (the 4s and the 6s). In clusters, the groups are heterogeneous "within"; each family has a tall, medium, and short member. The similarity in clusters is between groups, rather than within.
2.  In the use of strata, one individual (or name) was taken from each group. In the use of clusters, only one group was chosen, and all individuals within that group were studied.

Stratification might be used to study variables related to income, grouping people by high, middle, and low income, etc. Instead of sampling from the population as a whole, we first stratify (classify) the population on income, then sample from these strata. Clusters might be used to study customer reaction to a new product. Instead of taking a random sample from the stores in the 10 big cities we serve (the cities being roughly the same in distribution of income, type of work force, etc.), we might study a "cluster" of one or 2 cities, say New York and Boston. We extrapolate the results to the other 8 cities because of the similarity "across the 10 big cities," i.e., the similarity "between" cities.

One needs, however, to be cautious in the design of samples. Williams gives an example of how things can go wrong if one samples incorrectly. If one stratifies into the homogeneous groups

| | |
| --- | --- |
| Short: | 2,2,2 |
| Medium: | 4,4,4 |
| Tall: | 6,6,6 |

but then mistakenly selects one group as a naturally occurring cluster (e.g., the tall group), one will have reduced the variance to zero (all 6s), but at the expense of an inaccurate mean value (6). It is necessary to keep the sampling methodology clear, and, as usual, the advice of experts might be sought out in designing and implementing a particular research program.

We continue our analysis of the problem of estimating the height of the "average American" with simple random sampling. The use of simple random sampling is widespread and understanding the more powerful methods of sampling relies on understanding this simpler method. (The term *average American* is a misnomer, since we aren't studying one "typical" American, but the average of a wide variety of Americans.)

Besides simply being widely understood and used, simple random sampling must be used where stratification or clustering is not possible. It is not always possible to "find" (know) a relevant variable on which to stratify, or to find equivalent clusters. However, before going on to the discussion of random sampling and the estimation of data values, we examine the possibility that one might use a biased sample instead of a "fair" or representative one.

## Using a Biased Sample

It is interesting to note that even in this simple case of sampling people for the purpose of making a doorway, a departure from simple random sampling is indicated by the statement of the problem. We want most people to fit under the doorway, hence it might be better to study basketball players than to study the general population. If they fit, most others will. It is thus possible to desire a biased sample. (The sample would be biased with respect to the original target population of adult males. It should be representative of the population of basketball players.) The sampling methodology, like the statistical analysis and the means of measurement, must be selected with respect to the question we wish to answer. The ideal methodology is one that has a high likelihood of providing a correct answer at a low cost and in an adequate time frame.

TABLE 6.3

| ID | Person | Height in Inches |
|----|--------|------------------|
| 0 | Joe | 72 |
| 1 | Jim | 70 |
| 2 | Larry | 71 |
| 3 | Don | 72 |
| 4 | Bill | 62 |
| 5 | Kerry | 85 |
| 6 | Anthony | 74 |
| 7 | Chris | 75 |
| 8 | Josh | 71 |
| 9 | Cory | 67 |

Total   719 in., mean = 71.9 in. $\approx$ 6 ft

Differences Due to Chance

The fact that we are using samples instead of entire populations in order to make statements about the population introduces an element of chance. Samples, even "representative" ones, do not exactly represent the population. As indicated in the above discussion, the values obtained for the mean of the sample will vary with the sample chosen. In terms of the estimation of height, suppose that we have the population of 10 adult males shown in Table 6.3. Suppose that we draw a random sample including "subjects" 2, 1, and 9

| Larry | 71 in. |
| Jim | 70 in. |
| Cory | 67 in. |

The mean of this sample is 69.3 in., which is not equal to the mean of the population (71.9 in.). The standard deviation of the sample would also differ from the population value (the standard deviation of the population is about 5.5 in. in this example; we leave the calculation of the standard deviation of the population and of the sample to the reader). We could draw more samples. For example, using the random number table we might obtain the samples shown in Table 6.4. (Note that Don, person 3, height 6 ft, has not yet been included in a single sample. This is one manifestation of the role of chance in sampling.) The means of these samples are shown in Table 6.5.

Several things are noteworthy about the sample means. The first is that there is a distribution of the sample means. One does not get the same estimate of the mean from each sample one draws. Some sample means are closer to the true population mean, which we know to be 71.9 in. (but which we don't usually know); some are farther away. The second thing to note is that the "mean of the sample means" is 71.6 in., which is quite close to the "true" population mean. We did not draw all possible samples. However, if we did draw all possible samples of size three, and we did calculate the mean of all these sample means, we would find that the mean of the sample means would be identical to the population mean. This is what is meant by saying that the sample mean is an unbiased estimator of the population mean. Of course, we never take "all samples" of a given size; we take one, and one problem we will have to address is how accurate that one sample mean is as an estimate of the population mean.

Secondly, the sample means show some variation. This is what it means (English) to have a distribution of sample means. They are not all the

TABLE 6.4

| Sample Number | Subjects |
| --- | --- |
| 2 | 4, 5, 6 |
| 3 | 8, 1, 2 |
| 4 | 1, 4, 2 |
| 5 | 5, 0, 7 |
| 6 | 9, 6, 0 |

TABLE 6.5

| 1: | (2, 1, 9) | 69.3 in. |
|---|---|---|
| 2: | (4, 6, 5) | 73.7 |
| 3: | (8, 1, 2) | 70.7 |
| 4: | (1, 4, 2) | 67.7 |
| 5: | (5, 0, 7) | 77.3 |
| 6: | (9, 6, 0) | 71.0 |

Total   429.7   Avg. = 71.6 in.

same. However, this variation is less than the variation in the population of raw scores. The sample means range in value from 67.7 in. (sample 4) to 77.3 in. (sample 5). This is less than the variation in the raw scores, which ranged from 62 in. to 85 in., but it is still a variation. We can calculate a standard deviation for the sample means. Without doing the calculation, this standard deviation of the sample means would be in the vicinity of 3 in. This standard deviation of the sample means is called the standard error of the mean. Hence, we have three uses of the word mean and three uses of the word standard deviation

- Mean of raw scores in population
- Mean of a particular sample drawn from the population
- Mean of all possible sample means of a given size drawn from a population
- Standard deviation of raw scores in population
- Standard deviation of a particular sample
- Standard deviation of all possible sample means of a given size (called the standard error)

We use the mean of a particular sample (the one we actually draw) to estimate the mean of the population (which we usually do not know). We also use the standard deviation of a particular sample to estimate the standard deviation of the population. Finally, we use the theoretical distribution of all sample means (of a given size) to determine a numerical range around the sample mean within which we think the true population mean can be found.

For this example the population mean is known. It is the value of the mean for the 10 people listed, about 6 ft. This would be referred to as the "true population mean."

In this example we have not shown all possible samples of a given size, showing only six samples, but, if we did draw all possible samples of size three from this population, we would obtain a mean value for each sample (e.g., the values 69.3 and 73.7 for the samples shown above). We could then calculate *another mean* of all these sample means. It is this "mean of all sample means of a given size" that is theoretically equal to the true population value.

In practice we will draw only one sample (or a few), not "all of a given size," but theory tells us what the results would be of drawing all samples of a given size and taking first a mean of each individual sample, then a mean of all those sample means. The mean of the sample means would be exactly equal to the true population value; however, it is not the case that each individual mean will be equal to the population value, as the obtained means of 69.3, 73.7, and so on, indicate. There will be a distribution of the sample means, and we will be interested in examining the shape of this distribution.

## The Distribution of Sample Means

If the sample mean were always an "exact estimate" of the true population values, here about 6 ft, there would be no difficulty. We would simply use the mean of the single sample drawn and omit the following discussion; i.e., if the distribution of sample means were uniform (Table 6.6), there would be no doubt about our sample value being correct. We will still use the obtained sample mean of a single sample as our estimate of the population value. But we will do so with some caution. Since it is not the case that each obtained value is a correct estimate we will be aware of the possibility (probability) of being in error.

We will be in error more often than not. Most of the sample means are "off a bit." In the samples shown above we had "estimates" of 69.3 in. (or 5 ft, 9.3 in., 73.7 in., 70.7 in., etc.) None of the estimates listed were exactly 72 in., so our estimates (drawn from a single sample) are bound to be off a bit, despite the "unbiasedness" of the estimator, and the question becomes "How far off?"

The unbiasedness of the estimation process is "over the long run," i.e., if we draw all samples of a given size. We are interested in the "short run," drawing a single sample and using its results as an estimate of the population value.

There is a set of mathematical relationships between the variation in the samples drawn from a population and two other characteristics that either are known or can be estimated

- The sample size, which is known, since we choose it
- The population variance, which can be estimated from the variance of the single sample actually drawn

The relationship is

$$\sigma^2_{\bar{x}} = \frac{\sigma^2_{pop}}{n}$$

or

## TABLE 6.6

| | |
|---|---|
| Sample 1: | 6 ft |
| Sample 2: | 6 ft |
| Sample 3: | 6 ft |
| . | |
| . | |
| . | |
| Sample n: | 6 ft |

$$VAR_{\overline{x}} = \frac{VAR_{pop}}{n}$$

The relationship can also be stated in terms of the standard deviations of the population and the sampling distribution

$$\sigma_{\overline{x}} = \frac{\sigma_{pop}}{\sqrt{n}}$$

n is the sample size, and is known; $\sigma_{pop}$ is the population standard deviation and is not known; it will be estimated from the sample variation.

The term $\sigma_{\overline{x}}$ is the standard deviation of the sampling distribution. It is called the "standard error of the mean," since it gives an indication of the amount of error likely to be involved in our using the sample mean as the estimate of the "true" mean. It is the standard error that enables us to create the ranges within which we believe the true population mean to lie.

## The Standard Error

The standard error is the standard deviation of the distribution of sample means. It is calculated on the entire distribution. We did not draw all possible sample sizes of three from our population of 10 people, but we can nevertheless calculate the standard deviation of the six samples we did draw, and make some comments with regard to the values obtained from this incomplete data. The standard deviation of the distribution of six samples is shown in Table 6.7. In this case the deviations did not sum to zero (-9.3, 7.0). This is because we used 72 rather than 71.6 as the mean for ease of computation. However, the point is that the standard deviation of the means of the samples (3.2) is smaller than the standard deviation of the raw scores, which is approximately 5.5, calculated as shown in Table 6.8.

TABLE 6.7

| Sample | Sample Mean Value (in.) | True Population Mean (in.) | d | $d^a$ |
|---|---|---|---|---|
| 1 | 69.3 | 72 | −2.7 | 7.29 |
| 2 | 73.7 | 72 | +1.7 | 2.89 |
| 3 | 70.7 | 72 | −1.3 | 1.69 |
| 4 | 67.7 | 72 | −4.3 | 18.49 |
| 5 | 77.3 | 72 | +5.3 | 28.09 |
| 6 | 71.0 | 72 | −1.0 | 1.00 |

$$59.45$$
$$\text{Variance} = 59.45/6 = 10$$
$$\text{Standard deviation of means} = \sqrt{10} = 3.2$$

TABLE 6.8

| Person ID | Raw Score | Mean | d | d[a] |
|---|---|---|---|---|
| 0 | 72 | 72 | 0 | 0 |
| 1 | 70 | 72 | +2 | 4 |
| 2 | 71 | 72 | −1 | 1 |
| 3 | 72 | 72 | 0 | 0 |
| 4 | 62 | 72 | −10 | 100 |
| 5 | 85 | 72 | +13 | 169 |
| 6 | 74 | 72 | +2 | 4 |
| 7 | 75 | 72 | +3 | 9 |
| 8 | 71 | 72 | −1 | 1 |
| 9 | 67 | 72 | 5 | 25 |
| | | | | 313 |

$$313/10 = 31.3$$

$$\sqrt{31.3} = 5.5$$

of the samples (3.2) is smaller than the standard deviation of the raw scores, which is approximately 5.5, calculated as shown in Table 6.8.

We say "approximately" 5.5 since using 72 as the mean instead of 71.9 has introduced some error. The choice was "computationally convenient," and for our purposes, the error is negligible. The exact relationship between the standard error and the population standard deviation is given by the formula shown above, and is repeated below for convenience.

The main point here is that the variation in the sample means is smaller than the variation in the raw scores. The main point overall is that there is a mathematical relationship between the variation in the population of raw scores, the size of the sample, and type of sampling (e.g., replacement or not), and the resulting variation in the sample means. This mathematical relationship will allow us to establish the confidence intervals for our estimate of the population mean.

"The Formula"

The formula used to relate sample variation and popular variation is that shown earlier

$$\sigma^2_{\overline{x}} = \frac{\sigma^2_{pop}}{n}$$

It is convenient to state the formula in terms of the variance; however, an equivalent expression in terms of standard deviation can be derived by taking the square root of both sides of the equation.

The formula essentially says that the variance of the sample means will be smaller than the variance of the raw scores. It also tells "how much" smaller, i.e., it says that if we divide the population variance value by the sample size we will obtain the variance of the sample means.

If we then take the square root of this answer, we will have the standard error, $\sigma_{\bar{x}}$. The sigma is used because the standard error is a standard deviation of a population, the population of all samples of size n. The subscript $\bar{x}$ indicates that this population is a population of sample means, not a population of raw scores.

We have enclosed the descriptor "the formula" in quotes to indicate that slight variations on the theme are in order if the assumptions behind the derivation of the formula are not fulfilled. For example, the formula assumes sampling with replacement, which essentially gives an "infinite" population size. If the sampling is without replacement, a slight adjustment might be made for a sample that is very large relative to the population size, e.g., sampling 5 people from a population of 10. The formula also assumes normally distributed raw scores. However, if the sample size is large enough, it will be applicable to the sampling distribution regardless of the shape of the population distribution. Rather than concentrate on the difficulties, we look at the use of the relationship in the cases in which it is applicable. This applicability turns out to be quite frequent in practice.

We can use the relationship between the variance of the sample means and the population variance to "reduce" the variation of the distribution of samples to "any value we wish." We do this by noticing that the sample size n appears in the denominator of the right-hand side. Without regard to the value of the population variance, we can reduce the variance of the sampling distribution by increasing the value of n. The reader is cautioned, however, that in some studies this increase in sample size can result in a *less accurate* study. The reason is that an increase beyond a manageable size may introduce another source of error, measurement error, e.g., due to improperly conducted or "nonconducted" interviews. The author can remember one extensive survey that was carried out by hiring college students to interview people about their preference for various colors of a package (Do you prefer the red one? the silver and blue one?). The rationale was that the students would approach people at street corners, the bus station, etc., show people the packages, and record their responses, being paid $2 per interview. The reality was that many questionnaires (interviewing instruments) were filled out in dormitory rooms.

## The Shape of the Distribution of Sample Means

Given certain assumptions, the shape of the distribution of sample means is the normal curve. The mean of the distribution of sample means is the population mean. And two-thirds of the sample means can be found within the interval $-1\sigma$ to $+1\sigma$; 95% in the interval $-2\sigma$ to $+2\sigma$; and 99% in the interval $-3\sigma$ to $+3\sigma$.

## Intervals of the Distribution of Sample Means

The intervals with respect to the distribution of sample means are known. We can expect

68% of the sample means to be within one standard error of the true mean (above or below)
95% to be within two standard errors
99% to be within three standard errors

For our data, the standard error can be calculated from the formula

$$\sigma_{\bar{x}} = \frac{5.5}{\sqrt{3}} \quad \begin{array}{l} \text{(population standard deviation)} \\ (n = 3) \end{array}$$

$$= \frac{5.5}{1.7} = 3.2$$

which is the same as the calculation we obtained from the six samples. We would expect, then, 68% of the sample means to fall in the interval

72 ± 3.2 or 68.8 to 75.2 in.

95% to fall in the interval

72 ± 6.4 or 65.6 to 78.4 in.

and 99% to fall in the interval

72 ± 9.6 or 62.4 to 81.6 in.

However, we are not really interested in these values for their own sake. We are interested in the mean of the single sample we draw and the creation of a numerical range around this mean value that we think "captures" the true population value.

## The Confidence Intervals

The term *confidence interval* is really a misnomer. The phrase refers to a procedure by which we create a range that we expect contains the true population mean. The method of creating the confidence interval is based on the assumption that the distribution of sample means is normal. Knowing that the distribution of sample means is normal, we can rely on such statements as

68% of the sample means that could be drawn would fall in the one standard deviation interval bracketing the true population mean.

95% of the sample means that could be drawn would fall in the two standard deviation interval bracketing the true population mean.

99% of the sample means that could be drawn would fall in the three standard deviation interval bracketing the population mean.

This information can be summarized symbolically as

68% of $\bar{x}$'s in interval: $\mu_{pop} \pm 1\sigma$
95% of $\bar{x}$'s in interval: $\mu_{pop} \pm 2\sigma$
99% of $\bar{x}$'s in interval: $\mu_{pop} \pm 3\sigma$

The only drawback is that this is not the information we want. We want to estimate the population mean, not use it to set up confidence intervals. We can, however, use the confidence intervals to estimate a range in which the population mean should lie, we illustrate the procedure with respect to the 99% interval.

We know that the probability of a sample mean falling in the interval $-3\sigma$ to $+3\sigma$ is

$$99\%: \mu_{pop} - 3\sigma \leqslant \bar{x} \leqslant \mu_{pop} + 3\sigma$$

Statisticians manipulate this equation by subtracting the population mean throughout

$$-3\sigma \leqslant \bar{x} - \mu_{pop} \leqslant +3\sigma$$

then subtracting x throughout

$$-3\sigma - \bar{x} \leqslant -\mu_{pop} \leqslant +3\sigma - \bar{x}$$

then multiplying by a -1 (which reverses the inequalities)

$$+3\sigma + \bar{x} \geqslant \mu_{pop} \geqslant -3\sigma + \bar{x}$$

and turning the inequality around

$$\bar{x} - 3\sigma \leqslant \mu_{pop} \leqslant \bar{x} + 3\sigma$$

to estimate that the population mean will fall between three standard errors ($-3\sigma$) below the sample mean ($\bar{x}$) and three standard errors ($+3\sigma$) above the sample mean. The significance of the new form of the equation is that it takes a known value, the sample mean $\bar{x}$ in conjunction with another known (i.e., estimated) value, the standard error, to pinpoint the range in which the true population mean will lie. This range will not always "capture" the true population mean, but it will capture it 99% of the time (given the assumption of normality of the sampling distribution). This range is another estimate of what the value of the true population mean is. However, it is not a "point" estimate, (e.g., $\bar{x}$ = 69.3 in.), but a range in which we think the "true point" can be found.

The range is considered a more useful estimate in that it can tell us how much below or above our sample mean the true population might lie. It is like saying we think the true population mean is between 5 ft and 6 ft, and we are sure that this range will do unless we get a very rare sample, one that would occur only one in 100 times. (Similar statements can be made about the 68% and 95% intervals; only the number of samples that could have occurred outside the range changes: 5 in 100 and 32 in 100, respectively.)

We could, of course, just pick a large range. For example, we could say that the height of the average adult male is somewhere between 3 ft and 10 ft, and feel 100% confident that we were right. This is of course not of much help in using the estimated values. What is desirable is a fairly small range with a high confidence level, and this is accomplished by keeping the standard error low, e.g., by taking a larger sample size (within the constraints of manageability), since the bigger the denominator in the formula

$$\sigma_{\bar{x}} = \frac{\sigma_{pop}}{\sqrt{n}}$$

the smaller the standard error. It is also ensured by a small population variance, which is the case for the variable height.

## Turning the Equation Around

The initial development of the confidence intervals for sample means was developed with respect to a known population value and the spread of the samples. This resulted in such statements as

68% of the sample means will fall in the interval....

However, having turned our equation around we now make such statements as

68% of the time the true mean will be within one standard error of the obtained sample mean.

95% of the time the true mean will be within two standard errors of the sample mean.

99% of the time the true mean will be within three standard errors.

These are the statements we will use in building the doorway.

## Designing the Doorway

The person designing the doorway has several alternatives. Assuming that a sample has been drawn (say sample 1 above, reproduced here for convenience in Table 6.9), he or she can compute the sample mean and the sample variance and standard deviation (Table 6.10). He or she can then

• Use the sample mean as the estimate of the population mean, i.e., estimate the population mean to be 69.3 in.
• Create ranges within which the population mean can be expected to lie, using the sample standard deviation to create the 68%, 95%, and 99% ranges

Assuming he or she chooses to create the ranges, we would use the sample standard deviation to estimate the standard error

$$\text{Standard error} = \frac{1.7}{\sqrt{3}} = \frac{1.7}{1.7} = 1$$

then use the standard error to estimate the 68%, 95%, and 99% ranges

68% = 69.3 ± 1.0 = 68.3 to 70.3

95% = 69.3 ± 2.0 = 67.3 to 71.3

99% = 69.3 ± 3.0 = 66.3 to 72.3

## TABLE 6.9

| ID | Person | Height |
|----|--------|--------|
| 2  | Larry  | 71     |
| 1  | Jim    | 70     |
| 9  | Cory   | 67     |

TABLE 6.10

| Scores | Sample Mean | d | $d^2$ |
|---|---|---|---|
| 71 | 69.3 | +1.7 | 2.89 |
| 70 | 69.3 | +0.7 | 0.49 |
| 67 | 69.3 | -2.3 | 5.29 |

208 = total

Mean = 208/3 = 69.3

$\Sigma d^2 =$ 8.67

Variance = 8.67/3 = 2.89

S.D. = $\sqrt{2.89}$ = 1.7

We expect the interval from about 66 in. to 72 in. to contain the true mean, "not always," but 99 times out of 100. This is probably "enough," i.e., we "expect" (or hope) that our sample is one of the 99 falling within this range, not the 100th, the one that "misses."

We are building doorways, so we are interested in the "top end" of the interval used to estimate the mean. We can "take" the mean to be the highest value in this interval, 72.3, as a "safe value," and use it as our estimate of the population mean.

Estimated population mean = 72.3 in.

This is a "conservative estimate." The initial estimate of 69.3 in. is "lower," hence will fit fewer people than the 72-in. estimate.

The estimate of 72 in. is an estimate of the mean height of the American adult male. However, we are interested not only in the mean height, but in the distribution of heights. We want to build a doorway that will serve the needs of 99% of the population. We need, then, to examine the distribution of the raw scores. (Note here that the value 1.0 is the estimated variability of the *sample means*; it is used to set up the estimation ranges for the sample mean. The value we now need is the estimate of the standard deviation of the population *raw scores*.)

To study the distribution of raw scores we need their standard deviation. We saw earlier that this was 5.5 in., but we would be estimating this value from our sample values. Hence, we would estimate the population standard deviation at 1.7 in. We could then set up the intervals of raw scores as

68%: 72.3 ± 1.7 = 70.6 - 74.0 in.

95%: 72.3 ± 3.4 = 68.9 - 75.7 in.

99%: 72.3 ± 5.1 = 67.2 - 77.4 in.

Since we are interested in the top end of the 99% interval of raw scores, we would take the value of 77.4 in. as the height to make the door. Adding a 10% "contingency factor" (safety factor) we might calculate the desired height as

99% interval of raw scores: 77.4 in.
Contingency (10%): 7.7 in.
Height of doorway: 85.1 or 85 in.

We would expect this height, about 7 ft, to allow 99% of the population to pass through the doorway without difficulty.

## Human Factors

The study of the characteristics of human beings in order to design work spaces, environments, and equipment, is called "human engineering" or "human factors in engineering and design," and, more recently, "ergonomics." The design of video display units, work spaces, and the like relies heavily on the normal distribution of physical characteristics. In addition to physical characteristics, the study of communication patterns, the flow of data in an office, and the like, leads to variations in the placement of work stations. (The interested reader is referred to Kantowitz and Sorkin, 1983; McCormick and Sanders, 1982; and Van Cott and Kinkade, 1963.)

## Using Extant Data

It is possible that the samples need not be taken at all. Various data have already been collected on "things of interest," e.g., populations of cities, and heights and weights of certain groups. If one judges that this data is "good," i.e., collected and analyzed in a proper manner, it is natural and valuable to use it in place of taking a sample. For example, the American Institutes for Research published the *Human Engineering Guide to Equipment Design*, the results of studies sponsored by a joint Army-Navy-Air Force steering committee (van Cott and Kinkade, 1972). It has such data as the height of male and female military personnel, and civilians. The data is broken into several subgroups, but we will take a few representative examples.

Male College Students, Midwest, 18-24 Years Old:

Percentiles (in.)

| 1st | 5th | 50th | 95th | 99th | S.D. |
|------|------|------|------|------|------|
| 64.2 | 65.9 | 70.0 | 74.1 | 75.8 | 2.49 |

Female College Students, Midwest (No Age Breakdown):

Percentiles (in.)

| 1st | 5th | 50th | 95th | 99th | S.D. |
|------|------|------|------|------|------|
| 58.8 | 60.5 | 64.4 | 68.4 | 70.0 | 2.36 |

As the data indicates, the men and women have roughly the same standard deviations (2.49, 2.36), but the men are taller (50th percentile at 70 in.

versus 50th percentile at 64.4 in.). Assuming we want a door that both men and women fit under, we would design one for the men. The women, being "in general" shorter will also fit.

The data indicates that the men have a 99th percentile value of 75.8 in. We can use this directly, eliminating the calculation of the value from the mean and standard deviation of the raw scores. We make the doorway as follows:

99th percentile value: 75.8 in.
Contingency: 7.58 in.
Total: 83.38 in.
Make doorway: 84 in.

Our estimate of 85 in., obtained through sampling, gave a similar value.

Watching for Change

The previous sections have discussed the estimation of a value at a point in time. It is often the case that we are interested not only in the estimation of values at one point in time, but in their change over time. For example, if the average life span of the American male were 45 years in 1900 and 70 years in 1990, the change in this value would be relevant to the formation of life plans, as well as the development of insurance rates and social security programs. It is also the case that we are often interested in the deviation of values from certain expected values. For example, one expects one's temperature to be about 98.6°F. If it is not, action may be called for. The expected values may be naturally occurring, e.g., one's temperature, or they may be artificially set. The management technique called "management by exception" is an example. A manager may set certain values or a range of values, such as a sales quota. Values within this range are considered normal and do not require action. Values outside the range are considered exceptional and do require action. For example, if sales quotas are set as "between $1,900 and $2,100 monthly," with the

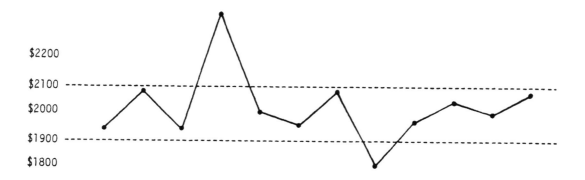

FIGURE 6.2

expectation of $2,000 as "average," but allowing for some deviation, the data of Figure 6.2 would cause "no action" in most months. Things are as expected. However, in April the manager might wish to commend the salesperson, say with a special dinner or a commmemorative watch. In August he or she may wish to take it back.

## Information and Control

Both the example of making the doorway and the example of using sales data to manage personnel are examples of the use of information to gain control of a situation. The function of information is to facilitate effective action. In some cases the action will be virtually certain to produce the outcome. This was the case in creating the doorway. The creation of the proper doorway is within the power of the agent attempting to produce it.

The case of the salesman is a bit different. The outcome "higher sales volume" is not completely within the power of the sales manager to produce. It requires "coproduction" on the part of the salesperson. Hence, any action the manager might take to increase sales, e.g., giving bonus incentives, is taken "under uncertainty" about the eventual outcome. He or she cannot be certain that the goal "higher sales" will be achieved by his or her action alone.

At this point we simply wish to examine the effect of information on the effectiveness of action in situations in which we have full control. We do so with the example of the test of flying ability developed earlier.

There are two ways in which we can control the outcomes of events. One is to produce the outcome directly. This was illustrated in the example of the doorway. Another is to control the outcome indirectly. This is illustrated by the example of the test to select pilots.

The results of the written test showed variability in the outcomes: some people passed the test, some did not (Table 6.11). We used these results, however, to remove variability in the outcome "flying success" by hiring only those people who passed the test. This resulted in no variability in the final outcome of pilots who were successful (Table 6.12).

The outcome of our hiring policy was not that we ourselves trained the pilots to fly better (though we might also do that), but that the pilots we selected were better pilots. Other common examples of the indirect control

## TABLE 6.11

| Applicant | Test Result |
| --- | --- |
| 1 | P |
| 2 | P |
| 3 | F |
| 4 | F |
| 5 | P |
| 6 | F |
| 7 | P |
| 8 | F |

TABLE 6.12

| People Hired | Flying Ability |
| --- | --- |
| 1 | G |
| 2 | G |
| 5 | G |
| 7 | G |

of outcomes are the use of umbrellas in rainstorms or suntan lotion at the beach. We do not control the rain directly or reduce the rays of sun; however, we influence their impact on us (i.e., by staying dry or not suffering overexposure) by taking an intermediary action that prevents (or accomplishes) a particular outcome. In either case, direct control or indirect, the information facilitated the action. In the one case the data value we estimated enabled us to produce the doorway of the proper size; in the other case, the data values on the tests enabled us to prevent potentially adverse outcomes by removing their cause.

The link between information and effective action gives us one means of evaluating an information system. If the result of our actions is consistently successful, one can assume that the information provided by the information system is accurate. If our actions are not generally successful, we need to examine one of two possible causes of the failure: (1) the information is incorrect, or (2) our control of the outcome is not complete. If the control is not complete, we need to take means to obtain control, either by obtaining the cooperation of the coproducer of an event, or by obtaining prior information about the actions the coproducer will take. A simple example is the use of predictions about the coproducer "nature." We cannot always control natural events, but, as indicated above, we can often control the outcome of our actions if we can predict the natural event. An example we will treat later is the decision to hold a bingo game or a picnic. We might have such situation/action rules as the following:

If rain is predicted, hold bingo.
If sun is predicted, hold picnic.

Given these rules and a prediction of good weather, the successful outcome of our action (holding a bingo or a picnic) is assumed. We will return to this example in the discussion of the value of information.

Desirable Lack of Control

In some situations we may not wish to have full control. For example, in such games as baseball, the player's objective is to control the outcome of each competitive event, i.e., to strike out the batter, or to hit a home run. However, interest in the game is caused by the lack of full control in the outcome.

It seems that in activities that are done for their own sake, such as playing checkers or solitaire, the attainment of full control over one's opponent (person or deck or cards) leads to lack of interest in the activity (although some people still cheat at solitaire). Hence, lack of control is preferable to control. In goal attainment problems, however (e.g., making a profit), control, either direct or indirect, is preferable.

## Related Readings

Alder, Henry L. and Roessler, Edward B., *Introduction to Probability and Statistics*, 4th ed. San Francisco: W. H. Freeman and Co., 1968.

Bierman, Harold, Jr., Bonini, Charles P., and Hausman, Warren H., *Quantitative Analysis for Business Decisions*, 4th ed. Homewood, IL: Richard D. Irwin, Inc., 1973.

Churchill, Gilbert A. Jr., *Marketing Research: Methodological Foundations*, 2nd ed. Hinsdale, IL: The Dryden Press, 1979.

Kantowitz, Barry H. and Sorkin, Robert D., *Human Factors: Understanding People-System Relationships*, New York: John Wiley & Sons, 1983.

Kerlinger, Fred N., *Foundations of Behavioral Research*, 2nd ed. New York: Holt, Rinehart & Winston, Inc., 1973.

Lewis, Edward E., *Methods of Statistical Analysis in Economics and Business*. Boston: Houghton Mifflin Company, 1953.

Li, Jerome C. R., *Statistical Inference I*, Ann Arbor, MI: Edward Brothers, Inc., 1964.

McCormick, Ernest J., *Human Factors in Engineering and Design*, 4th ed. New York: McGraw-Hill, 1976.

McCormick, Ernest J. and Sanders, Mark S., *Human Factors in Engineering and Design*, 5th ed. New York: McGraw-Hill, 1982.

Menyk, M., *Principles of Applied Statistics*, New York: Pergamon Press, Inc., 1974.

Siegel, Sidney, *Nonparametric Statistics for the Behavioral Sciences*, New York: McGraw-Hill, 1956.

Suppes, Patrick, *Introduction to Logic*, Princeton, NJ: D. Van Nostrand Company, Inc., 1957.

Tweney, Ryan D., Doherty, Michael E., and Mynatt, Clifford R., eds. *On Scientific Thinking*, New York: Columbia University Press, 1981.

Van Cott, Harold P. and Kinkade, Robert G., eds. *Human Engineering Guide to Equipment Design*, revised edition. New York: McGraw-Hill, 1972.

Williams, Bill, *A Sampler on Sampling*, New York: John Wiley & Sons, Inc., 1978.

# *IV*
# Coding the Data

Data is coded for several reasons. One is to prepare the data for manipulation by machine, e.g., using statistical packages to compute correlation values or summary statistics, or using specially written programs or packages to perform mathematical trnasformations. Another reason is to store and retrieve the data, and a third is to transmit it over data communications paths, be they books or electronic data communications, e.g., terminal to computer and back. We introduce the notion of codes here as a prelude to storage and retrieval. However, the section can conceptually be placed under the topics of data manipulation and data communication.

Chapter 7 introduces the notions of coding to represent items and to compact storage. It also treats the development of error detection and error correction techniques. Finally, comes a brief introduction to the use of appropriate "codes" or representations of data in order to aid human memory and understanding. The use of such codes is of interest to cognitive scientists in studying both human memory and human problem-solving behavior.

Chapter 8 presents a traditional data-processing approach to the representation of data. The concepts of data fields, records, and files are introduced. The differences between fixed length data and variable length data are illustrated, as are two techniques of handling variable length fields, records, or files: the use of prefixes, such as count fields, and the use of suffixes, such as special characters, to mark the end of fields.

There is no discussion of computers, disks, or magnetic tapes per se, although knowledge about these storage media and machine processors is assumed. Again, the reason for this is pedagogical; this text is not one on data processing, and focusing on the technologies in vogue would take the discussion astray. The concepts are presented so that data-processing background is not essential, although it is helpful. It is assumed either that the students will have some familiarity with computer-related technology from previous courses or experience, or that such experience is provided as an adjunct to the current course, i.e., as a parallel theme throughout the course. The latter is the situation at the University of Pittsburgh. In the introductory versions of the course, BASIC has been taught as a programming language and the characteristics of computers and storage technology, e.g., capacity, access time, and transfer rates of devices have been taught separately.

# 7
# Coding the Data

## Objectives

Upon completion of this chapter, the reader should be able to:

1. List and explain the properties of codes: representation, compaction, error detection, error correction
2. Recognize ambiguous and unambiguous codes
3. Construct an unambiguous code
4. Perform conversions between the decimal and binary number systems
5. Encode alphabetic data into a binary code
6. Explain the relationship of coding to human memory and understanding

Once data is collected, it can either be used immediately or stored for future use. If it is stored for future use, it is often coded. Codes serve several functions:

1. Representation
2. Compaction
3. Error detection
4. Error correction
5. Aid to human memory
6. Aid to understanding

## Representation

The primary usage of a code is to represent things. The things represented can be events, objects, attributes of objects, or entire statements. Thus, PGH can stand for the town Pittsburgh, and "PGH 500,000" can indicate the assertion that "the population of Pittsburgh is 500,000."

When devising a code to represent some person, thing, or event, one of the questions that arises is the ambiguity of the code. For example, if we choose "LA" to represent Los Angeles, the code will work as long as we don't also choose "LA" to represent Los Alamos. The problem of ambiguity arises not in the coding

Los Angeles ——→ LA

Los Alamos ——→ LA

but in the decoding. If we see the code

LA

how do we know if it stands for Los Angeles or Los Alamos? It's hard to tell.

Devising a code is really a problem in representing one set of symbols (e.g., the name Los Angeles) by another set of symbols (the abbreviation LA). In order to illustrate the concept of code, we devise an example that translates numeric digits into alphabetic characters. Suppose that our code consists of the rules in Table 7.1, where the arrow means "is replaced by." Then the number

469

would be "encoded" as EGJ. In order to interpret the coded message, we must "decode" it by reversing the arrows

E → 4

G → 6

J → 9

yielding

EGJ → 469

The table of rules tells us how to transform the symbol from one alphabet (numerals) into the symbols for the other alphabet (letters). Because of this "transformation" process, these rules are often referred to as a set of transformation rules. The entire set of rules *is* the code.

Very often, we need not list the entire set of rules. Rather, we determine one rule that summarizes the pattern for the entire set. For example, if we wished to transform each letter of the English alphabet into a numeral, we could devise the rule

Numeral = position of letter in the alphabet

## TABLE 7.1

0 → A
1 → B
2 → C
3 → D
4 → E
5 → F
6 → G
7 → H
8 → I
9 → J

TABLE 7.2

---

A → 01
B → 02
    ·
    ·
    ·
I → 09

---

so that A would be represented by a 1, Z by 26, and E by 5. To include the space, we could add the rule "Space = 27."

However, without one more restriction (one more rule), we would find decoding difficult here. This is because the two rules we have established result in ambiguous messages

15

Does this message represent two letters

1 = A

5 = E

so that we have

15 = AE

or does it represent one letter?

15 = O (letter "oh")

The answer is not clear.

Whenever a message can have two separate meanings, we call it ambiguous. The rules that generated the message (the code) are likewise ambiguous.

In our example we can eliminate the ambiguity by adding one more rule

Each numeral representation must be two digits long.

We implement this rule by adding a leading digit to the single-digit symbols (Table 7.2). Now, the message "AE" would be written

0105

while the letter O would be

15

and we have eliminated the ambiguity.

Our code now consists of three rules

1. Letter of alphabet = numeric position of letter in alphabet
2. Space = 27
3. All numeric representations are two digits wide.

An example of a message encoded in this code is

071515042712210311

To decode the message, we need to reverse the rules

TABLE 7.3

| | |
|---|---|
| A ↔ 01 | |
| B ↔ 02 | |
| . | |
| . | |
| . | |
| Z ↔ 26 | |
| D ↔ 27 | |

1. Read digits in pairs
2. Numeral = position of letter in alphabet
3. 27 = space

Applying these rules, we first divide the digits of the message into pairs

  07 15 15 04 27 12 21 03 11

then use rules 2 and 3 to translate the digit-pairs

  07 15 15 04 27 12 21 03 11

  G  O  O  D ɓ L  U  C K

where the symbol ɓ indicates a space.

## A Two-Way Street: Reversibility

Note that in order to be unambiguous, a code must be reversible. We must be able to first put the message into the code (called *encoding*) then retrieve the message from the code (called *decoding*).

  Since there is one set of rules for encoding, and another set for decoding, we could say that a code actually consists of two sets of rules. However, a more satisfying representation is simply to list the rules with reversible arrows, indicating that the rules "go both ways" (Table 7.3).

## 1-1 Correspondence

Note that in our code each symbol on the left is transformed into one and only one symbol on the right. Likewise, each symbol on the right is transformed into one and only one symbol on the left. This correspondence of exactly one symbol to exactly one symbol is called a "1-1 correspondence" (read one-to-one correspondence). A 1-1 correspondence is essential to have a completely reversible, unambiguous code.

  If more than one symbol on the left is transformed into the same symbol on the right (many to one)

TABLE 7.4

```
000
001
002
012
210
```

the code is ambiguous, and cannot be uniquely decoded. The code is not reversible. For example, the sequence

AAA

could represent any of the sequences in Table 7.4, as well as any of 22 other permutations (27 different sequences in all), which is not a desirable situation if your job depends on decoding the messages correctly.

Codes that are one to many (one item on the left to many on the right; Figure 7.1), are uniquely decodable, but not uniquely encodable. Thus, the sequence 100 could be encoded as AXX or as AYZ, but in either case, the decoding would result in AXX $\longrightarrow$ 100 and AYZ $\longrightarrow$ 100.

Codes that are one to many or many to one can be useful. An example of a code that is one to many is the representation of STOP signs: the message STOP is translated into several different representations

1.  The word STOP
2.  The octagonal shape of a STOP sign
3.  The red color of a STOP sign

The several encodings of the same message introduce redundancy into the system, insuring that the message gets across.

An instance of a code that is many to one is the phone dial (Figure 7.2). Three separate letters, e.g., A, B, and C are encoded as a single digit (2). Thus, if phone listings include letters, such as Yards 7-9149, where the first two letters of the word *YArds* are part of the phone number

YA7-9149

the number translation would be

927-9149

The prefix

Washington 7-9149

FIGURE 7.1

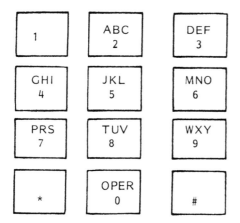

FIGURE 7.2

would give the same numerals

927-9149

so that care must be exercised in the choice of verbal prefixes.

The fact that the phone number cannot be uniquely decoded, e.g., determining whether

927-9149

came from

Yards 7-9149

or

Washington 7-9149

is not so important because the choice of verbal prefixes was made in order to aid in the memory of phone numbers. The purpose is to translate the words into numeric representation, but not vice versa. Thus, the code is expected to work only one way so that decoding is not critical.

Another example of a useful many-to-one code is the use of index terms in an information retrieval system. In order to retrieve data efficiently, it is often stored under "key words." Thus, such items as cheese, milk, and butter might be categorized as "dairy products" and stored under those key words. When someone retrieves the data on dairy products, data about all three items are retrieved. The fact that three items are stored under one term

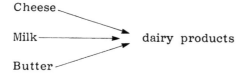

indicates that the code is many to one. The function of such a code in the information retrieval system is to reduce the number of key words. However, a by-product of this function is that the user of the system can no longer isolate "cheese" from "milk" or "butter" since the term dairy

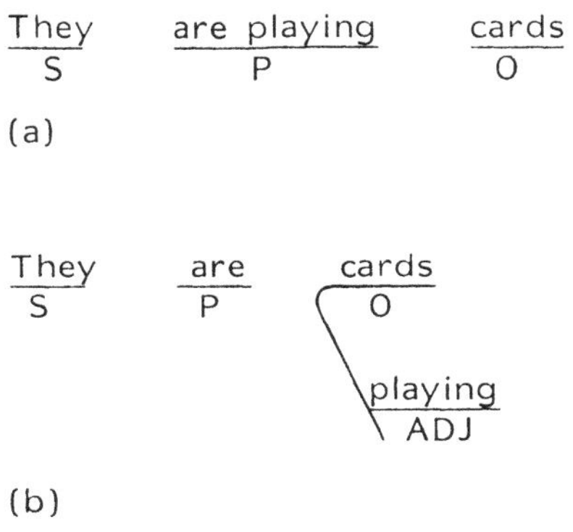

They    are playing    cards
 S         P            O

(a)

They    are    cards
 S       P      O

              playing
              ADJ

(b)

FIGURE 7.3

products cannot be uniquely decoded. By categorizing three different products under one term, we have reduced the number of categories in the information system. At the same time we have sacrificed the ability to differentiate among the items in that category at a more specific level.

### The English Language

The English language is neither perfectly decodable (unambiguous) nor perfectly encodable (unique encoding of each message). The fact that English is ambiguous can be seen from the consideration of the following sentence:

> They are playing cards.

Does this sentence mean "some people are playing cards," or does it mean "these cards are called playing cards because they are used to play games?" We cannot tell from the sentence alone.

The two separate meanings of the sentence can be illustrated by "diagramming" or "parsing" the sentence. In the diagrams we use the symbols S = subject, P = predicate, O = object, and ADJ = adjective.

The first meaning, "some people . . ." results in Figure 7.3a, while the second sentence, "some cards . . ." results in Figure 7.3b. However, this ambiguity does not leave us helpless. Very often the context in which the sentence occurs (e.g., previous sentences), can aid us in decoding the current sentence properly. Thus, if someone has asked "What are they doing?" and I reply, "They are playing cards," you will have no trouble determining that I mean sentence 1, "some people..." If you hold up a little packet of cards, and ask "What are these?" and I reply "They are playing cards," you immediately zero in on meaning number 2, "some cards...." The study of ambiguous sentences and the means by which we resolve the ambiguity is one of the considerations of linguistics.

The fact that ideas are not uniquely encoded in English, that there is more than one way to say something, is even more easily demonstrated. For example, if I see a child eat a cookie, and want to report the fact, I can say:

The child ate the cookie. (Active)

or

The cookie was eaten by the child. (Passive)

The two sentences represent the same event: a child (agent) eating (action) a cookie (object of the action). The two versions are equivalent in meaning. Linguists call different versions of one underlying idea "surface structures." The underlying idea is called the "deep structure."

In our first example, "They are playing cards," we had *one* surface structure (the sentence itself), but two underlying, or deep, structures (some people..., some cards...). This is the essence of ambiguity: one surface structure can be explained in more than one way, i.e., by more than one deep structure. One surface structure may be decoded in more than one way.

In the second example, we have two surface structures (active, passive), but one underlying structure (child, eat, cookie). Thus, we can rephrase our definitions of ambiguity and nonunique encodability to

1. Ambiguous—many deep structures to one surface (many to one)
2. Nonuniquely encodable—one deep to many surface (one to many)

## Natural Versus Artificial Languages

The languages of normal human communication, such as English, French, and Chinese, are referred to as "natural" languages. The term *natural* seems to describe the organic way in which they develop. While our far distant ancestors may have done so, we no longer sit around a table and discuss whether the word *dog* should describe a four-legged furry animal or a device for making coffee. With the exception of new words (laser, TV, computer), the words and their meanings are established; we merely learn and use them. Furthermore, new words are introduced "organically" as they are needed, by simple usage. One person or a few begin to use the word, and its usage spreads "naturally." In contrast to this "natural" language, we also devise "artificial" languages—codes—like our code for transforming letters of the alphabet into numeric digits.

All natural languages contain ambiguity and have more than one way to encode statements. In devising artificial languages, one of our aims is to eliminate the ambiguity and the nonunique encodability; we wish to devise codes that are 1–1 correspondences.

A subset of the artificial languages are the "machine languages." The symbols in them are interpreted, stored, retrieved, and manipulated by machines. In addition, in order for the machine to do its job properly, these machine languages should be unambiguous. Some examples of machine languages are the languages used for writing computer programs: FORTRAN, COBOL, BASIC, etc. Another example is the code used for storing data in the computer, the binary code. We shall frequently refer to the binary code in this text, so we take time out now to introduce it.

## Binary: The Language of the Computer

While the binary code can be used to represent alphabetic characters, we shall restrict our treatment here to the consideration of how to represent decimal numerals in binary. There are only two symbols in binary: zero and one

0

1

This is in contrast to the 10 symbols of the decimal code

0, 1, 2, 3, 4, 5, 6, 7, 8, 9

The fact that binary has only two symbols is reflected by its alternate name, the base 2. Decimal is called the base 10. Since binary has only two symbols, 0 and 1, a typical binary numeral looks like

101

A numeral like

212

could not possibly be a binary representation, because it contains an illegal digit, the 2.

There is a 1–1 correspondence for translating decimal numerals into binary, and binary into decimal. The essential ingredient for performing such conversions is an understanding of positional notation.

In the decimal number system, the positions have the values

100      10      1

Thus, a number like 749 stands for 7 100s, 4 10s, and 9 1s

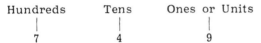

The positional notation for binary is

8  4  2  1

We convert decimal numerals into binary by placing 1s in the columns or positions of the binary representation that will sum to give the decimal numeral. Thus, the decimal numeral 10 would be represented in binary by placing 1s in the columns 8 and 2

8  4  2  1

1     1

and 0s in the remaining positions

8  4  2  1

1  0  1  0

since 8 + 2 = 10.

The binary representation of decimal 5 is 4 + 1

8  4  2  1

0  1  0  1

To convert binary to decimal, we simply reverse the process. For example, the binary numeral

1  1  1  0

can be converted to decimal by filling in the positional values

8  4  2  1

1  1  1  0

and summing the positions that contain a 1

8 + 4 + 2 = 14

The largest number that can be represented by four binary digits (bits) is 15

8  4  2  1

1  1  1  1

which yields 8 + 4 + 2 + 1 = 15.

However, larger numbers can be represented by adding more positions (bits) to the left. This is done by simply doubling the value of the previous bit, so that the next values are 16, 32, 64, etc.

64  32  16  8  4  2  1

This process can be extended indefinitely, so that the binary code is capable of representing integers of any size.

Using this extended representation, the number 100 (decimal 100, not binary) would be

64  32  16  8  4  2  1

1   1   0   0  1  0  0

and, reversing the process, the binary numeral

10010011

would be

128  64  32  16  8  4  2  1

1    0   0   1   0  0  1  1

which yields 128 + 16 + 2 + 1 = 147 in decimal.

## Some Terminology: Numbers and Numerals

A number is an abstract concept. For example, the number five represents the idea of so many items. In contrast, the representation of this idea is a concrete symbol called a numeral. The decimal representation for the number five is 5; the binary is 101. Thus, 5 in decimal and 101 in binary are two different numerals for the same number. Another example is the Roman numeral X, which is the representation of the number ten; the decimal representation is 10, while binary is 1010.

The distinction between number and numeral is a fine one. We have taken care to make the distinction here, but shall take the liberty of using the more common usage—number for numeral—in the rest of the text. The context will usually make it clear if the discussion is about numerals or numbers.

## A Matter of Notation

In order to avoid confusion between numerals in different bases, we often write the base of the numeral as a subscript to that numeral, thus

$$101_2$$

indicates that this is a base 2 numeral. Using the rules for converting from binary to decimal, we see that its value is five. The number

$$101_{10}$$

indicates a decimal number, and its value is one hundred and one.

## Representing the Alphabet in Binary

In order to explain the way alphabetic characters are translated into binary, we use the example of reading data on magnetic tape.

The magnetic tape is divided into several horizontal areas called "channels." In the tape we describe, there are seven channels. Only six of these are used for storing data, the seventh being used for error detection, so we will restrict our attention to these six channels.

The six channels are divided into two groups: the zone channels and the digit channels. There are two zone channels: channel A and channel B. There are four digit channels: channels 8, 4, 2, and 1. The channels are arranged as shown in Figure 7.4. It is on these channels that magnetic spots that represent data are placed. The presence of a spot is taken to mean "on," or the presence of a 1 in the binary code. The absence of a spot is "off" or 0.

In order to represent numeric values, only the digit channels are used. We use these channels in exactly the same way that was described above to translate decimal digits into binary ones: "Place dots where the digits will add to the value of the decimal number." The dots (magnetic spots) are placed vertically in columns for each character represented. Thus, if we wish to represent the decimal number 9, we would place spots in the 8

Zones $\left\{ \begin{array}{l} B \underline{\hspace{6cm}} \\ A \underline{\hspace{6cm}} \end{array} \right.$

Digits $\left\{ \begin{array}{l} 8 \underline{\hspace{6cm}} \\ 4 \underline{\hspace{6cm}} \\ 2 \underline{\hspace{6cm}} \\ 1 \underline{\hspace{6cm}} \end{array} \right.$

FIGURE 7.4

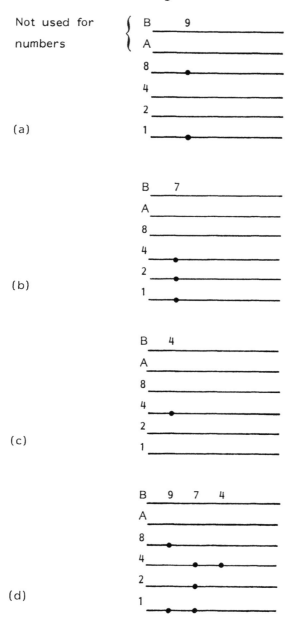

FIGURE 7.5

channel and in the 1 channel (Figure 7.5a). The number 7 is represented as 4-2-1, Figure 7.5b. The number 4 would result in a single dot in the 4 channel (Figure 7.5c), so that the number 974 would be represented in three successive columns of the tape (Figure 7.5d).

In order to encode alphabetic data on the tape, we make use of the two zones, B and A. We first divide the letters of the alphabet into three groups

TABLE 7.5

| Letter | Zone | Digit |
|--------|------|-------|
| A | B&A | 1 |
| B | B&A | 2 |
| . | . | . |
| . | . | . |
| I | B&A | 9 |
| J | B | 1 |
| K | B | 2 |
| . | . | . |
| . | . | . |
| R | B | 9 |
| S | A | 2 |
| T | A | 3 |
| . | . | . |
| . | . | . |
| Z | A | 9 |

1. A through I
2. J through R
3. S through Z

We then assign zones to these groups as follows:

1. A through I: zones B and A
2. J through R: zone B only
3. S through Z: zone A only

Within each zone there are at most nine letters: A through I, and J through R (groups 1 and 2) have nine letters apiece. The third group (S through Z), has only eight letters. (9 + 9 + 8 = 26 letters of the alphabet.)

We now assign the digits 1 through 9 to each letter in each group, according to the position of the letter in the group. Thus A will be assigned 1, as will J. B will be assigned 2, as will K in group 2. I, R, and Z will be assigned the digit 9. The only complication is that in group 3, we assign the digit 2 to S, so that this group of eight letters has the digits 2 through 9. The list of assignments, zones and digits, is shown in Table 7.5.

TABLE 7.6

| Zones | Digits | | | | | | | | |
|-------|---|---|---|---|---|---|---|---|---|
| | 1 | 2 | 3 | 4 | 5 | 6 | 7 | 8 | 9 |
| B&A | A | B | C | D | E | F | G | H | I |
| B | J | K | L | M | N | O | P | Q | R |
| A | | S | T | U | V | W | X | Y | Z |

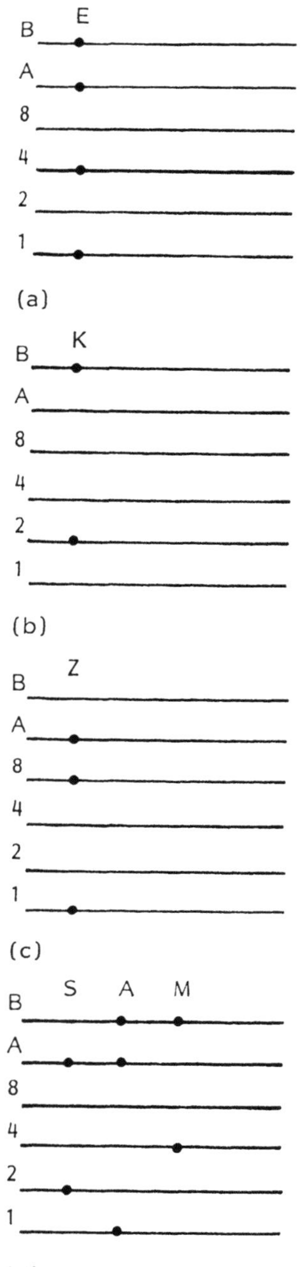

(a)

(b)

(c)

(d)

FIGURE 7.6

We can condense this list into a more compact form by creating a matrix (two-dimensional table) wherein the columns (across the top) represent the digits, the rows (along the side) represent the zones, and the intersection of a row and column contains the letter represented by that zone and digit (Table 7.6). Thus, the combination A-2 (A zone, 2 digit) represents the letter *S*. The letter *E* is represented by the combination B, A, 5, which would be represented by dots in the B, A, 4, and 1 channels, since 5 = 4 + 1 (Figure 7.6a). *K* would be B-2 (Figure 7.6b), and *Z* is A-9 or A-8 – 1 (Figure 7.6c). The name *Sam* can be stored on the tape by coding each character in successive columns (Figure 7.6d).

The student is encouraged to practice his or her mastery of this code (called "binary coded decimal" or "6-bit," because of the six channels, B, A, 8, 4, 2, and 1) by encoding his or her name and social security number on "a piece of tape."

## Compaction

The second function of a good code is data compaction. One of the most common operations we perform with data is to record it. The medium on which data are recorded is of limited size. For example, the card frequently used to store data in computerized data processing is called the Hollerith card, after Herman Hollerith, the inventor of punched card equipment. The Hollerith card has 80 positions for storing data. Suppose that we wish to store the following information about somebody:

Name
Address
State of residence
Status in school
Sex

We could keypunch the verbal representation of each item, so that the record would read:

Jones, Mary    717 Wolf Dr.    West Virginia    Junior    Female

However, by using some codes, we can shorten this record considerably. For example, sex can have the code

1 = male

2 = female

Status in school could have the code shown in Table 7.7, and state of residence could have the code shown in Table 7.8, where the states are listed in alphabetical order, and the code assigned to each is its position in the list. Now, our record looks like

Jones, Mary    717 Wolf Dr.    48    3    2

We've compacted 25 characters into 4, and the remaining space can be used to hold other data.

## TABLE 7.7

1 = freshman
2 = sophomore
3 = junior
4 = senior
5 = graduate

TABLE 7.8

| |
| --- |
| 01 = Alabama |
| 02 = Alaska |
| . |
| . |
| . |
| 48 = West Virginia |
| 49 = Wisconsin |
| 50 = Wyoming |

While the card is no longer used as in the past, other storage media such as magnetic disks, magnetic tape, and the main store of a computer have fixed sizes as well, making the compaction of data a continuing consideration.

### Accomodating the Medium

Not every code compacts, as a consideration of converting decimal numerals into binary makes evident. The decimal numeral

$$100_{10}$$

consists of three digits, while the binary equivalent

$$1100100_2$$

takes seven bits.

However, in cases where codes do not compact, the most common reason is that the longer code is an accommodation to the medium used to store the data.

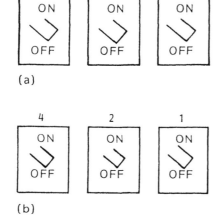

(a)

(b)

FIGURE 7.7

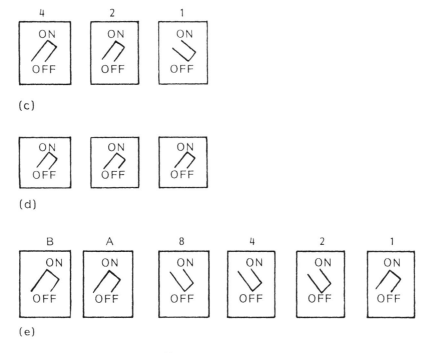

FIGURE 7.7 (continued)

In computerized data processing, the medium is usually electronic or magnetic, and the simplest method of representing items is to have "switches" that are either "on" or "off," a binary or two-state division. Thus, the binary code is used for this technology, with the "on" state representing a "1," and "off" representing a "0."

If we look at the inside of a computer as three light switches (Figure 7.7a), each switch representing a position in the binary code (Figure 7.7b), we can then represent the number 6 by turning the two leftmost switches on, and leaving the rightmost switch off (Figure 7.7c), to indicate 4 + 2. The number 7 would have all three switches on (Figure 7.7d). All switches in the off position would represent zero.

Adding three more switches, one each for the B-zone, A-zone and 8-digit (Figure 7.7e), we could store letters in a series of light bulbs! (What is the letter? Try it, then see the answer below.)*

### Error Detection

The third use of a code is in error detection. We can easily see this by considering our code for translating the letters of the English alphabet into numerals (Table 7.9).

We know that every symbol translates into two digits. Thus, if we receive the message

---

*Answer: The letter is A (BA-1).

TABLE 7.9

| | | |
|---|---|---|
| A | ↔ | 01 |
| B | ↔ | 02 |
| | · | |
| | · | |
| | · | |
| Z | ↔ | 26 |
| b̸ | ↔ | 27 |

080512121

and attempt to divide it into pairs

    08   05   12   12   1

we see that something has gone wrong. We have detected an error in the representation or transmission of the message.

However, we cannot correct the error, since we do not know which digit was lost. It could have been a 0 preceding the 1

    01 = A

or a 1 or 2 preceding the 1

    11 = K      21 = U

or any of the 10 digits as a successor to the 1

    10 = J      11 = K      12 = L      etc.

Another example of error detection can be seen in the parity bit used in coding data on magnetic tape. Besides the six "information" channels (B, A, 8, 4, 2, 1) the magnetic tapes are made with one other channel dedicated to detecting errors. This extra channel is called the parity or check channel (Figure 7.8a), and is used to adjust the number of magnetic spots in each column. The spots are counted as they are created, and the total number of spots is either all odd or all even. Our example will use "odd parity," which indicates that all columns will have an odd number of magnetic spots. If the number of dots in a column is odd already

Parity or
check channel ⟶

Information
channels

    B _____
    A _____
    8 _____
    4 _____
    2 _____
    1 _____

(a)

FIGURE 7.8

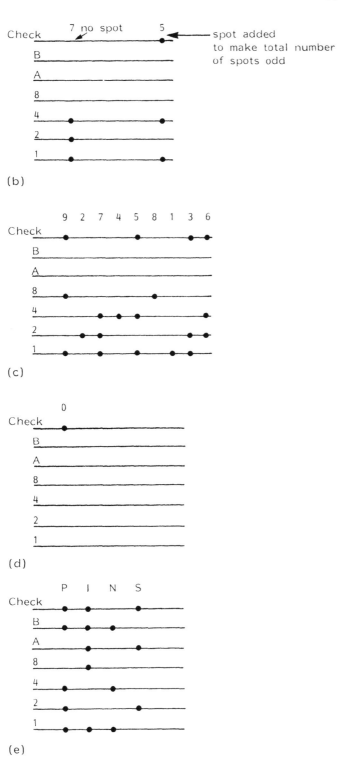

FIGURE 7.8 (continued)

(as in the case of storing a 7 that has spots in the 4, 2, and 1 rows), the check channel is left without a "bit." If the number of dots is even (as in the case of storing a 5 with spots in the 4 and 1 rows), a dot is added to the check channel (Figure 7.8b).

Note that the value of the number has no bearing on the use of the check bit. It is the total number of spots that counts. Thus, the number 5 is odd, but is represented by an even number of bits (4 and 1), so an extra bit is needed in the check row. To store the social security number 927-45-8136, we would have the representation shown in Figure 7.8c.

Note that if the number zero is stored, it would have zero dots in the 8, 4, 2, and 1 channels. Since zero is even (one being odd), this would require the use of a check bit (Figure 7.8d), resulting in every column having at least one bit in it, thus aiding in the timing necessary to read the tape.

The word *PINS* would be stored as shown in Figure 7.8e.

The way in which the parity bit is used to detect errors can be seen if the representation of the number 937 (Figure 7.9a) incurs the loss of a bit (Figure 7.9b). When the tape is read, the bits in each column are counted, and the column in which the 3 had been stored is "detected" as having an even number of bits (Figure 7.9c). The machine that reads the tape would indicate that the data is bad, e.g., by flashing a red light, so that the original data could be checked in order to correct the error.

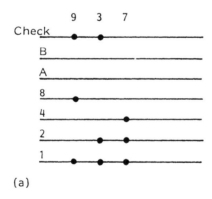

(a)

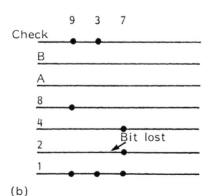

(b)

FIGURE 7.9

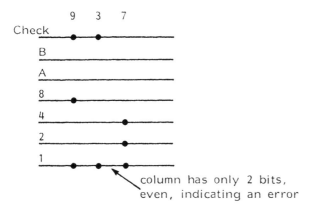

(c)

FIGURE 7.9 (continued)

Note that the detection of the error does not allow us to correct it, since we cannot tell which bit has been lost. When determining that the column has an even number of bits (Figure 7.10a), we cannot tell if the bit was lost in the 2-row (indicating a 3 had been the original number stored), the 4-row (indicating a 5 had been originally stored), the 8-row (indicating a 9), the A-row (indicating the /, which is stored as A-1), or the B-row (indicating a J). The problem of error correction is taken up later in the chapter. It is handled in a similar manner (counting the bits), simply involving more check bits.

Note also that the parity bit will not detect the loss of two bits in a single column, since this will result in the number of bits remaining odd (Figures 7.10b and 7.10c), so that the 7 is now incorrectly interpreted as a 1. What the systems specialist has to decide is the likelihood of losing two bits in the same column. Methods can be devised to detect the loss of more than one bit, but the question is whether or not the error detection methods necessary to do so are worth the risk. If the information is extremely important, and the likelihood of losing more than a single bit is high, these more powerful error detection methods might be employed. If

Check
B
A
8
4
2
1

(a)

FIGURE 7.10

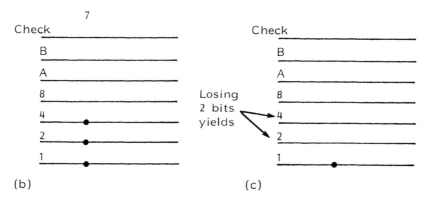

FIGURE 7.10 (continued)

either of these two considerations is not true, i.e., either the information is not that important, or the likelihood of losing two bits at once is low, the single parity bit may suffice.

The use of the parity bit in each column is called vertical parity. This is because the bits are counted in a vertical manner. The concept of horizontal parity will be considered under error correction. (Note: In some usages, based on a different representation of the data, the use of these terms, vertical and horizontal, is reversed, but the concepts are the same.)

## Machine Error Versus Human Error

The loss of bits on a magnetic tape is due to machine error. It is also possible for humans to err in entering data into a system. An example would be the incorrect keying of 73¢ as 37¢. One of the popular means of detecting human errors is the use of the check-digit.

## The Check Digit

In this age of massive, machine-processed data files, many of us are more recognized by such numbers as our social security number than by our facial features. It is important in dealing with these numbers that we "keep the numbers straight." For example, suppose that my social security number is 423-40-5961. My income tax is filed under this number; my grades are filed under this number; every time I get a job, I must submit this number. If it were to become accidentally changed in my file, I would become a nonentity. Or, less disastrous, but possibly even more frustrating, if I request some record of mine by this number, and the clerk handling the request keys in the wrong number, I do not get an answer to my query, or at best, I get an answer only after some delay. One of the most common forms of keying error is the "transposition" of two numbers. Thus, instead of keying in 423-40-5961, the clerk reverses the position of two numbers, keying 243-40-5961. Because transposition is such a common error, measures have been taken to detect such errors. One such method is the check-digit. The check-digit is an extra digit that is appended to the original number in order to catch such errors as the transposition of digits. Upon assigning a unique number to identify a person or transaction (called the "key" to that person's record or to the record of that transaction), we not only assign the original digits used for identification (423-40-5961), we assign an extra digit, usually appended at the right, which adds nothing to the identification process, but which will be used to check all transactions as to the correctness of the identification number, e.g., 423-40-5961-1 ⟵ (check digit).

There are several methods for calculating the check-digit. The one we will explain is particularly suited to detecting transposition errors. It is called the 2-1-2 method, for reasons that will become clear as we develop the algorithm (rule) for calculating the extra digit. Starting with the leftmost digit, we take alternate digits from the number

```
4   2   3   4   0   5   9   6   1
|       |       |       |       |
        ↓
    4   3   0   9   1
```

Then multiply each by 2 (the 2-digits)

    8   6   0   18   2

and add these numbers

    8 + 6 + 0 + 18 + 2 = 34

Now we take the remaining digits of the original number

```
4   2   3   4   0   5   9   6   1
    |       |       |       |
        ↓
    2   4   5   6
```

and simply add them, with no multiplication (the 1-digits)

    2 + 4 + 5 + 6 = 17

We then sum the two subtotals

    34 + 17 = 51

and use the rightmost digit (the 1 in 51) as the check-digit: 423-40-5961-1. We now store the entire number, ID-part plus check-part, as the identification of the person or transaction—the "record." Whenever we refer to this record, e.g., in fulfilling a request to see a transcript that is stored in a machine-readable form, the clerk keys in the entire extended number

    423-40-5961-1

and the algorithm for computing the check-digit is performed. If the computed check-digit agrees with the check-digit that has been keyed in, we accept the number as valid. If it does not agree, we immediately notify the operator that the number he or she has input is incorrect, and request a second input. For example, suppose the operator reverses the first two digits: the number 423-40-5961-1 is keyed in as 243-40-5961-1. Taking the "2" digits, which are 23091 in the number that was erroneously keyed in, then multiplying these by 2, we get 4 6 0 18 2. Adding these, we get the number 4 + 6 + 0 + 18 + 2 = 30, then taking the 1-digits and adding, we get $4 + 4 + 5 + 6 = 19$. Summing the results of the 2-digit and 1-digit processes, we get $30 + 19 = 49$, which indicates that 9 is the check-digit. This disagrees with the check-digit that has been keyed in as a 1 in 243-40-5961-1, so we ask the clerk to "try again." We have identified the error, so that the clerk may recover, and the customer be served without unnecessary delay or frustration. Note that the check-digit itself does not enter into the calculations; it is the result, not an ingredient, of the calculations.

To summarize, the process is:

1. Take every other digit, beginning with the leftmost digit, and "weight" these by 2 (multiply by 2).
2. Add these "weighted" digits.
3. Take the remaining digits and sum them (unweighted).
4. Add the two sums (steps 2 and 3 above).
5. Take the rightmost digit of the result as the check-digit.

## Security at a Price

Note that the check-digit adds no new identification information about the person or transaction. The person is completely identified by the original numbers, without the check-digit. However, the check-digit does help us in detecting errors made in handling the data, but only at a price—the price of some extra storage for the extra digit, and some computation time both in generating the original check-digit, as well as in processing any transaction that refers to this identification number.

## Other Algorithms

There are many different algorithms for computing check-digits, each geared to catching different types and different percentages of errors. Our particular algorithm catches the transposition of adjacent digits, one of the most common types of errors made by "keyboard" operators. That it does not catch 100% of all errors is evident from the following example, where the correct number, 423-40-5961-1 is keyed in as 324-40-5961-1 and the error goes undetected. The student is encouraged to calculate the check-digit for the incorrect number, and "see for him- or herself" that the error goes undetected. The various coding methods, and the types and percentages of errors each combats, are studied in the fields of systems analysis and design, as well as in the more specialized field of coding theory.

## Error Correction

In addition to detecting errors, a proper selection of codes can aid in correcting errors. While the following method of error correction will not work 100% of the time, it illustrates the idea.

Suppose that in our alphabetic example the original message is

08   05   12   12   15

## TABLE 7.10

$$0 + 8 = 8$$
$$0 + 5 = 5$$
$$1 + 2 = 3$$
$$1 + 2 = 3$$
$$1 + 5 = 6$$

Suppose further that we send some extra digits with our message, these digits being computed by taking the sum of the two digits in each pair. These extra digits will be called "check-sums." (The check-sums for each pair are shown in Table 7.10). We append these digits to the original message, taking care to separate the message digits from the check-digits by a pair of zeroes.

Now, if the message is adulterated

```
08   05   12   12   1   00   8   5   3   3   6
                      ↑
                   ─────── 5 is lost
```

not only can we detect the error by noting the odd number of digits, we can also look at the check-digits to correct the error.

The fifth check-digit is a 6, but the fifth pair of the message is "1." In order to attain a sum of 6, the missing digit must be a "5." We fill in the 5 and decode the message.

```
08   05   12   12   15
 H    E    L    L    O
```

The fact that our error-correcting algorithm is not foolproof is indicated by the fact that both 12 and 21 would sum to 3, so that if we received the message

    1   00   3

we would not know if the message letter was

    21 = U

or

    12 = L

Some algorithms (rules) for computing check-digits will catch 100% of some errors, but no check-digit can correct 100% of all possible errors; so this example is not unrealistic.

## The Check-Digit: Redundancy Applied

We take time out here to introduce the concept of redundancy. Notice that check-digits are redundant insofar as the message is concerned. They add no new information to the message

| 08 | 05 | 12 | 12 | 15 | 00 | 8 | 5 | 3 | 3 | 6 |
|----|----|----|----|----|----|---|---|---|---|---|
| H  | E  | L  | L  | O  |    |   |   |   |   |   |

           Message                 Check-digits

This is indeed wasteful of the storage medium. We have stored 7 extra digits (2 for end of message, 5 check-digits) in a message that originally had only 10 digits. These 7 extra digits could have been used to encode some other data. Redundancy leads to inefficiency in the use of the storage medium. However, with these extra 7 digits, we are able to correct the message that had been adulterated in transmission, so that redundancy leads to "safer" storage and/or transmission of data.

## Horizontal Parity

Another example of error correction is the storage of data on magnetic tape. In addition to computing a vertical parity bit, the bits in each row are counted horizontally, with an extra character (the "check character") being recorded after the data item. For example, in coding the social security number 927-45-8136, the vertical parity bits were as shown in Figure 7.11a.

If we now include a horizontal (or longitudinal) parity character, we must count the bits in each row horizontally, which results in the check character shown in Figure 7.11b.

Note that rows A and B get a parity bit in the check character because they have no bits recorded in them (with zero being even). Rows 8, 4, and 2 also have an even number of information bits, so that we record a parity bit in the check character for them. However, row 1 has 5 informa-

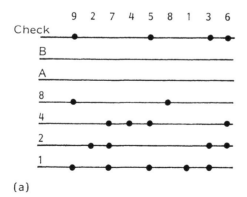

(a)

FIGURE 7.11

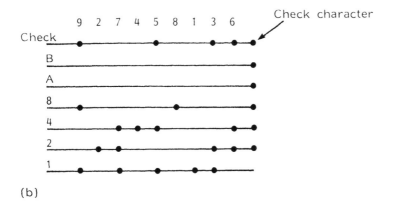

(b)

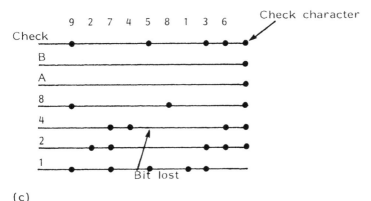

(c)

FIGURE 7.11 (continued)

tion bits recorded in it, so that it does not receive a bit in the check character.

If we now lose information by the loss of a single bit, not only can we detect the loss, but we can also correct it. For example, say that we lose the 4-bit in the column with a 5 recorded (Figure 7.11c). As the tape is read back, we count the bits in the columns, recognizing that the column where the 5 had been recorded is wrong (Figure 7.12a). By counting the bits in each row, we also detect the incorrect row (Figure 7.12b). Where the incorrect column and the incorrect row meet (Figure 7.12c), the bit is wrong. Since there is no bit, and this is wrong, we simply restore the bit (Figure 7.12d), and we have not only detected, but corrected the error.

The scheme described above can correct a single incorrect bit, and can detect, but not correct, two incorrect bits. More elaborate schemes can be devised to correct more complex errors.

A scheme similar to the above is used in computers and telecommunications equipment, where a code such as ASCII (American Standard Code for Information Interchange) is used to store information in binary; e.g., the letter A is

1000001

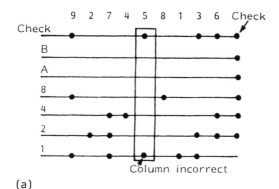

(a)

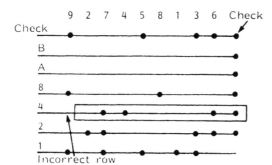

(b)

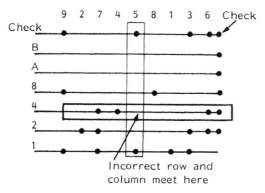

(c)

FIGURE 7.12

where the 1s indicate a bit is on, and the zeroes indicate a bit is off. If a parity bit is attached to the letter *A* at the leftmost position, and we use odd parity, the encoding of the letter *A* becomes

11000001

and we send eight bits per character instead of seven. The letter *E* has the ASCII code

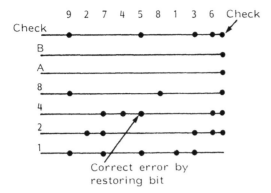

(d)

FIGURE 7.12 (continued)

    1000101

so that the parity bit would be a zero

    01000101

The reader should indicate the parity bits for even parity.

    With this treatment of error detection, we now turn to the uses of codes that enable humans to remember and process information more easily.

## An Aid to Human Memory: Chunking

The concept of recoding the data into "chunks" was introduced by George Miller (1956) in his treatment of the limitations of humans as information processors. Chunking is actually a type of compaction, and it is this compaction that leads to aiding memory. For example, if we wish to memorize the following string of binary digits

    1100101011110101

we might find the task somewhat difficult. However, if we divide the number into groups of four binary digits

    1100   1010   1111   0101

and translate these into decimal

    1100   1010   1111   0101

     12     10     15     5

we simplify the task. We now remember four decimal numbers

    12   10   15   5

and reconstruct the binary digits on demand.

    Dividing the original string into two parts

    11001010   11110101

and translating them into their respective decimal values

    11001010   11110101

      202        245

reduces the problem to remembering two decimal numbers, or, we can consider the entire number to be a single integer: 51957. Of course, to reconstruct the binary representation, we would have to create the positional
values and determine which bits would be on to give 51957

    32,768 16,384 8192 4096 2048 1024 512 256 128 64 32 16 8 4 2 1

      1      1     0    0    1    0   1   0   1   1  1  1 0 1 0 1

which involves quite a bit of processing. In general, a trade-off can usually be had between the amount of storage space used and the amount of
processing required. Using large amounts of storage will usually reduce
the need to process. On the other hand, storage space can be saved by
increasing the processing load. For example, storing the binary numeral

    1001

on this page takes four positions; storing the decimal equivalent

    9

takes one position. However, if the binary is stored, it can be retrieved
immediately, without a conversion process. If the 9 is stored, and the
binary is desired, the conversion must be performed

    $\frac{8}{1}$ $\frac{4}{0}$ $\frac{2}{0}$ $\frac{1}{1}$

Whether we wish to conserve memory (storage) or processing (thinking,
manipulating data) depends on the relative abundance of each. In the consideration of short-term memory, storage is being conserved.

   Applying the principle of chunking to the problem of remembering a
phone number, we could translate the number

    469-3279

into the letters that represent those numbers on a phone dial

    HOW-EASY

One car club used this method to choose a phone number that translated
into OUR-CARS. (Note that the translation of numbers into letters is not
uniquely encodable. For example the number 2 can be represented by A,
B, or C. However, the reverse process—letters to numbers—is uniquely
decodable. One might not remember the digits, but one could reconstruct
them. Take a look at a phone dial and see.)


## Regenerative Memory

One means of reducing the load on storage is to store only enough data
and rules for manipulating that data so that we can regenerate the details,
a sort of "regenerative memory." The essence of the regenerative memory
is that we do not store the details of everything; rather, we store a rule
for generating the details.

TABLE 7.11

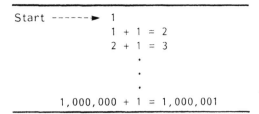

Start ------➤ 1
1 + 1 = 2
2 + 1 = 3
.
.
.
1,000,000 + 1 = 1,000,001

An example would be storing a rule for generating all the positive integers. Actually, the rule would be twofold

1. Store the starting symbol 1.
2. To get next symbol, add 1 to the current symbol.

Thus, we count as shown in Table 7.11.

Our example is somewhat simplified, since we must also store a list of the 10 decimal symbols, and a set of the rules for addition. However, the concept is the same.

That regenerative memory of some sort must take place is evident from the following argument:

1. There are an infinite number of positive integers.
2. The brain probably has a finite size.
3. Therefore, we cannot store the infinite set of positive integers in the finite brain.
4. But, we are capable, given enough time and energy, of generating as many integers as we wish.
5. Therefore, we need not store the details, the integers themselves; we store the rules for obtaining them when we need them.

Of course, we have actually stored two types of information—the list of decimal numerals and the name of the starting numeral (1)—which are "details," and the rules for handling these details (next = current + 1 and the rules for addition). We can refer to these two types of items as "instructions" (what to do) and "data" (with what), Figure 7.13. This representation is analogous to one of the models commonly used in explaining the computer and has led to the description of human processing in terms of computer processing. Whether the model actually represents the workings of our brain, or is just a convenient explanation, is not a settled issue.

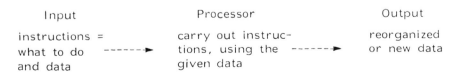

| Input | Processor | Output |
|---|---|---|
| instructions = what to do and data | carry out instructions, using the given data | reorganized or new data |

FIGURE 7.13

TABLE 7.12a

---

yellow on, red and green off

red on, green and yellow off

red and green on, yellow off

all lights on

green on, yellow and red off

all off

yellow on, red and green off

red on, green and yellow off

.
.
.

---

## An Aid to Understanding: Getting the Concise Picture

Even more significant than the contribution of proper coding to the memory process is its contribution to our ability to understand the encoded data. A good example is provided in Weinberg (1975). Suppose that we are studying the behavior of a machine. The machine indicates its internal status by turning three lights on and off. The three lights are colored red, green, and yellow. We do not understand how the machine works, but we are observing its activity in the hope of finding out some "law" of its behavior.

We take a comfortable chair, a notebook, and a pencil, settle down in front of the machine, and begin to jot down the state of each light—which one is on, which off—whenever its state changes. Our notebook might look like Table 7.12a. Is the pattern self-evident? Not exactly.

TABLE 7.12b

| R | G | Y |
|---|---|---|
| 0 | 0 | 1 |
| 1 | 0 | 0 |
| 1 | 1 | 0 |
| 1 | 1 | 1 |
| 0 | 1 | 0 |
| 0 | 0 | 0 |
| 0 | 0 | 1 |
| 1 | 0 | 0 |

TABLE 7.12c

| R | G | Y | Name |
|---|---|---|------|
| 1 | 1 | 1 | 7 |
| 1 | 1 | 0 | 6 |
| 1 | 0 | 1 | 5 |
| 1 | 0 | 0 | 4 |
| 0 | 1 | 1 | 3 |
| 0 | 1 | 0 | 2 |
| 0 | 0 | 1 | 1 |
| 0 | 0 | 0 | 0 |

Suppose we now arrange our method of taking notes. We set up three columns

R   G   Y

and place 1s in the columns of the lights that are on, 0s in the columns of the lights that are off. Our data now translates into Table 7.12b. Still not self-evident?

Suppose that we now redesign our system of taking notes. We list every possible state that the three lights can be in (8 in all), and give each state a numeric name. The numeric name is the decimal representation of the bits that are "on" in binary, the code being 4-2-1 (Table

1
4
6
7
2
0
1
4
.
.
.

(a)

(b)

FIGURE 7.14

7.12c). Our notes now look like Figure 7.14a. Furthermore, if we now graph the sequence of states, we get

$$1 \rightarrow 4 \rightarrow 6 \rightarrow 7 \rightarrow 2 \rightarrow 0 \rightarrow 1 \rightarrow 4$$

and, noting that the sequence seems to start over, we rearrange our graph into Figure 7.14b, and we see our machine is one with six distinct states that repeat themselves in cyclic fashion! A picture is indeed worth a notebook of words, at least in some cases.

## The Laws of Science

The process we have just gone through is essentially what a scientist does when he or she transforms such data as

An apple fell.
The bowling ball is harder to throw than the Ping-Pong ball.
Bumping into a person running hurts more than bumping into the
same person walking.

into a "law," such as

$$f = ma$$

or

Force = mass times acceleration

We have enclosed the word "law" in quotes to call attention to the fact that the law does not "dictate" reality; it describes reality. The law is an encapsulation, a supercode, for an entire set of events.

## Intelligence: Finding Order

If we watched two separate people performing the above experiment, both striving to ascertain the nature of this mysterious machine, we could compare the times at which each arrived at the solution. And, if one person took 2 hr to solve the problem, while the other took 2 weeks, we might conclude that the first person was more intelligent than the second.

Of course, many factors other than intelligence can enter into the race to solve a problem; for example, the resources, such as laboratory, time, and money of each person, as well as previous training. However, the point we wish to make is that intelligence can be viewed as the rate at which we are able to condense meaningless, disorganized data into meaningful, organized data; the speed with which we can compact the data into a concise code, a rule, a law. Of course, speed is a secondary factor, accuracy being the primary quality of interest with respect to our models.

## Summary

We close the chapter with a summary of the main points.

1.  Encoding is the process of putting a set of signals into another
    set of signals according to some transformation rules. Decoding

is simply the reverse process: taking the encoded message and recreating the original signals.

2. A good code is both unambiguous and reversible, which can be accomplished by creating a code that has a 1–1 correspondence.

3. Natural languages contain ambiguities; one of the goals of artificial languages is to avoid those ambiguities.

4. An ambiguous sentence in natural language can be recognized by the fact that two deep structures generate the same surface structure; the nonuniqueness of natural language encoding is demonstrated by two surface structures for one deep structure.

5. Both numbers and alphabetic characters can be represented in the code called "binary coded decimal" or BCD; the student is expected to know these.

6. Some properties of codes are representation, data compaction, error detection, error correction, aid to human memory, and aid to understanding.

7. Certain codes seem more suited to certain media than others.

8. The human memory seems to be able to store two types of data:
   a. Individual items and lists of items.
   b. Rules for regenerating data. This capability has led to the description of human information processing in terms of the computer's data processing.

9. The ability to digest unorganized data into a compact code is one way of defining intelligence.

10. The laws of science are concise codes for representing a mass of data that describes the workings of nature.

## Related Readings

Burch, John G., Strater, Felix R., and Grudnitski, Gary, *Information Systems: Theory and Practice*, 3rd ed. New York: John Wiley & Sons, 1983.

Cherry, Colin, *On Human Communication: A Review, A Survey, and A Criticism*, 2nd ed. Cambridge, MA: M.I.T. Press, 1975 (C1966).

Hamming, Richard W., *Coding and Information Theory*, Englewood Cliffs, NJ: Prentice-Hall, 1980.

Kent, Allen, *Information Analysis and Retrieval*, 1st ed. New York: John Wiley & Sons, 1971.

Miller, George A., "The Magical Number Seven, Plus or Minus Two: Some Limits on our Capacity for Processing Information," in *Psychological Review*, Vol. 63, no. 2, 1956, pp. 81–96.

Pierce, John R., *An Introduction to Information Theory Symbols, Signals and Noise*, 2nd ed. New York: Dover Publications, 1980.

Shannon, Claude E. and Weaver, Warren, *The Mathematical Theory of Communication*, Urbana: University of Illinois Press, 1980 (C1949).

Weinberg, Gerald M., *An Introduction to General Systems Thinking*, New York: John Wiley & Sons, 1975.

Various introductory texts in data processing.

*8*

# Fields, Records, and Files

## Objectives

Upon completion of this chapter, the reader should be able to

1. Distinguish among and define the concepts of field, record, file, and data base
2. State the trade-offs between fixed length and variable length fields
3. Distinguish between, and name the trade-offs involved, in using the prefix and suffix methods for storing variable length data
4. Explain the concepts of multiply occurring and optional fields
5. Describe a field, given the name, type of data, and length
6. Describe a record, given the number and types of data fields included in the record
7. Explain the trade-offs between coded and uncoded data
8. Explain the trade-offs between alphabetic and numeric codes
9. Define the concept of data access point, using an example
10. Define the concept of key field in a record, giving an example
11. Describe the role of human factors in designing a system

Once we have collected our data, we usually want to store it. This involves coding the data, formatting the data fields and records, selecting the file structures, and chosing the storage medium. We will consider each of these items, although not in that precise order. In this chapter we look at formatting fields and records, and choosing codes.

## Content of the Data Base

In order to concretize our treatment of the data base, we shall describe a specific example, a "wine data base," which will contain information on the generic type of wine: red or white; on the particular type of wine within these generic categories: Burgundy, Beaujolais, and Chianti for the red; Rhine, Moselle, Sauterne, and Chablis for the white; the brand name for each particular wine (only fictitious names will be used); and the price of the wine expressed in general terms: expensive, medium, or cheap.

| Wine-type (general) | Particular type | Brand name | Price |
|---|---|---|---|

FIGURE 8.1


## Fields and Records, Files and Data Bases

These four items—generic type of wine, particular type of wine, brand name, and price—are the four "fields" of our data. We can think of a field as the smallest "interpretable" unit of data. For example, a payroll data record might include the following fields:

> Social security number
> Employee number
> Rate of pay
> Pay to date
> Deductions
> Etc.

Some fields may be broken into subfields, e.g., the date field:

> Date
>   Month
>   Day
>   Year

However, we consider the entire date to be the field, since the day's date does not do us much good if we don't know the month in which it occurred. The entire date is interpretable, but the individual parts of the date—month, day, year—are usually not interpretable by themselves, and are considered subfields. All the fields pertaining to one person (as in an employee record), one item (as in a wine record), or one transaction (as in a checking account transaction) are called "records."

Our wine record consists of the four fields shown in Figure 8.1. Note the difference between the field name and the contents of the field: the name of the first field is "wine type (general)," while its contents will be the words *red* or *white*. The names of the fields, as shown in our record description, are the "blueprints" for the record. They show what data goes where. The actual values that go into the data field are the contents of that field. Thus, while the blueprint for our data records looks like Figure 8.2a, a particular record would look like Figure 8.2b or Figure 8.2c.

The distinction is most easily seen if we look at the record description as a title or "heading" to a report, which describes the meaning of the data; and the actual records as the data items:

| General Type | Particular Type | Brand Name | Price |
|---|---|---|---|
| Red | Burgundy | ABC Distilleries | Expensive |
| White | Rhine | U-Drink Inc. | Cheap |
| White | Moselle | ABC Distilleries | Medium |
| Red | Burgundy | U-Drink Inc. | Cheap |

| General type | Particular type | Brand name | Price |
|---|---|---|---|

(a)

| Red | Burgundy | ABC Distilleries | Expensive |
|---|---|---|---|

(b)

| White | Rhine | U-Drink Inc. | Cheap |
|---|---|---|---|

(c)

FIGURE 8.2

The entire set of records pertaining to one person (as in an employee file), one item (as in a wine file), or one type of transaction (as in a checking account file) is called a "file." Our file thus consists of a number of records as listed below. In fact, we could change the heading from "wine report" to "wine file," in order to show the file structure.

Wine File

| General Type | Particular Type | Brand Name | Price |
|---|---|---|---|
| Red | Burgundy | ABC Distilleries | Expensive |
| White | Rhine | U-Drink Inc. | Cheap |
| White | Moselle | ABC Distilleries | Medium |
| Red | Burgundy | U-Drink Inc. | Cheap |
| . | . | . | . |
| . | . | . | . |
| . | . | . | . |

A file may contain a few records, such as a file consisting of the presidents of the United States, or many records, such as the file of customers of a large department store chain. Some files are accessed very often, as the information file used by the phone company, others are accessed relatively infrequently, as the file of birth certificates kept by a city. We will speak more about these and other characteristics of files later.

One file (or more) pertaining to a single application is called a data base. An example might be a firm's data base, consisting of files of sales records, production records, accounting records, etc. In our simple application, the data base will consist of the single "wine file"; however, this is not the general case. In summary, the smallest item of the data base is the "data item" or "field"; groups of fields are called "records"; groups of records are called "files"; and groups of files are called a "data base." The progression is as shown in Figure 8.3. There are other more specific usages of the term data base, but we will consider them later.

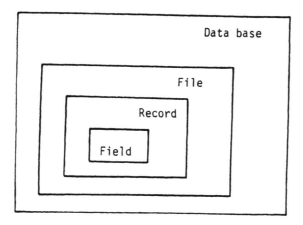

FIGURE 8.3

## Fixed Length Versus Variable Length Fields

One issue that must be faced when designing the data fields for any file or data base is the issue of fixed length versus variable length fields. The difference is easily illustrated by considering the problem of setting aside storage space for a person's surname. Let us take the two names Benson and Antonelli. As is obvious, the name Benson is considerably shorter than the name Antonelli, Benson having six characters, Antonelli having nine. And, of course, an even greater range could be found by searching through the phone book for both shorter and longer surnames.

Fixed length fields set aside a specified number of spaces for a data field, regardless of the length of the individual data values. Thus, if we employ a fixed length field to contain a person's last name, we would first decide on how many spaces would be necessary to contain the "longest"

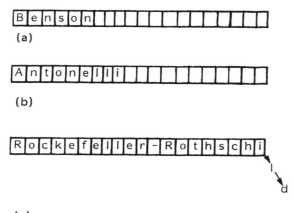

FIGURE 8.4

last name, and set aside that many spaces. For example, we might choose to set aside 20 spaces for the last name. In that case, Benson would be stored as shown in Figure 8.4a, in which only 6 of the 20 spaces are used, with the other 14 wasted. Antonelli would be stored as shown in Figure 8.4b, with 9 spaces used, and 11 wasted. A particularly long last name (e.g., a hyphenated surname resulting from the marriage of two prominent families, such as Rockefeller-Rothschild) would contain too many characters (22, including the hyphen), and would not fit in the space allotted (Figure 8.4c). The last two letters, the *l* and the *d*, would simply be "lost" or "truncated." A letter printed through automated means with this storage scheme would be addressed to: Mr(s). Rockefeller-Rothschi— not quite the personal touch necessary to induce a friendly attitude in the recipient.

The above two examples illustrate the major disadvantages of fixed length fields

1. If the data value is smaller than the space allotted, some space is wasted (Figure 8.4a).
2. If the data value is larger than the space allotted, some data is lost (Figure 8.4c).

To overcome the problems of wasted space (the more common) and insufficient space, we can design variable length fields.

### Variable Length Fields

In a variable length field, the size of the field is made to match the size of the data value. Thus, Benson, with 6 characters, would be allotted only 6 units of storage space (Figure 8.5a), while Antonelli would be allotted exactly 9 spaces (Figure 8.5b), and Rockefeller-Rothschild would be allotted 22 spaces (Figure 8.5c). There would be no wasted space and no overflow. Neat!

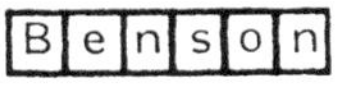

(a)

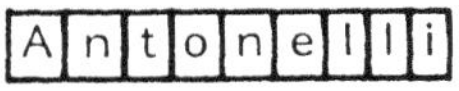

(b)

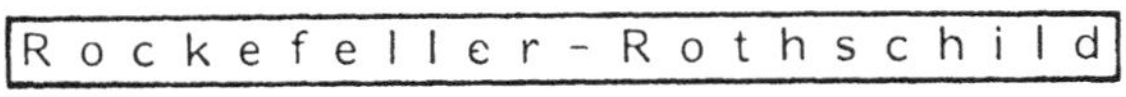

(c)

FIGURE 8.5

Columns numbered 1 through 80

FIGURE 8.6

## A Problem

As you might have guessed, designing and processing variable length fields is not quite as simple as we have described; otherwise, there would be no other kind of field. The very existence of fixed length fields should tip us off that there must be some drawback to using variable length fields, and there is. In order to understand the drawback, let us consider a particular type of storage medium: the Hollerith card, named after Herman Hollerith, the inventor of punched card machines, and founder of the company that grew to be IBM. While the punched card has given way to the technology of the CRT, it is a perfect example of a medium suited to fixed length

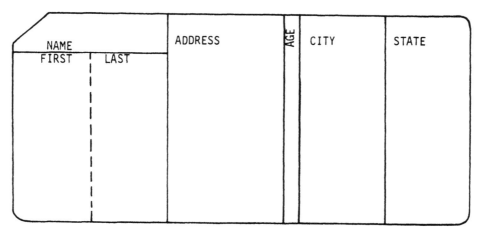

FIGURE 8.7

Surname-field - columns 1 through 20

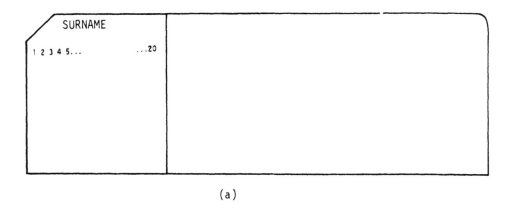

(a)

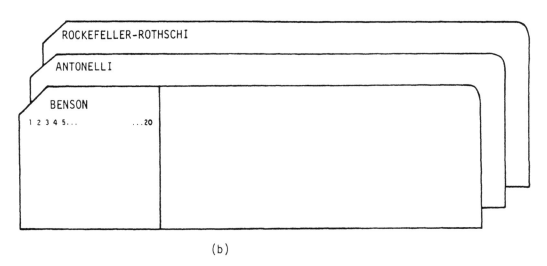

(b)

FIGURE 8.8

fields, and gives a visual example of what occurs when fixed length fields
are used on a disk or other storage medium. In fact, the trade-offs between fixed length fields and variable length fields generalize to situations
as disparate as the representation of character strings in memory, the
construction of queues to hold jobs waiting for a line printer, and the estimation of the number of seats to install in a theater or baseball stadium.
With minor flexibilities the latter are almost always "fixed length" applications.

The Hollerith card contained 80 columns in which information could be
recorded (Figure 8.6). Because the Hollerith card always had exactly 80
columns, it was a "fixed length" storage medium. These columns could be
subdivided into fields (Figure 8.7). To simplify the discussion we will begin to speak in the present, as if the Hollerith card still retained its pre-
eminent place in data processing.

Suppose that we are storing the surname in the first few columns of the Hollerith card. Using the fixed field format, we would simply set aside the first 20 columns as the "surname field" (Figure 8.8a). Then in punching in the names, we would have the data shown in Figure 8.8b. As we can see, the space set aside for "surname" is largely wasted. However, there is one distinct advantage: the surname *always* appears in the first 20 columns of the card; no more, no less, no maybes. This is exactly the situation that can be handled by a machine. We can either wire a machine to "read" these columns, or write a computer program to read them. In either case, the machines will have no problems, since the definition of the field is clear.

However, in a variable length field, the situation is not so definite. In fact, it is never definite, which is just what the word *variable* means. On one card, the machine is to read 6 columns, on another 9 columns, and on another 22. This is not a situation that is easily handled by a machine. Machines work best with standardized fields that are cut and dry in length; this is the fixed field. In order to handle variable length fields, we have to write a computer program to process the surname field. The program's sole job is to "look for the end of the field."

### Two Methods

There are two methods of "looking for the end of the field" when dealing with variable length fields. The first is called the "prefix" method; the second, the "suffix" method. The prefix method really does not "look for the end of the field"; it tells the machine exactly how long the field is. When the data item is stored, the number of characters are counted, and this number is stored as a "prefix" to the field. Thus, Benson, which contains 6 characters, would be stored as shown in Figure 8.9a, Antonelli as

| 0 | 6 | B | e | n | s | o | n |

(a)

| 0 | 9 | A | n | t | o | n | e | l | l | i |

(b)

| 2 | 2 | R | o | c | k | e | f | e | l | l | e | r | - | R | o | t | h | s | c | h | i | l | d |

(c)

Count field

Surname field

| 0 | 6 | B | e | n | s | o | n |

(d)

FIGURE 8.9

shown in Figure 8.9b, and Rockefeller-Rothschild as shown in Figure 8.9c. The computer (or other machine) would then be directed to read the "length field" or "count," and proceed to read exactly that many characters as the data value. Of course, this takes extra processing time, since it must now read two fields: the length or count field, and the surname field. In addition, at the time the data is originally stored, the characters must be counted in order to create the count field.

Thus, in the prefix method, we handle the problem of variable length fields by actually employing two fields, the count field and the actual data field (in this case, surname; Figure 8.9d). This involves counting the number of characters in the surname when we input the data, then storing this count along with the actual data. At output time, i.e., when we are retrieving the data, we must first read this count, then read exactly that many characters of data. (Note that if the count is wrong, for whatever reason, we will read either too much or too little data. Note also that the count field is itself "fixed length." This is necessary, since we must always ultimately revert to some standard size field that can be read "automatically." However, the count field is much smaller than the surname field, and thus will waste less space.)

Finally, note that even in variable length fields, we must use some "extra storage" in order to store the count field. Thus, it is never quite true that the name Benson would be stored in exactly six characters, Antonelli in nine, etc.

## The Suffix Method

In the suffix method of handling variable length fields, we use only one field (the surname), but signal the end of that field by some "special" character. For example, we might store Benson as shown in Figure 8.10a, Antonelli and Rockefeller-Rothschild as shown in Figures 8.10b and 8.10c. The crosshatch (#) is the special character signifying the end of the field. In choosing this character, we must be sure to choose a character that is not likely to occur in the middle of the surname. For example, if we had used the hyphen as our special character, the names would be stored as

    Benson-
    Antonelli-
    Rockefeller-Rothschild-

but in reading the names back, the machine would correctly read both Benson and Antonelli, but would misread Rockefeller-Rothschild as Rockefeller, since it would take the first occurrence of the hyphen as the end of the field.

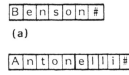

(a)

(b)

FIGURE 8.10

| R | o | c | k | e | f | e | l | l | e | r | - | R | o | t | h | s | c | h | i | l | d | # |
|---|---|---|---|---|---|---|---|---|---|---|---|---|---|---|---|---|---|---|---|---|---|---|

(c)

FIGURE 8.10 (continued)

## Extra Processing

The process of reading a name stored in this fashion is somewhat tedious. In effect, what the program must direct the machine to do is to read *every character* and "look for" the special character. When it finds the special character, it knows it has reached the end of the name. Thus, for the data shown in Figure 8.11a, the computer or other machine, would read the *B*, ask whether or not it was the special character "*," receive the answer "no," store the *B* as "part of the last name" (Figure 8.11b), then read the *e*, ask if this was the "*," get the "no" answer, store the *e*, (Figure 8.11c); and proceed in this fashion until it finally reads the "*," at which point it would get a "yes" answer in asking if this was the special character, and would stop processing, having already stored the name as shown in Figure 8.11d. As can be seen, this process involves a lot of extra "work" or processing time in reading the data.

## The Trade-Offs

In designing any system (and a data base is a system, or part of one), we are constantly faced with decisions between alternative methods of per-

| B | e | n | s | o | n | * |
|---|---|---|---|---|---|---|

(a)

Surname

| B |
|---|

(b)

Surname

| B | e |
|---|---|

(c)

| B | e | n | s | o | n |
|---|---|---|---|---|---|

(d)

FIGURE 8.11

forming some function. Each choice we make involves a trade-off: certain advantages gained at the cost of certain disadvantages. The contrast between fixed length and variable length fields is a classic example of these trade-off situations.

Contrasting the two methods, we have the following table, where a "+" indicates that the method excels in that particular point, and a "−" indicates that the method is deficient in that point

Storage Organization

| Feature | Fixed Length | Variable Length |
|---|---|---|
| Conserves storage | − | + |
| Less processing | + | − |

This table illustrates the point that fixed length fields waste storage, but save on processing time, while variable length fields excel in conserving storage, but involve more work (processing).

No general rule can be presented for making one choice over another. In any particular situation, our choice would be governed by such considerations as "Which is more convenient and/or less costly for us: space or processing?" Thus, a company with a lot of storage space, but little machinery for processing, might choose to stick with the fixed length field, while a company with a lot of processing power, but little space, might choose the variable length field.

If we choose to go with the variable length fields (sacrificing processing time in order to conserve storage), we have a further trade-off between the prefix and suffix methods of storage. In the prefix method, the extra processing time occurs at "input," i.e., when we are storing the data. It is at this input time that we must count the number of characters, which requires reading each character individually. In the suffix method, the extra processing occurs at "output," when we are reading back previously stored material. Thus, we have

Variable Length Implementation

| Feature | Prefix Method | Suffix Method |
|---|---|---|
| Input fast? | − | + |
| Output fast? | + | − |

Even within the fixed field, we have a trade-off, which revolves around the length of the fixed field. If we choose a long length, most names will fit (no truncation), but more space will be wasted when storing shorter names (Figure 8.12a). With a shorter length, we waste less storage, but

```
┌─┬─┬─┬─┬─┬─┬─┬─┬─┬─┬─┬─┬─┬─┬─┬─┬─┬─┬─┬─┬─┬─┬─┐
│B│e│n│s│o│n│ │ │ │ │ │ │ │ │ │ │ │ │ │ │ │ │ │
└─┴─┴─┴─┴─┴─┴─┴─┴─┴─┴─┴─┴─┴─┴─┴─┴─┴─┴─┴─┴─┴─┴─┘
```

FIGURE 8.12a

we truncate more names (Figure 8.12b). For example, choosing a surname field 10 spaces long, we would have to truncate as follows:

```
┌─┬─┬─┬─┬─┬─┬─┬─┬─┬─┐
│R│o│c│k│e│f│e│l│l│e│ ➤ r
└─┴─┴─┴─┴─┴─┴─┴─┴─┴─┘

┌─┬─┬─┬─┬─┬─┬─┬─┬─┬─┐
│S│m│i│t│h│s│o│n│i│a│ ➤ n
└─┴─┴─┴─┴─┴─┴─┴─┴─┴─┘

┌─┬─┬─┬─┬─┬─┬─┬─┬─┬─┐
│K│o│w│a│l│k│o│w│s│k│ ➤ i
└─┴─┴─┴─┴─┴─┴─┴─┴─┴─┘

┌─┬─┬─┬─┬─┬─┬─┬─┬─┬─┐
│B│i│e│n│v│e│n│u│t│o│ ➤ ni
└─┴─┴─┴─┴─┴─┴─┴─┴─┴─┘
```
   etc.

FIGURE 8.12b

The trade-off is

| Long Field | Short Field |
| --- | --- |
| Waste storage | Conserve storage |
| Less truncation | More truncation |

No decision is cut-and-dried in designing a data base, or any system for that matter, we are always balancing one alternative against another.

### Multiply Occurring Fields

In the above discussion, we have assumed that there is only *one* data value for each field. Thus, a wine is either red or white, but not both; Burgundy or Chablis, but not both; and a person has only one surname, not two or more (note that this does not take account of aliases). However, there are many occasions in which a particular data field may have more than one data value. A common example is the author field in a bibliographic data base. There are some books with a single author, e.g., *The Sound and the Fury* by William Faulkner, while other books have multiple authors, e.g., *The Final Days* by Woodward and Bernstein.

A field that may take on more than one data value, such as the author field, is called a multiply occurring field. We may have both singly occurring and multiply occurring fields in the same record. For example, in our bibliographic file, each book has only one title. Thus, the title is a singly occurring field. But there may be more than one author. Thus, the author is a multiply occurring field.

An example related to business would be an employee's work history file. The employee's name is a single occurring field, since we assume one name per employee. But the field set aside for "work history" is multiply occurring, since it may have several entries for some employees.

Multiply occurring fields are handled like variable length fields.

- Have a count field indicating the number of occurrences

  or
- Have a special symbol at the end of the set of fields

In fact, multiply occurring fields are a particular type of variable length field.

In handling multiple values in a data field, the methods may be mixed, as in the following:

Number of authors
03      Smith, Jones, Williams

where the number of authors is indicated in a prefix, the 03, but each author's surname is followed by a comma, or "delimeter" indicating one end of the field.

## Required Versus Optional Fields

One other distinction made in regard to data fields is the distinction of whether or not the field must appear in the record. For example, in a file on celebrities, we might have an optional field called "nickname." This field would not be necessary, since some celebrities do not have a nickname. Yet, some celebrities do (John "Duke" Wayne), and would have this field filled in. An optional field can be made a required one by stipulating that the word *none,* or some equivalent symbol (a zero, for example), be filled in if the field is not applicable. However, some applications allow the field to be omitted when not applicable. Another example of an optional field might be "business phone." While most people have a home phone, many do not have a business phone. Hence, we might treat the business phone as an optional field in storing such personal data as address, phone, and age. Both multiply occurring and optional data fields present problems not encountered when dealing with singly occurring, required fields. If a null value (i.e., zero or "none") is not used, each field may be tagged

AU: Smith, Jones, Williams
TI:  The Book to End All Books

so that we have some means of identifying which fields are indeed present (e.g., AU = author, TI = title).

## Variable Length Records

Just as there can be variable length fields, we have the possibility of keeping variable length records. Files with either multiple occurring or optional fields will contain variable length records. Records with variable length fields will also be variable in length.

The example of a "wine record" developed in this chapter will be fixed length. However, in the data on bibliographic records (Figure 8.14), the records are variable length. Variable length records may be handled in a fashion similar to variable length fields: by using either the prefix method, which "forecasts" the length of the record, or the suffix method, which gives a special signal at the end of the record.

## Multiply Occurring and Optional Records

We also have occasions in which there are multiply occurring records. An example of a singly occurring record might be the "master" record in the customer file of a department store. Presumably, each customer is listed only once, with his or her address, phone, credit card number, etc. However, in the transaction file, a particular customer may have several records, representing several different purchases on any given day or month. In fact, this transaction file is also an example of an optional record, since on a particular day a customer may have no transactions, having failed to shop on that day.

## Variable Length Fields

The concept of fixed length as opposed to variable length may also be extended to files. An example of a fixed length file is the list of the "top 40 hits" so popular with radio stations. There are 40 items listed; no more, no less. Other examples might be the top 10 best-selling books, or the top 20 football teams.

Much more common than fixed length files are variable length files. For example, the number of employees in a personnel file varies, decreasing with retirings and firings, increasing with hirings.

Again, we may use either the prefix or the suffix method to indicate the length of the file. If the prefix method is used, we normally give the number of records in the file. For example, in a file of employee records, we might list the number of employees as the first line in the file, fol-

```
05  ◄───────────────── Number of employees (prefix)
Flynn, 320-34-6003. . . ⎫
Anthony, 423-00-4239. . . ⎪
Moretti, 123-45-6789. . . ⎬ The employees
Williams, 232-44-5565. . . ⎪
Smith, 465-78-9012. . . ⎭

(a)

Flynn, 320-34-6003. . . ⎫
Anthony, 423-00-4239. . . ⎪
Moretti, 123-45-6789. . . ⎬ The employee file
Williams, 232-44-5565. . . ⎪
Smith, 465-78-9012. . . ⎭
##  ◄───────────────── End of the employee file

(b)
```

FIGURE 8.13

[#026
[A STRACHEY, CHRISTOPHER
[T SYSTEMS ANALYSIS AND PROGRAMMING
[C INFORMATION, SCIENTIFIC AMERICAN, FREEMAN & CO., 1966,   PP56-75
[D HOW TO PROGRAM A CHECKER GAME; SYSTEMS ANALYSIS & PROGRAMMING OF
A PROBLEM; IMPORTANCE OF DATA STRUCTURES; HUMAN ERROR AND DEBUGGING;
RECURSION; DEVELOPING A MATHEMATICS FOR COMPUTERS.
[I ANALYSIS, CHECKERS, COMPUTER PROGRAMMING, DEBUGGING, PLANNING,
PROGRAMMING, RECURSION, SYSTEMS ANALYSIS
#
[#027
[A WILKES,M.V.
[T TIME-SHARING COMPUTER SYSTEMS
[C TIME-SHARING COMPUTER SYSTEMS, AMERICAN ELSEVIER INC., 149PP.
[D COMPLETE EXPLANATION OF TIME-SHARING; EARLY SYSTEMS, GENERAL
PRINCIPLES, PROCESS MANAGEMENT, CORE MANAGEMENT, SCHEDULING,
SATELLITE COMPUTERS, GRAPHICAL DISPLAYS, FILING SYSTEMS, OPERATIONS
MANAGEMENT.
[I COMPUTER SYSTEMS, CONVERSATIONAL MODE, FILING SYSTEMS, ON-LINE SYSTEMS,
OPERATING SYSTEMS, SCHEDULING, TIME-SHARING
#
[#028
[A DESMONDE, WILLIAM H.
[T REAL-TIME DATA PROCESSING
[C COMPUTERS AND THEIR USES, PRENTICE-HALL, 1971, CH. 12.
[D EXAMPLES AND USES OF REAL-TIME DATA PROCESSING, INCLUDES SAGE,
BMEWS, SABRE, APPLICATIONS TO BANKING, INVENTORY, AND OTHERS, CONSIDERS
BACK-UP, QUEUING, RESPONSE TIME, SIMULATION.
[I BACK-UP SYSTEMS, BMEWS, DATA PROCESSING, EDP, ON-LINE SYSTEMS,
REAL-TIME, SABRE, SAGE
#
[#029
[A DESMONDE, WILLIAM H.
[T TIME-SHARING SYSTEMS
[C COMPUTERS AND THEIR USES, PRENTICE-HALL, 1971, CH. 14.
[D OVERVIEW OF OPERATING SYSTEMS FOR A TIME-SHARING SYSTEM, TREATS
TURNAROUND, DEBUGGING, CONVERSATIONAL USE, STORAGE ALLOCATION, MULTIPROGRAM
MEMORY ALLOCATION, SYSTEM CONFIGURATION, CONTROL, SCHEDULING,
OVERHEAD, PAGING, VIRTUAL MEMORY, OPERATING SYSTEMS, AND THE
TIME-SHARING INDUSTRY.
[I COMPUTER SYSTEMS, MEMORY ALLOCATION, MULTIPROGRAMMING,
OPERATING SYSTEMS, PAGING, SCHEDULING, TIME-SHARING, VIRTUAL MEMORY
#
[#030
[A GRUENBERGER, FRED (EIDTOR)
[T THE TRANSITION TO ON-LINE COMPUTING
[C THE TRANSITION TO ON-LINE COMPUTING, INFORMATICS, 1967.
[D VARIOUS ASPECTS OF TIME-SHARING: ON-LINE, TIME-SHARING, AND
MULTIPROCESSING; SOFTWARE AND HARDWARE; DISPLAYS; COST/EFFECTIVENESS;
CONVERSATIONAL COMPUTING; TERMINALS; HISTORY.
[I COMPUTER SYSTEMS, CONVERSATIONAL MODE, CRT, MULTIPROCESSING,
ON-LINE, REAL-TIME, TERMINALS, TIME-SHARING
#
##
FIGURE 8.14

lowed by the actual employee records (Figure 8.13a). Alternatively, we can use a special symbol to indicate the end of the file, e.g., a double cross-hatch (Figure 8.13b).

## An Example

An example involving all three—variable length fields, records, and files—is the excerpt from a bibliographic data base shown in Figure 8.14.

The fields are delineated by brackets ("["). These are called "delimeters," since they define the limits or "delimit" the boundaries of the field. The next letter to the brackets indicates the nature of each field, i.e., what it contains; it is a tag. For example, the first field is the numbered field, denoted by "[#"; the second field is the author field, denoted by "[A"; and the third field is the title field, denoted by "[T." The remaining fields are

[C : Citation, giving the name of the journal the article appeared in, year published, volume number, etc.

[D : Abstract of the contents of the journal article

[I : Index terms used to describe the subject content of the article

The entire set of six fields constitutes one record. The end of the record is signaled by the presence of the single crosshatch ("#"). The end of the file is signaled by the double crosshatch ("##"). This file thus consists of five records, each of which has six fields. Of course, a real file would contain many more records, but the principle would be the same. The fact that *the fields* are variable in length can be seen by noting that the abstract field ("[D") encompasses three lines in the first record, but only four lines in the second record, and five lines in the fourth record. The fact that *the records* are variable in length is indicated by the fact that the first record encompasses 9 lines in toto, while the second encompasses 10 lines, and the fourth encompasses 11 lines. The fact that the file is variable in length is not self-evident from the example, but can be surmised from the fact that the arrival of new books or journals shall assuredly add items to the file. Note that the accession number (which uniquely identifies each record) is the only fixed field in the record. Since it is only three spaces long (026, 027, 028 ...), the builders of the data base must believe they will never have more than 999 (or 1000 if we include ID 000) documents in the file.

## Left and Right Justification

When dealing with fixed length fields, a special problem arises whenever the data value does not fit the storage area exactly. Whenever the data value is smaller than the space allotted, we face the problem of "justification," which simply asks whether the data item should be aligned at the left or right of the storage area. When the data value is too large for the storage allotted, we face the problem of truncation, which simply asks "At which end are the characters lost?" The two problems are related in that items that are left-justified are truncated at the right, while items that are right-justified are truncated at the left; i.e., truncation always occurs at the end opposite justification. A couple of examples should make this clear.

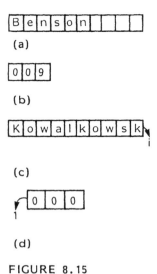

(a)

(b)

(c)

(d)

FIGURE 8.15

In fields that contain alphabetic items, data values smaller than the field are "left-justified," and blanks (empty spaces) fill in the remaining places (called "blank-fill"). Thus, in a 10-character field, the name *Benson* is stored as shown in Figure 8.15a. In fields that are numeric, the data values are "right-justified" and "zero-filled," i.e., leading zeroes fill up any unused spaces. Thus, in a three-digit numeric field, the number 9 is stored as shown in Figure 8.15b. If the data values are larger than the space allotted, we encounter the phenomenon of "truncation." As mentioned earlier in this chapter, alphabetic characters are truncated on the right. Thus, in a 10-space field, the name "Kowalkowski" is left-justified, and the characters that do not fit "fall out" of the right end of the storage space (Figure 8.15c).

With numeric values that are too large for the storage area, truncation occurs on the left. This is because the numbers are right-justified, so that the "overflow" digits are not "discovered" until we get to the left-hand side of the storage area. Thus, in a 3-digit storage area, the number 1,000 would be stored as shown in Figure 8.15d, and 1,000 becomes zero.

## Describing the Data

While several schemes are employed for describing data items, probably the simplest method is that employed in the COBOL programming language (COBOL is a business-oriented language that looks very much like English). COBOL recognizes three basic groups of characters:

Alphabetic: the letters *A* through *Z*
Numeric: the digits *0* through *9*
Alphanumeric: any alphabetic, numeric, or special characters, such as
. , $ * -

To describe a data field containing alphabetic information, the letter *A* is used; to describe a field containing numeric information, a 9 is used; and to describe a field containing alphanumeric information, an *X* is used.

The length of the data field is indicated by repeating the symbolic character as many times as is necessary. Thus, an alphabetic field that allows for three characters would be described as AAA. A numeric field that allows for five digits would be described as 99999, and an alphanumeric field that allows for four characters would be described as XXXX.

This method of description can get tedious for large fields. For example, an alphabetic field of 20 spaces would be: AAAAAAAAAAAAAAAAAAAA Furthermore, after a few characters, the exact number of spaces in the larger fields is not evident. Thus, we use a shorthand to handle such situations. We simply write the symbolic character followed by a set of parentheses that encloses the actual number of characters in the field. Thus, our 20-character alphabetic field would be described as A(20), a 7-digit numeric field would be described as 9(7), and a 13-character alphanumeric field would be X(13). There is no general rule as to when to use one method of description or another. However, they are entirely equivalent, so that XXXX and X(4) both describe the same type and size field. To fully describe a field, we must also include the name of that field. Thus, the full description of a data field includes

1. Name of the field
2. Data type (alphabetic, numeric, or alphanumeric)
3. Length (in number of characters or digits)

In COBOL, the "picture" of the field is also preceded by the word *Picture*: Picture 999. Thus, if we were describing a field containing a person's social security number, we might call the field "social-security," allow for only numeric values, and set aside nine spaces for the data item: Social-Security Picture 9(9). A typical data value for this field would be 234760981. If we wished to include hyphens between the three subfields of the number (234-76-0981), we would make the field alphanumeric (since the hyphen is a special character), and set aside 11 spaces for the data item: Social-Security Picture X(11). Note that with a data item of fixed size, such as the social security number, a fixed length field wastes absolutely no storage space, and is to be preferred over a variable length field. Variable length fields are desirable only for data values that vary in length, such as the surname.

## Designing the Data Fields

Having discussed certain general properties of fields and records, it is now time to turn to the design of our specific data, the "wine data." As we have mentioned before, this involves formatting fields, records, and files; choosing a storage medium; and coding data. It is this last item, coding data, to which we now turn.

## Coding the Data

We have already treated codes in an earlier chapter. However, the treatment in that chapter was more generic. Here we shall concentrate on more specific issues, e.g., should we use a code or not, and if we do, should it be numeric or alphabetic. Each choice provides certain advantages at the cost of certain disadvantages; i.e., there is always a trade-off.

Let us begin the discussion with the field "general type" of wine. We have only two values in this field, "red" and "white." However, a more complex application might yield several hundred possible values for a given field. For example, the field "employee number" might be represented by different values for each of several thousand employees in a major corporation. We would decline to use any code at all for this field. In this case, we would set aside enough space to fit the largest value, WHITE, which would require five spaces for the data item. The value "red" requires only three spaces, but we must set aside enough space to accommodate the largest possible value. If we choose to code the data field, we could choose a numeric code, e.g., RED = 1, WHITE = 2, in which case the data field would occupy only one space. Thus, our code would "compact" the data. Similarly, we could select an alphabetic code (RED = R; WHITE = W), which also takes up only one space, saving storage space and hence storage costs, and is also more mnemonic.

## The Trade-Off

We have said that each design decision involves a trade-off: an advantage gained, but only at the cost of also incurring a disadvantage. If we choose not to code the data, the disadvantage is extra storage space used. However, the advantage is that we do not have to "translate" the coded data in order to output it in a humanly readable form. If we choose to code the data, we must "translate" this code when outputting the data for human consumption. Thus, instead of printing a report such as

General Type
1
2
2
1

we would employ a "code-to-English" distionary (Figure 8.16) in order to "look up" the numeric values and substitute their English equivalents at output time.

Such "locking up" of values requires extra "processing" time during output, so that the trade-off we are incurring is storage space vs. processing time. In the noncoded representation, we use up more storage space, but our output operation is straightforward, with no "dictionary look-ups." The coded data conserves storage space, but causes the extra processing of the dictionary look-up before printing an output report. In large files, the dictionary look-up can be time consuming, increasing the time needed to respond to a request for data.

| Code Value | English Equivalent |
|---|---|
| 1 | Red |
| 2 | White |

FIGURE 8.16

## Alphabetic Versus Numeric Codes

We have also raised the question of whether we should choose an alphabetic code (RED = R; WHITE = W) or a numeric code (RED = 1; WHITE = 2) to represent our data. In this particular case, the choice is not crucial, since we have only two items to code. However, the example can illustrate the trade-off very neatly.

An alphabetic code is more easily translated by humans, e.g., it does not take a genius to translate "R" into "RED," and "W" into "WHITE." However, this "mnemonic" value of the code holds only as long as the code "fits" the actual data values, and it is easy to run into situations in which a simple alphabetic code does not fit. For example, suppose that we add *rosé* to our repertoire of wines. The code Red = R, White = W, Rosé = R will not work. It is ambiguous, since R can now stand for either "red" or "rosé." We could choose another letter to represent "rosé," e.g., S, but now we have lost the mnemonic value of the code, since it is not self-evident that S should stand for rosé.

An alphabetic code can thus serve as an aid to human memory, *if the data permit it*. But the range of data items that will permit such usage is not as great as the number of data items that do not lend themselves "easily" to a "simple" alphabetic code.

TABLE 8.1

| State name | Code | State name | Code |
|---|---|---|---|
| Alabama | AL | Montana | MT |
| Alaska | AK | Nebraska | NE |
| Arizona | AZ | Nevada | NV |
| Arkansas | AR | New Hampshire | NH |
| California | CA | New Jersey | NJ |
| Colorado | CO | New Mexico | NM |
| Connecticut | CT | New York | NY |
| Delaware | DE | North Carolina | NC |
| Florida | FL | North Dakota | ND |
| Georgia | GA | Ohio | OH |
| Hawaii | HI | Oklahoma | OK |
| Idaho | ID | Oregon | OR |
| Illinois | IL | Pennsylvania | PA |
| Indiana | IN | Rhode Island | RI |
| Iowa | IA | South Carolina | SC |
| Kansas | KS | South Dakota | SD |
| Kentucky | KY | Tennessee | TE |
| Louisiana | LA | Texas | TX |
| Maine | ME | Utah | UT |
| Maryland | MD | Vermont | VT |
| Massachusetts | MA | Virginia | VA |
| Michigan | MI | Washington | WA |
| Minnesota | MN | West Virginia | WV |
| Mississippi | MS | Wisconsin | WI |
| Missouri | MO | Wyoming | WY |

Zip code

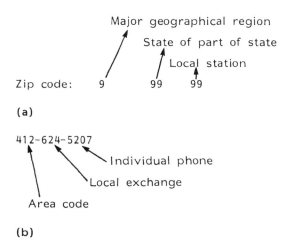

Major geographical region

State of part of state

Local station

Zip code:    9       99      99

(a)

412-624-5207

Individual phone

Local exchange

Area code

(b)

FIGURE 8.17

A numeric code is usually harder for humans to interpret. For example, we might forget whether a 1 stood for red or white. However, making additions to a numeric code is not a "special" problem. We simply assign another number. Thus, rosé would be assigned the code 3. The range of data items to which a numeric code applies is virtually unlimited. A common alphabetic code is the one used to identify the individual states of the United States (Table 8.1). Note that the code takes up only 2 spaces per name, whereas the full names of some states can reach as high as 13 characters, as in West Virginia or New Hampshire.

A numeric code used by the post office is the five-digit zip code. This code has the further characteristic of being a block code, in which different "blocks of digits" represent different concepts. In the zip code, the first digit represents a major geographical region of the country, the second two digits represent a state or part of a state, and the last two digits represent the local postal station (Figure 8.17a). Another familiar example of a block code is the numeric code used by the telephone industry (Figure 8.17b).

### The Actual Codes

For purposes of example, let us code the generic type of wine numerically: 1 = Red; 2 = White. In describing this field, we give its name, type, and length

GENERIC-TYPE PICTURE 9

which indicate numerical data, one character in length.

For the "particular type" field, let us leave the data uncoded. We could devise a numeric code (1 = Burgundy; 2 = Beaujolais; 3 = Chianti; 4 =

Rhine; etc.), but this code is not particularly easy to remember, and will involve a "lengthy" dictionary look-up when we wish to print a report. An alphabetic code like BU = Burgundy, BE = Beaujolais, CH = Chianti, and RH = Rhine also involves a "lengthy" dictionary look-up, with little advantage being offered by the mnemonic code. Since we do not expect to deal with wines that have long descriptor names, we can set aside 10 spaces for this field (Beaujolais demands 10 spaces). Since the field will contain only alphabetic characters, the description will be: Particular-Type Picture A(10).

We will also leave the brand name uncoded, but allow 20 spaces to handle the longer names involved (for example, ABC Distilleries has 16 spaces, including the blank). Also, since this field may contain special characters, such as the period in "Inc.," we shall use the alphanumeric description of the field: Brand-Name Picture X(20).

For the price, let us devise an alphabetic code. We could choose: E = Expensive; M = Medium; C = Cheap. However, the letters $E$, $M$, and $C$ hold no particular significance in other contexts (except $E = MC^2$), and thus are not particularly enlightening. It might be better to translate our description of the prices into other terms—Expensive, High priced; Medium, Medium price; Cheap, Low price—and use the codes H = High; M = Medium; L = Low, which are more in line with our everyday experience. The picture for this field is: Price Picture A.

## The Human Factor

A decision to choose one code over another because "it fits in with our previous experience" is employing one of the principles of human factors, which is the research done on the problem of "matching the human to the machine." It attempts to design technological devices and systems in a manner that facilitates, rather than hinders, human usage.

An example of a human factor-type decision would be to use a red light to indicate "trouble" with a machine, and a green light to indicate "A-okay," since this would take advantage of our long experience with red and green stop-and-go lights. A decision to use yellow for trouble, purple for A-okay might be more artistic, but would be flying in the face of common sense. While this example may seem trivial, the field of human factors is far from trivial. In fact, it received major emphasis during World War II, when diagnoses of plane crashes indicated confusion caused by the design and placement of both displays and controls. Human factors teams redesigned cockpit areas, and thus saved lives.

A less dramatic, but possibly more wide-reaching example, is the design of the typewriter keyboard. The current design of the keyboard, called the QWERTY design, because these are the first six letters starting from the left in the top row, is a human factor nightmare. Letters that occur quite frequently, such as the letter $A$, must be reached with the left pinky, while rarely occuring letters, such as $J$, are centrally located. In the early part of the century, a man named Dvorak redesigned the keyboard to take account of the frequencies of the letters, and people trained on his typewriter have consistently outperformed people trained on the QWERTY model. Yet, because of the inertia involved in retraining the thousands (millions) of people trained on the QWERTY system, the more efficient Dvorak method has never found wide acceptance. Of course, this widespread resistance to change is another example of the human factor entering into the use of technology.

| Field name | Generic type | Particular type | Brand name | Price |
|---|---|---|---|---|
| Type and length | 9 | A(10) | X(20) | A |

FIGURE 8.18

## Describing the Record

The record description is simply a concatenation of the data field descriptions. We can describe the record by simply giving the field names and their respective descriptions *in the order in which they will appear on the record* (Figure 8.18). Note that the order in which the fields are placed is also a design decision. We simply placed the fields in the same order in which we had discussed them. However, there is no intrinsic rationale for this order. Many different considerations can enter into ordering the fields. One might be importance, with the most important fields placed first. Another might be ease of input (i.e., ease of keying). In this light, we might place all the numeric fields together, so that the typist does not have to keep changing shifts on the keyboard. Or, we might consider human readability, with a view to interpreting the data easily and catching errors. With this reasoning, we might alternate numeric and nonnumeric fields, to avoid the confusion engendered by running similar type fields together. (For example, if we place the employee number, social security number, and phone number adjacent to each other, we could get an employee record looking like 3234567789017745201, which is not immediately interpretable to a human being, although a machine could be easily programmed to separate the fields as 323/456-77-8901/774-5201.)

## Access Points

In our particular file, we can ask for such information as "List all the red wines you have available"; "List all the burgundies you have"; "List all the wines made by ABC Distilleries"; and "List all the wines that are medium priced." We can also ask for combinations of fields, e.g., "List all the *red* wines that are *medium* priced," or "List the *chablis* manufactured by *ABC Distilleries.*" These fields that we can ask questions about are referred to as access points. In our file, we have four access points, which may be accessed individually or in combination with other fields (Figures 8.19a–d).

There is one difficulty with the file organization as it currently exists. If we ask for red wines, we get a list of several items (Figure 8.19a; 1 = red). Likewise, if we ask for wines by type (e.g., Burgundy; Figure 8.19b) or by brand name (e.g., all wines manufactured by ABC Distilleries; Figure 8.19c), or by price (e.g., all "cheap" wines; Figure 8.19d), we are always accessing more than one record.

Sometimes we might wish to access only one record. For example, our favorite brand might be the expensive red Burgundy of ABC Distilleries. Of course, we could access this particular record by asking for "red" wines, and sorting through the list. Or, we might try combinations of fields

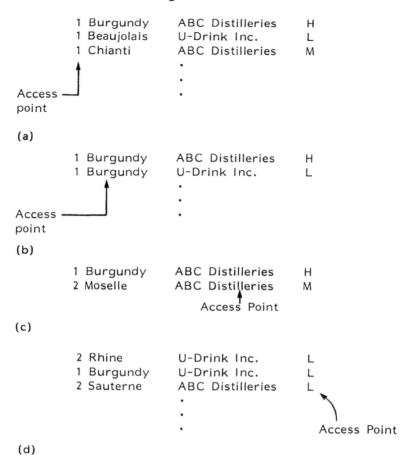

FIGURE 8.19

in order to narrow the output. However, it would be more convenient to have one field that uniquely identifies this record and no other. For example, we might assign a wine code to the record, assigning number 2482 to this particular brand, type, and price of wine. Such a field that "uniquely" identifies a record is called the key field, or simply the "key."

## The Key

The key field of a record uniquely identifies that record, distinguishing it from every other record in the file. Some examples of key fields are: the social security number in identifying employees; the purchase order number in a purchasing file; the book call number in a bibliographic file; the parts number in an inventory file; and the course number in a school registration file.

The primary quality of the key is that it uniquely identifies the record. Thus, the surname is usually not a good key, since several records may have the same surname (e.g., Smith or Jones). However, we can often

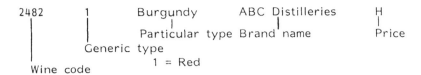

FIGURE 8.20

gain uniqueness by considering two fields in conjunction, e.g., surname plus first name, in which case John Smith would be distinguished from Mary Smith. If two fields were not enough, we could include a third field. e.g., middle initial, which would distinguish John P. Smith from John Q. Smith. Such keys are called "multiple field keys," and can conserve storage space, since they use the fields already present in the record. However, they often consume processing time in searching the file, since a much larger key must be looked at. Single field keys are normally an "additional" field, thus spending storage, but simplifying processing by the consideration of a more compact key.

For our file, we shall add the fifth field, the key field, using a numeric key four digits wide. The name of the field will be "wine code": Wine-Code Picture 9999. Thus, our complete file will contain records as shown in Figure 8.20, where the first 4 digits are the wine code (2482), the next digit the generic type of wine (1 = red), the next 10 characters the particular type (Burgundy), the next 20 characters the brand name (ABC Distilleries), and the final character the price (H = high or expensive).

Each wine record will have a different or unique key, so that now if we wish to access one particular record, we can simply give the record key, and *only* that record will be retrieved.

## Summary

In this chapter, we have distinguished between fields, records, files, and data bases. The field is the smallest interpretable data item. The record is a group of fields. The file is a group of records. And the data base is a group of files. We have also distinguished between fixed length and variable length versions of each of these data structures, and have noted that a trade-off exists when choosing between fixed and variable lengths: fixed length wastes storage but conserves processing, while variable length has the opposite effect.

In treating variable length fields, we distinguished between the prefix and suffix methods of indicating the length of the fields. The prefix method includes a "count" field by counting the characters at input time. The suffix method searches for a special character, which signals the end of the field, at output time.

We indicated that the concepts of fixed versus variable lengths apply not only to data fields, but more generally to fields, records, files, and data bases. We have treated multiply occurring versus singly occurring fields, as well as optional versus required fields, noting that both the multiply occurring and optional fields require extra processing. We describe the fields in a record by listing their names, data types, and lengths, e.g., Brand-Name Picture X(20), with the three data types being alphabetic (denoted by *A*), numeric (*9*) and alphanumeric (*X*). We then described our own data, choosing codes, data types, and field lengths. In choosing the codes, we distinguished first of all between coded and uncoded data, then between alphabetic and numeric codes. Uncoded data normally takes up more space, but avoids the processing involved in "dictionary look-ups"; coded data saves space, but requires processing dictionary look-ups. Alphabetic data is often "mnemonic," offering a special aid to human interpretation, but is not as widely applicable as numeric codes, which are less mnemonic in nature, but lend themselves quite readily to expansion for inclusion of new data values.

We took a slight digression into a discussion of human factors, as the topic applied to the selection of codes. We then treated the accession points in a record, which are defined as the "data fields we can ask questions about." Finally, we treated the concept of a record key, which uniquely identifies each record in the file, so that any record may be accessed individually, leaving the other records undisturbed and making the output more precise.

## Related Readings

Bradley, James, *File and Data Base Techniques*, New York: Holt, Rinehart and Winston, 1982.

Brainerd, Walter S., Goldberg, Charles H., and Gross, Jonathan L., *Introduction to Computer Programming*, New York: Harper & Row, 1979.

Burch, John G. Jr., Strater, Felix, R., and Grudnitski, Gary, *Information Systems: Theory and Practice*, 3rd ed. New York: John Wiley & Sons, 1983.

Forsythe, Alexandra I., et al., *Computer Science: A First Course*, New York: John Wiley & Sons, 1969.

Graham, Neill, *Introduction to Computer Science: A Structured Approach*, 2nd ed. St. Paul, MN: West Publishing Company, 1982.

Gustavson, Frances G. and Gear, C. William, *Introduction to Computers, Structured Programming, and Applications: Module as Applications and Algorithms in Business*, Chicago, IL: Science Research Associates, Inc., 1978.

Lefkovitz, David, *File Structures for On-Line Systems*, New York: Spartan Books, 1969.

Lewis, T. G. and Smith, M. Z., *Applying Data Structures*, Boston: Houghton Mifflin, 1976.

London, Keith R., *Techniques for Direct Access*, 1st ed. Philadelphia: Auerbach Publishers, 1973.

Martin, James, *An End-User's Guide to Data Base*, Englewood Cliffs, NJ: Prentice-Hall, Inc., 1981.

Shelly, Gary B. and Cashman, Thomas J., *Introduction to Computers and Data Processing*, St. Brea, CA: Anaheim Publishing Co., 1980.

# V
# Storing the Data

This section addresses the subject of file structures. The topic treats the physical organization of data in terms of speed of access, storage requirements, and flexibility of access. Chapter 9 treats storage organizations based on the value of the primary key: sequential organization (both unordered and ordered), random access, and indexed sequential. Trade-offs between storage space and access time are examined across all four organizations. In addition, the concepts of file activity, volatility, volume, frequency of access, and programming difficulty are introduced as one set of criteria for deciding the type of file organization to be implemented.

Chapter 10 introduces the notion of the inverted file, which offers access through secondary attributes. Topics relevant to searching, such as the use of the Boolean operators AND, OR, and NOT, are introduced, as well as the use of Venn diagrams to represent union (OR), intersection (AND), and set difference (NOT, as used in query language retrieval systems).

The two chapters in this section parallel the two types of question put to data bases.

- Tell me the value of attribute X for the object named such-and-such, e.g., the color of John's hair. The primary ID is used to identify the object, and the relevant attribute or attributes are named. The system returns the values for these attributes if the object is in the data base.
- An object ("goal object") is described by giving attribute values, e.g., "We need someone who has data processing and accounting experience," the request being entities that fulfill these requirements. The data base returns the IDs or names of the entities that have the attributes, if any exist.

The discussion of the means of access, by name or by attribute, as well as the efficiency of access leads naturally into the topics of Section VI, the use of bibliographic retrieval systems and the use of data base management systems.

# 9
# File Structures

Objectives

Upon completion of this chapter, the reader should be able to

1.  Distinguish between the three types of file structure: sequential, random access, and indexed sequential
2.  Explain the relative advantages and disadvantages of each of these file structures
3.  Explain the method of organization and addressing employed by each type of file structure
4.  Compute the best, worst, and average access times for each type of file organization
5.  List and explain five of the qualities to be considered in choosing a particular file structure
6.  Explain the trade-off between storage space and processing time in choosing file structures

In this chapter, we consider various ways in which a file can be structured. Placing records into a file is called *storage*. Accessing the data records to retrieve information is termed *retrieval*. Since the structure of the storage file is inherently related to the methods used to access the file, we shall treat both storage and retrieval in conjunction.

In this chapter, we treat three major types of file organization: (1) sequential, (2) random access, and (3) indexed sequential. These are the most common file structures. They are all based on a "key," which is used to both store and retrieve data. The "key" uniquely identifies each data record in the file. In Chapter 10, we will consider a file organization based on the content of the data fields: the inverted file.

The method of organizing the records in a file is referred to as its *structure*. The method by which we search the file in order to retrieve data is called the *access method*. Since the type of structure determines the possible means of access and vice versa, these two elements, structure and access method, become intertwined.

## Sequential Access

Sequential files are the most simply organized; they simply contain the records in a linear fashion, one after another. They are searched by starting at the beginning of the file and looking at each record until the desired record is found. There are primarily two types of sequential files: ordered and nonordered. We will first treat nonordered files.

## Nonordered Sequential Files

In a nonordered sequential file, new records are simply placed at the end of the file; no effort is made to keep the records in order. Thus, if we have three records already in the file

    Smith...
    Jones...
    Buck...

and we add a new employee (e.g., Filibuster), the person's record is simply placed "at the end of the line"

    Smith...
    Jones...
    Buck...
    Filibuster...

No attempt is made to keep the file in alphabetic order (if the file has an alphabetic key) or numeric order (for numeric keys).

A good example of a nonordered sequential file is the grocery list

    Eggs
    Bacon
    Tomatoes
    Lettuce
    Salami
    Milk

In constructing the list, we make no effort to "keep the items in order." Since the list is usually short, the extra effort to rewrite it in alphabetical order is not worth it. We can just as easily "scan" the unordered list. (This example of the grocery list was adapted from Lewis and Smith, 1976).

In order to search a nonordered sequential file, we simply start at the beginning, and proceed through each record until we find the record we are looking for. Thus, in our first example, if we wanted Buck's record, we would first have to look at Smith's record, decide that this was not the record we wanted, then look at Jones' record, decide this was also a "wrong record," and finally, come upon Buck's record on our third try, decide that this was "it," and retrieve the record

    Smith...
    Jones...
    Buck...    ← we find Buck on the third try
    Filibuster...

In the example of the grocery list, we keep scanning the entire list (possibly crossing off items) until we have found every item on it. The shortness of the list makes the time spent scanning insignificant. The non-ordered sequential file is especially useful with such short lists.

## Searching the File: Best, Worst, and Average Case

In the best case, i.e., our luckiest search, the record we are looking for will be the first record in the file. We will find it "right away," in one access. Thus, the best case in a nonordered sequential file is a search of 1 access.

In the worst possible case, the record we are looking for will be the last record in the file. We will have to search through every record in order to find the one we are looking for. If the file contains five records, the search will take five accesses. If the file contains 5,000 records, the search will take 5,000 accesses. We may generalize this situation by stating that: "In a file consisting of $n$ records (where $n$ represents the number of records in the file), the worst search will consist of $n$ accesses."

Besides the best and worst cases, we also have the "average case," i.e., we are seldom so lucky as to get the "best case," nor seldom so unlucky as to get the "worst case"; more often, the record we are looking for will be someplace "in the middle" of the file. In fact, the "average case" for a sequential search of a file is about "$n/2$," i.e., on the average, we find the item we are looking for after searching about "half" the records. Thus, in a file of six records, we normally search three times "on the average" in order to find what we are looking for. In a larger file, say 5,000 records, each search "averages" about 2,500 look-ups before we find the item we are looking for. (The exact number of searches is $(n+1)/2$, but for large files, this is close enough to $n/2$ to allow us to use the simplified calculation.) Thus, we can see that searching large files in a sequential mode is very time consuming. In fact, this long search time is the major drawback of sequentially ordered files.

## File Reorganization Versus Search Time: A Trade-Off

The major advantage of nonordered sequential files is that little effort is required to add new records to the file. Adding and deleting records are two operations involved in maintaining a file. While deleting records (e.g., if Buck quits) is a little more complex in sequential files (eventually the records have to be moved up to "fill the gap"), the ease of adding new records is the major attraction of using nonordered sequential files. In fact, if we have a small file, where the search time is never very long, even in the worst case, e.g., a class roster of 20-30 students, a nonordered sequential file may be the easiest method to use. The major drawback to the nonordered sequential file is the long search time for larger files. Thus, we have a trade-off: ease of adding records versus time-consuming search. We shall later see that "conservation of storage" is another benefit of nonordered sequential files, so that the trade-off becomes "storage conservation and easy insertion of records" versus "long search time." However, the long search time becomes such a prohibitive factor in large files, we really have little choice but to try some other method of structuring the file once we get beyond very small or very infrequently used applications.

## Updating the File: Insertions, Deletions, and Changes

The process of making changes to a file is called "updating" the file; we bring the file "up to date." Updating involves three major operations

1. The insertion of new records, e.g., a new employee is hired, so that his or her record must be added to the personnel file
2. The deletion of records that are no longer applicable, e.g., a person cancels his or her reservation for an airline flight, and the record of the reservation must now be removed from the file
3. Simple changes to one or more fields in the data record, e.g., the employee "pay-to-date" field is updated weekly in a payroll file

Processing simple changes in the data in a particular field causes little problem as far as file organization is concerned. Since one value merely replaces another value *in the same space*, there is no change in the size of the record, the number of records, or the sequence of the records in the file. Thus, we simply enter the new record in the same space formerly occupied by the old record. Changes that affect the length of the field are more complex to handle. (This assumes disk storage. On magnetic tape the update may require rewriting the entire file.)

Adding records to the file is simple enough in the nonordered sequential file: they are simply placed at the end of the file. However, if the file is "organized" by some field, the addition of new records will normally cause us to "move some records" in order to make room for the newcomer. The situation is similar to the addition of a new pupil (e.g., Grogan) to a classroom in which the students are seated alphabetically. While the students whose names precede Grogan (e.g., Baker) are undistrubed, everybody following Grogan must move one seat back in order to "make room." Because of the difficulties encountered in adding new records, these records are not always added immediately, but are "saved up" until we have a batch of new records to add. These records then are inserted together in one operation, known as "reorganizing the file."

Deletions also present special problems. If someone drops out of the class, everybody must move up to fill the gap. Likewise, in a sequential file, deletions will cause "gaps" that must be filled. However, as in the case of the additions, the deletions can be "saved up," and then processed in a batch at file reorganization time. This is done by reserving a special field of the record to indicate whether or not the record is "current." For records that are current, this field might be set to the value "1"; records that are deleted have this "flag" changed to a zero in order to indicate the deletion. These comments on insertions and deletions set the stage for our consideration of the ordered sequential file.

## Ordered Sequential Files

A variation on the nonordered sequential file is the ordered sequential file. In this case, the file is "sequenced" by the key. For example, our file, using a surname as the key, would be sorted into alphabetical order

Buck...
Filibuster...
Jones...
Smith...

Now, when adding a new name to the file (e.g., Olson), we would have to place the new record in its proper spot

    Buck...
    Filibuster...
    Jones...
    Olson...  ← Olson's "proper" place
    Smith...

Of course, this placement of Olson in a "special" place, rather than simply adding his or her record to the end of the file, makes the process of adding records to the file more complicated. In fact, we have to "re-sort" the file every time we add a new record, moving everybody after the new record "down a notch." In practice, the file may not be re-sorted for every new record we add. Rather, we save up a "batch" of new records, then add them all at once, and re-sort the file. This might be done on a daily basis, or weekly, monthly, or even once a year, depending on how many new records we get. (The new records are temporarily kept in a nonordered sequential file until it is time to "reorganize" the file.) The "re-sorting" procedure makes inputting new records a more complex task. Deleting records is still as difficult as it was previously, i.e., we have to move the records up in order to "fill in the gaps" whenever records are deleted.

However, the additional burden of sorting the input does offer a balancing advantage of permitting us to shorten the search time involved in retrieving records from the file.

Two methods can be used to "cut" the search time in an ordered sequential file: the first is called the "block search"; the second is called the "binary search."

## The Block Search

In the block search, we skip over blocks of data items. For example, if we had a file of 1,000 items sorted alphabetically (Figure 9.1a), we could divide the file into standard size blocks (e.g., the following division is into blocks of 200 records; Figure 9.1b). We could then search every 200th record. For example, suppose we are looking for the record for Peterson. We search only the "last name" in each block, to see if *Peterson* falls into that block or not. Searching the first block, we compare the desired record, Peterson, with the last record in the block, Davis, and conclude that our record must be further down the file. We next examine the last record of the next block, Gherlik, and again conclude that we must keep looking. We search the third block, finding Michaels as the last name in the block, and search again. Now we find Smith as the last name in the block. Since Peterson precedes Smith in alphabetical order, we now know that Peterson must be in this block of names (block 4), if it is in the file at all.

We now "backtrack" to the first name in the block, and start searching sequentially. Suppose that Peterson is about halfway through the block. Since the block is 200 names long, we would find Peterson after about 100 searches (accesses) of the 200 records in the block. If we now stop to count the number of accesses, we find that it took us: (1) 4 accesses to find the correct block, and (2) 100 accesses (estimated) to find the

|  | Block 1 | 000 Aaron |
|--|--|--|
| Aaron. . . | | : |
| Abner. . . | | 199 Davis |
| . | | : |
| . | Block 2 | 200 Dawson |
| Billings. . . | | : |
| . | | 399 Gherlik |
| . | | : |
| Dwight. . . | Block 3 | 400 Gladstone |
| . | | : |
| . | | 599 Michaels |
| Peterson. . . | | : |
| . | Block 4 | 600 Moriarity |
| . | | : |
| Smith. . . | | 799 Smith |
| . | | : |
| . | Block 5 | 800 Smithson |
| Zurkowski. . . | | : |
| | | 999 Zurkowski |

(a)                                     (b)

FIGURE 9.1

correct record within the block. Thus, we had 104 accesses. Comparing this with the "average" number of accesses in a sequential search, (about 500 for a file of 1,000 records) we can see that the block search has brought a savings of almost 400 accesses in this particular case.

### The Worst Case: Block Search

We can treat the block search as two sequential searches

1. One sequential search through the last names of each block
2. One sequential search through the correct block, once it has been identified

Both of these searches have a specified number of items in them. In our example, the "last name in the block" search has an n of five items, since there are five blocks (the n of this first search is always equal to the number of blocks in the file). The search within a block has an n of 200 items, since this is the "block size." We thus have two items to use in our calculations: (1) number of blocks: $n_1 = 5$; and (2) block size: $n_2 = 200$. In the worst case, when the item we are searching for is the last item in the file, we will have to search through both the "number of blocks" and the "records within a block" completely. This will involve simply adding the two n figures in order to get the calculation for worst case: $5 + 200 = 205$. Comparing this figure with the worst case for a sequential search, which would be 1,000 in our example, we see a substantial savings of almost 800 accesses in the worst case. (Note: In searching the last names of the blocks, we never have to search more than n-1 blocks, since if we do not find the name in the first n-1 blocks, it must be in the last block, if it is in the file at all. That is, in our example, if we find that *Thomas* does not fit into the first four blocks, it must fit into the fifth block, and we do not have to waste an access to find this out. However, if the item being searched for is larger than the largest name in the last block, say Zwiggy, indexing the last name can prevent an unfruitful block search.)

### The Average Case: Block Search

We can calculate the average case for the block search in a similar fashion. Using the two figures for n: (1) number of blocks: 5, and (2) block size: 200, along with the fact that the average search for any sequential search is (N + 1)/2, we get the individual averages

1.  Number of blocks, average search: 3, from [(5 + 1)/2 = 3]
2.  Block size, average search: 100.5, from [(200 + 1)/2 = 100.5]

Adding these together, we get the average block search length of 103.5 (3 + 100.5 = 103.5). Comparing this average with the sequential average of 500.5, we save an *average* of 397 accesses *per search*. Thus, if an access costs us 5¢, we save 5¢ times 397 accesses, or $19.85 per search. If we do 100 searches per day, we save $1,985 per day! *It pays to optimize.*

### Optimizing the Block Search

We can do better than the above figures by choosing our block size more judiciously. Mathematically, it can be shown that the "optimal" block size is the square root of the number of records in the file. Thus, in our file of 1,000 records, we would choose a block size of 32 records (32 * 32 is slightly large, giving 1,024 records; but 31 * 31 would be too small, giving only 961 records). Whenever a file does not admit of an exact square root, choose the larger figure in order to accommodate all the records in the file. The last block will be a little small, but that presents no problem.

If we choose a block size of 32 records, we will have 32 blocks of 32 records each (Figure 9.2). The worst case is simply the sum of the two n's: 32 + 32 = 64, or, in symbolic terms: $2\sqrt{n}$. The average case is simply

$$\frac{\sqrt{n} + 1}{2} + \frac{\sqrt{n} + 1}{2} = 2 \; \frac{\sqrt{n} + 1}{2} \; = \sqrt{n} + 1$$

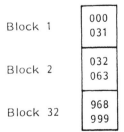

| | |
|---|---|
| Block 1 | 000 / 031 |
| Block 2 | 032 / 063 |
| Block 32 | 968 / 999 |

FIGURE 9.2

TABLE 9.1

| Case | Search Type | Search Length |
|------|-------------|---------------|
| Worst | Sequential | 1000 |
|       | block | 64 |
| Average | Sequential | 500 |
|         | block | 33 |

Thus, the average case in our example would be 33 searches.

Comparing these figures for the optimal block search with the figures for a sequential search, we have the data shown in Table 9.1, showing a savings of 936 accesses in the worst case, and of 467 accesses on the average. At 5¢ an access, we are now saving $23.35 *per search*, on the average. We are also saving time. The block search is over 15 times as fast as the sequential search in both the worst case (1,000 accesses divided by 64 accesses equals 15.6) and the average case (500 divided by 33 is 15.2).

## The General Comparison

The above figures apply only to our particular example. The general comparison is always made in terms of n. Thus, the table would be similar to Table 9.2. In order to see how these values vary as n becomes larger, we give the following table of average values for a sampling of n-values. We give the average value table because this is the most widely applicable value; it tells us how things are going to go "generally." The worst case is useful for estimating the longest wait, i.e., "how bad things can get," when we are unlucky. The average values for the sequential and block searches are shown in Table 9.3.

As is evident from the table, the sequential and block searches are "equivalent" for small files, but the block search rapidly surges forward as the best bet as the file grows larger.

TABLE 9.2

| Case | Search type | Search length |
|------|-------------|---------------|
| Worst | Sequential: | $n$ |
|       | block: | $2\sqrt{n}$ |
| Average | Sequential: | $(n+1)/2$ |
|         | block: | $(\sqrt{n}+1)$ |

TABLE 9.3

| | Average Search Length | |
|---|---|---|
| N | Sequential | Block |
| 1 | 1 | 1 |
| 4 | 2.5 | 3 |
| 9 | 5 | 4 |
| 100 | 50.5 | 11 |
| 10,000 | 5000.5 | 101 |

### The Binary Search

The binary search is another method by which search time can be cut. The essence of the binary search lies in dividing the file into two equal parts, then determining which part contains the item for which we are searching. Thus, in our file of 1,000 records, we would first divide the file into two sections of 500 records each (Figure 9.3a). If we are looking for Peterson, we now ascertain that Peterson is included in the second half of the file. We then disregard the first 500 records, and concentrate on the second half of the file as if it were a file of 500 records. Dividing this into two equal parts of 250 records each, we have Figure 9.3b.

We now determine that the top half of this file contains the name Peterson, and concentrate our efforts on that portion of the file, breaking it into the two parts (Figure 9.3c).

Proceeding in this fashion, we would locate the record for Peterson in approximately 10 accesses. Comparing this figure with the 500 accesses required in the sequential search, and the 32 accesses of the block search, we can see that the binary search offers us the best deal so far. In fact, if the cost per access is approximately equal for all three searches, the

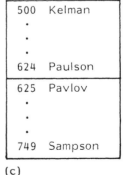

FIGURE 9.3

TABLE 9.4

| N | Worst Case |
| --- | --- |
| 1 | 1 |
| 10 | 4 |
| 1000 | 10 |
| 65000 | 16 |
| 1,000,000 | 20 |

binary search costs us one-fiftieth of the cost of a sequential search, and one-third the cost of the block search. Of course, the cost per access is not always equal for all three search methods, since the cost of the storage medium used as well as the cost of processing time might vary for each. For example, a sequential search can be performed with data stored on magnetic tape at a lower cost than the direct access storage required for a binary search.

### Worst Case, Average Case: Binary Search

The worst case in a binary search is approximately $\log_2 n$, where n is the number of records in the file. For example, we have the "worst case" values for a sampling of n-values shown in Table 9.4. We say the $\log_2 n$ is "approximately" the correct value.

### Complexity Analysis

The study of the number of instructions (or other operations) necessary to implement a given algorithm is called complexity analysis. We have informally performed such analysis on sequential files, but we concentrated on successful searches. A more thorough treatment would consider both successful and unsuccessful searches. For example, with unordered sequential files, the successful search (found the query) takes

Worst case $= N$

Average case $= \dfrac{(N + 1)}{2}$

The unsuccessful case always takes N accesses in an unordered sequential file because we do not know the item is *not there* until we get to the end of the file

Worst case $= N$

Average case $= N$

In ordered sequential files, both successful and unsuccessful searches can be done on the average of $(N + 1)/2$, since we can stop searching

Query     File

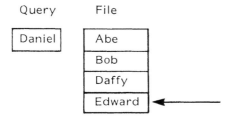

FIGURE 9.4

when the query, say *Daniel*, becomes "impossible," e.g., when we have not found it by the time we get to *Edward* (Figure 9.4).

For an ordered sequential file we have

Successful Search

$$\text{Average case } = \frac{(N + 1)}{2}$$

Unsuccessful Search

$$\text{Average case } = \frac{(N + 1)}{2}$$

## Complexity of Binary Search

The same type of analysis can be applied to the binary search. The mathematics is a little more complex (see Knuth, 1973), but the principle is the same. As in the sequential search, the calculations differ for successful and unsuccessful searches, but the maximum number of accesses is never more than

$$\lfloor \log_2 N + 1 \rfloor$$

where the notation $\lfloor \; \rfloor$ indicates "the floor." It truncates to the integer exactly equal to or lower than the number within the stilts. Thus, we have

$$\lfloor 2.1 \rfloor = 2$$

$$\lfloor 2.6 \rfloor = 2$$

$$\lfloor 2.0 \rfloor = 2$$

$$\lfloor 3.0 \rfloor = 3$$

This is in contrast to rounding, where

$$2.1 = 2$$

$$2.6 = 3$$

There is a third notation, the ceiling, in which the number is raised to the next higher integer if there is a fractional part

TABLE 9.5

| N | $\log_2 N$ | $\lfloor \ \rfloor$ | $\log_2 N+1$ |
|----|------|---|---|
| 15 | 3.9 | 3 | 4 |
| 16 | 4.0 | 4 | 5 |
| 17 | 4.1 | 4 | 5 |
| 31 | 4.9 | 4 | 5 |
| 32 | 5.0 | 5 | 6 |
| 33 | 5.1 | 5 | 6 |

$$\lceil 2.1 \rceil = 3.0$$

$$\lceil 2.6 \rceil = 3.0$$

$$\lceil 2.0 \rceil = 2.0$$

$$\lceil 3.0 \rceil = 3.0$$

Whether one wants to use the floor, ceiling, or rounding is application dependent. When dealing with money, we usually round. If we are computing the number of persons necessary to perform a task, we might use the ceiling, since a need for 5.3 persons can be filled by 6 persons, but not by 5, and we can never seem to locate exactly 5.3. In this particular calculation, the floor happens to be the appropriate number.

For various file sizes, the worst case would be as shown in Table 9.5. As the reader can see the cut-off points are the exact powers of two. For 16 items the worst case is 5 searches, not 4. For all values of from 16 through 31, the worst case is 5. Then, at 32, the worst case becomes 6. The respective maxima for worst cases for exact powers of two, irrespective of success or nonsuccess, are shown in Table 9.6. However, for any file "in between two powers of two," say 9 through 15, one can think of the exact log of the next higher power of two. For 9 through 15, the next

TABLE 9.6

| N | Worst case |
|----|------|
| 1 | 1 |
| 2 | 2 |
| 4 | 3 |
| 8 | 4 |
| 16 | 5 |
| 32 | 6 |
| 64 | 7 |
| . | |
| . | |
| . | |

TABLE 9.7

| N | Worst case |
|---|---|
| 1 | 1 |
| 4 | 2 |
| 8 | 3 |
| 16 | 4 |
| 32 | 5 |
| . | . |
| . | . |
| . | . |
| 1024 | 10 |
| . | . |
| . | . |
| . | . |
| 4096 | 12 |

higher number that is a power of 2 is 16; its log is 4, and that is the worst case.

In any event one would not go far wrong in thinking in terms of the powers of two (Table 9.7), and attempting to keep the file size at least one element smaller than the N listed in the table.

Another notation for the floor is the integer function

$$\text{INT } (\text{LOG}_2 N) + 1$$

which means that we take the integer part of the $\log_2 n$, then add 1 to the result. For example, a file of 1,000 items gives

$$\log_2 1,000 = 9.96$$

Integer part of $9.96 = 9$

$$9 + 1 = 10$$

TABLE 9.8

| N | Worst | Average |
|---|---|---|
| 1024 | 10 | 9 |
| 4096 | 12 | 11 |
| . | | |
| . | | |
| . | | |
| 65000 | 16 | 15 |
| . | | |
| . | | |
| . | | |
| 1,000000 | 20 | 19 |

TABLE 9.9

| N | Sequential search n/2 | Block search √n | Binary search $\log_2 n - 1$ |
|---|---|---|---|
| 4 | 2 | 2 | 1 |
| 16 | 8 | 4 | 3 |
| 64 | 32 | 8 | 5 |
| 1024 | 512 | 32 | 9 |
| 1,000000 | 500,000 | 1000 | 19 |

The average case for successful searches in the binary search "approaches" one less than the worst case. That is, if the worst case is 10, the average will be 9. If the worst case is 20, the average will be 19 accesses. Thus we have Table 9.8.

Using a file of size $n = 2^t - 1$, i.e., of files that have exactly one less element than a power of 2 (1, 3, 9, 15, etc.), Maurer (1977) develops the formula for the "average case" as

$$\frac{1}{n} \sum_{i=1}^{t} i2^{i-1} * i$$

for data items accessed with equal probability, then indicates how the formula can be simplified to the approximation $(\log_2 n) - 1$. For our purposes we can simply use the approximation.

## The General Comparison

We can now compare the three search methods in regard to the average and worst cases. We do so for a sampling of n-values. The first comparison is for the average case (Table 9.9). For the worst case, we have Table 9.10. Thus, the binary search is considerably superior to both sequential and block searches in both the average and worst cases.

TABLE 9.10

| N | Sequential search n | Block search 2√n | Binary search $\log_2 n$ |
|---|---|---|---|
| 4 | 4 | 4 | 2 |
| 16 | 16 | 8 | 4 |
| 64 | 64 | 16 | 6 |
| 1024 | 1024 | 64 | 10 |
| 1,000000 | 1,000000 | 2000 | 20 |

## The Trade-Off

Why do we not use only the binary search? Why do such things as sequential and block searches exist? One reason is that the binary search demands a direct access device (e.g., a disk), while both the sequential and block searches can be implemented on sequential access devices (e.g., magnetic tape). (The sequential search can be implemented with very little difficulty on a sequential access device; the block search with somewhat more difficulty; but both are feasible.) Thus, an installation lacking direct access devices would not implement the binary search for large files stored on sequential storage devices.

Another reason is that the binary search requires somewhat more effort to program. For example, the routine for the binary search might be three times as long as the routine for the sequential search, and require three to five times the amount of time to program and debug. However, the savings in processing time over the investment in programming time is so great that this reason is diminished in its force. Neither of these reasons is as important as the final reason we will examine: the nature of the search.

## Selective versus Complete Retrieval

Sometimes we process a file in order to retrieve only one record. This is the case, e.g., in a checking account file. When a customer cashes a check, we wish to deduct the amount from his or her balance, and no one else's. Thus, we would like to "select" this one person's "checking account record" from the entire file of checking account records, which might number in the thousands. This type of search to retrieve one (or a few) records from a file is called a "selective" search. The opposite of the selective retrieval of records is "complete" retrieval, which occurs when we are going to process each and every record in the file. This would be the case in a payroll file, e.g., where each and every employee gets a paycheck on payday. Since we are going to process every record in the file, we may as well access each record sequentially; i.e., we might as well begin at the beginning of the file, and proceed methodically to the end.

The binary search is particularly apropos for selective searching; the sequential search is particularly apropos for complete retrieval. Thus, we use different searches for different purposes. In fact, we can show the trade-off mathematically. If we are searching for 1 record out of 1,000 (selective search), the binary search will find that record in 9 or 10 accesses. The sequential search will take an average of 500 accesses, and might take the full 1,000 accesses. Clearly, the sequential search is inappropriate for selective searching. However, if we are going to retrieve every record in the file, as would be the case in computing a payroll, the sequential search will access every record in exactly 1,000 accesses! (It needs only 1 access per record, since it is taking each record in order.) The binary search, on the other hand, will take considerably longer. In fact, it will take about 9,000 accesses. This is because the binary search is set up to find one item at a time. It finds that item very fast (an average of 9 accesses for a 1000-record file), but it must look up each item *as if it were a new item!* Thus, in looking up the entire set of 1,000 records, it will perform 1,000 separate searches, at an average of 9 accesses per search, or a total of 9,000 accesses.

One solution to our problem would be to develop two search routines: the sequential search for projects demanding complete retrieval, and the binary search for projects involving selective retrieval.

## Random Access

Another mode of processing data that is particularly suited to selective retrieval is called *random access*. The name *random access* comes from the fact that any data item chosen "at random" can be accessed in the same amount of time as any other data item; the physical positioning of the item has no effect on our retrieval time. (This is certainly *not* true with the sequential and block searches, in which the last item takes longer to find than an item nearer the front of the file. Physical positioning has less effect in the binary search, but the number of accesses is greater than in most random access techniques.)

As we have seen, the tendency in searching files is to attempt to reduce the number of accesses per search. In our file of 1,000 records, the sequential search took an average of 500 accesses, the block search an average of 32 accesses, and the binary search an average of about 9 accesses. Furthermore, in the worst case, the sequential search took exactly 1,000 accesses, the block search only 64, and the binary search only 10. The ideal would be to reduce both the average and the worst cases to *1 access*; i.e., every time we looked something up in the file, we would find it on the *first try*. This is the somewhat lofty goal of the random access technique of coding and storing data.

## Hash-Coding

The random access technique that we shall next discuss is called "hash-coding." The essence of the technique lies in using the data *value* in order to *compute* a storage location address. For example, suppose that we have alphabetic data as our "key"

    ABEL
    BOB
    CHUCK
    ED

We would use these data values in order to compute a storage address. For example, we might chose to take the "alphabetic position" of each letter and add them together. Thus, ABEL would be: ABEL = 1 + 2 + 5 + 12 = 20, and we would store the data value "ABEL" in location 20 (Figure 9.5a). The storage addresses for the other items would be

Bob    = 2 + 15 + 2 = 19

Chuck = 3 + 8 + 21 + 3 + 11 = 46

Ed     = 5 + 4 = 9

so that all four data items would be stored as shown in Figure 9.5b.

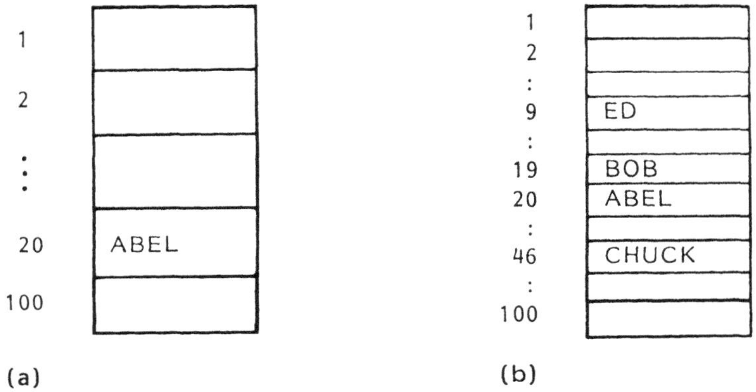

FIGURE 9.5

Note that the names *are not* stored in alphabetical order. This is one drawback to using a hash-code. However, this disadvantage is balanced by the advantage of "quick retrieval." For example, if we wish to locate Bob's record, we no longer have to begin at the top of the file and search down; we don't even have to divide the file into equal parts and ascertain which part contains the record for "BOB." We simply perform our "hashing" computation on the key (BOB = 2 + 15 + 2 = 19) to obtain the *exact* storage address, then proceed to retrieve the record from that address. It is a single access search.

The Hashing Algorithm

The computations we perform in order to arrive at the storage address are referred to as the "hashing algorithm." No one algorithm is applicable to all data values. As an extreme example, the algorithm of "alphabetic position" would not be applicable to a social security number, such as 321-32-3212, although an algorithm consisting of the simple addition of the digits might be: 3 + 2 + 1 + 3 + 2 + 3 + 2 + 1 + 2 = 19, in which case this record would be stored at location 19. (In practice, this might result in too many collisions.)

Collisions

There is one inherent difficulty with hash-coding schemes: the matter of "collisions," which occur when two or more data items "hash" to the same storage location. For example, take the names GINO and ANITA. Under our hashing algorithm of "adding the alphabetic positions of the letters," GINO would receive the storage location 45: GINO = 7 + 9 + 14 + 15 = 45; while ANITA would also receive location 45: ANITA = 1 + 14 + 9 + 20 + 1 = 45. That is, they both receive the *same storage location*. While this might work in real life (Gino and Anita are indeed married), it does not work in the world of data processing. In fact, one of the "colliding records" would have to be relegated to an "overflow" file.

## Two Methods of Handling Overflow

There are several methods of handling the problem of overflow, including (1) a separate overflow area, and (2) the next available location. In the method of a "separate overflow area," any records that "collide" are stored in a separate area (Figure 9.6a). Note that the overflow area, like the main file, has a fixed upper limit to its length (in this case, 25 records). Once this limit has been reached, the file must be reorganized. Note also that the overflow area is often searched sequentially, so that the access time for these items is considerably longer than the access time for items that did not collide.

In the method of the "next available location," the "colliding record" is placed in the next empty location in the main file (Figure 9.6b). In this method, the upper limit on space is the size of the main area. Thus, fewer records can be placed. However, we do not waste the extra storage space devoted to an overflow area.

In the case of the "next available location," we must again search for overflow records in a sequential fashion. Thus, in either case, the occurrence of overflow records increases the search time over the optimum of one access. Methods that "rehash" to the next available location avoid "clustering" records (45, 46, 47 above), but are similar in concept to the next available location.

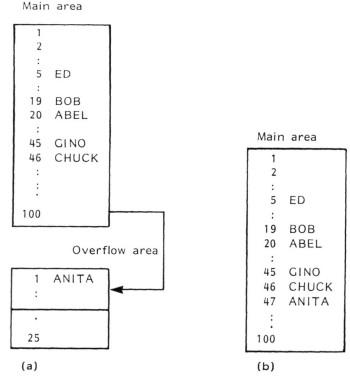

(a)  (b)

FIGURE 9.6

## Using Extra Storage

The number of collisions rises as the number of records already stored in the file increases. Thus, in an "almost full" file, we will have a greater number of collisions, and performance (in terms of access time) deteriorates.

This concept of more collisions as the file gets "fuller" can be easily illustrated with an example. Suppose that we have a file consisting of ten storage locations (Figure 9.7). The first record stored (when the file is initially empty) has a 100% chance of finding an empty spot on the first try. Conversely, there is 0% chance of a collision for this first record.

However, the second record stored has 9 chances in 10 of finding an empty slot (since 1 of the 10 slots is already filled). Conversely, it has 1 chance in 10 of resulting in a collision. The third record we store will have eight-tenths of a chance of finding an empty slot, and two-tenths chance of a collision. Proceeding in this fashion, we build Table 9.11. Thus, in a file that is 90% full, we have a 90% chance of having a collision in putting away the next record. In a file that is 50% full, we have only a 50% chance of a collision. In fact, if n represents the "fullness" of the file, we may say that for any file n% full, there is also n% chance of a collision occurring when we try to put away the next record, and we have 1-n chance of finding an empty slot (100% - n for percentages).

London (1973) gives the following theoretical distribution of record assignments for a 1,000-record file. We say "theoretical" distribution, since

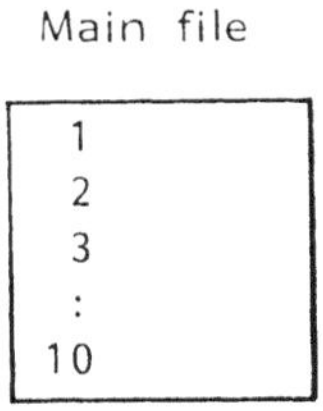

Main file

```
 1
 2
 3
 :
10
```

FIGURE 9.7

TABLE 9.11

| Record being stored | Chance of finding empty slot | Chance of having a collision |
|---|---|---|
| 1 | 10/10 | 0/10 |
| 2 | 9/10 | 1/10 |
| 3 | 8/10 | 2/10 |
| 4 | 7/10 | 3/10 |
| 5 | 6/10 | 4/10 |
| 6 | 5/10 | 5/10 |
| 7 | 4/10 | 6/10 |
| 8 | 3/10 | 7/10 |
| 9 | 2/10 | 8/10 |
| 10 | 1/10 | 9/10 |

TABLE 9.12

| | |
|---|---|
| 68 | addresses had no records assigned to them (empty spaces in the file) |
| 135 | addresses had one record assigned (no collission) |
| 135 | addresses had two records assigned (one collision) |
| 90 | addresses had three records assigned |
| 45 | addresses had four records assigned |
| 18 | addresses had five records assigned |
| 6 | addresses had six records assigned |
| 2 | addresses had seven records assigned |
| 1 | address had eight records assigned |
| no | addresses had more than nine records assigned to them |

the numbers were derived from statistical analysis rather than actual experience with the file. In files that are not perfectly random in the distribution of their keys, the actual assignments might differ from the theoretical distribution. In fact, if the data is biased in any way (e.g., more recent accounts are more active in a department store credit file), these biases can be used to improve performance. London's theoretical distribution for the 1,000 records is shown in Table 9.12.

It is also possible for the same record to encounter more than one collision before it gets placed. For example, Weiland (1970) gives the "number of collisions before placement" in a file using the algorithm of "next available location" shown in Table 9.13.

Because of the problem of collisions, and the fact that the number of collisions increases as the file gets fuller, the storage area allocated to the random access file is usually larger than the area actually needed; i.e., the file is kept between 70 and 90% full, with a wastage of 10 to 30%.

Optimizing the Hashing Algorithm

As we have pointed out, if the overflow file becomes too lengthy (i.e., if we have too many collisions), the efficiency of hashing is reduced, since these items will incur a longer search time. One method of combating this problem is to keep the file "somewhat empty." Another is to choose a hash-

TABLE 9.13

| %Full | Average number of collisions before placing item |
|---|---|
| 10 | 1.11 |
| 50 | 2 |
| 75 | 4 |
| 90 | 10 |

ing algorithm that "works well," by which we mean an algorithm that tends to distribute data evenly over the entire data area.

An example of an algorithm that would not work well is our "add-up-the-alphabetic-positions" algorithm, when working with surnames. If we restrict ourself simply to the surname, the numerous Smiths and Joneses would all wind up in the same position—JONES = 10 + 15 + 14 + 5 + 19 = 63; SMITH = 19 + 13 + 9 + 20 + 8 = 69—so that locations 63 and 69 would be somewhat overworked. In fact, we would probably have to switch to an algorithm that selected a few letters from the surname (possibly the consonants, since vowels are too common to be useful), a few letters from the first name, and the middle initial, in order to derive an algorithm that would distribute the data more evenly. The study of hashing algorithms is a subfield of data processing that has received much attention, and the interested student is advised to follow up on some of the references provided at the end of the chapter.

## Restricting the Algorithm to the Storage Space

Not every hashing algorithm may be applied indiscriminantly. For example, if we have 999 storage locations, our algorithm must produce values between 1 (or zero) and 999, since these are legal storage addresses; but exclude both negative values and values larger than 999. While the problem of negative values is seldom encountered, the problem of values "outside the range" of our storage area (i.e., values that are too large) is frequently incurred.

The problem is handled by dividing the "hash-total" by a suitable number, and using the *remainder* as the address. For example, if we had just 30 storage locations and 25 data records, an algorithm that simply added up the digits in the social security number would give too many large values (929-31-4683 = 45). However, a suitable algorithm would be the following:

1. Isolate the last three digits of the social security number.
2. Divide these three digits by 29.
3. Save the remainder of this division, and disregard the quotient.
4. Add 1 to the remainder.

Under this algorithm, the above social security number would be stored at address 17. The detailed calculation is

1. The last three digits are 683.
2. Divide 683 by 29, giving a quotient of 23 and a remainder of 16.
3. Retain the remainder of 16.
4. Add 1 to the value 16, yielding location 17.

The step involving the addition of one to the remainder usually occurs only in higher-level programming languages, e.g., COBOL, in which an address of zero is not allowed. Lower-level languages (e.g., assembly language at the system level) and some higher-level languages (e.g., arrays in BASIC) admit a "zero" address. That a zero address can occur in our remainder algorithm is evident from the following example: 058 are the last three digits of the social security number; dividing 058 by 29, we get a quotient of 2, with a remainder of 0. That is, 29 goes "evenly" into 58. The addition of 1 to the remainder will transform any zero remainders into the address "one."

The largest address in our scheme is 29. This is because the largest possible remainder is 28; adding 1 to 28 would give us the address 29. Thus, the range of values encompassed by our hashing algorithm is 1 through 29, or 29 distinct storage locations. If our algorithm distributed the data records "perfectly," we could assign storage locations to 29 records without a collision. A thirtieth record would inevitably collide with some other record, since we have only 29 distinct addresses. The choice of a divisor should allow a range of addresses greater than or equal to the number of records to be stored, and less than or equal to the number of physical locations in the file.

Choosing a divisor larger than the storage area will result in illegal addresses. For example, using the divisor 31, we would generate addresses from 1 thorugh 31. However, we would now have the problem of making sure that we never assign address 31 to any record, since our storage area consists of only 30 locations, numbered 1 thorugh 30. Hence, address 31 is "illegal." We can choose the file size to be exactly equal to the divisor, here 29, as long as we choose the divisor as a number larger than the total records to be stored, here 25.

## Choosing the Divisor: Primary Numbers

In order to insure an even distribution of addresses, the divisor in a numeric-hashing algorithm is usually a "primary number." Primary numbers have no "factors" (divisors) other than 1 and the number itself. Thus, 29 is primary, since its only divisors are 1 and 29. Thirty-one is also primary, its only divisors being 1 and 31. However, the number 30 is not primary, since it has divisors 1, 2, 3, 5, 6, 10, 15, and 30; considerably more than "1 and the number itself."

Primary numbers generate fewer "clusters" than nonprimary divisors, i.e., they give an even distribution of addresses. For example, suppose we have the following "keys" (perhaps the last three digits of a social security number):

Key
703
456
121
713
345
073
375
036

Dividing these keys by the numbers 30, 29, and 31, respectively, we get the remainders shown in Table 9.14. Thus, dividing by 30 yields 3 collisions, dividing by the primary number 29 yields 1 collision, and dividing by the primary number 31 yields no collisions. Primes do not eliminate collisions entirely (any multiple of 29 will result in a collision when dividing by 29), but they do reduce the frequency of their occurrence.

A good rule of thumb is to choose a primary number larger than the number of data items we want to store, and equal to or smaller than the storage area allocated to hold these items. Choosing a primary number

TABLE 9.14

| Key | Remainder | | |
|---|---|---|---|
| | ÷ 30 | ÷ 29 | ÷ 31 |
| 703 | 13* | 07* | 21 |
| 456 | 06** | 21 | 22 |
| 121 | 01 | 05 | 28 |
| 713 | 23 | 17 | 00 |
| 345 | 15*** | 26 | 04 |
| 073 | 13* | 15 | 11 |
| 375 | 15*** | 27 | 03 |
| 036 | 06** | 07* | 05 |
| | 3 collisions | 1 collision | 0 collisions |

larger than the number of data items insures that the file will be "a little empty," thus minimizing the number of collisions.

Thus, in storing 25 data items we choose to divide by 29, and would allocate 29 different storage locations to this file. In a particular installation, we may not be allowed to allocate exactly 29 locations. For example, we may have to allocate space in "blocks of 6." In that case, we would allocate 30 locations to the file, the nearest number greater than 29.

### The Trade-Offs in Random Access Files

The primary advantage of random access files is the "quick access." With a minimum seek time of one access, and an average and worse case not far from one, the random access provides an alluring incentive. Some of the disadvantages to random access lie in the processing involved in developing and implementing the "hashing algorithm," as well as in the "wasted" storage involved in keeping the file a certain amount "empty." However, the major drawback to random access files is that they are not readily amenable to the production of sequential lists. As we have seen, the data in random access files are not stored in sequential order. Thus, we had the key names stored in the order

    ED
    BOB
    ABEL
    GINO
    CHUCK
    ANITA

which is not even close to alphabetic order. Numeric keys provide no better results.

If the production of sequential lists (e.g., a list of customers, produced alphabetically, or a list of account numbers, produced in ascending numerical order) is of importance, the use of random access files presents a problem. Ascending means the numbers get larger, e.g., 3, 7, 19, 52;

descending means successive numbers get progressively smaller, e.g., 52, 19, 7, 3. In regard to alphabetic data, ascending is alphabetic order: A, B, C, ...Z; while descending is the reverse order: Z, Y, X, ..., A.

Thus we have a dilemma

1. Sequential files can produce sequential lists easily, but they have a slower access time.
2. Random access files have a fast access time, but they cannot easily produce sequential lists.

What we need is a type of file organization that can produce sequential lists and still have a decent access time; what we need is a compromise. Such compromise is achieved by the file organization called "indexed sequential."

## Indexed Sequential Files

The problem with sequential files is the search time; it just takes too long to find the item we are looking for. Random access files reduce the problem of search time, but they have the drawback of the data not being organized in some sorted sequence (e.g., alphabetically), which makes it somewhat difficult to print an alphabetic listing of our customers.

The trade-off is

| Feature | File Structure | |
| --- | --- | --- |
| | Sequential File | Random Access |
| Fast search? | — | + |
| Easy sequential handling? | + | — |

The concept of an indexed sequential file can be used to strike a compromise between the two poles of this trade-off. While index sequential files have a longer search time than random access files, the search time is considerably better than that involved in sequential files. Yet, while the random access file has its data scattered in an unorganized manner, the indexed sequential file is *sequential*, thus permitting easy printing of such things as alphabetic listings.

## Two Files

The indexed sequential file is not really a single file, but a combination of at least *two* files: the data file and the index. The data file contains the actual data items. For example, in our 1,000-record file, the data file would consist of the exact same records as our sequential file, in exactly the same alphabetic order (Figure 9.8a).

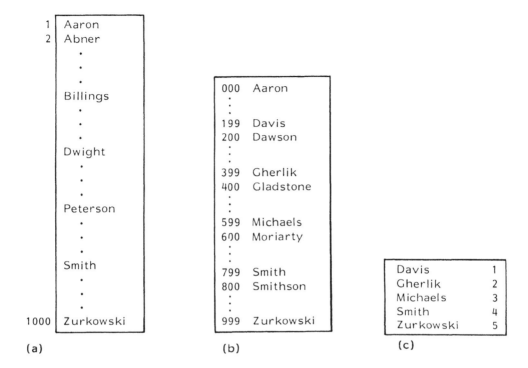

FIGURE 9.8

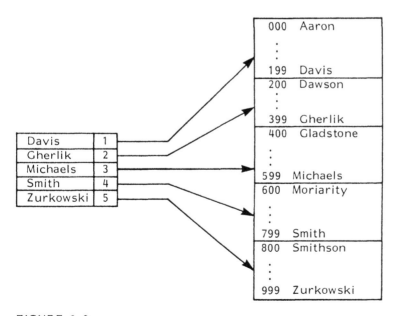

FIGURE 9.9

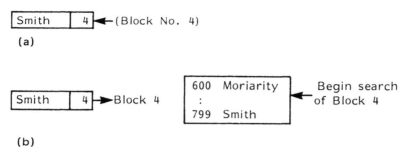

FIGURE 9.10

However, in addition to this data file, we would have a separate "index" file that acts as a pointer into the data file. For example, we might divide our 1,000 records into the five 200-record blocks that we used in explaining the block search (Figure 9.8b). We would then also construct a five-value index, consisting of the last data item in each block and the block number (Figure 9.8c). Again, only four index entries would be sufficient for successful searches, but not for unsuccessful ones.

This index would then be used to "point to" the correct block of data for any item we are retrieving (Figure 9.9). Now, if we wish to look up Peterson, we would first search the index to find the proper block. Our criterion is: "Is Peterson 'larger' [comes later in alphabetic order] than the last name in the block?" If the answer to this question is "yes," then we have to keep searching the index for a later block; if the answer is "no," we are in the correct block. Thus, in searching for Peterson, we would first match it against Davis. Asking whether Peterson is larger than Davis, we continue on to the next block. Again, Peterson is larger than Gherlik, so we move on to the next item in the index. Michaels is also smaller than Peterson, so we move on to Smith. Smith is larger than Peterson, so that the data record for Peterson must be situated in the block that ends with Smith. We take a look at the block number (Figure 9.10a), and proceed to search block 4 in the data file for the exact record (Figure 9.10b).

In the simplest case, we would search the data file sequentially, so that with a 200-record block, we will find the desired record within about 100 accesses of this data file. Explained in this fashion, the indexed sequential search is exactly the same as the block search, except that two files are involved, since we keep the index as a separate file. Thus, the mathematics we employed for the block search are applicable here: the optimum block size is $\sqrt{n}$, where n is the number of records in the file.

## Why Use an Indexed Sequential File?

At least one answer to this question comes from a consideration of storage media and their sizes. With a large file, the records are kept on some auxiliary storage medium, e.g., a disk. The size of each record and the size of the entire file would prohibit bringing the entire file into the main memory of the computer to be worked on. However, access to the main memory is much faster than access to auxiliary storage devices. Thus, we would like to have at least the "keys" in main memory, if not the entire file. Since the key is normally much smaller than the entire record, keeping the file of keys in main memory is entirely feasible. And, by including the disk address of the record along with the key

| Key | Disk address |
|-----|--------------|
| 783 | 10289 |

we have an indexed sequential organization. The index (or parts of it, if it is very large) is stored in main memory. The data file is stored on the auxiliary storage device.

With a block search, there is only one file, so that it is either in main memory in its entirety (if it is a small file), in which case we do not need an index; or on the auxiliary storage device in its entirety, in which case searching the keys takes considerably longer than searching an index in main memory. The benefit of the block search over the indexed sequential is that the block organization consumes no extra storage, having one file only in place of the two files constituting an indexed organization.

Improving Access Time: Levels of Indexing

Apart from the above discussion about the locus of the index, the search times of the indexed sequential approach can be improved by adding "extra indexes." The idea is to "cascade" the indexing, so that we have an index into the index into the data (Figure 9.11a).

With this scheme of indexing, we choose the cube root of the file size as our "block" instead of the square root. Thus, in our file of 1,000 items, we would have 1 index of 10 blocks pointing to another index of 10 blocks, which points to a data file of 10 records (Figure 9.11b).

In searching the file, if we are looking for record 256, we would search index 1 until we found the interval 201-300. This would direct us to the third block of index 2. We now search this block until we find the interval 251-260, which would direct us to the twenty-sixth block of the data file, which block consists of the following keys:

251
252
253
254
255
256
257
258
259
260

We would now search this block until we found record 256.

In our particular example (searching for record 256), it would take 3 accesses to find the correct interval (201-300) in index 1; 6 accesses to find the correct interval (251-260) in index 2; and 6 accesses to find the exact record (256) in the data file. Thus, we have expended 15 accesses in all.

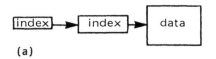

(a)

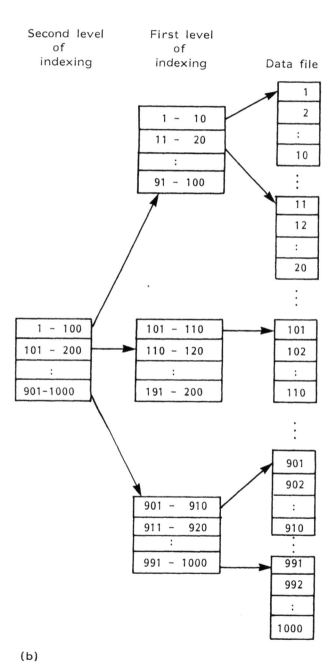

(b)

FIGURE 9.11

## The General Case

We can find the general formula for the worst case by an extension of the reasoning applied with a single level of index. With two levels of indexing, we simply use the cube root of the file size

$$\sqrt[3]{n}$$

To find the "worst case," we simply multiply this by 3

$$3 * \sqrt[3]{n}$$

Thus, for our example, we have a worst case of

3 * 10 = 30 accesses

The average case is

$$\frac{3 * (\sqrt[3]{n} + 1)}{2}$$

For our example, we have

$$\frac{3 * (10 + 1)}{2} = \frac{3 * 11}{2} = \frac{33}{2} = 16.5$$

The same reasoning can be applied to three, four, and even higher levels of indexing.

## Increased Minimal Seek Time

Besides the fact of extra storage consumption, cascading indexes also in-increases the minimum seek time. In both the sequential and the random access times, the minimum seek time is one access. This happens in the sequential file when the first record we look at happens to be the one we want (which is not very frequently). This happens as the normal rule in random access files, being violated only when collisions have occurred.

In indexed sequential files, we *never* get a minimum access time as low as one. In single-level indexing, our "luckiest" search would be a single access to the index, and a single access to the data file, for a minimum of two accesses. With two levels of indexing, our minimum is three accesses.

One method of attaining a faster access is "complete indexing," in which every record has an index entry. We may use such methods as hash-coding or the binary search in order to access the index, which would then direct us to the exact record on the secondary storage device.

## Some Practical Examples

The indexed sequential approach has been the organization employed by our library systems for years. The data files are the books on the shelf. The index is the card catalogue.

London (1973) gives an example of the cascading index used by the Greater London telephone directory. There are three levels of indexes into the data file, which consists of about 2 million subscibers.

The first level of indexing consists of four volumes, labeled A-D, E-K, L-R, and S-Z. These break down the list of 2 million people into 4 chunks of approximately 500,000 each. The next level of indexing consists of tabs within each volume, indicating the beginning of each alphabetical letter. Thus, volume A-D would have 4 tabs: A, B, C, and D. This would cut the 500,000 subscribers into blocks of approximately 125,000. The final level of indexing consists of page headings (Adams-Adamson), which list the first and last names on each page. This breaks our search into a block of a few hundred names, which we then search sequentially. (Actually, many people seem to take advantage of the alphabetical listing to perform a sort of block search, when they "scan" the page, others seem to flip "back and forth," somewhat like a binary search. In any case, the search is seldom strictly sequential until we get to a very small portion of the page, e.g., scanning P. Smith, Q. Smith, R. Smith, etc.)

## The General Trade-Offs: Storage Versus Processing

One of the major trade-offs in choosing a file structure is between storage space and processing time. For example, the sequential file wastes no extra storage. Both the random access and the indexed sequential organizations waste storage space: the random file uses extra storage to keep the file "a little bit empty"; the indexed sequential file uses storage for the extra index file. However, the search time for the sequential file involves more processing at the time of the search, accessing hundreds, even thousands of records. Both the random and the indexed sequential approaches result in less processing at search time, at least in the case of selective search.

In terms of maintaining the file, the unorganized sequential file presents fewer processing problems than any other organization (we simply add records to the end of the file; deletions are handled by moving everything up). The ordered sequential file requires somewhat more processing to keep the file in order (we must re-sort the file after adding new records; deletions are handled as in the unordered sequential, by simply moving the items up every now and then); however, the added organization allows us to find items more quickly. The random access file results in fewer maintenance problems than the ordered sequential when it does not encounter collisions; the only processing involved is the computation of the hash-code. However, if the file encounters a lot of "overflow," the processing problem can become much more complex. The indexed sequential approach requires the most work to "keep the file in order," since two files must be updated whenever new records are added to the file. However, the indexed sequential organization gives a "flexibility" (in both fast access and sequential processing) that is not present in the random organization (no sequential processing).

Insertions are particularly troublesome in the indexed sequential organization. They cause blocks to overflow and index entries to change. Several methods have been developed to handle this. One is to keep the blocks a little bit empty (see Martin, 1975). More complex techniques involve strategies that keep the index entries static (see Ullman, 1980).

The cost of the storage medium employed is another major factor. Sequential files may be stored on a sequential medium, such as magnetic tape; and may be searched sequentially, perhaps in a "batch" mode, at a lower cost than random access files. The random access files require direct access devices (usually at a higher cost), and are often searched "on-line" (also at a higher cost) in order to produce an "immediate" response, as in an airline reservation system.

The trade-offs encountered in designing the file structures for a data base are varied and numerous. We offer these considerations as samples of the problems to be faced. However, certain "general guidelines" for choosing file structures are available. These are discussed in the next section.

## Qualities to Be Considered in Selecting a File Structure

There are several qualities in any file that can give indications as to the type of structure we might choose. We will consider five of them

1. Activity
2. Volatility
3. Frequency of access
4. Volume or size
5. Response time required

## Activity

*Activity* refers to the question of how many of the records in a file are accessed whenever the file is processed? It is the quality we referred to when discussing "selective" versus "complete" retrieval.

A high-activity file is one that has complete or nearly complete retrieval whenever the file is processed. An example of a high-activity file is the "payroll" file, which is processed for every or almost every record in the file (someone may be laid off, on vacation, etc.; although these records would most likely be accessed to note this fact). Another example would be billing students for the courses they are taking; every student who is registered gets billed.

A low-activity file is one in which "selective" records, either one or a few, are accessed, while the rest of the records are not processed. An example is a checking account file: when you withdraw or deposit, only your record is selected to be processed out of all the bank's customers. Another example is the telephone "information" file. When someone asks for a person's phone number, we wish to select only that one record out of the myriad of telephone subscribers.

Files that have a "high activity," like the payroll file, are likely candidates for sequential access. This is because the entire file has to be processed anyway, so why not start at the beginning, and proceed to the end?

Files that are "low activity," like the checking account file, are likely candidates for random access. We would like to access the one single record, without accessing any other record. The "1 access" is the *raison d'etre* of random access files.

As usual, the indexed sequential is "in between." Its sequential organization allows for "high-activity" sequential processing, yet its lower access time makes it amenable to the selective processing characteristic of the random access files.

## Volatility

*Volatility* refers to the number of records deleted and added to a file. The records added are called *insertions*; the records deleted are simply called *deletions*.

Both the sequential and indexed sequential files are better in *low-volatility* situations (stable files; such as the file of bibliographic holdings in a library, or a file of data that has been collected in a scientific experiment), in which the amount of data is not expected to grow or diminish at all, but is simply being stored in order to be processed. This is because the files must be rearranged (re-sorted) whenever new records are inserted. Files that are high in volatility (additions and deletions occur frequently), such as a library circulation file (people taking books out are added to the file; people retruning books are deleted) are candidates for random access, since the records can be added and deleted "in any order," as the random access files do not preserve sequential order.

## Frequency of Access

The frequency of access refers to the question of how often we "query" the file. Some files are queried relatively infrequently, e.g., the payroll file, which might be queried only once a week, or the city-tax billing, which might be processed only twice a year. These "low-frequency-of-access" files are likely candidates for sequential processing, since we have an entire week (or six months) to get the file processed; we don't need a fast access.

Other files are queried very frequently. For example, an airline reservation file might be queried several times in a few minutes, likewise, a stock quotation file during the hours the market is open. If we are frequently accessing the file, an indexed sequential or random access approach is preferable, since we wish each of these frequent accesses to be as efficient as possible.

## Volume

The size of the file (number of records or number of characters) also is a strong determinant of type of file structure. Large files, like the New York directory of phone subscribers, cannot afford to waste much space. Hence, a sequential file, which wastes virtually no space, is indicated. Both the indexed method and the random access method waste storage; the indexed wastes it in building the extra index file, the random organization wastes it in keeping the file "a certain amount empty." Hence, if space is precious, sequential is the way to go.

In considering volume, another consideration is the "growth rate" of the file. If the file increases in size over time, both the size of the storage medium selected and the type of file organization must be selected with this in mind. The growth rate is also a consideration in the selection of codes, e.g., the choice of a 3-digit employee number allows for a maximum of 1,000 employees. Adding a fourth digit allows for expansion to 10,000 employees.

## Response Time

The time within which the file must respond to the user, i.e., the time it takes for us to get an answer, is also crucial to file design. For example, a fast answer (quick response, or "low response time") is just not possible with large sequential files (the average find rate of n/2 is too long). Both the indexed and the random approaches provide relatively fast response. Hence, if response time is critical (as in the telephone information service, or in the airline reservation system), we must go with indexed or random files. If the response can be somewhat slower, e.g., we ask for a person's resume, but don't need the answer for "a day or two," sequential access would be permissible. A good rule of thumb is that any response over a day would be considered for sequential access; in fact, any response over 10 or 15 minutes probably can be considered for sequential access.

## Conflicting Qualities

Very often the contents and processing of a particular file may lead to conflicting requirements. For example, the bank's checking account file might be huge (indicating sequential access), but the response required for a waiting customer must be immediate (indicating random access). In this particular example, the service to the customer (fast response) would probably overrule the factor of size (sequential, so no storage waste), and we would go with a random access organization. However, no general rule can be given; each case must be handled on its own unique characteristics.

## Programming Time

As we indicated earlier, another factor to be considered in choosing a file structure is the human time expended by the developer of the system. Complex file structures, such as indexed sequential and random access, require more programmer time than the simpler sequential organizations. In this day of rising human cost versus declining computer costs, a decision might be made to sacrifice searching efficiency (performed by machine) in order to optimize programming time (human effort). However, the development of software packages, such as ISAM (indexed sequential access method), by the hardware and software vendors has somewhat alleviated the programming problems. These packages are "ready-to-go," so that each organization does not have to develop all of its software from scratch.

## One-Time Versus Repeated Applications

In one-time applications, emergency jobs, or unique requests, the efficiency of the most elaborate file structures is not enjoyed often enough to justify the extra development time involved. These situations might best handled by a "quick and dirty" solution, often involving sequential storage structures.

However, repeated applications, e.g., the personnel file, which might be run weekly for years, will pay a hefty dividend in saved processing time if extra effort is expended in designing the files. These applications certainly justify the use of indexed sequential or random access methods. The rule of thumb is: "The more you use it, the better you should build it."

## Postscript: Equiprobable Versus Nonequiprobable Data

In this chapter, we have considered all the data items as if each was retrieved with equal probability. In fact, this is not always the case. Most often, certain data items are retrieved very frequently, other data items are retrieved less frequently. This nonequiprobable distribution of retrieval requests can be used to place the items requested most often at the front of an unordered sequential file. These items will be found more quickly, and the average search time will decrease. The worst search will still be incurred for some infrequent requests, but those will not hurt as badly because of their infrequency.

The same strategy can be applied to random access, not in accessing the file, since each item is to be accessed "independently of its physical location," but in its loading. When loading the file (putting in the initial records), we can insure that the frequently accessed items are loaded first. They will then reside in the "home" area, with the less frequently accessed records being relegated to the overflow area.

One example of a file that has "differential access" is the credit file of a department store. New recipients of credit cards seem to do much more buying than the older holder of a card. Thus, the data records for the new recipients should be placed at the head of the file; the older card holders placed at the rear. Another example is the "request for transcripts" by students who have graduated. Recent graduates may request more transcripts than older alumni, so their records should be kept more readily available. The redundancy in the request pattern enables us to optimize the file organization.

## Summary

In this chapter we have examined the three major styles of file organization: sequential, random access, and indexed sequential. We have seen that the sequential file can be divided into "ordered" and "unordered." The unordered organization requires very little effort in keeping the file organized, but it results in a long search time. The ordered organization (e.g., alphabetically sorted, ascending order) requires some extra effort in keeping the file organized, but enables us to take advantage of such search techniques as block or binary searches, which reduce the search time to a considerable extent.

The random access file attempts to reduce the search time to one access. It does this by performing some transformation on the key in order to "compute" the address at which the record will be (or is) stored. The only difficulty with maintaining the search time of "one access" is presented by collisions, i.e., when two or more records "hash" to the same address. In order to minimize the number of collisions, the data file is kept a "little bit empty," and research into "good algorithms" is carried out. A good algorithm is one that distributes the data evenly. One technique used in deriving such algorithms is a divisor consisting of a primary number. The major drawback of the random access file organization is that the data is not stored sequentially, so that the production of sequential lists is not an easy task.

The indexed sequential file organization attempts to compromise between the slow access time of the sequential file, and the nonsequential storage of the random access file. It consists of two files: the data file and the index. The data file is organized sequentially, so that the production of sequential reports is "routine"; furthermore, using the index reduces search time well below the sequential search. In fact, with some optimizing, a single-level index can approach a minimum seek time of "two accesses" as an average (if the file is fully indexed).

We have compared the best, worst, and average times for each type of organization. The best times are

| | |
|---|---|
| Sequential | 1 |
| Random | 1 |
| Indexed | 2 (for single-level; add 1 for each additional level) |

The worst times are

| | |
|---|---|
| Sequential | n |
| Random | about 10 for a file 90% full |
| Indexed | $2\sqrt{n}$ (single level) |

The average times are

| | |
|---|---|
| Sequential | $(n + 1)/2$ |
| Random | 2-3 or less for a file 70-90% full |
| Indexed | $\sqrt{n} + 1$ (single-level) |

We also gave figures for the block and binary searches

| Block: | minimum | 1 |
|---|---|---|
| | average | $\sqrt{n} + 1$ |
| | worst | $2\sqrt{n}$ |

| Binary: | minimum | 1 |
|---|---|---|
| | average | $(\log_2 n) - 1$ |
| | worst | $\log_2 n$ |

We have indicated that the choice of any one file organization involves trade-offs, e.g., storage space versus processing time. For example, the sequential file takes up less space than the indexed sequential, but involves more processing when retrieving records from the file. The indexed approach involves more processing in "maintaining" the file, since both the data file and the index must be "maintained" in order as new records are added. Maintenance of a sequential file involves only one file. The random access organization involves processing in computing the "hash-code," as well as in handling the overflow areas; however, it compensates for this by the faster access time.

All three file organizations face the problem of "overflow" records that do not fit into the main storage area. These records are usually handled by a separate storage area, although other techniques, e.g., the "next available location," are also possible.

We then considered some of the factors that influence us in the choice of a particular file organization: activity, volatility, frequency of access, volume, and response time. A highly active file is a candidate for sequential organization; a low-activity file is a candidate for the "selective" searching employed in the random access and indexed approaches. Volatile files tend toward random organization; nonvolatile toward sequential or indexed. Files that are frequently accessed tend toward random or indexed organization; less frequently accessed files may be sequential. Large files may require sequential organization, since it does not waste space, while both the random and indexed methods do. A fast response time indicates random access for the best response, with indexed being a possibility, but sequential files definitely ruled out. Programming time also enters the picture, as well as whether or not the application will be used repeatedly.

Finally, the distribution of requests for the data can be analyzed in order to take advantage of differential frequencies in designing the file.

## Related Readings

Beidler, John, *An Introduction to Data Structures*. Boston: Allyn and Bacon, Inc., 1982.

Bradley, James, *File and Data Base Techniques*. New York: Holt, Rinehart and Winston, 1982.

Flores, Ivan, *Data Structures and Management*, 2nd ed. Englewood Cliffs, NJ: Prentice-Hall, 1977.

Freeman, Donald E. and Berry, Olney R., *1/0 Design: Data Management in Operating Systems*. Rochelle Park, NJ: Hayden Book Company, Inc., 1977.

Gear, C. William, *Introduction to Computers, Structured Programming, and Applications: Module A: Applications and Algorithms in Computer Science*. Chicago: Science Research Associates, 1978.

Knuth, Donald E., *Sorting and Searching: The Art of Computer Programming*, Vol. 3. Reading, MA: Addison-Wesley, 1973.

Lefkovitz, David, *File Structures for On-Line Systems*. New York: Spartan Books, 1969.

Lewis, T. G. and Smith, M. Z., *Applying Data Structures*. Boston: Houghton Mifflin Company, 1976.

London, Keith R., *Techniques for Direct Access*. 1st ed. Philadelphia: Auerbach Publishers, 1973.

Martin, James, *Computer Data-Base Organization*. Englewood Cliffs, NJ: Prentice-Hall, Inc., 1975.

Martin, James, *Principles of Data-Base Management*. Englewood Cliffs, NJ: Prentice-Hall, Inc., 1976.

Maurer, Hermann A., *Data Structures and Programming Techniques*. Englewood Cliffs, NJ: Prentice-Hall, 1977.

Reingold, Edward, and Hansen, Wilfrid J., *Data Structures*. Boston: Little, Brown and Company, 1983.

Sedgewick, Robert, *Algorithms*. Reading, MA: Addison-Wesley, 1983.

Tenenbaum, Aaron, M. and Augenstein, Moshe J., *Data Structures Using Pascal*. Englewood Cliffs, NJ: Prentice-Hall, 1981.

Tremblay, J. P. and Sorenson, P. G., *An Introduction to Data Structures with Applications*. New York: McGraw-Hill, 1976.

Ullman, Jeffrey D., *Principles of Data-Base Systems*, 2nd ed. Potomac, MD: Computer Science Press, Inc., 1980.

Weiderhold, Gio, *Database Design*. New York: McGraw-Hill, 1977.

Weiland, Richard J., *Non-Numeric Methods: Phase 2 IS 202*. Chicago: Information Science Center, Illinois Institute of Technology, 1970.

# 10
# The Inverted File

## Objectives

Upon completion of this chapter, the reader should be able to

1. Explain the principle of the inverted file.
2. Given a data file, invert it on a specified field.
3. Explain the operations of the modifiers AND, OR, and NOT.
4. Perform various types of searches on the file, using the inverted indices.
5. Draw the Venn diagrams illustrating these searches.
6. Be familiar with the terminology of Boolean logic.

The three types of file organization we have studied so far (sequential, random, indexed) were based primarily on the key field. For example, in the sequential file, the data is searched by key. In the random access file, the key is used to compute the address of a storage location. In the indexed sequential file, the index is made up of the key and the address at which the data bearing that key is stored. In this chapter, we shall look at a file structure that emphasizes the content of the data over the key. What is important is the value stored in the data fields, rather than the address at which the data may be found. This type of file organization is referred to as an "inverted file."

## The Inverted File: Two Files

Like the indexed sequential approach, the inverted file consists of two or more files

1. The data file
2. One or more indexes into the data file

The major difference from the indexed sequential file is in the nature of the index, which is based on content rather than key.

## Storing the Data File Using the Traditional Methods

The data file is stored in any one of the three methods we have already treated: sequential, random, indexed sequential. For the sake of simplicity, we will assume that our data file is stored sequentially by key, i.e., in an ordered sequential organization.

The index will also be stored in one of the traditional methods. Again, we will assume an ordered sequential method, but this matter is best deferred until we see what the index looks like.

## Creating the Data File: An Example

The concept of an inverted file is best illustrated with an example. In order to create the example, we must start with a data file. The data file we will use is a variation of our wine file (Table 10.1), in which we have introduced certain simplifications in the interest of presenting a clear example. For example, the key field is now a three-digit numeric field, with consecutive values ranging from 001 through 006. Besides the key field there are four data fields: color, type, manufacturer, and price.

The key field will be used to store the data file. Using the ordered sequential method, with ascending key sequence, the file will be stored exactly as we have shown it.

One or more of the data fields may be selected to create an inverted index into the data file. One index is created for each data field chosen. We will begin with just one index, then expand to a more complex organization.

## Choosing the Data Field to Invert:
## What Questions Do You Want to Ask?

The data field that we choose to invert depends on the type of questions we will ask of the file. The inverted index facilitates quick access to the data file, so that the most frequently asked questions should have their "answers" inverted. We will assume that most people want the name of a red wine to go with meat or a white wine to go with fish, so that the average request will be on the order of "I want a white wine," or "What

TABLE 10.1

| Key | Color | Type | Manufacturer | Price |
|-----|-------|------|--------------|-------|
| 001 | Red | Burgundy | ABC | H |
| 002 | White | Chablis | U-Drink | H |
| 003 | Red | Beaujolais | U-Drink | L |
| 004 | Red | Burgundy | XYZ | H |
| 005 | White | Chablis | U-Drink | M |
| 006 | Red | Chianti | U-Drink | L |

red wines do you have?" Of course, connoisseurs might ask for such wines
as a Burgundy or a Chablis; economy-minded people might ask for "low-
priced" wines; and shareholders might patronize only one manufacturer,
e.g., U-Drink. However, we anticipate that these questions will be less
frequent than the questions about the color of the wine, so we will invert
on "color."

### Inverting the File

The process of inverting the file begins with a notation of each data value
that occurs in the field we are inverting. For our file, this consists of two
values: red and white. We now create one entry for each data value, noting
the data records that contain that value for that field. For example, in our
file, the value "red" appears on records 001, 003, 004, and 006

```
Key Color

001 Red    ←
002 White
003 Red    ←
004 Red    ←
005 White
006 Red    ←
```

We note this by creating the record Red 001, 003, 004, 006, where the
first field represents the data value, and the second field represents the
keys of documents in which the data value is found (Figure 10.1a). Note
that the number of records in which the data value appears can vary.
This field is "multiply occurring" (e.g., it appears four times here). However, the key itself is fixed length, since each record key is three digits
wide. Thus, we may have anywhere from one to many occurrences of a
fixed length numeric field.

   The record created for the data value "white" will have two record
occurrences: 002 and 005 (Figure 10.1b). The index thus looks like Figure
10.1c.

| Red | 001,003,004,006 |

Data value　　　　Records in which the data value is found

(a)

| White | 002,005 |

(b)

| Red | 001,003,004,006 |
| White | 002,005 |

(c)

FIGURE 10.1

288 · Section V: Storing the Data

If we look at a book as a data file, the index at the back of the book listing subjects and the pages on which those subjects are found, e.g.

Elephants 2, 103, 250-255

is an inverted index. (Note: Some refer to a single index on secondary values as a secondary index, reserving the term *inverted* for a file that has an index for each secondary field, i.e., is completely inverted.)

### The Number of Postings

The number of records attached to a particular data value is called the "postings" to that data value. Thus, the data value "red" has four records posted to it, and the data value "white" has two records posted to it. Because of the varying number of the multiply occurring field, it is useful to know how many postings are present for each data value.

We can use the "prefix" method of denoting variable length fields to do this. We simply add one more field to the index record: the postings field. Normally, this field will precede the rest of the record, as shown in Figure 10.2a. Because the record numbers are fixed length, and we know the number of postings, we can dispense with the commas in storing the record numbers (Figure 10.2b). We know that each group of three digits in the record numbers represents a new record number. However, for purposes of readability, we will include the commas in our discussion.

### Querying the File

The process of directing questions to our file now consists of the following four steps:

1. Formulate the question in terms of the values stored in the index file.

| Postings | Data value | Record number |
|---|---|---|
| 04 | Red | 001,003,004,006 |
| 02 | White | 002,005 |

(a)

| Postings | Data value | Record number |
|---|---|---|
| 04 | Red | 001003004006 |
| 02 | White | 002005 |

(b)

FIGURE 10.2

| Postings | Data value | Record number |
|----------|------------|---------------|
| 04 | Red | 001,003,004,006 |
| 02 | White | 002,005 |

(a)

| Key | Color | Type | Manufacturer | Price |
|-----|-------|------|--------------|-------|
| 001 | Red | Burgundy | ABC | H |
| →002 | White | Chablis | U-Drink | H |
| 003 | Red | Beaujolais | U-Drink | L |
| 004 | Red | Burgundy | XYZ | H |
| →005 | White | Chablis | U-Drink | M |
| 006 | Red | Chianti | U-Drink | L |

(b)

| Key | Color | Type | Manufacturer | Price |
|-----|-------|------|--------------|-------|
| 002 | White | Chablis | U-Drink | H |
| 005 | White | Chablis | U-Drink | M |

(c)

FIGURE 10.3

2. Look up the data value in the index file.
3. Use the record numbers listed in the index file to find the appropriate records in the data file.
4. Output these records as the response to the question.

For example, if someone asks "What white wines do you have?" look up "white" in the index (employing a random or sequential search; Figure 10.3a). This tells us that there are two postings for white: records 002 and 005. We next look for these records in the data file (employing a random search; Figure 10.3b). Having found the two relevant records, we output them as the response to the question (Figure 10.3c), whereupon the user of our system finds out that we have two white wines, both Chablis, both made by U-Drink, with one being expensive, the other medium-priced. Of course, in a real file, we might get many more "answers" to such a broad question, with several Chablis, several Sauternes, and several Rhines, each made by several manufacturers, with a variety of prices. The combinations are limitless, but the basic idea is sufficiently clear in the example.

We have chosen to use the sequential search in the index file, but would normally search the data file randomly, using the record number provided by the index as the key (address of the record.) The search of the index for "white" took two accesses

| 04 | Red | 001,003,004,006 |
| 02 | White | 002,005 (found in two accesses) |

and outputting the results would take two accesses (one for each record).

The search of the index can be optimized by choosing a more efficient search method. For example, in a larger index file we could choose to use a block search or a binary search. The index file would be stored in ordered sequential mode to allow this. As indicated, the data file could be accessed through random access. In fact, the determination of the record location from the key is extremely straightforward, in that the keys are numbered sequentially, beginning at one. Thus, the key and the relative position of the record are *exactly the same*. This enables us to go "directly" to the proper record once we know the key. That is, for key 004, we access the fourth record in the file. For key 006, we access the sixth record in the file. If the records are fixed length, this random access is quite straightforward, although it can also be achieved with variable length records. Using improved searches will shorten the response time.

## Some Terminology

The data items that we output in response to a question are called *hits*. Thus, in the previous example, we had two "hits," since two records were output. The question that is asked is called the *query*. The process of searching a data base is

1. Collecting the queries
2. Searching the index for data values matching the query
3. Outputting the "hits" corresponding to the records posted in the index item that matched

If no index item matches the query, we have no information in our file corresponding to that query. Or, we may not have indexed that information, although it might exist in the file. For example, if someone asks for a "high-priced wine," the information is in our file, but it is not indexed. Items that are not indexed cannot be easily accessed. However, they could be found by a thorough sequential search of each field in the file. This search would be time consuming, but would produce results. We will temporarily restrict ourselves to accessing the files only through the index, so that information not found in the index "does not exist in the file" for our purposes. When we ask a question, and the information is not there, we say that there are "zero hits."

## A Flowcharting of the Process

We can draw a simplified flowchart of the entire search and retrieval process, as shown in Figure 10.4.

## Questions About the Postings

In Figure 10.3, the user of the file asked for "white wines." If the question were phrased somewhat differently, i.e., if the user wanted to know

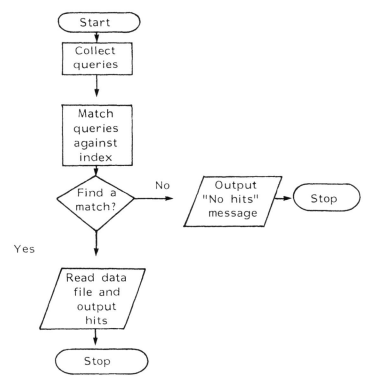

FIGURE 10.4

how many white wines we had, we could answer the question without ever consulting the data file. We would simply look up the index entry for white

    02      White        002,005

note that the number of postings is two

    02      White        002,005
    ↑
    Postings

and answer "two."

    The number of postings can be a guide to deciding whether or not we want to see the full output of the data items posted to our query. For example, in querying the *New York Times* data base about Conrail, I discover there are well over 300 postings. This would provide more output than necessary, and indicates that I should narrow my question to a more restricted topic. Of course, a low number of postings, e.g., zero or one, might indicate that I have asked too narrow a question and should broaden it.

### Increasing the Access Points: Creating More Indices

The data fields by which we can access the data file are called *access points*. In our example, we currently have one access point: the color of

| Postings | Data value | Record number |
|---|---|---|
| 01 | Beaujolais | 003 |
| 02 | Burgundy | 001,004 |
| 02 | Chablis | 002,005 |
| 01 | Chianti | 006 |

(a)

| Postings | Data value | Record number |
|---|---|---|
| 03 | H | 001,002,004 |
| 02 | L | 003,006 |
| 01 | M | 005 |

(b)

FIGURE 10.5

the wine. We can ask only one type of question, concerning whether the wine is red or white. This is somewhat restrictive. We would like to allow questions about the type of wine (Burgundy, Chablis, etc.) and the price of wine (high, medium, or low). In order to do so, we simply create another index for each additional access point.

The inversion of the field called "type" would result in the index shown in Figure 10.5a, in which the index is ordered sequentially by the type of field, using the alphabetical (or ascending) order. The index will be searched on this field (key). Note that the construction of the index converts multiply occurring values in the data file (e.g., Burgundy) into single (unique value) records in the index.

The inversion of the price field consists of only three index records, one for each possible price (Figure 10.5b). This file is also organized alphabetically by the data value (H, L, and M). (Note that in all inversions the total of the postings column equals the total number of documents. This is true in our example because no data item is posted to more than one index item. However, it is not true in the general case.)

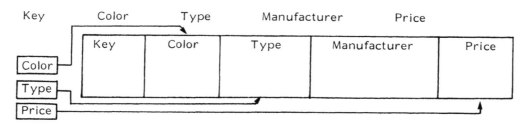

FIGURE 10.6

## Flexibility

We now have three indexes into the data file (Figure 10.6). Furthermore, we can access the data by key (if we know the key of the wine data we wish to access). In this case—access by primary key—we do not even have to consult the indices, which makes the access that much quicker.

Thus, we can request four types of information from the file. For example, we can make such requests as

1.  Please retrieve the data on wine 005.
2.  Create a list of the red wines.
3.  Which Burgundies do you carry?
4.  Do you have a cheap wine?

and get quick answers to all our questions. The addition of the extra indices has given us flexibility; we can attack the data from various points of view.

## Storage Versus Processing: A Recurring Theme

Of course, the flexibility and faster access time provided by the extra indices must somehow be paid for, and again, one expense is in the form of the extra storage space taken up by the indices. We have four files instead of one, which is like having four apartments spread throughout the city just so that we can lay our head wherever we happen to be; it's convenient, but the rent gets a little high. Furthermore, these indices have to be updated as we add or delete items from our stock, so that there is an overhead in organizing the files.

We still cannot readily answer questions about the manufacturer of the wines. As we have indicated, we can look up the manufacturers by searching the data file sequentially, but this is time consuming. Thus, the storage space saved in not inverting the manufacturer field is paid for by processing time incurred if someone asks "Which wines do you carry from ABC Distilleries?"

As an exercise, the student is encouraged to invert the file on the manufacturer field. This fourth and final index will give our file the ultimate in flexibility; we can ask questions about any field in the file. Of course, this ultimate in flexibility comes at the cost of the ultimate in storage expense: we have five files in order to access the five fields that were originally stored in a single file (Theoretically, we could dispense with the data file, since all field values are contained in the indices and are associated with the appropriate records. However, this is not usually done in practice, because the data files holds the attribute values in one place.)

## Combining the Questions

If we inverted the files simply to gain access to each field singly, i.e., to ask questions about only one field, the extra effort and storage space invested in the indices would really not be paying a good return. The main benefit of the inverted file comes when we begin to phrase questions that "combine the fields," i.e., when we ask such questions as

Searching
Color and Price

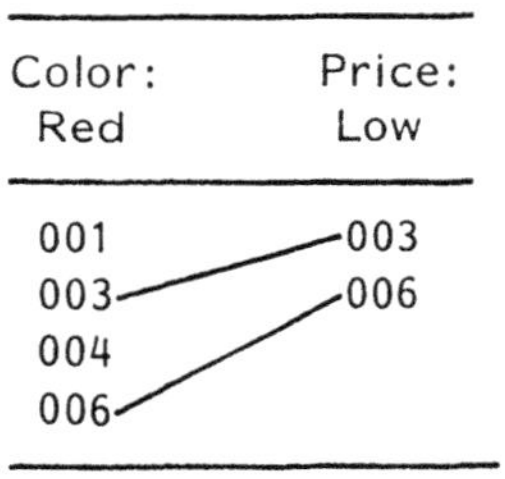

Color:          Price:
  Red             Low

  001          ─003
  003─         ╱006
  004      ╱
  006╱

FIGURE 10.7

1. Do you have a cheap red wine?
   or
2. Do you have a medium-priced Burgundy?

In order to answer such composite questions, we consult more than one in-dex. For example, in considering the first question we would first consult the index for color, then for price, and combine the results.

In consulting the index for color on the data value "red," we find four wines posted (i.e., there are four red wines)

    04      Red        001,003,004,006

We "save" the record numbers

    001
    003
    004
    006

and proceed to an examination of the index for price. Under the value "L" for "low" price, we find two wines posted

    02      L        003,006

We now compare these record numbers (003,006) with the record numbers for red wines (001,003,004,006), and find that two of the numbers occur in both lists (Figure 10.7). These two records, 003 and 006, are the an-swers to the request. We would output the records

    003     Red      Beaujolais    U-Drink    L
    006     Red      Chianti       U-Drink    L

and the user has a choice between Beaujolais and Chianti.

In handling the second request ("Do you have a medium priced Bur-gundy?"), we first examine the type of wine for Burgundy, finding

    02      Burgundy      001,004

We note the record numbers (001,004), and then proceed to consult the price file. Looking up "M" for medium, we find

    01      M        005

Comparing the two lists of record numbers

| Type: Burgundy | Price: Medium |
|----------------|---------------|
| 001<br>004 | 005 |

we see that they have *nothing in common*. No record in our data file satisfies both parts of the request; there are "no hits." We inform the person of the fact that we don't have a medium-priced Burgundy, and encourage him or her to try again.

## AND, OR, and NOT

The three most common ways in which fields are combined within questions are through the operators AND, OR, and NOT. The above questions

1. Do you have a cheap red wine?
2. Do you have a medium-priced Burgundy?

were both examples of AND questions. Although AND did not explicitly appear, it was implied. This can easily be seen by rephrasing the questions

1. Do you have a wine that is *both* red *and* cheap?
2. Do you have a Burgundy that is *also* medium priced?

In an AND question, *both* qualities must be present in order to satisfy the request. Thus, if we order "ham *and* eggs," we will not be satisfied with eggs alone, nor will we be satisfied with just ham; we must have *both* items in order to be satisfied.

The condition of both items being true for AND is sometimes summarized in the AND truth table (Figure 10.8a), where T stands for true, and F stands for false. The rows represent the "truth value" of item 1: thus, row 1 represents situations in which item 1 is true. Row 2 represents situations in which item 1 is false.

Item

Item 2

| And | T | F |
|-----|---|---|
| T | T | F |
| F | F | F |

Item 1

(a)

Item 2

| Or | T | F |
|----|---|---|
| T | T | T |
| F | T | F |

Item 1

(b)

FIGURE 10.8

The intersection of the row and column represent the truth value of the entire statement. Thus, the intersection of row 1 and column 1 indicates that both items are true. In this case, the truth value of the entire statement is true. This would be the case of both ham and eggs being present.

The intersection of row 1 with column 2 represents a case in which item 1 is true, but item 2 is false. Thus, we would have ham, but no eggs; in this case, the entire statement is false. The intersection of row 2 and column 1 means that item 1 is false, but item 2 is true. We have eggs, but no ham; in this case, we are not satisfied, and the entire statement is false.

Finally, the intersection of row 2 and column 2 represents a case wherein neither item is true. We have neither ham nor eggs, and we are certainly not satisfied. The entire statement is false.

In the AND truth table, the only true condition occurs when both items are true. Whenever one, or both, items are false, the entire statement is false.


## Combining Statements: OR

Besides the conjunction *and*, we can form compound questions with the connective *or*. OR statements are true if either one or both of the items involved are true. They are false *only* when *both* items are *false*. For example, if we say that we are going to have steak *or* lobster for dinner, our forecast is true if we have steak, but not lobster; it is also true if we have lobster, but not steak; and it is preeminantly true if we have "surf-and-turf" (both steak and lobster). The only condition under which our forecast would be false is if we have neither steak nor lobster, e.g., being forced to settle for peanut butter (Figure 10.8b).

In regard to our data file, a typical OR question might be "Do you have a Beaujolais or a Burgundy?

In order to answer this question, we would first examine the "type index" for Beaujolais, finding

    01       Beaujolais     003

We note the record number (003), and proceed to examine the type field for Burgundy. In looking up Burgundy, we find

    02       Burgundy     001,004

We note these record numbers (001,004), and combine these numbers with the numbers for Beaujolais (Figure 10.9). *All* of these records satisfy the

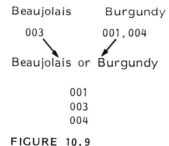

FIGURE 10.9

request. *None* contain both items, but the OR request does not demand that both items be present in every record; one is enough.

In fact, in our particular example, Burgundy and Beaujolais cannot possibly occur in the same record. However, other questions, such as "Do you have a wine that is either red or cheap?" might have instances of both items being true. In fact, this particular example does have such an instance.

In looking into the file for the query "red or cheap," we begin by consulting the color file, and finding

04      Red      001,003,004,006

We then look up cheap, and find

02      L      003,006

Wines 001 and 004 satisfy only one condition (red) and they are part of the "answer." Wines 003 and 006 satisfy both conditions, and they are also part of the answer. We would output all four wines: 001, 003, 004, and 006. Note that when one record key is repeated in the hit list, as in 003 and 006, we do not really repeat it; there is no surprise to outputting the same answer twice in a row.


## Narrowing Versus Broadening: AND Versus OR

We have mentioned earlier that sometimes we find too many hits, other times we find too few. When we find too many hits, we wish to "narrow" the output. When we find too few hits, we wish to "broaden" the search.

The conjunction *and* serves to narrow the search. This is because we are "imposing more restrictions" on the "hits." This can best be seen with an example. Suppose we are a personnel manager advertising a job opening. We advertise for a "body," any body. This might bring thousands of applicants (millions in hard times). However, we can narrow the number of applicants by adding that we want a "body with a college degree." We can further narrow the number of applicants by saying the college degree must be in engineering. We might now have 100 applicants. If we add the condition "female," this might dwindle to 50. Now we have a workable number.

The danger in adding AND conditions is that we can narrow the search so much as to exclude all hits. For example, if we add the condition that the "female, engineer, college graduate" must also have experience as a juggler in a carnival, all 50 applicants may disappear.

The principle is

1.  If there are too many hits, narrow the output by adding conditions in the AND mode.
2.  Do not add too many conditions, or there will be zero hits.

The connective OR works in the opposite direction. It *broadens* the search. If we have too few hits, we can turn to OR. Again, an example will illstrate the principle.

Let us suppose that our personnel manager asks for a person who has experience in both electrical engineering *and* art history. He might get one applicant, if he is lucky. But, suppose he now changes his ad to read "electrical engineering *or* art history"; now thousands of electrical engineers may apply; and so may thousands of art history majors. The personnel manager has broadened the scope of his search.

For OR, the principle is

1. If the output is too small, broaden the search by adding OR conditions.
2. Beware of too many OR conditions, or you will be deluged with output.

### Narrowing the Search: NOT

Another method of narrowing a search is to use the exclusion NOT. For example, we may have something against ABC Distilleries; maybe they once sold us a spoiled wine. Thus, we wish to exclude their wines from our list. We are seeking a red wine, so that we ask, "Do you have a red wine, *but not* one made by ABC?"

In order to answer this request, we first consult the index for red wines, and find

    04       Red       001,003,004,006

We then check the list of manufacturers (which the student has built), and find the entry for ABC

    02       ABC       001

We now compare the lists of record numbers, crossing off any of the "red" record numbers that are also found on the ABC list (Figure 10.10), so that we output only records 003, 004, and 006 as "hits" for this request.

| 003 | Red | Beaujolais | U-Drink | L |
| 004 | Red | Burgundy | XYZ | H |
| 006 | Red | Chianti | U-Drink | L |

As in the case of AND, the modifier NOT narrows the search. Thus, the general rule is

1. If there are too many hits, use AND or NOT to narrow the search.
2. If there are too few hits, use OR to broaden the search.

The truth table for NOT is somewhat different from the truth table for AND or OR. This is because NOT involves only one item. The truth table is shown in Figure 10.11.

Thus, if item 1 (the only item) is true, NOT makes it false. If item 1 is false, NOT makes it true. NOT always turns the truth value of an item to its opposite.

```
    Searching
RED NOT ABC

  Color                     Manufacturer
  RED                           ABC

 001    ◄------------------ 001
 003
 004
 006
```

FIGURE 10.10

|        | Not | Final truth value |
|--------|-----|-------------------|
| Item 1 | T   | F                 |
|        | F   | T                 |

FIGURE 10.11

The truth table for NOT is less useful in interpreting information retrieval applications than the tables for AND and OR. A better model is
"subtraction," since we "subtract out" the hits that we do not want. However, we can interpret this process as "turning the hits into nonhits,"
i.e., changing the "hit value" of the record number into its opposite. In
practice, query languages allow such queries as "red not high" (R-H),
but not simply "not high" (-H) since the use of NOT as a prefix to a
single term will usually result in too many hits.

**Another Example**

In the wine file, the set of data values is mutually exclusive, i.e., if a
wine is red, it cannot be white; if it is cheap, it cannot be medium or high
priced; if it is a Burgundy, it cannot be a Beaujolais; if it is made by U-
Drink, it is not made by ABC. Not every file of data is so arranged. Very
often, the data values for a particular field "overlap." In order to illustrate
this, let us consider another example, a modified "personnel" file. The file
shows the employee's number, name, and work experience. Thus, a typical
record looks like

      Field 1: Emplyee number:   001
      Field 2: Employee name:    Smith, Roger
      Field 3: Work experience:  Engineer, computer operator, accountant

Notice that this record "grows vertically" rather than horizontally. There
is no inherent reason why the fields of a record must be presented horizontally, as in the wine file, although this is a common case.
    We will consider our file to comprise only three records. These records
are separated from each other by the symbol #, denoting the "end of the
record." The symbol ## indicates the end of the file. The entire file of
three records looks like Figure 10.12. Note that we have abbreviated the
field descriptors to F1, F2, and F3, for field 1, field 2, and field 3. We
have also eliminated the "descriptor name" of the field, i.e., the words
*employee number, employee name,* and *work experience.* These names would
not be stored with the data, but would be described in separate documentation or a separate file.
    Field 1 is the "key" to this data file. In fact, we have stored the file
in ascending order on this key. There are two data fields: employee name
and work experience. We can invert the file on either or both of these
fields.
    If we choose to invert on the "last name" only, the inversion would be

Last Name Index

| 01 | Jones | 002     |
|----|-------|---------|
| 02 | Smith | 001,003 |

```
F1)   001
F2)   Smith, Roger
F3)   electrician, computer operator, accountant
#
F1)   002
F2)   Jones, William
F3)   electrician, carpenter
#
F1)   003
F2)   Smith, Mary
F3)   accountant, foreman
#
##
```

FIGURE 10.12

which indicates that we have one employee named Jones, and two employees named Smith. Note that if we are inverting on the last name only, we cannot distinguish between Roger Smith and Mary Smith in the index.

In the last name index, each employee has only one entry, one last name. This is not true of our work experience index. A single employee may have experience in any number of occupations; it is a multiply occurring field. Thus, employee 1 was an electrician; he was also a computer operator. Having one experience does not exclude the other experience; thus, we can have overlapping data values in the field for work experience.

Creating the inverted index for work experience, we take each job in order, and see how many employees fit that job description. Thus, the first type of experience is electrician (since this is the first job description listed under employee 1). We see that two employees have experience as electricians, employees 001 and 002, so that electrician will have two postings:

    02      Electrician       001,002

The next job description, computer operator, has only one employee

    01      Computer operator      001

We then have accountant, with two postings

    02      Accountant       001,003

We have now considered all of employee 1's work experiences, and move on to employee 2. The first work experience listed under employee 2 is electrician, which has already been considered. We do *not* consider it again. We move on to the second job description, carpenter, which has one posting:

    01      Carpenter       002

This finishes employee 2, so we move on to employee 3. Under employee 3, the job description "accountant" has already been handled, so we move on to foreman, which has one posting:

    01      Foreman       003

Thus, our entire index now looks like Figure 10.13a.

| Work experience index |
|---|
| 02  Electrician 001,002 |
| 01  Computer Operator 001 |
| 02  Accountant 001,003 |
| 01  Carpenter 002 |
| 01  Foreman 003 |

(a)

| Work experience |
|---|
| 02  Accountant 001,003 |
| 01  Carpenter 002 |
| 01  Computer Operator 001 |
| 02  Electrician 001,002 |
| 01  Foreman 003 |

(b)

FIGURE 10.13

While we could search the index in this order, it is more customary to sort the index on the field that is the key. Since this is "work experience," our sorted index would look like Figure 10.13b. Note that in this index, a record number may be repeated on more than one index entry. This is what we mean by "overlap." In the wine file, this "overlap" was not present. For example, we have the index for color

Color

| 04 | Red | 001,003,004,006 |
| 02 | White | 002,005 |

The trait "color" *partitions* the wine file. This means that a wine in one "part" of the file (e.g., red) *cannot* also be in another part of the file (e.g., white). The work experience index is *not* a partition. Thus, the fact that a person was an electrician does *not exclude* that same person from having experience as a computer operator. This "nonexclusivity" of the descriptors enables us to use the modifiers AND, OR, and NOT within the same index (in the wine file, we used the operators AND and NOT only to combine the results from *two or more* indices).

Let us proceed with an example. Suppose management has a need for an employee who has been both a computer operator and an accountant (possibly to keep the books in the data processing center). We can query our work index for

Computer operator "and" accountant

Searching the index for "computer operator," we find that employee 1 fills the bill for this requirement (Figure 10.14a). Now, consulting the

```
   02  Accountant 001,003
   01  Carpenter 002
→ 01  Computer Operator 001
   02  Electrician 001,002
   01  Foreman 003
```

(a)

```
→ 02  Accountant 001,003
   01  Carpenter 002
```

(b)

| Computer Operator | Accountant |
|---|---|
| 001 | 001 |
|  | 003 |

(c)

FIGURE 10.14

Computer
Operator                      Accountant

   001                              001
                             003

Computer Operator or Accountant

         001
         003

FIGURE 10.15

same index for "accountant," we find that employees 1 and 3 fill this half of the bill (Figure 10.14b). Thus we have the result shown in Figure 10.14c.

Since AND demands what is "common" to both lists, only employee 001 fills the bill, and we would output his record

F1)   001
F2)   Smith, Roger
F3)   electrician, computer operator, accountant

and management can give Roger Smith a call.

If we had asked for computer operator OR accountant, both records 001 and 003 would have been output (Figure 10.15).

The request for computer operator but NOT accountant would result in *no output*, since the only computer operator (employee 1) is also an accountant. However, a request for "accountant but NOT computer operator" would result in outputting the name of employee 3, since she appears on the accountant list, but not on the computer operator list.

### Some Terminology: Mathematics and Logic

The process of information retrieval is very often described in a mathematical way. This type of representation facilitates a formal study of the field that is not so readily possible with a verbal description. Because of this fact, an acquaintance with the various mathematical and logical systems used to describe the information retrieval process is a necessity for anyone seriously interested in the field. We close this chapter with a consideration of some of these representations.

### Arithmetic Versus Logical Operations

The modifiers AND, OR, and NOT have many similarities to the arithmetic operations of addition, subtraction, multiplication, and division. For example, in addition, the form of the basic operation is

$$5 + 4 = 9$$

where the + is called an *operator*, because it does something, or "operates" on some data items. The numbers, 5 and 4, that are operated on are called the *operands*, and the operation of the operator on the operands causes a result, the sum 9.

The situation is parallel in the case of AND. We have an operator and two operands

Ham and eggs

with a resulting "truth value," which is either "true," if both operands are true, or "false," if one or both operands are false.

The major difference between the arithmetic operations and the operators AND, OR, and NOT is in the nature of the items operated on. The arithmetic operators act on "numbers." The operators AND, OR, and NOT act on "truth values." Because of this difference in the nature of the operands, the operators like + are called *arithmetic operators*, while the operators like AND are called *logical operators*.

In fact, our example of "ham and eggs," simplified for pedagogical reasons, somewhat clouds the nature of the logical operations. The logical operators do not act on simple items like ham and eggs, but on entire statements (or expressions), such as

"I was served ham" AND "I was served eggs."

Thus, each operand is a statement that is either true or false. If the waiter or waitress brought the ham, the first statement is true; if he or she did not bring the ham, it is false. If he or she brought the eggs, the second statement is true; if not, it is false. Thus, each statement has its own "truth value." The operator AND then combines the two truth values of the individual statements. It does this according to the rules of the AND truth table. Thus, only if both individual statements are true will the truth value of the resulting combined statement also be true.

In dealing with our wine data base, a question such as

"Which cheap red wines do you have?"

is actually a condensation of the request: "I want a wine about which both of the following statements are true":

"This wine is red." AND "This wine is cheap."

Only data items that satisfy both parts of the request are retrieved from the file.

In dealing with OR, only one of the two individual statements must be true. Thus, if the OR statement is composed of the two parts

"This wine is good." OR "This wine is inexpensive."

the combined truth value will be "true" if "The wine is good," "The wine is inexpensive," or "The wine is both good and inexpensive." The combined truth value will be "false" if both individual statements are false, i.e., if we can say both of the following:

"The wine is not good." AND "The wine is not inexpensive."


## Binary Operators Versus Unary Operators

The operators AND and OR operate on *two* operands, *two* individual statements

| Statement 1 | Operator | Statement 2 |
|---|---|---|
| The wine is good. | AND, OR | The wine is inexpensive. |

For this reason, they are called *binary* operators.

The arithmetic operators of addition, subtraction, multiplication, and division are also binary operators, acting on two operands

| Operand 1 | Operator | Operand 2 |
|---|---|---|
| 4 | + | 5 |

The operator NOT acts on only one statement. For this reason, it is called a *unary* operator. For example, if we have the statement

"It is raining."

The operation NOT on this statement

| Operation | Statement |
|---|---|
| NOT | "It is raining." |

will yield the final statement

"It is not raining."

Thus, NOT reverses the truth value of the statement.

Because it is a unary operator, NOT is similar to the negative sign in arithmetic

$-4$

which "changes" the value of the number 4, a "positive value," to its opposite, the negative 4. Both the positive and negative signs of arithmetic are unary operators.

It is because of the fact that NOT is a unary operator, while AND and OR are binary operators, that the truth table for NOT appears different from the truth tables for AND and OR. The truth table for NOT involves only one data item, while the truth tables for AND and OR involve two data items.

## Boolean Algebra

Just as there is an arithmetic and an algebra for dealing with ordinary numbers, there is an arithmetic and an algebra for dealing with truth

AND (*) TABLE

1 * 1 = 1
1 * 0 = 0
0 * 1 = 0
0 * 0 = 0

FIGURE 10.16

values. The name of this "algebra of truth" is Boolean algebra, or Boolean logic. The name derives from George Boole, a mathematician who developed the concept of Boolean algebra in the nineteenth century.

As we have multiplication tables in arithmetic

1 * 1 = 1
1 * 2 = 2
1 * 3 = 3
   .
   .
1 * 9 = 9

there is a multiplication table for AND in Boolean algebra. The table is exactly the same as the "truth table" for AND, with the exception that the symbols used are 1 and 0 instead of T and F. The 1 can be interpreted as "true," the 0 as "false." Also, the AND is replaced by the multiplication symbol, the asterisk (*). The table is shown in Figure 10.16. The parallel between the Boolean 1, 0, and *, and the truth table composed of T, F, and AND can be easily seen by placing the two in adjacent tables (Figures 10.17a and b).

The table for OR is similar to the truth table for OR, using the symbols 1, 0, and the plus sign (+) for OR. Again, we place the tables in parallel, Figures 10.17c and d. Thus, AND is seen as related to multiplication (*), while OR is seen as related to addition (+). In fact, the Boolean multiplication table is exactly the same as the traditional arithmetic table, if we restrict the arithmetic table to the two symbols (1 and 0). The Boolean OR is similar to the addition table of arithmetic, with one exception

"*" Table           "And" Table

1 * 1 = 1           T "and" T = T
1 * 0 = 0           T "and" F = F
0 * 1 = 0           F "and" T = F
0 * 0 = 0           F "and" F = F

(a)                 (b)

"+" Table           "Or" Table

1 + 1 = 1           T "or" T = T
1 + 0 = 1           T "or" F = T
0 + 1 = 1           F "or" T = T
0 + 0 = 0           F "or" F = F

(c)                 (d)

FIGURE 10.17

$$1 + 1 = 1$$

in Boolean algebra, whereas it equals 2 in traditional arithmetic. The symbol 2 does not exist in Boolean arithmetic.

The symbol used for NOT in Boolean logic is the negative sign (−). The Boolean table and the truth tables for NOT are

| "−" Table | NOT Table |
|---|---|
| −1 = 0 | NOT T = F |
| −0 = 1 | NOT F = T |

The mathematics of Boolean algebra is often used to study information retrieval in a formal manner, and the interested student is encouraged to pursue its study through references at the end of the chapter.

## Combining Operations: The Order of Operations

Just as in arithmetic, we can create statements that involve more than one operation

$$6 + 5 * 3 = 21$$

We can likewise create statements involving more than one Boolean operator

I want a wine that is red and cheap or medium-priced.

Before answering this request, we must know which operation to perform first. If we do the AND first, we will get a different answer than if we do the OR first. In fact, doing the AND first is equivalent to asking for a wine that is

(Red and cheap) or medium-priced

Consulting our files for red and cheap, we would find records 003 and 006. Then, consulting our files for "medium," we find a white Chablis, record 005. Since, in an OR question, all possible answers are included in the output, we would output

| 003 | Red | Beaujolais | U-Drink | L | (red and cheap) |
| 005 | White | Chablis | U-Drink | M | (medium priced) |
| 006 | Red | Chianti | U-Drink | L | (red and cheap) |

If we perform the OR operation first, the question is equivalent to requesting a wine that is

Red and (cheap or medium priced)

i.e., our question is restricted to only red wines.

In consulting our file for cheap or medium-priced wines, we find 003, 005, and 006. Consulting the file for red, we find records 001, 003, 004, and 006. Since AND demands that we look for what the lists have in common (Figure 10.18), we would output only the records for the cheap Beaujolais and the cheap Chianti, not outputting the medium-priced Chablis.

The use of parentheses can eliminate any questions about the order in which operations are done. The item enclosed in parentheses is done first. However, not every retrieval system allows such use of parentheses, and in that case, we need to know the order of operations. The traditional order in Boolean algebra is

```
Cheap or
Medium          Red

003             001
005             003
006             004
                006
```

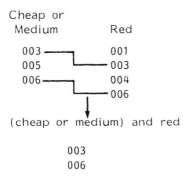

```
Cheap or
 Medium         Red

  003 ──────┐   001
  005       └── 003
  006 ──────┐   004
            └── 006
            │
            ▼
(cheap or medium) and red

      003
      006
```

FIGURE 10.18

1. NOT is done first
2. then AND
3. OR is done last

However, this order is frequently changed by a particular implementation. For example, one bibliographic retrieval system developed at the University of Pittsburgh executes the operations in the order:

1. OR
2. AND
3. NOT

The order in which the Boolean operations occur should be part of the documentation of any information retrieval system, and the user of such a system is encouraged to consult that documentation.

## Venn Diagrams: Another Representation

Another representation used to discuss information retrieval is the Venn diagram, which can supply a pictoral representation, either of the entire data base or of parts of the data base. For example, in the wine data base,

Wine Data Base

```
┌─────────────────────────────────────────────┐
│           001           003                   │
│  005             006             002          │
│           004                                 │
└─────────────────────────────────────────────┘
```

FIGURE 10.19

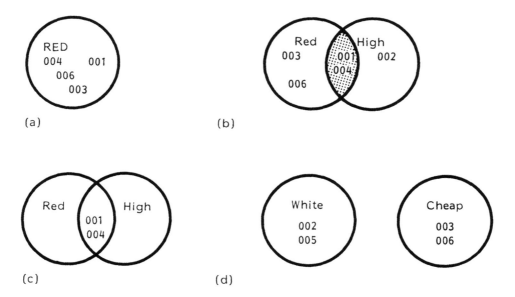

FIGURE 10.20

the picture of the entire data base would be as shown in Figure 10.19, in which the numbers represent the records in the data base. The representation of the entire data base is called the "universe" in the terminology of Venn diagrams. The universe consists of all the items we are talking about.

Besides depicting the universe, we can depict any one part of the data base. This is often done with circles, in contradistinction to the rectangle used to describe the universe. For example, the depiction of that portion of the data base described by the adjective "red" would be as shown in Figure 10.20a, which indicates that record numbers 001, 003, 004, and 006 contain information about red wines.

By combining more than one diagram, we can illustrate the operations of AND and OR (e.g., Figure 10.20b). The circle labeled "red" indicates that records 001, 003, 004, and 006 are red wines. The circle labeled "high" encompasses records 001, 002, and 004, indicating that these are all high-priced wines.

The operation of AND demands that we find what both circles have in common. This is represented by the "intersection" of the two circles (Figure 10.20b). Thus, records 001 and 004 represent wines that are both red and high priced (Figure 10.20c). Note that the shaded area indicates the hits, a common practice in dealing with Venn diagrams.

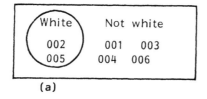

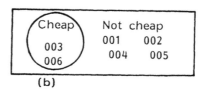

FIGURE 10.21

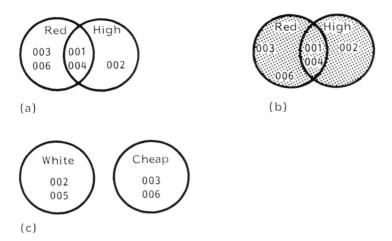

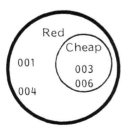

FIGURE 10.22

If the two circles have nothing in common, the response to AND would be "There is nothing in the data base satisfying your request," or "no hits." For our wine data base, this would be exemplified by Figure 10.20d. Wines 002 and 005 are white; wines 003 and 006 are cheap; but there is no wine that is both "white and cheap." We say that the intersection of the two circles is "null," i.e., it contains no "elements."

The concept of NOT is shown by using both the universe and one "subject" circle (Figure 10.21a). Of course, in our data base, "not white" represents "red." This is because this field has only two values. However, we also can have the categories shown in Figure 10.21b.

Like AND, the concept of OR requires two circles, because it is a binary operator. However, the results of combining the areas is different. If we return to the two circles we used to illustrate AND (figure 10.22a), we find the OR condition by including *every* number included in either one of the circles or both. The entire area of each circle is a "hit" (Figure 10.22b). Thus, all the records

001
002
003
004
006

FIGURE 10.23

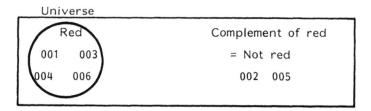

FIGURE 10.24

are correct responses to the query. The record 005 is the only record not included, since it is neither "red" nor "high priced." (Note that the records in the intersection are listed only once.)

In the OR condition, even circles that do not overlap result in hits. Thus, in our second example (Figure 10.22c), records 002, 003, 005, and 006 are all hits. We can get "zero hits" in the OR condition only if both circles are empty.

One final example will show the relationship of Venn diagrams to the branch of mathematics and logic called "set theory." If we depict the circles for both "red" and "cheap," we will find that all the records contained in "cheap" are also contained in the circle for "red" (Figure 10.23). Thus, records 001 and 004 are red, but not cheap. Records 003 and 006 are both "red" and "cheap." There are *no* wines that are "cheap" and "not red." This is evidenced by the fact that the entire circle for "cheap" is included in the circle for "red." We say that the wines that are "cheap" are a *subset* of the wines that are "red."

The term *subset* is borrowed from set theory, as are the terms *intersection*, *universe*, *null set*, and *element*. Two further terms are *union* and *complement*. The union denotes the joining of all elements of one "set" (one circle) with the elements of another set (OR). The set is the circle. Complement denotes the concept of NOT in set theory. The complement is the piece of the universe that fits with our set in order to make the entire universe (Figure 10.24).

The disciplines of Boolean logic, Venn diagrams, and set theory are *homomorphic*, homo- meaning the same, and -morphic meaning form. They have the "same form." Thus, results gleaned in any one of the three studies can be applied to the other two. The results of information retrieval are often expressed in any one, or any combination, of the three different representations.

## Single Aspect Versus Multiple Aspect Searches

Questions that enquire about a single data value, such as

"Do you have a *red* wine?"

are called "single aspect" searches.

Questions that involve more than one data value, such as

"Do you have a wine that is *red and cheap*?"

are termed "multiple aspect" searches.

Questions that involve the modifiers AND and OR are necessarily "multiple aspect," since these operators are *binary*.

Questions that involve either no modifier, or involve the *unary* operator NOT, with no other modifiers

"Do you have a wine that is *not red?*"

are single aspect.

## Summary

In this chapter, we have examined the inverted file organization. We have seen that the inverted file consists of two or more files: one, the data file, and the other(s), the index (or indices) into the data file.

The file may be inverted on any data field. However, the question of which data field to invert is answered by determining which questions we wish to ask of the data. The most frequently asked questions are the likely candidates for inverting the file on that data field.

Once the file is inverted, we can ask various questions of it, using either a "single" aspect or a "multiple" aspect search. The single aspect search inquires about one data value, e.g., "Do you have a *red* wine?" The multiple aspect search inquires about more than one value, e.g., "Do you have a wine that is *red and cheap?*" or "Do we employ someone who has experience as either an *electrician or* an *accountant?*"

The modifiers AND, OR, and NOT are called Boolean operators, or "logical" operators. The word *logic* comes from the fact that these operations work on truth values rather than numbers.

There is an entire area of logic and mathematics that deals with Boolean algebra, and this area is homomorphic to the study of both Venn diagrams and portions of set theory.

## Related Readings

Boole, George, *The Laws of Thought*, New York: Dover Publications, Inc., 1953.

Bradley, James, *File and Data Base Techniques*, New York: Holt, Rinehart and Winston, 1982.

Hafstrom, John E., *Basic Concepts in Modern Mathematics*, Reading, MA: Addison-Wesley, 1961.

Heaps, H. S., *Information Retrieval: Computational and Theoretical Aspects*, New York: Academic Press, 1978.

Hoernes, Gerhard E. and Heilweil, Melvin F., *An Introduction to Boolean Algebra and Logic Design: A Program for Self-Instruction*, New York: McGraw-Hill, 1964.

Hughes, John L., *Digital Computer Lab Book*, Nashua, NH: Digital Equipment Corporation, 1968.

Jackson, Ken, *Primer: System 1022: Data Base Management System*, Cambridge, MA: Software House, 1982.

Kemeny, John G., Snell, J. Laurie, and Thompson, Gerald L., *Introduction to Finite Mathematics*, 3rd ed. Englewood Cliffs, NJ: Prentice-Hall, 1974.

Kent, Allen, *Information Analysis and Retrieval*, 1st ed. New York: John Wiley & Sons, 1971.

Kertz, George J., *The Nature and Application of Mathematics*, Santa Monica, CA: Goodyear Publishing Company, 1979.

Kinsolving, May Risch, *Set Theory and the Number Systems*, Scranton, PA: International Textbook Company, 1967.

Lancaster, F. W. and Fayen, E. G., *Information Retrieval On-Line*, Los Angeles, CA: Melville Publishing Company, 1973.

Lefkovitz, David, *File Structures for On-Line Systems*, New York: Spartan Books, 1969.

Lewis, T. G. and Smith, M. Z., *Applying Data Structures*, Boston: Houghton Mifflin Company, 1976.

London, Keith R., *Techniques for Direct Access*, 1st ed. Philadelphia: Auerback Publishers, 1973.

Martin, James, *Computer Data-Base Organization*, Englewood Cliffs, NJ: Prentice-Hall, 1975.

Martin, James, *Principles of Data-Base Management*, Englewood Cliffs, NJ: Prentice-Hall, 1976.

Reingold, Edward M. and Hansen, Wilfrid J., *Data Structures*, Boston: Little, Brown and Company, 1983.

Salton, Gerard and McGill, Michael J., *Introduction to Modern Information Retrieval*, New York: McGraw-Hill, 1983.

Theodore, Chris A., *Boolean Algebra and Digital Computers*, Columbus, OH: Charles E. Merrill Publishing Co., 1969.

Tremblay, J. P. and Sorenson, P. G., *An Introduction to Data Structures with Applications*, New York: McGraw-Hill, 1976.

Ullman, Jeffrey D., *Principles of Database Systems*, 2nd ed. Potomac, MD: Computer Science Press, Inc., 1980.

Weiland, Richard J., *Non-Numeric Methods: Phase 2 IS 202*, Chicago: Information Science Center, Illinois Institute of Technology, 1970.

Whitesitt, J. Eldon, *Boolean Algebra and Its Applications*, Reading, MA: Addison-Wesley, 1961.

Wiederhold, Gio, *Database Design*, New York: McGraw-Hill, 1977.

# VI
# Retrieving the Data

The purpose of storing data is retrieval; i.e., we anticipate that the data will need to be retrieved at some future date. Such future needs may be predictable and periodic, in which case standard programming approaches to data processing are applicable (e.g., the development of software to do payroll, yearly financial reports, and inventories). These uses fall in the category of data manipulation, which is discussed in Section IX. Other future needs are less predictable and require data or information on demand. In this section we look at two types of query systems that have been developed to produce information on demand: bibliographic information retrieval systems and data base management systems (DBMSs).

Both types of systems interact with data bases, but the type of data held in the data base varies. Bibliographic information retrieval systems provide access to journal literature and research reports. They are analogous to online libraries. The user of the system describes a topic of interest, say articles on the use of light wave technology in medicine, and the system attempts to produce documents or "document surrogates" (abstracts) on the subject. The documents are often described by index terms, i.e., descriptors of "key words," and the user of the system must phrase his or her requests in the language of the system. Questions of relevance arise in that some retrieved documents are judged to be "about" the topic of interest, and are called "hits," while others are judged to be either peripheral to those interests or not relevant at all, and are called "noise." Systems are judged in terms of the relevance of the output and its completeness (in terms of the number of relevant documents returned). Several query languages are examined (PIRETS, a University of Pittsburgh "local system," and three commercial query languages, ORBIT, DIALOG, and BRS) in order to show the common features of such query languages.

The use of numerical data bases by the vendors traditionally involved in supplying bibliographic data bases has increased to the point that these have become topics of concern in themselves. However, we treat only the use of more fact-oriented data bases in the discussion of DBMSs as they are found in computer science and business applications.

DBMSs are treated from the user's of view. The theory of the various data models (hierarchical, network, relational) is left to a later course. The use of the DBMS is addressed in two stages, corresponding to the data description language (DDL) and the data manipulation language (DML). The DDL is used to describe the data (data types and lengths, key fields). Then, when the data has been described, records are added, either in batches or interactively "one at a time." Besides "loading" the data base (batch phraseology) or adding records (online additions), the query language (DML) can be used to find or delete data or to update (change) data values. Finally, most DBMSs allow for numerical manipulation of the data, obtaining totals, averages, standard deviations, and minima and maxima, as well as user-defined calculations.

# 11
# Information Retrieval Systems

## Objectives

Upon completion of this chapter the reader should be able to

1. Distinguish between query languages and data bases
2. Use an information retrieval system, if at all possible
3. Distinguish between the "hits" reported by a system and truly relevant documents
4. Define relevance and recall and explain the relationship between the two
5. Calculate the recall and precision for a given set of search results
6. Explain the term *growth of knowledge*
7. Illustrate the common elements among search systems, e.g., formulating search strategies, selecting data bases, obtaining a history of strategies, looking at the index terms or key words, and printing the results

We have necessarily begun the study of information retrieval while considering the storage of data. This is because the selection of the storage structure is made in conjunction with the selection of the retrieval mechanisms. We now concentrate on two methods of retrieving data that have become popular: information retrieval systems and data base management systems (DBMSs).

## Information Retrieval Systems

An information retrieval system, in the sense considered here, is a computer program that allows a person ("user") to search a data base by submitting terms that describe the information need. These terms can usually be combined with the Boolean operators AND, OR, and NOT. Several commercial systems exist, as well as a multitude of private systems. Some of the commerical systems are System Development Corporation's ORBIT, Lockheed's DIALOG, and the Bibliographic Retrieval System's BRS. Examples of these will be given, although the focus of our treatment will be

on the noncommercial system PIRETS of the University of Pittsburgh.
PIRETS stands for the Pittsburgh information retrieval system. It is similar
in concept to the commercial systems, although it uses a "guided" mode of
dialogue.

## PIRETS: An Information Retrieval System

The term *guided mode* comes from the fact that the computer program guides
the user through a process of searching.

The guiding begins with a set of instructions that explain the system.
After the instructions, PIRETS begins the search process by asking the
user if he or she wants to search now

    DO YOU WANT TO SEARCH NOW?
    →

The arrow after the question indicates to the user that it is his or her
turn to answer, and is called the "prompt." The user types "yes"

    DO YOU WANT TO SEARCH NOW?
    → YES

The system proceeds to ask if the user wants the short or long form of
the messages

    DO YOU WANT THE SHORT OR LONG FORM
    OF PIRETS MESSAGES. PLEASE RESPOND
    'SHORT' OR 'LONG'

Experienced users tend to take the short form of the messages so that
the entire interaction is shortened; inexperienced users take the long form
in order to more fully understand the messages

    DO YOU WANT THE SHORT OR LONG FORM
    OF PIRETS MESSAGES. PLEASE RESPOND
    'SHORT' OR 'LONG'
    → LONG

As can be seen from these two examples, PIRETS is an "interactive"
computer program, the interaction being between the user and the computer. Another term for such systems is *conversational*, since the computer
and the user hold a conversation. The computer program prompts the user,
the user responds, and the pattern is repeated again with a new question.
A typical interaction is shown in Figure 11.1.

After prompting for the short or long forms, the PIRETS program next
prompts the user as to whether the search desired is "current awareness"
or "retroactive." The data bases provided by PIRETS are bibliographic;
they contain abstracts of journal articles. Current awareness searches the
most recent month of the data base, while retroactive searches as far back
in time as the data base has articles, usually a period of years. The current awareness searches are usually done online, in the interactive mode,
because they are short, and thus suitable to online searching. The retroactive searches are usually done offline in batch mode, because they take
longer to accomplish. For purposes of illustration, we will assume an online,
interactive current awareness search.

After selecting the search mode (current awareness, interactive), the
user must choose the data base that he or she wishes to search. PIRETS

```
DO YOU WISH TO SEARCH NOW?
→ YES

INTERACTIVE SEARCH MODULE   9-12-80

DO YOU WANT THE SHORT OR LONG FORM OF
PIRETS MESSAGES?  PLEASE RESPOND 'SHORT'
OR 'LONG'
→ LONG

DO YOU WISH TO SEARCH A 'CBIS' DATA BASE?
→ YES     (CBIS stands for Campus Based Information
                                   Systems)
DO YOU WISH CURRENT AWARENESS SEARCH OF RETRO SEARCH?
RESPOND 'CA' OR 'RETRO'
→ CA

DO YOU WISH CA-INTERACTIVE MODE OR CA-BATCH MODE
OR SDI-BATCH MODE:

RESPOND 'INTER' 'BATCH' OR 'SDI'
→ INTER

SELECT YOUR DATA BASE AND FILE PLEASE

.....PSY-ABS ──────→ YES
..................(PSY-ABS-COPYRIGHT)OCT/82     YES

DO YOU WANT TO SEARCH USING A PROFILE WHICH
YOU HAVE STORED?
→ NO

BEGIN YOUR PROFILE.
        .
        .
        .
```

FIGURE 11.1

offers only two data bases: psych-abstracts, which contains articles in the area of psychology; and ERIC (Educational Research Institute Center), which contains articles in the area of education. For purposes of illustration, we will assume we choose to search the psychological data base, psych-abstracts.

After selecting a data base, the user must now indicate the type of articles he or she wishes to "find" in the data base, i.e., the topics of interest. This is done by entering "key words" that describe the topic. For example, if we are looking for information on the use of achievement tests in mathematics, we might select as the key words

ACHIEVEMENT
TESTING
MATHEMATICS

We wish articles that include all these terms, so that the "search strategy" we would formulate would incorporate these terms in the AND condition. The search strategy might then look for something like the following:

ACHIEVEMENT
AND

        TESTING
        AND
        MATHEMATICS

which indicates that we wish articles in which all three terms occur. If we wished to indicate synonyms for any of the words, we could do so by entering the synonyms in the OR condition (e.g., the word *testing* might have a synonym, such as *test*, or *tests*), so that the strategy would now look like the following:

        ACHIEVEMENT
        AND
        (TESTING OR TESTS OR TEST)
        AND
        MATHEMATICS

If any one of the three variations contained in the parentheses occurs in the article, it may be of use to us. Thus, if the abstract of a particular article were

        *Achievement tests* were developed for the eighth grade.
        Subjects tested included *mathematics* and English.

We would get the article as a "hit." Note, however, that if the abstract were written as follows:

        *Achievement tests* were developed for the eighth grade.
        Subjects tested included math and English.

We would *not* get a hit, since the word *math* does *not* match our search term *mathematics*. Thus, the match is not based on the meaning of the term, but on a character-by-character match of the word(s) in the search strategy with the word(s) used in the description of the article. Fields other than the abstract may be searched, e.g., the title of the article, the title of the journal in which the article appeared, the author's name, and key words selected by the person who indexed the article, but the principle is the same: there must be a character-by-character match of the terms in the search strategy (profile, query terms) against the words in the article.

        If the article's abstract had been written as follows:

        *Achievement testing* in the eighth grade showed an increase
        in scores in *mathematics* and English.

the article would still be a "hit" since the variation "testing" is acceptable (TESTING or TESTS or TEST). If we also wished to allow for variations in the word *mathematics*, we could have entered this term in an OR relationship

        (MATHEMATICS OR MATH)

Most retrieval systems allow for the specification of variant forms of a word by a special mechanism called truncation. For example, if we wish the forms

        TESTING
        TESTS
        TEST

to be valid, we could specify this with the single entry

TEST*

where * indicates that all words beginning with *test*, regardless of their endings, should be taken as acceptable. The * is taken as a wild card symbol, standing for "any character or characters." Thus, * matches the *ing* in *testing*, the *s* in *tests*, and "nothing" (the null character) in *test*. However, its use can introduce some matches that we did not wish, for example, testy and testosterone would also match, although neither was intended.

The use of the asterisk on the right side of the word is called right truncation. It indicates that all possible suffixes are acceptable. The use of the truncation symbol on the left

*MYCIN

indicates that all possible prefixes are possible, and is called left truncation. In the example *MYCIN, possible hits would include

ACTINOMYCIN
STREPTOMYCIN

The use of left truncation results in a longer search than the use of right truncation. This is because the use of left truncation involves a search of the *entire index*, since all alphabetic characters are possible prefixes. The use of right truncation does not involve a search of the entire index, since the first part of the word (TEST in TEST*) restricts the search to one portion of the alphabet (the *T*'s in the case of TEST*). Thus, the use of right truncation is usually more economical than the use of left truncation.

## The Hits

The "hits" comprise the articles that are returned in response to our query. The author submitted the query shown in Figure 11.2a to the PIRETS retrieval system, and received the output shown in Figure 11.2b. This search

```
        ACHIEVEMENT
        AND
        (TESTING OR TESTS OR TEST)
        AND
        MATHEMATICS

            (a)

----------SEARCH SUMMARY-------------

NUMBER OF DOCUMENTS:        3,196
TOTAL HITS FOR SEARCH:          8

TIME          0 MINS.     14.42 SECS.

            (b)
```

FIGURE 11.2

-----------------------

DOCUMENT:   P640408780

   SEQ.:     P640408780 8010

   TITLE:     A COMPARATIVE STUDY OF YOUNG CHILDREN'S CLASSROOM
       ACTIVITIES AND LEARNING OUTCOMES.

  AUTHOR:     EVANS, MARY A. (U WATERLOO, CANADA)

  SOURCE:     BRITISH JOURNAL OF EDUCATIONAL PSYCHOLOGY, 1979 FEB VOL
      49(1)   15-26.

 KEY-WDS:   ELEMENTARY SCHOOL STUDENTS, CLASSROOM ENVIRONMENT, CHILDHOOD
     PLAY BEHAVIOR, CLASSROOM BEHAVIOR, TEACHER STUDENT INTERACTION,
     INTERPERSONAL INTERACTION, ACADEMIC 〈 ACHIEVEMENT.〉

LANGUAGE:   ENGL.

ABSTRACT:   COMPARED 10 "INFORMAL' (I.E. A PLAY-BASED, CHILD-CENTERED
     PROGRAM WITH SELF-DIRECTED ACTIVITIES) 1ST- AND 2ND-GRADE
     CLASSROOMS WITH 10 COMPARISON CLASSROOMS MATCHED ACCORDING TO
     SOCIOECONOMIC NEIGHBORHOOD, GRADE, AND INSTRUCTIONAL ORGANIZATION
     USING THE PUPIL ACTIVITY SCAN.  ANALYSIS OF THE DATA INDICATED
     THAT SS. IN THE COMPARISON CLASSROOMS, WORD ANALYSIS ACTIVITIES,
     PRINTING ACTIVITIES, INDEPENDENT SILENT READING, AND TEACHER-LED
     GROUP EXPERIENCES WERE MORE PREVALENT.  SUBSTANTIAL VARIATION IN
     CURRICULA WAS ALSO OBSERVED ACROSS ALL CLASSROOMS. 〈 TESTING 〉 OF SS
     AT THE END OF THE SCHOOL YEAR INDICATED NO DIFFERENCES BETWEEN THE
     GROUPS IN LANGUAGE DEVELOPMENT, PROBLEM SOLVING, FINE MOTOR-FIGURAL
     PERCEPTION, ROLE-TAKING, OR UNDERSTANDING OF CLASSIFICATION,
     BUT SS' PERFORMANCE IN INFORMAL CLASSROOMS APPEARED LOWER
     WITH RESPECT TO READING AND〈 MATHEMATICS.〉 (30 REF)

FIGURE 11.3

summary indicates that there were 8 documents in the file matching my
query, out of a total of 3,196. The search that produced this information
took 14.42 sec, which is considerably faster than leafing through the tables
of contents of several journals. One of the eight articles was that shown in
Figure 11.3. Eight fields are listed in this document description: (1) the
document number and (2) the sequence number, both of which are used to
identify the document; (3) the title of the article; (4) the author; (5) the
title of the journal in which the article appeared; (6) some key words,
which are selected by an indexer in order to describe the contents of the
article (in this case the article was seen as being about "elementary school
students," "classroom environment," "teacher-student interaction," and
"academic achievement," among other things); (7) the language in which
the article is written (in this case English); and (8) an abstract of the
article's contents, which gives a brief description of what the author has
to say.

    Because of variable length fields, such as the abstract and key word
fields, the description of the article is a variable length record. Another
hit was that shown in Figure 11.4. Note that in both descriptions the words
of the query that caused the retrieval of the articles are enclosed in brack-

-------------------------------

DOCUMENT:   P640408892

   SEQ.:   P640408892 8010

   TITLE:   PREDICTIVE VALUE OF SAT SCORES AND HIGH SCHOOL ACHIEVEMENT
        FOR SUCCESS IN A COLLEGE HONORS PROGRAM.

  AUTHOR:   MCDONALD, RITA T. GAWKOSKI, ROMAN S. (MARQUETTE U)

  SOURCE:   EDUCATIONAL PSYCHOLOGICAL MEASUREMENT, 1979 SUM VOL 39(2)
        411-414.

KEY-WDS:   COLL ENT EXAM BD SCHOLASTIC APT ⟨ TEST, ⟩ PREDICTIVE VALIDITY,
       COLLEGE STUDENTS, ACADEMIC ⟨ACHIEVEMENT,⟩ HIGH SCHOOL STUDENTS,
       COLLEGE ACADEMIC ACHIEVEMENT, HUMAN SEX DIFFERENCES, TEST SCORES,
       SUBTESTS.

LANGUAGE: ENGL.

ABSTRACT:   STUDIES THE ACADEMIC RECORDS OF 206 MALE AND 196 FEMALE UNDER-
       GRADUATES IN AN HONORS PROGRAM.  THE VERBAL AND ⟨MATHEMATICS⟩ PORTIONS
       OF THE COLLEGE BOARD SCHOLASTIC APTITUDE TEST (SAT) AND HIGH SCHOOL
       GPA HAD MODERATE PREDICTIVE VALIDITY FOR THE ENTIRE GROUP. FOR WOMEN,
       ONLY THE MATHEMATICS PORTION OF THE SAT WAS USEFUL IN PREDICTING
       SUCCESS IN THE HONORS PROGRAM. (12 REF)

FIGURE 11.4

ets. The first article hit on the words *achievement* (in the key word field),
*testing* (in the abstract), and *mathematics* (in the abstract). The second
article had the words *test* (in the key words), *achievement* (in the key
words), and *mathematics* (in the abstract). The fact that both "testing"
and "test" caused hits indicates that our use of alternate terms through OR
was fruitful. In fact, in the eight hits, the variants of the term test occurred as follows:

| | |
|---|---|
| TESTING | 1 |
| TEST | 5 |
| TESTS | 2 |
| | 8 |

so that if we had used only the variation "testing," we would have received
only one hit and missed seven other articles on the subject.


BUT-NOT

In the above search we have used both AND and OR to search the data.
We will now illustrate the use of BUT-NOT. BUT-NOT is PIRETS' way of
expressing the Boolean operator NOT. It is used to exclude certain terms,
and hence certain articles containing those terms from the output. For example, if we did not wish to see articles involving achievement testing of
mathematics in elementary school, we could have eliminated such articles
with the phrase

```
ACHIEVEMENT                          ------SEARCH SUMMARY------
AND
(TESTING OR TESTS OR TEST)           NUMBER OF DOCUMENTS:      3,196
AND                                  TOTAL HITS FOR SEARCH:        4
MATHEMATICS
BUT-NOT ELEMENTARY                   TIME      0 MINS.    14.34 SECS.

(a)                                  (b)
```

FIGURE 11.5

### BUT-NOT ELEMENTARY

The search strategy (query, profile) would now read as shown in Figure 11.5a. Articles containing the word *elementary* would be excluded from the output. Hence, the first hit shown above would be eliminated, since the word *elementary* occurs in the key words ("elementary school students"). The second article would not have been eliminated, since the word *elementary* does not appear in any of the fields that summarize the article.

Submitting the search strategy with BUT-NOT ELEMENTARY resulted in only four hits (Figure 11.5b), which indicates that four of the articles contained the word *elementary*. A perusal of the output indicated that the remaining articles were on the following topics:

1. A study of various factors in relation to mathematics achievement at the college level
2. A study of sex differences in mathematics achievement in junior high school
3. A study of the predictive ability of SAT scores and mathematics achievement in high school for success in college
4. A study of the predictive value of SAT tests on success in college among freshmen in law and justice.

Thus, there are no articles containing studies carried out in elementary schools. The exclusion operator BUT-NOT has done its job.

### Relevance

Information retrieval systems allow the user to examine his or her output while searching, mainly to determine whether or not the articles are on the topic requested. Because the terms are matched on a character-by-character basis rather than meaning, it is possible either to get matches that are not of interest, or to fail to retrieve articles that are of interest but for which we have not chosen the proper terms. We treat the problem of articles that we do not want because of an accidental matching of our search terms to the terms used in the article. This mismatching involves the problem of relevance. Relevant articles are articles that are truly of interest; nonrelevant articles are not of interest. Hence, the articles that are reported as "hits" must be examined to determine if they are "truly hits," and thus "relevant" to our request.

An example in which both relevant and irrelevant items were retrieved follows. The search strategy was

DOCUMENT:  EJ 197517                          `RELEVANT`

SEQ.:  EJ197517  CG515837

TITLE:  SOCIAL INFORMATION PROCESSING ANALYSIS (SIPA) CODING ONGOING
⟨HUMAN⟩ COMMUNICATION.                     `HUMAN HIT HERE`

AUTHOR:  FISHER, B. AUDREY; AND OTHERS

SOURCE:  SMALL GROUP BEHAVIOR; V10 N1 P3-22 FEB 1979; FEB79
                                          `INFORMATION HIT HERE`
KEY-WDS:  *COMMUNICATION (THOUGHT TRANSFER) ⟨*INFORMATION⟩
PROCESSING; *INTERACTION PROCESS ANALYSIS; INTERCOMMUNICATION;
RESEARCHERS; *SOCIAL RELATIONS

LANGUAGE:  ENGLISH

(a)


DOCUMENT:  EJ 198690                        `NOT RELEVANT`
                                            `= NOISE`
SEQ.:  EJ198690  S0507071

TITLE:  WOMEN'S LIVES IN THE ASIAN TRADITION.

AUTHOR:  CROWN, BONNIE R.

SOURCE:  SOCIAL EDUCATION; V43 N4 P248-57 APR 1979; APR79

KEY-WDS:  *ASIAN STUDIES; *BELIEFS; CHANGING ATTITUDES; CIVIL
RIGHTS; *CULTURAL AWARENESS; *FEMALES; *LIFE STYLE;
MINORITY ROLE; SECONDARY EDUCATION; SOCIAL CHANGE

LANGUAGE:  ENGLISH
                                            `HUMAN HIT HERE`
ABSTRACT:  REVIEWS DEPICTION OF ASIAN WOMEN IN LITERATURE BY ASIAN
WRITERS WITHIN THE CONTEXT OF DEVELOPMENT OF BASIC ⟨HUMAN⟩
RIGHTS FOR MEN AND WOMEN. ⟨INFORMATION⟩ IS PRESENTED TO
HELP STUDENTS ANALYZE THE LITERATURE SELECTIONS.  (AUTHOR/DB)
                                            `INFORMATION HIT HERE`

(b)

FIGURE 11.6


INFORMATION
AND
HUMAN

The intent was to gather articles on human information processing, such as
thinking, problem-solving, and the organization of memory. The search retrieved two articles (Figure 11.6). The article in Figure 11.6a is in the
area of human information processing, as indicated by both the title and the

content of the article (social information processing in human communication) as well as by the fact that the indexer selected the key term *information processing* to describe the article.

The article in Figure 11.6b, however, is not on the topic of human information processing, but is an article about Asian women. This article was retrieved because of the accidental confluence of the terms *human* and *information* in the abstract:

HUMAN RIGHTS
    AND
INFORMATION IS PRESENTED


## Precision and Recall: Measures of the System's Effectiveness and Efficiency

Two terms are frequently used when assessing the effectiveness of an information retrieval system: *recall* and *precision*. Recall refers to the fact that an information system may not retrieve all the relevant articles it should. Failure to retrieve relevant articles could occur because of poor indexing, inadequately written abstracts, a poor selection of search terms by the user, or simply because of the great variety of terms that can be selected in order to describe a concept.

Precision refers to the fact that while only relevant articles should be retrieved irrelevant documents are sometimes retrieved as well. A perfect information system would retrieve all relevant articles (perfect recall) and no irrelevant ones (perfect precision), but this rarely happens in reality.

The concepts of recall and precision can be understood more fully if we construct a two-by-two table that describes the activities of the information system (Figure 11.7a). The boxes that indicate correct action on the part of the information system are those labeled 1 and 4. The information system should retrieve all articles that are relevant (box 1) and should not retrieve those that are not relevant (box 4). Boxes 2 and 3 indicate incorrect action on the part of the information retrieval system. Box 2 indicates that the system failed to retrieve articles that were relevant (called misses). Box 3 indicates that the system retrieved some articles that were not relevant (called false drops or noise). The relevant articles retrieved in box 1 are "hits." As can be seen from the previous discussion, the system itself may call certain "hits" that are not truly hits. The system refers to all articles that are retrieved as "hits," but in evaluating the output of the system, only relevant retrieved articles are considered hits. Box 4 does not have a commonly accepted name, but might be considered to be the "rightly rejected" box. Hence, our diagram, including the names attributed to each box, is shown in Figure 11.7b. The boxes labeled "hits" and rightly rejected represent "good work" on the part of the information system. The boxes labeled "misses" and "noise" represent malfunctions in the search process. We purposely say the search process, since the malfunction could be due to either the information system or the user. If the system is being evaluated, only its own failures should be considered. Of course, some failures on the part of the user may be due to the system as well. For example, the user might choose terms poorly because the designers and/or operators of the system have not made the proper terms clear. Some systems assist the user by publishing a list of terms to be used for certain concepts, such as a thesaurus (see the ERIC thesaurus). If such an aid is

|  | Articles Retrieved | Articles Not Retrieved |
|---|---|---|
| Articles that are relevant | 1 | 2 |
| Articles that are not relevant | 3 | 4 |

(a)

|  | Articles Retrieved | Articles Not Retrieved |
|---|---|---|
| Articles that are relevant | Hits | Misses |
| Articles that are not relevant | False drops or noise | Rightly rejected |

(b)

FIGURE 11.7

not published, or is published in a manner that is not clear to the user, the fault for the selection of poor search terms is at least partially attributable to the system. However, if the user chooses to ignore a well-done thesaurus, the system should not be faulted.


## Calculating Recall and Precision

If we know how many articles are in the data base, how many are relevant to our question, how many documents were retrieved, and how many of those retrieved were relevant, we can calculate percentages to reflect the recall and precision achieved on a particular search. Suppose that the figures are as shown in Figure 11.8a. The table may be read as follows: eight documents were retrieved by the information retrieval system in response to the user's query (see total retrieved). Of these eight documents, the user judged six to be relevant (see relevant-retrieved) and two were considered not relevant (retrieved-not relevant). Furthermore, four documents that were relevant to the user's query were not retrieved (see relevant-not retrieved). There were 10 relevant documents in the system (total relevant), but only 6 were actually retrieved (six true hits). There were 990 irrelevant documents in the system (total not relevant) of which 988 were rightly passed over in the search (not relevant, not retrieved), but 2 turned up as "noise." There were a total of 1,000 documents in the system. Note that the totals of relevant (10) and not relevant (990) add to 1,000, as do the totals of retrieved (8) and not retrieved (992).

|  | Retrieved | Not Retrieved | Totals |
|---|---|---|---|
| Relevant | 6 | 4 | 10 |
| Not Relevant | 2 | 988 | 990 |
| Totals | 8 | 992 | 1000 |

(a)

|  | Retrieved | Not Retrieved | Totals |
|---|---|---|---|
| Relevant | 10 | 0 | 10 |
| Not Relevant | 0 | 990 | 990 |
| Totals | 10 | 990 | 1000 |

(b)

FIGURE 11.8

Both recall and precision use the numbers of hits (6) in the calculations of their percentages. Precision is the ratio of the true hits to the total documents retrieved

$$\frac{\text{Hits}}{\text{Total retrieved}}$$

For our example, this is

$$\frac{\text{Hits}}{\text{Total retrieved}} = \frac{6}{8} = .75 \text{ or } 75\%$$

A perfectly precise system would have a precision of 100%, since all documents retrieved would be hits

$$\frac{\text{Hits}}{\text{Total retrieved}} = \frac{6}{6} = 1.00 \text{ or } 100\%$$

The recall is calculated as the ratio of the true hits (relevant, retrieved) to the total relevant documents in the system. For our example this is

$$\frac{\text{Hits}}{\text{Total relevant}} = \frac{6}{10} = .60 \text{ or } 60\%$$

A perfectly working retrieval system would have a recall of 100%; i.e., it would retrieve all of the relevant documents

$$\frac{\text{Hits}}{\text{Total relevant}} = \frac{10}{10} = 1.00 \text{ or } 100\%$$

Thus, if the above search had resulted in perfect results, the figures would have been as shown in Figure 11.8b. Our search was not perfect, achieving a recall of 60% (6 of 10) and a precision of 75% (6 of 8).

It is usually difficult to increase both the precision and the recall together. To increase recall, we normally broaden a search, using more terms in an OR relationship, but this also usually results in more noise, thus decreasing precision. In order to increase precision, we normally narrow a search (by using AND or BUT-NOT) to restrict the number of hits. However, this winnowing of the output often causes a few more relevant articles to be missed (e.g., because they lack one of the terms in the AND statement).

The user often sees precision as the more important of the two measures. This is true because the user seldom needs complete recall. What is often wanted is a representative sample of articles on a topic. However, the user almost always wishes to avoid retrieving irrelevant articles, since they simply detract his or her attention from the relevant ones (hence the term *noise*); they interfere with processing the "good" data.

Precision is also the only measure that the user can calculate. The user usually has no idea of how many relevant articles are in the system, so that a measure of recall is impossible (it is not impossible for those who operate the information system). However, the user does know how many articles were retrieved (reported by the system as hits), and he or she also knows how many of these are truly relevant, so that the calculation

$$\frac{\text{Hits}}{\text{Total retrieved}}$$

is possible.

## Measuring Recall

Various systems have been developed to estimate the recall of a system (Lancaster and Fayen, 1973), but only one method is presented here. The choice of this particular example was made because it is readily comprehended, if not readily implemented. The idea is to perform parallel searches, e.g., one through the information system, the other through manual indices to the literature. The process involves the following steps:

1. Perform search on information system for a particular topic. Say 10 are retrieved, of which 8 are considered truly relevant.
2. Perform manual search to find relevant documents for the same topic. Say the total in this search is 15.
3. Search information system's data base for these 15 documents. Suppose 12 are in the data base.
4. Confine further evaluations to the 12 documents that are in the information system data base.
5. Compare the 8 relevant documents that were retrieved (in step 1) by our search strategy with the 12 relevant documents now known to be in the system.

Suppose that all 8 are included in the 12. Then, the recall of the system was

$$\frac{\text{Hits}}{\text{Total relevant}} = \frac{8}{12} = 67\%$$

Of course, this entire procedure would have to be repeated for a representative sample of topics and of searches on each topic, which indicates why it is not easily implemented.

A measure of recall that can be implemented and that can be useful is Lancaster's "comparative measure of recall." One of the controversies about information retrieval systems concerns the question of whether the user should perform the search (since he or she presumably understands the problem most intimately) or whether a third party, the information specialist, should perform the search (since he or she can presumably devote more time to understanding the system). Given a representative sample of users (say some psychologists, school educators, counselors, etc.) and a representative sample of topics (say testing, teaching, and advising), we can compare the number of true hits returned by the subject specialist (the psychologists, educators, and counselors) with the results achieved by a sample of information specialists. Say the results are

| Searcher | Average Number of Hits |
|---|---|
| Subject specialists | 8 |
| Information specialists | 10 |

we would then know that the information specialists achieve better recall than the subject specialists. Of course, this greater recall would have to be balanced against the greater expense in employing information specialists as searchers. If the subject specialists achieve better results, we might dispense with the information specialists, although this decision might not be taken if the time that the information specialist saves for the subject specialist were important. Finally, if no significant difference were found between the results, the question would remain open, with considerations of relative salaries and time constraints outweighing considerations of recall.

## Coverage and the Growth of Knowledge

Several other measures of system performance can be considered. One measure that is quite important to the user is the average response time, which is defined as the period lasting from the time at which a command is entered to the time at which the system responds to the command. Another is the cost of the search. However, the above discussion brings to mind the concept of coverage. In the example we constructed, the manual search uncovered 15 relevant documents. Of these 15, 12 were found in the information system's data base. The coverage for this total would be computed as

$$\frac{\text{Relevant documents in system}}{\text{Relevant documents in literature}} = \frac{12}{15} = \frac{4}{5} = 80\%$$

so that this system is "covering" 80% of the literature on the topic. The measurement of coverage is as difficult as the measurement of recall; however, the question of coverage brings up the question of whether or not 100% coverage is possible or even desirable.

One of the topics that has generated much discussion in modern times is the "growth of knowledge" (see Price, de Solla, 1963, and Lukasiewicz, 1972). The growth of knowledge refers to the increase in the number of scientists and the number of journal articles in modern times. While such increases do not guarantee a growth in knowledge, they are taken as indicators of such growth. De Solla Price has calculated that the number of scientists, as well as the number of articles in a field, doubles approximately every 15 years. This results in a 10-fold increase every 50 years.

To consider how this affects the growth of knowledge, let us assume that we begin with a total of 100 scientists. In a period of 15 years, this number becomes 200, and in another 15 years it becomes 400. If all the scientists are producing new knowledge, we will have a much more difficult time keeping up with the work of 399 others than we initially had in keeping up with the work of 99 others. In fact, if our career lasts another 15 years (not unheard of, since a career of 45 years would make us 70 years old if we had begun our career at the age of 25), we must keep up with the work of 799 other scientists (since the population has again doubled from 400 to 800). As is readily seen, the process of "keeping up" quickly becomes impossible. In fact, it was just such a growth in the number of scientists and the number of journal articles that led to the emphasis on bibliographic retrieval systems, as well as abstracting services and other means of keeping abreast of scientific developments.

The question now arises as to whether or not an information system should attempt to cover all the literature. Some observations by Bradford (1948) indicate that attempting to achieve 100% coverage may not be a wise strategy. Bradford noted that given a particular topic, the number of journals that had to be consulted in order to cover all articles grew in a fashion similar to the following:

| 25% coverage | 50% coverage | 75% coverage | 100% coverage |
|---|---|---|---|
| 4 journals or issues | 16 journals or issues | 256 journals or issues | 65,536 journals or issues |

i.e., every increment of 25% in coverage resulted in *squaring* the number of journals to be consulted. Thus, to cover 25% of the articles, we need consult only 4 journals (or issues), which is feasible; however, to achieve 100% coverage, we need to consult about 65,000 journals (or issues), which would be quite costly and time consuming. The numbers in this example are simulated, but the idea is there.

If we consider the process by which scientific articles become published, the phenomenon described by Bradford becomes understandable. The initial article on a topic is usually considered a "breakthrough," and is sent to the leading journals in the field. Assuming the article really is a breakthrough, it will be accepted, and subsequent articles will also be accepted

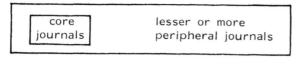

(a)

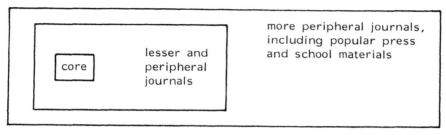

(b)

FIGURE 11.9

by these leading journals. However, over time, the topic will become known among readers of these journals, so that subsequent articles will be submitted to "lesser" journals, or to journals that treat the topic "peripherally." These journals will normally outnumber the initial core of journals (Figure 11.9a). This process of saturation and spread into a new area will continue until the articles reach even the popular journals, such as *Time* and *Newsweek*, and the school journals, such as *Junior Scholastic*. Again, the number of journals in this outer area is quite large (Figure 11.9b). Hence, the topic appears in an ever-widening number of sources, making the figure of 65,000 seem quite realistic, even if we start with a core of 4 journals (or issues of a single journal).

This phenomenon of coverage being concentrated in a small number of publications is seen in studies of library usage, the library being the traditional means of information storage and retrieval. In a study of some of the University of Pittsburgh libraries, data about the physics library indicated that 11 journals accounted for 46% of journal usage during the study period. Since the entire collection consisted of approximately 300 journal titles, this meant that 3-4% of the available titles accounted for almost 50% of the usage in that period.

In the case of books, the problem of the librarian is further complicated by the fact that he or she must predict usage with very little data to go on. Some data is possible (e.g., certain authors may be read more than others), but in a large number of cases, the decision to buy or not buy a book has to be made without a strong history of performance data. Thus, we find books in the collection that are seldom used, as well as frequently requested books that are not in the collection. The case of books in the collection that are not used is akin to the problem of precision (several books have been purchased, but not all of them are truly relevent). The second problem, not having a requested book, is akin to the problems of recall (we cannot recall all of the material on a given topic because it was not purchased) and coverage (it was not purchased because we can't buy everything).

Libraries have recently given the problem of coverage increasing attention. In a time in which the cost of books and journals have escalated and
budgets have not, the decision to acquire a book or subscribe to a journal
is looked at more closely. In fact, several libraries have joined in resource-
sharing groups, so that decisions about whether or not to buy can be made
in light of the fact that another library may already have the book or journal in question and can share it, thus retaining "access to materials" without actually purchasing each item.

## Effectiveness and Efficiency

We have called recall and precision measures of effectiveness and efficiency.
Effectiveness can be defined as the measure by which we determine whether
or not a system has met its goal. Did it achieve what it set out to do?
For an information system, this would be a measure of the retrieval of infor-
mation. Did the system retrieve (bring back) the documents it should have?
Recall would be a measure related to this.

Efficiency tries to ascertain whether or not the system achieved its
goal within a reasonable cost and time frame. In regard to the cost to the
user, precision would be a measure of efficiency, the reason being that it
is not efficient, timewise or effortwise, to sort through a batch of unwant-
ed documents. Coverage would be related to cost efficiency, since an attempt
at too wide a coverage would certainly add to the cost of the system. Response time (and search time) would also be measures of efficiency, since a
quick response would be more efficienct to the user than a slow response.
Search time, as mentioned earlier, is a function of the storage structures,
computer programs, and technology used to implement the system. All of
these involve costs, so that an efficiency in regard to user time may cause
an increase in system dollar costs. These are trade-offs that the system
analysts must consider in planning, building, and operating the system.

## Learning from the Key Words

In using an information retrieval system that employs key words, we can
often benefit by using these terms again in future searches. For example,
in the search for achievement testing in mathematics, some of the key words

```
---------------------------------
DOCUMENT:  P640408816

SEQ:       P640408816 8010

TITLE:     RELATIONSHIP BETWEEN SELECTED VARIABLES AND STATISTICS ⟨ACHIEVEMENT:⟩
           BUILDING A THEORETICAL MODEL.

               ↓        :                      ↓
KEY-WDS:   MATHEMATICS EDUCATION, ⟨MATHEMATICS⟩ ACHIEVEMENT, HUMAN SEX
           DIFFERENCES, MASCULINITY, FEMININITY, STATISTICAL ANALYSIS,
           SPATIAL PERCEPTION, COLLEGE STUDENTS.
```

FIGURE 11.10

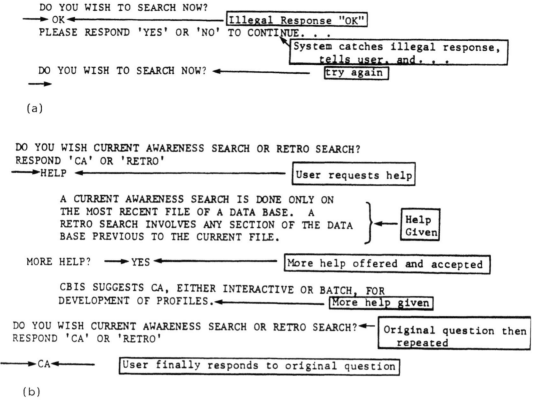

FIGURE 11.11

on the hits we obtained were *mathematics education* and *mathematics achievement* (Figure 11.10), so we might also use these phrases in future searches. Furthermore, we can see that if we are interested in studies done at the college level, the term *college students* can be used. Thus, we can become more proficient in using the information system as we go along.

### Catching Errors and Helping the User

One of the problems in doing a search with a computer program is that the user does not always know what to do, nor does the user always type in the correct responses. Most retrieval systems are written in such a way that incorrect responses are caught, the user is made aware of them, and the question is repeated (Figure 11.11a). Furthermore, the systems often have HELP commands, which the user can use whenever he or she feels a need for clarification (Figure 11.11b).

### Searching Selected Fields

In a single aspect search this author submitted the query term

SKINNER

The intent was to get articles either about or by B. F. Skinner, the psychologist. Three articles were output

1. One specifically about Skinner, a true hit
2. One by Nicholas F. Skinner, considered noise in this search
3. One that mentioned the Skinner box, but was not really about B. F. Skinner himself

However, the question arises: "What if I wish to distinguish articles by Skinner from articles about Skinner?" The answer is that most systems allow the user to specify that the search be restricted to certain fields. Thus, if I am looking for articles by Skinner, I would search the author field. If I am looking for articles about Skinner, I might search the title or abstract fields, but exclude the author field.

On the PIRETS system this is called level searching. Other systems, such as ORBIT or DIALOG, have special indicators for the various fields (e.g., AU = Skinner for author), and keep separate indices for the various fields.

## Commercial Systems

Several commercial information retrieval systems exist, among them the systems referred to as ORBIT, DIALOG, and BRS. We will give a representative example of each in order to show the similarity among systems. (The searches shown here were actually performed on emulators of these commercial systems, which were developed by Daniel Strick at the University of Pittsburgh, with partial support from the Buhl Foundation.)

All three of the systems shown here are "command driven," rather than guided mode; i.e., the user, not the system, takes the initiative. The assumption is that the user has been trained in using the system.

## ORBIT

ORBIT is an information retrieval program (query language) provided by Systems Development Corporation (SDC). Numerous data bases are available. Of course, a fee is charge for use of both the query language and the data base. (A particular fee may have both components combined into, say the data base fee, but it represents charges for both.) The fees for the data bases vary widely, say from $25 an hour to $150 an hour, and are based on the cost of developing or acquiring the data base. Fees for using the system are based on connect time and the type of communication line and distance involved. Charges are also levied for citations printed, either online (at the terminal) or offline. The online printing costs may be subsumed in the connect fee or processing costs (CPU time), but the offline costs will be added on. The fee structure differs from organization to organization, so that each must be individually studied by the potential subscriber. Also, package details, such as 600 searches for a set fee, are possible. We will be interested here in the technique of searching rather than in the fee.

A somewhat simplified but typical interaction with ORBIT is shown in Figure 11.12. In the ORBIT system, the user first selects a data base,

```
)FILE INFORM
INFORM (ABI/INFORM)
SS 1/C
USER:
Information
PROG:
SS   1  PSTG (163)
SS   2/C?
USER:
storage
PROG:
SS   2  PSTG (33)
SS 3/C
USER:
retrieval
PROG:
SS   3  PSTG (15)
SS 4/C
USER:
1 AND 2 AND 3
PROG:
SS   4  PSTG (10)
SS 5/C
PRINT  SS 4
   ⋮
```

FIGURE 11.12


then begins to enter search terms. In this particular example, the user
has chosen the file INFORM (ABI/INFORM), which is a data base for business, covering such topics as management, accounting, and banking. The
user selected the file with the command

   FILE INFORM

The system (computer program) responds by indicating that the file has
been selected, and then prompting for the search terms. The prompt to the
user is

   SS  1/C?
   USER:

where the SS stands for search strategy; the 1 indicates that if a strategy
is selected, it will be the first such strategy entered by the user; the /C
gives the option of combining previous strategies (if they exist) rather than
entering a new search term; and the ? indicates that the statement is really
a question about two alternatives

   1.  Entering a search term
   2.  Combining previous search terms

The computer is effectively saying

   "Do you wish to enter a new term or do you wish to
   combine some terms that you previously entered?"

The phrase

   USER:

is the actual prompt to the user, saying "it's your turn" to enter data.

In this particular search, the user chose to enter the search term *information*

```
SS  1/C
USER:
information
```

where the user's entry of data is marked by lowercase letters, uppercase being used to print the system messages.

In response to the query term *information*, the system typed

```
PROG:
SS  1  PSTG (163)
```

where the abbreviation PSTG stands for *postings*, and the number in parentheses gives the number of documents described by this term. Thus, there were 163 postings for the term *information*. Note that the system message was preceded by the term PROG:, which indicated that this message originated from the program, not the user.

The user next entered the term *storage*

```
SS  2/C?
USER:
storage
```

which had 33 postings

```
PROG:
SS  2  PSTG (33)
```

The third search term entered was *retrieval*, with 15 postings

```
SS  3/C?
USER:
retrieval
```

```
PROG:
SS  3  PSTG (15)
```

Upon being asked for the fourth search strategy, the user elected to combine the terms from several strategies

```
SS  4/C?
USER:
1 AND 2 AND 3
```

which indicates that the user wished to combine search strategies 1, 2, and 3 in the AND relationship

```
1 AND 2 AND 3
```

Thus, the user is looking for information on "information storage and retrieval." The system indicates that there are 10 documents on this subject

```
PROG:
SS  4  PSTG (10)
```

and then prompts the user again. However, having narrowed the search to a particular topic, and wishing to see the documents listed under this topic, the user now asks for a printout (online) of the articles that were found in search strategy 4. He or she does this by typing

```
- 1 -
AN - 78-01141
TI - Integrating Reference Material into CAI
AU - James, Vaughn
SO - Jrnl of Systems Mgmt (JSYMAS, JSM), v28n12, PP.24-25, ISSN 0022-4839,
     December, 1977
DT - J (Journal)
LA - English

- 2 -
AN - 78-01127
TI - Auditing in a Data Base Environment
AU - Reneau, J. Hal
SO - Jrnl of Accountancy (JACYAD, JAC). v144n6, PP.59-65, ISSN  0021-8448,
     December, 1977
DT - J (Journal)
LA - English

- 3 -
AN - 78-01079
TI - Distributed Real Time Data Processing for Manufacturing Organizations
AU - Kochhar, Ashok
SO - IEEE Transactions on Engineering Mgmt (IEEMA4,IEE), VEM-24n4, PP.119-124,
     ISSN 001809391, November 1977
DT - J (Journal)
LA - English

- 4 -
AN - 78-01033
TI - A Look Inside NCIC
AU - Kashey, Daniel R.
SO - Computerworld (CMPWAB,COW), v11n50, PP.15-19, ISSN 0010-4841, December 12
     1977
DT - J (Journal)
LA - English

- 5 -
AN - 78-00975
TI - Micrographics at Kemper Insurance Company
AU - Kavanaugh, David D.
SO - Jrnl or Micrographics (JMGPBN,JMG), v11n2, PP.94-95, ISSN 0022-2712,
     November/December, 1977
DT - J (Journal)
LA - English
```

FIGURE 11.13


PRINT  SS 4

which causes the program to list the contents of the first five documents.
In our particular example, these were the documents (document surrogates
or descriptions) shown in Figure 11.13. The fields listed in this printing
of the "documents" are: the accession number (AN), which is a unique
number assigned to each document; the title of the document (TI); the
author (AU); the source (SO), which indicates the journal (or other type
of document) in which the article appeared; the document type (DT),

which might be "journal" or "research report" or other types, depending on the file searched; and the language in which the article was written (LA), which will be a natural language (e.g., English, Russian, or Spanish). In referring to the "documents" in the data base, we have enclosed the word *document* in quotes to indicate that we are not dealing with the full text of the document, but with a document "surrogate" or summary of the original document's contents.

If the user requests a term that is not included in the index to the data base, e.g.,

    SS  1  /C?
    USER:
    zzzz

where zzzz is a nonexistant word, the system simply responds

    PROG:
    NO PTSG (ZZZZ)

indicating that no documents are described by the term. Because this result is "null," it is not saved, and the program will again prompt for search strategy 1

    SS  1  /C?
    USER:

Besides combining terms in the AND relationship

    1 AND 2 AND 3

the user may use the Boolean operators OR and AND NOT:

    1 OR 2
    1 AND NOT 2

or a combination of operators

    (1 AND 2) AND NOT 3

The system treats a combination of terms as a separate search strategy.

The PRINT command used in the above example indicates that we want the results of a search strategy printed. Since the user did not specify which documents were to be printed, the system used the default value of printing the first five documents. We can alter this default value if we wish. For example, the command

    PRINT SS 2  3

indicates that we wish to see the third document from the results of search strategy 2. The user may also indicate various formats for printing the documents. In the above example, we accepted the default fields (AN, TI, AU, SO, DT, LA); however, means are available for specifying either fewer fields or a more complete listing. For example, PRINT FULL prints the full content of the document surrogates (more fields).

Three other commands that are of frequent use in the ORBIT system are NEIGHBOR, HISTORY, and EXPLAIN. NEIGHBOR is used to see terms that are alphabetically near to the term we cite. HISTORY gives a listing of all the search strategies we have entered. EXPLAIN is used to obtain help messages.

```
        PROG:

Postings                          Term
    2                             INFORMALLY/BI
    1                             INFORMATION/BI
  163                             INFORMATION/BI
   10                             INFORMATION/IT
   57                             INFORMATION/IW
UP N OR DOWN N?
```

(a)

```
        PROG:

Postings                          Term
   16                             INFORMATION/TI
    2                             INFORMATION CENTERS/IT
    1                             INFORMATION CONTROL/IT
    3                             INFORMATION DESSEMINATION/IT
    2                             INFORMATION FLOW ANALYSIS/IT

    UP N OR DOWN N?
```

(b)

FIGURE 11.14


One of the problems that occurs in doing automated information retrieval is when the message NO POSTINGS is received and we do not know  what to ask for next.  Assuming we still wish to look for the same topic, we may use the command NEIGHBOR to obtain a listing of terms that are "alpha- betically close" to the term we have entered.  In the following example, the user asked to see the "neighborhood" of the term *information*

    SS  11  /C?
    USER:
    neighbor information

The program responded with a list (Figure 11.14a), which gives the term (e.g., INFORMALLY), and the number of postings for that term (in this case two for INFORMALLY). It also indicates the index in which the term is found, BI (standing for basic index). ORBIT has several indices, and several types of terms within an index, such as BI, IT (index terms), and IW (index term words), which can aid the searcher in ascertaining the importance of the term to this particular search. We are primarily interested in the terms and the postings.

As the reader can see, the listing of terms is followed by the question

    UP N OR DOWN N?

where N stands for an integer, such as 2 or 5. If the user chooses to look "down" the list five more words

    USER:
    down 5

```
PROG:
SS  1:  INFORMATION (163)
SS  2:  STORAGE (33)
SS  3:  RETRIEVAL (15)
SS  4:  1 AND 2 AND 3 (10)
SS  5:  COMPUTER (106)
SS  6:  CRIME (5)
SS  7:  5 AND 6 (1)
SS  8:  COMPUTER (106)
SS  9:  SECURITY (46)
SS 10:  8 AND 9 (7)
```

(a)

```
PROG:
THE HISTORY COMMAND, ABBREVIATED HIS, DISPLAYS ACTIVE SEARCH STATEMENTS AS
FOLLOWS:
HISTORY                       (ALL PREVIOUS ENTRIES ARE DISPLAYED)
HISTORY 5                     (DISPLAYS SEARCH STATEMENT NUMBER 5)
HISTORY 4-7                   (DISPLAYS SEARCH STATEMENTS 4 THRU 7)
HISTORY REVERSE               (DISPLAYS FROM LATEST TO EARLIEST ENTRY)
```

(b)

FIGURE 11.15

the system responds with the next five terms in alphabetical order (Figure
11.14b). If the user had chosen "up 5," the program would have shown
the preceding five terms in alphabetical order. Whenever the user wishes
to stop viewing the index terms, he or she simply issues a command, such
as PRINT or a search term.

The HISTORY command was instituted to help the user "remember" all
the search strategies employed so far. ORBIT allows up to 30 search strategies to be active, so frequently we do not remember what transactions
have already transpired. When we type HISTORY

```
SS  11  /C?
USER:
history
```

the system reproduces all the search strategies, along with their postings,
in numerical order (Figure 11.15a). We see that search strategy 1 was a
single aspect search for the term INFORMATION, and had 163 postings.
Search strategy 4 was a combination, using AND, of the first 3 strategies
(INFORMATION, STORAGE, RETRIEVAL), and received 10 postings.

Very often in online searching, we are not sure what a particular command does, or how it works. The command EXPLAIN is used to solve this
problem. EXPLAIN, as might be expected, obtains explanations for the user.
For example, in the following interaction, the user wished to have the
HISTORY command explained

```
SS  1  /C?
USER:
explain history
```

PROG:
THE FOLLOWING GROUPS OF EXPLANATIONS ARE AVAILABLE:

| | |
|---|---|
| EXPLAIN EXPLAIN | (COMPLETE LIST OF EXPLANATIONS) |
| EXPLAIN COMMANDS | (LIST OF COMMANDS AND ABBREVIATIONS) |
| EXPLAIN PROGRAM MESSAGES | (LISTS PROGRAM MESSAGES IN SHORT AND LONG MESSAGE LENGTHS) |
| EXPLAIN ONLINE TUTORIALS | (LISTS SEARCH-RELATED EXPLANATIONS) |
| EXPLAIN INFORMATION | (LISTS EXPLANATIONS FOR SYSTEM INFORMATION |

IF YOU ENCOUNTER PROBLEMS, DISCONNECT PHONE FROM TERMINAL AND CALL AN ACTION
DESK FOR HELP:

| | |
|---|---|
| SANTA MONICA, CALIFORNIA | 213/829-9463 |
| TOLL FREE OUTSIDE CALIF. | 800/421-7229 |
| TOLL FREE IN CALIF. | 800/352-6689 |
| | |
| MCLEAN, VIRGINIA | 703/790-9850 |
| TORONTO (INFOMART) | 416/598-4000 |
| TOKYO (INTERNATIONAL-DENTSU) | (03)  461-5261 |
| PARIS, FRANCE | 33(1)  575-5775 |

FIGURE 11.16

to which the program responded that there are several alternatives in using
HISTORY, only one of which was illustrated here (Figure 11.15b).

One of the most important parts of an interactive system is this ability
to get "help." ORBIT allows for help from the very first message after the
user logs on. Upon entering ORBIT the user sees the following greeting:

PROG:
YOU ARE NOW CONNECTED TO THE ORBIT DATA BASE.
FOR A TUTORIAL, ENTER A QUESTION MARK. OTHERWISE
ENTER A COMMAND.

If the user enters a question mark

USER:
?

a tutorial results (Figure 11.16). This tells the user how to obtain information both online (e.g., EXPLAIN EXPLAIN) or offline (e.g., by calling a
staff member in Paris). In order to exit the system, the user types STOP

USER.
stop

the program asks for a confirmation

PROG:
ALL DONE? (Y/N)
USER:
y

and, upon receiving such confirmation, terminates the session

```
PROG:
TERMINAL SESSION FINISHED 2/21/81   10:52 A.M.   (PACIFIC TIME)
ELAPSED TIME ON INFORM:   0.15 HRS.
TOTAL ELAPSED TIME:   0.24 HRS.
```

PLEASE HANG UP YOUR TELEPHONE NOW.   GOOD-BYE!

Many other commands are supported by the ORBIT system, for example, RESTART, which erases all search strategies and starts over again, or TIME, to obtain the current date and time (in Pacific time). These are explained in the ORBIT user manual, and are left to those who wish to search in a more dedicated fashion than our discussion allows. The commands illustrated here should suffice to show the parallels between ORBIT and PIRETS. The one major distinction between the two systems is that PIRETS is a guided mode system, requiring very little training and memory on the user's part, while ORBIT is a command language, requiring some training but allowing for more efficient (i.e., faster, more concise) dialogue.

## DIALOG

The use of DIALOG (Lockheed) is similar to the use of ORBIT, with minor variations such as the use of the terms *select* and *combine* in creating search strategies, *type* instead of *print* to see the output, *expand* for *neighbor* in looking at alphabetically close terms, and *display sets* instead of *history* to see past search strategies. As the term *display sets* indicates, DIALOG looks at the "set" of documents retrieved in response to the search terms as the element of interest. The term to get off DIALOG is *logoff* rather than *stop*.

A typical search occurs as follows. After logging in, the user types "BEGIN" to start the search process

    ?begin

The system responds by requesting information (Figure 11.17a). As can be seen from this interaction, a common occurrence is for the actual searcher to be an intermediary, searching a topic for another person, called the

```
                                      Accessible files:

                                       7    SOCIAL SCISEARCH - 75/WK 1-3
                                       8    COMPENDEX - 1975
SEARCH TITLE                          11*   PSYCH ABS - MAR 78
?  Sample                             14    ISMEC-MECH ENGR - 80?May
SEARCHER NAME                         15    ABI/INFORM - 80/Apr
?  Flynn                              28    OCEANIC ABS - 80/Mar
REQUESTOR NAME                        41    POLLUTION ABS - 80/May
?  Ziegler                            42    PHARM NEWS INDEX - 80/Apr
MAIL ADDRESS                          56    ART MODERN - 1977
?  4200 S. Mozart                     77    CONFERENCE PAPERS INDEX - 80/may
SEARCH FILE
?  8                         ?8

(a)                         (b)
```

FIGURE 11.17

```
?FILE 8
?select information
1  92  INFORMATION
?select technology
2  80  TECHNOLOGY
COMBINE 1 AND 2
3  4  1 AND 2
?type 3
   ⋮
```

FIGURE 11.18

"requestor." The prompt in DIALOG is the question mark, so that each request for information is concluded by a question mark, which tells the user
"it's your turn."

Files in DIALOG are selected by using a number. If the user does not
remember the name or number of the files available, he or she may request
the system to explain the files

?explain files

which will generate a list of the files now available online (Figure 11.17b).
The number preceding the file is its "id," the information following the file
name concerns the data that is available. Thus, POLLUTION ABSTRACTS
is file 41 and the data available online is from May 1980. Our user selected
file 8, Compendex, which is an engineering data base.

The listing of the files after the request "explain files," in which
each file and its identifying number is listed, is called a "menu." The user
selects a file from the menu, a procedure called "menu selection." The use
of menus is another example of methods designed for infrequent or "casual"
users. It is very popular in 24-hr banking operations, in which the user
cannot be expected to know the entire system (is "untrained").

A shorter version of file selection consists in the user simply typing

?>FILE 8

if he or she already knows the number of the file desired. This is usually
done by trained users, and is "command" mode. An abbreviated sample interaction in DIALOG is shown in Figure 11.18.

In order to enter a term the user types the key word *select*, followed
by the word to be searched for

?select information

the system simply responds

1  92  INFORMATION

where the *1* stands for search strategy 1, the 92 is the number of postings,
and the word *information* repeats the search strategy. In this example, the
user next chose *technology*, which had 80 hits

?select technology

2  80  TECHNOLOGY

then chose to combine the first two search strategies

COMBINE 1 AND 2

which resulted in only 4 hits.

| 3 | 4 | 1 AND 2 |
|---|---|---------|
| ↑ | ↑ | |
| Search strategy three | Postings or hits | The strategy combined strategies 1 and 2 |

Thus, although there were 92 articles in the data base that contained the word *information* and 80 articles that contained the word *technology*, there were only 4 articles that contained both words.

The user begins scanning the output by saying

?type 3

which requests the system to type the first document surrogate from set 3. The system responded with the printout shown in Figure 11.19a. The numbers 3/2/1 indicate that the document printed was from set 3, that the format used was format 2, and the document printed was the first one in the set

3/2/1

    Set       Format     Document

→ 3/2/1
```
    565250          ID NO. - EI751065250
    SPEICHERSCHALTUNGEN   MIT  MNOS-TRANSISTOREN.    $left bracket$ Storage
Arrays with MNOS Transistors $right bracket$ .
    Horninger, Karlheinrich
    Siemens, Munich, Ger
    Siemens Forsch Entwicklungsber Res Dev Rep  v 4  n  4 1975 p 213-219
CODEN: SFEBBL
    DESCRIPTORS:  (*DATA STORAGE, SEMICONDUCTOR,  *Storage Devices),
TRANSISTORS, FIELD EFFECT,
    IDENTIFIERS: MNOS MEMORY DEVICES, MNOS TRANSISTORS, CCD MEMORIES
    CARD ALERT:  714,721
```

  (a)

```
?type
3/2/2
    569078   ID NO.  - EI751069078
    CHARGE-COUPLED DEVICES AND RADAR SIGNAL PROCESSING.
    Upton, Lee O.; Mayer, Gerard J.
    RCA, Moorestown, NJ
    RCA Eng  v 21  n 1  Jun-Jul 1975 p 30-34   CODEN: RCAEBC
    DESCRIPTORS:  *RADAR,  SEMICONDUCTOR DEVICES, CHARGE COUPLED, SIGNAL
PROCESSING
    IDENTIFIERS: MOVING TARGET INDICATORS
    CARD ALERT: 716, 714
```

  (b)

FIGURE 11.19

```
3/5/4
   567895    ID NO. - EI751067895
   MINING TECHNOLOGY IN 1974 $EM DASH$ A YEAR OF UNCERTAINTY.
   Kennedy, Bruce A.: Edey,  Anthony;  Niermeyer, Karl E.; Clews, K.
Malcolm
   Goler ASsoc, Inc, Seattle, Wash
   World Min  v 28  n 7  Jun 25 1975 p 87-97  CODEN: WOMIAI
   1974 afforded the mining industry time to consider the future.  It
was evident that a great deal of thought was being given to the possible
development of new concepts and improved technologies for both open pit
and underground mining, to handle the ever-increasing demand for minerals
and energy.  However, the continuing restrictive economic and political
climate worldwide generated so much uncertainty that little action has
been taken by the industry to develop or test many of these sorely needed
technological improvements.  This reduction in the rate of development of
new equipment has, however, afforded the manufacturers time to improve
existing equipment and technology.  The modification of the design of ex-
isting equipment with particular emphasis on reducing and improving the
ease of maintenance, and in simplifying the operation of equipment, was
evident from the information released by mining equipment manufacturers
in 1974.  In certain areas of the industry, some major equipment breakthroughs
have been achieved; however, little information has been released by the
various manufacturers about the new developments.  In order to economically
exploit oil shale deposits, deep thick coal reserves and the like, new
mining concepts must be developed utilizing highly automated, large capacity
mining equipment.  Because of the highly competitive nature of the energy
business, the public announcement of such new equipment and technology to
meet these requirements is likely to be slow.
   DESCRIPTORS:  (*MINES AND MINING, *Equipment),
   CARD ALERT:  502, 504, 505
```

FIGURE 11.20

The user can select other formats and other document numbers. However, if he or she wishes, the next consecutive document can be seen by simply inputting "type" again (Figure 11.19b).

The default format does not have an abstract of the article. However, the user can get such an abstract by choosing format 5

?type 3/5/4

Set 3        Document 4
    Format 5

which gives the results shown in Figure 11.20. To see a great number of documents, the user might first use format 6, which gives a very abbreviated output (Figure 11.21), then use the longer format for titles that indicate articles of interest.

If the user has forgotten what search strategies have been used, he or she can command the system to "display sets"

?display sets

which results in the "history" of search strategies (Figure 11.22a). To see items that are alphabetically near to a given term, we use "expand" (Figure 11.22b). To see more terms, the user types "page"

?page

```
?type 4/6/1-3
4/6/1
   566943    ID NO. - EI751066943
NATIONAL AND INTERNATIONAL NETWORKS OF LIBRARIES, DOCUMENTATION AND
INFORMATION CENTRES.
   AGARD Conf Proc   n   158, Mar 1975, for Meet, Brussels, Belg, Oct 2-3
1974, 84 p

4/6/2
   566058    ID NO. - EI751066058
ACCIDENT SURVEYS A GUIDE FOR AGRICULTURAL SAFETY ENGINEERING AND
EDUCATION.
   ASAE  Pap, Annu Meet, 67th, Okla State Univ, Stillwater, Jun 23-26
1974 and Winter Meet, Chicago, Ill, Dec 10-13 1974 Pap 74-5001, 10 p.
Publ by ASAE, St.   Joseph, Mich, 1974

4/6/3
   565182    ID NO. - EI751065182
UNIVERSAL DATA RECORD.
   IBM Tech Disclosure Bull   v 18   n 1 Jun 1975 p 191-198
```

FIGURE 11.21


which gives the terms following the last term in the first list (Figure
11.22c). The use of page in DIALOG is similar to the use of UP and DOWN
in ORBIT and allows the user to "scroll" through the index terms.

A term from the expand list may be selected for searching by using
its reference number

   ? select e8

which results in

   4   3   Information Retrieval Systems

which indicates that e8 and Information Retrieval Systems are synonymous.

As in both ORBIT and PIRETS, the user can combine terms in the OR
and NOT relationships, as well as in the AND relationship

   ? COMBINE 2 OR 5
   ? COMBINE 2 NOT 5

Finally, to terminate a session, we "logoff," which is computer jargon for
getting off the system


| Set | Items | Descriptions |
|-----|-------|--------------|
| 1 | 92 | Information |
| 2 | 80 | Technology |
| 3 | 4 | 1 and 2 |

(a)

FIGURE 11.22

```
?expand information
Ref            Index-term            Type Items RT
E1              INFLUENCES-----------      1
E2              INFLUX--------------       2
E3              INFOLGE-------------       1
E4              INFORM--------------       1
E5              INFORMAL------------       2
E6             -INFORMATION----------     92
E7              INFORMATION DISSEMINATION  1
E8              INFORMATION RETRIEVAL
                  SYSTEMS------------      3
E9              INFORMATION SCIENCE--      1
E10             INFORMATION THEORY---     12
E11             INFORMATIONEN--------      1
E12             INFORMATIONS---------      1
E13             INFORMATIQUE---------      1
E14             INFORMATSII----------      1
E15             INFORMTION-----------      1
E16             INFRAKRASNOM---------      1
E17             INFRARED-------------     17
E18             INFRARED HEATING-----      1
                                      -more-
```

(b)

```
?page
Ref            Index-term            Type Items RT
E19             INFRARED IMAGING ----      1
E20             INFRARED RADIATION---      1
E21             INFRAROUGE-----------      2
E22             INFREQUENTLY---------      1
E23             ING-----------------       2
E24             INGENIEUR------------      1
E25             INGENIORAKAD---------      2
E26             INGENUITY------------      1
E27             INGESTED-------------      2
E28             INGOT----------------     16
E29             INGOT CASTING--------      3
E30             INGOT MOLDS----------      1
E31             INGOTS---------------     16
E32             INGREDIENTS----------      4
E33             INHERENT-------------     15
E34             INHERENTLY-----------      6
E35             INHERENTS------------      1
E36             INHIBIT--------------      1
E37             INHIBITED------------      3
E38             INHIBITEURS----------      1
                                      -more-
```

(c)

FIGURE 11.22 (continued)

? logoff

The system responds to our logoff with an accounting of the time spent on the system, the cost in dollars and cents, as well as the date

```
    ? logoff
              21feb81  14:02:28  User7449
    $1.63  0.109 Hrs  File8  3 Descriptors
```

so that we have a record of our activity.


## BRS

In BRS, the search is again similar to ORBIT and DIALOG. We first select
a file, e.g.,

    ENTER DATA BASE NAME____:  ERIC

where the user has selected the ERIC data base. We then enter terms by
simply typing

    1___:  PRIMARY AND EDUCATION

to which the system responds with the number of postings


```
10__:    root herbicide
         HERBICIDE$

         HERBICIDE                    IO  DOCUMENTS

         HERBICIDES                   50  DOCUMENTS
```

(a)


```
..display all
1 DEATH OR DYING
RESULT   1057

2 1 AND (CHILD OR ADOLESCENT)
RESULT      99

3  CHILDREN
RESULT  37758

4  ADOLESCENT
RESULT    1407

5  YOUTH
RESULT    6169

6  CAT OR DOG
RESULT     139

7 (CAT DOG) AND FARM     (implied or)
RESULT       1

     ****   END OF DISPLAY   ****
```

(b)

FIGURE 11.23

> 1___ :   PRIMARY AND EDUCATION
>           RESULT 150

where the system prompt is

> 1___ :

with the 1 representing search strategy 1. The user entered the terms *primary* and *education*, and the system returned the result of 150 postings. To combine terms, we can do so directly, as above (primary and education) or we can make the sets (here 1, primary; 2, education) and then create the relationship we want between the sets

> 1 AND 2
> 1 OR 2
> 1 NOT 2

To see alphabetically near terms, we ask for the root, e.g.,

> 10___ :   ROOT HERBICIDE

which resulted in the list shown in Figure 11.23a. To print our output, BRS uses the command PRINT preceded by two periods

> ..PRINT

The two periods are used to indicate a switch from "search" mode to "print" mode. BRS distinguishes between search mode (selecting terms) and print mode (typing the output). ORBIT and DIALOG left this distinction "invisible" to the user. Again, arguments are provided, e.g., to get the full format, we say

> PRINT
> ALL

Documents may also be specified

> PRINT
> ALL
> DOC=1,3

which indicates that we want all fields printed (ALL) for documents 1 and 3 (DOC=1,3) of the most recent search. The user can also specify printing documents from sets other than the most recent by saying

> ..PRINT 4

where the 4 indicates that we wish documents printed from set 4. To see the old search strategies, BRS employs the command

> ..DISPLAY ALL

which results in output such as that shown in Figure 11.23b. To get off BRS, the user types ..OFF, which results in the BRS logoff message about connect time, date, and time of day.


### The Same Old Story

In order to show the parallels among systems, we include a list of the commands in the three languages (Table 11.1). Because of the similarity among systems, knowledge in one system allows the user to easily begin to use other systems.

TABLE 11.1

---

1) To choose a file

      ORBIT – FILE ERIC
      DIALOG – FILE 1
      BRS – ERIC

2) To enter a term

      ORBIT – just enter term
      DIALOG – SELECT term
      BRS – just enter term

3) To combine terms

   a)  AND      ORBIT – 1 AND 2
                 DIALOG – COMBINE 1 AND 2
                 BRS – 1 AND 2

   b)  OR       ORBIT – 1 OR 2
                 DIALOG – COMBINE 1 OR 2
                 BRS – 1 OR 2

   c)  NOT      ORBIT – 1 AND NOT 2
                 DIALOG – COMBINE 1 NOT 2
                 BRS – 1 NOT 2

4) To see the dictionary

                 ORBIT – NEIGHBOR term
                 DIALOG – EXPAND term
                 BRS – ..ROOT term

5) To print output

      ORBIT – PRINT SS 2 FULL
      DIALOG – TYPE 2/5/1-3
      BRS – ..PRINT
             ALL
             DOC=1,3

6) To see old searches

      ORBIT – HISTORY
      DIALOG – DISPLAY SETS
      BRS – ..DISPLAY ALL

7) To get off the system

      ORBIT – STOP
      DIALOG – LOGOFF
      BRS – ..OFF

---

| Subject | Data base |
|---|---|
| Art | Art Modern |
| Business | Accountants Index |
| | Inform |
| | Predicasts |
| Chemistry | Chemline |
| Computer Science | Compendex |
| Information Science | Lisa |
| Law | Locis (Scorpio) |
| Medicine | Medicine |

(a)

| | |
|---|---|
| *Art Modern* | Cover publications in the field of modern art and design in the period of 1800 to the present. Corresponds to *Artbibliographies Modern*. Prepared by American Bibliographical Center (ABC-Clio, Inc.). Coverage: January 1974 to present. |
| | File size: 48,000 records |
| | Unit record: citation, abstract. |
| *Accountants Index* | International coverage of the English-language literature related to accounting, auditing, taxation, data processing, investments, and management. |
| | Prepared by the American Institute of Certified Public Accountants. |
| | Coverage: 1974 to present. |
| | File size: 77,906 records |
| | Unit record: citation. |
| *Compendex* | The computerized *Engineering Index* data base covering engineering literature from over 2,000 serials. |
| | Prepared by Engineering Index, Inc. |
| | Coverage: January 1970 to pesent. |
| | File size: 915,083 records |
| | Unit record: citation, abstract. |

(b)

FIGURE 11.24

## Special Purpose Systems

Several other information retrieval systems are available, e.g., the National Library of Medicine's (NLM) Medline Systems, the Mead Corporation's Lexis System (legal data base), and the *New York Times* (NYT) data base (morgue) of newspaper articles. However, the user quickly finds that all of these systems are pretty much alike, and that once you have mastered searching one, the others are easier.

## Data Bases

Just as there are several information retrieval systems, so there are several data bases available. For example, some are listed in the *Directory of On-Line Information Resources* (1981); see Figure 11.24a. The guide lists descriptions for each data base (see Figure 11.24b). Furthermore, each data base will usually have a more detailed description of its contents (e.g., which index terms are used, what fields of information are kept, and what policies are pursued in acquiring documents), so that the study of the data bases and their contents can be quite extensive.

Not all data bases are offered by every vendor (e.g., SDC through ORBIT, Lockheed through DIALOG, or BRS) and one of the criteria for choosing a vendor is the range of data bases available. As indicated above, the vendors charge for using the data base by hourly fees, often ranging from $25/hr to $150/hr. These charges reflect the costs in developing the data bases, as well as how much these costs can be amortized over several users. Not all vendors create their own data bases. For example, almost all vendors offer ERIC, the educational data base, which is prepared under the auspices of the National Institute of Education (NIE), but is available at a price. Some of the data bases, e.g., ERIC, are available not only "online," but in tradtional paper and/or microfilm form.

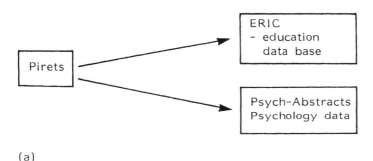

(a)

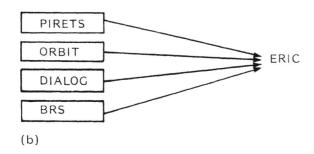

(b)

FIGURE 11.25

## The Distinction Between Query Languages and Data Bases

The data base, as the name implies, contains the data. In our example, the data have been summaries of journal articles in various subject areas. The query language is a means of interacting with the user, a means of getting the search terms from the user, so that the data base might be searched. Thus, the query language (PIRETS, ORBIT, DIALOG, or BRS) is an access mechanism to the data base. A single query language may access several data bases (Figure 11.25a). Furthermore, the same data base (same in content, although physically different copies) may be accessed by various query languages (Figure 11.25b).

## Time Delay in Creating a Data Base

If we perform a search in December, we may find that the most recent data in October's journal articles. Because of the delay involved in reading, indexing, and abstracting the articles, then keying the summaries into machine-readable form, the data base is seldom up to the minute, although some data bases are updated online, thus ensuring current data.

## Statistical Data Bases

We have used bibliographic data bases for our illustrations. However, there are not only the data bases available through the commercial firms, Numerical and/or statistical data bases are also available, containing, e.g., census figures, sales data, prices of goods, forecasts, etc. These data bases are accessed in a manner similar to the bibliographic data base. However, the layout of their fields is somewhat different, and they allow for greater facility in manipulating the data, e.g., providing totals, finding regression equations, and displaying graphs.

## Related Readings

Borko, Harold and Bernier, Charles L., *Abstracting Concepts and Methods*, New York: Academic Press, 1975.

Bradford, S. C., *Documentation*, London: Crosby Lockwood, 1948.

Campus Based Information System, *Users Manual for Interactive PIRETS*, 3rd ed. Pittsburgh: University of Pittsburgh, November 1981.

Chen, Ching-Chih and Schweizer, Susanna, *Online Bibliographic Searching: A Learning Manual*, New York: Neal-Achuman Publishers, Inc., 1981.

*Directory of Online Information Resources*, 7th ed. Kensington, MD: CSG Press, March 1981.

Duncan, Elizabeth E., Klingensmith, Patricia J., and Ross, Nina, M., *Manual for On-Line Training Center Number 1—DIALOG*, May 1982.

Duncan, Elizabeth E., Klingensmith, Patricia J., and Ross, Nina M., *Manual for On-Line Training Center Number 2—ORBIT*, April 1982.

Duncan, Elizabeth E., Klingensmith, Patricia J., and Ross, Nina M., *Manual for On-Line Training Center Number 3—BRS*, February 1982.

Flynn, Roger R., "The University of Pittsburgh Study of Journal Usage: A Summary Report," *The Serials Librarian*, Vol. 4(1), 1979, pp. 25-33.

Hayes, Robert M. and Becker, Joseph, *Handbook of Data Processing for Libraries*, 2nd ed. Los Angeles: Melville Publishing Co., 1974.

Heaps, H. S., *Information Retrieval Computational and Theoretical Aspects*, New York: Academic Press, 1978.

Kent, Allen, *Information Analysis and Retrieval*, New York: John Wiley & Sons, 1971.

Kent, Allen, et al., *Use of Library Materials: The University of Pittsburgh Study*, New York: Marcel Dekker, Inc., 1979.

Lancaster, F. Wilfred, *Information Retrieval Systems Characteristic, Testing and Evaluation*, 2nd ed. New York: John Wiley & Sons, 1979.

Lancaster, F. W. and Fayen, E. G., *Information Retrieval On-Line*, Los Angeles: Melville Publishing Company, 1973.

Lukasiewicz, J., "The Ignorance Explosion: A Contribution to the Study of Confrontation of Man with the Complexity of Science-Based Society and Environment," *New York Academy of Sciences Transaction*, (Series II), 34(5), May 1972, pp. 373-391.

Martin, James, *Desing of Man-Computer Dialogues*, Englewood Cliffs, NJ: Prentice-Hall, 1973.

Meadow, Charles T., *Man-Machine Communication*, New York: John Wiley & Sons, 1970.

Meadow, Charles T. and Cochrane, Pauline A., *Basics of Online Searching*, New York: John Wiley & Sons, 1981.

Price de Solla, D. J., "Prologue to a Science," *Little Science, Big Science*, New York: Columbia University Press, 1963, pp. 1-32.

Salton, Gerard, *Automatic Information Organization and Retrieval*, New York: McGraw-Hill, 1968.

Salton, Gerard and McGill, Michael J., *Introduction to Modern Information Retrieval*, New York: McGraw-Hill, 1983.

Saracevic, Tefko, ed. *Introduction to Information Science*, New York: R. R. Bowker Co., 1970.

*Thesaurus of ERIC Descriptors*, 9th ed. Phoenix: Oryx Press, 1982.

Various articles in the "Journal of the American Society for Information Science" (JASIS).

# 12
# The Use of Data Base Management Systems

## Objectives

Upon completion of this chapter the reader should be able to

1. Use a query language of a data base management system (DBMS) to access a data base that already exists
2. Use the data description facilities of a DBMS to create a data base
3. Discuss the problem of redundancy in regard to data consistency, the efficient use of storage space, and most important, in terms of access to data, i.e., the ability to ask questions and receive answers "across files"
4. Distinguish between the operations of insertion (adding records), deletion, and "update" (in the sense of changing values)
5. Indicate how the operation of finding a given record is related to each of the above operations
6. Indicate some of the physical operations (e.g., sort) as well as the mathematical operations (e.g., take totals, compute means and standard deviations), that can be accomplished with certain DBMSs, and use them if available
7. Distinguish between the data base description language (DDL) and the data manipulation language (DML)
8. Distinguish between a "stand alone" query language and access through a "host language," e.g., FORTRAN, COBOL, or Assembly Language.

While we have placed this chapter in the section on retrieving data, the use of DBMSs spans activities from collecting, coding, organizing, and storing data to retrieving and displaying it. The activities of collecting, coding, organizing, and storing data are involved in building a data base. The purpose, of course, of building a data base is to retrieve the data when necessary, and this involves displaying the data for the user. Most systems also allow for data manipulation, hence, the use of DBMSs creates a focus for the entire data cycle.

Student ID
  (e.g., social security number)
Student name
Student address
Student phone number
Count field for number of courses taken
  (prefix method for variable length list)
The actual list of courses, the credits for
  the courses, and a grade for each

(a)

729123064
Christopher Wise
1514 Bellefield St.
Pittsburgh, PA 15217
7274198
3
IS 10-Introduction to Information Science, 3 credits, A
CS 1 - Introduction to FORTRAN, 4 credits, A
Math 3-Algebra, 3 credits, B

(b)

FIGURE 12.1

## Data Base Management Systems: How Did They Arise?

The original approach to data processing was file oriented and single application oriented. For example, if we wished to have data on student grade
reports, we would get somebody to write a program to collect that data
and store it in a file, the "student grade file." This file might be arranged
sequentially, or it might be arranged for random access, etc. The contents
of the file would be several student records, with each record following a
standard pattern of fields. For example, the student grade file might include
the information shown in Figure 12.1a. A record might look like Figure
12.1b. The techniques of storing data might vary, e.g., instead of storing
the entire name of a course, we might store a code for each course, say
0001 = Introduction to Information Science, and look up the codes in a table
(dictionary) when outputting the data. Whatever the exact format of the
records, the programmer would be intimately aware of this format, and
would design his or her program to fit the physical organization of the
data. The program would be written for this application, with little worry
about other applications involving students, e.g., student accounts, housing, or medical records. The program itself might read in the student name
and ID, read in the grades and credit hours to compute a quality point
average (QPA), then print out a list of students and their QPAs. This list
might be organized alphabetically (sorted on name) or by QPA (sorted on
QPA), depending on whether we wished to use it in advising students (we
would know the student name, and would access the QPA by finding the
name in the alphabetic list) or in creating a class ranking (the QPAs would

Student ID
Student Name
Student Address
Student Phone Number
Count of Courses Taken
List of Courses and Credits for Each

(a)


729123064
Christopher Wise
1514 Bellefield St.
Pittsburgh, PA   15217
7274198
3
IS 10, 3 credits
CS 1, 4 credits
Math 3, 3 credits

(b)

FIGURE 12.2


be listed in descending order, and the question "Who was first in the class?" would be answered by looking at the top QPA and accessing the name through the QPA). In fact, the program might be written in such a way that a "user" of the program could specify which list he or she desired by submitting a piece of data, say N for name and Q for QPA, or else both lists might be produced each time the program were run, whether we needed them or not. The first method, i.e., specifying whether we want the name or the QPA to be primary, would allow flexibility at little (but some) cost to the user, i.e., the submission of the request Q or N. The second method, producing both lists on each run, does not involve the user, and is often easier to implement operationally, so that it is often done to avoid "complications," with a resultant stack of paper that may or may not be consulted.

Another programmer might be concerned with student accounts, and would design a file around the record layout shown in Figure 12.2a. A record for the same student, Christopher Wise, would be included in the students accounts file (Figure 12.2b). The program would read the student's name and address, compute a bill from the credits taken and the price per credit (information that might be contained in the program or in a separate data file), and print a bill.

The program for student housing might have the data fields shown in Figure 12.3a, so that Christopher's record would be as shown in Figure 12.3b. Without going into too much detail, the reader can surmise that the medical records file might contain the data fields shown in Figure 12.4, among other things.

Student ID
Student name
Student home address
Student home phone
Student campus address
Student campus phone
Year in school
Yearly housing fee
Status of bill (paid or unpaid)
Count of housing infractions (0 if none)
List of infractions

(a)

729123064
Christopher G. Wise
1514 Bellefield St.
Pittsburgh, PA 15217
7274198
124 Connecticut Ave.
Washington, Illinois
8235197
Junior
3500
Paid
2
Missed Bed Check
Rowdy Party

(b)

FIGURE 12.3


Some Observations

The above description of the files can serve to indicate several problems
with the independent file approach to data processing

- Duplication of data
- Inconsistency of data
- Difficulty of updating files


Student ID
Student name
Student address
Student phone
Count of records in medical history
Medical history
Count of records on visits to the Student Health Center
List of visits, diagnosis, actions taken, cost of visit
Status of account (balance due)

FIGURE 12.4

- Difficulty of maintaining application programs
- Difficulty of answering certain reasonable questions

## Duplication of Data

While the above programs and files may not be completely realistic, a simple perusal of the files indicates the duplication of

- Student ID
- Student name
- Student address
- Student phone number

in all four files, and the duplication of

- Courses taken
- Credits per course

in two files.

The duplication of data increases storage costs. For example, if the last name field were fixed length (say, 20 characters), and the first name field were fixed length (say, 10 characters), we would reserve 30 characters for the name field. If we had 3000 students, this is 90,000 (30 × 3,000) characters of storage space needed to hold the names in a single file. With four files, we have 36,000 (90,000 × 4) characters devoted to the name field. Similar calculations can be done with the ID (9 characters for a social security number), address (say 25 for street, 20 for city, 2 for state, 5 for zip code), and phone (7 characters without area code, 10 with). The reader should calculate the total space taken by the

- ID
- Name
- Address
- Phone

in a single file. This is the amount of storage necessary to hold the information. The remaining three files triple this amount in duplication.

## Inconsistency of Data

Even worse than duplication of data is inconsistency of data. In the above files, Christopher is listed as

Christopher Wise

in two files (student grades, student accounts), while another file (student housing) has

Christopher G. Wise

While this particular inconsistency seems trivial, it could become nontrivial, as in a case where there are two Christopher Wises, and no social security number to separate the two. In fact, such a case arises in using the phone book, where there may be two listings of Christopher Wise

| Christopher Wise | 1514 Bellefield St. | 727-4190 |
| Christopher Wise | 328 Forbes Avenue | 591-2847 |

People who have seen Christopher recently, and know his address, can choose correctly. However, people who have been "out of touch" and do not know his current address may have to call both numbers to resolve the problem.

A more subtle inconsistency in the data on Christopher is the distinction between "home" address and "campus" address in the student housing file, and the lack of such a distinction in the other files.

In all the above instances, the student has filled in his "home" address (1514 Bellefield St., Pittsburgh, PA) when asked for an address without specification. Even this amount of consistency is not to be expected. The student could easily have filled in his home address in the form for the student accounts file (since he hopes his parents will take care of it), but his campus address for the grade file (since he wishes to see the grade report first). In fact, even with the consistency of the data on the home address, the lack of a campus address makes the student relatively inaccessible to the school. If there is a question about a bill, e.g., the only phone number available to student accounts is the "home phone." Since the school is in Illinois, and his home is in Pennsylvania, this is obviously not the needed phone number, which can be obtained only by calling the student's home. If his parents are away on vacation, it could be a week or two before contact with them is made.

## Difficulty of Updating the File

The problem of consistency leads directly to the difficulty of updating the files. (The reverse is also true.) Suppose that Christopher changes his last name (as a result of getting married and taking his wife's name, or some other reason). We must update four files. If Christopher does not file the forms with all four units of the university (grades, student accounts, student housing, and medical records), the updates may not be consistent. For example, if Christopher notifies the registrar (for grades) and medical records, these two files will have his new last name

Christopher Daye

while the remaining files have the old last name

Christopher Wise or Christopher G. Wise

If medical records has Christopher's middle initial as well, we have four versions of his name:

Christopher Daye (grades; updated)
Christopher Wise (student accounts; not updated)
Christopher G. Wise (housing; not updated and including G)
Christopher G. Daye (medical records; updated and middle initial included)

If we add a single keying error to the process, we could wind up with an even worse mess

Christopher Daye (grades)
Christopher Wise (student accounts)
Christopher G. Wise (housing)
Christopher G. Dale (medical records)←(mistyped *l* for *y* in Daye)

The very difficulty of updating several records leads to inconsistency of the data.

## Difficulty of Maintaining Application Programs

In addition to the difficulty of maintaining consistent files, there is an additional problem of maintaining the application programs that were written to process the data. Suppose that the school decides to avoid using the social security number as a student ID because its use could lead to invasions of privacy, and issues a new student ID. Suppose further that the new student ID is 6 digits long (since the school never has more than a few thousand students at a time, and anticipates recycling the IDs after some period of time). Each of the four applications programs must be changed. If each were changed by the programmer who wrote the original program, this might not be difficult, although it might be time consuming. However, suppose we have since centralized our data processing operations, so that the maintenance of all four programs is being carried out by a single programmer, one who wrote none of the original programs. It might be the case that each original programmer used a different variable name (identifier) for the social security number. For example, in the grade report, the programmer may have used SOC-SEC; in student accounts we find SS-NUM; while student housing has SSN; and medical records has STUDENT-ID. Tying all variants to a single data element is not easy. The simple change of the physical size of a data element has caused a maintenance problem of rather large dimensions. In fact, since it is inevitable that the maintenance programmer will miss at least one occurrence of the variable in at least one program, one or more of the previously running programs may no longer run after the changes have been made!

## The Difficulty of Answering Certain Reasonable Questions

Even more serious than the above problems is the difficulty of answering certain questions in a file-oriented system. For example, suppose that Christopher Wise becomes ill, and is sent to a local hospital. The administration wishes to notify his teachers and the residence supervisors so that they will understand his sudden absence from his classes and from the dormitory.

The first step in the process would be to obtain Christopher's social security number, since this is our primary method of identifying him. In order to do this we consult a recently printed list of "users of student health." If none is available, we run the student health program to obtain it. Once obtained, we must phone the registrar's office to obtain a list of the courses in which Christopher is enrolled. If the system is not designed to answer individual questions, this may involve printing a list of *all* students enrolled (not a rare occurrence in data processing). Of course, this list tells us Christopher's courses, but it does not mention the faculty member, or his or her office phone or classroom number, either of which could be used to contact the faculty member. The list of courses, faculty teaching them, and rooms assigned are in another file, the "course listing file," so that we access this file to obtain a printout of all courses, and *manually* obtain the name of each instructor associated with Christopher's courses, as well as his or her address. Finally, we repeat the process to obtain the name and address of Christopher's residence advisor, by consulting the "housing allocation and supervision file." Of course, by this time Christophe may have returned.


## A Diagnosis

The list of difficulties presented above was due to several considerations

- Multiple copies of the same data item
- Multiple names for the same data item
- A close reliance on the physical layout of data by the applications programs
- A lack of *overall logical* organization of the data
- An inability to access the data from several points of view
- Inability to conveniently access a few data items

These are the issues that DBMSs address.


## A Data Base Management System: The User View

The DBMS consists of three major components:

- The data base itself
- A set of programs to create and access the data base
- A query language to interface the user of the system with the data base

We begin with a description of the user interface, the way in which a person uses the DBMS to store data and to obtain answers to his or her questions.

In the interests of simplicity, let us start with an example with which we are all familiar, a "phone book." Instead of a book, our data will be stored on a disk, but the "record layout" will be the same:

| Last Name | First Name | Address | Phone Number |
|-----------|-----------|--------------|--------------|
| Smith     | John      | 727 Forbes   | 442-2194     |
| Williams  | Joe       | 1408 Pocusset| 512-6894     |
| Canasta   | Mary      | 2701 Phillips| 412-6203     |

The system we will use to store and retrieve the data will be system 1022. This choice is made for convenience (it is used at the author's installation). Many other systems are available from computer manufacturers and software houses.


## Describing the Data

The first step in using a DBMS is to get the data into the system, and the first step in storing the data is to describe it to the system. In system

```
.TYPE PHONE.DMD
ATTRIBUTE    LNAME          TEXT      LENGTH    15    KEYED
ATTRIBUTE    FNAME          TEXT      LENGTH    10
ATTRIBUTE    ADDRESS        TEXT      LENGTH    25
ATTRIBUTE    PHONE          TEXT      LENGTH    8
```

FIGURE 12.5

1022 this is done by creating a data description file. This can be done with an editor (the details are not as important as the concept of what the file does). For this application, the author created the file shown in Figure 12.5. The file is named PHONE.DMD: PHONE for our purposes (to remind ourselves that the file contains data on phone numbers); DMD (data management description) for system 1022's sake. The DMD is the "default extension" used to indicate to 1022 that this is the data description file. The details of naming files vary greatly from system to system. The important thing is that there is some way to identify the description file.

Each line labeled "attribute" indicates a data field; thus there are four data fields. The name of the data field is indicated in the second column. The four data fields are named

> LNAME      (for last name)
> FNAME      (for first name)
> ADDRESS
> PHONE

The third column defines the data type. Typical data types are character or text (any characters are valid), integer (whole numbers like 5, -2, 0, 4), and real (numbers like 4.3, 6.0, -5.2). Sometimes, special data types are available. For example, in 1022, there is a type "date," which accepts data in the form MM/DD/YY. In this example, all the data has been declared "text," which indicates the field can hold any valid character. Next we give the length of the field, here 15, 10, 25, and 8, respectively. The fields are "fixed length." Finally, the last name field is marked "keyed." This indicates that this is the field we will later search, and that we wish to have a table of keys built to facilitate fast retrieval. Other fields can be searched sequentially, but that would be a slower process. In 1022 the command "keyed" results in an inverted index. Find operations on the entire data base can be performed only for such keyed fields. Sequential searches must be performed on previously selected (found) sets of records. More than one field may be designated as keyed. The keyed fields are not necessarily unique, i.e., not necessarily primary keys (identification fields).

## Storing the Data

Once the data has been described, we add the actual data to the file. This can be done in "batch" mode, with an entire file of data elements, or interactively, with a human being at the terminal adding a few names at a time. For large batches of data, the batch mode is preferred. However, for the addition of one or two persons (or the updating of one or two records), the interactive mode would be preferred. We first illustrate the interactive mode. In system 1022, the first step is to load the description of the file. This is done by a command

      LOAD PHONE

where PHONE is understood to be the file PHONE.DMD described above. This is what is meant by calling the extension DMD the default; it does not have to be explicitly designated in commands that "expect" it.

    When the LOAD statement is executed, the DBMS builds a special file of its own, using the data description file as a guide. This file is called the data set file, and consists of the data and the tables that enable the system to search the data. It is this file that the system uses to add, find, change, and delete records, and it receives a special extension of its own

      PHONE.DMS

the *S* indicating "set" in data set, or "searchable" data set. Once this file is created, it must be opened

      OPEN PHONE

where the extension is understood to be DMS. Again, the details vary from system to system, but the concepts are basically the same

1.   The user describes the data.
2.   The system uses this description to build a special "searchable" file.
3.   The user then accesses this searchable file to add, find, change, and delete records.

The system is "loaded" only once. From then on, the file is "opened" whenever we wish to use it.


## Adding Records

In order to store data, the user opens the "data set," then commands the system to "add." For the three records in our phone data set, the entire interaction would be as shown in Figure 12.6. The user types OPEN PHONE. (Note: the asterisk is the 1022 system prompt to the user indicating a *command* is expected.) When 1022 has opened the data set, it gives another prompt and the user responds with "add" since he or she wishes to add a record to the data set. At this point, the system responds

      SUPPLY ATTRS

which stands for supply attributes. It then lists each field that was described in the data description file, the first field being LNAME

      LNAME--

the two hyphens are a prompt to the user, indicating that data should now be entered. Since the last name of our first record is SMITH, we enter SMITH

      LNAME--SMITH

the system then prompts for FNAME

      FNAME--

and the user types in JOHN

      FNAME--JOHN

```
* OPEN PHONE ◄--- open phone data set
* ADD ◄---------- add record

SUPPLY ATTRS
  LNAME--SMITH        ⎫
  FNAME--JOHN         ⎪
  ADDRESS--727 FORBES ⎬   actual data entry
  PHONE--442-2194     ⎪
* ADD                 ⎭

SUPPLY ATTRS
  LNAME--WILLIAMS
  FNAME--JOE
  ADDRESS--1408 POCUSSET
  PHONE--512-6894
* ADD

SUPPLY ATTRS
  LNAME--CANASTA
  FNAME--MARY
  ADDRESS--2701PHILLIPS
  PHONE--412-6203
* QUIT

EXIT
```

FIGURE 12.6

and the address and phone number

```
    ADDRESS--727 FORBES
    PHONE--442-2194
    *
```

Note that using the hyphen in the phone field forced us to do two things

1. Declare PHONE to be data type "text"
2. Declare PHONE to have a length of 8

Upon receiving the data for the phone field, the system "knows" that it has received the last data item. Hence it prompts with an asterisk again, indicating it is waiting for a command

```
    PHONE--442-2194
    *
```

The systems uses two kinds of prompts

- The asterisk, when it is expecting a command, like ADD or FIND
- The pair of dashes, when it is expecting data, like a last name, address, or phone number

When the user sees the asterisk, he or she can enter any valid command, e.g., ADD, FIND, DELETE, and CHANGE. In this example, we are attempting to enter the three data records, so we again say ADD, then enter the data for Joe Williams, and repeat the process for Mary Canasta. On receiving the asterisk for Mary Canasta, the user said QUIT, since all three records had been entered, and he or she wished to "exit" the system. The system responded with the word *EXIT* to indicate that the QUIT command was successfully retrieved, and the session terminated.

## Add, Find, Change, Delete

While there are commands to manipulate data, probably the most common activities are

> Adding new records (insertions)
> Finding (and displaying) the data values in a record
> Changing a particular value in a record (e.g., the bank balance), called updating
> Deleting records (deletions)

The operation of adding involves the storage of data. The remaining operations involve the retrieval of data: in order to display or change the values of a record, or to delete a record, we must first locate (or find) it. In fact, the find operation is also implicit in adding records: in order to store the record, we must find a suitable location at which to store it, and then either remember that location (e.g., in a table of addresses, like an index), or recompute the same address (as in hashing) at a later time. Thus, the "find" operation might be considered basic, with the add, delete, and update operations all relying on it. Displaying a data record is simply a matter of transferring it from storage to a display unit (such as a teletype or video terminal). We can, of course, manipulate records (e.g., in updating them) without displaying them. This would involve transferring the record from secondary storage to the main memory of the computer, changing the data field, and returning the record to secondary storage. Hence, the display command is often separate from the find command. The process of moving the record from secondary storage to the main memory of the computer is sometimes allocated a separate command (e.g., GET), since we may choose to find records (e.g., obtaining addresses) without wishing to manipulate them. However, we will consider the basic operations to be

- Finding records in order to display them
- Adding new records (insertions)
- Deleting old records (deletions)
- Changing values in records (update)

All these basic operations are provided in DBMSs.

## Answering Questions: Find and Print

In order to find a record in system 1022, we simply say find, and give the name of the key field and the value of the key for the record we wish to access. Hence to find the phone record of Williams, we say

> *FIND LNAME WILLIAMS
> FOUND

to which the systems responds FOUND if it has indeed located the record. If the system could not locate the record (e.g., if Williams did not have a phone, and thus was not in our phone data set), the system would have responded NOT FOUND

```
*FIND LNAME WILLIAMS
NOT FOUND
```

In fact, the record does not have to be "missing" in order to be "not found." If we had misspelled Williams

```
*FIND LNAME WILLIANS
```

or given the wrong data value

```
*FIND LNAME JOE
    (mistakenly entering the first name instead of the last name)
```

the system would respond NOT FOUND.

In requesting the system to find the record, we named the key field as well as giving a value for the field

```
*FIND LNAME WILLIAMS
```

The reason for naming the key field (LNAME) is that system 1022 allows us to have more than one key field. For example, in the wine file, we were interested in not only the color of the wine (red or white), but its particular type (Chablis, Burgundy) and, for quick access, if we know it, the wine number (002 or 006). All of these fields could be "keyed" in the DBMS. Of course, some fields might not be "good keys" (e.g., color), since there are too many records with the same value (e.g., 409 red wines, and 321 white wines). The wine identification number is unique to each wine and could be keyed to allow direct access to that wine record (e.g., by the clerk, who might know the keys of certain wines). This could be done by hashing or by keeping a table of addresses. Key fields that have more than one record posted to them (e.g., Burgundy: 001, 004) would use some method other than hashing (e.g., the inverted file). The point here, however, is that there may be more than one key field; hence, we must tell the system the name of the particular key field in which we are searching

```
FIND LNAME WILLIAMS
       |
       name of key field
```

as well as the value of the key

```
FIND LNAME WILLIAMS
             |
             value of key for record we want
```

If a single field had to be designated as the key, we could simply give the value of that field for the record we want

```
FIND WILLIAMS
```

The distinction between the name of the field and the value of that field is crucial. While all records will have a last name field, here called LNAME, each will have different values in that field, and these are the values that distinguish one record from another

```
LNAME
WILLIAMS←—— identifies record for Williams
SMITH    ←—— identifies record for Smith
CANASTA←—— identifies record for Canasta
```

Some fields will have a unique value for each record (e.g., the wine ID or a person's social security number). Other fields will have "repeating values." For example, there may be two or three employees who have experience as accountants, which might be called the work-experience field, and could be keyed in 1022, which uses the term for "create an inverted index." The way in which this repeating value fields are handled will distinguish different data base "architectures."

The use of the term key has two different senses

- As a field that uniquely identifies a record
- As a field for which an inverted index (secondary index) has been created

The reader will have to keep the distinction in mind and use the context to tell which meaning is intended. In system 1022 keyed fields are not necessarily unique IDs.

The fact that the system simply replies found instead of displaying the record indicates that we must explicitly ask for the record to be displayed. The automatic display of records is avoided because we may not want to see the record, or at least not all of it. An instance in which we might not want to see the record at all is one in which we just want to know if the record actually exists in the data set (e.g., "Has the Williams data been added yet?"). Of course, the more common situation is that we do not want to see all the data fields. A record may have several data fields, consisting of hundreds of characters (alphabetic characters, not people), which would take time to display, and the display would be cluttered with items of no interest. Hence, instead of automatically displaying all the data, the system allows the user to request the data he or she wishes to display. On system 1022, this can be done with the print command

    *PRINT PHONE
    512-6894

where the user typed PRINT PHONE and the system replied with 512-6894, which is the phone number for Williams. The entire transaction was

    * FIND LNAME WILLIAMS
    FOUND
    * PRINT PHONE
    512-6894

If the user had wished to find Mary Canasta's address, the sequence would be

    * FIND LNAME CANASTA
    FOUND
    * PRINT ADDRESS
    2701PHILLIPS

where we first find the record by giving the name and value of the key field, then request that the value of the address field be printed. Note that in the print command, one simply names the field to be printed. The system returns the value. Presumably, we would not be searching for the record if we already knew the value (in the find and display situation).

Of course, if we wish, we can display more than one field

    * FIND LNAME CANASTA
    FOUND
    * PRINT ADDRESS PHONE        412-6203
    2701PHILLIPS

and the order in which the data is displayed does *not* have to be the same as the order in which it was entered

    * PRINT PHONE ADDRESS
    412-6203  2701PHILLIPS

where we printed the phone number before the address, even though these data were entered in the reverse order.

If we do wish to see all the data fields, we simply say PRINT ALL

    * PRINT ALL
    CANASTA      MARY      2701PHILLIPS      412-6203

in which case the data values are printed in the same order as they were entered.

## Changing Records

You may have noticed that the address for Mary Canasta is mistyped

    2701PHILLIPS

with no space between the street number and the street name. We would want to correct this by changing or updating that data field. In order to do so, we first locate the record

    * FIND LNAME CANASTA
    FOUND

then issue the command to change the data field

    * CHANGE  ADDRESS "2701 PHILLIPS"
    *

which gives the name of the field we wish to change, address, and the *new* value we want assigned to that field. The data value "2701 Phillips" is enclosed in quotes because of the space within the data value. If we did not enclose it in quotes, the system would see two data values where it expected one. If we were changing the phone number, we would not need the quotes

    * CHANGE PHONE 624-5200
    *

The *new* phone number would be 624-5200. Similarly for the last name

    * CHANGE LNAME MILLER
    *

the change command does not "echo" the change. The fact that the new value has been accepted (and the old value lost) is indicated by the appearance of the prompt (*) on the next line. If a command was *not* successful, an error message would have been printed. For example, in the find command

    * FIND WILLIAMS
    ? (CS18) Needed an attribute name

where the user forgot the attribute name (LNAME) of the key field, the system responds with a question mark and the error message. The question mark is a fairly standard way of saying "what?", indicating the system's lack of understanding of the command. The error message itself ("needed an attribute name") tries to pinpoint the problem. Here the message actually makes sense. We will see that this is not always the case. Here, we are concentrating on the error message as a basic form of feedback, simply indicating a yes-no decision on the successful reception of our command, where

- The reception of the asterisk indicates "Yes, the command was accepted."

  and

- The reception of the error message means we should look at the command to see if something is misspelled, missing, or otherwise awry.

If we do receive the asterisk, i.e., our command has been successful, we may still wish to list the new data value to see that it is what we intended

```
* PRINT PHONE
624-5200
*
* PRINT LNAME
MILLER
*
```

Printing out the data we just entered is called "echoing" the data. It guards against errors made in keying the data into the system. For example, if we had echoed the record for Mary Canasta when it was originally entered, we might have noticed the mistyping of the address at that time, and corrected it then, instead of carrying the bad data in the system. For something like a missing blank in the address, the entry of bad data is not a serious problem. However, if the data value misentered is a "reasonable but wrong" value, e.g., entering the phone number as 412-6023 instead of 412-6203 (a transposition error), the error would not be obvious at a time other than the time of entry. In fact, we would never know of the incorrect data entry until we actually had to call Mary Canasta and got a wrong number. At this time, it might be more difficult to track down the correct number (e.g., if the source data forms had been discarded), so that it is beneficial to echo and check the data at the time it is entered. Of course, echoing also takes time; there is a trade-off between accuracy and "throughput," i.e., the amount of data entered per hour. The characteristics of each situation will determine which factor is more important.

## Error Messages

As indicated above, the system sometimes gives error messages when we mistype a command. These error messages are meant to be a "diagnostic aid," so that we may know exactly what is wrong with the command. In the message

```
* FIND WILLIAMS
? (CS18) Needed an attribute name
```

the message "needed an attribute name" indicated that the user had forgotten to name the key field (LNAME). The CS18 in parentheses is the "error message number," which can be used to look up "diagnostic hints" in the manual that explains the system. In this example, the CS (command scanner) indicates a generic error type. The number in the code (18 in CS18) indicates which particular error of this type occurred. For example, in this version of system 1022, there are 156 CS-type errors, with CS18 being "needed an attribute name."

On this particular system, there are several generic categories of errors. The CS code indicates that the system has read the command and did not understand it. Another generic type of error occurs when opening files (OP). For example, if we mistype the name of the file, we get the following message:

    * OPEN PHONEE
    1022 LOOKUP error (0) File not found File:   PHONEE.DMS
    ? (OP2) Dataset not found

which has the code OP, indicating that the error occurred in opening the files. In practice the error message is not always as helpful for diagnosing the error as it is for indicating that an error occurred. For example, receiving the error message FILE NOT FOUND, we simply look at the open statement to see that we misspelled PHONE as PHONEE, so that the system looked for a file called PHONEE.DMS, which, of course, it did not find.

An example of a misleading error message is the following:

    * CHANGE ADDRESS 2701 PHILLIPS
    ? (CS18) Needed an attribute name

where the system tells us that we need an attribute name, when we actually have one (address), and the real error was that we forgot the quote marks around the data value "2701 Phillips." As the reader can see, error diagnosis by a computer program is not a completely solved problem.

As indicated above, many users treat the error message as a "yes-no" form of feedback. An error message indicates the command was not carried out. No error message indicates success. If an error message occurs, the user simply looks at the command to see if the reason is obvious. If the reason is not immediately obvious, he or she might then consult the user manual for further help. If the user manual approach does not succeed, another person (e.g., a user consultant at the installation, or a supervisor), would be consulted.

## Deleting Records

In order to delete records from the data set, we find the record, then say DELETE

    * FIND LNAME WILLIAMS
    FOUND
    *DELETE
    *

Again, the system simply replies with an asterisk. To assure ourselves that the record has been deleted, we can issue another find

    * FIND LNAME WILLIAMS
    NOT FOUND
    *

where the system's reply of NOT FOUND indicates that the record for Williams has indeed been deleted.

Note that the delete command takes "no arguments," i.e., we do not need to name a data field or give a value for a data field; the record found is deleted in its entirety. Thus, some commands take zero arguments

DELETE

one argument

PRINT PHONE

or two arguments

CHANGE LNAME MILLER

The "arguments" are the pieces of information that the command needs in order to be executed successfully. In a sense, the command is like a computer program, consisting of instructions and data. The instruction tells the machine "what to do," and the data tells it "with what." Thus in PRINT PHONE, the instruction is to PRINT, and the data to be printed is the value of the phone field. In

CHANGE LNAME MILLER

the command is to update a data field. The information needed is

• The name of the field
• The new value that is to replace the current value of the field

The DELETE command has no explicit arguments. The data to be deleted is understood to be the last record accessed.


## Various Applications

The reasons for adding, deleting, changing, and finding records vary from application to application. For example, in a department store, we would add records when a new account is opened, delete them when an account is closed, and change them when payments or purchases are made. We might find a record in order to check a credit rating when a customer wishes to make a purchase, or to check the balance in an account if the customer wishes to make a payment. In a banking application, we would add and delete records to open and close accounts, update for deposits or withdrawals, and use "find" to check balances, e.g., in cashing a check. In a library circulation application, we might add records as books are taken out (indicating the book title, borrower's name, date due, etc.) and delete them as they are returned. We might update the record if the book was renewed, and we might simply display the record if we wished to see who had a particular book out. If we wished to see how many books a particular individual had taken out, we would retrieve all the records with that borrower's name in the borrower field.


## More Than One Key: The Wine File

In the phone application, there was a single key field, the name, which was assumed to be unique. It is possible, however, to have more than one

| Key | Color | Type | Manufacturer | Price |
|-----|-------|------|--------------|-------|
| 001 | Red | Burgundy | ABC | H |
| 002 | White | Chablis | U-Drink | H |
| 003 | Red | Beaujolais | U-Drink | L |
| 004 | Red | Burgundy | XYZ | H |
| 005 | White | Chablis | U-Drink | M |
| 006 | Red | Chianti | U-Drink | L |

(a)

```
.TYPE WINE.DMD
ATTRIBUTE  WINE_ID    ABBREV   ID  INTEGER LENGTH 3 KEYED
ATTRIBUTE  COLOR    ABBREV C  TEXT   LENGTH 5 KEYED
ATTRIBUTE  PARTICULAR_TYPE   ABBREV  TYPE TEXT LENGTH 15 KEYED
ATTRIBUTE MANUFACTURER  ABBREV  MFR TEXT LENGTH 10
ATTRIBUTE  PRICE  ABBREV P   TEXT LENGTH 1 KEYED
```

(b)

FIGURE 12.7

field "keyed" in 1022. In the wine file (Figure 12.7a), we were interested in the color of the wine (red or white), the particular type of wine (Burgundy, Chablis, etc.) and the price (H, L, M). In addition, we wished to be able to access the record by the wine identification number, when it was known. Hence, all of these fields would be "keyed." A data description file to do this is shown in Figure 12.7b. Again, there is one "attribute entry" for each field in the record. The first field is named the WINE_ID; it is an integer of length 3, and it will be keyed. Also, for convenience of typing, this field may be abbreviated as ID. The use of ABBREV in system 1022 allows us to enter long names for data fields into the data description file (e.g., WINE_ID), but use shorter names (e.g., ID) in interacting with the system. The use of long names in the data description file serves as "self-documentation"; we can tell what each field contains by its name. However, to use the long name in a number of commands, e.g.,

*FIND WINE_ID   002

might prove tedious. Hence, we can abbreviate

*FIND   ID   002

The user may use either the long name or the abbreviation in his or her queries, so it is not necessary to know all the abbreviations. Casual users (people who use the system once in a while) might use the long name; dedicated users (people who enter data and/or search the system frequently) might use the abbreviations. Also, 1022 allows field names to contain the underscore (_). This can improve readability, by allowing names to consist of two or three words

WINE_ID
RATE_OF_PAY

```
* OPEN WINE
* ADD

SUPPLY ATTRS
  ID--001
  C--RED
  TYPE--BURGUNDY
  MFR--ABC
  P--H
* ADD

SUPPLY ATTRS
  ID--002
  C--WHITE
  TYPE--CHABLIS
  MFR--U-Drink
  P--H
* ADD

SUPPLY ATTRS
  ID--003
  C--RED
  TYPE--BEAUJOLAIS
  MFR--U-DRINK
  P--L
* ADD

SUPPLY ATTRS
  ID--004
  C--RED
  TYPE--BURGUNDY
  MFR--XYZ
  P--H
* ADD

SUPPLY ATTRS
  ID-005
  C--WHITE
  TYPE--CHABLIS
  MFR--U-DRINK
  P--M
* ADD

SUPPLY ATTRS
  ID--006
  C--RED
  TYPE--CHIANTI
  MFR--U-DRINK
  P--L
*
```

FIGURE 12.8


PARTICULAR_TYPE
HOURS_WORKED

The names are really not two words, but appear so. If the underscores were omitted, the field name would actually be two words, and would be picked up as an error.

In the example, four of the five fields have been keyed

WINE_ID             (ID)
COLOR               (C)
PARTICULAR_TYPE     (TYPE)
PRICE               (P)

These are all "searchable" fields. In order to illustrate how we would search the file, we must first add (insert) the wine records (Figure 12.8). (Note: The entire process of creating the wine file description, as well as adding the six records took a matter of minutes. To prepare a program to read and store this data might take half an hour or so; a program to store the data in such a manner that we could later search it efficiently might take hours, days, weeks, months or years, depending on the complexity of the data and the queries we wish to make.)

### Answering Questions: Searching the Wine File

Once the data has been inserted into the data base, we can search it in order to answer various questions. For example, if we are looking for a red wine, we ask the system to

* FIND COLOR RED

```
* FIND COLOR RED
4 RECS FOUND.
* PRINT ALL
1 RED    BURGUNDY      ABC        H
3 RED    BEAUJOLAIS    U-DRINK    L
4 RED    BURGUNDY      XYZ        H
6 RED    CHIANTI       U-DRINK    L
*

(a)


* PRINT ID
1
3
4
6

(b)

* PRINT TYPE
BURGUNDY
BEAUJOLAIS
BURGUNDY
CHIANTI
*


(c)
```

FIGURE 12.9

```
*
* FIND COLOR RED
4 RECS FOUND.
* GETREC 3
* PRINT ALL
4 RED   BURGUNDY       XYZ           H
*
```

(a)

```
* FIND COLOR RED
4 RECS FOUND.
* SEARCH PRICE L
2 RECS FOUND.
* PRINT ALL
3 RED    BEAUJOLAIS         U-DRINK       L
6 RED    CHIANTI            U-DRINK       L
*
```

(b)

FIGURE 12.10


It will retrieve all records that have the value "red" in the color field,
and tell us how many there are

> * FIND COLOR RED
> 4 RECS FOUND.

at which point we can choose to print the records found. The entire transaction is shown in Figure 12.9a, where PRINT ALL indicates we wish to see
all the fields. If we wished to see only the wine identification numbers,
we could type PRINT ID (Figure 12.9b), or we could select the PARTICU-
LAR_TYPE field (abbreviated "type"; Figure 12.9c).

If not told differently, the system types the values for all records just
found (called the "set of selected records"). To tell the system "differently,"
we can use the GETREC command to specify a particular record in the set
(Figure 12.10a), which retrieves the third record in the selected set. Or,
more usefully, we can search for other field values within the selected set
(Figure 12.10b), where the FIND command found four records with color
red, and the search command

> * SEARCH PRICE L

then found two records within this set that were low in price.

We can also focus our search with the Boolean operators, as in bibliographic information retrieval systems. The AND relationship is illustrated
in Figure 12.11a, where we have selected all high-price red wines.

The OR relationship is illustrated in Figure 12.11b, where we have
found all wines that are low or medium priced ("not high" would have
worked as well). In this illustration, we have used OR on a single field.
In that case an abbreviated form may be used, omitting the second field

```
*
* FIND PRICE H AND COLOR RED
2 RECS FOUND.
* PRINT ALL
1 RED     BURGUNDY     ABC        H
4 RED     BURGUNDY     XYZ        H
```
              (a)

```
* FIND PRICE L OR PRICE M
3 RECS FOUND.
* PRINT ALL
3 RED     BEAUJOLAIS      U-DRINK   L
5 WHITE   CHABLIS         U-DRINK   M
6 RED     CHIANTI         U-DRINK   L
```
              (b)

```
* FIND PRICE M OR L
3 RECS FOUND.
* PRINT ALL
3 RED     BEAUJOLAIS      U-DRINK   L
5 WHITE   CHABLIS         U-DRINK   M
6 RED     CHIANTI         U-DRINK   L
```
              (c)

```
* FIND COLOR RED OR PRICE H
5 RECS FOUND.
* PRINT ALL
1 RED     BURGUNDY      ABC         H
2 WHITE   CHABLIS       U-Drink     H
3 RED     BEAUJOLAIS    U-DRINK     L
4 RED     BURGUNDY      XYZ         H
6 RED     CHIANTI       U-DRINK     L
```
              (d)

FIGURE 12.11

name (Figure 12.11c). In other applications, we might use OR across fields, in which case the second field name would be necessary (Figure 12.11d), although it is not really a practical query in this instance.

NOT is illustrated in Figure 12.12a, which, of course, gives different results than the query in Figure 12.12b. Finally, if we wish, we can search

```
* FIND PRICE H NOT COLOR RED
FOUND.
* PRINT ALL
2 WHITE CHABLIS        U-DRINK          H
*
```
              (a)

FIGURE 12.12

```
* FIND COLOR RED NOT PRICE H
2 RECS FOUND.
* PRINT ALL
3 RED        BEAUJOLAIS       U-DRINK      L
6 RED        CHIANTI          U-DRINK      L
```

(b)

```
* FIND ID 004
FOUND.
* PRINT ALL
4 Red      BURGUNDY       XYZ         H
*
```

(c)

FIGURE 12.12   (continued)

```
* PRINT ALL
1 RED      BURGUNDY       ABC          H
3 RED      BEAUJOLAIS     U-DRINK      L
4 RED      BURGUNDY       XYZ          H
6 RED      CHIANTI        U-DRINK      L
```

(a)

```
* VALUES PRICE
H (2)
L (2)
*
```

(b)

```
*
* PRINT ALL SYSID
1 RED      BURGUNDY       ABC          H 1
3 RED      BEAUJOLAIS     U-DRINK      L 3
4 RED      BURGUNDY       XYZ          H 4
6 RED      CHIANTI        U-DRINK      L 6
```
system ID

(c)

FIGURE 12.13

```
.R 1022

1/18/83
System 1022A 115A(207)

* OPEN WINE
* ADD

SUPPLY ATTRS
  ID--8◄---ID 8, but 7th record entered
  C--RED
  TYPE--CHIANTI
  MFR--ABC
  P--L
*
* ADD

SUPPLY ATTRS
  ID--7◄---ID 7, but 8th record entered
  C--WHITE
  TYPE--SAUTERNE
  MFR--ABC
  P--M
*
```

FIGURE 12.14

on the ID number (Figure 12.12c), if we know it. This would provide the most direct access of the record.

    If we are interested only in the number of records "posted" for each value in a particular field, there is a specialcommand VALUES. For example, given the selected set of Figure 12.13a, we can use VALUES to see how many wines are listed for each price (Figure 12.13b), which indicates that this set contains two high-priced wines and two low-priced ones. The system also allows us to see the system ID of each record (Figure 12.13c), which indicates that these records have been stored in the order entered; this was the same order as the wine ID number. The fact that the records are ordered by order of entry (and not by hashing on the ID field) can be seen by adding two records in an order different from their ID (Figure 12.14).

```
          * FIND ALL
          8 RECS FOUND.                                  System ID
          * PRINT ALL SYSID
   Key    1 RED     BURGUNDY       ABC          H 1 ↵
    ↳     2 WHITE   CHABLIS        U-Drink      H 2
          3 RED     BEAUJOLAIS     U-DRINK      L 3
          4 RED     BURGUNDY       XYZ          H 4
          5 WHITE   CHABLIS        U-DRINK      M 5
          6 RED     CHIANTI        U-DRINK      L 6
   keys  ⌈8 RED     CHIANTI        ABC          L 7 ⌉ order
entered  ⌊7 WHITE   SAUTERNE       ABC          M 8 ⌋ entered
          *
```

FIGURE 12.15

We can select all records in the file with the command

    * FIND ALL

then print their data values and the system ID (Figure 12.15). The records are listed in the order stored, which reflects the system ID (7 before 8), but not the key (wine ID 8 listed before wine ID 7). While the user often has no need for the system ID, it can give us a glimpse into the internal structuring of the data base.


## Primary and Secondary Keys

In discussing keys, a field that is used to uniquely identify a record, like the WINE_ID, is called a primary key. In some applications, there may be more than one candidate for a primary key. For example, if we assume all our employees have unique last names and unique social security numbers, we could use either field as the primary key. Both fields would be "candidates" for the designation "primary key." The one actually selected would be the primary key.

All keys other than the primary key are called secondary keys or secondary attributes. The term *secondary attribute* is probably better, since the phrase "secondary key" connotes a unique identifier. Some attributes may be unique; e.g., if we chose the last name to be the primary key, the social security number would be a unique secondary attribute. Other secondary attributes may be "non-unique" in that several records may have the same value for that field. An example is the color field in the wine file, or the price field.

In 1022 the phrase key refers to "indexed" or not. Hence, secondary attributes that are not "keys" in the identifier sense are sometimes called secondary keys. Some keyed fields are unique, others are not. Some fields may not be keyed at all, e.g., the manufacturer field in the wine file. Keyed fields may be searched quickly. The system builds tables—inverted indices—to aid in searching the file. These are the fields accessed by the command FIND in 1022

    * FIND PRICE H
    3 RECS FOUND.

If we attempt to FIND a nonkeyed field, the system will issue an error message

    * FIND MFR ABC
    ? (CS62) UNKEYed attribute
      FIND MFR
    *

where the system tells us that the field is UNKEYed, and repeats our erroneous command (FIND MFR). System 1022 provides a facility for searching nonkeyed fields, the SEARCH command

    * SEARCH MFR ABC

The search on a nonkeyed field is a sequential search, hence slow; for this reason, system 1022 does not allow it to be used to search the entire data set. However, as we indicated above, it is often used to search through a selected set of records on a nonkeyed (or keyed) field (Figure 12.16).

```
* FIND COLOR RED
4 RECS FOUND.
* SEARCH MFR XYZ
FOUND.
* PRINT ALL
4 RED     BURGUNDY        XYZ         H
*
```

FIGURE 12.16

    The keyed fields offer a faster search, but incur the overhead of the search tables. Nonkeyed fields do not incur the overhead, but are not capable of quick searching. Whether a field is keyed or not will depend on the frequency and type of access. In system 1022, a search can be performed on the entire data set if preceded by the command FIND ALL, but this will be time consuming for a large data base.

    In some systems, the key fields can only be created at the time the data base is loaded. On others, such as 1022, they can be created dynamically

    * KEY MFR

    System 1022 Keying Program
    keying attributes:
    MANUFACTURER (1 Block, 1 new)
    *

Keys can also be removed dynamically

    *UNKEY MFR

The dynamic keying and unkeying of fields enables us to change the structure of the data base as our needs change. Some systems also make the user distinguish between primary keys and secondary keys. In 1022, we distinguish only between keyed and nonkeyed fields.


Manipulating the Data

Most DBMSs offer some means to manipulate data. In order to illustrate some of the simpler commands in 1022, we will create two new files

- A file of data
- A data description file for this data

The data file contains a list of people and their respective ages (Figure 12.17a). This data file will replace the insertion of records online. When the file is loaded, it will be initialized to the data in this file. The data file has the extension DMI with the *I* indicating "input" to the data base (data management input). The second file is the data description file (Figure 12.17b).

    When the data base is loaded (Figure 12.17c), the system will use the data description file (DMD) to load the data from the data file (DMI) to create the data set (DMS). The system indicates that it has loaded the data by typing "4 records processed." It also indicates that there were two keyed fields (NAME and AGE). In the absence of the data file, the system

```
.TYPE AGE.DMI
FLYNN       22
WILLIAMS    21
MARINO      33
BOOSKE      28
```

(a)

```
.TYPE AGE.DMD
ATTRIBUTE NAME TEXT LENGTH 10 KEYED
ATTRIBUTE AGE INTEGER LENGTH 2 KEYED
```

(b)

```
.R 1022

1/17/83
System 1022A 114E(46)

* LOAD AGE
System 1022 Data Loading Program
No errors in DESCRIPTION file
4 records processed, 4 blocks written on phase 2
processing keyed attributes:
NAME (1 block, 4 values)
AGE (1 block, 4 values)
2 blocks written on phase 3
*
```

(c)

FIGURE 12.17

loads the description of the data, but does not put actual data into the data set, and indicates this by saying that it loaded zero records. This was the case in our earlier examples.

The use of the DMI file is "batch" loading as opposed to "online data entry." The system allows us to manipulate the data physically, e.g., in sorting, to perform calculations, such as totals, as well as to calculate some simple statistics, such as the mean and standard deviation. In order to sort data, we use the SORT command and name the field to be sorted

```
    * SORT BY NAME
```

The sort command works on a selected set of records. In order to have the selected set consist of the entire file, we can use the command

```
    * FIND ALL
```

The entire interaction would be shown as in Figure 12.18a. In the absence of a qualifier, the sort is in ascending order. To obtain descending order, we type the commands shown in Figure 12.18b. If we are interested in the persons' ages instead of their names, we can sort on AGE (Figure 12.18c),

```
* FIND ALL
4 RECS FOUND.
* SORT BY NAME
* PRINT ALL
BOOSKE      28
FLYNN       22
MARINO      33
WILLIAMS    21
*
```

(a)

```
* SORT BY NAME DESCENDING          * SORT BY AGE ASCENDING
* PRINT ALL                        * PRINT ALL
WILLIAMS    21                     WILLIAMS    21
MARINO      33                     FLYNN       22
FLYNN       22                     BOOSKE      28
BOOSKE      28                     MARINO      33
*                                  *
```

(b)                                (c)

FIGURE 12.18

where the word *ascending* is not necessary, but might be used for completeness.

As above, we can find a particular age (Figure 12.19a). We can also search for values that are greater than (Figure 12.19b), less than (Figure 12.19c), or not less than (Figure 12.19d) a particular value, or other logical combinations.

```
                                                      * FIND AGE LT 30
                        * FIND AGE GT 25              3 RECS FOUND.
* FIND AGE 33           2 RECS FOUND.                 * PRINT ALL
FOUND.                  * PRINT ALL                   FLYNN       22
* PRINT NAME            MARINO      33                WILLIAMS    21
MARINO                  BOOSKE      28                BOOSKE      28
*                       *                             *
```

(a)                     (b)                           (c)

```
                                  * FIND AGE BETWEEN 21  25
* FIND AGE NOT LT 30              2 RECS FOUND.
FOUND.                            * PRINT ALL
* PRINT ALL                       FLYNN       22
MARINO   33                       WILLIAMS    21
*                                 *
```

(d)                               (e)

FIGURE 12.19

One can also search on a range of values (Figure 12.19e), where the term *between* is interpreted as being inclusive of the end points (21 through 25, inclusively) rather than its more customary meaning of "exclusive of" the end points. We can print minimum values

```
* PRINT MIN AGE
21
```

maximum values

```
* PRINT MAX AGE
33
*
```

or combine the two to get a range

```
* PRINT MIN AGE MAX AGE
21    33
*
```

A total can be obtained by the key word TOT

```
* PRINT TOT AGE
104
*
```

although this particular application might not warrant a total. To obtain an average or arithmetic mean we type the key word MEAN

```
* PRINT MEAN AGE
26.000000
*
```

and the standard deviation by

```
*
* PRINT STDEV AGE
5.5976185
*
```

In an application involving students and their QPAs (Figure 12.20a), we could use the sort command to create a class ranking (Figure 12.20b),

```
.TYPE QPA.DMD
ATTRIBUTE NAME TEXT LENGTH 10
ATTRIBUTE QPA REAL LENGTH 4

.TYPE QPA.DMI
DRAGO      3.86
DRUMM      2.49
BAILEY     3.99
HUITT      2.75
BRYAN      3.51
ALLAN      3.01
STEPHEN    2.88
```

(a)

FIGURE 12.20

```
* SORT BY QPA DESCENDING
* PRINT ALL                              * PRINT QPA NAME
BAILEY        3.9900000                  3.9900000  BAILEY
DRAGO         3.8600000                  3.8600000  DRAGO
BRYAN         3.5100000                  3.5100000  BRYAN
ALLAN         3.0100000                  3.0100000  ALLAN
STEPHEN       2.8800000                  2.8800000  STEPHEN
HUITT         2.7500000                  2.7500000  HUITT
DRUMM         2.4900000                  2.4900000  DRUMM
*                                        *
```

(b)                                      (c)

FIGURE 12.20 (continued)

printing either the names first (Figure 12.20b), or the QPA first (Figure 12.20c).

In a sales record application, we could key data on items purchased and their respective prices (Figure 12.21a and b). We could use total to compute the balance due

```
* PRINT TOT PRICE
66.900000
*
```

The output of the total is not esthetic, so we might use the system-formatting capabilities to change it

```
* PRINT TOT PRICE FORMAT F6.2 END
66.90
*
```

where the formats follow the FORTRAN programming language conventions, and are signaled by the key word FORMAT. The format F6.2 stands for floating point (F), which is another term for real numbers; the 6 indicates a maximum total field width of 6 (counting the decimal); and the 2 indicates

```
.TYPE BILL.DMD
ATTRIBUTE ITEM_BOUGHT ABBREV ITEM TEXT LENGTH 10 KEYED
ATTRIBUTE AMOUNT_PAYABLE ABBREV PRICE REAL LENGTH 5
```

(a)

```
.TYPE BILL.DMI
SHOES      21.75
SHIRT      14.25
PANTS      28.95
SOCKS       1.95
```

(b)

FIGURE 12.21

2 places after the decimal, which gives us the dollar and cents format. The FORMAT statement is variable length, hence the need for a key word (END) to end it.

### Relating Data Sets

In the above examples, we used the DBMS as a "file system," but this is not its best use. The examples, however, did serve two purposes

- They introduced us to a DBMS.
- They indicated the ease with which data can be described, stored, retrieved, changed, and manipulated with a DBMS.

However, the primary use of a DBMS is to relate data in a way that is not file oriented. As an example, we will develop a miniature information system for a school. The example is an adaptation of one given in Kroenke (1977). The portion of the school system we wish to study will have

- A list of students enrolled in the school
- A list of courses offered in the school
- A registration list of courses offered this term and the students registered for them

The data for the students will consist of the fields shown in Figure 12.22a. The data description file for student records is shown in Figure 12.22b, which has only one student number keyed. The course record will

Student number (SNUM)
Last name (LN)
First name (FN)
Address (ADDR)
Phone number (PHONE)
City (CITY)
State (STATE)
Zip Code (ZIP_CODE)

(a)

```
.TYPE STUDNT.DMD
ATTRIBUTE STUDENT_NUMBER ABBREV SNUM INTEGER LENGTH 3 KEYED
ATTRIBUTE LAST_NAME ABBREV LN TEXT LENGTH 15
ATTRIBUTE FIRST_NAME ABBREV FN TEXT LENGTH 10
ATTRIBUTE ADDRESS ABBREV ADDR TEXT LENGTH 25
ATTRIBUTE PHONE_NUMBER ABBREV PHONE TEXT LENGTH 8
ATTRIBUTE CITY TEXT LENGTH 15
ATTRIBUTE STATE TEXT LENGTH 15
ATTRIBUTE ZIP_CODE TEXT LENGTH 5
```

(b)

FIGURE 12.22

Course Number      (e.g., IS 10)
Course Name       (Introduction to Information Science)
Room Number      (324 CL)
Days Class Meets   (M-W-F)
Start Time        (9AM)
End Time         (10AM)

(a)

```
.TYPE COURSE.DMD
ATTRIBUTE COURSE_NUMBER ABBREV CNUM TEXT LENGTH 5 KEYED
ATTRIBUTE COURSE_NAME ABBREV CNAME TEXT LENGTH 25
ATTRIBUTE ROOM_NUMBER ABBREV ROOM TEXT LENGTH 6
ATTRIBUTE DAYS_COURSE_MEETS ABBREV DAYS TEXT LENGTH 5
ATTRIBUTE TIME_OF_START ABBREV START TEXT LENGTH 7
ATTRIBUTE TIME_FINISHED ABBREV END TEXT LENGTH 7
```

(b)

FIGURE 12.23

have the fields shown in Figure 12.23a. The data description file is shown in Figure 12.23b, which indicates course number as the only key. The actual data used for the student file will be that shown in Figure 12.24a.

In system 1022, the absence of a field can be indicated by simply hitting the return key when prompted (Figure 12.24b), although a better

```
001                002                003              004
Estep              Beshears           Blundon          Pepprey
Fred               Ralph              Donna            Lisa
207 N. Portland    412 Oakland St.    1511 Edison      402 N. Craig
442-8167           319-8208           422-7513         No Phone
Oconomowoc         Oconomowoc         Milwaukee        Pewaukee
Wisconsin          Wisconsin          Wisconsin        Wisconsin
99771              99773              45458            87690
```

(a)

```
    SUPPLY ATTRS
      SNUM--004
      LN--PEPPREY
      FN--LISA
      ADDR--402 N. CRAIG
----  PHONE--
      CITY--PEWAUKEE
      STATE--WISCONSIN
      ZIP_CODE--87690
```

(b)

FIGURE 12.24

| IS10 | IS14 | IS114 |
|------|------|-------|
| INTRO INFO SCIENCE | PROGRAMMING LANGUAGES I | INTERACTIVE PROGRAMMING |
| 324CL | 503LIS | 409LIS |
| M-W-F | T-H | M |
| 9AM | 9:30AM | 5PM |
| 10AM | 11AM | 8PM |

(c)

FIGURE 12.24  (continued)

design might be to enter a data value, such as NONE or NOPHONE. If no value is entered, the field will be blank when printed out. If a value is entered, it will not be blank, and can even be searched (e.g., for a list of students who have no phone, if we wish to encourage them to obtain one). The data for the course file is shown in Figure 12.24c. The interesting file will be the one that links student data and the course data—the registration file. It will have only two fields

- Student number
- Course number

which are the primary keys of the other two files. Its data description is shown in Figure 12.25a. Both attributes are keyed, so that we can access the file by student (to see his or her schedule) or course number (to get a class listing). The data used for this application will be that shown in Figure 12.25b.

The data indicate that student 001 (Estep) is registered for two courses (IS10, IS14), student 002 (Beshears) one course (IS114), etc.; or, reading it another way, that course IS10 has two students registered (Estep, Pepprey). The student name will not appear in the registration file, but is included here to indicate which student is attached to each number.

We have three data sets

```
.TYPE STUCRS.DMD
ATTRIBUTE STUDENT_NUMBER ABBREV SNUM INTEGER LENGTH 3 KEYED
ATTRIBUTE COURSE_NUMBER ABBREV CNUM TEXT LENGTH 5 KEYED
```

(a)

| SNUM | | CNUM |
|------|------|------|
| 001 | (ESTEP) | IS10 |
| 001 | (ESTEP) | IS14 |
| 002 | (BESHEARS) | IS114 |
| 004 | (PEPPREY) | IS10 |
| 004 | (PEPPREY) | IS14 |
| 004 | (PEPPREY) | IS114 |

Note: Data in parentheses will not be entered

(b)

FIGURE 12.25

STUDNT
COURSE
STUCRS

In order to illustrate how the data sets may be accessed in a related fashion, let us assume we wish to ask such questions as

• What are the names of the students registered for a particular course?

or

• What are the course names for which a student is registered?

Assuming that we have opened all three data sets

* OPEN STUDNT COURSE STUCRS

we may access any particular data set by first selecting it

*DBSET STUCRS

and then giving the commands we wish to be carried out on that data set. Thus, to search the student course data set, we simply say

*DBSET STUCRS
*FIND CNUM IS10

This will result in the selection of all records having IS10 as a member, which is synonymous with having all students registered for the course, since one record exists for each student in the course. If we wish to see only the student numbers, we can do so without reference to any other data set (Figure 12.26a). However, seeing the student numbers 1 and 4 is not very enlightening; we would rather see their names. To do this, we must access the student data set for the names associated with these numbers. In 1022 this is referred to as mapping from the STUCRS data set to the STUDNT data set, and is accomplished with the MAP command

*MAP TO STUDNT VIA SNUM

which indicates that we wish to map from the selected set of records in STUCRS (the data set we are currently in) to the data set STUDNT, matching on the value of SNUM. Since the student numbers found for IS10 were 1 and 4, the command will find records in the data set STUDNT with values 1 and 4 (Figure 12.26b).

A class listing is thus available daily, even hourly, on demand, with very little effort on the part of the user of the data base. (In a real system, much effort may have gone into building the data base, i.e., into its design and data entry.)

To get a list of courses for which a student is registered (his or her class schedule), we could find simply the course numbers (without mapping; Figure 12.26c), or the names of the courses (with mapping to the COURSE data set; Figure 12.26d), or a complete listing showing the time and place at which the course meets (Figure 12.26e), in which there should be little excuse for not being there on the first day of class. (The date of the first day of class is not included in this data set, although it has been presumably announced elsewhere.)

If the student course data set is searched for a particular student number, and a match is not found (Figure 12.27a), the student is not registered. In this case, we cannot map to the student file because no records

```
* OPEN STUDNT COURSE STUCRS
* DBSET STUCRS
* FIND CNUM IS10
2 RECS FOUND.
* PRINT SNUM
1
4
```

(a)


```
*
* OPEN STUDNT COURSE STUCRS
* DBSET STUCRS
* FIND CNUM IS10
2 RECS FOUND.
* MAP TO STUDNT VIA SNUM
2 RECS FOUND.
* PRINT SNUM LN FN
1 ESTEP           FRED
4 PEPPREY         LISA
*
```

(b)


```
* DBSET STUCRS
* FIND SNUM 4
3 RECS FOUND.
* PRINT CNUM
IS10
IS14
IS114
*
```

(c)

```
* DBSET STUCRS
* FIND SNUM 4
3 RECS FOUND.
* MAP TO COURSE VIA CNUM
3 RECS FOUND.
* PRINT CNUM CNAME
IS10   INTRO INFO  SCIENCE
IS14   PROGRAMMING LANGUAGES I
IS114  INTERACTIVE PROGRAMMING
*
```
(d)

```
* DBSET STUCRS
* FIND SNUM 4
3 RECS FOUND.
* MAP TO COURSE VIA CNUM
3 RECS FOUND.
* PRINT ALL
IS10   INTRO INFO SCIENCE           324CL  M-W-F  9AM      10AM
IS14   PROGRAMMING LANGUAGES I       503LIS T-H    9:30AM  11AM
IS114  INTERACTIVE PROGRAMMING       409LIS M      5PM     8PM
*
```
(e)

FIGURE 12.26

```
* DBSET STUCRS
* FIND SNUM 3
NOT FOUND.
```

(a)

```
* DBSET STUDNT ◄---- switches data sets from STUCRS to STUDNT
* FIND SNUM 3
FOUND.
* PRINT LN FN
BLUNDON        DONNA
*
```

(b)

FIGURE 12.27

were found. In order to find the name of the student, we would "switch data sets" (Figure 12.27b). Similarly, if a course were not found in STUCRS, it would mean that nobody had yet registered for it (not illustrated in this example).

If the last name were keyed (Figure 12.28a), we could begin the search with the student name, obtaining his or her number from the student file, then mapping from the student number to the registration file (student course file) to obtain the course numbers for his or her schedule, and mapping again, this time to the course file to obtain the names of the courses (Figure 12.28b).

It is this ease of querying single files as well as cross-referencing files on demand that makes DBMSs attractive. Of course, the amount of programming that goes into the development of the DBMS package and the computer-related hardware to support it may make the use of DBMS expensive as well. (Some smaller systems are relatively inexpensive.) In addition, once the system is purchased, the data must be described, entered, and maintained. The purchaser of such a system must balance the ease of using

```
* DBSET STUDNT
* KEY LN

System 1022 Keying Program
Keying attributes:
LAST_NAME (1 Block, 0 new)
*
```

(a)

```
* FIND LN ESTEP
FOUND.
* MAP TO STUCRS VIA SNUM
2 RECS FOUND.
* MAP TO COURSE VIA CNUM
2 RECS FOUND.
* PRINT CNUM CNAME
IS10   INTRO INFO SCIENCE
IS14   PROGRAMMING LANGUAGES I
*
```

(b)

FIGURE 12.28

the system, the timeliness and accessibility of the data, as well as the flexibility of the questions that can be asked of the system against these costs.

## Building the Data Base

The user of the data base adds, finds, deletes, and changes records without regard to the actual layout of the data; i.e., the user is usually unaware of such details as the DMD file. However, someone must be involved in designing the data records. This "someone," whether it be a single person or a group of people, is usually referred to as the data base administrator (DBA). The administrator of the data base decides such things as which fields will be included in a record, their type and length, and whether or not they are keyed. In addition, he or she will usually decide who has access to the data. Some data fields may be considered "private," to be accessed only by a select group of people. For example, the salary field in an employee record may be accessed by the payroll department, but not by clerical help who change addresses, phone numbers, etc. One method of effecting such security measures is the use of a password. For example, in 1022 the DBA can designate a password for the entire file by opening the file and using the ADMIT command

*ADMIT CLASS PASSWORD ACF

which indicates that the password for the file is ACF and any member of the CLASS of users knowing this password may access the file. The entire transaction is shown in Figure 12.29a, where the CLOSE command closes this data set, but does not exit 1022. This allows the DBA to access other data sets and set the security restrictions on them. The QUIT command closes the current data set and also exits 1022.

Anyone subsequently attempting to open the data set will be prompted for the password (Figure 12.29b). If an incorrect password is entered, access will be denied (Figure 12.29c). The password entered (here XXX) is not echoed for security reasons. A user who knows the correct password will obtain access (Figure 12.29d).

Passwords may also be issued for different types of access, e.g., READONLY, where a user knowing the password can read the data but not change it, or UPDATE where the user may read or write (change) the data. In fact, different groups can be given different types of access to the same data set (Figure 12.30a). A user using the password XYZ will be able to read the data, but not change it (Figure 12.30b). A user using the password ABC will be able to change the data (Figure 12.30c). The DBA must see to it that the proper groups have the proper passwords. For example, people producing paychecks may access the salary field of the personnel file in READONLY mode to produce the proper amount, but need not have write access (i.e., to give a raise). A salesperson may need to see the price of a given item, but the marketing department might be assigned to set the prices.

A password may be designated for the entire data set, as above, or for particular fields within a data set. In 1022 this is done with the FOR qualifier

* ADMIT CLASS PASSWORD BOSS FOR SALARY UPDATE

```
* OPEN PAYROL
* ADMIT CLASS PASSWORD ACF
* CLOSE
```

(a)


```
* OPEN PAYROL
Password for PAYROL in PAYROL.DMS
```

(b)


```
* OPEN PAYROL
Password for PAYROL in PAYROL.DMS
              ◄---user types XXX instead of ACF
? (OP3) Wrong Password
* ADD          ◄---user attempts to add data
? (CS31) Dataset not OPEN◄---but data set is not open
```

(c)

```
* OPEN PAYROL
Password for PAYROL in PAYROL.DMS
              ◄---- user typed ACF, the correct password
* ADD

SUPPLY ATTRS
  LN--LEE
  FN--JAMES
  EN--923
  ADDR--7017 S. MOZART           and obtained access
  CITY--CHICAGO
  STATE--IL
  ZIP--60629
  PHONE--682-2914
  SALARY--10000.00
* CLOSE
```

(d)


FIGURE 12.29


which indicates that anyone knowing the password BOSS can update the salary field. We can indicate that others are "locked out" of the salary field by giving them a different password and using the keyword LOCKED for the salary field

    * ADMIT CLASS PASSWORD ANYONE FOR SALARY LOCKED

The entire interaction is shown in Figure 12.31a, after which we give the boss the password BOSS and everyone else the password ANYONE. When the boss accesses the data set, he or she can print (or change) the salary field (Figure 12.31b), while all others will be locked out of the salary field (Figure 12.31c).

```
* OPEN PAYROL
* ADMIT CLASS PASSWORD XYZ READONLY
* ADMIT CLASS PASSWORD ABC UPDATE
* CLOSE
*
```

(a)

```
* OPEN PAYROL
Password for PAYROL in PAYROL.DMS
                    ◄---user types XYZ
* FIND LN LEE
FOUND.
* PRINT LN FN EN        ⎫
LEE      JAMES 923      ⎬ allowed to see (read) data
* CHANGE EN 622◄━ but not change (write) it
? (CS88) Unauthorized attribute -- ADMIT protected
 CHANGE EN
*
```

(b)

```
* OPEN PAYROL
Password for PAYROL in PAYROL.DMS
          ◄----user typed ABC
* FIND LN LEE          ⎫
FOUND.                 ⎪
* PRINT LN FN EN       ⎬ can read
LEE      JAMES 923     ⎭
* CHANGE EN 226        ⎫
* PRINT LN FN EN       ⎬ and write
LEE      JAMES 226     ⎭
*
```

(c)

FIGURE 12.30

The DBA also makes decisions as to the physical layout of the data, e.g., whether a particular data set is to be on disk or tape, or which disk it is on. He or she (or they) consider the system performance and use the data on performance to restructure the data base as necessary. Thus, the administrator must be cognizant of user needs (who needs what data and

```
* OPEN PAYROL
* ADMIT CLASS PASSWORD BOSS FOR SALARY UPDATE
* ADMIT CLASS PASSWORD ANYONE FOR SALARY LOCKED
* CLOSE
*
```

(a)

FIGURE 12.31

```
* OPEN PAYROL
Password for PAYROL in PAYROL.DMS
        ◄-----typed boss
* FIND LN LEE
FOUND.
* PRINT SALARY
 10000.000
*
```

(b)


```
* OPEN PAYROL
Password for PAYROL in PAYROL.DMS
          ◄----·typed anyone
* FIND LN LEE
FOUND.
* PRINT SALARY
? (CS88) Unauthorized attribute -- ADMIT protected
 PRINT SALARY
*
```

(c)

FIGURE 12.31 (continued)


when), the logical layout of the data (the data description files), and the physical configuration of the system.


## Data Description Language Versus Data Manipulation Language

In 1022 there are really two different languages we use

- A language to describe the data, called the data description language (DDL)
- A language to manipulate the data, called the data manipulation language (DML)

This is true in general of DBMSs. The DDL is of most interest to the DBA and to programmers, both of whom must describe data sets. The DML is of interest to the end user who must query and manipulate the data sets.

In 1022, the DDL consists of system words, such as ATTRIBUTE, TEXT, LENGTH, user-defined words, such as LNAME and FNAME, and constants, such as 10

ATTRIBUTE FNAME TEXT LENGTH 10

The DDL language is interpreted by the portion of the DBMS that builds the system tables and data files.

The data manipulation language consists of the verbs (commands), such as FIND, CHANGE, PRINT, DELETE, and the arguments given to these commands, usually attribute names and/or attribute values

FIND LNAME WILLIAMS

as well as the verbs to SORT, take TOTals, etc. Each command usually has a separate routine in the data "processing" module of the DBMS.

In comparing DBMSs, we are usually concerned with the ease of use and the power of both the DDL and the DML languages. There are three basic models of DBMS

- The relational model
- The hierarchical model
- The Codasyl data base task group (DBTG) model

The particular model used will affect both the DDL and the DML.

## Query Languages and Host Languages

We have illustrated the use of a query language that "stands alone," i.e., is not incorporated into a programming language. Commands may also be "embedded" in a programming language such as FORTRAN, COBOL, PL/I, Pascal, or assembly language. The programming language so used is called the host language. In this case, commands to the DBMS are issued as subroutine calls

CALL DBOPEN ("Phones")

and programmers create application programs to read input data and commands, create interfaces with the data base to carry out the commands, and output the results (often in report form, although output to a terminal is also possible).

## Building the Data Base Management System

The DBMS itself is a set of programs developed by the people who market the system. This is usually a different group than that which builds and uses the data base. The producers of a DBMS package must be intimately aware of the physical placement of the records and the manipulations necessary to respond to such commands as FIND, PRINT, CHANGE, and ADMIT. The producers of the DBMS create the programs to store and access the data, as well as the query language to interface with the user and the language used to interface with the host language (which may or may not be the same as the query language). In systems that permit access through a host language, there is a need for programmers to create the programs that access the data base, hence the division of responsibilities is

| End user | • Accesses the data base through the query language |
| | • Has a logical view of some portions of the data base |
| Programmers | • Write "host language" programs to access the data base |
| | • Have a logical view of some portions of the data base |
| | • May need some knowledge of the physical layout of the data in order to make programs efficient |
| Data base administrator | • Has knowledge of logical layout of the entire data base |

- Has knowledge of user needs for data and controls user access
- Has knowledge of physical layout of data
- Acts as coordinator of user needs, logical layout, and physical layout in order to provide the end user with convenient access to the data in an efficient manner.

DBMS producer

- Creates programs that interface with the user and data, and indicates the hardware necessary to support the system (in fact, may produce a single package consisting of both hardware and software)

## Related Readings

Atre, S., *Data Base: Structured Techniques for Design, Performance, and Management,* New York: John Wiley & Sons, 1980.

Haseman, William D. and Whinston, Andrew B., *Introduction to Data Management,* Homewood, IL: Richard D. Irwin, Inc., 1977.

Inmon, William H., *Effective Data Base Design,* Englewood Cliffs, NJ: Prentice-Hall, 1981.

Jackson, Ken, *Primer: System 1022: Data Base Management System,* Cambridge, MA: Software House, 1982.

Kroenke, David M., *Database Processing: Fundamentals, Design, Implementation,* 2nd ed. Palo Alto, CA: Science Research Associates, 1983.

Lyon, John K., *The Database Administrator,* New York: John Wiley & Sons, 1976.

Martin, James, *An End-User's Guide to Data Base,* Englewood Cliffs, NJ: Prentice-Hall, Inc., 1981.

Martin, James, *Computer Data-Base Organization,* Englewood Cliffs, NJ: Prentice-Hall, Inc., 1975.

Martin, James, *Principles of Data-Base Management,* Englewood Cliffs, NJ: Prentice-Hall, Inc., 1976.

Maurer, Hermann A., *Data Structures and Programming Techniques,* Englewood Cliffs, NJ: Prentice-Hall, Inc., 1977.

Ross, Ronald G., *Data Base Systems: Design, Implementation, and Management,* New York: AMACOM, 1978.

*System 1022 Data Base Management System: User's Reference Manual,* Cambridge, MA: Software House, 1980.

Ullman, Jeffrey D., *Principles of Database Systems,* 2nd ed. Potomac, MD: Computer Science Press, Inc., 1980.

Wiedernold, Gio, *Database Design,* New York: McGraw-Hill, 1977.

# VII
# Displaying the Data

The display of data is a relatively new field of study in information science. It concerns such questions as the use of numerical displays versus the use of graphic displays. Each display has functions the other does not, with complementary disadvantages. For example, graphic data displays are useful for presenting the overall "form" of relationships or trends. The graphical displays are not usually useful for computational purposes. Numerical displays lend "exact values" to analytical computations, but often lack the ready comprehensibility.

Since the computational manipulation of data values is treated in a later section, we focus primarily on graphical displays in this section. Chapter 13 concentrates on the use of packages to create standard display forms, e.g., graphs (plots), bar charts, and pie charts.

Chapter 14 is more technical in nature, indicating how one goes about writing graphics programs. This is one of the few instances of technology being highlighted in this text. One reason for this is the relative newness of the graphics technology and terminology, e.g., bit map graphics, vector graphics, raster scans, and the like. Another is the widespread availability of graphics capability in the microcomputer market. Finally, we have the infinitely more pleasing use of color, shape, and sound in place of monochromatic data lists, a user-oriented development that will be exploited more fully as the use of such systems increases and the research into the design in terms of design/impression (or effect) principles increases.

# 13
# Data Display

Upon completion of this chapter the reader should be able to:

1. Explain the trade-offs between numerical presentation and graphic display of data.
2. Discuss the organization of data in regard to the purpose of the recipient of the report.
3. List and explain some of the means of highlighting data values.
4. Explain how displays can be made misleading.
5. Use a package to create displays if one is available. Create a
   a. Bar graph
   b. Plot
   c. Pie chart
   or other designs available with the package.

The primary consideration in the display of data is the facilitation of the user's understanding of that data—the transfer of meaning. The physical characteristics of the display can have either a beneficial or a detrimental effect on that understanding. One of the fundamental concerns of a display is the choice between numerical and graphic displays of the same data. Other choices involve the use of color and sound, the size of the characters or objects displayed, and the sequence in which things are presented. We begin with a consideration of numerical versus graphical displays.

## Numeric Versus Graphic Displays

One of the most basic distinctions in considering displays is the use of numeric versus pictorial displays. For example, in considering data on sales for a swimwear company, we might have the following data for a given department store (Figure 13.1a). While the numbers give an idea of increasing sales as we approach the summer months, with a high of 1,250 in July, then declining sales during the fall months, a graph of the same data might

Jan, 123, Feb, 135, Mar, 207, Apr, 321, May, 512,
June, 1047, July, 1250, Aug, 1123, Sept, 517,
Oct, 312, Nov, 152, Dec, 119

(a)

Jan     *
Feb     *
Mar     **
Apr     ***
May     *****
June    *********
July    ***********
Aug     **********
Sep     *****
Oct     ***
Nov     *
Dec     *

(b)

FIGURE 13.1

present a "better picture" (Figure 13.1b, in which the number of asterisks
represents the number of sales).

Of course, the graph is not entirely accurate. We have used one asterisk for each 100 sales, truncating portions of 100, hence, both January
(123) and February (135) are shown with a single asterisk. The problem
is that our "resolution" of the data into single asterisks for each 100 sales
makes our system incapable of representing smaller quantities. Of course,
we would obtain a finer resolution by placing an asterisk for each 25 sales

Jan     ****       (123------→100 or four 25s)
Feb     *****      (135------→125 or five 25s)

But this scheme would require 50 asterisks for July

July    **************************************************

which makes our display unwieldy. An exact resolution could be achieved
by printing one asterisk for each swimsuit sold, in which case January
would have 123 asterisks and July's 1,250 asterisks would certainly run
off the page.

Diagrams of the sort shown in Figure 13.1b are sometimes referred to
as histograms by nonstatisticians. Technically, the term *histogram* is used
to refer to displays in which the variable being depicted has its "class intervals" depicted along the X-axis, the relative frequencies of these intervals represented on the vertical axis, and the "bars" of the diagram are
contiguous, so that the horizontal axis is depicted as a continuous scale
(Figure 13.2).

Graphs in which the bars are not contiguous are referred to as bar
charts. Graphs using asterisks might be called pictographs (Freund, 1981).
We will refer to such graphs by the term bar chart or histogram, used in

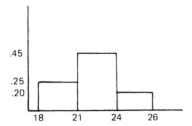

FIGURE 13.2

the less technical sense of a linear representation of the data, either counts or relative frequencies, whether depicted vertically or horizontally.

## A Trade-Off

Graphic displays, such as the histogram shown in Figure 13.1b are often used to give a summary picture of the data, sacrificing some accuracy. The use of numeric data can provide accuracy, but with some sacrifice of the "immediacy" of the display.

We will concentrate primarily on graphical techniques; however, first let us consider some of the ways in which simple numeric or alphanumeric displays can be manipulated in order to enhance the transfer of meaning.

## Organizing Numeric Data

Even in the consideration of numeric data, the choice of a display can be made judiciously. In the above example, we listed the data on sales as

Jan,123,Feb,135,Mar,207,Apr,321,May,512,
June,1047,July,1250,Aug,1123,Sept,517,
Oct,312,Nov,152,Dec,119

| Jan | 123 | | | | |
|-----|------|-----|------|-----|-----|
| Feb | 135 | | | | |
| Mar | 207 | | | | |
| Apr | 321 | | | | |
| May | 512 | Jul | 1250 | | |
| Jun | 1047 | Aug | 1123 | | |
| Jul | 1250 | Jun | 1047 | Dec | 119 |
| Aug | 1123 | Sep | 517 | Jan | 123 |
| Sep | 517 | May | 512 | Feb | 135 |
| Oct | 312 | • | | • | |
| Nov | 152 | • | | • | |
| Dec | 119 | • | | • | |

(a)                     (b)                     (c)

FIGURE 13.3

with the items interspersed in a cluttered fashion. We also allowed some
of the names of the months to be printed in full (June, July) and some to
be abbreviated. A neater display might list each month on a separate line
and require that each name be abbreviated in a uniform fashion or written
out in full (Figure 13.3a). If we are interested not in the year as a whole,
but only in the busy months, we could sort the data in descending order
on the sales field (Figure 13.3b). Of course, if we wanted to know the
months with poorest sales, e.g., in order to plan when to hold sales, we
could sort the data in ascending order on the sales field (Figure 13.3c),
so that it becomes obvious that a pre-Christmas "Santa's Swimwear" sale
might be in order in the off-season.


## Color, Reverse Video, and Blinking Fields

Another technique to facilitate the understanding of alphanumeric displays
is the use of color. For example, if we wished to emphasize the cutoff point
between those passing a course and those failing it (say 70%) we could
print the names and averages of those passing in black, those "below"
the line in red (Figure 13.4).

The use of red and black for "not satisfactory" and "satisfactory"
parallels the use of these colors in profit-and-loss statements, in which "in
the black" indicates a profit, "in the red" a loss. This is a good example
of the use of human factors in creating the display. We use colors for
which a standard meaning already exists. Green (go) and red (stop) might
have been just as effective in terms of meaning, although they might have
given an undesirable "Christmas" effect.

On some devices, such as some CRTs, only one color is available (monochrome display), so the effect of using different colors is achieved in other
ways. For example, there is usually a means of displaying data in a "blinking field," in which the characters of interest turn on and off, much as in
a neon sign. In a bowling tournament, we might list the winner's name
in a blinking field (Figure 13.5a). Note that a similar effect can be achieved
in a printed text with the use of quotation marks (Figure 13.5b) or arrows
(Figure 13.5c). The point is that the data of interest is highlighted in some
way.

An alternative means of highlighting on a CRT is to use reverse video,
where the normal background (dark) and foreground (light) colors are
reversed. In fact a myriad of techniques exists for designing displays in
both printed form and on computer-related devices. Much has been written
about noncomputer-related techniques in the literature on art and design.
Little research has currently been applied to computer-generated displays,


| Smith | 98 | |
|---|---|---|
| Jones | 84 | black |
| Phillips | 82 | |
| Forester | 71 | |
| Billings | 69 | red |
| Worthmore | 52 | |

FIGURE 13.4

| Bill | 152 | | Bill | 152 | | | Bill | 152 |
| „Joe | 275„ | | Joe | 275 | | | Joe | 275 |
| =Mary | 290= | | "Mary | 290" | | -----> Mary | 290<----- |
| "Harry | 175" | | Harry | 175 | | | Harry | 175 |
| Ann | 212 | | Ann | 212 | | | Ann | 212 |
| (a) | | | (b) | | | (c) | |

FIGURE 13.5

although it is becoming an area of great interest, and some cross-fertilization between the arts and the use of computer displays may be expected, as well as research more specifically related to computer displays.

With this brief introduction into the general use of displays, we begin an examination of the use of displays in a computer environment. We begin with alphanumeric displays, then move on to the consideration of graphics and graphics packages.

## Alphanumeric Displays

Various graphical applications can be done in computerized applications. On the simplest level these involve the use of normal CRTs, Teletype

```
HIST                    .09:46

 10 READ M$,S
 20 IF M$="DONE" THEN 100
 30 LET N=INT(S/100)
 40 PRINT M$;
 50 FOR J=1 TO N
 60 PRINT "*";
 70 NEXT J
 80 PRINT
 90 GOTO 10
100 PRINT
110 PRINT "END OF REPORT"
120 STOP
130 DATA JAN,123
140 DATA FEB,135
150 DATA MAR,207
160 DATA APR,321
170 DATA MAY,512
180 DATA JUN,1047
190 DATA JUL,1250
200 DATA AUG,1123
210 DATA SEP,517
220 DATA OCT,312
230 DATA NOV,152
240 DATA,DEC,119
250 DATA DONE,0
260 END
```

FIGURE 13.6

```
HIST                     09:46              26-MAR-83

JAN*
FEB*
MAR**
APR***
MAY*****
JUN**********
JUL***********
AUG**********
SEP*****
OCT***
NOV*
DEC*
END OF REPORT
```

**FIGURE 13.7**

terminals, or printers. More sophisticated applications require the use of special equipment, such as plotters and/or specialized display terminals (graphics terminals).

The simplest applications of computer graphics involve the use of alpha-numeric characters, using a standard keyboard for input and a standard output device. For example, the histogram of asterisks illustrating swimsuit sales can be produced by having the computer generate the required number of asterisks on a Teletype terminal or CRT. A BASIC program to do the job would be that shown in Figure 13.6. The output from the program is similar to that shown in Figure 13.7.

The program itself simply reads in the name of the month and the total sales, then computes the sales in terms of "100s." This computation is done in the line

    LET N=INT(S/100)

where the division S/100 produces such numbers as 1.23 from (123/100). The function INT (convert to integer) then converts the result (1.23) to its integer part (1) by truncating. The truncated result is used to control a loop that prints nothing but asterisks

    FOR J=1 TO N
    PRINT "*";
    NEXT J

The function of the semicolon in the PRINT statement is to "turn off the line feed" at the end of the PRINT statement, so that the asterisks can be printed on a single line. The PRINT statement after the loop (line 80) "turns the line feed back on" (as well as printing a blank line) so that the next month is printed on a new line.

The data was treated as a variable-length list, terminated by the line

    DATA DONE,0

While the "monthly sales" could be treated as a fixed-length list, the use of the form for variable-length lists is suitable for various applications. Treating the list as fixed length would result in an "outer loop"

```
FOR K=1 TO 12
READ M$,S
    ·
    ·
    ·
PRINT
NEXT K
```

but the program would be restricted to applications consisting of 12 data items.

One problem with the program occurs if the sales are less than 100

$$INT(57/100)=INT(0.57)=0$$

which causes problems for the loop to print asterisks, since the expression

```
FOR J=1 TO N
```

will be evaluated as

```
FOR J=1 TO 0
```

The programmer could handle this by explicitly testing for N=0 and skipping the loop

```
IF N=0 THEN _____
```

However, the month will look like it had no sales. Since the character set does not provide "half asterisks," the dilemma is really between representing 57 sales as 1 asterisk or none, which again brings up the question of "resolution." It also introduces the notion of the choice of a character set, since a more elaborate character set could include half an asterisk. However, the expense involved in implementing the character set with a nonstandard printer might not be justified for our application.


Computer Drawn Pictures

One application with which the reader may be familiar is the use of computers to draw pictures, such as Snoopy or the Mona Lisa. For example, the following Christmas card, sent out by one of the programmers at the University of Pittsburgh, was computer generated (Figure 13.8). Such pictures require inputting the entire picture as data, i.e., the programmer must draw the picture, then input the data as an explicit replica of the drawing. Other less detailed applications can "compute" the picture. For example, the program shown in Figure 13.9a, adapted from Nahigian and Hodges (1979), also generates a Christmas tree. The output of the program is the tree shown in Figure 13.9b.

The program uses the tab function to create the tree. For example, the statement

```
PRINT TAB(25);"*"
```

prints the very top asterisk, which is not only at the top, but on the center axis of the tree. The loop

```
  ||        ||      *                       m     m  eeee  rrr   rrr   y   y
  |||||||||||     ((*))                      mm    mm  e       r r   r r   y y
                    *                        m mmm m  eee   rrr   rrr    y
___xxxx_____   ^^^                       m  m  m  e       r r   r r    y
___xxxx_____    ^^^^^                      m     m  eeee  r  r  r  r    y
|| ||||           ^(*)^^^
|| \\\\\\)        ^^^^^^^^^^                  xx    xx  m     m    a      ssss
||   ---        ^^^^^^^(*)^                    xx  xx  mm   mm   a a    s
||            ^^^(*)^^^^^^^^                    xxxx  m mmm m  a   a   ssss
||           ^^^^^^^^^^(*)^^^                  xx  xx  m  m  m aaaaaaa      s
||          ^^^^^(*)^^^^^^^^^^                xx    xx  m     m a      a  ssss
_____   ^^(*)^^^^^^^^^^(*)^^
            ^^^^^^^^^^^^^^^^^^^^^^^
     //          |||  /CHO \\
     ||          |||  /CHOO  ||
     \_____() ()__//          Tom, Cheryl, and Tao Neuendorffer
      -------------------
```

FIGURE 13.8

```
FOR J=1 TO 5
PRINT (25-J);"*";
PRINT (25+J);"*";
NEXT J
```

prints the asterisks along the sides of the tree. The left side is designated by

```
25-J
```

which takes on the values 25-1 or 24, 25-2, 25-3, 25-4, and 25-5, making the placement of the asterisk progressively more "leftward" (Figure 13.10a). The calculation

```
XMAS            15:38          31-MAR-83

10 PRINT TAB(25);"*"
20 FOR J=1 TO 5
30 PRINT TAB(25-J);"*";
40 PRINT TAB(25+J);"*"
50 NEXT J
60 FOR J=1 TO 11
70 PRINT TAB(20+J-1);"*";
80 NEXT J
90 PRINT
100 FOR J=1 TO 2
110 PRINT TAB(24);"*"·
120 PRINT TAB(26);"*"
130 NEXT J
140 PRINT TAB(25-1);"***"
150 STOP
160 END
>
```

(a)

FIGURE 13.9

XMAS         15:39         31-MAR-83

```
TIME:  0.06 SECS.
>
>LIST
```

(b)

FIGURE 13.9  (continued)

        25+J

places the asterisk at tab positions 26, 27, 28, 39, and 30, or progressively
more "rightward" (Figure 13.10b), and the conjunction of the two statements
creates the body of the tree (Figure 13.10c).

The bottom of the tree is printed in the loop

    FOR J=1 TO 11
    PRINT TAB(20+J-1);"*";
    NEXT J

where 20 is the leftmost asterisk and the asterisks step along by adding
J-1, i.e.

    20+1-1=20
    20+2-1=21
    20+3-1=22
       .
       .
       .
    20+11-1=30

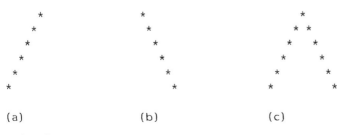

(a)              (b)              (c)

FIGURE 13.10

The semicolon at the end of the print statement

```
PRINT TAB(20+J-1);"*";
                    ↑
```

suppresses the line feed. The result is the line of asterisks that forms the base of the tree

```
**********
```

The loop

```
FOR J=1 TO 2
PRINT TAB(24);"*";
PRINT TAB(26);"*"
```

prints the sides of the trunk of the tree. Note that the first print statement

```
PRINT TAB(24);"*";
                ↑
```

suppresses the line feed, since it prints the left "bark" and we want the "right bark" on the same line. However, the second print statement

```
PRINT TAB(26);"*"
```

leaves the line feed "on," so that the next pair of asterisks is printed on the next line.

Finally, the statement

```
PRINT TAB(25-1);"***"
```

prints the three asterisks that form the base of the trunk, beginning with one to the left of center (24,25,26). This could be generalized to any width (i.e., other than 1) which is the reason we wrote 25-1 instead of 24. The earlier tabs at 24 and 26 could also be written as 25-1 and 25+1.


## Generalizing the Programs

The above program draws a tree centered at 25, and 5 dots high (actually 6 counting the top dot), but the size is explicitly stated as 5 high in the loop

```
FOR J=1 TO 5
PRINT TAB(25-J);"*";
PRINT TAB(25+J);"*"
NEXT J
```

It would be more desirable to allow a tree of arbitrary height to be drawn, and to be able to place it at an arbitrary point on the page. A program to do this is shown in Figure 13.11.

The first change is that the user is prompted for the

- Center axis of the tree (C)
- Height of the tree (H)
- Height of the trunk (H2)
- Half-width of the trunk (W)

XMAS2          16:01          31-MAR-83

```
10 PRINT "ENTER CENTER AXIS OF TREE"
20 INPUT C
30 PRINT "ENTER HEIGHT OF TREE"
40 INPUT H
50 PRINT "ENTER HEIGHT OF TRUNK"
60 INPUT H2
70 PRINT "ENTER HALF-WIDTH OF TRUNK"
80 INPUT W
90 PRINT TAB(C);"*"
100 FOR J=1 TO H
110 PRINT TAB(C-J);"*";
120 PRINT TAB(C+J);"*"
130 NEXT J
140 LET L=2*H+1
150 LET T=C-H
160 FOR J=1 TO L
170 PRINT TAB(T+J-1);"*";
180 NEXT J
190 PRINT
200 LET L=C-W
210 LET R=C+W
220 FOR J=1 TO H2
230 PRINT TAB(L);"*";
240 PRINT TAB(R);"*"
250 NEXT J
260 FOR J=L TO R
270 PRINT TAB(J);"*";
280 NEXT J
290 PRINT
300 PRINT TAB(C-7);"MERRY CHRISTMAS"
310 STOP
320 END
```

FIGURE 13.11

We could have prompted for the width of the trunk instead of the half-width and computed the half-width. To ensure that the width is symmetrical, however, we would have to ensure that the user enter an odd number or make it odd by adding one in the program. This is a result of the center dot in the trunk base

Width 5

.  .  .  .  .
         ↑
Center dot makes width odd

We avoid the check for oddness by asking for the half-width, i.e., the number of dots to the left (or right) of the center axis

.  .     .  .

Half-width is 2

90   Print top asterisk at C (center)

100  Use height of tree (H) to control loop that prints sides of tree

110, Tab is still offset from center (C) by value of J(1,2...H)
120

140, We must now compute the tab positions for the base line of tree
150  statement 140:

$$LET\ L = 2*H+1$$

Counts the number of asterisks in the base (or length of the line).
In the non-general program this was simply listed as 11, but the
11 was a summary of the value 2*5+1, where the height of the
tree (5) determines the number of dots to each side of center (hence 2*5) and the center dot adds 1 more asterisk, giving
2*H+1

Statement 150:

$$LET\ T=C-H$$

computes the leftmost starting point of the line. The leftmost
point was 5(H) to the left of center in the original program
(25-5=20) so that the generalized program simply subtracts the
height (H) from the center (C) to give the starting point of the
base line (that is, it starts H dots to the left of center).

160  The loop controls the number of asterisks printed, L

170  The tab begins at the leftmost point (T) and adjusts this by J−1
     (that is when J is 1, add 0 to T, when J is 2, add 1 to T,
     et cetera)

200, These statements are used to compute the left position (left
210  bark) and right position (right bark) of the tree trunk. Using
     the half-width makes this easy. The left bark is:

$$C-W$$

and the right is:

$$C+W$$

220  The height of the trunk is governed by the user set parameter H2

230  Print a dot at TAB(L), the left bark, suppress line feed

240  Print a dot at right bark (R), turn on line feed

(a)

FIGURE 13.12

Having prompted the user for values C,H,H2, and W, we now use these
rather than the numeric values in the appropriate lines, i.e., we replace
"25" with "C," and "FOR J=1 TO 5" with "FOR J=1 TO H." A line-by-line
summary is given in Figures 13.12a and 13.12b.
    The run of the program with the parameters

260 The base is printed from left bark to right bark

FOR J=L TO R

using line 270 (tab at J) to "step along" the line. This technique could also have been used to print the base line of the tree:

```
        L=C-H
        R=C+H
FOR J=L TO R
PRINT TAB(J);
NEXT J
```

Which is probably simpler to compute than the method used above. (Lines 140-180).

190, These PRINT statements simply turn on the line feed, since it
290 had been turned off throughout the loops

300 The message "Merry Christmas" is written beneath the tree. The tab value:

C-7

is computed with a constant (7) because the string "Merry Christmas" is exactly 15 characters wide, so that we center it at C by having the leftmost point at C-7. (C=center of tree, although by accident "C" is the seventh letter in the string "Merry Christmas.") Note that this routine could also be generalized to accept an arbitrary message from the user:

```
PRINT "ENTER MESSAGE"
INPUT S$
```

in which case we would compute the length of the message

LET N=LEN(S$)

then use that length to compute the "half-width":

LET W2=INT(N/2)

where the INT function ensures an integer result, so that the leftmost point of the string (its "anchor point") would be:

C-W2

(b)

FIGURE 13.12   (continued)

```
C =25
H =5
H2 =2
W =1
```

gives the same tree as the nongeneral program. The actual run, including prompting the user, is shown in Figure 13.13a. A second run, "doubling the size of the tree," is shown in Figure 13.13b.

XMAS2             16:01          31-MAR-83

ENTER CENTER AXIS OF TREE
?25
ENTER HEIGHT OF TREE
?5
ENTER HEIGHT OF TRUNK
?2
ENTER HALF-WIDTH OF TRUNK
?1

```
        *
        * *
       *   *
      *     *
     *       *
    *         *
    ***********
        * *
        * *
        ***
      MERRY CHRISTMAS
```

TIME: 0.15 SECS.
>LIST

(a)


XMAS2             16:02          31-MAR-83

ENTER CENTER AXIS OF TREE
?50
ENTER HEIGHT OF TREE
?10
ENTER HEIGHT OF TRUNK
?4
ENTER HALF-WIDTH OF TRUNK
?2

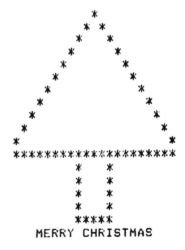

```
          *
          * *
         *   *
        *     *
       *       *
      *         *
     *           *
    *             *
   *               *
  *                 *
  *********************
        *     *
        *     *
        *     *
        *     *
        *****
      MERRY CHRISTMAS
```

(b)

FIGURE 13.13

## How to Lie with Statistics

The reason we enclose the word *doubling* in quotes in the above description of the tree program is that the size of the tree *more* than doubled, it
quadrupled. In fact, this quadrupling can be used to "lie with statistics"
(see Huff, 1954). If we are illustrating the relative incomes of two people
as a bar graph (histogram), we would do so as a straight line. For example, if one person is currently making $20,000, the other $30,000, we
could use the two bars (Figure 13.14a), where the relative height of the
bars is 3/2, indicating the ratio of Mary's salary to John's (30,000/20,000
= 3/2). The bars are represented as a single dimension (conceptually, 1-D
since they do have "some width," the width of the ink). The ratio could
also be illustrated with 2-D bars (Figure 13.14b), in which each bar is one

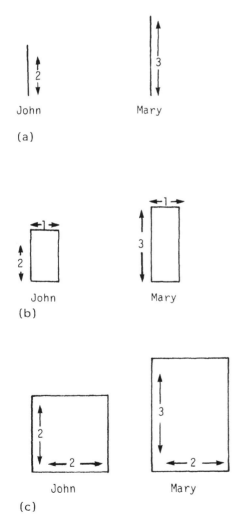

FIGURE 13.14

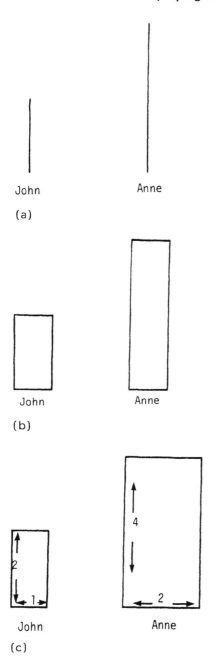

FIGURE 13.15

unit wide. The overall area of the rectangle is 2 for John (2*1) and 3 for Mary (3*1). This would hold even if the bars were more than one unit wide. For example, with a two-unit width, we have (Figure 13.14c) areas of 4 (John) and 6 (Mary), for a ratio of 6:4 or 3:2.

The "lying" comes in when we wish to illustrate such concepts as "double the income" and we change two dimensions instead of one. For example, suppose Anne makes $40,000 and John $20,000. True representations of the ratio are given in Figure 13.15a and Figure 13.15b. However, if we take the term *double* too literally and change the dimensions of *both* the base and the height for Anne (Figure 13.15c), where we have Anne's height as double John's (4 to 2) *and* Anne's width as double John"s (2 to 1), the actual ratio of the two figures is 4 to 1 instead of 2 to 1

| | |
|---|---|
| John's area | 2*1=2 |
| Anne's area | 4*2=8 |
| Ratio | 8:2=4:1 |

which is the reason John feels "dwarfed" by Anne's rectangle. Whenever we double both dimensions, we quadruple the ratio of the areas. If we had tripled them, we would have generated a nine-fold increase in area, so that the "visual impact" would be much greater (misleadingly so) than "tripling the salary." Anne would overwhelm John with a nine-fold increase in area.

To show such concepts as doubling and tripling, we obtain a true picture if we show the difference or change in one dimension only (Figure 13.16). If we show the change in two dimensions, the actual result is an increase in area corresponding to the *square* of the increase we were trying to show

Double = increase of 2
Shown in 2-D $\longrightarrow 2^2 = 4$

Triple = increase of 3
Shown in 2-D $\longrightarrow 3^2 = 9$

Thus, a "fourfold" increase, shown by making *each* dimension of a 2-D diagram increase in a fourfold manner would actually depict a ratio of 16

$$4^2 = 16$$

The power of the increase in 2-D is 2 because the area is a multiple of two dimensions (L*W of the rectangle). If we are depicting 3-D, the exponent is 3, thus, if income is shown as a pile of dollars (Figure 13.17a), and we show Anne's doubling of salary in all three dimensions (Figure 13.17b), the actual effect is to show an eightfold increase in Anne's volume.

If we tripled each side, the effect on volume would have been

$$3^3 = 27$$

| | |
|---|---|
| 2 | 3 |
| 1 | 1 |

Same width for
both rectangles

FIGURE 13.16

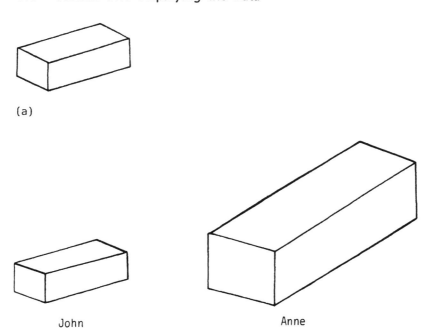

(a)

John          Anne

(b)

FIGURE 13.17

so that we can give some fairly large deceptive perceptions. Huff's work discusses not only these difficulties with areas and volumes, but many other topics, such as the gee-whiz graph, the little figures that are not there, and much ado about practically nothing. The reader interested in statistical displays should find these discussions fascinating as well as enlightening and caution-inducing.

## Setting Parameters

In the generalized program, the values set by the user for the height and central axis of the tree, as well as for the height and half-width of the trunk, are referred to as the "parameters" of the program. The program generates a tree. However, the exact location of the tree to the right or left of the paper is set by the value of the central axis. The size of the tree is set by its height. Various computer packages exist to create graphs. They too are "generalized" programs in the sense that they accept various parameters, and yet special purpose in that they produce drawings of a particular type.

## Checking the Parameters

Besides obtaining the parameters from an end user, a more sophisticated program would check that the parameters make sense. For example, in the program for generating a Christmas tree, setting the parameters to

```
XMAS3            16:12        31-MAR-83
ENTER CENTER AXIS OF TREE
 ?2
ENTER HEIGHT OF TREE
 ?10
ENTER HEIGHT OF TRUNK
 ?2
ENTER HALF-WIDTH OF TRUNK
  ?4
    *
  * *
 *    *
 *     *
 *      *
 *       *
 *        *
 *         *
 *          *
 *           *
 *            *
************************
*          *
*          *
********
MERRY CHRISTMAS
```

(a)


```
        Center = 2

              *
Room for      *
2 dots to     *
the left      *
              *
              *
```

(b)

FIGURE 13.18


```
    C =2
    H =10
    H2 =2
    W =4
```

results in the output shown in Figure 13.18a. The left half of the tree has gone off the left of the page, and the base of the tree and the base of the trunk have gone too far to the right. All of these problems stem from the choice of 2 as the center axis and the choice of 10 as the height of the tree. There is simply not enough room to the left of the center of the tree to accommodate 10 dots (Figure 13.18b). The fact that two dots fit to the left is due to BASIC's interpreting positions on the line as starting at zero, with tab (0) being the first physical column, tab (2) being the second physical column, etc. Without error-checking, the calculation.

Tab (C-J)

becomes negative at J=3

Tab (2-3)=Tab (-1)

and BASIC interprets the negative value as "the leftmost position" (equivalent to tab [0]). On equipment other than a terminal or programming languages other than BASIC, the effect might be different, but distortion will enter into the picture if the parameters "don't make sense."

## Using Graphic Displays

With standard equipment, such as Teletype terminals or nongraphic CRTs, the use of alphanumeric techniques is dictated by the equipment. In order to obtain better quality graphical output, we must use terminals that are designed for graphical displays. The simplest of these is a CRT that is equipped to draw lines and/or curves (which may be approximated by a series of short lines) or a hard-copy plotter that can do the same. Using equipment of this sort, it is possible to make line drawings of simple objects, such as bar charts or histograms, plots, and/or pie charts. In fact, much more sophisticated figures, such as contour maps, can be drawn. We begin with a simple graphics package to generate the above figures, i.e., histograms or bar charts, plots, and pies.

## TELL-A-GRAF

TELL-A-GRAF is a graphics package that enables the quick construction of figures commonly used in business, e.g., bar charts, plots, and pie charts. The name TELL-A-GRAF comes from the procedure of "telling" the computer what graph we want. We will illustrate the types of commands given to the package with examples of all three figures: bar charts, plots, and pie charts.

## Generating a Bar Chart

In order to generate a bar chart using TELL-A-GRAF, we issue a general command

GENERATE A BAR CHART

where the command "generate" indicates that we wish to create a graph, and the term *bar chart* indicates the type of graph we wish to generate.

We must also include the data for the bar chart. For example, for the "sales volume" of swimsuits, we would enter the data as

INPUT DATA:

1,123   2,135   3,207   ...

where the first digit of each pair (1 in 1,123; 2 in 2,135) indicates the "first" time period, the "second" time period etc., or, more precisely, the X-value of an X,Y pair. The second number of each pair is the Y-value, so that 1,123 represents the point

X = 1
Y = 123

For the swimsuit sales there would be 12 data points, each expressed in terms of X-Y coordinates.

Besides the command to generate a bar chart and the data points, we might enter commands to label the chart itself as well as each axis. The label for the entire chart is its "title" and the command is

TITLE IS "SALES VOLUME"

where the key word is TITLE and the title is enclosed in quotes. To label the Y axis we say

LABEL THE Y AXIS "MILLIONS."

to indicate that the sales actually represent "millions of swimsuits sold," e.g., 123 million or 135 million (which may not be a completely realistic figure). We can cause the X-axis to have month names (or abbreviations of month names) by including the statement

X AXIS IS MONTHLY.

or by including the adjective MONTHLY in the command to generate the bar chart

GENERATE A MONTHLY BAR CHART.

The entire program is shown in Figure 13.19. The statement GO causes execution of the program. The QUIT command exits TELL-A-GRAF. The command INPUT DATA signals the beginning of the data, and END OF DATA signals its termination. The output of the run is shown in Figure 13.20.

We can further refine the picture by "framing it," i.e., enclosing it in a rectangle, and putting in a "grid" to aid in reading the Y-values. The resulting program is shown in Figure 13.21. The output is shown in Figure 13.22, where the dotted lines are the grid, and the frame "outlines" the graph.

```
.type sales.prs
GENERATE A MONTHLY BAR CHART.
THE TITLE IS 'SALES VOLUME'.
LABEL THE Y AXIS 'MILLIONS'.
INPUT DATA.
1,123 2,135 3,207 4,321 5,512 6,1047
7,1250 8,1123 9,517 10,312 11,152 12,119
END OF DATA.
GO.
QUIT.
```

FIGURE 13.19

SALES VOLUME

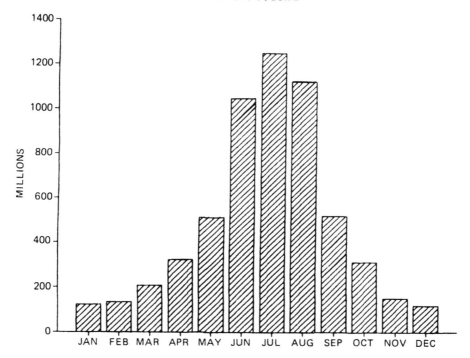

FIGURE 13.20

An example of a bar chart with two sets of data values might be a comparison of tourist spending in New York and Paris on a monthly basis. With data for 4 months, a program to generate the bar chart would be that shown in Figure 13.23. Note the X axis has a label "1970"

LABEL Y AXIS "DOLLARS"
AND X AXIS "1970"

in addition to the abbreviations for the names of the months

X AXIS IS MONTHLY

The data is preceded by the command SEQUENCE DATA, which indicates that the X-values should be generated "in sequence." Hence

150     125     350     375

will be read as

1,150     2,125     3,350     4,375

There are two sets of values, one for New York, the other for Paris, and each is preceded by the "label" for that data

"NEW YORK"     150     125     350     375
"PARIS"     100     100     175     250

```
.type sales3.prg
GENERATE A MONTHLY BAR CHART.
THE TITLE IS "SALES VOLUME".
LABEL THE Y AXIS "MILLIONS".
```
---> `TURN ON GRID Y.`
---> `FRAME THE PICTURE.`
```
INPUT DATA.
1,123 2,135 3,207 4,321 5,512 6,1047
7,1250 8,1123 9,517 10,312 11,152 12,119
END OF DATA.
GO.
QUIT.
```

FIGURE 13.21

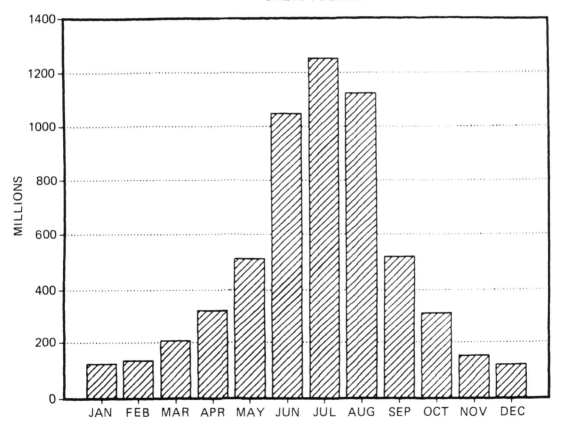

FIGURE 13.22

```
.type bar.prg
generate a barchart.
label y axis "dollars"
and x axis "1970".
x axis is monthly.
title is "Tourist Spending".
frame the picture.

sequence data.
"New York" 150 125 350 375
"Paris" 100 100 175 250
end of data.
go.
quit.
```

FIGURE 13.23

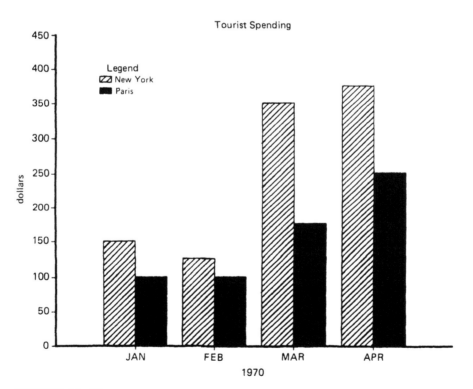

FIGURE 13.24

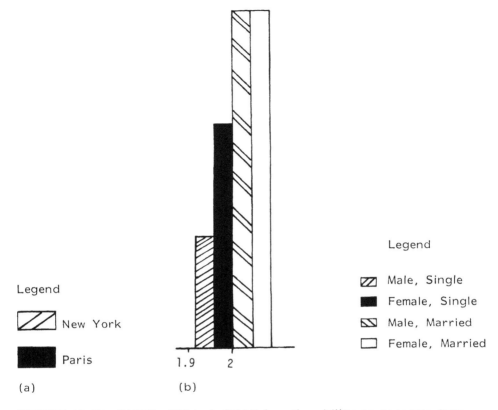

FIGURE 13.25 (NOTE: TELL-A-GRAF has the ability to generate true colors, but these graphs were produced on a monochromatic terminal, then painted on a monochromatic printer.)

```
.TYPE BARS3.PRG
GENERATE A BAR CHART.
INPUT DATA.
--- "MALE,SINGLE"
    1,50 2,45
--- "FEMALE,SINGLE"
    1,65 2,60
--- "MALE,MARRIED"
    1,75 2,80
--- "FEMALE,MARRIED"
    1,75 2,80
END OF DATA.
GO.
QUIT.
```

4 labels =
4 sets of data =
4 separate bars in chart

(Note: The hyphens just point to the
lines with labels in this example.
They are not part of TEL-A-GRAF)

FIGURE 13.26

The output is shown in Figure 13.24, where TELL-A-GRAF has chosen two different "colors" for the two sets of data and included the labels of the data sets in a legend (Figure 13.25a). More variables result in more "colors" and a longer legend (Figure 13.25b), which is a portion of the output generated by the program shown in Figure 13.26. The user does not have to indicate the number of data items other than by listing the various labels for the data (Figure 13.26).

### Submitting the Program

TELL-A-GRAF programs may be run in either the interactive or batch mode. The use of interactive graphics packages enables the user to adjust designs dynamically; the batch mode allows less convenient modification. However, because graphics packages often consume a considerable amount of main memory, and in some cases, of processing time, they are often run in the batch mode. This can be accomplished for TELL-A-GRAF by simply enclosing the name of the file containing the program in the job control language (Figure 13.27a). The JOB command simply signals that this is a job. The parentheses will include a "user number" and the "project programmer number" (PPN) on this system. The switch on the JOB command

```
$JOB (PPN)/CORE:75K
.COPY PRG:TAGPRO.DAT
$RUN PRG:TAG
BAR.PRG(XEQ)
$EOJ
```

(a)

```
$JOB (PPN)/CORE:75K
$RUN PRG:TAG
BAR.PRG(XEQ)
$EOJ
```
(b)

```
.TY TAGPRO.DAT
PRIMARY DEVICE IS CALCOMP.
SECONDARY DEVICE IS PRINTER
SECONDARY DEVICE UNIT NUMBER IS 6.
PAGE LAYOUT IS HRH.
ECHO IS ON.
ERROR REPORTING LEVEL IS 2
EXIT.
```

(c)

FIGURE 13.27

indicates that 75K of main memory is necessary to run TELL-A-GRAF. The copy command copies a default data file from the system disk area (PRG:). This file gives certain parameters to TELL-A-GRAF, primarily describing the devices. The next command, $RUN, requests execution of the TELL-A-GRAF package. It will execute the program that is indicated by the (XEQ) command. The $EOJ ends the job.

The line

BAR.PRG(XEQ)

is a command to TELL-A-GRAF. It gives the name of the file containing the program, here BAR.PRG, created by using one of the system editors. The XEQ indicates that we wish the program to be executed.

If the file TAGPRO.DAT has already been copied onto one's own disk area, the copy command can be eliminated. In this case the form of the batch invocation of TELL-A-GRAF would look like Figure 13.27b. The default data file specifies devices, page layout, error reporting, etc. (Figure 13.27c).

The primary device, CALCOMP, indicates the type of plot routine to which the output will be submitted. The secondary devices indicate where information about the outcome of the job (successful or not, and error messages) should be directed. These are the line printer and the Teletype terminal, respectively, depending on whether the job was entered in batch mode (printer) or interactive mode (Teletype). These parameters are set by the nature of the devices used at the installation (type of plotter) and the nature of the interaction (batch, interactive). The remaining commands can be set by the user to other values. The EXIT simply "exits" this parameter-setting file.

When TELL-A-GRAF executes, it examines the TAGPRO.DAT file to get the parameters that will influence the manner in which it produces the output, then executes the user program. The .DAT file sets "the environment"; the user program is the program of main interest. While the details of the .DAT file and the JCL used to submit a program will differ from installation to installation, the user programs will be formed in the same manner across installations (with some restrictions, such as the inability to effectively implement color commands in monochromatic displays).

The output of the TELL-A-GRAF program is a file named something like

Q9AS7.PLT

where the first part of the file name (Q9AS7) is randomly generated by the operating system. The extension (PLT) indicates that this is a file containing data meant for the plotter. It must be submitted by the PLOT command

PLOT   Q9AS7.PLT

## Plots

Probably the graph most well known to people who have taken algebra is what TELL-A-GRAF calls a "plot," and which we usually refer to as the "graph" of a straight line or curve.

The same swimsuit data can be "plotted" by replacing the command

```
.TYPE SALES4.PRG
GENERATE A PLOT.
TITLE IS "SWIM SUIT SALES"
INPUT DATA.
1,123 2,135 3,207 4,321 5,512 6,1047
7,1250 8,1123 9,517 10,312 11,152 12,119
END OF DATA.
GO.
QUIT.
```

FIGURE 13.28


### GENERATE A BAR CHART

with the command

### GENERATE A PLOT

A program to do so is given in Figure 13.28. The output is shown in Figure 13.29. Note that in the absence of a command such as "X AXIS IS MONTHLY," the X-axis is labeled numerically, just as the Y-axis. Of course, the units on each axis are different, reflecting the numerical values of the data (range of 1 to 12 on X, 123 to 1250 on Y).

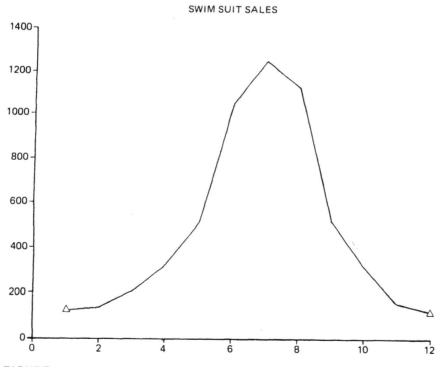

SWIM SUIT SALES

FIGURE 13.29

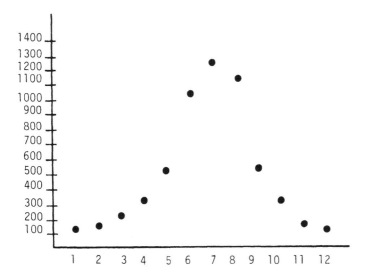

FIGURE 13.30

Note also that the actual data points do not warrant a curve. They would simply be plotted as 12 discrete points (Figure 13.30). Connecting the dots gives a "better" visual display. Of course it also implies continuity between the points, which is not the case. We would expect the viewer to realize that the connectivity is for purposes of display, not a statement about the nature of the data. However, in cases where this might be in doubt, we might explicitly state that the data is discrete, or use a program that draws "points."

Finally, note that the "curve" of swimsuit sales is really approximated by a series of straight lines between the data points. It is often the case that curved figures, such as arcs and circles, are approximated by a series of short lines.

```
.type proft.prg
GENERATE A PLOT.
TITLE IS "PROFIT PICTURE"
X AXIS LABEL IS "MONTHS".
X AXIS IS MONTHLY.
Y AXIS LABEL IS "MILLIONS."
INPUT DATA.
"SALES"
1,750 2,1020 3,1472 4,1802 5,2621
"EXPENSES"
1,500 2,630 3,720 4,1029 5,1248
END OF DATA.
GO.
QUIT.
```

FIGURE 13.31

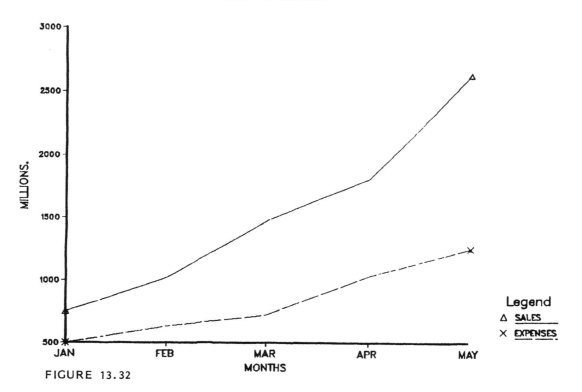

FIGURE 13.32

## Plotting Two Sets of Data

Plotting two sets of data, such as "sales revenue" and "expenses" in order to give a "picture" of profits (sales-expenses) yields two curves. For example, the program of Figure 13.31 results in the output of Figure 13.32, in which each line has its own symbol (triangle and cross, and the legend explains the symbols, again using the labels for the data). As in the case of the bar chart, this process generalizes to an arbitrary number of data sets.

## Beautifying the Picture

In the graph of profits, the fact that the picture is unframed gives it an "open" effect. We can "close" the picture with a frame, the code shown in Figure 13.33, which results in the output shown in Figure 13.34. The profit itself is the area between the two curves. We can highlight this area by shading it. The command to do so is

    CURVE 1 SHADE PAIR IS 2.

which says that curve 1 is to be shaded, and its partner in the "pair" is curve 2, i.e., "shade from curve 1 to curve 2." The program is shown in Figure 13.35, and the output is shown in Figure 13.36.

```
.type proft2.prs
GENERATE A PLOT.
TITLE IS "PROFIT PICTURE"
X AXIS LABEL IS "MONTHS".
X AXIS IS MONTHLY.
Y AXIS LABEL IS "MILLIONS."
--->FRAME THE PICTURE.
INPUT DATA.
"SALES"
1,750 2,1020 3,1472 4,1802 5,2621
"EXPENSES"
1,500 2,630 3,720 4,1029 5,1248
END OF DATA.
GO.
QUIT.
```

FIGURE 13.33

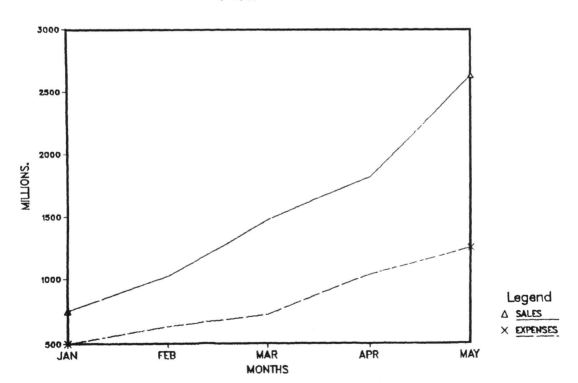

FIGURE 13.34

```
.type proft3.prs
GENERATE A PLOT.
TITLE IS "PROFIT PICTURE"
---> CURVE 1 SHADE PAIR IS 2.
X AXIS LABEL IS "MONTHS".
X AXIS IS MONTHLY.
Y AXIS LABEL IS "MILLIONS."
FRAME THE PICTURE.
INPUT DATA.
"SALES"
1,750 2,1020 3,1472 4,1802 5,2621
"EXPENSES"
1,500 2,630 3,720 4,1029 5,1248
END OF DATA.
GO.
QUIT.
```

FIGURE 13.35

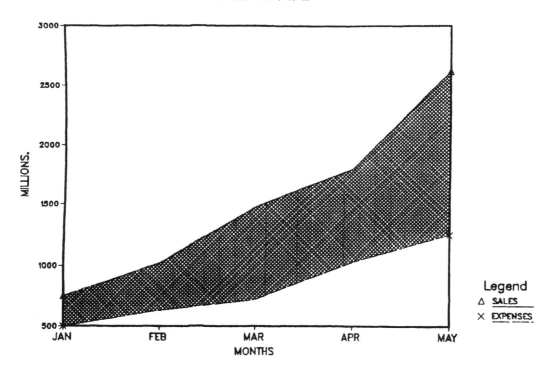

FIGURE 13.36

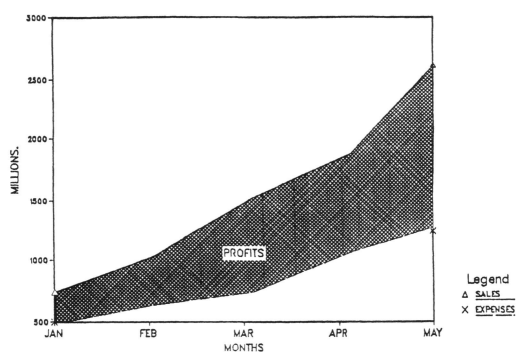

FIGURE 13.37

```
.type proft4.prs
GENERATE A PLOT.
TITLE IS "PROFIT PICTURE"
CURVE 1 SHADE PAIR IS 2.
X AXIS LABEL IS "MONTHS".
X AXIS IS MONTHLY.
Y AXIS LABEL IS "MILLIONS."
---> MESSAGE 1 IS "PROFITS",
CONNECT BC TO X=3, Y=1000,
IN COORDINATE UNITS,
HEIGHT 0.15,
---> BLANKING ON.
FRAME THE PICTURE.
INPUT DATA.
"SALES"
1,750 2,1020 3,1472 4,1802 5,2621
"EXPENSES"
1,500 2,630 3,720 4,1029 5,1248
END OF DATA.
GO.
QUIT.
```

FIGURE 13.38

```
.TYPE PROFT5.PRG
GENERATE A PLOT.
TITLE IS "PROFIT PICTURE"
CURVE 1 SHADE PAIR IS 2.
X AXIS LABEL IS "MONTHS".
X AXIS IS MONTHLY.
Y AXIS LABEL IS "MILLIONS."
MESSAGE 1 IS "PROFITS",
CONNECT BC TO X=3, Y=1000,
IN COORDINATE UNITS,
HEIGHT 0.15.
FRAME THE PICTURE.
INPUT DATA.
"SALES"
1,750 2,1020 3,1472 4,1802 5,2621
"EXPENSES"
1,500 2,630 3,720 4,1029 5,1248
END OF DATA.
GO.
QUIT.
```

FIGURE 13.39

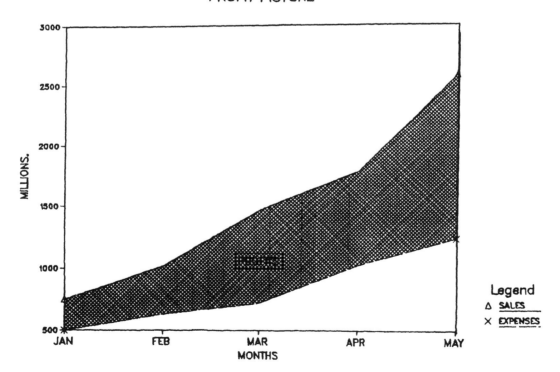

FIGURE 13.40

Finally, we can label the shaded area by including a message (Figure 13.37), so that it is quite clear that

- Sales are rising
- Expenses are rising
- Expenses are not rising as quickly as sales, so that profits are rising
- There is no doubt about the fact that we are talking about PROFITS

The program to generate the labeled profit area is shown in Figure 13.38, in which the message is named in the phrase

MESSAGE 1 IS "PROFITS"

The reason for the number 1 is that we can include more than one message if we so wish. The phrase

CONNECT BC TO X=3,Y=1000

indicates that the bottom center of the message (BC of profits) is to be positioned at X=3, Y=1000 of the graph (where 3 and 1,000 should be expressed in the same coordinate units as those generated for the X- and Y-axes. The height of the message box is .15 of an inch (not coordinate units). The phrase

BLANKING ON

causes the area around the word profits to be whited out. To indicate what benefit that is, consider the program shown in Figure 13.39, which omits the phrase BLANKING ON and results in the output shown in Figure 13.40, in which the word *profits* is obscured by the shading between the curves. The phrase "BLANKING ON" removes the shading from this area before writing the word *profits*. It does so by putting blanks in the area, hence the name.

## Pie Charts

Another common data representation is the pie chart, which is used to show relative percentages. The pie is a circle, which is divided into "pieces," with the size of each piece representing a given portion of the

| Year in School | Number of students |
|---|---|
| Freshman | 200 |
| Sophomores | 150 |
| Juniors | 125 |
| Seniors | 100 |
| Total | 575 |

(a)

FIGURE 13.41

| Year in School | | Proportion of School Population |
| --- | --- | --- |
| Freshman | 200/575 | .35 |
| Sophomores | 150/575 | .26 |
| Juniors | 125/575 | .22 |
| Seniors | 100/575 | .17 |
| | | 1.00 |

(b)

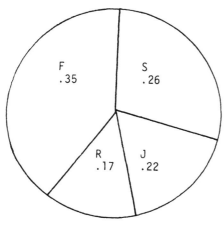

(c)

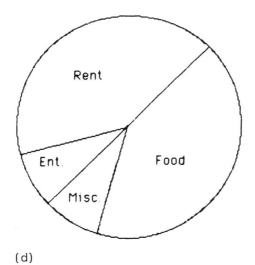

(d)

FIGURE 13.41 (continued)

```
     .TYPE STUPIE.PRG
---> GENERATE A PIE,
---> DIVISION LABELS "FR", "SO", "JU", "SE".
     TITLE IS "DISTRIBUTION OF STUDENTS".
     INPUT DATA.
     1,200 2,150 3,125 4,100
     END OF DATA.
     GO.
     QUIT.
```

FIGURE 13.42

total pie. For example, if the data on enrollment in our school is that given
in Figure 13.41a, we would create a pie chart by first creating a list of the
relative proportions of the students (Figure 13.41b), then arranging the
pie chart according to these proportions (Figure 13.41c), where the circle
or pie is divided according to the proportions. When the proportions are
relatively equal, the difference in size of the pieces is not as dramatic as
when the proportions vary. For example, a budget pie for the data

| | |
|---|---|
| Rent | $300 |
| Food | $300 |
| Entertainment | $ 50 |
| Miscellaneous | $ 50 |

would give the proportions

DISTRIBUTION OF STUDENTS

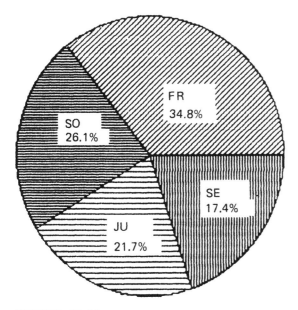

FIGURE 13.43

| Rent | 3/7 |
| Food | 3/7 |
| Entertainment | 1/14 |
| Miscellaneous | 1/14 |

and the pie shown in Figure 13.41d, which indicates that entertainment is just a "sliver" of our budget.

A TELL-A-GRAF program to generate a pie chart is shown in Figure 13.42, in which the generic command is

GENERATE A PIE

The line

DIVISION LABELS "FR","SO","JU","SE"

gives the number of pieces in the pie (4), as well as the label for each pie.

In the data

1,200    2,150    3,125    4,100

the first number of each pair is not taken as the X-value, nor is the second number the Y-value. The first number is taken as the "piece number" and the second number is the "amount" or value for that piece. TELL-A-GRAF does the addition of the values and the computation of the relative percentages. The output is the pie shown in Figure 13.43, where TELL-A-GRAF has again selected four different modes of shading, one for each piece of the pie.


Choosing Graphs Appropriate to the Data

The example on profits, in which we had two variables to compare—sales and expenses—enables us to consider the choice of various graphic displays for various sets of data. While the data can be generated with pie charts, this may not be a suitable form for our purposes. Using slightly different data, a program to illustrate profits in pie chart form is given in Figure 13.44.

The user does not need to explicitly indicate that two pies must be drawn. The nature of the pie is that it is suitable for a single set of data, thus, two sets of data automatically result in two pies (Figure 13.45).


```
.type prfpie.prs
GENERATE A PIE
INPUT DATA.
"SALES"
1,985 2,1121 3,1368 4,1737 5,2361
"EXPENSES"
1,836 2,960 3,1139 4,1441 5,1963
END OF DATA.
GO.
QUIT.
```

FIGURE 13.44

PROFIT PICTURE

SALES

PROFIT PICTURE

EXPENSES

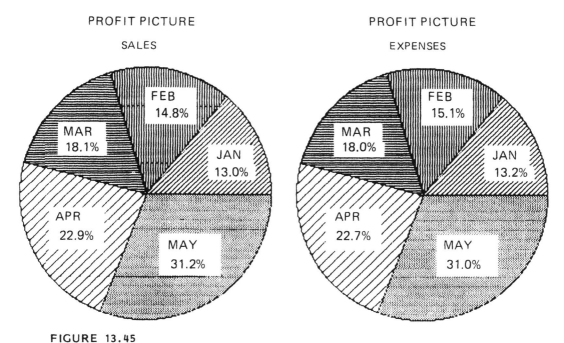

FIGURE 13.45

In order to "see" profit, we have to compare the corresponding pieces of each pie, but this is not even possible! The percentages reported in each slice are relative portions of expenses or sales *within that category*, hence, February accounted for 14.8% of all sales in the 5 months consider- ed. February also accounted for 15.1% of all expenses. But the numbers 14.8% and 15.1% are *not* comparable to each other. If they were, we would seem to have a loss

| | |
|---|---|
| February sales | 14.8% |
| February expenses | 15.1% |
| Net profit | -0.3% |

When the actual data show a profit

```
.type prfbar.prg
--> GENERATE A BAR.
    INPUT DATA.
    "SALES"
    1,985 2,1121 3,1368 4,1737 5,2361
    "EXPENSES"
    1,836 2,960 3,1139 4,1441 5,1963
    END OF DATA.
    GO.
    QUIT.
```

FIGURE 13.46

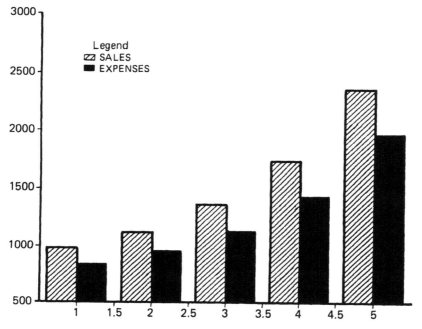

FIGURE 13.47

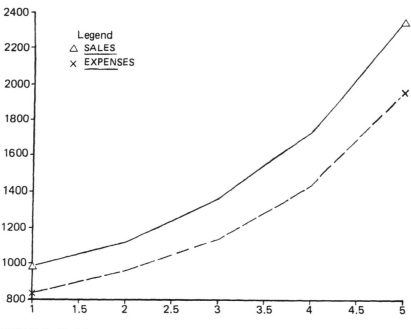

FIGURE 13.48

```
.type prfplt.prg
GENERATE A PLOT.
INPUT DATA.
"SALES"
1,985 2,1121 3,1368 4,1737 5,2361
"EXPENSES"
1,836 2,960 3,1139 4,1441 5,1963
END OF DATA.
GO.
QUIT.
```

FIGURE 13.49

| | |
|---|---|
| February sales | 1121 |
| February expenses | 960 |
| Net profit | 161 |

The use of pie charts for comparing sets of data is thus not generally applicable.

A bar chart will allow the comparison. For example, the same data, coupled with the program shown in Figure 13.46 gives the output of Figure 13.47, which does show sales (////) continually higher than expenses, although not as directly as the plot given in Figure 13.48.

The plot of Figure 13.48 was generated by the code given in Figure 13.49. Embellishing the program by framing the picture, shading the area between the curves, and adding the message "PROFIT" with blanking on, will serve to make the effect even greater.

## 3-D

Packages are available to create the effect of 3-D. One example is the contour maps produced by geological graphic packages. The diagrams are produced in 2-D, but give the effect of 3-D by using the principles of perspective. The use of the packages is similar to the use of TELL-A-GRAF: picking a "type" of program and giving parameters to that program.

## Summary

In this chapter we have considered the use of numeric versus graphic displays. We have concentrated on some primitive programs, such as the BASIC program to draw Christmas trees and the BASIC program to print histograms, and on the use of graphics packages, such as TELL-A-GRAF, in order to create standard graphs: bar charts, plots, and pies. In Chapter 14, we will look at the technology involved in computer graphics and at the procedures involved in writing graphics programs at both a more primitive level and at a higher level.

## Related Readings

Demel, John T. and Miller, Michael J., *Introduction to Computer Graphics,* Monterey, CA: Brooks/Cole Engineering Division, 1984.

Freund, John E., *Statistics: A First Course,* 3rd ed. Englewood Cliffs, NJ: Prentice-Hall, 1981.

Harrington, Steven, *Computer Graphics: A Programming Approach,* New York: McGraw-Hill, 1983.

Huff, Darrell, *How to Lie with Statistics,* New York: W. W. Norton & Company, 1954.

Kreitzberg, Charles B., and Shneiderman, Ben, *FORTRAN Programming: A Spiral Approach,* 2nd ed. New York: Harcourt Brace Jovanovich, 1982.

Mufti, Aftab A., *Elementary Computer Graphics,* Reston, VA: Reston Publishing Company, 1983.

Nahigian, J. Victor and Hodges, William S., *Computer Games for Businesses, Schools, and Homes,* Cambridge, MA: Winthrop Publishers, Inc., 1979.

Newman, William, M. and Sproull, Robert F., *Principles of Interactive Computer Graphics,* 2nd ed. New York: McGraw-Hill, 1979.

*TELL-A-GRAF User's Manual,* ISSCO Graphics.

# 14
# Writing Graphics Programs

Objectives

Upon finishing this chapter the reader should be able to

1. Distinguish between bit map graphics and vector graphics
2. Explain the need for refreshing screens that do not hold a permanent display
3. Explain the trade-offs between dot matrix quality output devices and those using continuous characters
4. Explain how the number of pixels affects resolution and the use of color
5. Explain the use of escape sequences to manipulate a graphics terminal
6. Indicate how these escape sequences are incorporated into higher level languages, e.g., BASIC
7. Use a programming language, e.g., BASIC, to create a graphic display involving text output, color, blinking, and sound
8. Explain the relationship between the CRT screen coordinate system and the Cartesian coordinate system
9. Explain the need for scaling data points to accommodate the non-symmetrical horizontal and vertical resolution in many commonly used terminals
10. Distinguish between high-resolution graphics and low-resolution graphics
11. Create at least one program that combines the drawing of points and lines into the production of more complex figures

The method of writing graphics programs varies with the type of technology used (e.g., vector graphics versus bit map graphics), the method in which points on the screen are described (e.g., X-Y coordinates or polar coordinates), and the applications for which the graphics programs have been written (e.g., computer aided design, referred to as CAD; computer aided manufacture, or CAM; display of business statistics, as found in bar charts or pie charts; and production of animated pictures, as in computer games or the simulation of real world situations, such as flying airplanes). The discussion here presumes an X-Y coordinate system.

## Various Technologies

Two distinctions made in the categorization of graphics devices are (1) the method in which objects are drawn on the screen, and (2) the permanence of the figures on the screen. The methods by which objects are drawn can be placed into two general categories

- Vector graphics
- Bit map graphics

The considerations of image persistence results in the subdivision

- Refresh devices
- Storage tube (or similar) devices

## Vector Graphics Versus Bit Map Graphics

In vector graphics devices, the display unit is capable of drawing straight lines on the screen. In bit map graphics, the straight line is approximated by lighting a set of dots (called *pixels* for picture elements). Thus, in vector graphics, the line drawn between two points would be continuous (Figure 14.1a). In bit map graphics, it would consist of a discrete number of spots (Figure 14.1b).

The lines drawn by vector graphics devices are usually of a better quality than those of the bit map devices, although the quality of the latter is quite good if the screen has a high resolution.

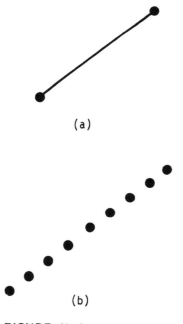

(a)

(b)

FIGURE 14.1

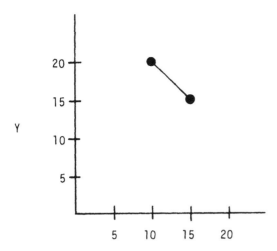

FIGURE 14.2

## Programming in Vector Graphics

The essence of writing a program in vector graphics consists in identifying two points in the X-Y plane, then drawing a line between them. The line can be drawn as an "offset" to the initial points. For example, we might have

    Point      10,20
    Line       +5,-5

which indicates that an initial point is selected at coordinate position 10,20 (X=10, Y=20), then a line is to be drawn to the point obtained by increasing the X-coordinate value by 5 (+5) and decreasing the Y-coordinate by 5 (-5). The resulting point is 15,15, so that the line would be drawn from 10,20 to 15,15 (Figure 14.2). The line itself would be a continuous "stroke" from 10,20 to 15,15, which sometimes gives rise to the name "stroke graphics" for vector graphics devices and/or programs.

The specification of the second point as +5,-5 is called "relative addressing." The second point is identified "relative to" the first point (five units to the right, five units down from the first point). We can also use "absolute addressing" by giving the exact coordinates of the second point

    Point      10,20
    Line to    15,15

where the command "line to" indicates that a line should be drawn from the first point (10,20) to the point 15,15. The point 15,15 is identified in exact or "absolute" coordinate values rather than values relative to the first point.

## Bit Map Graphics

In bit map graphics, the screen is seen as a matrix of dots (or pixels), each of which can be turned on or off. Figure 14.3a would be the repre-

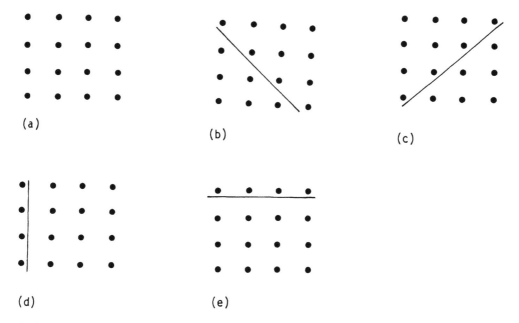

(a) (b) (c)

(d) (e)

FIGURE 14.3

sentation of a 4*4 matrix of pixels (a small screen indeed). In order to draw a line, we must "turn on" certain pixels. For example, by turning on the dots (pixels), a diagonal line can be drawn in one direction, (Figure 14.3b), or it could be drawn in the other direction (Figure 14.3c). A vertical line would be as shown in Figure 14.3d, and a horizontal would be as shown in Figure 14.3e. It is the method by which the dots are turned on that gives rise to the term *bit map graphics*.

Internally, there is a storage buffer that represents the screen. Thus, for a 4*4 screen, we would have a situation (Figure 14.4a) in which each position in the buffer represents a pixel position on the screen. In order to turn a pixel on, a 1 is placed in the position in the buffer representing

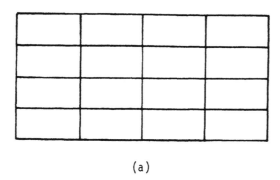

(a)

FIGURE 14.4

| 0 | 0 | 0 | 1 |
|---|---|---|---|
| 0 | 0 | 1 | 0 |
| 0 | 1 | 0 | 0 |
| 1 | 0 | 0 | 0 |

(b)

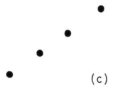

(c)

FIGURE 14.4 (continued)

the pixel. In order to turn a pixel off (or leave it off), a zero is placed in that position in the buffer. Thus, for the diagonal line slanting upward (left to right), we would have the distribution shown in Figure 14.4b, which would result in the screen output shown in Figure 14.4c, with four bits "on," the rest "off." The controller of the graphics device scans the buffer in order to direct the lighting or nonlighting of pixels on the screen. An "electron gun" scans the screen, turning on at positions where a 1 is placed in the buffer, turning off where a zero exists in the buffer. The screen itself is called a "raster" and the scanning of the raster is called a "raster scan." The buffer gives a "map" of the screen, giving rise to the term *bit map graphics*.

### Raster Scan Versus Random Scan

Video display devices that read bit map buffers in order to display the graphics on the screen are referred to as raster scan devices. The screen matrix is the "raster" and a gun scans left to right, top to bottom, across the screen in order to light or not light the pixels (Figure 14.5). The "gun" is switched on for the scan left to right, turned off for the return to the left margin, then turned on again. At the end of the "page" (bottom of the screen) the gun is turned off and repositioned at the uppermost left-hand corner of the screen (called vertical blanking or vertical retrace). In order to avoid flicker, this process must be repeated over 30 times a second.

The raster scan is the method used to produce pictures on a standard TV screen. The number of scan lines per screen varies with the equipment. In American TV, the number of scan lines is 525. European sets have 625

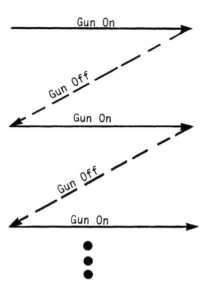

FIGURE 14.5

lines per screen. A raster of 1024*1024 pixels must scan 1024 lines, light-ing 1024 pixels on each line, over 30 times a second.

In practice the scan is not always performed "line by line." Rather, the even lines are scanned in one pass over the screen, the odd lines on the next pass, and the number of passes is doubled. The time in which the gun is returned from the right-hand side of the screen to the left-hand side (called horizontal retrace) is "idle time." So is the time in which the gun is returned from the lower right-hand corner of the screen to the up-per left-hand corner, the vertical retrace. In videotext systems, which use standard TV screens to display information as well as the normal TV fare, the TV-scan time (left to right, gun on) is used to transmit the video sig-nals for the normal TV fare; the idle time (vertical blanking) is used to transmit data and control signals for the videotext displays. Individual users govern the reception of normal TV versus videotext by the controls

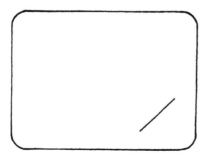

FIGURE 14.6

they set on the receiving unit. If the TV switch is on, they watch TV programs and the videotext signals are ignored, if the videotext switch is on, they receive the videotext displays and the TV signal is ignored.

Vector graphics devices use what is called a random scan; i.e., they can scan the screen in a random rather than a uniform fashion. The scan is really not random, but directed by the graphics program. However, the term *random* is used in contrast to the "deterministic" scanning in raster scanning. In drawing a line on the screen (or any other figure), the random scan device traverses only the area necessary to draw the line (Figure 14.6), it does not repeatedly scan the entire raster.

## Refresh Devices Versus Storage Tube

In devices that "light up" a CRT or TV screen by spraying "electron bullets" onto a phosphorous coating, the phosphorescent material retains its brightness for only a short period of time. Hence, if the image is to remain on the screen, it must be "refreshed," usually about 30 times a second. In storage tube devices, the image, once drawn, remains until it is explicitly erased; there is no need to refresh the screen. The permanence of the image in storage tube devices saves processing time (by eliminating the constant refreshing), and allows for building a picture in modular fashion. However, it does not allow for easy erasure and is not very suitable for animation or interactive modification of designs. The use of refresh devices that use a bit map allow for easier modification of the image by modification of the bit map. In refresh devices that do not use a bit map (vector refresh devices), the program driving the electron gun can also be modified to cause movement across the screen, e.g., in "landing a plane" in a simulation of flight patterns.

Vector devices, whether refresh or permanent display, will usually be used to create line drawings (Figure 14.7a), while the use of a bit map allows for shading figures in a manner that makes the objects look "solid" (Figure 14.7b). Of course, lines can be used to "shade" the figure but not as smoothly as the bit map techniques.

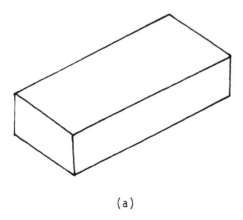

(a)

FIGURE 14.7

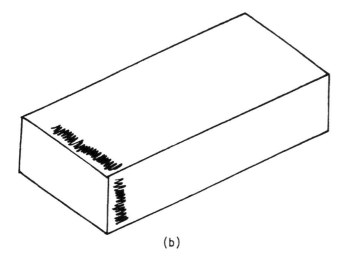

(b)

FIGURE 14.7 (continued)


## Refresh Rate

As indicated above, in any "nonpermanent" display, e.g., a CRT, the screen must be "refreshed," i.e., the picture must be redrawn several times a second (usually about 30 times).

The reason for refreshing is that the phosphorous coating of the screen does not retain its glow indefinitely. Thus, a pixel that has been activated will eventually lose its brightness; in order to maintain it in a steady bright state, one must continually reactivate it. The reason for the 30 times a second cycle of refreshing is due to the qualities of human perception. At rates of 30 refreshes a second or faster, the human eye will see the refreshed screen as a "steady state." At slower rates, the eye will detect fading in the phosphorescent glow, and then its rebrightening, fading, and rebrightening, causing the picture to seem to "flicker."


## The Screen Plane

In both vector graphics and bit map graphics, the screen plane is seen as a rectangular coordinate system.(It may also be described in polar coordinates, or any other suitable coordinate system, however we restrict our discussion here to the X-Y coordinate system typical of the Cartesian plane.) The screen plane is not continuous, like the "abstract" X-Y plane; rather, there are a finite number of positions in the horizontal and vertical directions. The number of positions available in the horizontal (X) direction and the vertical (Y) direction determines the "resolution" of the device. This varies from device to device.


## The Standard CRT Screen

The standard CRT screen, operating in "text" mode, consists of 24 rows with 80 characters in each row, a 24*80 "raster" or "matrix." The CRT

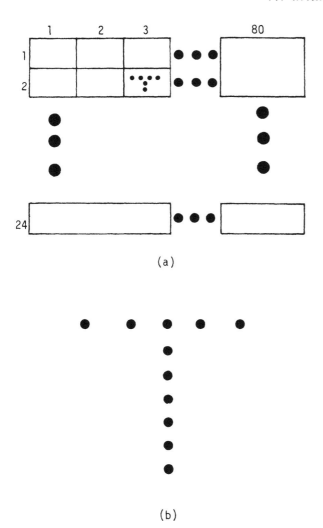

(a)

(b)

FIGURE 14.8

screen itself is capable of having more than 24*80 positions resolved, but if we use the standard character set, the space allotted to each character is predetermined and consumes several "physical dots" on the screen. For example, a character displayed in a 5*7 matrix consumes 35 dots to display the single character. Thus, a 24*80 matrix (1,920 positions) of 5*7 dot matrix characters really consists of 24*80*35 (67,200) "dots."

However, only the 1,920 character positions are "individually address-able." The individual positions (pixels) lit by the characters placed in each addressable position of the grid are predetermined. We can cause the letter T to be typed in row 2, column 3 (Figure 14.8a), however, we cannot re-quest that the individual "dots" in that character position be turned on or off when in text mode. The reader will note that the letter T is not contin-uous, but composed of individual pixels (Figure 14.8b). The top row of pixels is "lit," along with the middlecolumn. These pixels are selected from the 5*7 (or 7*10, or other dimensions) grid.

The situation of characters created with pixels as opposed to straight lines is analogous to the use of dot matrix printing versus "solid" printing characters.

### The Quality of Printed Output

Hard copy devices that print solid characters, e.g., daisy wheel or drum printers, are analogous to vector graphics; those that use a dot matrix are analogous to bit map graphics. The use of a solid continuous letter is similar to the technology used with the wooden printer block (Figure 14.9a).

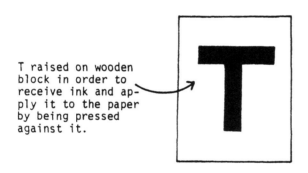

T raised on wooden block in order to receive ink and apply it to the paper by being pressed against it.

(a)

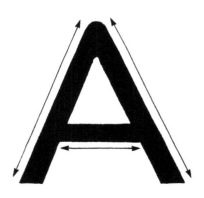

(b)

FIGURE 14.9

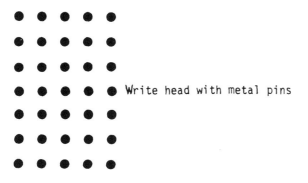

Write head with metal pins

FIGURE 14.10

Vector graphics devices would create similar continuous letters, although they might be composed of several linear pieces (Figure 14.9b).

As indicated earlier, CRT displays use a series of dots to create a letter. Dot matrix printers use the same methodology, substituting wire pins and ink for the electron gun and phosphorous (Figure 14.10). The pins of the write head can be selectively "pushed out" against the print ribbon, causing the character to be typed. The characters are predefined and only those predefined patterns can be delineated in the 5*7 matrix. We cannot turn on the individual 35 dots in an independent fashion, although we may be allowed to define some of our own characters. (In programs that use dot matrix printers to copy images from a graphics screen, the individual pins are manipulated.)

## Quality Versus Flexibility

The quality of characters printed in dot matrix form is not as good as the characters printed by a single solid continuous letter (Figure 14.11a and b), however, the lack of quality is balanced by the flexibility of the meth-

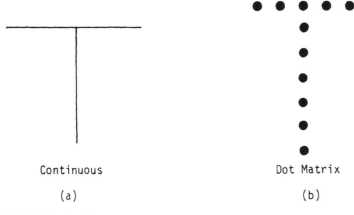

Continuous

(a)

Dot Matrix

(b)

FIGURE 14.11

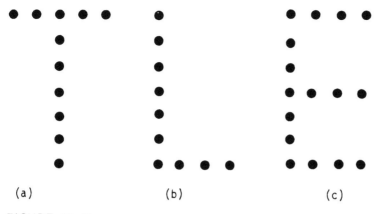

(a)                    (b)                         (c)

FIGURE 14.12

od. We can use a single printing mechanism (single write head) to create any character in the character set (Figures 14.12a, b, and c). With a single solid continuous character, we need a different physical "mold" for each character in the character set (Figure 14.13a, b, and c). This is the method used on chain printers or drum printers. Chain printers have the entire character set on a chain that revolves past the write head (Figure 14.14a). The head simply strikes against the chain (or the ribbon) at the proper time to select the proper character. On a drum, the situation is similar; each print position has a copy of the entire character set (Figure 14.14b).

The difference between the chain and the drum is that the chain prints one character position at a time (called a character printer), with the head moving along the line. The drum can be set to print all 132 (or some other number, like 120 or 144) positions at once, printing an entire line (called a line printer). Hence, the line printer is faster than the character printer. They both will produce "quality output" if a single continuous mold is used for each character. However, they are correspondingly more expensive in that the chain or drum has more "parts" (the characters) and a complex

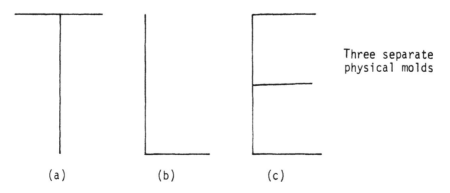

Three separate physical molds

(a)          (b)          (c)

FIGURE 14.13

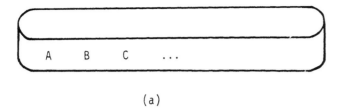

(a)

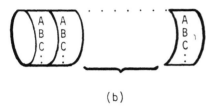

(b)

FIGURE 14.14

system of selecting the proper character (rotating chain or setting the print wheels for each position) than the dot matrix printer.

With this brief digression into the types of "print characters," we return to the consideration of graphics devices. The primary interest here has been the ability or inability of a given device to turn on each dot or pixel in a screen. When displaying characters, we cannot turn on each pixel in the 5*7 matrix individually, although we can select the "proper character" to cause a given pattern of dots to turn on. And, on some systems, we can predefine characters of our own, giving us some flexibility in manipulating the dot matrix. The considerations of continuous characters versus dot matrix characters are analogous to the consideration of lines drawn with vector graphics devices (continuous) versus bit map graphics devices (discrete).

### The Staircase Effect

The lines drawn by vector graphics devices are usually "straighter" than the lines drawn by bit map graphics devices. For example, if the points 1,1 and 2,3 are connected on a vector graphics "scope," we would have the line shown in Figure 14.15a. In a bit map graphics device, we would have the dots shown in Figure 14.15b or Figure 14.15c, in which the extra dot (2,2 in the first diagram; 1,2 in the second diagram) "fills in the line." As the reader can see, neither of the lines drawn with dots is straight. This is called the "staircase" effect of drawing lines with dots or pixels (see Newman and Sproull, 1979). If the screen has a sufficient number of pixel positions, the staircase effect is less noticeable, although it is still there.

Using pixels, straight lines can be drawn only along lines parallel to either axis (i.e., horizontal or vertical lines) and the 45° direction (either

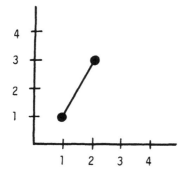

(a)

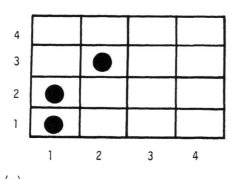

(b)

(c)

FIGURE 14.15

diagonal; Figures 14.16a, b, c, and d). All other line orientations (e.g., 60°, 30°) will exhibit the staircase effect.

On a vector graphics device, straight lines can be drawn at a large number of angles, so that the quality of the lines drawn in most pictures is superior to that found in bit map graphics. Thus, vector graphics devices are good for "line drawings." The lines are usually monochrome or

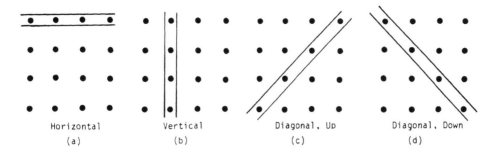

| Horizontal | Vertical | Diagonal, Up | Diagonal, Down |
| (a) | (b) | (c) | (d) |

FIGURE 14.16

restricted to a relatively small number of colors. "Shading" between the lines is difficult to achieve. By allocating more than a single bit to the description of a pixel, bit map graphics devices allow for more subtle shading and a wider range of color than vector graphics devices.

### How Many Bits Per Pixel?

In the above bit map, we assumed a single bit was turned on or off in the bit map buffer, causing a corresponding pixel to be turned on or off on the screen. This on-off method is the simplest bit map available. It will result in a monochrome image (whatever color the screen uses for drawing characters or lighting pixels, e.g., green, white, or orange) that has dots either lit at a given intensity or not lit at all. More complex schemes can vary either the intensity (brightness) of the pixels or the color of the pixel (or both).

### Varying the Intensity

In order to vary the intensity of the pixels, we set aside more than a single bit for each pixel position. Thus, if we wish four intensities

    Bright
    Medium bright
    Dull
    Off

we would set aside 2 bits for each pixel position

    11 = Bright
    10 = Medium bright
    01 = Dull
    00 = Off

and a map might look like that in Figure 14.17a, which would have the center pixels "bright" (3), some surrounding pixels "medium bright" (2), and some dull (1). The resulting figure would have a bright center, with a less bright "surrounding halo," much as a picture of the sun. Although the example did not show the use of the off value, it too can be used to

| 1 | 2 | 2 | 1 |
|---|---|---|---|
| 2 | 3 | 3 | 2 |
| 2 | 3 | 3 | 2 |
| 1 | 2 | 2 | 1 |

(a)

| 2 | 1 | 1 | 2 |
|---|---|---|---|
| 1 | 0 | 0 | 1 |
| 1 | 0 | 0 | 1 |
| 2 | 1 | 1 | 2 |

(b)

FIGURE 14.17

| 4 | 2 | 1 | |
|---|---|---|---|
| 0 | 0 | 0 = 0 = off |
| 0 | 0 | 1 = 1 = very dim |
| 0 | 1 | 0 = 2 | . |
| 0 | 1 | 1 = 3 | . |
| 1 | 0 | 0 = 4 | . |
| 1 | 0 | 1 = 5 | . |
| 1 | 1 | 0 = 6 = very bright |
| 1 | 1 | 1 = 7 = brightest |

(a)

| 8 | 4 | 2 | 1 | |
|---|---|---|---|---|
| 0 | 0 | 0 | 0 = 0 = off |
| 0 | 0 | 0 | 1 = 1 = very, very dark |
| | . | | |
| | . | | |
| | . | | |
| 1 | 1 | 1 | 1 = 15 = brightest |

(b)

FIGURE 14.18

good effect. For example the map in Figure 14.17b might indicate a "black hole" (four inner zeroes) in the midst of a relatively brighter universe.

The number of intensity levels is directly related to the number of bits set aside for the description of intensity. Three bits gives 8 levels (Figure 14.18a), and 4 bits gives 16 levels (Figure 14.18b). The trade-off is between the amount of storage in the bit map buffer and the quality of the screen display. Fewer bits in the buffer saves memory but gives a binary on-off display. More bits in the buffer gives a "smoother" display, allowing for various "shadings" of the picture. As memory gets cheaper and processing faster, there is a tendency to choose quality of display as the desirable feature by increasing the size of the bit map buffers.

## Color Graphics

Certain display screens can support the use of color graphics. Not all screens are capable of doing so, some having a single color, or mono-chrome, coating. However, assuming that the video display unit can support the use of color, this too is implemented by a set of extra bits for each pixel.

Video display units (VDUs) that support graphics are based on some basic set of colors, usually three: red, blue, and green. These colors can

| R | G | B | |
|---|---|---|---|
| 0 | 0 | 0 | = Black |
| 0 | 0 | 1 | = Blue |
| 0 | 1 | 0 | = Green |
| 0 | 1 | 1 | = Cyan |
| 1 | 0 | 0 | = Red |
| 1 | 0 | 1 | = Magenta |
| 1 | 1 | 0 | = Yellow (or Brown) |
| 1 | 1 | 1 | = White |

(a)

| R | G | B | |
|---|---|---|---|
| 1 | 0 | 0 | = Red |
| 0 | 1 | 0 | = Green |
| 0 | 0 | 1 | = Blue |

(b)

| R | G | B | |
|---|---|---|---|
| 0 | 1 | 1 | = Cyan |
| 1 | 0 | 1 | = Magenta |
| 1 | 1 | 0 | = Yellow |

(c)

| R | G | B |
|---|---|---|
| 1 | 1 | 1 |

(d)

| R | G | B |
|---|---|---|
| 0 | 0 | 0 |

(e)

**FIGURE 14.19**

| R | G | B | |
|---|---|---|---|
| 00 | 00 | 00 | = all off |
| 00 | 00 | 01 | = red, green off, blue dull |
| . | | | |
| . | | | |
| . | | | |
| 11 | 01 | 10 | = red bright, green dull, blue medium bright |
| . | | | |
| . | | | |
| . | | | |
| 11 | 11 | 11 | = all three bright, which yields bright white |

FIGURE 14.20

be turned on and off in various combinations to produce eight different colors (Figure 14.19a). The pure colors are red, green, and blue (Figure 14.19b), while cyan, magenta, and yellow are combinations of two colors (Figure 14.19c). White is "all colors" on (Figure 14.19d), and black is "none on" (Figure 14.19e). If we have a simple on-off system of representing the colors, the three bits are sufficient. In this case the above eight colors are all that are possible.

If extra bits are added to vary the intensity of each color, the range of colors produced by mixing values can be extended indefinitely. A scheme with 2 bits used for intensity would be that shown in Figure 14.20. Note that 6 bits are "dedicated" to each pixel, 2 for each color. Since four levels of intensity can be chosen for each of three colors represented, we have

$$4^3 = 64$$

various possibilities of color and brightness as indicated in the tree shown in Figure 14.21. If three bits were set aside for intensity, there would be eight levels of intensity

0,1,2,3,4,5,6,7

and 8**3 = 512 different possible variations of color and intensity. (The two asterisks indicate exponentiation.)

In practice, systems have been developed with various bit configurations, e.g., 8 bits, divided unevenly

| 3 bits | 3 bits | 2 bits |
|--------|--------|--------|
| Red | Green | Blue |

or 24 bits, divided evenly into 8 bits (256 levels of intensity) for each color

| 8 bits | 8 bits | 8 bits |
|--------|--------|--------|
| Red | Green | Blue |

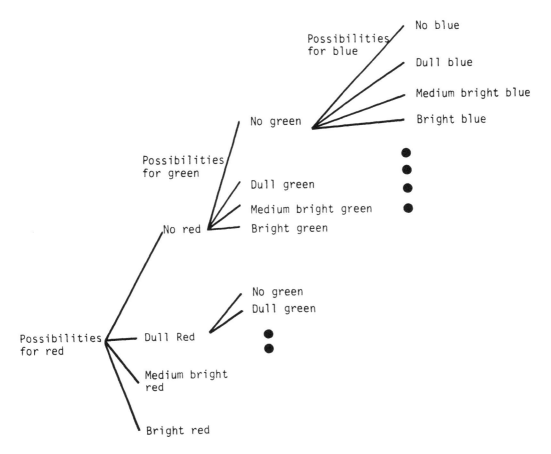

FIGURE 14.21

In the case of 8 bits (256 levels) set aside for each color, there are 256**3 (or approximately 16 million) possibilities

$$256^3 = (2^8)^3 = 2^{24} = 2^4 * 2^{20} \approx 16 \text{ million}$$

### The Cost of Storage

In a display screen with a grid of 1024*1024 (over 1 million) pixels, setting aside 3 bits per pixel yields over 3 million bits per screen surface (for simple on-off intensity, three basic colors). Setting aside 24 bits per pixel consumes in the vicinity of 25 million bits. For purposes of comparison, 1 million bits is equal to 125,000 bytes (1,000,000/8 = 125,000) or half of a single-sided floppy disk. This memory must be readily accessible to the display unit controller in order for it to refresh the screen in a reasonably fast fashion. These bits must also be capable of being updated in a fraction of a second (1/30 sec) if the screen is to change dynamically, leading to complex techniques in both hardware and software design.

## Color Vector Graphics

Most vector graphics screens are monochrome. However, this is not inherent to vector graphics. In using hard copy plotters, a printed form of vector graphics, various colors and widths of pens can be used to produce multi-colored displays and shading, respectively. In video vector displays, the shading can be achieved by spacing the lines as well as changing their orientation in space, as in the bar charts and pie charts of Chapter 13. In fact, the graphs reproduced in Chapter 13 were initially produced on a display that emulated the Tektronix storage tube display and then copied onto paper with a special printing device. An alternative to the screen copying printer would have been to send the data to a Calcomp plotter, a type of pen plotter similar to vector graphics devices.

## Higher Resolutions

While a standard CRT can address 1,920 character positions (in text mode), high-quality graphics devices often have a screen with a matrix of 1024* 1024 positions, a higher resolution than the screen capable of addressing 24*80 positions. The higher resolution will allow finer representation of objects.

## The Graphics Character Set

Some VDUs have only the alphanumeric character set (letters, numbers, special characters); others (e.g., Digital Equipment's VT 100 series) have a special graphics character set. If such a graphics character set is available, the terminal may be programmed to produce graphical output with these characters alone. This is a more restricted use of graphics capability than the use of bit map or vector graphics techniques. We will refer to it as "character graphics."

The user of the terminal chooses between the alphanumeric character set and the graphics character set by choosing the "mode" of the terminal: text or graphics. The mode is selected by a given character sequence, e.g.

    ESC     ( 0

to select graphics mode, and

    ESC     ( B

to select "ASCII," or text mode. These sequences vary from device to device and are described in the manual for the terminal. They may be sent to the terminal directly, if the terminal is placed in "local" mode (a physical switch or button) or through a program (BASIC, FORTRAN, Pascal) if the terminal is in nonlocal mode. The ensuing discussion assumes that the terminal is in local mode. A reader with access to a VT 100-compatible terminal is encouraged to read the text at the terminal and watch the results.

In a high-level language the same results can be achieved by using WRITE (PRINT) statements (Figure 14.22). In many versions of BASIC for microcomputers, special high-level commands (e.g., screen or beep) are

```
      WRITE (6,15)
15    FORMAT ('ESC (0')        (FORTRAN)

      PRINT "ESC (0"           (BASIC)

      WRITE ('ESC (0')         (PASCAL)
```

FIGURE 14.22

supplied to produce the results without the "low-level" knowledge of the exact escape sequence.

## An Example

One of the commands directed to the terminal itself is the command to select the graphics character set

    ESC       (0

Note that the commands consist of sequences of characters. The above command is "given" by the user typing the keys

- Escape
- Leftparen
- Zero

in that order, with no spaces in between. Once the graphics character set has been chosen, the normal keys take on a "different meaning." For example, in the graphics mode, when a lowercase *a* is printed on the screen, the results are as shown in Figure 14.23.

Not all the characters are different in the graphics mode. For example, the entire uppercase character set is the same as it is in standard ASCII mode

    A   B   C   ...   Z

So are periods, commas, quotation marks, arithmetic operators, and other symbols useful for generating messages. Retaining these symbols allows us to print messages in the graphics mode as well as to draw pictures. Of course, if one wants the complete ASCII character set, one could do graphics in graphics mode, switch to ASCII for characters, then back to graphics, etc. The command to switch back to ASCII is

    ESC       (B

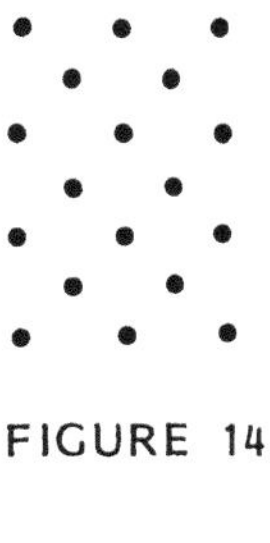

FIGURE 14.23

where the uppercase *B* (as opposed to lowercase) is essential, and is achieved by hitting the shift key simultaneously with the B key.

The user can make the screen "blink" by typing

    ESC      [5m

and reverse video can be obtained by

    ESC      [7m

The use of blinking and reverse video can be used to indicate errors to the user or to highlight portions of the screen. Either blinking or reverse video (or both) can be turned off by typing

    ESC      [0m

where the 0 is a zero and the *m* is lowercase.

Some other useful commands are

    ESC      [2J      • clear screen
    ESC      [H       • place cursor at "home" position (Row 1, Column 1)

To move the cursor up and down, the commands are

    ESC      [A       • up
    ESC      [B       • down
    ESC      [C       • right
    ESC      [D       • left

These cursor movements, as well as "home" and other common movements, are often supplied by function keys on the VDU. To move the cursor to an arbitrary position, the command is

    ESC      [n1;n2H

where n1 and n2 indicate the row and column numbers and are to be replaced by numerical values; the remaining characters (ESC,[ ,H) are typed as is. Thus, the command

    ESC      [12;40H

will move the cursor to the center of a 24-by-80 screen.

To type the word HELLO in reverse video at the center of the screen, we execute the following commands (i.e., type these keys):

    ESC      [12;40H    • move to center screen
    ESC      [7m        • select reverse video
    HELLO               • type word

To type HELLO at the "home" position with "blinking," we first "clear" reverse video, then move the cursor, select blinking, and type HELLO

    ESC      [0m        • clear reverse video
    ESC      [H         • go home
    ESC      [5m        • select blinking
    HELLO

Note that the original HELLO in reverse video is still on the screen. To remove it, one would have to clear the screen before the blinking program with the command

    ESC      [2J

f    displays a little o, two will make eyes

o    prints a straight line at the top of
     the "character rectangle" or "box"

s    prints a straight line at the bottom of
     the character rectangle

q    prints a straight line at the middle of
     the character rectangle

x    will print a vertical line

**FIGURE 14.24**

To place HELLO in the lower left corner in both reverse video and blinking, we leave "blinking on" (by not issuing ESC [0m), select reverse video, move the cursor to 24,1, and type HELLO

```
ESC      [7m
ESC      [24;1H
HELLO
```

Of course we can erase all our work with ESC [0m.

Some other useful characters are those given in Figure 14.24. The lowercase letters o, p, q, r, and s all print straight lines, but each prints the line at a different height in the character rectangle. Try it and see. Other characters, such as t, u, and v, print shapes that wind up being useful in conjunction with other characters. In fact, such combinations of characters are used to draw figures (e.g., the sequence given in Figure 14.25 will print a rectangle in the center of the screen). Note that the edges of the rectangle do not meet, a problem due to the low resolution provided by a 24*80 grid. Adding the commands

```
ESC    [12;40H
ff
```

will place a pair of eyes in the rectangle to peer out at the user. The eyes will replace part of the base of the rectangle. The reader can adjust this with a program that makes the rectangle out of three rows of the CRT screen. The reader is encouraged to play with the primitive graphics commands at his or her installation. A booklet that explains the commands for that terminal is usually obtained when purchasing the terminal.

| | |
|---|---|
| ESC  [2J | clear screen |
| ESC  [11;37H | go to line 11, column 37 |
| xooooox | vertical line, top lines, vertical line |
| ESC  [12;37H | go to line 12, column 37 |
| xsssssx | vertical line, bottom lines, vertical line |

**FIGURE 14.25**

## Using a Personal Computer

The devices used in both vector graphics and bit map graphics have historically been relatively expensive. They normally consist of a video display screen, possibly a hard copy printer or plotter, a storage area for the bit map in bit map graphics or the computer program that drives the vector drawing mechanism, and a control unit to interpret the commands (the bit map or the program), and they cause the device to act appropriately (either turning pixels on and off in a raster scan or moving the electron gun in a specified "random scan"). Input devices range from the keyboard to lightpens, joysticks, "mice," and digitizing devices. The advent of microcomputers has made many of these capabilities available at a much lower cost. The personal computers have limitations on quality and power of the display when compared to the more specialized systems, but they are ideal for the beginning study of graphics because of their ease of use (commands are embedded in such high-level languages as BASIC) and their relative availability.

## Text Mode and Graphics Mode

The personal computer with graphics capability is usually able to operate in at least four modes

- System-level command mode
- Program level
  - a. Text mode
  - b. Low-resolution graphics
  - c. High-resolution graphics

At the system level the programmer can select a language or a system utility, such as the sort routine. Assuming we are going to write graphics programs in BASIC, this is the language that would be selected at the system level. Then, within BASIC we have three choices

- Text mode
- Graphics mode, low resolution
- Graphics mode, high resolution

In text mode one uses the normal ASCII (or EBCDIC) character set. This is the default mode and is the mode in which programs are created and modified.

In addition to the standard character set, the language may allow certain primitive graphics operations, e.g.

- Blink cursor
- Reverse video
- Use color
- Make cursor larger or smaller
- Make cursor appear or disappear
- Cause a beep
- Clear the screen

While some systems do not consider these to be true graphics capabilities, they afford a level of graphics, especially the use of color and sound, that is sufficient for such applications as data entry, and provides a pleasing display.

For example, on the IBM personal computer, the commands

```
COLOR      14,1,0
CLS
LOCATE     12,40
INPUT "NAME?",N$
```

will cause the screen to have a blue background, a black border, and a yellow foreground. Prompts and other text are printed in the foreground so that the message "NAME?" will appear in yellow on a blue background, the background being surrounded by a black border about an inch wide. Because of the locate command, the prompt will appear at the center of a 24*80 screen. The effect is quite dramatic when contrasted to the usual display of white on black with prompting always at the left-hand column of the screen.

The locate command is a "high-level" facility that creates the necessary escape sequences to move the cursor; i.e., it is translated into commands of the type discussed under the graphics character set of the VT 100. Similar comments apply to the use of the commands to cause the output to blink. On the IBM PC, blinking is accomplished through the color command by adding the value 16 to the foreground color

```
color      30,1,0
```

which is still foreground yellow (30-16) = 14, but yellow blinking. A command for reverse video is not explicitly included since the color command can accomplish even more extensive changes that simply reversing the color combination of the screen, and subsumes reverse video.

The format of the color command is

```
color foreground, background, border
```

and the "palette" of colors is as follows. For foreground, 16 colors can be selected (Table 14.1). For both background and border, eight choices are provided, those numbered 0 through 7. Blinking (add 16) can only be done with the foreground colors. Using the above information, we can see how the command

```
color      14,1,0
```

is decoded into the yellow foreground on blue background (screen color) with black border. If one wanted no border, the command

```
color      14,1,1
```

TABLE 14.1

| 0 | Black | 8 | Gray |
|---|---|---|---|
| 1 | Blue | 9 | Light blue |
| 2 | Green | 10 | Light green |
| 3 | Cyan | 11 | Light cyan |
| 4 | Red | 12 | Light red |
| 5 | Magenta | 13 | Light magenta |
| 6 | Brown | 14 | Yellow |
| 7 | White | 15 | High-intensity white |

would do, since the background and border will be identical in color, hence indistinguishable.

If the normal screen is white on black

color        7,0,0

or

color        15,0,0

reverse video can be achieved with the commands

color        0,7,7

or

color        0,15,15

as well as a host of other options.

## Visual Versus Audial Signals

While the use of such visual signals as reverse video are suitable for displays that are being visually monitored, they are not usually sufficient for data entry or other applications where the person is not monitoring the display visually. This is where the BEEP command (translated to ASCII 7, ring bell) is convenient. Assuming that the allowable responses to the menu

1. Deposit
2. Withdraw
3. Check Balance

are 1, 2, or 3, the code shown in Figure 14.26 displays the menu, then accepts and checks the user response. If the response is correct, the appropriate subroutine is selected; if incorrect, a beep and a reprompt result.

The subroutines at 1000, 2000, 3000, and 4000 process the respective transactions (deposit, withdraw, balance, quit) by prompting for other data, searching for data, or simply stopping. All but the quit routine will return (it has stop in it). Upon returns, line 100 checks to see if the re-

```
10   LOCATE 8,25  (Line 8, Column 25)
20   PRINT "1.  DEPOSIT"
30   PRINT "2.  WITHDRAW"
40   PRINT "3.  CHECK BALANCE"
45   PRINT "4.  QUIT"
50   LOCATE 12,25
60   INPUT "ENTER CHOICE",C
70   IF C = 1 GOSUB 1000
80   IF C = 2 GOSUB 2000
90   IF C = 3 GOSUB 3000
95   IF C = 4 GOTO 4000
100  IF C >= 1 and C <= 4 GOTO 10
110  BEEP
120  GOTO 50
```

FIGURE 14.26

sponse was valid; if so, it goes back to the menu level. If the response was invalid, none of the routines would have been triggered, and the test at line 100 would fail, causing execution to "fall through" to the beep and the subsequent transfer of control to the prompt for a choice.

## Similar Commands in Other Systems

The use of the IBM PC in the previous example was merely a convenience. Many systems have similar commands at the "character graphics" level. For example, in one version of BASIC used with the Apple II computer, the command to reverse video is INVERSE

```
10      INVERSE
20      PRINT A
```

This will cause the value of A to be printed in reverse video. To "turn off" the INVERSE printing of the characters, one uses the command NORMAL. Normal mode is defined as white-on-black characters (inverse being black on white).

In printing an error message, one might use INVERSE temporarily

```
50      INVERSE
60      PRINT "YOU MUST ANSWER 'YES' OR 'NO'"
70      NORMAL
```

returning to normal video for the rest of the interaction.

In order to cause blinking of the printed characters, the command is FLASH

```
10      FLASH
20      PRINT "LOOK HERE"
```

Again NORMAL returns the terminal to "regular" nonflashing white-on-black mode.

Other commands to the screen are

HOME, which clears the screen, then positions the cursor to the "home" position (the uppermost left-hand corner).

HTAB, which causes "tabbing" in the horizontal direction, e.g., HTAB 15 moves the cursor to column 15. (The columns are numbered 1 through 40.)

VTAB, which moves the cursor to a specified row, e.g., VTAB 10 moves the cursor to line 10. (The lines are numbered 1 through 24.)

Hence the sequence of commands

```
10      VTAB 12
20      HTAB 18
30      PRINT "HELLO"
```

will cause the word *HELLO* to be printed in the center of the screen. The sequence

```
10      VTAB 12
20      HTAB 18
30      INVERSE
40      PRINT "HELLO"
```

will cause the printing of *HELLO* at center screen in reverse video. If the screen had other things previously printed on it, it would be desirable to first clear the screen with the HOME command before issuing the remaining commands

```
10      HOME
20      VTAB 12
30      HTAB 18
40      INVERSE
50      PRINT "HELLO"
```

Note that the placement of the HOME command after the tabs would not work

```
10      VTAB 12
20      HTAB 18
30      HOME
40      INVERSE
50      PRINT "HELLO"
```

since the effect of HOME, repositioning of the cursor to line 1, column 1, after clearing the screen, would invalidate the use of the TAB commands.

The commands to the terminal, e.g., INVERSE and FLASH, are translated into such commands as ESC [5m or ESC [7m, as appropriate for the video unit at hand. They are "higher-level" commands that must be translated into their technical forms. Of course, the human user will normally find it easier to say INVERSE than ESC [7m.

## Hardware and Software

While we have associated the BASIC command language with a particular system, e.g., the IBM PC or APPLE II, the features offered are a function of the software, the BASIC interpreter, or compiler. In the case of the IBM PC, the BASIC language was Microsoft BASIC. On the APPLE II it was Applesoft. However, the hardware will also limit the utility of certain features. For example, with a monochrome CRT, the use of 16 colors can result in various shades of gray, but certainly not 16 colors.

## Graphics

With this brief discussion of character graphics, we now turn to a brief discussion of "true" graphics. The complete treatment requires a text (or texts) of its own, but we will give enough of the commands and concepts to illustrate the general idea.

There is usually a choice between low-resolution graphics (LRG) and high-resolution graphics (HRG). In low- (or medium-) resolution graphics, fewer pixels are addressable, but more colors are available. In HRG there are more pixels addressable, but fewer colors. In the IBM PC (model XT, Microsoft BASIC) the two modes offer the following resolutions:

```
Medium:     320 by 200
High:       640 by 200
```

On the Apple II described here, the two modes are

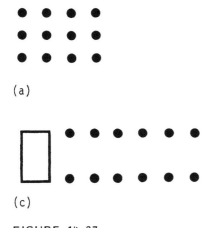

(a)

(b)

(c)

FIGURE 14.27

| Low:  | 40 * 40   |
| High: | 280 * 160 |

The first number quoted is the number of dots in a row (the resolution in the direction of the X-axis). The second number is the resolution in the vertical direction. This is a characteristic of the technology used. The horizontal direction of such monitors as that of the TV is wider than the vertical dimension, usually 4:3 (called the aspect ratio).

The pragmatic effect is that figures described in normal X-Y coordinates will not always appear in the same fashion on the screen. Whether or not they appear similar in both the abstract X-Y system and the screen systems depends on the density of the dots or number of pixels per inch. If the pixels are evenly spaced in both directions (Figure 14.27a), the dimensions of a regular figure, such as a square, will be the same in both coordinate systems, say 2*2.

However, if the pixels are not spaced evenly in both directions (Figure 14.27b), then a square cannot be formed with 2 Y's and 2 X's (Figure 14.27c), since the sides will not be equal, In this particular example, there are four pixels per unit in the X-direction, and two in the Y-direction, i.e., twice as many X's as Y's. Hence, for a square of given dimensions, we should light twice as many X-values as Y-values; i.e., given the dimensions 2*2 (X,Y), we create a display that is 4*2, having doubled the X-value. This doubling is a "scaling factor" that should be invisible to the end user of a graphics program, i.e., invisible to the user of the program we write. Other scaling factors might be dictated by the user, such as doubling a figure's size or "zooming" in on a portion of a drawing. However, the technical features of the equipment are the programmer's concern only. We would prompt for the size of the square

```
PRINT "ENTER LENGTH OF SIDE"
INPUT X
```

then adjust it internally. Since this requires the use of the ability to draw points and lines, we address these issues first. We also address the issues of the colors available in each resolution mode.

## Some Sample Commands

The commands to plot points and draw lines vary with the graphics mode used in the Apple graphics system. In low resolution, the commands are

PLOT - draw point
HLIN - draw horizontal line
VLIN - draw vertical line

In HRG, the command to draw both lines and points is HPLOT, where the *H* signals high resolution. The parameters given to PLOT will determine whether a point or a line is being drawn.

## Selecting the Graphics Mode

In order to select the graphics mode two commands are available

RG - to select LRG
HRG - to select HRG

One of these commands (but not both) would be entered before entering any graphics routine

5 GR

or

5 HGR

If we wish to reenter "normal mode" later in the program, the command

TEXT

may be given to return to "text" mode, preceded, of course, by a line number

100 TEXT

These commands are analogous to the commands available on the VT 100, e.g.

ESC (0

to enter graphics mode, and

ESC (B

to return to normal ASCII or "text" mode. The BASIC interpreter translates the commands from their current "high-level language form" (GR, HGR, TEXT) to the "machine level" commands for the device (the VDU).

## Low Resolution Graphics

As indicated above, there are three commands available for plotting points and drawing lines in LRG: HLIN, VLIN, and PLOT. HLIN draws a horizontal line (H), parallel to the X-axis. The values required are the value of the Y-coordinate for the line (e.g., Y=3 for the line shown in Figure 14.28a), and the values of the X-coordinates, at which the line begins and ends. For example, the command

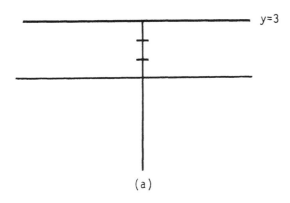

(a)

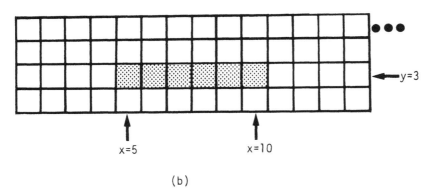

(b)

FIGURE 14.28

    HLIN 5,10 at 3

will draw a horizontal line on the third row of the screen (Y-value=3); the line will be drawn from X=5 to X=10. Thus, the line would be as shown in Figure 14.28b. The syntax of the command is

    HLIN    FROM X-VALUE, TO X-VALUE AT Y-VALUE

Thus, the command

    HLIN 18,21 at 19

draws a horizontal line from columns 18 through 21 at row 19.

    In order to use the commands effectively one must know the position of the origin, and the direction in which lines are numbered. On the Apple II in LRG mode, the screen is a 40*40 matrix. The origin is considered to be the upper left-hand corner of the screen, and is numbered 0,0 (Figure 14.29a). The X-axis goes left to right, with the points numbered 0 through 39. This is similar to conventional usage. The Y-axis, however, is numbered 0 to 39, increasing in downward direction (Figure 14.29b), which is unconventional in terms of the Cartesian coordinate plane, but useful in counting lines.

    A line that covers the screen from left to right, drawn at the bottom of the page, would be designated by the command

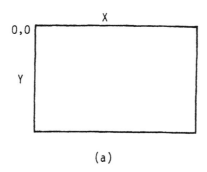

(a)

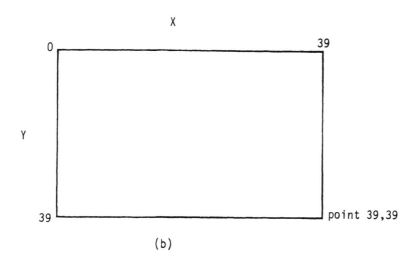

(b)

FIGURE 14.29

    HLIN    0,39 AT 39

The same line (side to side, full screen) at the top of the page would be

    HLIN    0,39 AT 0

    Vertical lines have a similar format in the command designation

    VLIN FROM Y-VALUE, TO Y-VALUE AT X-VALUE

Thus, the command

    VLIN    0,39 AT 0

would draw a vertical line the length of the screen at the left-hand side (Figure 14.30a). A similar line at the right-hand side of the screen would be drawn with the command

    VLIN    0,39 AT 39

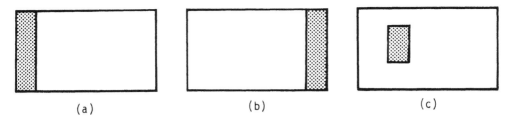

FIGURE 14.30

yielding the line shown in Figure 14.30b. A vertical line near the middle of the screen (in left-right terms) extending vertically through the middle would be obtained with the command

        VLIN     15,24 AT 15

which yields the line shown in Figure 14.30c. Note that the "at-value"

        HLIN         5,10 AT  15
        VLINE       20,30 AT  5

is equivalent to the equation of the line in algebraic terms

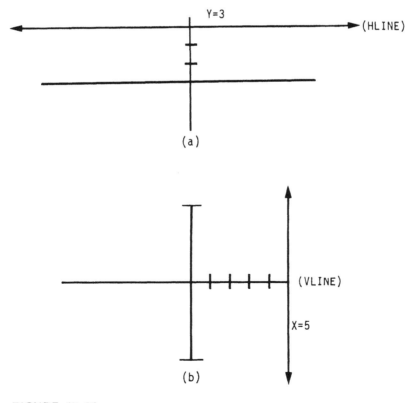

FIGURE 14.31

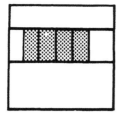

FIGURE 14.32

Y = 3   (for horizontal lines)
X = 5   (for vertical lines)

The lines are considered infinite in the Cartesian plane (Figures 14.31a and b). However, in terms of the video display terminal, the line has finite length, delineated by the FROM,TO values of the respective axis.

Note that the lines themselves are drawn on the screen by filling in the entire character position (Figure 14.32), so that the term *dot* is quite relative indeed. A theoretical point is dimensionless; however a "point" on the video screen has considerable height and breadth—the height and breadth of the addressable region (of which there are 1,600 in the 40*40 screen).

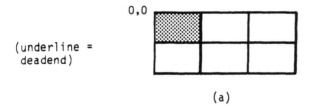

(a)

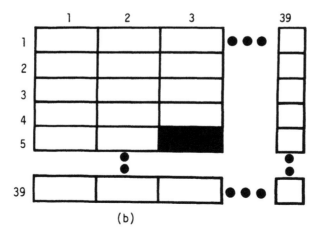

(b)

FIGURE 14.33

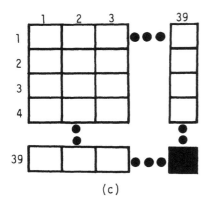

(c)

FIGURE 14.33 (continued)

## Plotting Points

The command to plot a point in LRG is PLOT. The syntax is

    PLOT X-VALUE, Y-VALUE

Thus the command

    PLOT 0,0

colors in the origin (Figure 14.33a). The command

    PLOT 3,5

colors column 3 (X-value) in row 5 (Y-value; Figure 14.33b), and

    PLOT 39,39

colors the lower right-hand corner (Figure 14.33c).

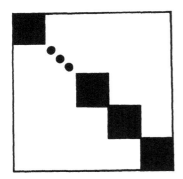

FIGURE 14.34

TABLE 14.2

| X=J | Y=39-J |
|-----|--------|
| 0 | 39 |
| 1 | 38 |
| 2 | 37 |
| · | · |
| · | · |
| · | · |
| 39 | 0 |

Diagonal Lines

Note that the Apple II graphics commands allow easy plotting of vertical or horizontal lines. Diagonal lines would have to be plotted individually by the user. For example, a line on the diagonal could be drawn by using a loop to generate values

```
FOR J = 0 TO 39
PLOT J,J
NEXT J
```

This line goes in the "downward" direction, from the upper left-hand to the lower right-hand corner (Figure 14.34), and is certainly not "straight." A line going diagonally from lower left to upper right is more complex

```
FOR J = 0 TO 39
PLOT J, 39-J
NEXT J
```

where the Y-value is the "complement" of the value of J (Table 14.2). Lines other than those at a 45° angle are yet more difficult to plot, as indicated above. The user must determine the values of X and Y from the equation of the line. For example, the line

$$Y = 2X + 1$$

yields the values given in Table 14.3. To plot these, we use the code shown in Figure 14.35. Of course the line may not be perfectly "straight"

TABLE 14.3

| X | Y |
|---|---|
| 0 | 1 |
| 1 | 3 |
| 2 | 5 |
| 3 | 7 |
| · | · |
| · | · |
| · | · |

```
 5  GR
10  LET X=0              ; initialize X
20  LET Y=2*X+1          ; get value of Y
30  PLOT X,Y             ; plot the point
40  X=X+1                ; bump X to get next point
50  IF X < 19 THEN 20    ; keep getting points until outside
                           range of screen; Y goes out of
                           range first

60  STOP
70  END
```

FIGURE 14.35

(Figure 14.36), which is a result of the restriction to draw lines in a plane consisting of discrete points rather than a continuous plane as in the algebraic conception of the plane.

Color

In LRG, the Apple II offers a "spectrum" of 16 colors (Table 14.4). These can be "turned on" by the color command

    COLOR = 3

where the number indicates the selected color (here purple). The number may be replaced by a variable. For example, the loop

    FOR J= 0 TO 15
    COLOR = J
    NEXT J

selects each color in turn. Of course, in order to see the effect of the color, we would have to plot a point, or a line. For example, the code

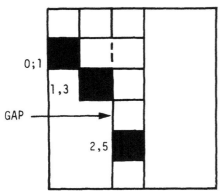

FIGURE 14.36

TABLE 14.4

| 0 | Black | 8 | Brown |
|---|-------|----|--------|
| 1 | Magenta | 9 | Orange |
| 2 | Dark blue | 10 | Gray |
| 3 | Purple | 11 | Pink |
| 4 | Dark green | 12 | Green |
| 5 | Gray | 13 | Yellow |
| 6 | Medium blue | 14 | Aqua |
| 7 | Light blue | 15 | White |

```
FOR J=0 TO 15
COLOR = J
PLOT J,J
NEXT J
```

will print a diagonal line approximately a third of the way down the screen with each "dot" a different color. Some interesting programs manipulating the color commands and the commands to draw lines are given by Culp and Nickles (1983).

## The Background Color

The normal background color of the screen is black. This can easily be changed by first selecting a color and then coloring in each point on the screen. For example, to select a pink background we have

```
GR
COLOR=11 (GET PINK)
FOR J=0,39
FOR K=0,39
PLOT J,K
NEXT K
NEXT J
```

A similar effect can be gained with simple loops and HLIN or VLINE

```
GR
COLOR=11
FOR J=0 TO 39
HLIN 0,39 AT J
NEXT J
```

or

```
GR
COLOR=11
FOR J=0 TO 39
VLIN 0,39 AT J
NEXT J
```

If you have access to an Apple II, try these commands and "see."

High-Resolution Graphics

As indicated earlier, the HRG interpreter has a single command with which to draw points and lines: HPLOT. However, HPLOT has three syntactic forms, one each for

- Drawing points: HPLOT 15,10
- Drawing a line between "any" two points: HPLOT 5,3 TO 4,9
- Drawing a line from the current line to another point: HPLOT TO 25,20

In order to plot a point anywhere in the screen (labeled 0 to 279 on the X-axis, 0 to 159 on the Y-axis, for a total of 280*160 points), we simply name the coordinates. Hence, the following would plot points at the given positions

    HPLOT 0,0 (home, upper left corner)
    HPLOT 279, 159 (lower right corner)
    HPLOT 139,79 (approximate center of screen)
    HPLOT 3,5 (column 3, row 5)

In order to draw lines, we may explicitly name both points

    HPLOT 1,3 TO 4,9

which draws a line from (1,3) to (4,9), part of the line designated by the equation

    Y = 2X + 1

Alternatively, we may draw a line from the current position of the cursor to a single other point

    HPLOT TO 4,9

which means draw a line from "here" to the point 4,9. If "here" were the point 1,3, we would obtain the same line as above. In fact, the sequence of commands

    HPLOT 1,3
    HPLOT TO 4,9

is equivalent to the single command

    HPLOT 1,3 TO 4,9


Color in High-Resolution Graphics

The range of colors available in HRG is more restricted than the "rainbow" available in LRG. There are six colors available

    0 = Black          4 = Black
    1 = Green          5 = Orange
    2 = Violet         6 = Blue
    3 = White          7 = White

where both white and black are represented by two codes each (0,4; 3,7). The bits devoted to varying intensity, hence allowing for a greater "mixing" of colors, have been devoted instead to the extra pixels on the screen. The HRG screen has 280*160 pixels as opposed to the 40*40 LRG screen

$$\frac{\overset{7}{280} * \overset{4}{160}}{40 * 40} = 28 \text{ times as many pixels}$$

The extra 43,200 bits (44,800-1600) were originally distributed among the 1600 LRG pixels

$$\frac{43200}{1600} = 27 \text{ bits per pixel}$$

These 27 bits were used to vary the intensity and color of each pixel, allowing for a greater mixture of colors. Now they are devoted to addressing extra pixels.

The trade-off for the decrease in color is the increased performance in drawing straight lines. While LRG allowed "good" straight lines in only the horizontal, vertical, and 45° positions, the HRG allows "straighter" lines in a variety of directions. The extreme in trading off color for line quality is in the use of monochrome vector devices, which use a single color (possibly at varying intensities) to draw straight lines at virtually any angle.

## Similar Commands on the IBM PC

While the commands available in the Microsoft version of BASIC available with the IBM PC/XT are "different" in the sense that they use different words, the effects of the commands are virtually the same. Because graphics commands are not standardized, and various types of systems are becoming increasingly available, the programmer of such systems must become flexible in transferring from one to the other. The task is not difficult if one concentrates on the goals

- How do I select the graphics mode?
- How do I draw points?
- How do I draw lines?
- What colors are available?

rather than on the commands themselves. In fact, it is these questions that guide us in looking through the manual rather than the manual "driving us."

## Selecting Graphics Mode

On the IBM system the selection of the graphics mode is made through the screen statement

| Screen 0 | (Text) |
|---|---|
| Screen 1 | (Medium-resolution graphics) |
| Screen 2 | (High-resolution graphics) |

This command can also be used to enable or disable color. (One might disable color if the monitor was monochrome.) We will assume that color is enabled for text and medium-resolution graphics (MRG). In HRG, the IBM system allows only black and white images (stealing bits from color and intensity to address more pixels).

Selecting Colors

We indicated how to select colors in text mode with the color command (e.g., color 14,1,0 yields yellow foreground, blue background, black border). In MRG the color command is used but its interpretation is different. The format of the command is

Color        Background,        Palette

Background may be any of the 16 colors listed earlier, and the codes are the same. Hence, "color 1" would yield a blue background. The argument "palette" is interpreted as selecting from one of two predefined palettes of color

| Number of Color | Palette 0 | Palette 1 |
|---|---|---|
| 1 | Green | Cyan |
| 2 | Red | Magenta |
| 3 | Brown | White |

We can work with only one palette at a time, hence four colors at a time. In commands that reference the colors, we will refer to a specific color by its color number, e.g., number 2 for red in the palette 0, number 1 for cyan in palette 1. The palette must be selected prior to referencing the colors. The default is palette 0. When referred to by a palette number (1,2,3), the foreground color (color in which messages are written and figures drawn) will be the corresponding color of the palette that has been selected. The background color is whatever color has been selected. The system will keep track of what color (0-15) this was.

Drawing Points

Points can be drawn in the Microsoft BASIC by the command PSET, which has two forms, one indicating the X,Y coordinates only, the other indicating both the coordinates and the color of the point. The first form is

PSET (X,Y)

where the values for X,Y can be constants or variables, respectively. In medium resolution (320 by 200) the command PSET (319, 199) will light a pixel in the lower right-hand corner of the screen. (The Y-coordinates are numbered 0 through 199, X are numbered 0 through 319). If no color is specified, the color of the point will be color 3 of the palette in current use. Thus, if palette 0 is being used, the default will be brown. The color of the point can be set to some other value by including it explicitly as a second argument

PSET (319, 199), 2

which gives the color red for palette 0, magenta for palette 1.

```
 5  SCREEN 1
10  COLOR 1,0  background blue, palette 0
15  FOR Y = 0 TO 199
20  X = Y
30  PSET (X,Y),2
40  NEXT
```

FIGURE 14.37

A point can be erased by rewriting it with the background color. This is indicated in the argument by the numeric value zero rather than the actual color code chosen for the background. With our background of blue, the statement

PSET (319,199),0        "use background color

should write over the pixel with blue, effectively erasing it. (The single quote begins a comment.) The program shown in Figure 14.37 will draw a red slanted line across the blue screen. The diagonal will not be "corner to corner" across the screen, since not all 320 X-values will be used. In medium resolution, there are 320 horizontal pixels, and 200 vertical, a ratio of 8 to 5. We cannot light a horizontal pixel in each column while lighting a vertical pixel in each row because there are more columns than rows. We would have to light eight horizontal pixels for each group of five vertical to fill the screen. In order to create a true diagonal, we must "spread the X-pixels out," i.e., we will light all 200 Y-pixels (all 200 rows) but only 200 of the 320 columns. This can be done in several ways. The code segment

```
FOR Y = 0 TO 199
X = INT (1.6*Y)
PSET (X,Y)
NEXT Y
```

accomplishes the feat by multiplying each Y-value by 1.6 (8/5), then "truncating" this value by using the function INT. The values produced are those shown in Table 14.5. An alternative would be to "round" rather

TABLE 14.5

| Y | 1.6*Y | X |
|---|-------|---|
| 0 | 0 | 0 |
| 1 | 1.6 | 1 |
| 2 | 3.2 | 3 |
| 3 | 4.8 | 4 |
| 4 | 6.4 | 6 |
| 5 | 8.0 | 8 |
| . | . | . |
| . | . | . |
| . | . | . |

TABLE 14.6

| Y | 1.6 * Y + 5 | X |
|---|---|---|
| 0 | .5 | 0 |
| 1 | 2.1 | 2 |
| 2 | 3.7 | 3 |
| 3 | 5.3 | 5 |
| 4 | 6.9 | 6 |
| 5 | 8.5 | 8 |
| . | . | . |
| . | . | . |
| . | . | . |

than "truncate." This can be accomplished by adding .5 to the expression 1.6*Y before using INT

$$X = INT(1.6 * Y + .5)$$

which gives the values shown in Table 14.6. Fractional values originally less than .5 (e.g., 3.2), remain in the "3 range" after adding; fractional values of .5 or larger "rise to the next integer" (e.g., 1.6 + .5 yields 2.1, which truncates to 2). We will have more to say about the need to adjust values when drawing figures.

In HRG, with 640 pixels in the horizontal direction and 200 in the vertical, the multiplication factor would be 3.2 (640/200). For the truncation of values, this gives the values in Table 14.7.

The reader should create the program for a diagonal across the HRG screen. If color has been used in MRG, the programs will have to be modified. In HRG there are only two colors: black, background; white, foreground. With a black background, points should be set in white

PSET (639,199),1

which is the default. They can be erased with

PSET (639,199),0

or with the PRESET command.

TABLE 14.7

| Y | 3.2*Y | X |
|---|---|---|
| 0 | 0 | 0 |
| 1 | 3.2 | 3 |
| 2 | 6.4 | 6 |
| 3 | 9.6 | 9 |
| . | . | . |
| . | . | . |
| . | . | . |

## Preset: Erasing

As indicated above, a point (or line) can be erased by rewriting it with the background color. This version of BASIC gives a special command to accomplish this

    PRESET (X,Y)

which stands for "point reset" or "reset point." When PRESET is used, the background color is used to draw the point, so that the point (or line or figure if the command is used in some routine, such as a loop) is erased.

The terms *set* and *reset* are routinely used in computer jargon for "create" and "uncreate." Thus, setting a bit makes it a "1"; resetting it makes its value "0."

## Relative Addressing

The commands PSET(0,0) or PRESET(319,199) use absolute addressing. Points may be set or reset in relative form as well, the increment of the X- and Y-values being indicated by the keyword *step*, e.g.

    PSET STEP (+5,+5)

which would create a point 5 to the right (X-increment) and 5 above (Y-increment) the current value. The signs and magnitudes of X and Y can be manipulated independently, with their usual meanings. The command

    PSET STEP (+2,-3)

will draw a point 2 pixels to the right, 3 below the current position.

## Preset Versus Clear

One could use CLS (clear screen) to erase, but this erases the entire screen. With PRESET (or PSET using the background color) we can selectively erase parts of a drawing, while retaining other parts.

The program

```
PSET (160,0)      TOP MIDDLE
FOR J=1 TO 199
PSET STEP (0,+1)
NEXT J
```

draws a vertical line down the middle of the screen. Following this with the code

```
Y=99
PRESET (160,Y)      MIDDLE MIDDLE, I.E., CENTER OF SCREEN
FOR J=1 TO 100
PRESET (160,Y+J)
PRESET (160,Y-J)
NEXT J
```

erases it from the middle out. The reader should write a program to draw a single vertical line from top to bottom at the middle of the screen, then a single horizontal line across the middle, so that the lines intersect at the

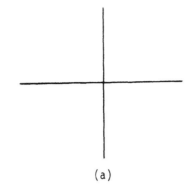

(a)

(b)

FIGURE 14.38

center of the screen (Figure 14.38a). Then use PRESET to erase the vertical line above, and there will be a "hole" in the horizontal line at the point of intersection (Figure 14.38b). This is because we erased the "intersection dot" when erasing the vertical line. Finding intersection points so that they can be handled by redrawing the single dot (e.g., PSET 160,99) is one of the classic problems of writing graphics programs that allow the user to modify the picture.

## Drawing Lines

Lines may be drawn by creating our own loops, as above, or by using a special command (LINE). There are many formats of the line command. We examine a few. One of the simplest forms is

    LINE (10,20)

which says draw a line from wherever "we are," i.e., from the last point drawn, to the point 10,20. Hence, the diagonal line from (0,0) to 199, 199) could be drawn as

    PSET (0,0)
    LINE (199,199)

and the line from (0,0) to (319,199) can be drawn as

    PSET (0,0)
    LINE (319, 199)

letting the BASIC graphics package worry about which pixels to turn on and off (Should we truncate? Round? Use some other algorithm?).

Another format names both "end points"

LINE (0,0)-(319,199)

which again prints the diagonal, but eliminates the need for the separate PSET command.

Color may be designated in the line command in the same manner as PSET, as another argument

PSET (0,0),2
LINE - (319,199),2

or

LINE (0,0)-(319,199),2

Keeping in mind the different uses of color in MRG and HRG, relative addressing can be used to specify the second end point of the line, relative to the first

LINE (10,20) - STEP (+50,+150)

which draws a line from (10,20) "absolute" to (10+50,20+150) or (60,170). Because the second point needs a reference point, the first end point is specified in absolute terms.


Drawing Figures

One of the common purposes of drawing points and lines is to create figures: squares, rectangles, circles. The simplest of these are the regular polygons, such as squares and rectangles. However, even in so simple a figure as a square, problems can arise. The code given in Figure 14.39 would obstensibly draw a square. The square is 100 pixels on a side

```
10   TOP = 50
20   BOTTOM = 149
30   LEFT = 100
40   RIGHT = 199
50   XPTR = 0
60   YPTR = 0
70   FOR N=1 TO 100
80   PSET (RIGHT + XPTR,TOP)
90   PSET (RIGHT + XPTR,BOTTOM)
100  PSET (LEFT,TOP + YPTR)
110  PSET (RIGHT,TOP + YPTR)
120  XPTR = XPTR + 1
130  YPTR = YPTR + 1
140  NEXT N
```

FIGURE 14.39

```
     BOTTOM - TOP +1
   = 149 - 50 + 1
   = 100
```

where the need for adding 1 to the result of subtracting the value of top from bottom can be seen in counting the numbers from 4 through 6

6 - 4 + 1 = 3, namely 4, 5, and 6

The value of bottom - top + 1 gives the height of the polygon. The value of right - left + 1 gives its width; with the numbers given 'this is also 100

199 − 100 + 1 = 100

so that the figure being described is indeed a square. A simpler, yet more powerful program would prompt for a single point, say the top left-hand corner and the length of one side, then compute the other points. However, that is not the point here.

If the program is run in MRG (by preceding the code with the command screen 1), the square "appears" square (it is not exactly square). However, if it is run in HRG (screen 2), it will appear roughly as shown in Figure 14.40—a rectangle in which the height is the longer dimension. This is due to the distribution of pixels.

The statements of the loop

```
80      PSET (LEFT + XPTR,TOP)
90      PSET (LEFT + XPTR,BOTTOM)
100     PSET (LEFT,TOP + YPTR)
110     PSET (RIGHT,TOP + YPTR)
```

step across the screen in the horizontal and vertical directions. Lines 80 and 90 step horizontally, keeping the value of Y constant (at top or bottom, respectively), starting at the left border and incrementing the value of XPTR by one each time through the loop. Statements 100 and 110 increment Y, starting at the top and working down the left and right borders, keeping these border values as a static X-value.

The result is that 100 pixels are lit horizontally, 100 vertically, But this will cover less of a distance horizontally, since there are 16 pixels in a unit distance horizontally, and only 5 per unit vertically (Figure 14.41a). To get 16 pixels vertically, we have to traverse 3 1/5 vertical units (Figure 14.41b). One solution would be to light more pixels horizontally (3.2 times as many); the other is to space the 100 pixels more widely, using a multi-

FIGURE 14.40

. . . . . . . . . . . . .
.                       .
.                       .
.                       .
. . . . . . . . . . . . .

(a)

(b)

FIGURE 14.41

plication factor of 3.2 as in the creation of the diagonal lines. The code to space the pixels would be that shown in Figure 14.42. If this program is run in HRG on most conventional screens, the square will be too wide! It will appear similar to that shown in Figure 14.43a, although not quite as pronounced. This is because of the "aspect ratio" of the screen. Most conventional monitors are wider than they are tall (Figure 14.43b).

The ratio of the width to the height is called the "aspect factor" of the screen. Here the aspect factor has the value 4/3, which is common for TV monitors.

With a screen that is wider than it is high, either more pixels are required in the X-direction, or the pixels must be more spread out. The

```
N = 100
YTOP = 50
YBOTTOM = 149
XLEFT = 100
XRIGHT = 199
YNEXT = 1
XNEXT = INT(3.2*YNEXT)
PSET (YTOP,XLEFT)
FOR J=1 TO N-1
PSET (XNEXT,YTOP)
PSET (XNEXT,YBOTTOM)
PSET (XLEFT,YNEXT)
PSET (XRIGHT,YNEXT)
YNEXT = YNEXT + 1
XNEXT = INT(YNEXT * 3.2)
NEXT J
```

FIGURE 14.42

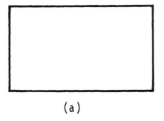

(a)

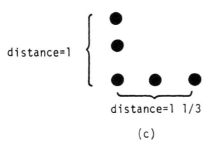

3 units

4 units

(b)

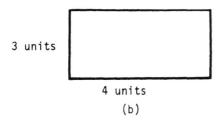

distance=1

distance=1 1/3

(c)

FIGURE 14.43

latter is the case on most conventional screens. If we had the same number of pixels in each direction, they would extend over a longer distance in the X-direction (Figure 14.43c). The screen aspect ratio of 4/3 would require more pixels to be lit in the Y-direction to achieve a square effect, namely "light 3 X's for every 4 Y's."

Unfortunately, there are not an even number of pixels in each direction. Hence, the calculation is not quite as straightforward. The screen aspect ratio (screen wider than it is tall) must be considered in conjunction with the unequal resolution ratio (more pixels in the horizontal direction than in the vertical direction); i.e., the aspect ratio of 4 to 3 (ratio of horizontal to vertical distance between pixels) must be combined with the distribution of pixels in the 8-to-5 ratio per "unit distance." The actual calculation is

Inverse of aspect ratio * resolution ratio

or

$$\frac{3}{4} * \frac{8}{5} = \frac{24}{20} \text{ or } \frac{6}{5}$$

for MRG and

$$\frac{3}{4} * \frac{16}{5} = \frac{48}{20} = \frac{12}{5}$$

for HRG. This indicates that one must light 6 horizontal pixels for every 5 vertical pixels to achieve the appropriate "balance" in the visual effect in MRG, 12 to 5 in HRG. These values are called the scale factors, and are the values by which the X-pixels should be "spread out," either 6 to 5 or 12 to 5, respectively.

The calculation deserves a bit of explanation. The aspect ratio gives the distance between pixels. The horizontal pixels are further apart. Hence, to achieve a given distance, one needs to light fewer horizontal pixels. However, the resolution factor indicates the "density" of pixels. Since the pixels are more dense in the horizontal direction one needs to light more horizontal pixels in a given distance than vertical pixels. If the screen were square, the resolution

$$\frac{8}{5}$$

would give the number of horizontal to vertical pixels that must be lit. However, because the aspect ratio (4/3) indicates "fewer horizontal" to be lit, we adjust the ratio 8/5 by this reduction factor (3/4 or the inverse of the aspect ratio)

$$\frac{3}{4} * \frac{8}{5} = \frac{24}{20} = \frac{6}{5}$$

to obtain the ratio of horizontal to vertical pixels to be lit to achieve balance. The results, scale factors of 6 to 5 in MRG and 12 to 5 in HRG are those given for the IBM system used in this chapter's examples.

Rewriting the second program to compute the square with the calculations

        XNEXT = INT(YNEXT * 1.2)

or

        XNEXT = INT(YNEXT * 2.4)

reflects the scale factors of 6 to 5 and 12 to 5, and should produce a "true square."


## Line B and Line BF

Drawing rectangles and squares is facilitated by a special form of the LINE command, either

        LINE (0,0) − (50,50),1,B

or

        LINE (0,0) − (50,50),1,BF

where the first point is the upper left-hand corner, the second the lower right-hand corner; the number 1 is the color selection; and the B or BF stands for "box" and "box filled." If "box" is chosen, a rectangle is created, with only the border "filled in"; i.e., the box is empty. With "BF," the box is filled in (either all white, in HRG, or with the chosen color in MRG). While the statement

    LINE (0,0) - (50,50),1,B

may look like the box should be a square, the discussion of pixel distribution and aspect ratio indicates that the command to achieve a square should be

    LINE (0,0) - (60,50),1,B

in MRG, and

    LINE (0,0) - (120,50),1,B

in HRG.

## Draw: Picture Subroutines

A special command

    DRAW A$

exists, in which the value of the string A$ determines the picture to be drawn. For example, the string

    "U  80  R  96  D  80  L  96"

will draw a square (the ratio 96 to 80 is 6 to 5) from a given point. The commands U, D, R, and L indicate up, down, right, and left. Diagonals use the letters *E* through *H*

    E = right, up
    F = right, down
    G = left, up
    H = left, down

To draw an isosceles triangle, we can use geometry (Figure 14.44), and the Pythagorean theorem

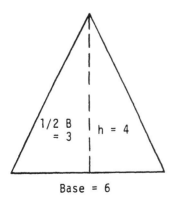

Base = 6

FIGURE 14.44

$$c^2 = a^2 + b^2$$

$$c = \sqrt{a^2 + b^2}$$

to obtain the diagonal distance in "abstract" terms (i.e., not considering distribution of pixels and the aspect ratio). For a total base of 6 (half base = 3) and height of 4, this results in a diagonal of 5 units

$$c = \sqrt{3^2 + 4^2}$$

$$= \sqrt{9 + 16}$$

$$= \sqrt{25}$$

$$c = 5$$

without considering the distribution of pixels and the aspect ratio, the string

"E   5   F   5   L   6"

would produce a triangle. If the square box is described with a length of 6 and a slightly different order of drawing operations

"R   6   D   5   L   6   U   5"

so that the last pixel lit is on the upper left, and the strings assigned as

A$ = "E   5   F   5   L   6"
R$ = "R   6   D   5   L   6   U   5"

the concatenation of the strings in the draw command

DRAW A$ + B$

(a)

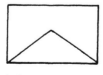

(b)

FIGURE 14.45

should produce a primitive house (Figure 14.45a). The reversal of the string references in draw

    DRAW B$ + A$

will place the roof in the living room (Figure 14.45b).

In considering the aspect ratio and pixel distribution, the commands for triangles of certain sizes and shapes may not always agree with the Pythagorean theorem. This version of BASIC allows the user to specify scale factors calculated as shown above.

The complexity of drawing realistic pictures within the constraints of the technology illustrate why graphics packages are used rather than original programs for most applications. The creators of the package assume the burden of matching geometry to technology. The task is compounded with the provision of animation, 3-D, hidden lines, rotating figures, perspective of the observer, portions of the picture that "go off" the screen (are "clipped"), and so on.


Circles, Ellipses, and Arcs

The creation of such linear figures as rectangles and squares is more easily approximated in the rectangular grid of most graphics technology. However, circles can be created by approximating them with short, straight lines or with many dots correctly positioned. Fortunately, even at the level of graphics available with personal computers, commands exist that aid the process. The command

    CIRCLE (120,50),10,1

causes the following:

- Center of circle at 120,50 (used in calculations, not drawn)
- Radius will be 10
- Color 1 of applicable palette (or white in HRG) will be used to draw border

Ellipses can be drawn by giving other parameters. To draw arcs, a starting point and an end point can be given, and the aspect ratio can be given to alter the manner in which the circle or ellipse is drawn.


Paint

Given a box, circle, or other figure, the inside can be "painted" by specifying a point within the figure and a specification of "how far" to paint. The indication of how far to paint is given in the language by specifying some color (usually that of the border) at which to stop. The color "to paint with" must also be specified. To paint the circle drawn above, one could use the command

    PAINT (120,50),2,1

where the point (120,50) is certainly inside the circle, being the center. The paint "applied" will be number 2 of the palette chosen, and painting will stop at color 1, which was used, above, to create the border.

```
SCREEN 1
COLOR 1,0
LINE (0,0) — (0,199),2
FOR J=1 TO 319
LINE (J-1,0) — (J-1,199),1
LINE (J,0) — (J,199),2
NEXT J
```

FIGURE 14.46


## Animation

Animation can be accomplished by drawing a figure, erasing it, then redrawing it at another location. For example, the program given in Figure
14.46 will cause a vertical line to sweep across the screen.

    In a generalized animation program—one that will "move" any figure—it
is a good idea to save the initial description of the figure (pixels lit and
unlit) from the screen itself, then use this description to produce the
"erasure" and the "movement." This version of BASIC provides two commands to do so: GET and PUT. GET saves the pixel "bit values" in an
array (the programmer must provide the array with a dimension statement).
PUT will take data out of the array, "putting" it on the screen. If PUT
puts the data "in the same place" (redraws the figure in exactly the same
place), but with the background color, or with a special command XOR,
the figure is erased. If it is "put" in a new place, it is drawn again;
hence, the sequence to cause animation is as shown in Figure 14.47.

    The syntax of GET is

    GET (X1,Y1) — (X2,Y2),ARRAYNAME

where (X1,Y1) and (X2,Y2) are the opposite corners of a quadrangle, as
explained earlier, and array name is the place where the bits describing
the pixels are stored. To store the square created by

    LINE (0,0) — (60,50),1,B

we could say

    GET (0,0) — (60,50),ARRAYNAME

The size of the array must be calculated from the size of this rectangle.
The calculation is


               —Draw the figure initially
               —Get "figure"
               —Save initial location, say in old J
Begin loop    —Put figure in initial location, i.e.,
                  old J, using XOR (causes erasure)
               —Calculate new address, say new J
               —Put figure in new J
               —Assign value of new J to old J
               —Repeat loop as long as desirable

FIGURE 14.47

4 + INT((X * bits per pixel) + 7)/8) * Y

with the result in bytes, not words. The formula requires a bit of explanation.

The initial 4 represents 4 bytes that are used to store the values of the X-dimension and the Y-dimension (2 bytes each). The remainder of the formula stores the data. We are particularly interested in this part of the formula.

The value of bits per pixel in medium resolution is 2, which is why there is a four-color palette: 2-squared = 4. In HRG the value is 1, which is why HRG has only two colors, black or white. The intensity of the pixels is "static," preset at one given level.

Since there are 640*200 pixels in HRG, the memory size of the bit map is exactly 128,000 bits, which translates into 16,000 bytes or 8,000 words of 16 bits (2 bytes) each, a good deal of space. The same space is used in MRG but the use of 2 bits per pixel means that the 128,000 bits can be assigned to only 64,000 distinct pixels. Dividing this value by the 200 vertical pixels (the value is the same in both resolution nodes), we have 320 vertical pixels! The mystery of screen sizes is calculable.

The value of +7 is used to "catch" leftover pixels. The pixels in a row are described by continuous bytes. These must be allocated in 8-bit chunks, hence, 10 X-pixels must be described in 2 bytes (Figure 14.48), with 6 bits of the second byte "wasted." When 7 is added to the number of pixels it "rounds" to the next higher byte when the entire expression is divided by 8 and the integer (INT) of the result is taken. For example, 1 X-pixel in HRG gives

$$\frac{(1 * 1 + 7)}{8} = \frac{2 + 7}{8} = \frac{9}{8} = 1.125 = 1$$

Eight X-pixels give

$$\frac{8 * 1 + 7}{8} = \frac{9 + 7}{8} = \frac{16}{8} = 2$$

and so on.

One row of bytes is stored for each Y-value, the row size being the same for each Y-value. Hence, once we have the size of the row storage area, we merely multiply by the number of Y-pixels.

For our square

LINE (1,1) - (60,50)

the number of X-pixels is 60, the number of Y-pixels is 50. The total storage area needed in HRG is

INT ((60 * 1 + 7)/8) * 50
= INT (67/8) * 50
= 8 * 50 = 400 bytes

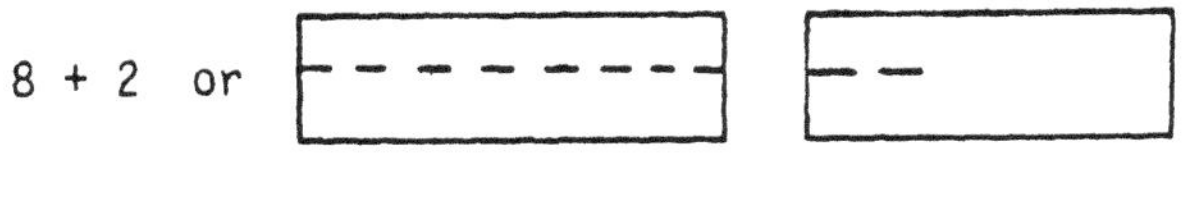

8 + 2 or

FIGURE 14.48

In MRG, this would be doubled. The 400 bytes translated into 200 words on a 16-bit word size machine, so that the array would be dimensioned as

    DIM    SAVE(200)

The BASIC interpreter will take care of translating this linear representation into rows and vertical positions and vice versa.


## PUT

The format of PUT is similar to that of GET. In its simplest form this is

    PUT (X,Y),ARRAYNAME

where the values of X,Y tell BASIC where to put the top left-hand corner of the figure to be drawn. The array will supply the data on the figure itself. Hence, the program given in Figure 14.49a will cause the square to move vertically down the screen. The FOR loop can be adjusted to have "steps" (Figure 14.49b) to make the move go faster.


## Summary

While we have shown the commands of an actual programming language, the purpose of this chapter was not to teach programming, but to give an idea of the operations, calculations, and storage manipulation involved in creating graphics effects on a computer. The application of the Microsoft BASIC was bit map graphics, although many of the commands, such as PSET and LINE, are similar to the commands used in a vector graphics system. However, the quality of lines in the vector graphics system might be better, though the technology is changing rapidly.


```
DIMENSION SAVE AREA, (200)
GET (1,1) - (60,50),SAVEAREA
FOR J=2 TO 149
PUT (1,J-1), XOR
PUT (1,J)
NEXT J
```

(a)


```
FOR J=4 TO 149 STEP 5
PUT (1,J-5),XOR  ·ERASE
PUT (1,J)        ·DRAW
NEXT J
```

(b)

FIGURE 14.49

The primary consideration to keep in mind is that after all the technical expertise is gained we still have to attack the area of actual design: form and placement of figures, choice and interaction of colors, sizes of figures, characters in messages, etc. This is an area that is in the infancy or pre-birth stage, hence one of oppotunity to the adventurous.

## Related Readings

Barnett, Michael P. and Barnett, Graham K., *Personal Graphics for Profit and Pleasure on the Apple II Plus Computer*, Boston: Little, Brown and Company, 1983.

Culp, George H. and Nickles, Herbert, *An Apple for the Teacher: Fundamentals of Instructional Computing*, Monterey, CA: Brooks/Cole Publishing Company, 1983.

Demel, John T. and Miller, Michael J., *Introduction to Computer Graphics*, Monterey, CA: Brooks/Cole Engineering Division, 1984.

Foley, James D. and Van Dam, Andries, *Fundamentals of Interactive Computer Graphics*, Reading, MA: Addison-Wesley, 1982.

Hampshire, Nick, *VIC Graphics*, Rochelle Park, NJ: Hayden Book Company, 1982.

Harrington, Steven, *Computer Graphics: A Programming Approach*, New York: McGraw-Hill, 1983.

IBM, ASIC by Microsoft, (Personal Computer Hardware Reference Library), 2nd ed. Boca Raton, FL: International Business Machine Corporation, 1981.

Mutti, Aftat A., *Elementary Computer Graphics*, Reston, VA: Reston Publishing Company, 1983.

Newman, William, M. and Sproull, Robert F., *Principles of Interactive Computer Graphics*, 2nd ed. New York: McGraw-Hill, 1979.

Sikonowitz, Waiter, *Guide to the IBM Personal Computer*, New York: Micro Text/McGraw-Hill Copublication, 1983.

Tydeman, John, et al., *Teletext and Videotext in the United States: Market Potential Technology Public Policy Issues*, New York: McGraw-Hill, 1982.

Wadsworth, Nat, *Introduction to Computer Animation*, Rochelle Park, NJ: Hayden Book Company, 1979.

Wadsworth, Nat, *Graphics Cookbook for the Apple*, Rochelle Park, NJ: Hayden Book Company, 1980.

# VIII
# The Communication of Data

The use of the term *communication of data* is a bit of a misnomer, but is used in uniformity with other sections in the text. The communication discussed embraces not only data but also the communication of commands, queries, and error messages. The focus is on human-to-machine dialogue rather than human-to-human dialogue, although human/computer dialogue must, at least in some respects, follow the same principles as human-to-human dialogue. Chapter 15 examines the distinction between systems that are oriented toward dedicated or expert users (command languages) and those oriented toward infrequent or casual users and beginners (menu systems). The initial discussion assumes a traditional alphanumeric keyboard with a paper output or video display (CRT). Then alternate technologies for input and output are discussed (e.g., the use of mice or joysticks or touch on input or voice on output). A discussion of machine capabilities for recognizing patterns follows from consideration of alternative means of input (e.g., optical character recognition or voice input).

Chapter 16 examines the communication model: messages, senders of messages, receivers of messages, and the protocols of conversation. The levels of communication are also presented: physical transmission, the transmission of meaning, and the "pragmatic level" of action taken on the message. These levels are discussed primarily in relation to human/computer conversation, with parallels drawn between such human/machine conversation and human/human conversation, but the emphasis is on the former. In regard to the level of meaning (semantic level), the roles of a lexicon (dictionary of words) and syntactical rules (structure of the language) are discussed in a relatively informal way. More formal study of grammars for artificial languages, as well as the study of natural language input and output, is deferred to a second (or later) course.

# 15
# Human/Computer Dialogue

**Objectives**

Upon completion of this chapter the reader should be able to:

1. Distinguish between computer-initiated dialogue and human-initiated dialogue, as instantiated in menu selection and command mode dialogue forms
2. Explain the concepts of echoing the input, performing limit and reasonableness checks, and bullet-proofing, showing the need for each
3. Distinguish between end user manipulation of the system and the use of an intermediary
4. Explain the trade-off between time to train personnel and expected length of employment
5. Explain the use of function keys, as well as the use of special technology for input, e.g., light pens or bar code readers
6. Explain the effect of light pen input on time to input data and number of data keying errors
7. Indicate how techniques of pattern recognition can be used to recognize input optically
8. Explain how techniques similar to those used in some aspects of artificial intelligence can be used to take an "educated guess" about the user's intentions

The communication of data to the user in a display is a type of communication; it is "one-way" in that the display is the final step in outputting the answers to our questions. However, the display is usually produced in response to a command from the user of the system. For example, in searching the wine data base, the user could issue a command, such as

FIND ALL COLOR RED AND PRICE HIGH

The output to the command would be

| 001 | Red | Burgundy | ABC | H |
| 004 | Red | Burgundy | XYZ | H |

The set of statements (the command and the reply) is often called a "dialogue pair," which indicates that we are having a conversation with the computer. In this section, we examine some of the characteristics of human/ computer dialogue. The dialogue we will consider will involve

- Input to a computer program
- Output from a computer program
- Dialogue used in normal processing
- Dialogue used when errors occur

In regard to the input to the computer, the user may be involved in giving commands or in entering text or data. The output will also normally consist of either data or instructions to the user.

## Menu Selection Versus Command Mode

One of the most basic distinctions in the consideration of human/computer dialogue is the mode in which the user presents commands to the computer (really to the computer program, a distinction we will not always make explicit). One of the most basic distinctions in the manner of giving commands is the distinction between "command mode" and "menu selection." Command mode is usually used by "experienced" users, menu selection by "casual" users. Because menu selection is the simpler of the two modes, we will discuss it first.

## Menu Selection

Menu selection is a form of "computer-initiated" dialogue. A typical example is the way one interacts with a 24-hr banking machine. When the machine is turned on (by a customer inserting a banking card and typing his or her password), the system begins the dialogue. For example, the system might type

DO YOU WISH TO:
1. WITHDRAW
2. DEPOSIT
3. CHECK YOUR BALANCE

This is the list of top-level commands. The purpose of the list is to relieve the user of the need to memorize the commands.

Assuming that we wish to withdraw some money, we would enter the number *1* (by typing it on the keyboard). The system might then respond with another "second level" menu

FROM WHICH ACCOUNT?
1. SAVINGS
2. CHECKING
3. VISA

Assuming we wish to withdraw from our checking account, we would type in a *2*.

The system might then "guide" us to enter the proper amount

ENTER A MULTIPLE OF 5.00

at which point we might type

    50.00

The system would then count out our money (after checking our balance to
see if sufficient funds were available) and give it to us (through some
mechanical system of dispensing the proper bills). It might then say

    TRANSACTION OVER
    THANK YOU

and "log us off the system." The name *menu selection* comes from the fact
that the computer gives us a menu of items

    1.  WITHDRAW
    2.  DEPOSIT
    3.  CHECK BALANCE

from which to select the command we wish executed. The benefit of the menu
selection is that we do not have to remember the commands. It is for this
reason that we say menu selection is suited to casual users. The user is
not expected to be so familiar with the system as to have the commands
memorized. Menu selection systems normally take a longer period of time to
complete a transaction than "more direct" systems would. For example, if
we typed in the single command

    WITHDRAW CHECKING     50.00

we could accomplish in a single line what the menu-driven system accomplished with two menus and a "guiding" message (ENTER A MULTIPLE OF
5.00). In the menu system, there were three "dialogue pairs" (Figure
15.1a). In the command system, there was the single command (Figure
15.1b) followed by the system's production of the dollar bills. If one uses
the system frequently, as might a teller in a bank, the use of menu selection as the form of dialogue can be both time-consuming and annoying. It is

SYSTEM:   MENU 1 (TOP LEVEL MENU)

USER:     SELECTION (E.G., NUMBER 1)

SYSTEM:   SECOND LEVEL MENU

USER:     SELECTION (E.G., NUMBER 2)

SYSTEM:   ENTER MULTIPLE OF 5.00

USER:     50.00

SYSTEM:   PRODUCE MONEY (final response)

(a)

WITHDRAW CHECKING 50.00

(b)

FIGURE 15.1

for this reason that "experienced" and "dedicated" users employ command systems.

## Command Mode

Command mode is "human-initiated" dialogue, as opposed to the computer-initiated dialogue of menu-driven systems. Once "logged on" or "on the system," the user initiates all action by entering commands. A good example is the use of an editor, such as UPDATE (on Digital Equipment's DEC-10) or ed (one of the editors used in UNIX). There are a relative handful of commands necessary to input text and edit it. If a user makes use of the system on any frequent basis, it is relatively easy to remember these commands, hence, most editors are "command driven." Another example is the use of a programming language, such as BASIC, or an operating system. It had been the case that operating systems (or monitors) were command driven, although recent systems designed for the users of microcomputers are often menu driven.

## Another Example

An example of command mode that might be more familiar to the "noncomputer specialist" is the case of a bank teller or an airline reservationist. Both tellers and reservationists are "dedicated users." They use the system day in and day out, many times a day. If they enter commands in menu selection mode, a typical transaction (one reservation or one deposit to or withdrawal from the bank) would take several dialogue pairs. For example, we might have the transaction shown in Figure 15.2. As the reader can see, this would result in a transaction time of 5 to 10 min per customer. The last person in a line of six would wait approximately half an hour (if transaction time is 5 min) or an hour (if transaction time is 10 min). If the interarrival time of customers (time between customers) is less than our service time (say customers arrive every 4 min, but it takes us 5 min to serve them), queueing theory indicates that the line will be infinite. Good business practice indicates that we will soon be bankrupt.

Martin (1972, 1973) describes a command mode method for an airline reservation system.* The reservation agent types commands such as

    A 12MAR ORDNYC 500P

where the symbols have the meaning indicated in Figure 15.3a. The system responds with the available flights that most closely match the request (Figure 15.3b). The first line

    12 MAR    F 52.30    S 48.00    Y 43.70

echoes the departure date (12 MAR) and also gives the fares for first class (F; $52.30), second class (S; $48.00), and tourist (Y; $43.70). The system anticipates our needs (i.e., questions we will likely want answered, and answers them without our explicitly asking). The information on the flights

---

*The author has used Martin's figures: his texts were some of the first in the field, and are valuable resources.

```
DO YOU WISH TO:
    1.  MAKE A RESERVATION
    2.  CANCEL A RESERVATION
    >   1

ENTER DESTINATION
    >   LOS ANGELES

ENTER CITY OF DEPARTURE:
    >   PITTSBURGH

ENTER DATE OF DEPARTURE FROM PITTSBURGH:
    MONTH:
    >   APRIL
    DATE:
    >   24
    YEAR:
    >   1983

ENTER DATE OF RETURN FROM LOS ANGELES:
    MONTH:
    >   APRIL
    DATE:
    >   30
    YEAR:
    >   1983
AVAILABLE FLIGHTS ON DATE OF DEPARTURE FROM
PITTSBURGH ARE:

    1.   9 A.M., ARRIVE LA 12 NOON
    2.  11 A.M., ARRIVE LA 2:30 P.M.
    3.   3 P.M., ARRIVE LA 6:00 P.M.

CHOOSE ONE

etc.
```

**FIGURE 15.2**

is also coded. For example, in line 1 of the flights, we have the interpretations shown in Figure 15.4. Note that the list of coded items is extensive and that nonobvious meanings, such as "number of intermediate stops," are not indicated in headings over the columns. The lack of headings is an attempt to speed up the transaction. However, it does require a certain amount of training for the user of the system (the ticket agent).

While we have spent several lines explaining this dialogue pair, the actual time taken to execute it would have been less than a second. Having seen the available flights, the agent would now interact with the customer, telling him or her what was available, and obtain his or her selection. Assuming the customer wishes the 6 PM departure, since it is nonstop and has two first-class seats (flight 2 at 5 PM, also nonstop, has only one first-class seat), the agent would type

N 2 F 3

where the codes are

A — availability request, that is, "please show the available flights that fulfill the following request"

12 MAR — date of departure, 12 of March (the year is assumed to be the current year for months after "this month", since people seldom make reservations a year ahead of time and *almost never* a year late. Months "before this month" are next year. Hence, if it is now July, August is this year, June is next year.)

ORD NYC — is a "city pair" where each code is fixed length (three characters). In this example, ORD is the abbreviation for O'Hare Airport in Chicago (city of departure) and NYC is New York City (destination).
Note that the order in which the agent enters the city names makes quite a difference.

500 — is the time of day in hours

P — indicates P.M. (A would indicate A.M., indicating that the position of the code letter A alters its meaning:

A in first position is a command (show the available flights)

A in hour field is A.M. (a data value rather than a command)

(a)

```
12 MAR  F52.30  S 48.00  Y43.70
1.  264  S7    ORDJFK  420P  800P  727  D  1
2.  212  FS    ORDJFK  500P  751P  DC8  D  0
3.  144  F7Y4  ORDJFK  600P  852P  747  D  0
4.  262  S6    ORDJFK  610P  955P  727  D  1
```

(b)

FIGURE 15.3

N - Need, i.e., I need a seat or seats
2 - Two seats
F - First class
3 - On the flight listed on line 3, i.e., flight 144, the 747 to JFK

At this point the system responds with the reply

1.    144F    12 Mar    ORDJFK    HS2    600P    852P

264        – flight number

S7         – number and type of available seats (seven second class seats);
           note that flight 3 has 7 first class seats (F), 4 tourist
           (Y).

ORDJFK  – departure airport (ORD as requested) and destination
           (JFK). The destination for New York City varies,
           since there is more than one airport (JFK, LaGuardia,
           Newark) available.

420P       – time of departure. Note that it is "in the vicinity" of the
           requested 500 PM time. The request involved searching on
           this field as well as on departure airport, arrival airport
           and date, a search involving four separate fields (or three
           if one considers the departure/destination airport pair as
           a single field with two subfields. The output of the search
           would be sorted on the time field in ascending order, starting
           with the flight at 4:20pm and going on through the flight at
           6:10pm. The system must decide what is "near 500"; for example
           is it one hour early (start outputting values at 4:00pm)
           or two (start at 3:00pm). Some values are definitely not
           close (8am), others definitely close (4:50pm), but there
           is a large grey area in between. In fact, if a single flight
           existed on MAR 12, at 8am, even this would be "close" since
           it is our only chance to fly at all. The system designers
           and builders have a non-trivial task on their hands.

800P       – time of arrival at JFK

727        – airplane type

D          – meal served, e.g.,  D=dinner
                                  L=lunch
                                  B-breakfast

1 = one intermediate stop (0=non-stop, 3 or 4=the "milk train")

**FIGURE 15.4**

where it echoes

- The flight number (144)
- The fact that we are talking about first-class seats (F)
- The date (12 MAR)
- The airports (ORDJFK)
- The times (600P, 852P)

and gives one new data item

     HS2

where "HS" indicates that the system has the seats and 2 indicates the
quantity of seats available. The actual "booking" or reservation of the seats
will not be done until the entire transaction is completed. This might involve booking other flights (e.g., a return flight, or a side journey to
San Francisco). For simplicity, we will assume that this is a one-way flight,

so that the transaction can now be completed. The agent must enter the name of the persons receiving the seats

   -Anderson, Jacob/Meyers, Marjorie

where the first character (-) indicates that this is the name field. The system responds that it has received the data by typing in a special symbol, e.g., the prompt. An error in the reception of the data would result in an error message, e.g., if the agent had typed a phone number instead of the name, the system might respond: "invalid. name. Please reenter." After entering the name, the agent may enter other information, using a special code to indicate the type of information being entered. For example, in order to enter the phone field, the agent uses the code 9 and types the phone number

   94126245203B

where the code (9) is always a single character (fixed length field) followed by the data for that action, here the phone number 412-624-5203, and the B, which indicates business phone. The phone field (or any data field following the single character action code) is variable length, terminated by the carriage return, hence, an agent might type the phone number as

   4126245203

or as

   412-624-5203

with an extension or without

   412-624-5203    EXT 32

This facilitates easy data entry of items that have a variable format in common usage. We simply read in all characters typed and, if later requested to display them, we type them out as they were typed in. This is often easier than training users to type the data in a fixed format, e.g.

   4126245203    [no hyphens]

or

   412-624-5203    [hyphens always]

When we "force" a fixed format—say no hyphens—we often "force" the commission of data entry errors. The agent will often type the hyphens

   412-624-5203

be informed of the error

   NO SPECIAL CHARACTERS IN PHONE NUMBER

and have to retype the data in the correct format

   4126245203

This can lead to much frustration and delay on the part of the agent.
   On the other hand, some errors should be checked. For example, a phone number consisting of fewer than seven digits

   625203

is useless, since some portion of the number is missing. If the area code is necessary (e.g., when we cannot assume the customer lives in the same area code region as the agency's location), 10 digits are necessary. The proper balance between the consideration of human factors (allows hyphens or no hyphens, in accord with common usage variability), along with the assurance of collecting correct data, is a difficult area to control.

Besides the passenger's name and phone number, the agent might wish to enter special messages (5 code)

5 PASSENGER IS DIABETIC

When the entry is complete, the agent types the *E* action key (end transaction or *enter* data) to effect the reservation of the seats. The agent can request to see the record (R code)

R

which would result in the message

ANDERSON, JACOB/MEYERS, MARJORIE
1.   144F    12MAR    ORDJFK    HS2    600P    852P

or update records (X code). For example, to change the date of the flight, the agent could enter

X1   144F    14MAR    ORDJFK    HS2    600P    852P

where X1 indicates a change (X) to line 1 of the display, and the remainder of the line is new data. Of course, the system would have to check that the seats are available on the 14th of March on this flight.

The use of such special codes as -, 9, or X enables the agent to input the data in any order that he or she wishes. This is usually more satisfactory than forcing the order of the input. The system can then use the codes to format the record internally. For example, note that in retrieving the record, the user's name comes first. If a particular field is necessary (e.g., the name or hyphen field), the system can check at the end of the transaction (when the agent types the special *E* key) to see that this field (or fields) has been entered. If it has not been entered, it can prompt the agent

NAME FIELD PLEASE

before allowing the transaction to terminate.

The entire transaction, including talking with the end user (the customer) can be completed in a minute or two, thus shortening our queues and reducing our chances of going out of business.

## Updating the Data Base

The system is required to update the data base in the above example, reducing the number of available first-class seats on flight 144 from F7 to F5

144 F5Y4   ORDJFK...

This is not a simple task in a system accessed by many users (several agents) in a "simultaneous" mode. For example, suppose there is only one first-class seat on flight 82 from Pittsburgh to LA on a particular day

82 F    PGHLAX...

and that two customers are inquiring about flights on that day, but talking to two different agents, one agent at the downtown office, another at the airport. Say that both agents have inquired and have seen that there is one seat available. Say also that each customer "takes it"

Agent 1 types:   N1F4 (where we assume flight 82 is on line 4)
Agent 2 types:   N1F4

and each agent issues a ticket to the customer with whom he or she is interacting. We have two people booked for the same seat, and a "collision" on the horizon. The system may allow several users to "read" (access, inquire into) the data base at one time. However, it must allow only one user to update (write into) the data base at a given time. Thus, only agent 1 or agent 2 may effectively issue the command

N1F4

thus reserving the seat. The means by which one user is allowed write access to the data base and others are "locked out" is a central concern in the study of data bases that are updated from several locations. Using a lockout mechanism, the system would inform the second agent who requests control that he or she must wait. Upon getting control (eventually), this second agent would be informed that there are no seats available, so that the command

N1F4

cannot be carried out (or is never issued).


Echoing the Input

In the example of the airline reservationist, the command indicating a need for two seats

N2F3

was followed by an "echo" of much of the data that had already been entered

1.   144F   12MAR   ORDJFK   HS2   600P   852P

where the entry HS2 for "have two seats," the confirmation of the ability to fulfill our needs, was the only really new data. It might seem at times that this echo is wasteful (and, indeed, in certain systems designed for experienced users, it might be). However, there are occasions, especially with either novice or casual users, where the user truly does not know what he or she has input, and the echo is quite beneficial. An example is found in the design of 24-hr banking systems. At one time, there were two different systems in the Pittsburgh area, one that required the user to input both dollars and cents; e.g., to enter $50 one typed four digits

5000

and the system supplied the period

50.00

In the second system, the banking machine supplied not only the period but the two "cents digits" as well, so that the user typed

50

to obtain $50, with the system filling in the rest:

50.00

System supplies

Suppose now that a particular user has used bank A (type 5000) for several years, then for some reason (possibly an argument over an error in processing the account), the user switches to bank B (type 50). Having several years of "training" in typing four digits to obtain $50, the user types

5000

and the system adds the decimal point and the cents

5000.00

and we have a different sum than we thought!

It is for reasons such as these that the banking systems often force us to "explicitly review our input" by requesting us to hit either the Enter key or the Cancel key, as appropriate. The user has a chance to either confirm or disaffirm the amount.

## Checking the Data: Limit Checks and Reasonableness Checks

The input data values should also be checked for accuracy. When a user requests money from a banking system one check is to compare the requested amount to the current balance. If the request exceeds the balance it must be rejected. In fact, if it equals the balance, usually a sign that the account is being closed, it may require special handling. If the amount requested is less than the balance, the request can be granted, but whether or not it should be is another story. At a 24-hr banking machine a request for $5000 is probably not reasonable; usually customers use such machines for smaller amounts of ready cash, say $50 or $100. The machine may want to query the user as to his or her intent. In practice, some machines may not have enough cash on hand to honor such a large amount. And, for security reasons, much smaller upper limits, say $100 or $200, are placed on a transaction at automatic money machines. However, the issue here is with reasonableness and limit checks.

For an amount as large as $5000, the request would not be "reasonable." The program or system should have reasonableness checks built into it, so that certain amounts are flagged as questionable, and not acted upon automatically. Checking the balance in our account is a "limit" check, i.e., we are checking the amount requested against an exact limiting number, the known balance in our account. The difference between a reasonableness check and a limit check is in the ability to set an exact number as the limit. If such an exact number exists, as in the months of the year (12) or days in the week (7), the check is called a limit check. If the number is not exact by nature, e.g., the oldest customer of our store, a "reasonable" number (say 100 years old) may be selected as the limit; this selection of the number (somewhat but not wholly in an arbitrary fashion) is a reasonableness check. Thus, a date entered in the format

MMDDYY

with the value

150183
⊤
Month

would be flagged as *definitely wrong*. The data entry person would have to investigate the cause of the error (i.e., was the real data 12/1/83? or 1/15/83?), but we *know* that the month number 15 *can't* be right. In terms of age, an age entered as 102 would be flagged as "not reasonable" or "possibly wrong," and the data entry person would still have to check the value. However, it is possible that the age *is* correct, that someone shops in our store who is 102 years old. On the other hand, it could be that the shopper was 12 (which may or may not be reasonable) or 52, and that the data must be corrected. It is this lack of certitude as to the rightness or wrongness of the data that distinguishes limit checks from reasonableness checks.

## Upper and Lower Thresholds

In the above examples we gave data values that exceeded some upper threshold (12 in the case of months, a check in excess of $200, say, in the banking example). Normally incorrect data can be detected at a lower threshold as well, e.g., a month value that is less than or equal to zero, a check value that is negative. The concepts of both limit checks and reasonableness checks apply to the lower threshold as well.

## Checking Commands

In the above examples we considered checking data values for appropriateness. Since the user can enter both data and commands, we must also involve ourselves in checking the commands entered. For example, in one editor used by the author, the command

n

is meaningless. If the user types such a command, he or she must be notified of the fact that the command is nonexistent with a message such as "ILLEGAL COMMAND."

Commands can be entered incorrectly in two ways

- The misspelling of a valid command
- The entry of a nonexistent command

For example, if we consider the commands to the BASIC programming language, the command to print the value of a variable

PRINT A

is a legal command. However, if the user misspells the word *print*

PRNT A

the command will not be recognized. This is a "syntax error" in computer terminology, and is usually indicated by an explicit error message, e.g.

ERROR IN LINE 1

The user could also enter what appears to be a valid command

    SHOW A

in the sense that the word *show* is spelled correctly and could mean "show me the value of A." However, the command SHOW does not exist in the BASIC language. This too will be signaled as a syntax error

    ILLEGAL COMMAND, LINE 10

but is really indicative of a conceptual error on the part of the user.

Checking user commands is done by a part of the system called the command interpreter, which reads commands entered by the user, and checks them against a list of valid commands. If the command entered by the user is on the list, it is a "valid command" and will be passed to the part or parts of the program that must execute (take action on) the command. If the command is not on the list, whether this is due to a typing error or a conceptual error, the command will be flagged as illegal and no action will be taken. In some systems the user will be given a chance to reenter the command; in other, more severe systems, the transaction will be aborted.

### Bullet-Proofing the System

Checking the user's responses to the system, especially in relation to conversational systems, is called *bullet-proofing* by Martin. The purpose of bullet-proofing is to ascertain if a response is legal or not, and if not, to give the user an appropriate message and a chance to try again. An example might be the code shown in Figure 15.5. The user is asked if he or she wants to enter another transaction

    100  PRINT "ANOTHER TRANSACTION (Y/N)?"
    110  INPUT R$

where the print statement "prompts the user," i.e., tells the user what response is being requested. Note that it also has a list of the legal commands (Y/N). The input statement actually collects the data from the user (by printing a question mark, then pausing to accept the response); the end of the response is signaled by the carriage return. This response is then stored in the location R$. Thus, an instance of the dialogue might look like

    ANOTHER TRANSACTION (Y/N)?
    ?Y

```
100   PRINT "ANOTHER TRANSACTION (Y/N)?"
110   INPUT R$
120   IF R$ = "Y" THEN 50 (GET COMMANDS AND DATA)
130   IF R$ = "N" THEN 900 (END OF JOB ROUTINE)
140   PRINT "PLEASE ANSWER Y OR N"
150   GOTO 100
```

FIGURE 15.5

in which the computer program caused the printing of the prompt message and question mark, but the user supplied the letter Y.

The user's response, stored in R$, is now checked against the list of "legal" responses (here two, but in general any number)

```
IF R$ = "Y" THEN 50 (GET COMMANDS AND DATA)
IF R$ = "N" THEN 900 (END OF JOB ROUTINE)
```

where the phrases "GET COMMANDS AND DATA" and "END OF JOB ROUTINE" indicate the types of routines at the locations named by the line numbers. These are parenthetical to the example and would be included as comments in an actual program.

If the user's response is "Y" the program will "branch" to the routine that gets the commands and data; if the response is not "Y," the branch will not occur. If the user's response is "N," the branch will be taken to the end of the job routine; if the value is not "N," the branch will not be taken. If the user's response was neither "Y" nor "N," neither of the branches (new transaction or EOJ) will be taken, hence the program will be executing at line 140. But if "Y" and "N" are the only legal responses, and the user's response was neither, the user's response was illegal. Hence at line 140, we tell the user he or she is wrong

```
PRINT "ANSWER Y/N"
```

at the same time repeating the correct usage (Y/N), and branch to line 100 in order to ask the question again. No matter what the user responds, the system can handle it.

### Nonbullet-Proofed Dialogue

In dialogue that is not bullet-proofed, not all user responses can be handled by the system (the system crashes) or they are handled inappropriately. For example, the code shown in Figure 15.6 handles a "Y" response correctly, by going to the routine for another transaction. In fact, it will also handle a "no" response correctly, by stopping at line 130. However, it will handle "blunders" inappropriately. For example, if the user types in the whole word *yes*, or types *okay*, the program terminates. The action of program abortion on a typing error is probably more extreme than is warranted.

```
100  PRINT "ANOTHER TRANSACTION (Y/N)?"
110  INPUT R$
120  IF R$ = "Y" GOTO 50 (ANOTHER TRANSACTION)
130  STOP
140  END
```

FIGURE 15.6

## Intermediaries Versus End Users

We have been using the term *user of the system* somewhat ambiguously until now. In the example of a 24-hr banking system, we referred to the "customer," the person actually withdrawing or depositing his or her funds, as the "end user." In the example of an airline agent, we referred to the agent as the "user" and the person actually buying the ticket as a "customer." In the discussions of interactive programming, a distinction is often made between the person who physically operates the system and the person "using" the system (i.e., the customer). The actual beneficiary of the system's action—the customer—is referred to as the end user. A person who operates the system on behalf of another is referred to as an "intermediary" or "third party," and the use is referred to as use through a third party, the other two parties being the computer system and the customer.

There are several reasons why we might want to employ a third party as an intermediate user. One of these reasons is the security of the system or the environment in which the system is housed. In computer systems an instance of protecting the system from the end user is the use of the operating system to perform reads or writes to the disk. The operating system ensures that we don't write over someone else's (maybe our own) data. Examples in applications programs are less plentiful, since a well-designed system will include enough error-checking of commands and data to protect the system from user interference without a third party, at least in terms of the software (programs) and data. In terms of equipment, the system is vulnerable to the end user, as well as to the elements, such as rain, snow, and extreme cold. However, most applications placed in the public domain will have hardware designed for "heavy" or "rough" use and physical protection mechanisms to preserve the equipment or other valuables (e.g., the money in the 24-hr banking systems).

An example of providing security for the work environment is the use of third party tellers in "indoor banking." We do not wish to have customers coming behind the counter, so we have tellers operate the equipment instead of the end user. That this arrangement is not necessary for the integrity of the system is evidenced by the very existence of 24-hr banking systems. Another example is the use of a clerk at a grocery counter using bar code readers. Not trusting the end user (customer) to mark every item, we employ someone else to do the checking.

Besides security measures, a factor that often enters into the choice of a third party as the operator of the system involves the expertise or lack thereof of the true end user. This lack of expertise may be physical, mental, or both.

People who use a system frequently gain a physical dexterity with the system that enables them to process transactions more quickly. Allowing the end user to enter the commands and data directly would slow things down (although it would also save the extra expense of the trained operator). The dedicated operator will also have a better grasp of the technical aspects of the system, knowing what codes are allowable, what commands are legal, and what data is expected and in what format. An end user might have no knowledge of these things, or have the knowledge perfunctorily, but make more errors in executing the sequence of operations. Again, this would slow matters down. A choice to design a system for the true end user, when this end user is untrained in the mechanics of the system, is often what leads to the choice of menu selection over command mode, which we have shown to have a large cost in terms of transaction time. As shown above, the cost pays for the benefit of ease of use of the system.


## Intellectual Expertise

The more interesting question, however, comes into play when the proper use of the system involves intellectual expertise other than that required by the technical elements of the system. A typical example is the use of information retrieval systems to search bibliographic data bases. The issue is discussed extensively in such works as Lancaster and Fayen (1973). We give a brief summary of the trade-offs here.

A typical scenario has an end user with a subject-related problem or question (e.g., a question about the use of laser beams in producing digital recordings). Presuming that the end user is an expert in the field, he or she probably has a better conceptual grasp of the problem as well as a better ability to recognize potential approaches and solutions to it (data that answers or might answer the question). These factors all point to the true end user or customer performing the search personally. However, the customer probably has less grasp than the expert of the data bases accessible through the system, their contents and indexing structure, and the techniques involved in formulating effective queries on the system. These factors presumably lead to the use of an intermediary to search for the end user.

In practice, this trade-off is often solved either by having both parties present during the search, or by having both parties "dialogue the problem" before and after the search, though not necessarily requiring both to be present during the search itself. If both parties are present during the search, they interact in a cooperative manner, with the end user formulating questions in the language of the subject matter, the third party user translating these requests into the language of the system, and the end user judging the relevance of the results. The intermediary adjusts the search strategies according to the relevance judgments of the end user, and the end user attempts to move from subject-oriented descriptions of the problem to verbalizations closer to the language of the system. The system of formulating questions and judging results is interactive between end user and intermediary, as well as between the system and the human operator in the dialogue pairs.

In a system in which the user and intermediary interact before and after the search but not during, the system is again interactive, but less so, since the time delay from one version of the statement of the problem to the next is greater. The end user is interviewed by an "information counselor" as to his or her needs. The counselor then translates these needs into the necessary search strategy, and an "operator" later performs the search. The search is often run retroactively, in a batch mode, rather than online. After receiving the output, the information counselor reviews it with the client (at some later date). If the search results are satisfactory, the session is over; if not, the question or problem is refined and the process of searching and reviewing the output is repeated.

The information counselor is a liaison between the end user and the system. He or she must ascertain the needs of the user, then interact with the system and/or systems people in order to translate these needs into an end product.

The concept of an information counselor has been paralleled by the role of an information broker, an individual (or more likely, a group of individuals) who takes a client's needs, researches the areas of knowledge related to these needs through manual searches, online and/or retroactive searches, and/or personal interviews, then prepares a finished report.

In the subsequent material we will assume that the person operating the system is the user. The reader can make the necessary transitions between ultimate customer and actual operator. The third party discussion is primarily relevant to information retrieval with query systems and data bases and the brokers that perform an "information service" for an individual or organization (e.g., the puclic library or the information systems group of an organization).

## Training

In the example of the airline reservationist, the agent had several codes to memorize

- The codes for the airports, such as ORD for O'Hara
- The codes for the commands, e.g., -, X, 9
- The codes for other data fields, such as the class of seat (F, S, Y) and the stop/nonstop field (0, 1)

as well as having to learn to manipulate the system. Learning these skills requires training, and the more complex the system the more complex the

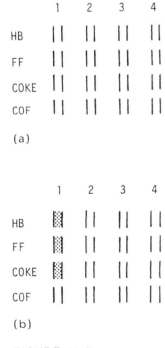

FIGURE 15.7

training. In considering the training of dedicated personnel, one aspect that is important to consider is the expected length of employment. For employees who are expected to work for a firm for several years, the investment of a few weeks, even a few months, is justified. However, if the expected length of employment is shorter, the time of training must be shortened correspondingly. In an automated system, the choice of the design of the human/computer interface can facilitate training the personnel. An example is training checkout clerks in a fast food chain. The expected length of employment for an order clerk might be 6 months or less, so that the time spent in learning to accept and place orders must be minimal. A design that facilitates both obtaining of the customer's order and entering it quickly into the computer system is the use of "mark sense" paper or cards. For example, a card might have entries such as those shown in Figure 15.7a. One clerk obtains the order from the customers in line, marking the card appropriately (Figure 15.7b) and another enters it into the cash register, which reads the marks, computes the cost, and sends the order to the kitchen. Each order has an identifying number, so that as it is filled the number is displayed and the clerk who delivers the order matches that number with the customer holding the proper receipt. In regard to the matter of learning the codes, the designers of the system have relied on the clerk's years of experience in eating fast food to know the meaning of the abbreviations HB and FF.

## Special Keys and Special Equipment

The introduction of the topic of mark sense cards leads naturally to the consideration of special keys and equipment to facilitate the human/computer interface. A common example of such special equipment is the use of function keys.

## Function Keys

In the case of the airline agent, the reservationist used the normal keyboard for entering the command for the action codes (A for availability, E for end transaction, X for update transaction). It is the position of the typed character (column 1) that distinguishes it as a command to the system rather than a data value. Hence, an *E* typed in column 2 or thereafter would be taken as data, as in the entry of a special message

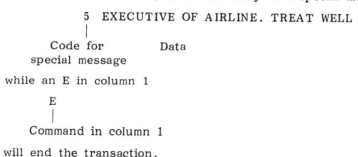

5  EXECUTIVE OF AIRLINE. TREAT WELL
   |
   Code for          Data
 special message

while an E in column 1

     E
     |
 Command in column 1

will end the transaction.

In some applications, it is useful to have a special key dedicated to a commonly executed function. For example, in data entry systems, a common

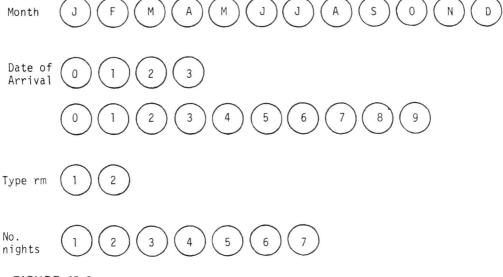

FIGURE 15.8

function key is "Enter." The person keying the data types an entry, then depresses the Enter key to send it. In an airline reservation system, the command to "reserve" a seat could be implemented as a special key

RESERVE

Other examples are the use of a reset key to clear the screen on a CRT, or a cancel key to abort a transaction in a banking system. The use of function keys reduces the number of keystrokes required of the typist (hit one key instead of seven in typing *reserve*), which reduces both the time required to input the data or commands and the number of errors.

Martin (1972) gives an example of a specialized keyboard for a hotel reservation system. Figure 15.8 gives an adaptation of his example. There are special keys for the selection of a month

as well as for selecting the date

where the fact that 31 is the largest possible date allows the use of only four keys for the first digit. There might also be a panel of control lights to indicate the status of the hotel rooms, e.g., a light out for available and on for not available.

The reader will note that the code for the months is ambiguous if we consider only the letters used

January

J  June

July

However, the position of the letter in the keyboard distinguishes among these occurrences

   J    J   J
January · · · June  July

Of course, if we thought the user of the system would be confused by the single letters, we could include three-letter abbreviations (Jan, Jun, Jul). Note that June and July force three as the number for "minimal character recognition" rather than two (likewise May and March).

The use of specialized keyboards is more costly than the use of standard keyboards. However, the cost is often justified by the benefit of faster and more accurate data entry.

One other drawback to special-purpose terminals is their incompatibility with other systems. The hotel keyboard could not be used to interact with a general-purpose computer system, e.g., to create a BASIC program, since the keys generate codes that do not have the standard meaning (e.g., there are three *J*'s and not enough of some other characters). In order to use a normal keyboard for some special functions, we could adapt certain infrequently used keys, such as the ampersand

  &

into function keys. To make the *&* stand for "reserve," we simply label the key

  RESERVE

and include a test for the ampersand in the program receiving commands from the terminal

   IF A$="&" THEN (RESERVATION ROUTINE
         OR ITS ADDRESS)

The program "searches for the ampersand," and, upon finding one, transfers control to a routine to do reservations. Various schemes have been developed to adapt standard keyboards to specialized ones by using overlays on the keyboard (to relabel the keys) and switches or commands to select the program to interpret the codes generated by the standard keys in a fashion compatible with the overlayed meaning.


## Light Pens and Bar Code Readers

Another popular method of interacting with an interactive display unit is the light pen. A user points to a menu of commands with the pen (Figure 15.9a), then points to an object on the screen (Figure 15.9b) and to a new location (Figure 15.9c), "dragging" the object along with it. The light pen senses light on the screen and the computer program interprets the signals generated to "know the position" of the pen. If the position is the same as the command "move," we know that the user wants us to move the object. After giving the "move" command, the program "expects" to receive a command telling it which object to move; hence it again looks for signals from

1. MOVE OBJECT
2. ADD OBJECT
3. DELETE OBJECT
4. QUIT

(a)

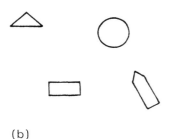

(b)

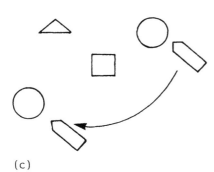

(c)

FIGURE 15.9

the light pen, which will be interpreted as indicating the position of the object on the screen. The user points to commands and objects by placing the pen close to the screen, and stops pointing by pulling it away.

### The Time/Error Curve

In such applications as data collection (data entry), the use of a device like the light pen or a "bar code reader" can facilitate both the speed and accuracy of the transaction. For example, in the University of Pittsburgh bookstore, a wand is used to input the name of textbooks and their prices from a magnetic bar code on the back of the book. The process for entering the data is to

- Find the strip of paper with the bar code
- Wave the wand back and forth across the code

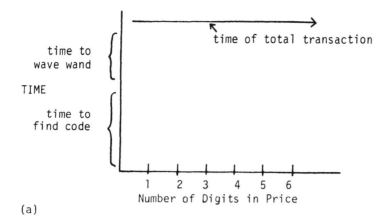

(a)

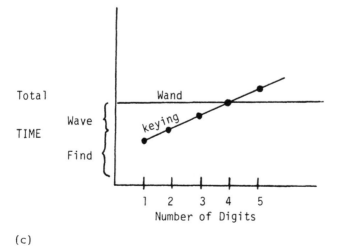

(b)

(c)

FIGURE 15.10

The thing to note about these actions is that they are relatively constant in terms of time to execute the actions, irrespective of the number of digits in the price of the book (or the number of digits in its identification number, called the ISBN or International Standard Book Number). Thus, if we were to graph the activities, we would have the diagram shown in Figure 15.10a. The horizontal nature of the line indicates that the time to enter the price is constant across the number of digits in the price. This is not true of input through the keyboard. In keying the data, each digit adds an increment to the total time of the transaction. The diagram of time versus number of digits would be something like the one shown in Figure 15.10b, in which the ascending nature of the line indicates that the more digits we key, the longer it takes. If we now superimpose the two diagrams (Figure 15.10c), we can see that the trade-off point between using the wand and using a keyboard is at four or five digits. Of course, other considerations, such as the reliability of the equipment, its cost, etc., will enter into the decision. However, in terms of time alone, the wand becomes beneficial at four or five digits. Actually, the label "time" on the Y-axis could be replaced by the label "number of errors" as well. The number of errors generated by the wand will be fairly constant, a function of its reliability. The number of errors generated by keying the values will increase as the number of digits increases. The crossover point may not be the same, but the general shapes of the curves will be similar (Hanes, 1975).

## Using the Human Body

Besides standard keyboards, function keys, specialized keyboards, light pens, and wands, a host of different devices has arisen for interacting with a computer system. One such display unit is the plasma display used by the PLATO system (a computer-aided learning system) at the University of Illinois. This unit makes use of the standard equipment of the human body. A user selects items by pointing to them on the screen. The plasma display is heat sensitive, and lights up (in orange) as the person's finger comes close to a particular item. The coordinates of the display can be checked to determine the position of the finger.

Other systems attempt to use voice input and output for the human/computer interaction. Handling output is somewhat simpler than handling input. If the output is well delineated, as in the selection of one message from a predefined set of messages, e.g.

- Today's movie is "The Adventures of Pearl." The starting times are 1 p.m., 3 p.m., 5 p.m., and 7 p.m.

the messages can be prerecorded. If the messages are not predefined, but the characters are, e.g., in reporting the value of a bank balance

    342.98

where the balance itself can be any combination of digits, but the fact that digits are used is a constant of the system, the sounds for each digit (three-four-two...) can be prerecorded or generated dynamically by combining the proper sound frequencies for each digit. Inputting commands and data by voice is somewhat trickier, in that the sound wave frequencies generated by various persons for the same syllables differ widely. In fact, considering only a single person, the sounds made when vocalizing a single word, e.g., *going*, are different from the sounds generated for the same word when used in a sentence, e.g., "I'm going downtown." A person may pronounce the single word *going* quite distinctly, then say the sentence so that it sounds like: "Ahm gowan dahntahn." The recognition of words pronounced "alone" is referred to as speech recognition. The recognition of continuous utterances, such as entire sentences or commands, is referred to as "speech understanding." Research is progressing in both areas (see Barr and Feigenbaum; 1981).

If the complexity of various persons speaking various words in an unlimited fashion is considered, modern technology cannot reliably recognize all inputs to the system. However, for a restricted range of commands (deposit, withdraw, or commands given by numerical value) systems can be devised to work "across people." And, in considering input from a single person (when vocal characteristics can be input into the system), a considerable range of words can be recognized by matching the voice input to a dictionary containing the various features expected for the selected vocabulary.

## Mice, Joysticks, and Other Creatures

In addition to using the human body, other mechanical/electronic devices are used to collect data in ways that are more natural to users of the system in particular applications. One of these is the use of a "mouse" to manipulate a cursor on the screen. The mouse is a boxlike device that is moved by hand along a table in front of a terminal. The underside (belly) of the mouse has wheels in the horizontal and vertical directions; the movement of these wheels is sensed and the screen cursor is moved in a similar direction. The use of the mouse is a continuous or analog motion, as opposed to the discrete movement necessary in using a keyboard to move the cursor, and is "more natural" in the sense of allowing the user to concentrate on the screen rather than on the keyboard. Of course, a mouse cannot be used to enter such commands as "1"

1. MOVE OBJECT
2. ADD OBJECT
3. DELETE OBJECT

by typing the characters. These commands must be presented as a menu on the screen. The mouse is used to position the cursor to that place on the screen, and a button is pressed to actually select the command. (The

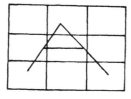
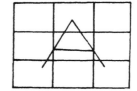

FIGURE 15.11

A    ᐳ  ᐊ

FIGURE 15.12

movement of the mouse only positions the cursor; pressing a button acti-
vates the command or object selection portion of the program.)

A joystick is a vertical bar that can be moved in the forward/backward
and right/left directions, and is popular in the manipulation of objects in
video games. Other common devices are digitizers, in which a person draws
a picture on a plane surface and the coordinates of the picture are sensed
(by pressure, sound, or some other physical means) and transmitted to the
computer in digital form (binary digits of the analog pencil strokes); and
character recognition devices, machines that "read" the reflections of light
waves off typed or handwritten characters and that match features of the
characters detected (see, e.g., Figure 15.11a) against a template of the
characters stored in the system (e.g., features representing a "perfect
A"; Figure 15.11b).

## Pattern Recognition

Recognition of letters such as the A is one aspect of the field of study
called pattern recognition. Humans are particularly adept at recognizing
patterns in various orientations. The letters shown in Figure 15.12 can all
be easily recognized by humans as the letter A; machines are less adept.
However, several techniques have been developed to recognize predefined
patterns in standard orientations.

## Feature Analysis

Newman and Sproull (1979) explain a methodology for recognizing characters by defining their "features" and looking for these features in the

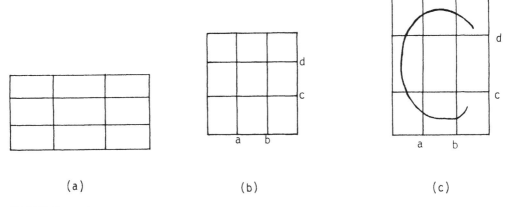

(a)                    (b)                    (c)

FIGURE 15.13

character presented as input. The model is based on recognizers developed both by Ledeen (1973) and Teitelman (1964).

The essence of the system is in the creation of a grid on which characters are to be drawn (Figure 15.13a). This grid has the internal horizontal and vertical lines labeled as shown in Figure 15.13b. A character drawn on the screen will have certain of its portions in different portions of the screen. For example, the letter C would be similar to the one shown in Figure 15.13c, where the letter appears in the area above d, the area below c, and the area to the left of a.

The features of interest to the recognizer are

1. The regions in which the character starts (left of a, left of b, below d, below c) in terms of each stroke drawn
2. The number of times a given stroke crosses each of the four dividing lines
3. The stroke's position in relation to other strokes of the character

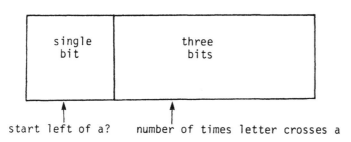

start left of a?     number of times letter crosses a

(a)

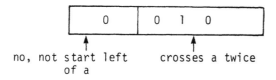

no, not start left     crosses a twice
of a

(b)

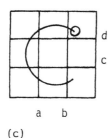

(c)

FIGURE 15.14

We will concentrate on features 1 and 2. The features of the character are encoded in 4-bit fields, where the leftmost bit of the field stands for the starting position of the stroke, and the remaining 3 bits stand for the number of crossings in regard to that particular line. One 4-bit code exists for each of the lines a, b, c, and d. Thus, the first bit in the descriptor for line a would be 0 (does not start left of a) or 1 (starts left of a). The remaining 3 bits stand for the count of crossings of a (allowing values from 0 through 7; Figure 15.14a).

For the letter *C*, assuming the stroke was begun in the upper right-most region of the character, the encoding in regard to line a would be as shown in Figure 15.14b. In considering the single stroke for the letter *C*, one must know where the stroke began. In interactive graphics this can be determined by the initial placement of the light pen or other device. We

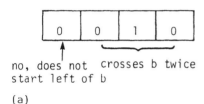

no, does not      crosses b twice
start left of b

(a)

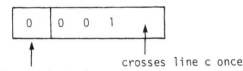

crosses line c once

does not start
below c

(b)

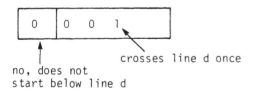

crosses line d once

no, does not
start below line d

(c)

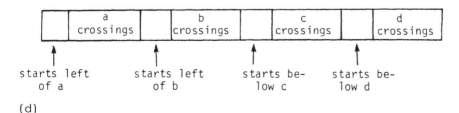

(d)

FIGURE 15.15

| 0 | 010 | 0 | 010 | 0 | 001 | 0 | 001 |

(e)

FIGURE 15.15   (continued)

assume that the stroke began in the uppermost, rightmost corner (Figure 15.14c). In noninteractive systems, the place where the stroke actually began cannot be determined. In such cases, descriptors based on the static properties of the character are used.

The encodings for line b, with the letter $C$; are as shown in Figure 15.15a. For line c, letter $C$, we have the encodings shown in Figure 15.15b. Finally, for line d, letter $C$, we have the encodings shown in Figure 15.15c. The four fields are encoded as a unit in the format shown in Figure 15.15d, so that the code for letter $C$ is as shown in Figure 15.15e. This is usually summarized in four decimal numbers (not always single-digit numbers)

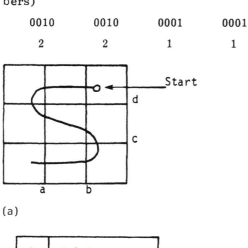

```
0010        0010        0001        0001
 2           2           1           1
```

(a)

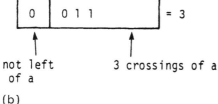

| 0 | 0 1 1 | = 3

not left     3 crossings of a
of a

(b)

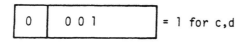

| 0 | 0 0 1 | = 1 for c,d

(c)

FIGURE 15.16

where each set is understood to be in the 8-4-2-1 code

$$\frac{8}{0} \quad \frac{4}{0} \quad \frac{2}{1} \quad \frac{1}{0} = 2$$

The letter $S$, with the starting point at the top right (Figure 15.16a) would be encoded as shown in Figure 15.16b in regard to line a. The description

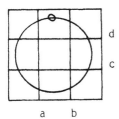

(a)

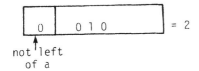

not left
of a

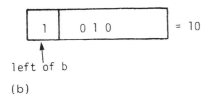

left of b

(b)

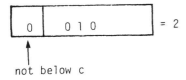

not below c

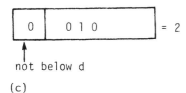

not below d

(c)

FIGURE 15.17

for b is the same. In regard to lines c and d, we have: not below c, not below d, and cross each once, so that the code is that shown in Figure 15.16c, so that the letter *s* is described as

3-3-1-1

The letter *O*, starting in the circled position shown in Figure 15.17a, has the character starting to the left of b, but not to the left of a. The character crosses both a and b twice, so that the encodings for a and b would be as shown in Figure 15.17b. In regard to c and d, we have not below c, not below d, and crossing each twice (Figure 15.17c), so that the code for the stroke is

2-10-2-2

If a hexadecimal code were used, this would be 2-A-2-2.

The letters *C*, *S*, and *O* consist of a single stroke. An example of a character consisting of more than a single stroke is the letter *F* (Figure 15.18a), which has three strokes, one vertical and two horizontal, so that it would be described by defining all three strokes.

The vertical stroke would be encoded as shown in Figure 15.18b, in regard to line a, since it starts to the left of a and never crosses it. (Con-

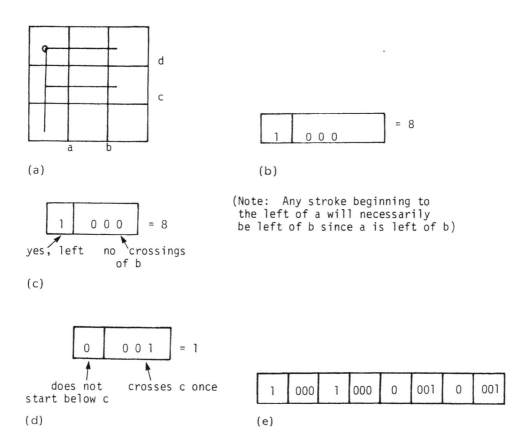

(a)

(b)

(Note: Any stroke beginning to the left of a will necessarily be left of b since a is left of b)

(c)

(d)

(e)

FIGURE 15.18

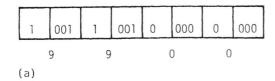

(a)

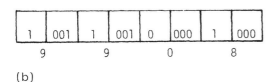

(b)

FIGURE 15.19

sider the vertical stroke to be drawn top down, from the uppermost point; consider the horizontal strokes to be drawn left to right.) It would be described similarly for line b, since it also lies to the left of b and never crosses it (Figure 15.18c). For line c, vertical stroke, we have the encoding shown in Figure 15.18d, and the same is true for line d, vertical stroke. Thus, the vertical stroke is described as shown in Figure 15.18e, or

8-8-1-1

The topmost horizontal stroke (beginning on the left) is

- Left of a, cross a once
- Left of b, cross b once
- Not below c, never cross c
- Not below d, never cross d

so that we have the code shown in Figure 15.19a: 9-9-0-0.
 The lower horizontal stroke is

- Left of a, cross a once
- Left of b, cross b once
- Not below c, never cross c
- Below d, never cross d

| Number of Strokes | Features | Letter |
|---|---|---|
| Single stroke: | 2-2-1-1 | C |
| | 3-3-1-1 | S |
| | 2-10-2-2 | O |
| Double stroke: | . . . . , . . . . | L |
| | . . . . , . . . . | T |
| Triple stroke: | 8-8-1-1, 9-9-0-0-, 9-9-0-8 | F |
| | . . . . ,, . . . . ,, . . . . | A |

FIGURE 15.20

so that the code is 9-9-0-8 (Figure 15.19b).

The values of features for a prototype character are stored in a dictionary. For example, a simplified dictionary might contain the entries shown in Figure 15.20. The reader should attempt to fill in the entries for L, T, and A.

Upon "seeing" a character, the character recognizer would extract the recognized features, then match them against the dictionary. For example, if the extracted features are 3-3-1-1, it would recognize the letter O. If an exact match cannot be found, it might guess the closest character. For example, in the abbreviated dictionary, the code 3-3-1-2 might generate the "guess" S.

Feature analysis is a technique used in many domains. For example, linguists use it to distinguish between the sounds of various letters (vowels or consonants), using features such as nasal (m, n) or non-nasal, closed lips (p, b, m) or open lips (a, o). Psychologists consider feature analysis in discussing the way in which humans recognize or assign objects to categories, e.g., a chair "has four legs, a flat surface, a back" where some features are considered essential, say the sitting surface, others optional, say the back. Controversy exists over whether the process of categorization involves feature analysis or other methods (template matching; prototype matching) or combinations of methods.


Artificial Intelligence

While the methods of recognizing patterns and making "intelligent guesses" can become quite complex in the field of artificial intelligence (diagnosing diseases, understanding human language), a simple example of the types of techniques used is the recognition of "intended user responses" in misspelled responses. In the earlier example of "yes" and "no" as the legal responses to the prompt "again?", a user might type

"ys"

The response is not intelligible, but a guess can be hazarded. If we keep track of the length of the legal responses

| Response | Length |
|----------|--------|
| Yes | 3 |
| No | 2 |

and the individual characters of each, we can count the matches between the actual responses and the correct responses

| Template | Actual | Match Ratio |
|----------|--------|-------------|
| Yes | ys | 2/3 |
| No | ys | 0/2 |

The denominator of the match ratio is the length of the template; the numerator is the number of matching characters.

A match ratio of one indicates the input response is an exact match; a ratio of zero indicates a response that is unintelligible. For values between zero and one, we can choose the response for which the input response produces the highest match ratio. Criteria other than 0, 1, and highest match ratio might be developed, but the principle is the same. For a good example of matching student responses with "prototype essay answers" in computer correction of exams, the reader should see Meadow (1970).

## Summary

In using a computer (or other machine) to collect and process data, to make inquiries, or to update data, we are engaged in a dialogue. The form of the dialogue usually consists of commands and data values entered by the human and prompts and responses supplied by the machine. This involves both a technology (input devices, output devices) and a form of the dialogue (a protocol or set of protocols) to control the generation of legal (intelligible) commands, and legal data values (by using limit checks, etc.), as well as their recognition. Both parties to the dialogue must be able to generate and recognize certain categories or statements. For example, in 24-hr banking, the human generates commands, such as "withdraw" or "deposit," and queries (polite commands), such as "show me my balance"; the computer generates declarative statements, such as "The menu of commands is..." and "your balance is...." In addition to the "normal conversation" of the user and system, some means of detecting errors (limit checks, command dictionaries), talking about them (error messages), and recovering from them (please reenter) must be devised.

The purpose of the dialogue is the production of the correct action on the part of the system, e.g., dispensing $50 or recording a sale. This "action" will be correct only if the message has been received properly in a physical sense (entered and received as an $a$, recognized as the response "yes"). These are the levels of physical transmission of signals and the interpretation of the message. The interpretation is based on the "words" used (the lexicon), e.g., *yes* and *no* or "letter $E$ in column 1," and, in applications requiring more than a single word or symbol, the syntactic ordering of these symbols. The syntactic ordering concerns the physical arrangement of the words, e.g., the command

  BASIC run

will not be as effective as the command

  run BASIC

While both symbols exist in the lexicon (dictionary), the syntactic ordering of the symbols is incorrect in the first example, just as the syntax of the sentence

  To the store go

is incorrect in standard English. We will treat these concerns (physical transmission, legal symbols or words, syntactic ordering of words, semantic interpretation of the entire phrase [i.e., what the phrase means], and action taken upon the command) in considering the communication model.

## Related Readings

Barr, Avron and Feigenbaum, Edward A., eds., *The Handbook of Artificial Intelligence: Volume I*, Los Altos, CA: William Kaufman, Inc., 1981.

Barr, Avron and Feigenbaum, Edward A., eds., *The Handbook of Artificial Intelligence: Volume II*, Los Altos, CA: William Kaufman, Inc., 1982.

Card, Stuart K., Moran, Thomas P., and Newell, Allen, *The Psychology of Human-Computer Interaction*, Hillsdale, NJ: Lawrence Erlbaum Associates, 1983.

Clark, Herbert H. and Clark, Eve V., *Psychology and Language: An Introduction to Psycholinguistics*, New York: Harcourt Brace Jovanovich, 1977.

Cohen, Paul R. and Feigenbaum, Edward A., eds., *The Handbook of Artificial Intelligence: Volume III*, Los Altos, CA: William Kaufman, Inc., 1982.

Hanes, Lewis. Class notes, 1975.

Lancaster, F. W. and Fayen, E. G., *Information Retrieval On-Line*, Los Angeles: Melville Publishing Company, 1973.

Ledeen, K. S., "Recognizer developed at Harvard University for DEC PDP-1," in Newman, William M. and Sproull, Robert F., *Principles of Interactive Computer Graphics*, New York: McGraw-Hill, 1973.

Martin, James, *Design of Man-Computer Dialogues*, Englewood Cliffs, NJ: Prentice-Hall, 1973.

Martin, James, *Systems Analysis for Data Transmission*, Englewood Cliffs, NJ: Prentice-Hall, 1972.

McCormick, Ernest J. and Sanders, Mark S., *Human Factors in Engineering and Design*, 5th ed. New York: McGraw-Hill, 1982.

Meadow, Charles T., *Man-Machine Communication*, New York, John Wiley & Sons, 1970.

Newman, William, M. and Sproull, Robert F., *Principles of Interactive Computer Graphics*, 2nd ed. New York: McGraw-Hill, 1979.

Rosch, Eleanor and Lloyd, Barbara B., eds., *Cognition and Categorization*, Hillsdale, NJ: Lawrence Erlbaum Associates, 1978.

Salton, Gerard and McGill, Michael J., *Introduction to Modern Information Retrieval*, New York: McGraw-Hill, 1983.

Solso, Robert L., *Cognitive Psychology*, New York: Harcourt Brace Jovanovich, 1979.

Teitelman, W., "A Display Oriented Programmer's Assistant." Xerox Palo Alto Research Center, CSL, 77-3, 1977.

Teitelman, W., "Real Time Recognition of Hand-drawn Characters." *EJCC*. Baltimore, MD: Spartan Books, p. 559, 1964.

Van Cott, Harold P. and Kinkade, Robert G., eds., *Human Engineering Guide to Equipment Design*, revised edition. New York: McGraw-Hill, 1963.

# 16
# The Communication Model

## Objectives

Upon completion of this chapter the reader should be able to:

1. List and explain the various components of the communication model, giving one or more examples of each.
2. List and explain "the" three levels of communication. (These three are not the only possible hierarchy; a particular model developed by Weaver [1980] is discussed.)
3. Give examples of commands, questions, and statements in human/computer dialogue.
4. Distinguish between the lexicon, syntax, and semantics of a language.
5. Distinguish between terminal and nonterminal symbols (words) in discussing languages.
6. Explain the use of the term *protocol* in regard to human/computer conversation.
7. Distinguish between the evaluation of a computer system (hardware and software) and the evaluation of the information system it serves.
8. Discuss the terms *mean time between failures* and *mean time to repair* in terms of hardware reliability.
9. Distinguish between the concepts of reliability and availability.
10. Discuss some of the issues in language design in regard to lexical and syntactic issues.
11. Indicate how noise can interfere with the message transmitted and how redundancy in the message can be used to combat noise.
12. Explain the use of ciphers and the means of using probabilities of letters, letter pairs (or sequences), and words to decipher encoded messages.
13. Distinguish between simplex (one-way) and duplex (two-way) transmission.
14. Explain the use of feedback in controlling conversation.

When discussing communication between two "points" (whether these be two humans, terminals, or a human and a computer program), use is often

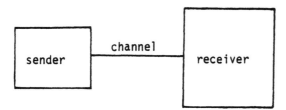

FIGURE 16.1

made of the communication model developed by Shannon and Weaver (1980). The simplest form of the model involves the two "terminal points" or "end points" of the communication process and the channel between them (Figure 16.1). The sender or "source" is the originator of the message. The receiver (or "destination" or "sink") is the target of the message. The channel is the physical medium by which the message is sent.

The message itself is intended to convey information: a statement being made by the sender (the sender "generates" the message), or a request or command. The means by which the message is imposed on the medium varies with the channel used. The task of the receiver is to "decode" the message, i.e., to physically receive it, to recognize it, and, ideally, to understand and act on it.

## Levels of Transmission

The tasks delineated for the receiver of the message are summarized in a three-level hierarchy by Weaver (1980), which can be represented graph-

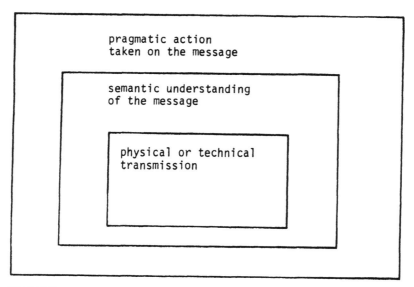

FIGURE 16.2

ically as shown in Figure 16.2. Weaver and Shannon caution the reader that the mathematical theory of communication addresses only the innermost level, the physical transmission of messages. However, others have found both the theory and the model to be useful in a variety of applications.

## Meaning of the Levels

The lowest level of transmission is the physical level, the transmission of signals from here to there. This is in part a technical consideration, concerning the development and use of suitable communication channels. However, it can be a behavioral issue, e.g., in influencing a person to turn her television set to a certain channel (by having excellent programs) so that she might see our commercial.

This latter influence, the persuasion to "tune in" to a given television channel or radio program, or to buy a certain newspaper or magazine, is usually the result of "prior messages," the action taken as a result of receiving, understanding, and being influenced by such messages. Hence, we will restrict our discussion to the physical media and the "modulation" of those media at the "technical" or "physical" level of communication. The modulation of the medium refers to the changes imposed on the medium in order to "convey" a message. The term *convey* is appropriate because the medium "carries" the message from the sender to the receiver.

## Physical Media

One of the simplest media to consider in the conveyance of messages is a beam of light, such as that used by Paul Revere. The beam carries the message from sender to receiver. There is no other "physical medium" in that the light could just as well be traveling through a vacuum as through the air.

The modulation of the beam is to turn it on or off. Hence, it might be more accurate to say that the "presence or absence" of the beam, its existence or nonexistence, is the "true" carrier. It will be simper, however, to simply refer to the beam as the carrier.

The use of an on-off mechanism of modulation is not the only possible means of "changing the value of" (modulating) the beam. We could have varied the intensity (very bright equaling "the British are coming"; dim equaling "they are not coming"). Or, if we had plastic coverings of various colors, we could have sent "red" for "coming," "green" for "not coming."

We will return to a consideration of messages, the codes that represent the messages, and the physical media in which these codes are represented later in the chapter. For our purposes at this time, it is enough to realize that the physical transmission of the message involves the "movement" of physical signals from one point to another. In terms of human speech, we would have sound waves moving from the speaker to the receiver of the spoken utterance.

## The Second Level: Understanding

The second "level of transmission" is understanding the message. This involves the recognition of the signal that has been received as a meaningful word or phrase (several signals may be needed to create a "word" and several words may be needed to create a phrase or sentence).

The words used in a dialogue may be as simple as a single letter (or symbol) or they may consist of a group of symbols. In devising a code, the single digits 1, 2, 3, or 4 may stand for the statements "This person is a freshman," "This person is a sophomore," etc., so that a single symbol represents an entire sentence. On the other hand, in considering the words of a natural language, such as English, or those of an artificial language, such as the programming languages Pascal or FORTRAN, a sequence of symbols may be necessary to form a single word. Hence, the word *balloon* requires seven symbols; the "begin" of the begin-end pair in compound statements of Pascal requires five characters, yet is considered a "single symbol"; identifiers, such as the variable name ISUM are composed of several symbols, but are considered to represent "a single thing," so that they are more like English words.

Thus, we may have

- Single symbol "words" (+ in Pascal)
- Multicharacter "single symbols" (begin)
- Multisymbol words (balloon, ISUM)

The entire set of words of a given language is called its "lexicon." These words are constructed from the legal symbols of the language. Hence, we need to know both

1. The legal symbols
2. The rules for constructing (and recognizing) words made from these symbols

and, in order to "understand" the word, we need to know the correspondence between the word and the "real world" entity or event that it represents.

## The Domain of Discourse

We enclose "real world" in quotes because what is considered the real world may vary from one arena to another. It is defined by the "domain of discourse," the things we have agreed that we are "talking about."

## Restricted Domains

In everyday conversation, the real world comprises "things and happenings in general," and words such as *dog* and *running* are used to represent commonly known things and events (at least to older children and adults). In the conversation between a "phone caller" and the operator of the phone company staffing the information desk, the domain of discourse is much more restricted, with such requests as "What is John Doe's number, please?" being acceptable, such statements as "I feel great" being a little surprising.

The restriction of the domain of discourse usually enhances our ability to understand an utterance, since only a fairly well defined set of utterances are allowed to have meaning (or allowed to be spoken). Hence, in the context of a phone number information system, the question "What is John

Doe's number?" is fairly unambiguous. In general discourse, it might mean "John's locker number," "his age," "his phone number," "his lucky number," and so on. In the context of watching a football game, an activity that implicitly delineates a domain of discourse, the phrase "his number" presumably would refer to the number on John's jersey.

Most human/computer conversations occur in "restricted domains." Hence, in talking to the editor ed, legal commands are

p
a
d

Each has a well-defined meaning (i.e., print a line, go into append mode, delete a line of text).

## Type of Utterances

We have not yet distinguished between the various types of discourse. The menu of utterances in human dialogue includes declarative statements, questions (or interrogatives), exclamations, commands, and requests (polite commands). Of these, the ones more commonly encountered in human/machine dialogue are the command, the question, and the statement. For the most part, the human gives commands

ed my file   (request to use editor)
Let A=5   (assign value 5 to variable A)

and questions

Find red not high

which might be interpreted as a command, but is most often looked upon as a question posed by the human.

The computer, on the other hand, is usually involved in making such statements as

003, 006   (the list of wine IDs)

or performing such operations as

5 + 6 $\longrightarrow$ 11

It "does work" or "makes statements."

## Understanding

In examining the second level of transmission, the level of understanding or extracting meaning from the signals transmitted, we must consider the rules by which statements are generated and recognized (the sender generates, the receiver recognizes). The first requisite is the recognition of the legal words. This may be done in a table lookup, e.g., matching the input words against a list of "key words" (Table 16.1), in which the "external" key word (e.g., *while*) may be replaced by an internal code (the "token") for convenience of processing. Alternate methods, such as a hardwired connection between a function key (say "reserve") and the program or hardware corresponding to that key may also be devised.

TABLE 16.1

| Pascal Keywords | Code |
| --- | --- |
| Program | 0 |
| Cons | 1 |
| Type | 2 |
| Var | 3 |
| Begin | 4 |
| End | 5 |
| If | 6 |
| While | 7 |
| . | . |
| . | . |
| . | . |

In addition to recognizing the words, the receiver must recognize the order in which the words are arranged, e.g.

To store go the

vs.

Go to the store

This is referred to as the "syntactic order" or syntax of the statement. While humans are often forgiving of such displaced words as "to store go the," computers are less capable of flexible meaning extraction. Hence, in BASIC, the command

GOTO 100

will cause a transfer of control to line 100. But, the command

TOGO 100

will generate only a *what?* The recognition of the words is called lexical analysis. The recognition of larger constructs derived from the ordering of the words is called syntactical analysis.

Lexical Analysis

In terms of a computer language, the assignment statement

AVE = SUM/3.0

would result in the recognition of the words shown in Table 16.2. As the results of the lexical analysis indicate, the words of the language belong to certain categories or classes of things: variable, constant, operator. These are similar to the general categories used to describe the role of English words: subject, predicate, object, sentence. These descriptor words are not part of the language itself, but used to "talk about" or define and describe the language. They are often called "nonterminal symbols," because they must eventually be transformed into a word of the "target language." Thus, they never appear in the "end result" and are "nonterminal." The actua words of the language are considered terminal in that they are the "end result.

TABLE 16.2

| Computer language | Words |
|---|---|
| AVE | variable |
| = | assignment operator |
| sum | variable |
| / | division operator |
| 3.0 | numeric constant |

The words used to describe a language are often referred to as a "metalanguage," a language "above" or "outside" the language we are describing. The author prefers the interpretation "outside" since "above" seems to imply superiority. The intent is simply to show "distinctness" or "differentness" between the two languages. The one, target language, speaks about "real world objects"

He hit the ball.

The other—the metalanguage—speaks about the terminal language itself. Hence, to parse "He hit the ball"

<subject><verb><article><object>

The metalanguage has simply categorized the words according to their role in the sentence

*He* is the subject; *hit* is the verb, etc.

In the computer language that was used in expressing the assignment statement

AVE = SUM/3.0

the "real world" objects are locations in the computer, and the "events" are operations performed on the contents of these locations, e.g., moving objects to them (store), fetching objects from them, and passing values through an adder or multiplier.

### Syntactic Analysis

The syntax of a language imposes restrictions on the manner in which the words of the language may be arranged. These restrictions are normally phrased in terms of the categories of objects rather than in terms of the words themselves. This allows for a few rules to account for or regulate a large number of cases. Thus, we do not say

"John hit the ball." is OK
"Mary hit the ball." is OK
"John painted the house." is OK

but that the "form"

<subject><verb><article><object>

is OK. This covers not only the above subjects, actions, and objects, but ones that might arise "anew" as people are born, new activities (twirling a Frisbee) initiated, and new objects (television in the early part of the century, the Frisbee itself) created.

## The Prerequisites of Meaning

The level of physical transmission is a prerequisite to the level of understanding. We cannot understand a message if we do not receive it. This
"link" between sender and receiver is provided by the channel: the air
waves in human speech done face to face, the communication lines in telephone usage. As the examples indicate, the distance over which a message may be successfully carried (it gets to the destination and the destination can recognize it) varies with the physical implementation of the channel. Face-to-face conversation is limited to few hundred feet (even when
yelling), and is usually done within a few feet. Human conversation carried
on over the phone can be done around the world, and as the conversations
with astronauts indicate, throughout the universe.

The use of a mutually agreed upon code (language) is also a prerequisite for the transference of meaning. This implies the use of the correct
symbols and words, arrayed in the proper order. However, none of the
elements alone, nor their conjunction, can ensure the transfer of meaning.
That physical transmission alone is not sufficient is obvious to any traveler
in a foreign country. The fact that I utter "I wish a platter of bagels,
lox, cream cheese, and capers," and the waiter in a Milanese restaurant
"hears" the message, does not ensure that he understands it. And, lacking
understanding, it is doubtful that he will provide the desired dish.

The difficulty in the English-Italian example is the lack of a mutually
agreed upon code. However, even with such a code, we can run into difficulties. For example, the phrase "random access files that use a hashing
scheme may result in collisions that can be resolved by looking for the next
available location with some disadvantage in the creation of primary clusters'
may not be intelligible to all speakers of English.

The exact nature of "meaning" and how "we know the meaning of a
word, sentence, or phrase," and even the question of "how we know that
we know the meaning" are lively areas of research and debate. Fortunately,
we need not wait for their resolution in order to send, receive, and understand messages. Presuming that the sender and receiver can agree on a
common meaning for a set of messages, we can look for the conditions that
are prerequisite to or necessary for such comprehension by the receiver:
(1) physical transmission (the modulated signal), or (2) the correct symbols
or words (the lexicon), and (3) these words being arranged in the "proper
order" (the syntactic order designated by the language or code).

## Semantics

The term *semantics* is used to refer to the level of meaning. The use of the
term varies somewhat when applied to natural languages as opposed to computer languages. In natural languages, the usage is what we intuitively
expect. Such statements as "John hit the ball" are taken to refer to real
world objects (John, the ball) and real world events (hitting the ball).
Declarative statements are usually descriptive, or in some cases, explana-
tory in content: "The window broke because the ball hit it." Statements
such as the imperatives: "Please, pass the salt"; and interrogatives: "What
is your name?" can be transformed into declaratives of the sort

"I wish that you would pass the salt."

or

"It would please me if you would pass the salt."

"I wish to know your name."

or

"It would please me if you would tell me your name."

However, it will be useful to distinguish between the three types of utterances

Command:  print myfile
Question:  find all red wines
Declaration:  the red wines are 1, 3, 4, 6

When discussing computer languages, the term semantics refers both to straightforward cases of manipulating data and to "context-dependent" situations, e.g., the rules against multiply defined variables.

In the straightforward case, an assignment statement, such as

A = B * C

has the "meaning"

1. Fetch the value of B.
2. Fetch the value of C.
3. Multiply these two values.
4. Place the result in the location A.

With one exception, the meaning of the statement is a straightforward translation of the symbols (or tokens) in the sentence. No other statements have to be taken into account in order to derive the meaning of the assignment statement. The sentence is a command, not a description, although the command does describe what actions are commanded. Barring hardware or software failures, the command will be carried out, which is not always the case in statements directed to humans, such as "Please pass the salt." The one exception in considering the assignment statement is the consideration of data types. The variables A, B, and C have to be of compatible data types, e.g., all reals or all integers, or B and C real, A integer, etc., or be converted into compatible types.

In computer programming languages, there is usually some means by which to declare the type of variable. The type of declaration indicates that a variable is of a certain type

Integer A
Integer B
Integer C

or

Integer A,B,C

both of which say that the variables A, B, and C will be interpreted as holding integral values (whole numbers) rather than "reals" (with decimal or fraction parts, such as 3.14).

Rules are imposed on the declaration of variables, such as "A variable can be declared only once." Rules are also imposed on the manipulation of variables, such as "only variables of the same type (or compatible types) can be added together." These rules require the examination of the "history" of prior statements (which is kept in a table of variables and their types, called the symbol table) in order to see if the rules are being kept.

Hence, in examining the sequence

Integer A
Integer B
Integer C
Real    A

the compiler (translator of a computer language) must "flag" the second declaration of A as illegal. Similarly, in examining the assignment statement

A = B * C

the compiler must check that the variables A, B, and C are all integers or all reals. If not, then they must be converted to compatible types (integers can be promoted to reals or reals truncated to integers) or the computation will be disallowed.

These considerations of "history" or "context" are applicable to natural language statements as well. For example, if someone uttered the sentences

Because of his sprained ankle John did not play today. John hit the winning home run.

we would protest the speaker "is not making sense."

In most cases, however, the derivation of meaning in computer languages is more constrained than the derivation of meaning from natural language utterances. The statement

A = 5

means store the value of 5 in A. The effect of "context" is less broad. Natural languages are "richer in meaning" while computer languages, due to the limited number of statements and contexts, are easier to handle.

## The Rules of Discourse: Protocols

In human-to-human conversation, as in human/machine conversation, there are rules of discourse, called "protocols," which govern such things as who can speak when. There is also some agreement on the things being talked about, the "domain of discourse." While linguists refer to the rules of discourse when discussing the pragmatics of language, they are not what Weaver (1980) had in mind in his three-tiered hierarchy at the level of pragmatics. Weaver was referring to actions taken on the messages received. The "pragmatics" or "rules" of discourse discussed here, protocols, would apply more to the levels of successful transmission (if two people talk simultaneously, the message is garbled), and the level of meaning (the common domain of discourse enables correct interpretation of the messages). Later discussion will address the actions taken on messages, i.e., the pragmatics of the Weaver model. In order to discuss the transmission of messages in a more detailed fashion, we expand the communication model to include the encoding and decoding of the messages being sent and received.

## Expanding the Model

The model encompassing the encoding/decoding process is shown in Figure 16.3. At the physical level, this might represent sending the letter *a* from

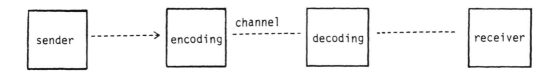

FIGURE 16.3

the user's terminal to the computer. The process would involve the hitting of the key (A); its being encoded into a series of 1s and 0s (different frequencies or different amplitudes of a carrier signal)

A        1000001
            $\longrightarrow$

the transmission of the signals (physical movement) across the medium (electric wire pair, microwave "path," or other communications channel); the physical reception at the receiving end, with the "bit stream" being decoded into the letter A

1000001 $\longrightarrow$ A

and the interpretation of the A by the receiver.


## Interpreting the A

The interpretation of the letter A by the receiver depends on the context in which the message is being sent. The letter A may have a meaning in itself, say "place the editor in append mode," or it may be part of a larger construct, say part of the command "Archive," which might be used to save disk files on a magnetic tape.

The interpretation must be made according to the "rules" in force at the time. This is why a command to print the table of contents of a disk directory (group of files), such as DIR, is intelligible when "speaking to the monitor," but not intelligible when speaking to the basic editor and interpreter. Similarly, the command LIST is intelligible to the basic editor and interpreter, but not to the monitor (the command interpreter of the operating system).

In order to converse, we need

1.  A common language
2.  A domain of discourse
3.  The protocols for speaking at the right time

The common language may be a natural language or it may be an artificial one, such as COBOL or the command language of the monitor.

## Choosing the Language

The choice of a language is usually explicitly made in using a computer. The choice is actually a combination of choices made by the provider of the computer, computer services, and the user of these facilities. For example, when one "logs on," one "chooses" to use the command language of the computer. This might be considered an implicit choice in that we do not "explicitly agree" to use the language. However, one can look at the choice of a particular computer and operating system as an explicit choice. Subsequent choices are explicit in the sense of choosing a programming language: R BASIC, a utility, R SORT, or some other facility of the system, each having its predefined language.

While we do not always think of it, such choices are also made in using natural languages. They might be done tacitly, as when I speak English (because I am living in an English-speaking country) and you respond in English. Or, they might be done explicitly, as when we agree to practice our French. Some families vary the language with the context, speaking one language at home (say Italian), another in public (say English). The only difficulties arise when one person speaks in a given language, say English, and the other responds in a second language, say Dutch, and, going through a process of trial and error, no common language is attained. Conversation stops; while the physical signals are getting through, mutual comprehension is blocked by the lack of a common code.

## The Protocols

In using a computer language, the rules for "who speaks when" are controlled by the use of "prompts." The prompt tells us it is our turn to speak. As indicated earlier, in menu driven languages, the computer will normally initiate the conversation by listing our choices

1. Withdraw
2. Deposit
3. See balance

then prompt us for our response

Please enter number

In command languages, the prompt appears first

?

indicating that it is our turn right away; we speak first and the computer responds.

In either case, the computer must know when it is its turn to speak. Its turn comes when we are done speaking, which is usually indicated by the carriage return (or new line or enter) key (character) that we transmit at the end of our response. In fact, the computer being quite polite, if we forgot to type the return, will wait indefinitely for us to "finish speaking," unless some "timeout" mechanism has been implemented.

These activities of human/machine dialogue reflect similar processes in human-to-human conversation. For example, "switching" from my turn to your turn is often accomplished by pauses at the end of the utterance. In casual conversation, say on the bus, the initiator of the conversation may be arbitrary (whoever asks about the weather first) although it is not guaranteed that the other will agree to participate in the conversation. In more structured environments, such as calling the phone company's information service, we initiate the conversation by dialing the number. In terms of the actual dialogue, the called party may initiate the conversation

"May I help you?"

Although a curt

"Yes."

is a prompt to us, telling us it is our turn (or duty) to initiate the dialogue.

## Choosing the Domain

The choice of a domain of discourse in human/machine dialogue varies with the facility used. For example, in the use of a data base, we select a retrieval system (DIALOG, ORBIT, BRS, or PIRETS), which specifies the language (find, combine, etc.); and we select a data base to choose the domain of discourse. The contents of the data base and its indices will dictate the terms (index terms, words in the document) that will be "recognizable." In choosing a "sort package," the domain of discourse is restricted to specifying file names, columns on which to begin and end sorting, directives as to the direction of the sort, and the like.

In choosing a programming language, the objects referred to by the language are the variables and constants of the language, and the storage locations are designated by these. Statements are usually restricted to describing these objects (declaring data types and structures) as in the statements

Integer A

or

A:  Array [1..10] of characters

and to declaring operations that should be performed on these objects, such as

Multiply A by B giving C

or

A = 5
Call SQRT (X)

## Assymetry in Conversation

In human discourse (between two or more humans) we often have symmetrical discussions. All parties are equal and the types of statements are varied among declarations, requests, and questions

Please pass the salt.
Here you are.
Thank you.

What did you do at school today?
.
.
.

Of course, some situations give rise to asymmetrical situations. For example, in classroom lecture mode, the instructor gives declarative statements (explaining topics) and commands (homework); the students are usually relegated to asking questions, or to answering declaratively to a "command performance" requested by the instructor. This asymmetry is usually dropped outside of class, say in conversation in the student union, although considerations of status (based on position, age, etc.) may dictate certain forms of address

    Hello, Mrs. Jones  (student speaking)
    Hello, Johnny  (teacher speaking)


Asymmetry of Conversing With a Machine

Conversations between human and machine are usually asymmetric. While a machine may be programmed to give us a pithy comment or cheery hello when we "log on," the conversation usually settles into the format shown in Figure 16.4. The human can also indicate noncomprehension, not usually by a beep on a "what?", but by using a "help" command.


Formats of the Various Statement Types

Since we are considering statements that are of various types

    1. Declarative
    2. Imperative
    3. Interrogative

it will be useful to consider the formats of each. We begin with the type of statement most frequently transmitted from human to computer, the command.


- Operator gives commands (for action) or requests for information (polite commands, but commands for data)

- The computer responds by:

    a. performing the requested action (response to a command, e.g., loading the Basic interpreter in response to R BASIC)
    b. providing the requested information (data), e.g., a list of all wines that are "red" and "not high priced"
    c. indicating its lack of comprehension of the command (error messages, beeps, blinking displays)

FIGURE 16.4

## The Format of Commands

Since commands usually require the computer to "do something" "with something" (i.e., they consist of an instruction part [what to do] and a data part [with what]), we need to indicate "which is which." The rules for indicating instructions (or operations) and data (or operands or arguments) vary with the language being used. Hence, in arithmetic or algebra, we have

    5 + 7
    a + b

to indicate the sum of 5 and 7 or the sum of a and b. The expression is referred to as "infix," because the operator is on the "inside." Other rules are possible. The expression

    ab+

is in "postfix," a notation popular in the interpretation and evaluation of arithmetic expressions by a compiler. There is also "prefix"

    +ab

with the operator coming first. The terms prefix, infix, and postfix all refer to the position of the operator

    Prefix:   operator first
    Postfix:  operator last
    Infix:    operator in the middle

The interested reader is referred to texts on data structures or compilers for further study.

The command or request to use the editor

    $UPDATE
      or
      ed

is usually followed by the name of the file to be edited

    ed    myfile

Since the command (operation) comes first (ed) and the argument second (myfile), the format is prefix. Most commands to the monitor are in prefix

    type myfile
    compile myfile
    execute myfile

The length of the argument list may vary. For example, the command

    DIR

requesting the printing of the file names in the directory can take on zero arguments, indicating "this directory," "all file names."

The type command takes one or more arguments

    type onefile
    type filea, fileb

The conventions as to number and position of arguments must be known by both user and system, i.e., a protocol must be set.

Arguments to functions or subroutines are often given in parentheses attached to the subroutine name in the "call"

    CALL SQUARE (a,b)

and "received" by the subroutine in its "parameter list" (formal argument list)

    SUBROUTINE SQUARE (X,Y)
    Y = X*X
    RETURN

The value of the variable a will be associated with X; the value of b will be associated with Y. In this routine, b may be initially undefined; the value of Y will be computed in the subroutine, and will be "returned" to b on completion.

Note that the position of the variables makes a difference in the communication between the main routine and the subroutine. The call

    CALL SQUARE (b,a)

will give different results than the call

    CALL SQUARE (a,b)

In fact, if b is undefined, the first call will either generate an error message or produce garbage as a result.

Arguments that are given "positionally" are often more difficult to remember than "tagged" arguments. For example, the job control language (JCL) statement

    $JOB(PPN) (30,2,32)

may indicate

    Time:  30 seconds
    Priority Class:  2
    Core Requested:  32K

where the position "first" indicates time, "second" indicates priority, and "third" indicates core size. If one does not wish to designate a priority, accepting the "default," one needs to indicate this by two adjacent commas

    $JOB(PPN) (30,,32)

This is the sort of thing that leads to JCLs being considered "mysterious." The mystery can be removed by adding tags to the fields

    $JOB(PPN) (Time=30,Priority=2,Core=32)

where the tags remove the necessity for placing the arguments in a given physical order. The command

    $JOB(PPN) (Priority=2,Core=32,Time=30)

is as easily interpreted as the first version. And the absence of a field can be indicated by the absence of the tag.

Tagged fields are somewhat more difficult to handle by a programmer (the systems programmer). He or she must "look for" the tags and keep a list of which ones have been set and which have not. However, they are usually more palatable to the end user.

An example of commands given in postfix is the print command in the editor (ed) that is used with the UNIX system. (UNIX is an operating system, not an editor, but ed is one of the editors that often "comes with" UNIX.) The format of the command is

1,3 p

where the command is p (print) and the arguments are the line numbers, here 1 and 3, indicating print lines 1 through 3.

## Format of Questions

The format of commands gives an instruction (what to do) and arguments or data (with what). The format of the interrogatives gives a descriptor, the thing being sought, and requests information about the entity. The two primary forms of asking questions are the following:

- Give ID, request attributes
- Give attributes, request ID

The former is illustrated in retrieving data on an employee, a student, a wine, etc., by giving the identification field: social security number, employee number, student number, wine number, and the like. The item retrieved would normally be unique, and the record would include the secondary attributes of the entity. This is the type of retrieval suitable to files organized by key: indexed sequential, random access, ordered sequential, and even unordered sequential. The assumption is that the key "is available" to the user or application program. This is the case in a large number of applications: e.g., requesting graduate transcripts, processing payroll files, processing transactions in a bank or department store, and accessing books by the catalogue number. The problem is not one of "identifying" the necessary information, but of accessing it, i.e., considerations of file organization and retrieval methods are important in regard to performance, but the consideration of finding "an answer" to our question is not particularly problematic. "Questions" of this sort can be thought of as commands

| Operation | Argument |
|-----------|----------|
| Retrieve  | ID       |

The more interesting and difficult problem of retrieval comes in the questions that describe an abstract entity or a "goal entity," requesting the system to find concrete entities that match the description. The procedure involves two distinct processes

- The formulation of the question
- The recognition of the answer

The question must be formulated in a manner that specifies the domain of entities (or subjects) that are being "searched through." Hence, in looking for someone with work experience in data processing and electronics, we must specify whether the set of individuals being considered is "our own personnel," "all the people in Pittsburgh," "all the people in the United

States," and so on. This is the selection of the data base. The second part of formulating the question is the specification of the attributes, say "data processing experience" and "electronics experience," that identify the type of person or entity we seek. These are the queries that are put to the data base.

The specification of the question often involves an interplay between user needs and system design in that the attributes "recorded" may constrain our choice of descriptors. In searching a 1022 data base, the attributes described in the DDL are the only ones that may be queried. In systems that allow full text searching, and that match query words against words in a document using "all words" in the document as searchable text, more flexibility is permitted in specifying the request.

In using automated query systems, the recognition of the answer is often considered the task of the system: if the system can find a record with secondary attributes that match our request. However, in the broader picture, it is the task of the person retrieving the data to recognize appropriate responses to his or her questions, rejecting inappropriate data and possibly reformulating the question.

While much work has been done in the area of implementing information retrieval systems, the theory of question formulation and answer recognition is relatively unexplored. Some work is being done in the areas of logic (Belnap and Steel, 1976) and artificial intelligence (Lehnert, 1978), but the area is in need of more work in terms of formal analysis to guide the implementation efforts.

## Declarative Statements

The use of declaratives is made in presenting the data to the user. As indicated earlier, the response to a query

Red wines are 1, 3, 4, 6

is a declarative statement. So is the output from a program. For example, the response

11

to the "program"

```
LET A = 5
LET B = 6
LET C = A + B
PRINT C
```

is interpreted as the statement

The sum is 11.

While the output is "obviously" a declaration, the same analysis can be performed on input data.

The formulation of the attributes input into a query system are descriptions of the thing desired

It is red and high priced.
(Description by categories or attributes)

or

It has name 001.
(Description by unqiue name or ID)

While these descriptions are of an entity other than oneself, there are several occasions in which one describes oneself. For example, in "logging in," the use of a "user number" and "password" is a description of oneself as a legal user: "I am so-and-so, and you will find me on the 'guest list.'" In some speculation about retrieval systems, it is expected that future systems will be able to accept statements describing the user and adjust the system to his or her needs.

Input data submitted to programs (computational programs instead of query languages) can also be considered as declarative statements. The placement of a value in a data file (or on a card)

Data 5

in conjunction with the command to read

Read A

is interpreted as the statement

The value of the variable A is 5.

As the example indicates, the interpretation of the data is provided by the program. The data itself

40,5

is uninterpreted. However, if the program segment for reading and computation is

Read Hours-Worked, Rate-of-Pay
Gross Pay=Hours-Worked * Rate-of-Pay

the interpretation is

- 40 is the number of hours worked
- $5 is the rate-of-pay

## Instructions and Data

In general, there are really two forms of statements put to the computer

- Commands
- Declarations

the commands indicate operations to be performed

- Compute the sum
- Find the value of the attribute "price" for the entity "wine ID=001"

The arguments (data values) given to the commands are the declarations naming or describing the objects (or events) to be manipulated (computed) or found out about (the object of the query).

## Data Lists

Lists of data, such as

| City | Population |
|------|-----------|
| Pgh | 500,000 |
| NY | 250,000 |
| . | |
| . | |
| . | |

are "implicit" declaratives, summarizing such statements as "The population of New York is 250,000," as well as implicitly defining the domain of discourse: "The cities of interest are...." The study of "assertions" is well developed in the study of logic (manipulating and combining statements), the study of science (generating and verifying statements), and the study of communication (linguistics, rhetoric, psychology). Some of these principles have been transferred to the area of human/machine communication. However, this is another area needing research.

## The Pragmatic Level: Action

The third level of communication in the Weaver model is the level of pragmatics, which is interpreted as the action taken upon reception of the message. This level is applicable to various means of control: the control of a computer through the appropriate commands; control of human behavior through overtly persuasive techniques, such as advertising, and through less overt techniques, such as education; and the control of group behavior or "abstract entities," such as the economy. A full treatment of the various means of control is beyond the scope of this text; it is treated in texts on general systems theory and cybernetics. In terms of the model, the receiver of the message is expected to execute the action; the sender is attempting to control the production of the action by means of the message sent.

In controlling a machine such as a computer, the realm of action is limited, just as the realm of meaning was quite restricted compared to the variety of meaning in human-to-human discourse. When a command such as

```
.R BASIC
   or:
LET A=5
```

is given, we expect the machine to "do the appropriate thing": load the basic interpreter or place the value 5 in the location A.

## Advertising

In human-to-human discourse the realm of possible actions (responses) to the stimulus of the message is broader in scope. However, in most situations the sender has some well-defined action that he or she wishes to "bring about," e.g., the purchase of a product, say orange juice. It is in such situations that the "hierarchy" of the model becomes evident. Without the successful physical transmission of the message, it can never be understood, and without the intellectual comprehension of the message, it cannot be acted upon. In many situations, the physical transmission requires "cooperation" on the part of the receiver, e.g., turning to a particular chan-

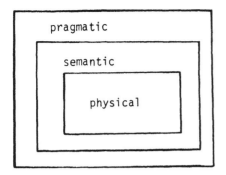

FIGURE 16.5

nel on the television set. This is where such ratings schemes as the Nielsen ratings or "market shares" become important to the advertiser. A heavily watched show, such as the Academy Awards or the Super Bowl, ensures that a greater portion of the audience will physically receive any advertisement broadcast during the show. Hence, these shows are priced more highly than a less popular presentation.

However, physical transmission alone is not sufficient to generate either comprehension or action. Hence, consideration of the format of the display, the dialogue used, etc., is necessary to ensure the "transfer of meaning." If the message is persuasive, considerations of "effective" stimuli are also a concern. Hence, we have the hierarchy shown in Figure 16.5.

The physical transmission is essential to any understanding of the message. I can't understand you unless I hear you, so the noise of a construction project next door may hinder our having a meaningful conversation.

However, hearing you is not enough. If you are speaking English and I understand only Russian, our conversation is hindered. While this level of understanding is labeled "semantic," it subsumes the lexical level (use of the "right words," i.e., the words of the language) and the syntactic level (use of proper structure, i.e., ordering of the words).

Finally, understanding a message is not the same as acting upon it, as any parent knows. I can understand your request that I open a window (or issue a grade of A) but I may not comply with the request.

## Conversation Versus Persuasion

The three-tiered communication model explicitly brings the concept of action into the model. It may be the case that the communication (i.e., the transfer of information) between people or between people and machines, is a goal (end result) in itself. This seems to be the case in many human conversations. It is less often the case in human/computer conversation. As we indicated earlier, most interactions with a computer involve commands (explicit, as in "Type my file," or in "polite form," as in queries). Hence, the three-tiered model is appropriate to these interactions.

While it may be difficult in some cases to motivate another human to "see our way" and perform some activities we designate, this should not be a difficulty in interacting with a computer. The computer is in the position of servant, slave, or subordinate agent to the human, i.e., it is designed to carry out human commands. Hence, if the physical transmission occurs correctly, and the commands have been entered with proper syntax and argument lists, we can expect our requests to be fulfilled.

## Evaluating Information Systems

In evaluating information systems, we can perform the analysis at each level. At the first level, such questions as

- Did the message get through in an error-free manner? (quality of transmission)
- Is the system up? (availability and reliability)

are applicable to the physical level. The first question, regarding quality of transmission, is a question pertinent to data communications (or voice/video communications)—a purely technical question.

The question of reliability is one of quality of equipment, i.e., a "hardware" question. In assessing reliability, such questions as "mean time between failures" (MTBF) and "mean time to repair" (MTTR) are applicable.

## MTBF and MTTR

The MTBF and the MTTR are averages computed on data about when the system was "up," when "down." Given the data

|       |       |
|-------|-------|
| Up:   | 40 hr |
| Down: | 2 hr  |
| Up:   | 20 hr |
| Down: | 1 hr  |

The MTBF would be 30 hr

$$\frac{(40 + 20)}{2} = \frac{60}{2} = 30$$

The mean time to repair would be 1.5 hr

$$\frac{2 + 1}{2} = 1.5 \text{ hr}$$

The MTBF tells us how long we are up on the average. The MTTR tells us how long we are down when we go down. A "good" MTBF is large; a good MTTR is small. These concepts apply to a variety of situations. For example, the MTBF for a car owner is the average time between trips to the mechanic. The MTTR is the average time in the repair shop. An owner with an MTBF of 6 months and an MTTR of 1 day, is better off than one with an MTBF of 1 day and an MTTR of 6 months.

## Availability

Availability of the system is tied to reliability. If a system is "down a lot," it is unavailable. However, the question of availability is a broader issue than that of reliability. It can be affected by other concerns, such as hours available. This is especially noticeable in using systems that are in another time zone. For example, if a system is "up" (in the sense of "open") from 9 to 5, daily, i.e., business days, in California, it is available only from noon to 8 P.M. in New York, due to differences in time. In terms of normal business hours, this means that the system is up only from noon to 5 in New York, so that it is less available on the East Coast.

The ultimate in availability is 24-hr 7-day-a-week availability, something the convenience grocery stores know well. This availability requires

- Reliable equipment, possibly with backup equipment
- Full operating hours, necessitating personnel round the clock

Hence both the hardware costs and the personnel costs will increase as we increase availability.

## Evaluation at the Semantic Level

The interpretation of commands (and argument lists) is a system function. Presumably, if the system's programming has been done correctly the system will understand such commands as

- type myfile
- dir

If it does not, we have a software problem (a program bug).

However, correct interpretation of commands is not enough. The system can be evaluated in terms of ease of use

- The choice of words and syntax in entering commands

and in terms of comprehensibility of output

- The format and display of results, whether computational results or data lists

## Ease of Use

In terms of ease of use (i.e., the ease with which commands and data may be entered), there are various levels of evaluation. We have already mentioned the differences between menu systems, that list the commands and prompts for data values, and command driven systems, in which the user initiates both the entry of commands and of data values. Some conclusions were that menu systems are preferable for either new users or casual users, command mode for trained, dedicated users. As the discussion indicated, this evaluation is "user dependent"; some systems are better for one type of user, others for another type. Similar considerations apply to the use of technology, e.g., the use of function keys versus the use of an alphanumeric keyboard. The function keys are "special purpose, but efficient"; the alphanumeric keyboard is "flexible, but less efficient." However, some considerations apply "across the board," i.e., to users of various types. Some of the following discussion will be technology dependent, e.g., assuming the use of an alphanumeric keyboard. However, many of the considerations apply "across technologies" as well. These questions concern the design of the language used in the dialogue and are answered in the terms of this language, primarily the syntax, although questions of lexicon do arise.

## The Design of Artificial Languages

The most common questions in the design of artificial languages are syntactic. With few exceptions, the size of the lexicon is limited, and the choice of words to represent a particular concept is also limited. Hence, in order to print a data value, one may say

- PRINT
- WRITE
- TYPE
- OUTPUT

or something similar to the "short list." Almost any of the commands will be suitable.

Exceptions do occur. For example, in the UNIX system, one says "cat" to cause the contents of a file to be typed. This is an historical accident. The program used to concantenate files (CAT) was found useful to print them as well. The original name was retained.

An instance of lexical "overuse" is the use of the plus (+) sign. It is commonly used to refer to the processes of

- Integer addition (e.g., 5 + 6)
- Floating point addition (e.g., 5.2 + 6.3)
- Concatenation of strings (e.g., "hot" + "dog")
- The Boolean OR (e.g., A + B)

Each of these operations involves either different parts of the computer (regular accumulators and adders versus floating point registers and adders) or different operations entirely (addition of numbers, concatenation of strings, combination of truth values).

Another instance is the use of the equal sign (=) to denote both assignment

LET C = A + B

and the comparison of values

IF (A = B) THEN C = 5

This use has been addressed in recent times by using such symbols as := or ← to indicate assignment

C: = A + B

reserving the equal sign for its proper use among the relational operators $(<,>,=)$.

Despite these instances of lexical choices that seem inappropriate or ambiguous, the primary difficulties in using systems seem to arise from syntactical matters.

## Syntactic Issues

We have already looked at one syntactic question, the form of delineating arguments. We compared a positional notation

(30, 2, 32)

with a tagged notation

(Time = 30, Priority = 2, Core = 32)

and indicated that the latter has more flexibility.

## Describing the Language

We can use a notation similar to BNF (Backus Naur form or Backus normal form) to describe the syntax and lexicon of the language (BNF was developed in conjunction with the ALGOL-60 report, which described the ALGOL "publication" language, a language later implemented as a programming language).

The notation uses "production rules" of the form

<sentence>⟶<subject><predicate><object>

which indicates that a subject "goes to" or "is formed from" a subject followed by a predicate followed by an object. Of course, there would be other forms of English sentences, but this will do for our current purposes. The words *sentence, subject, predicate,* and *object* are all "nonterminals"; they are words used to describe the language. The first rule takes one nonterminal (sentence) into a set of three nonterminals (subject, predicate, object). Other rules would take these nonterminals to terminals, e.g.

<subject> ⟶ John
<predicate> ⟶ kisses
<object> ⟶ Mary

finally yielding the sentence

John kisses Mary.

In this notation the nonterminals appear in angle brackets, the terminals without angle brackets. Also, the nonterminals always appear on the left of some rule (they go to something). The terminals never appear on the left (they don't go to anything).

With this rudimentary explanation we would describe the positional notation as

<argument-list>⟶(<time>,<priority>,<core>)

where the lefthand side (LHS) indicates that we are describing an argument list. The right-hand side (RHS) indicates that the list consists of a left parenthesis (a terminal symbol), followed by the time requirements (a nonterminal), followed by a comma (terminal), and so on. The nonterminal symbol on the right, such as "time," will eventually "go to" terminals, in this case integers, e.g.,

<core>⟶ integer in range 01-96

For our purposes, the point is that the syntax describes a strict ordering of the values for time, priority, and core

<time>,<priority>,<core>

A description of the tag fields would allow more flexibility. Using a notation similar to that in describing the COBOL language, we would have

<argument-list> ⟶ <tag>=<value>
                  { ,<tag>=<value>...}

where the word <tag> would eventually be replaced by words such as *core* or *priority*

       <tag>⟶   time
       <tag>⟶   priority
       <tag>⟶   core
       <value>⟶   integer in range 00-99

However, now the word core is "terminal," part of the language. The braces ({ }) indicate optional items, and the ellipsis (...) indicates "as many as we wish," i.e., we can repeat the pattern

       <tag> = <value>

as many times as we like, separating entries by a comma.


## Formal and Informal Descriptions

The formal description of a language is useful for an unambiguous description. In terms of programming languages, they are especially useful to compiler writers, who have to generate the language translator. They are also useful to programmers in order to determine the rules of the language, although it has been the experience of the author that they are not always consulted by programmers, possibly because of the symbolism. For our purposes in this chapter, we indicated the formal description to show how the positional notation "locked the order in," in contrast more flexible syntax. However, in discussing the remaining issues we abstract from the formal notation.


## Other Syntactic Issues

One issue that has been a thorn in the author's programming side is the placement of the semicolon in such languages as ALGOL and Pascal. The semicolon is considered a separator in Pascal. It separates statements

    WRITE ("HELLO");
    WRITE ("THERE")

If there is no statement "following," no semicolon is needed

    WRITE ("DONE")
    END.

    The "END." indicates the end of the program and is not a "statement" (not an executable statement). Since the write statement is the last statement, it does not require a semicolon "after it."
    This use of the semicolon as a separator is analogous to the use of a comma in a print statement

    PRINT A,B,C

However, while its usage in the print statement seems natural, the usage in a program to separate statements does not always "seem so natural." Both the list of variables in the print statement

    A,B,C

and the list of statements in a program

```
BEGIN
  WRITE;
  WRITE;
  WRITE
END.
```

are being treated as just that, lists of elements, with separators between the elements. It may be that a "list" on one line

```
PRINT A,B,C
```

is easier to visualize than a list "across lines"

```
BEGIN
  WRITE;
  WRITE;
  WRITE
END.
```

at least when the longer list becomes as complex as a program.

Languages such as COBOL require a period after every "complete" statement

```
MOVE A TO B.
ADD B TO C GIVING D.
```

Statements can be "combined," as in

```
MOVE A TO B
ADD B TO C GIVING D.
```

But each "sentence," simple or complex, ends in a period. This parallels our usage in forming English sentences.

Research into the use of language, especially in the area of the influence of syntax on ease of use (less mental effort) and correctness of use (fewer errors) is another area of "current interest." It is one that combines technical considerations with questions of language (linguistics) and psychology (especially cognitive psychology).


## Prefix, Postfix, and Infix

The question of the placement of the semicolon is one of "low-level" syntax. Although the form of the "terminating" symbol is one of concern to someone who has trouble "getting it right," it is not a very "substantive" question. At a somewhat "higher level," the question of postfix, prefix, and infix is one of syntax. The "forms" in question are

```
<operand><operator><operand>
        (infix)
```

```
<operator><operand><operand>
        (prefix)
```

```
<operand><operand><operator>
        (postfix)
```

where the forms shown represent binary operations (two operands, e.g., 5 + 6).

In forming arithmetic expressions it certainly seems simpler to write

5 + 6

than

5,6+

However, this may be due to the conditioning of the educational process. In considering commands of the form

<operator><operand-list>

or

<operand-list><operator>

the command is considered a "unary operator," taking a single operand, the argument list.

The question arises as to whether it is easier to use a form such as

print (lines 1-3) (prefix)

or

(lines 1-3) print (postfix)

Research has begun in this area (Cherry, 1983), but the surface has only been scratched.

## The Copy Command

The other question that has interest for programmers (and sometimes disastrous results) is the placement of the input and output files in a copy command

copy        file 1        file 2

Some operating systems (e.g., DEC-10) use the form

copy        output        input

with the output file on the left, as in an assignment statement

copy output ⟵ input

others (e.g., UNIX, IBM PC/XT) do the opposite

copy        input        output

following English phraseology

copy "this" to "that"

Which is easier to use is not clear, but the order does matter, and a standard form may help.

## Standardization

While complete standardization will never be the rule, the "variance" among language forms can be annoying and sometimes painful (e.g., when one copies an empty file "into" a full one, ending up with two "empties" due to getting the form of the copy command wrong). Research into the area of human/machine conversation can remove some of these difficulties.

## Semantics in Artificial Languages

As indicated earlier, the question of semantics is not as crucial in the design of artificial languages as that of syntax, at least at the present time. A "do-loop" has the syntax

> DO 10    J = 1,5
>     .
>     .
>     .
>   10 CONTINUE

in FORTRAN. The meaning of the statement is to repeat the body of the loop as many times as the "do-statement" indicates. The "continue statement" tells where the body ends (it is "purely" syntactic). The meaning of the statement (repeat body five times) is tied quite closely to the syntax

> DO . . . 1,5 $\longrightarrow$ Repeat 5 times

This may not be the case in more elaborate dialogues with machines, say using natural language (English, Russian, or French) to input our commands, and possibly, receiving our output in natural language (Kukich, 1983).

If there is a failure at the semantic level, it is a software or hardware failure, i.e., if the do-loop

> DO 10   J =1,5

is "understood" to mean "repeat the body 10 times," the FORTRAN compiler or the computer is "sick."

## Pragmatics of the Computer System

In most artificial languages the use of such commands as

> DO 10 J = 1,5

or

> FIND COLOR RED

cause a prescribed sequence of actions

> The body loop is executed five times.

and

> A file lookup is performed, possibly using an inverted index.

If there is failure at the pragmatic level, it may be a software error (the compiler is incorrect or the application program is incorrect). If the problem is not software, the computer is "very sick," i.e., the hardware is not interpreting the instructions correctly, and a maintenance person should be contacted.

## Semantics of the Information System

While the questions of semantics and pragmatics are relatively straightforward in the computer system itself, they are not so in the larger picture of the information system.

In regard to semantics we have already indicated that the question of ease of use and minimization of errors is a concern in inputting commands. With regard to the inputting of data we would wish to know if the data display (form for entering data) is clear, and if the data values are checked for accuracy. In regard to output from computer to human, we are also concerned with the format and context of the data displays. Are they easy to interpret? Can they easily be related to the real world objects and events they are meant to represent?

## The Pragmatics of the Information System

The pragmatic question in regard to an information system concerns the efficiency of the actions we take based on the models and data provided through the system. If our actions are effective, the system is deemed successful. If our actions are not effective, one must ascertain the cause of the failure. The cause may be physical; i.e., the means necessary to implement the action are lacking (e.g., the lack of reliable "working" equipment or the "physical inability" of the agent). If this is the case, the information system may or may not be adequate. This question cannot be answered until the physical means of implementation are secured. However, if the physical means to implementation are available, but our actions are ineffective, the presumed fault lies with the information system

- The model used in the application may be inappropriate.
- The "threshold values" (i.e., goal values) of the variables in the model may be inappropriate.

It is even possible that both may be inappropriate. The question of why the model or values are inappropriate is addressed by considering two possibilities

- The model (and/or values) was never appropriate (we had an incorrect world view).
- The model had been appropriate at one time, but changes in the environment or in the agent (person, organization) have caused the model to become invalid (the world changed).

In either case, the information system must be adjusted to implement a new (or adjusted) model. We must identify the relevant variables affecting our actions and the relationship of our actions to the goal outcomes.

## Noise

The model of sender-encoder-channel-decoder-receiver is expanded to include one final element, noise that may interfere with the physical transmission and hence the comprehension of the message (Figure 16.6). The presence of noise is analogous to audible noise (e.g., a worker drilling) while someone is holding a conversation, electrical interference while trans-

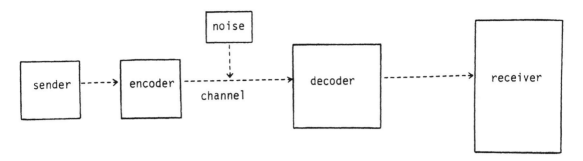

FIGURE 16.6

mitting a message over a data communications channel, printer's errors in a book, and the like. In the storage and transmission of data, these are handled by encoding schemes that incorporate error detection or error correction.

In terms of human communication, such as written text, a good bit of error detection and correction is "built into the language." As Shannon (1980) and others have illustrated (e.g., Pratt, 1939), there is a good bit of redundancy in the English language. For example, when confronted with the following phrase:

The U***** S***** of A******

Most Americans can fill in the blanks

The United States of America

even though 16 of the 28 letters (counting blanks), over 50%, was obliterated.

### Redundancy as Constraint

Redundancy can be looked upon as a constraint in what can be said. For example, in considering the English language, such constructions as

BOOK
BARK
BILL
BALK
BUCK

are legal, but such constructions as

BIJK
BJIK
BKJI
BKIJ
BZOK
BOZK

are not. Not every possible configuration of letters (or words or sentences) is realized. In terms of Shannon's theory, we would say that the possible configurations are not equally likely.

## Redundancy and Predictability

Redundancy in a message enhances predictability. Faced with the message

He hit the _____.

it is more likely that the missing word is *ball, car, crook,* or *books* than *apple, flower,* or *Necktie*. This predictability enhances the successful transmission of messages. Faced with noise in human conversation, we can often "fill in the blanks."

In terms of data transmission, the value of a parity bit is completely redundant information. Given the ASCII sequence

1000001

and the decision rule "even parity," the parity bit must be a zero

10000010
↑
parity

The value of the parity bit is completely specified or "known" by the value of the "information" bits. This redundancy reduces the efficiency of the transmission, since only seven of the eight bits (87.5% of the "channel") are being used to transmit information. This price is paid to ensure that we can detect the errors in transmission and take means to correct them, e.g., by retransmitting. At a further cost in efficiency (adding more parity bits) we can not only detect but correct errors, avoiding the need for retransmission.

## Some Examples

One of the common examples of redundancy is the shape and color used in street signs, such as the stop sign shown in Figure 16.7. The redundancy lies in encoding the message in several ways: written text, shape, and color. The text STOP would be sufficient for a reader of English. However, in addition to the text, the color and shape help get the message across, even to a person unable to read English.

Services that transmit messages, such as the telegraph company, often use the redundancy of English to send the text of messages without any error detection scheme. They rely on the receiver's capability to detect and correct such errors as

Will arrive at airpert
at 10 on April 21.

FIGURE 16.7

However, the dates are often transmitted twice, since there is less redundancy "built into" the numerical values. Both 12 and 21 are legal dates, so that a transposition error, say from April 21 to April 12

> Will arrive at airport
> at 10 on April 12.

could go undetected, at least until the person greeting the traveler became tired of waiting during the 9-day period from the 12th to the 21st.

The numbers in dates do exhibit some restraint. For example, the date 32 is illegal in any month, and the values of 29, 30, and 31 are illegal in some months and years. In general, however, numbers exhibit no redundancy, all combinations being possible, e.g.

> 12345
> 53214
> 41325

While certain applications will show some numbers more often than others, the number system allows each combination to occur with equal likelihood. It is this lack of constraint that indicates the lack of redundancy. When constraint exists, there is some redundancy in the system, some "information" built into the system. When there are no constraints, there is more potential variety in the system. Messages carry more information but are also more subject to errors in transmission.

## Foreign and Domestic Intrigue: Cracking Ciphers

In the spirit that some things should be done "for the fun of it," we close this section on redundancy with an example that is becoming more and more relevant in business, but is also fascinating for its own sake: the encoding of messages—secret messages—in ciphers, and the efforts of experts to "crack the code." (A fascinating book about this subject is *Secret and Urgent*, by Fletcher Pratt, from which the following example has been adapted.)

A cipher is a method of writing a message so that it cannot be read by anyone ignorant of the method used to encode it. One of the simplest types of ciphers is the "substitution" cipher, wherein one character is merely substituted for another character according to some rule. This type of cipher was allegedly used in the movie *2001* to derive the name of the computer: HAL. The rule used in encoding is: Take the letters of the original message, and replace each by its "predecessor" in the alphabet

> Code = original - 1

In order to decode the encoded message, we simply reverse the rule. Take the encoded message, and replace each letter by its "successor" in the English alphabet

> Original = code + 1

Thus, *H* will be replaced by *I*; *A* by *B*; and *L* by *M*, so that we have the code

> H   A   L
> ↓   ↓   ↓
> I   B   M

A cryptogram is a message written in cipher. Thus, the name HAL is a cryptogram. The original message is called the "clear," so that IBM was the clear. A cryptographer is a person who tries to decipher a cryptogram, deriving the clear without knowing the cipher. He or she deduces the cipher by whatever ingenious methods possible. Among the most powerful tools of the cryptographer is the redundancy inherent in natural languages.

## English: The Probability of Letters

As we alluded above, the frequency distribution of the different sequences of letters in the English language is not equiprobable. For example, if we see the group of letters *th_*, where the underline indicates a missing letter, and wished to fill in the blank, the odds would be pretty high for it being an *e*. The odds on the letter being a *q* or a *z* are nil. We know this because the frequency of the combination *the* is very high, while the frequencies of the combinations *thq* and *thz* are zero in *English*. (Note that the frequencies of different combinations differ from language to language. For example, the combination *aa* occurs much more in Dutch [waar = where, naar = to, bezienswaardigheden = sightseeing] than in English.) In fact, these differences in physical structure alone can aid us in distinguishing text in one language from text in another.

The sequence *qu* is an even better example. With the exception of acronyms (e.g., QED for *quod erat demonstrandum*), there is not a single instance in the *American College Dictionary* (1958) of an English word beginning with q that does not have a *u* following the *q*. Thus, we *always* know that an initial *q* means an initial *qu*. If we were sending messages by telegraph, we could send the *q*, and skip the *u*, making the line more efficient. Or, as one professor advocated, don't send the *u* unless it *doesn't* occur after the *q*, which can be translated into something like "only send the exceptions to the rule," not the rule itself.

Not only sequences of letters, but the individual letters themselves have different frequencies of occurrence. As Samuel Morse knew so well, the letters *e*, *t*, and *a* occur much more frequently than *j*, *z*, and *b*. It is this quality that leads to puzzles such as the following being printed in magazines like the *Reader's Digest*:

> What is different about the following paragraph?
>
> "Who hit a ball against a wall?" said a man from Whithall. "A man from Aspinwall hit a ball against a wall. It took a fall, a spin, and a roll, this ball hit against a wall; so that this man from Aspinwall ran round all, and did stand tall," said a man from Dunwall.

The thing that is different about the paragraph is that it contains no instance of the letter *e*, a fact that does not occur often, and indeed, takes some unnatural contrivances to accomplish. (The author read the example on a mimeographed copy years ago and no longer remembers the origin of the text.)

## Monograms, Digrams, and Trigrams

The frequencies of the individual letters of the English alphabet are called monogram frequencies. A list of these monogram frequencies (relative fre-

## TABLE 16.3a

| | | | | | |
|---|---|---|---|---|---|
| Space | .187 | I | .051 | R | .055 |
| A | .066 | J | .001 | S | .050 |
| B | .011 | K | .003 | T | .085 |
| C | .022 | L | .027 | U | .020 |
| D | .031 | M | .020 | V | .007 |
| E | .107 | N | .058 | W | .016 |
| F | .024 | O | .065 | X | .001 |
| G | .016 | P | .016 | Y | .016 |
| H | .043 | Q | .001 | Z | .001 |

## TABLE 16.3b

| | | | | | |
|---|---|---|---|---|---|
| Space | .187 | H | .043 | W | .016 |
| E | .107 | D | .031 | Y | .016 |
| T | .085 | L | .027 | B | .011 |
| A | .066 | F | .024 | V | .007 |
| O | .065 | C | .022 | K | .003 |
| N | .058 | M | .020 | J | .001 |
| R | .055 | U | .020 | Q | .001 |
| I | .051 | G | .016 | X | .001 |
| S | .050 | P | .016 | Z | .001 |

(Figures taken from "The Man-Made World," Polytechnic Institute of Brooklyn, adapted from Pratt's figures.)

quencies or proportions) is given in Table 16.3a. Listing the letters in order of occurrence, we get Table 16.3b. Note that the space is considered a letter. As indicated earlier the space does provide a distinguishing function as illustrated by the words: *befit* and *be fit*, or *together* and *to get her* (*befit*, as in "The suit befits you" [is becoming to you]; and *be fit*, as in "eat a good breakfast and do 20 push-ups every morning to be fit" [healthy]; and *to get her*, as in "I'll drive down to get her," and *together*, as in "So we can go to the movies together."). A list of frequencies of the letters, omitting the space (from *Man-Made World*) is given in Table 16.4. We will refer to both lists, with and without the space, so we include both here.

## TABLE 16.4

| | | | | | |
|---|---|---|---|---|---|
| E | .132 | H | .053 | Y | .020 |
| T | .104 | D | .038 | W | .019 |
| A | .082 | L | .034 | B | .014 |
| O | .080 | F | .029 | V | .009 |
| N | .071 | C | .027 | K | .004 |
| R | .068 | M | .025 | J | .001 |
| I | .063 | U | .024 | Q | .001 |
| S | .061 | G | .020 | X | .001 |
| | | P | .020 | Z | .001 |

TABLE 16.5

| Diagrams | Frequency |
|----------|-----------|
| TH | .168 |
| HE | .132 |
| AN | .092 |
| RE | .091 |
| ER | .088 |
| IN | .086 |
| ON | .071 |
| AT | .068 |
| ND | .061 |
| ST | .053 |
| ES | .052 |
| EN | .051 |
| OF | .049 |
| TE | .046 |
| ED | .046 |
| OR | .045 |
| TI | .043 |
| HI | .043 |
| AS | .042 |
| TO | .041 |

Pairs of letters are called "digrams." A partial list of the digrams and their frequencies is given in Table 16.5. A more complete list is given in Pratt. A full list would contain 26 * 26 = 676 items, if we do not include the space (26 possible first characters, each combined with 26 possible second characters); and would have 27 * 27 = 729 items, if we included the space.

Groups of three letters, e.g., *thi*, *the*, and *thr*, are called "trigrams." A list of these is also included in Pratt. A full list would have 17,576 items (26 * 26 * 26) if we exclude the space; 19,683 (27 * 27 * 27) if we include the space.

TABLE 16.6

| Word | Frequency |
|------|-----------|
| a | 108 |
| about | 11 |
| an | 16 |
| be | 43 |
| by | 42 |
| for | 49 |
| he | 31 |
| I | 16 |
| of | 222 |
| the | 420 |
| we | 12 |

Instead of going on to "quadgrams," "quintgrams," etc., researchers usually move from trigrams into the frequencies of words. The frequencies of single words are called "first-order" word frequencies. Monograms are first-order letter frequencies. Letters listed as equiprobable (or without frequencies) are considered zero-order letter frequencies. The first-order word frequencies of some common English words (based on 10,000 words of normal text, adapted from Pratt) are given in Table 16.6.

The frequencies of pairs of words, for example, *the book, a house,* and *black cherries,* are called "second-order" word frequencies. Again, we can see that certain sequences, e.g., *the book,* occur more frequently than other sequences, *book the,* although both sequences are possible

That is *the book.*
That is the very *book the* boy brought.

Groups of three words are "third-order" word frequencies, four words are "fourth-order," and so on.

## Using the Frequencies: An Example

Suppose that a cryptographer is faced with a cryptograph (letters grouped and numbered for convenience; Figure 16.8a). The first step in deciphering the message is to count the frequency with which each letter appears (Figure 16.8b).

The cryptographer now turns to his or her table of single letter frequencies (monograms), and finds that *E* is the most frequently used letter, with *T* next. (In the subsequent text "he" is used as "he or she," i.e., in its generic sense of "someone." The choice is one of convenience in

| 1 | 2 | 3 | 4 | 5 | 6 | 7 |
|---|---|---|---|---|---|---|
| SZPQP | ERJKQ | PCRKJ | VZXPU | PJSZP | GKRSC | GCSPT |

| 8 | 9 | 10 | 11 | 12 | 13 | 14 |
|---|---|---|---|---|---|---|
| QIQXL | SKNQC | LZPOR | ZKTFM | ZPRES | CSPFK | JNKUP |

| 15 | 16 | 17 | 18 | 19 | 20 |
|---|---|---|---|---|---|
| QCREG | LFPRT | HRSES | TSEKJ | IELZP | Q |

(a)

| | | |
|---|---|---|
| P—13 | J—5 | N—2 |
| S—10 | L—4 | M—1 |
| Q—8 | T—4 | H—1 |
| K—8 | F—3 | V—1 |
| R—8 | G—3 | |
| Z—7 | I—2 | |
| C—6 | U—2 | |
| E—6 | X—2 | |

(b)

FIGURE 16.8

| 1 | 2 | 3 | 4 | 5 | 6 | 7 |
|---|---|---|---|---|---|---|
| SZPQP | ERJKQ | PCRKJ | VZXPU | PJSZP | GKRSC | GCSPT |
| t.e.e | ..... | e.... | ...e. | e.t.e | ...t. | ..te. |

| 8 | 9 | 10 | 11 | 12 | 13 | 14 |
|---|---|---|---|---|---|---|
| QIQXL | SKNQC | LZPQR | ZKTFM | ZPRES | CSPFK | JNKUP |

| 15 | 16 | 17 | 18 | 19 | 20 |
|---|---|---|---|---|---|
| QCREG | LFPRT | HRSES | TSEKJ | IELZP | Q |

(c)

**FIGURE 16.8** (continued)

writing.) The space is not considered since cryptograms normally omit the space as being "too helpful" in distinguishing words. Thus, he hypothesizes that

P = E

S = T

He replaces the letters P and S in the cryptograph with his hypothesized values (Figure 16.8c). Now he takes a look at the trigram frequency table, and finds that *the* is overwhelmingly the most frequent trigram. In the present message, the combination *szp*, which we have translated as *T_E*, occurs twice, once in group 1 and once in group 5. Our cryptographer surmises that the blank is to be replaced by an *H*. But if *Z* is *H*, then *Q* is either *R* or *S*. We deduce this from the combination *SZPQP* of group 1, which is now thought to be *THE_E*, so that *THESE* and *THERE* seem to be the possibilities.

Looking at group 10, *ZPQ* translates as *HE_*. Consulting the table of trigrams, our cryptographer finds that *HER* occurs much more frequently than *HES*, so he concludes that the *Q* is to be replaced by *R*, yielding *THERE* for group 1, and *HER* for the *ZPQ* sequence of group 10. We now have assigned four letters

P = E

S = T

Z = H

Q = R

In groups 17 and 18, our cryptographer recognizes a "pattern" word, *SESTSE*, the repeated *S* establishing the pattern. He has already substituted the letter *T* for *S*, so that the hypothesized pattern is

T   T   T

Consulting a table of pattern words (see Pratt; 1939), he determines that this pattern is *TITUTI* (as in restitution), and fills in

E = I

T = U

| 1 | 2 | 3 | 4 | 5 | 6 | 7 |
|---|---|---|---|---|---|---|
| SZPQP | ERJKQ | PCRKJ | VZXPU | PJSZP | GKRSC | GCSPT |
| there | i ... r | e .... | .h.e. | e.the | ...t. | ..teu |

| 8 | 9 | 10 | 11 | 12 | 13 | 14 |
|---|---|---|---|---|---|---|
| QIQXL | SKNQC | LZPQR | ZXTFM | ZPRES | CSPFK | JNKUP |
| r.r.. | t..r. | .her. | h.u.. | he.it | .te.. | ....e |

| 15 | 16 | 17 | 18 | 19 | 20 |
|---|---|---|---|---|---|
| QCREG | LFPRT | HRSES | TSEKJ | IELZP | Q |
| r..i. | ..e.u | ..tit | uti.. | .i.he | r |

(a)

| 1 2 | | 3 | 4 | 5 | 6 |
|---|---|---|---|---|---|
| SZPQP/ER/JK/Q | | PCRKJ/ | VZXPU | PJ/SZP/ | GKRS/C |
| there/is/no/r | | eason/ | .h.e. | en/the/ | .ost/a |

| 7 | 8 | 9 | 10 | 11 | 12 | 13 |
|---|---|---|---|---|---|---|
| GCSPT | Q/IQXL | SKNQC | LZPQR | ZKTFM/ | ZPRES | CSP/FK |
| .ateu | r/.r.. | to.ra | .hers | hou../ | hesit | ate/.o |

| 14 | 15 | 16 | 17 | 18 | 19 | 20 |
|---|---|---|---|---|---|---|
| JNKUP | Q/C/REG | LFP/RT | HRSES | TSEKJ/ | IELZP | Q |
| n.o.e | r/a/si. | ..e/su | .stit | ution/ | .i.he | r |

(b)

FIGURE 16.9

The partially solved cipher now looks like Figure 16.9a.

Of the characters in the cipher that were "high frequency," we have not "solved" *K*, *R*, *C*, and *J*. Of the English characters that are high frequency, we have not used *A*, *O*, *N*, and *S*. Looking at the *TITUTI* combination in groups 17 and 18, we see that the *K* and *J* occur in the cipher

    SES  TSEKJ
    tit  uti

and since *TITUTI* can be a part of *TITUTION* (restitution, substitution), he chooses to assign

    K = O

    J = N

so that *A* and *S* are the only two "high-frequency" English letters not yet accounted for. Looking at groups 1 and 2, he sees the sequence

    SZPQP ER
    there i

and decides that this is probably "there is," so he assigns

    R = S

Now we have only one high-frequency cipher letter, *C*, and one high-frequency English letter, *A*, so that he arbitrarily attempts the substitution

C = A

Filling in the message, we now have Figure 16.9b, and we are very close to a solution.

Looking at groups 10 and 11, he sees

```
R   ZKTFM
s   hou
```

which certainly looks like it should be *should* (pun intended), and he assigns

F = L

M = D

Group 6 is

```
GKRS
  ost
```

which is most likely to yield *most,* so that

G = M

and groups 13 and 14

```
FK  JN
lo   n
```

yield *long* with

N = G

The *U*'s in groups 4 and 14

```
PU   PJ  KUP  Q
e    en  o e  r
```

seem to fit nicely as *V*, yielding *even* and *over* (*U* = *V*). Groups 16, 17, and 18

```
RT   HRSES  TSEKJ
su   stit   ution
```

seems to give *H* = *B*. Groups 2, 3, and 4

```
Q  PCRKJ  VZXPU  PJ
r  eason     h ev  en
```

seem to say *reason why even,* so that

V = W

X = Y

And we have only two more letters to "solve": *I* and *L* in the cipher, *C* and *P* in English. The last word (groups 19 and 20) contains both the *I* and the *L* of the cipher letters

SZPQP/ER/JK/QPCRKJ/VZX/PUPJ/SZP/GKRS/CGCSPTQ/IQXLSKNQCLZPQ/RZKTFM/
there/is/no/reason/why/even/the/most/amateur/cryptographer/should/

ZPRESCSP/FKJN/KUPQ/C/REGLFP/RTHRSESTSEKJ/IELZPQ/
hesitate/long/over/a/simple/substitution/cipher/

FIGURE 16.10

 

    IELZP  Q
     i  he  r

which can be either *picher* or *cipher*, and, since only the latter is a legal
English word, we assign

    I = C

    L = P

so that the final message is as shown in Figure 16.10.


**A Final Look at the Model: Two-Way Transmission**

While we have talked about "conversations," a two-way dialogue, the model
developed has really been a model of one-way communication (Figure 16.11a).
This model is appropriate to one-way transmissions (called simplex transmissions) such as television broadcasts, books, magazine articles, speeches,
and some lectures. Two-way conversation requires that both "parties" be
capable of transmitting and receiving, encoding and decoding (Figure
16.11b). Such two-way conversation is called duplex transmission in data
communications. If both parties can transmit and receive simultaneously, it

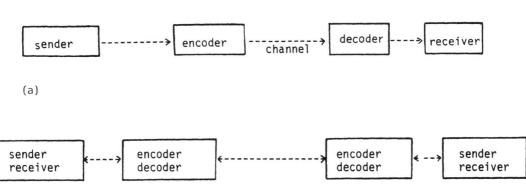

(a)

(b)

FIGURE 16.11

is called "full duplex" or "duplex." If the parties must "take turns," one transmitting, the other receiving, then "turning the dialogue direction around," the transmission is called half-duplex. Half-duplex transmission is defined as "two-way transmission but only one way at a time."

In human-to-human verbal conversation, both people can send messages, encoding them with their vocal cords, and both can receive, physically receiving the signals with their ears, and decoding them at the higher neural centers. While full duplex conversation is possible (everybody talking, everybody or possibly nobody listening), polite, intelligent conversation normally requires half-duplex transmission.

In human-to-computer communications, full duplex lines allow the user to type in messages while the computer is outputting data or messages. These can speed up the entire transaction. Of course, when the reaction of the user to the output of the computer requires thought, the interaction will take place in "half-duplex" mode despite the full-duplex capabilities.

Simplex transmission might be used in the collection of data or in its transfer to a central location. However, in these cases, a "smaller" channel (less capacity) may be used to transmit control signals (commands) and feedback signals (acknowledgment of successful reception). In human communications, simplex transmissions, such as radio broadcasts, can be made duplex by providing an alternate channel, say a telephone line, for listener feedback. Newspapers provide the same service with letters to the editor.

## Forms of Feedback

In any successful conversation, there are various forms of feedback. One of the simplest is the periodic nod of the head or the "uh-huh" utterance used to indicate that we are still listening. In human/machine conversations, the need for feedback is just as prevalent from the human's point of view. When a command is entered, such as

.R SORT

the system usually indicates the transfer of control (the loading and executing of the sort program) by the prompt. When commands are issued to compile and execute programs, successful compilation is indicated by a message, such as

End of compilation

or

Compilation complete

Successful execution is usually indicated by the presence of output. However, a message such as "end of execution" may also be issued to take care of cases in which the output is not visible, as in the tranference of data from one disk file to another.

Lack of comprehension, hence lack of execution, is indicated by the various error messages, ranging from the use of question marks, the word *What?*, to full-blown diagnostics: "symbol table overflow."

## Related Readings

Belnap, Nuel D. Jr. and Steel, Thomas B. Jr., *The Logic of Questions and Answers*, London: Yale University Press, 1976.

Cherry, Colin, *On Human Communication A Review, A Survey and a Criticism*, 2nd ed. Cambridge, MA: Massachusetts Institute of Technology, 1975 (c1966).

Cherry, Joan M., *Command Languages: Effects of Work Order on User Performance*, Ph.D. thesis, University of Pittsburgh, 1983.

Clark, Herbert H. and Clark, Eve V., *Psychology and Language: An Introduction to Psycholinguistics*, New York: Harcourt Brace Jovanovich, 1977.

Gannon, John D. and Horning, James J., "Language Design for Programming Reliability." *IEEE Transactions on Software Engineeering*, June 1975.

Grice, H. P., "Logic and Conversation." In *Syntax and Semantics: Speech Acts*, P. Cole and J. L. Morgan, eds. New York: Academic Press, 1975, pp. 41–58.

Jeffrey, Richard C., *Formal Logic: Its Scope and Limits*, New York: McGraw-Hill, 1967.

Kukich, Karen, Knowledge-based Report Generation: A Knowledge Engineering Approach to Natural Language Report Generation. Ph.D. dissertation, University of Pittsburgh, August, 1983.

Ledgard, Henry and Marcotty, Michael, *Programming Language Landscape*, Chicago: Science Research Associates, 1981.

Lehnert, Wendy G., *The Process of Question Answering*, Hillsdale, NJ: Lawrence Erlbaum Associates, Inc., 1978.

Lehnert, Wendy G. and Ringle, Martin H., eds., *Strategies for Natural Language Processing*, Hillsdale, NJ: Lawrence Erlbaum Associates, 1982.

Lindsay, Peter H. and Norman, Donald A., *Human Information Processing: An Introduction to Psychology*, 2nd ed. New York: Academic Press, 1977.

*The Man-Made World: Engineering Concepts Curriculum Project*, New York: McGraw-Hill, 1971.

Martin, James, *Design of Man-Computer Dialogues*, Englewood Cliffs, NJ: Prentice-Hall, 1973.

Meadow, Charles T., *Man-Machine Communication*, New York: John Wiley & Sons, 1970.

Minsky, Marvin, ed., *Semantic Information Processing*, Cambridge, MA: Massachusetts Institute of Technology, 1968.

Naur, Peter, ed., "Revised Report on the Algorithmic Language Algol 60," in *Communications of the ACM*, January 1963.

Pierce, John R., *An Introduction to Information Theory Symbols, Signals and Noise*, second revised ed. New York: Dover Publications, Inc., 1980.

Pratt, F., *Secret and Urgent*, Indianapolis, IN: The Bobbs-Merril Co., 1939.

Raphael, Bertram, *The Thinking Computer: Mind Inside Matter*. San Francisco: W. H. Freeman and Company, 1976.

Shannon, Claude E. and Weaver, Warren, *The Mathematical Theory of Communication*, Urbana: University of Illinois Press, 1980 (c1949).

Solso, Robert L., *Cognitive Psychology*, New York: Harcourt Brace Jovanovich, 1979.

Suppes, Patrick, *Introduction to LOGIC*, Princeton, NJ: D. Van Nostrand Company, Inc., 1957.

Thomas, Norman L., *Modern Logic: An Introduction*, New York: Barnes & Noble, Inc., 1966.

Weaver, Warren, "Recent Contributions to the Mathematical Theory of Communication," in *The Mathematical Theory of Communication*, Claude E. Shannon and Warren Weaver, eds. Urbana: University of Illinois Press, 1980 (c1949). pp. 1–28.

# IX
# Data Manipulation

The reader may be surprised to see data manipulation relegated to a position so far down the road. It has traditionally been considered a primary concern of information processing. In fact, books labeled as being about information processing are often introductory texts in data processing. It is precisely for this reason that the subject has been deferred; the intent was to show other aspects of information systems that receive less emphasis in the data processing literature, at least at the introductory level. However, the placement of the section on data processing adjacent to that on decision-making and problem-solving has a conceptual foundation as well.

The use of data manipulation techniques assumes a model of the situation at hand. And, in many instances, the model is one in which we have control over both our actions and the outcomes of these actions; i.e., we act "under certainty."

Much of the literature in information science (or the study of information) has emphasized the use of data to reduce uncertainty. This is a result of the mathematical communication model's treatment of the amount of information in a message as a measure of uncertainty in the system of messages from which the particular message is selected. It is also a result of the intuitive notion of information needs reflecting a lack of knowledge, translating "lack of knowledge" into uncertainty. The intent in this section is to distinguish between a lack of information and the multiple uses of uncertainty. The phrase "decision-making under uncertainty" refers to actions over which we have partial control over outcomes that we do not fully control, e.g., outcomes that are coproduced by the agent (with guidance by the agent's information system) and someone other than the agent, e.g., "acts of nature" or other agents. These decisions under uncertainty are studied in the last section of the text, just prior to the topic of problem-solving. In this section we examine the use of data within models in which we have control of the outcomes (e.g., the linear programming model) or in which the outcomes are probabilistically determined (e.g., queuing theory) but the lack of control is not attributable to some known force of nature or known "other agent."

The three models chosen (forecasting, queuing theory, and linear programming) have been chosen because they are relatively widely applicable and interesting in themselves. However, they are not meant to be even loosely representative of the wide variety of models that are applicable to the topic of data manipulation. The variety of models follows the variety of situations we face. Some models, such as those used in business, are more salient in the literature. However, each information system much be "about something," so that the models used to guide data manipulation will be application dependent. We indicate only general types of manipulations and uses of the output data.

The second chapter introduces the notion of text processing, a use of computation facilities that is essentially noncomputational, prompting views of the computer as symbol processor rather than number cruncher, the symbols being either numeric or textual.

The initial concerns of Chapter 18 are physical processing activities, e.g., sorting data to present the more salient items first or to impose an order on the data; using editors to input text and/or programs/data; and using text formatters to prepare documents. The last consideration of the chapter indicates how text processing techniques (such as finding and sorting the words in a document) can be combined with numerical techniques (e.g., counting the words and comparing the count to "meaning thresholds") to extract meaning.

# 17
# Numerical Techniques

## Objectives

Upon finishing this chapter the reader should be able to:

1.  Discuss the purpose of data manipulation
2.  Give forecasts based on the three simple models presented here and compare them in terms of variability of forecast, storage consumed, and processing required
3.  Compute the average length of a waiting line as well as the average number of people "in the system" with the queuing model presented here
4.  Define the load and indicate how it affects performance, e.g., average length of the queue or average waiting time
5.  Discuss the trade-off between services and cost of servers, as well as that between time spent waiting and cost of personnel
6.  Apply the linear programming model to both a problem of profit maximation and a problem of cost minimization
7.  Explain the graphic representation of the linear programming problem
8.  Explain the algebraic solution of a linear programming problem

Very often the data we are able to collect is not in the exact form that we wish. There are numerous methods in which the data can be manipulated in order to present a relevant answer to our question, i.e., an answer in the form in which we can obtain a direct answer to our questions. We will examine two major categories of data manipulation

1.  Numerical manipulation
2.  Text processing

The reasons for which we process data are as varied as the techniques to process it; some of these are

1.  Prediction. Our data is usually about the past or present, yet our questions are about the future. We need methods of forecasting the future from the past. One example, the moving average, is presented in this chapter. The regression equation presented in Chapter 4 is another.

2. Summarization. Very often the data we have is too bulky to be digested readily, and some form of data compaction is necessary. The use of the mean and standard deviation, as well as the median, mode, and range, are examples, as are tabular displays of frequency counts.

3. Operations management. The data on operations is used to manage more effectively, e.g., in hiring or laying off personnel, or reorganizing the workplace or the flow of information. The techniques of linear programming (to guide resource allocation) and queuing theory (to plan for and handle workloads) are examples, both presented in this chapter. In earlier chapters, we saw the use of statistical measures in design (the door) and planning (the number of tellers in a bank).

4. Extracting meaning. The data are simply symbols organized in a particular way; however, to a human interpreter, they have a meaning. One of the questions facing the information scientist is a method by which we may extract this meaning using such technology as a computer. In earlier chapters, we considered the analysis of numerical data to extract relationships (correlation, chi-square) and make evaluations (the test of flying ability is good or bad, my standing on the achievement test was above/below normal) and guide decisions (this football player is fast; therefore, we will hire him). In Chapter 18 we will examine the use of text processing techniques in conjunction with numerical processing to extract meaning from written text.

5. Data display. Both numerical and textual data are physically manipulated in order to present the data in a more intelligible or accessible form. An example is sorting data, presented in Chapter 18. Other examples, also included in Chapter 18, are the use of editors to create files of data, programs, or other "documents" in electronic form, and the use of text formatters in preparing such documents as letters, chapters of a book, and journal articles.

In this chapter we examine mathematical data manipulation. The mathematical models used to describe the data, as well as the computations (operations) performed on the data vary with each application field, as well as within each field. We give a "nonrepresentative" sample of three commonly used techniques in the areas of

1. Forecasting
2. Queuing theory
3. Linear programming

The techniques are nonrepresentative in that they do not sample all areas of numerical data manipulation, a task that is beyond the scope of this text, possibly any single text. However, they are representative in that they display the process of developing and using mathematical models to produce answers to our questions.

## Forecasting

The first problem we attack is the problem of forecasting demand for goods. Suppose that we are manufacturing automobiles or selling hamburgers. One of the problems we face is the estimation of the amount of goods to pur-

TABLE 17.1

| Year | Sales (in 1000s of items sold) |
|------|------|
| 1990 | 15 |
| 1989 | 12 |
| 1988 | 16 |
| 1987 | 14 |
| 1986 | 18 |
| 1985 | 12 |
| 1984 | 11 |
| 1983 | 12 |
| 1982 | 14 |
| 1981 | 13 |

chase for the next time period, say a year or a week. If we order too few goods (e.g., automobiles), we may lose some profit by being unable to satisfy customer demand. On the other hand, if we order too many goods, we may increase our costs by having some things left over. The problem is to order "just the right amount."

One source of data we have about our company's operations is the record of past sales. We wish to use these past sales as indicators of future sales. The question is how to make the best use of this data. Many sophisticated techniques exist in regard to forecasting problems. We will show some of the simplest. The reader is referred to forecasting texts for further study.

## An Example

In order to illustrate the techniques of forecasting, let us assume that our company has data on sales for the past 10 years (Table 17.1), and that we are attempting to predict sales for 1991. Three relatively straightforward strategies come to mind

1. This year (1991) will be exactly like last year (1990).
2. This year (1991) will be like the average of all years (1981-1990).
3. This year (1991) will be like the average of some number of years, but not all (say the average of 1990, 1989, and 1988).

Let us examine each of these strategies in turn.

## This Year Will Be the Same as Last Year

If we assume that this year will be the same as last year, we would predict 1991 sales as 15,000 items, since this was the number of items sold in 1990. The use of this strategy simplifies both our storage requirements and our processing requirements. We need to store only one number (last year's sales) and we simply read that number to determine our new prediction, so that no computation is involved.

TABLE 17.2

| Year | Predicted Sales | Actual Sales | Prediction over (+) or Short (−) |
|---|---|---|---|
| 1986 | 12 | 18 | −6 |
| 1987 | 18 | 14 | +4 |
| 1988 | 14 | 16 | −2 |
| 1989 | 16 | 12 | +4 |
| 1990 | 12 | 15 | −3 |

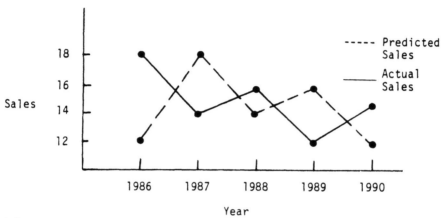

(a)

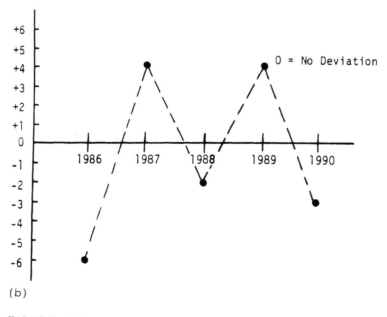

(b)

FIGURE 17.1

However, the question that arises is "Does this method of predicting give satisfactory results?" In order to examine the results of predicting in this manner, let us consider the data from the last few years

    1990: 15,000
    1989: 12,000
    1988: 16,000
    1987: 14,000
    1986: 18,000

If we had used the simple rule of "this year will be the same as last year" to predict sales in 1987, we would have predicted 18,000 (the number of sales in 1986). Since actual sales in 1987 were 14,000, we would have over-stocked by 4,000 items. Then, predicting 1988, we would have predicted 14,000 items (actual sales in 1987). Since actual sales in 1988 were 16,000, we would have been "short" two items. If we examine the data for this 5-year period, we see that we would consistently be short or over by a relatively large amount (Table 17.2); we are successively short 6, over 4, short 2, over 4, and short 3. This is a relatively "bumpy" record, the bumps reflecting actual fluctuations in sales, as can be seen if we graph the data on predicted and actual sales (Figure 17.1a). The dotted line showing predicted sales follows the same pattern as actual sales, one time period later, so that the predictions suffer all the fluctuations in the data on actual sales. (To see the pattern more clearly, ignore the leftmost piece of the predicted sales and the rightmost line of actual sales. Within the vagaries of drawing accuracy, the lines are identical.) The fluctuations in deviation of predicted values from actual values are shown in Figure 17.1b. It is in an attempt to "smooth" out these fluctuations that forecasters turn to averaging techniques.

## This Year Will Be the Same as the Average of All Years

The average of a set of numbers is less extreme than the endpoints of the original data. Thus, in considering the data from 1986 (18,000) and 1987 (14,000), the range is four items, but the average (16,000) is less extreme than either of these two numbers. If we use an average to predict sales, we would encounter less extreme fluctuations than if we use the individual numbers themselves. The question is "How many year totals should we average?" A first thought might be to include "as much data as we have," which would result in taking an average of all years. The average of our 10-year data is 13.7 items per year. If we use the average of all years to predict the coming year, we would predict 13,700 items for 1991. (Note: In determining averages, if a fraction occurs, the interpretation depends on the type of object we are considering. For example, 10.2 cars does not make sense, and would be truncated to 10 or increased to 11; 10.2 tons of steel would make sense, since we can have fractions of a ton).

In using the method of "averaging all years," we have increased both our storage costs and our processing costs. We must store data on all 10 years, and we must add all these numbers then divide by 10 in order to obtain the average. The hope would be that this investment in storage and processing is offset by better predictions. Let us see what the predictions for each year would have been under this rule, as well as the deviation of our predictions from the actual data (Table 17.3).

TABLE 17.3

| Year | Years Used to Predict | Prediction | Actual Sales | Deviation* |
|------|----------------------|------------|--------------|------------|
| 1981 | ---- | --- | 13 | ----- |
| 1982 | 1981 | 13 | 14 | -1 |
| 1983 | 1981-1982 | 13.5 | 12 | +1.5 |
| 1984 | 1981-1983 | 13 | 11 | +2 |
| 1985 | 1981-1984 | 12.5 | 12 | +0.5 |
| 1986 | 1981-1985 | 12.4 | 18 | -5.6 |
| 1987 | 1981-1986 | 13.3 | 14 | -0.7 |
| 1988 | 1981-1987 | 13.4 | 16 | -2.6 |
| 1989 | 1981-1988 | 13.8 | 12 | +1.8 |
| 1990 | 1981-1989 | 13.6 | 15 | -1.4 |
| 1991 | 1981-1990 | 13.7 | ? | ? |

*- = prediction is short; + = prediction is over.

In the early years of our company (1981-1985), the predicted values fluctuated between the positive and the negative, and stayed in the vicinity of 12,000-13,000 units. However, in the later years (1986-1990), the predictions are consistently short, with the single exception of 1989, which seems to be an extraordinary year—extraordinarily bad.

The reason that the predictions consistently fall short in the latter years is that there was a "turning point" in 1986. In the years prior to 1986, our company had been selling in the range of 11,000-14,000 units per year. In the years from 1986 to the present, the range is 12,000-18,000, and, if we "take out" the data on 1989 (abnormally low sales of 12,000 units), the range in the time span 1986-1990 is 14,000 through 18,000. If we graph these ranges, we obtain the results shown in Figure 17.2. We see that sales have been significantly greater from 1986 to the present. It may be that we had a particularly successful advertising campaign in 1986, attracting and keeping many new customers. Note that the elimination of a data point, such as 1989's 12 units sold, is a controversial matter. On the

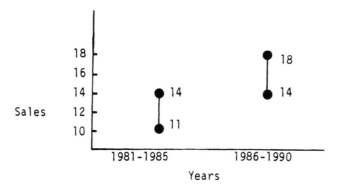

FIGURE 17.2

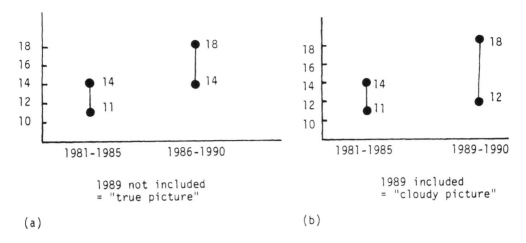

FIGURE 17.3

one hand, we wish to use the data as is. On the other, it would seem that 1989 was a unique year, perhaps a time of economic difficulty for reasons other than a dislike of our product, so that total sales in this year do not reflect the "true pattern." Such data is called "outlying data," extreme points that should be examined individually. In computing the averages for the tables, we have used the data for 1989. However, in drawing the ranges we have not, since the "true picture" is clearer without including the data on 1989's 12 units (Figure 17.3a). The first graph (Figure 17.3a), clearly shows the dichotomy of the two time periods, whereas the second graph (Figure 17.3b), is more difficult to interpret.

The use of the "average of all years" weights the past too greatly, especially with dichotomous data such as this, so that the low sales years of 1981-1985 are influencing predictions in the high sales years of 1986-1990. We are taking too much data into account. In order to combat this phenomenon, forecasters turn to what is called a "moving average."

## Moving Average

The moving average is similar to the average of all years, except that we average a limited number of years. The forecasters attempt to determine the number of years that is relevant to the prediction of this year's sales, call it "n" years, then use the average of those n years to predict the following year's sales; n might be 2, 3, 4, or any number greater than 1 and less than the total number of years in business. In fact, the moving average is the more general model, with both other models being special cases. The model of this year being the same as last is the special case of n = 1. The model of using the average of all years is the special case of n = all years.

To illustrate the method of the moving average, let us assume that we have chosen n = 3, i.e., we will base our prediction of this year's sales on the average of the data from the previous 3 years. For 1991, we must average sales for 1988, 1989, and 1990

1988: 16,000
1989: 12,000
1990: 15,000

The average is 14.3 [from (15+12+16)/3], thus we would predict sales for 1991 as 14.3 thousand units.

The reason why this method is called a moving average can be seen in predicting sales for 1992. In order to do so, we will need data from 1989, 1990, and 1991. The data from 1988 can be discarded

| Predict 1991 From | Predict 1992 From |
|---|---|
| 1988 | ---- |
| 1989 | 1989 |
| 1990 | 1990 |
|  | 1991 |

so that the group of 3 years has "moved up" one slot in the list of data. Each year we discard the oldest year of the n years, and add data from the most recent year.

Using this method of averaging 3 years, we can calculate predictions and deviations of predictions from actual data for our 10-year period. In the first years of the company's existence, only as many years as are available will be used. The data are as shown in Table 17.4.

In using the method of moving averages, only 2 years have relatively large deviations

1986: the year in which we launched our marketing effort, and presumably a year in which we desired to cause a greater deviation

TABLE 17.4

| Year | Years Used in Prediction | Predictions | Actual Sales | Deviation* |
|---|---|---|---|---|
| 1981 | ---- | ---- | 13 | ----- |
| 1982 | 1981 | 13 | 14 | -1.0 |
| 1983 | 1981-1982 | 13.5 | 12 | +1.5 |
| 1984 | 1981-1983 | 13 | 11 | +2.0 |
| 1985 | 1982-1984 | 12.3 | 12 | +0.3 |
| 1986 | 1983-1985 | 11.7 | 18 | -6.3 |
| 1987 | 1984-1986 | 13.7 | 14 | -0.3 |
| 1988 | 1985-1987 | 14.7 | 16 | -1.3 |
| 1989 | 1986-1988 | 16.0 | 12 | +4.0 |
| 1990 | 1987-1989 | 14.0 | 15 | -1.0 |
| 1991 | 1988-1990 | 14.3 | ? | ? |

*- = prediction short; + = prediction over.

TABLE 17.5

| Year | Actual Sales | Deviation Prediction Based on 1 Year | Deviation Prediction Based on Average of All Years | Deviation Prediction Based on Previous 3 Years |
|------|------|------|------|------|
| 1981 | 13 | — | — | — |
| 1982 | 14 | −1.0 | −1.0 | −1.0 |
| 1983 | 12 | +2.0 | +1.5 | +1.5 |
| 1984 | 11 | +1.0 | +2.0 | +2.0 |
| 1985 | 12 | −1.0 | +0.5 | +0.3 |
| 1986 | 18 | −6.0 | −5.6 | −6.3 |
| 1987 | 14 | +4.0 | −0.7 | −0.3 |
| 1988 | 16 | −2.0 | −2.6 | −1.3 |
| 1989 | 12 | +4.0 | +1.8 | +4.0 |
| 1990 | 15 | −3.0 | −1.4 | −1.0 |
| 1991 | ? | Predict: 15 | Predict: 13.7 | Predict: 14.3 |
| Average absolute deviation | | $24 \div 9 = 2.7$ | $17.1 \div 9 = 1.9$ | $17.7 \div 9 = 2.0$ |

in the direction of more sales than would be warranted by past performance, and may have compensated by adjusting the calculated prediction upwards

1989: the year of the "outlying" or "funny" data, which we have attributed to economic factors in general rather than to loss of interest in our product

For all other years the deviations do not exceed 2, whereas the deviations based on last year alone (Table 17.2) had a range of 2 to 6 deviation units, in the limited number listed, with *none* of these 5 years having a deviation *fewer* than two units. For purposes of comparison, we show the entire range of deviations in Table 17.5. As the table clearly indicates, both averaging methods perform better than the predictions based on a single year. In this particular data, the predictions based on all data perform better than the moving average in some instances, worse in others. However, one would have to consider the costs of keeping and processing the data as well as the benefit of better predictions. The method of the moving averages stores less data (3 to 10 years) and requires less mathematics (three additions to ten) in comparison with the average of all years. In addition, from the pattern of data given here, a prediction of 14.3 for next year seems closer to the mark than 13.7, although this remains to be seen.

Of course, the average of 3 years' data might not be the best predictor. A forecaster might try 2 years, 4 years, 5 years, or other combinations in order to find the most suitable "cycle of history" to maintain in the data base.

TABLE 17.6

| Hour | Arrivals | Cumulated Arrival | Serviced | Cumulated People Served | Queue |
|---|---|---|---|---|---|
| 1 | 10 | 10 | 5 | 5 | 5 |
| 2 | 10 | 20 | 5 | 10 | 10 |
| 3 | 10 | 30 | 5 | 15 | 15 |
| 4 | 10 | 40 | 5 | 20 | 20 |
| 5 | 10 | 50 | 5 | 25 | 25 |

Queuing Theory

Another application of mathematical techniques to management problems is "queuing theory" or the theory of waiting in lines. Queuing theory is a study of systems that offer a "service" to people (or other entities) who "arrive" at the service facility, and of lines that form at the service facility as the people who arrive "queue up" until it is their turn.

Two numbers are of particular interest in queuing theory

1.  The service rate, or the rate at which we can dispense customers. We will call this S.
2.  The arrival rate, or the rate at which customers arrive. We will call this A.

If the arrival rate (A) is greater than the service rate (S), i.e., if customers arrive faster than we can handle them, the line will eventually become infinite. For example, if people arrive at a rate of 10 an hour, and we can service only 5 and hour, the line will grow in the fashion indicated in Table 17.6, in which case we see that the queue is growing at a rate of 5 persons an hour. If we run a 24-hr business (such as an answering service, in which "calls received" are the arrivals, or a computer systems servicing "jobs"), the queue would consist of 120 persons at the end of the first day, 240 persons at the end of the second day, 840 persons at the end of a week, 3,600 persons at the end of 30 days, and approximately 43,200 persons (12*3600) at the end of the year. Of course, this is unrealistic. A business with such a service rate would soon have no lines, since the customers would no doubt have moved elsewhere. However, the example serves to point up the fact that the service rate must exceed the arrival rate if we are even to begin considering the study of queues (lines).

One of the more useful formulas in queuing theory is the formula for the average length of the queue. If we assume a Poisson arrival rate (the Poisson distribution is a theoretical probability distribution that we will not explain here, but will take for granted in this application) and a service rate that follows an exponential distribution, the formula for the average length of the line (number of persons waiting) is

$$L_{AVE} = \frac{A^2}{S(S-A)}$$

Thus, if we own a store in which customers arrive at a rate of 10 an hour and we employ one clerk who can service 15 persons an hour, the average length of the line will be

$$L_{AVE} = \frac{10^2}{15(15-10)} = \frac{100}{15*5} = \frac{100}{75} = 1\frac{25}{75} = 1\frac{1}{3}$$

There will also be 1 person being "serviced." Of course, there will never be exactly 1 1/3 people in line; sometimes there will be no one in line, other times there will be 1 person in line, other times 2 or 3, but the average number will be 1 1/3.

The formula for the total number of persons in the system is

$$Q_{AVE} = \frac{A}{S-A}$$

For an arrival rate of 10 customers per hour and a service rate of 15 customers per hour, we have

$$Q_{AVE} = \frac{10}{15-10} = 2$$

This is the total number of people "in the system" on the average, although it is also referred to as the number of people "in the queue."

The terminology used in queuing theory deviates a bit from common usage. While one might expect "people in the queue" to refer to the people "waiting," it usually refers to "those waiting plus those being serviced." We say "those" being serviced because queues with more than one server, e.g., several bank tellers, can service more than a single person at a time.

The reader will note that the number of persons waiting "on average" (1 1/3) and the total number in the system (2) do *not* follow the relationship

$$Q_{AVE} = L_{AVE} + 1 \longleftarrow \text{not true}$$

This is because there are times when nobody is in the system (number in the queue is zero), bringing the average "down" from 2 1/3 to 2.

## The Load Factor

The relationship between A and S, i.e., their ratio, is referred to as the load factor, and is usually called "rho"

$$rho = \frac{A}{S} = \frac{10}{15} = .67$$

For our case, the load factor is 2/3. We are busy two-thirds of the time, idle one-third of the time. The formulas given in terms of A and S can be rewritten in terms of rho. For example, the total number of people in the queue is

$$Q_{AVE} = \frac{rho}{1-rho} = \frac{\frac{2}{3}}{1-\frac{2}{3}} = \frac{\frac{2}{3}}{\frac{1}{3}} = 2$$

Systems operating near a rho of 1.0 are very busy, systems near 0.0 are idle. The value of rho can exceed 1.0, but this indicates an arrival rate faster than the service rate, with the resultant infinite lines. A load factor exceeding .8 or .9 is usually considerd "dangerous" in that a slight increase in the arrival rate will cause a large deterioration in service. For example, at rho = .8, we have a queue size (total persons in the system) of

$$\frac{.8}{1-.8} = \frac{.8}{.2} = 4$$

But if the demand for our product increases so that rho moves to .9, we have more than doubled the average number of persons in the system

$$\frac{.9}{1-.9} = \frac{.9}{.1} = 9$$

and the people in line will start becoming restless. It is at this point that queuing theory (and management theory) "tells us" to put on another server.

## Relationship Between Q and L

The relationship between $Q_{AVE}$ and $L_{AVE}$ is given in terms of the load factor or rho. For a "single-server facility," we have

$$Q_{AVE} = L_{AVE} + rho$$

For our data, this is

$$2 = 1\frac{1}{3} + \frac{2}{3}$$

which is indeed true.

## The Longest Line

One other question we might want to ask is "What will be the longest length the line becomes?" That is, how bad will the wait be in the worst case? This value cannot be computed exactly, because there is no limit to the number that can *possibly* be in the queue. However, we can compute a probability of the number of persons in the system (waiting in line and being serviced) being a particular value. The formula for doing so is

$$\text{Probability } (n = x) = \left(\frac{A}{S}\right)^x \left(1 - \frac{A}{S}\right)$$

where the n stands for "number of people in the system" and the "=x" stands for "n takes on the particular value of x." Hence, we might say n = 0, n = 1, or n = 5, and compute the probability of that many people being in the system. Note that the value of x is used in the formula as the power to which the term A/S is raised

$$\left(\frac{A}{S}\right)^x$$

To solve for any particular number of persons in the system, we simply substitute the necessary values in our formula. Hence, the probability of having no one in the system (x = 0) is

$$P(n = 0) = \left(\frac{10}{15}\right)^0 \left(1 - \frac{10}{15}\right)$$

and since any number raised to the zero power is equal to 1, this reduces to

$$P(n = 0) = 1 * \left(1 - \frac{A}{S}\right) = \left(1 - \frac{10}{15}\right) = 1 - .67 = .33$$

That is, 33% of the time the system will be empty. This is a direct result of the load factor being .67; if we are "busy" .67 of the time, we must be idle .33 of the time. The probability of having five persons in the system is

$$P(n = 5) = \left(\frac{A}{S}\right)^5 \left(1 - \frac{A}{S}\right) = \left(\frac{10}{15}\right)^5 \quad 1 - \frac{10}{15}$$

$$= \left(\frac{2}{3}\right)^5 \quad 1 - \frac{2}{3}$$

$$= \frac{32}{243} * \frac{1}{3} = \frac{32}{729} = .04$$

so that five persons will be in the system (one being waited on, four waiting) about 4% of the time. The probability for six persons being in the system is

$$P(n = 6) = \left(\frac{10}{15}\right)^6 * \left(1 - \frac{10}{15}\right)$$

$$= \left(\frac{2}{3}\right)^6 * \left(1 - \frac{2}{3}\right)$$

$$= \frac{64}{729} * \frac{1}{3}$$

$$= \frac{64}{2187}$$

$$\approx .03$$

and larger values for n get progressively smaller, so that the probability of having 10 or 15 persons in the system is extremely small or "negligible."


## The Queuing Curve

The relationship between the load factor (or utility factor) and queue size is indicated by a curve in the shape shown in Figure 17.4, which shows that at low load factors, there are relatively few persons in the system (not good for the proprietors), but that at high load levels, the size of the queue "takes off," again not good for business. The goal is to achieve a balance between being too idle (no profits) and too busy (poor service). This can be done in several ways

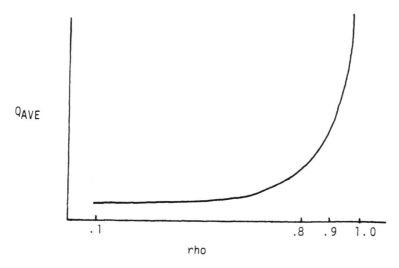

FIGURE 17.4

- Reduce arrival rate
- Increase service rate
- Add more servers

In most profit-making applications we do not wish to reduce the arrival rate, since this means a reduction in profits. However, there are instances in which it does make sense to reduce the arrival rate. A particular intersection of the city may be quite congested. One way to reduce the congestion would be to reduce the number of cars arriving. Say they "arrive" at the intersection on their way to buy groceries. We could reduce the load at the intersection by encouraging private enterprise to build a store in the area near the homes of these commuters. Of course, this is a "second server" in terms of grocery suppliers, which indicates that a problem can be modeled in more than one way.

An increase in the service rate can be accomplished by making organizational or technological changes. An example of an organizational change is the change in a bank from several lines (say 6; one at each teller referred to as single-server queues), to a single queue serviced by all tellers (one six-server queue). The formulas of queuing theory indicate that the latter organization is preferable in terms of performance. Technological changes can be had by training the servers to be faster, or by providing faster equipment, e.g., using high-speed data communication lines to move the data more quickly. The technological changes will usually involve some cost. The organizational changes may or may not involve a dollar cost. The switch from six independent queues to one six-server queue in a bank usually requires the placement of a rope and a sign to route the customers, a minimal investment for the increased performance.

There are limitations to the increased performance resulting from organizational and technological changes. Hence, the final solution to problems of "overload" is the addition of more servers, e.g., more tellers at the bank, more grocery stores in the area, and more CPUs at the computing center.

## Adding Servers

In the first example, the load factor was two-thirds, arising from an arrival rate of 10 persons per hour, a service rate of 15 per hour. However, suppose that our reputation for good service gets around so that the number of customers coming into our store more than doubles, arrivals now coming in at a rate of 25 per hour. Since we can service only 15 an hour, we must put on an extra clerk or two and the question becomes one of how many. If we add one checker, we now have two service facilities. Let us assume that each server has the same service rate of 15 customers per hour (if this is not the case, we would compute an average service rate). We can then double the service rate in our formulas from 15 customers per hour to 30 (15 customers/server * 2 servers = 30), so that the expected number of people waiting in line is

$$L_{AVE} = \frac{A^2}{S(S-A)} = \frac{25^2}{30(30-25)} = \frac{625}{30*5} = \frac{625}{150} = 4.2$$

We have an *average* of four persons waiting. This is not the great service that we built our reputation on. The relatively poor service is due to a higher utility factor

$$\frac{A}{S} = \frac{25}{30} = 83\%$$

which indicates that our clerks are busy over 80% of the time!

We might consider hiring a third clerk, so that our service rate triples and our utility factor becomes

$$\frac{A}{S} = \frac{25}{45} = \frac{5}{9} = 56\%$$

and the expected length of the waiting line is

$$L_{AVE} = \frac{A^2}{S(S-A)} = \frac{25^2}{45(45-25)} = \frac{625}{45*20} = \frac{625}{900} = .7$$

so that "less than 1 person" is waiting *on average*, and our reputation is restored. (We reused the formula for the single-server queue. This assumes that there are two or three single-server queues. A better organization is to have a single multiserver queue. A different set of formulas pertains to the multiserver queue, but the idea is the same.)

## Translating Time Into Money

Several authors have developed the idea of queuing theory in relation to business applications. Those who have proved to be particularly useful to this author have been Bierman, Bonini, and Hausman (1973) and Gustavson and Gear (1978). The analysis presented here is similar to that found in Gustavson and Gear.

Suppose that we have a set of accountants who keep our books. These accountants are paid $10/hr. Each accountant uses a desk calculator to perform his or her computations. Every once in a while the calculator breaks, and the accountant must take it to a central repair facility. There is one person at the repair facility, and this person is paid $6/hr. Suppose, further, that the rate at which the accountants arrive at the repair facility is 5/hr, while the rate at which the repairperson can service the accountant (repair the calculator) is 6/hr. The average number of accountants in the system (having a calculator repaired or waiting in line) is

$$N_{system} = \frac{A}{S-A} = \frac{5}{6-5} = 5$$

(The use of N rather than $Q_{AVE}$ is more common in the literature of queuing theory.) At $10/hr, we have $50 tied up in accountants who are idle while their calculators are being fixed. If we now examine the possibility of a second repairperson, working as fast as the first, we could reduce the number of accountants in the system to

$$N_{system} = \frac{A}{(S-A)} = \frac{5}{12-5} = \frac{5}{7} = .7145$$

where the new service rate (12/hr) is double the service rate with one repairperson. At $10/hr, we are investing approximately $7.15 (.7145*$10) per hour in accountants getting their calculators repaired. This is a savings of $42.85 ($50 − $7.15) per hour, which must be balanced against the cost of an additional repairperson at $6/hr. Since we are saving more than we are spending, a net of $36.85, we decide to hire the new repairperson. A savings of $36.85/hr projects into $294.80 in an 8-hr day, or $1,474 in a 40-hr week, which certainly would justify the time spent in reading a chapter or two on queuing theory.

Of course, other options are open to us. We could reduce the arrival rate by buying more reliable calculators. If the more reliable calculators reduced the arrival rate to one accountant per hour, we would have the following number of accountants in the repair system

$$N_{system} = \frac{A}{S-A} = \frac{1}{6-1} = \frac{1}{5} = .2$$

which is a better rho than that achieved by the use of a second repairperson. Of course we would now have to calculate the cost of the more reliable calculators. If we assume that we spend $50,000 a year on calculators now, and that the increased reliability model will add a cost of 10%, the cost of the added reliability is $5,000 year. At $6/hr, the repairperson will make approximately $9,600 a year (200 days * 8 hr * $6/hr), so that the increased reliability is cheaper than hiring another repairperson. If the increased reliability had cost 20% more, or $10,000, we might hire the repairperson.

Another alternative would be to have a cache of "backup" calculators, so that accountants could use calculators from this reserve while their own are being repaired. This would result in a much faster service time in terms of servicing the accountant (time to exchange calculators), so that we might service 30 accountants per hour and our average number in the system becomes

$$N_{system} = \frac{A}{(S-A)} = \frac{10}{30-10} = \frac{10}{20} = .5$$

Of course, we now have to calculate the cost of the extra calculators, and we still have to repair the calculators, though not while the person is waiting.

As indicated here, there are several ways to attack a queuing problem. They all revolve around the idea of decreasing service time (increasing service rate) or decreasing arrival rate. Service times can be decreased by adding more servers (up to a point), using new technology (e.g., automation rather than manual methods), or streamlining procedures (e.g., using task analysis to see the sequence in which actions are performed and arranging the necessary tools in this order). Arrival rates can be reduced by similar methods, e.g., using more reliable technology, safer procedures (e.g., to reduce arrivals at an infirmary), or other means. In any case, we can use the data we have (on arrival rates, service rates, and salaries) to

- Calculate the expected queue length
- Calculate the cost of this "waiting" time
- Instigate a study of methods to make the system more efficient or more cost effective

## Linear Programming

Another application of mathematical techniques to management decisions is the use of linear programming in order to maximize profits or minimize costs. The essence of linear programming can be exemplified by an example in which we manufacture at least two products that sell at different profits. These two products require the use of two or more machines in varying amounts of time for each product (our resources). We wish to allocate the resources so as to maximize profits. For the purposes of example, let us assume that we make two types of denim pants: fashionable and durable. These two types of pants require the use of two different machines, a cutting/sewing machine and a pressing machine. The fashionable pants, priced slightly higher, sell at a profit of $12 a pair. The durable denims, priced slightly lower, sell at a profit of $8 a pair.

If we had unlimited resources, and were motivated solely by profit (i.e., consideration of the social needs of the working community for durable denims were not a factor to us), we would make only the fashionable denims, since these would generate a greater profit per pair sold ($12 to $8). However, it is seldom the case that there are unlimited resources (even resources that were once considered to be virtually unlimited, such as pure water and clean air, have been found to be remarkably finite). We must now consider the "constraints" on our clothing manufacturing operation. These constraints are

1. The total number of hours the machines are available
2. The number of hours required on each machine in order to manufacture a given pair of pants

We have already said that each pair of pants requires the use of two machines. (We could have required three, four, or more machines; the mathematics becomes more extensive, but the concept is the same. The requirements are determined by the application.) Let us assume that we own these machines and that our operation runs 24 hr/day. Let us further suppose that machine 1, the cutting/sewing machine, can be used 6 days a week (the union allows work on Saturday, but not on Sunday), so that we have 144 hr available to us on machine 1. The union for pressers forbids work on both Saturday and Sunday so that we have only five 24-hr days, or 120 hr/week, available on machine 2. (We will abstract from the question of "downtime" when the machines are broken and being repaired.) Finally, let us assume that the fashionable denims require 2 hr on the sewing machine, 1 on the presser; the durable denims, requiring less stitching, require only 1 hr on the sewing machine and 1 hr on the pressing machine.

## Possible Solutions

There are four possible "mixes" available to us. We could

1. Make no denims at all
2. Make only fashionable denims
3. Make only durable denims
4. Make a mixture of fashionable and durable denims

If we designate the fashionable denims by the letter $F$, durable by the letter $D$, choice 1, make no denims at all, corresponds to the values of $F = 0$, $D = 0$. This choice renders no profit at all, so that we will look at the other three possibilities to see if they generate a higher profit.

## The Pure Solutions

Choices 2 and 3, make all fashionable and make all durable, respectively, are "pure" solutions in that they involve the manufacture of only one product. Let us see how many of each product we could make.

Considering the fashionable denims first, we see that we could press 120 pairs a week, and the pressing machine is available for a total of 120 hr/week. However, we can make only 72 pairs of the fashionable denims on machine 1, the sewing machine, since the fashionable denims require 2 hr on this machine for each pair, and there are only 144 hr available (144 hr * 1 pair/2hr = 72 pairs). Since we can't press more denims than we can sew, the lower figure of 72 pairs is the maximum number of fashionable denims we can create.

If we assume that we sell every pair we make, this would generate a total profit of $864 ($12 per pair * 72 pairs). This is certainly better than the profit of $0 if we make nothing, so we would rather "specialize," making all fashionable denims, than not be in business at all. However, we still have two more cases to consider: make all durable denims, and make a mixture of fashionable and durable denims.

If we specialize in durable denims, we can make 120 pairs. This figure is arrived at as follows: on machine 1 we can sew 144 pairs of durables a week (1 hr each pair, 144 hr available); however, on machine 2 we can press only 120 durables a week, since 120 is the total number of hours available and we need 1 hr per pair. Since there is no point in sewing more pairs than we can press (we would never sell an unfinished, wrinkled pair), we produce the lesser number of denims, 120.

If we produce and sell 120 pairs of durable denims, we can make $960 ($8 per pair * 120 pairs), which is better than both the $0 of not producing and the $864 of producing only fashionable denims. If there were no more choices, we would make only durable denims. However, we must consider the case of a mixture of fashionables and durables.

## The Mixed Case

The question we now ask is if we can do better not by specializing, but by producing a mixture of fashionable and durable denims. In order to investigate this possibility, we have to "systematize" our data. We will create equations that describe the constraints of our problem. With the two machines, we will have at least two equations; however, since there are other constraints on our system, such as the fact that we cannot make "a negative number of denims," there will be more than two equations involved. The equations we develop are called a "system of equations" and the solution to our question is found by "solving" these equations for values that satisfy all constraints on the system.

## The Equations of Constraint

The first constraint on our system is that concerning machine 1, the cutting/sewing machine. This machine can be used 144 hr/week at most (it can be used fewer hours, such as 72 or even 0, if we decide to go out of business, but the total hours used cannot exceed the 144 available). Whenever this machine is used to make fashionable denims, 2 hr of use are consumed; thus if we make 10 pairs of fashionable denims, we consume 20 hr of machine time. If we make 25 pairs of fashionable denims, 50 hr are consumed on this machine. The number of fashionable denims we make is considered a variable, so we represent it by a letter, say $F$, which is assumed to take on such values as 10 or 25 pairs. Whatever value F takes on, the number of hours consumed on machine 1 is 2 times F, i.e., 2 hr for each pair. We represent this relationship as 2F, which indicates that whatever number we substitute for F, the number of hours on machine 1 will be twice that figure.

In a similar fashion, we will designate the number of durable denims by the variable D. We know that these consume only 1 hr on machine 1: 10 pairs, 10 hr; 25 pairs, 25 hr. This relationship is designated as 1D, which indicates that whatever value D takes on, the number of hours consumed on machine 1 will be exactly the same (or 1 time as many).

Finally, if we add the total hours spent making fashionable denims and the total hours making durable denims, the total number of hours spent making both types of denims cannot exceed 144. We indicate the total number of hours consumed by

$$2F + 1D$$

which says "total hours fashionable" plus "total hours durable," and indicate that this sum cannot exceed 144 by the expression

$$2F + 1D \leqslant 144$$

where the symbol $\leqslant$ means that the expression on the left (total hours actually consumed) must be less than or equal to the expression on the right (total hours available, i.e., potential for consumption). The equation says that the total units actually consumed must be within the limits of the potential consumption, which makes sense, since our system cannot do the impossible.

On machine 2, we need 1 hr for each pair of fashionable denims

1F

and 1 hr for each pair of durable denims

    1D

so that the total hours needed is

    1F + 1D

We have 120 hr available on machine 2 (since we don't use it on Saturday or Sunday), so that the inequality becomes

    1F + 1D ≤ 120

again indicating that actual use must be made less than or equal to our capacity.

    These two inequalities

    2F + 1D ≤ 144 (for machine 1)

    1F + 1D ≤ 120 (for machine 2)

indicate what "can be made." They have to be considered together ("simultaneously") since *both* conditions must be satisfied. Thus, even though inequality 2 could be satisfied by values of 100 for F and 20 for D

    1F + 1D =

    1*100 + 1*20 = 120

which is less than *or equal* to 120; these same values cannot satisfy equation 1

    2F + 1D =

    2*100 + 1*44 = 244

which is *not* less than or equal to 144. Because the inequalities have to be considered together, they are called "simultaneous inequalities" or a "system of inequaltiies."


Restriction to Positive Values

In theoretical mathematics, numbers such as negative 1 could be substituted into the equations for F and D and still satisfy the equations

    1F + 1D =

    1*(-1) + 1*(-1) =

    -1 + -1 = -2

which is less than 120. However, in this "applied" use of mathematics, such numbers do not make sense. We can make some denims or we can make none, but we can't make minus one. Therefore, two more inequalities are added to our system

    F ≥ 0

    D ≥ 0

which indicate that F and D must take on positive values or zero, but that they cannot be negative.

Although the "positiveness" relations (inequalities) are often present, they are not always explicitly stated, since the "logic of the situation" will restrict our attention to the region of feasible answers.

## Conditions for Solving the Inequalities

The expressions

$$2F + 1D \leqslant 144$$

$$1F + 1D \leqslant 120$$

are called inequalities, since they allow the unequal relationship of "less than" as well as the "equal" relation between the expression on the left and the expression on the right-hand side of the relation. It will be convenient, however, to consider them as equalities for our current discussion. In this case, we will write only the equal sign, and refer to the equations as "simultaneous equations."

The justification for changing the inequalities into equations is that we wish to maximize profit and thus the use of our resources. While the inequality

$$2F + 1D \leqslant 144$$

can be satisfied by such numbers as $F = 1$ and $D = 1$, we would have hours "left over" (called "slack") that we could use to make more denims. In a more rigorous treatment of linear programming, the inequalities are changed into equalities by introducing a "dummy variable" into each equation to take up any "slack" if the results are less than the total number of hours. We will present a simplified example that gives the flavor of the calculations and their purpose.

We have two equations

$$2F + 1D = 144$$

$$1F + 1D = 120$$

in two unknowns (F and D). One of the essential requirements for solving simultaneous equations is that we have at least as many equations as we have unknowns. Since we do have "two equations in two unknowns," they can be solved. In fact, we have four equations in two unknowns, with the solutions being restricted to positive values of F and D. If we had two unknowns and only one equation, we could not solve the equation for a *unique* set of values. Thus if we have the equation

$$2F + 1D = 144$$

values of $F = 72$ and $D = 0$ will work, as will $F = 10$, $D = 124$; $F = 25$, $D = 94$, etc. It is the second equation that will specify which single pair of values for F and D (out of the myriad that satisfy equation 1) will satisfy both equations.

By comparing the number of equations with the number of unknowns we can tell if the system of equations is "solvable." Whenever the number of independent equations equals the number of unknowns, the equations can be solved (if the equations are consistent and distinct). If the number of equations is less than the number of unknowns, they cannot be solved in the sense of producing a unique solution. Thus, three equations in five unknowns is not solvable. Five equations in three unknowns may be, if the extra equations do not make the system inconsistent. In our case, two unknowns and two equations, we have a soluble case.

## The Solution

The method of solving the simultaneous equations is to manipulate them arithmetically in order to eliminate all but one of the variables, then solve for that variable. For example, in our case

$$2F + 1D = 144$$

$$1F + 1D = 120$$

the coefficient of the D terms is the same in each equation. Thus, we can subtract equation 2 from equation 1 in order to eliminate the D term from the expression

$$2F + \phantom{-}D = \phantom{-}144$$
$$-1F + -D = -120$$
$$\overline{\phantom{2}1F \phantom{+ -D} = \phantom{-}24}$$

so that F = 24 is one answer, and substituting this value into equation 1, we solve for D

$$2*24 + D = 144$$

$$48 + D = 144$$

$$D = 144 - 48 = 96$$

which indicates that we could make

F = 24  pairs of fashionable denims

D = 96  pairs of durable denims

If we do so, our total profit will be

$$\$12 * 24 + \$8 * 96 =$$

$$288 + 768 = \$1056$$

since we will make $12 on each of the 24 pairs of fashionable denims sold and $8 each for the 96 pairs of durable denims.
   This is a greater profit than any of the "pure" solutions

1.  Make all fashionable denims
    Total made = 72
    Total profit = 72 * $12 = $864
2.  Make all durable denims
    Total made = 120
    Total profit = 120 * $8 = $960

so that our "mixture of products" is worthwhile. Of course, this mixture will require some management of activities; the cost of these activities should be compared to the difference between the best pure solution ($960) and the best mixed solution ($1,056), which is $96, to see if the additional costs are less than the additional profits.

## Multiplying By a Constant

The solution of another set of simultaneous equations may require the multiplication of one or more of the equations by a constant value in order to make the coefficients of a given unknown alike. For example, with the equations

$$3x + 2y = 12$$
$$x + 3y = 11$$

we might multiply equation 2 by 3 in order to get the form

$$3x + 2y = 12$$
$$3x + 9y = 33$$

so that we can subtract to obtain

$$3x + 2y = 12$$
$$-3x - 9y = -33$$

$$-7y = -21$$
$$y = 3$$

and substitute our result back into equation 1

$$3x + 2*3 = 12$$

to solve for x

$$3x + 6 = 12$$
$$3x = 12-6$$
$$3x = 6$$
$$x = 2$$

The student is advised to review an introductory algebra text for the necessary calculations.

## Summary of the Process

The above procedure is the algebraic method of solving a system of linear equations. A summary of the method is given in Figure 17.5. It will *not* be the case that the mixed solution will always be optimal. An example of a "pure" solution is given later in the chapter. Thus, all cases must be examined.

## Maximal Utilization of Resources

In producing

$$F = 24$$
$$D = 96$$

pairs of denims, our machines are allocated as shown in Figure 17.6. In each case, we have consumed the total number of hours on each machine; we have maximized the use of our resources.

1.  Consider the case of D=0, F=0, that is no production, with profit $0

2.  Consider the pure cases. To do so, take each case separately:

    a.  D=0, F=maximum

        1.  Find maximum
            To find maximum, substitute D=0 into *each* of the constraint equations and solve for F:

            EQ1: 2F + 1*0 = 144
                        F =  72
            EQ2: 1F + 1*0 = 120
                        F = 120

            Choose the least of these numbers as the maximum number to be produced. The rationale for choosing the least number is that we need *both* machines to create a *complete* product, and we are creating only complete products.

        2.  Calculate profit

            $12 F   + $8D = P
            $12(72) + $8(0) = $864

    b.  Do same for F=0, D=maximum

        1.  Find maximum

            EQ1: 2*0 + 1*D = 144
            EQ2: 1*0 + 1*D = 120
               Maximum      = 120

        2.  Find profit

            $12F   + $8D = P
            $12(0) + $8(120) = $960

3.  Solve simultaneous equations for mixed case:

            2F + 1D = 144
            1F + 1D = 120
            ─────────────────
                 F =  24
                 D =  96

        Find profit:

        $12F    + $8D = P
        $12(24) + $8(96) = $1056

4.  Choose highest profit

            $1056 > $960 > $864 > $0

    so produce F = 24
               D = 96

FIGURE 17.5

Machine 1:      $2F + 1D \leq 144$
             $2*24 + 1*96 = 144$
                       No Slack

Machine 2:      $1F + 1D \leq 120$
             $1*24 + 1*96 = 120$
                       No Slack

FIGURE 17.6

## A Graphic Solution

The two constraint inequalities can be depicted graphically. In graphing the inequalities, we will use only the first quadrant, since this is the area in which both F and D will be positive. We will place the F variable (num-

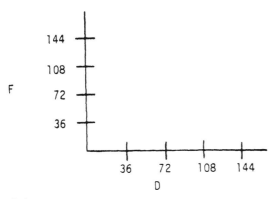

(a)

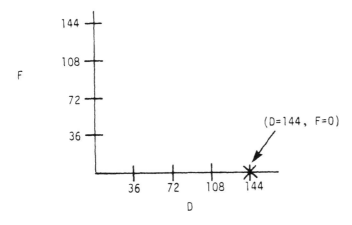

(b)

FIGURE 17.7

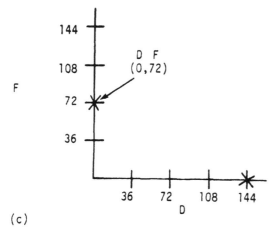

(c)

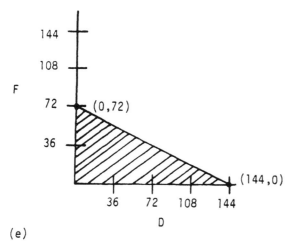

(d)

(e)

FIGURE 17.7 (continued)

ber of fashionable denims sold) on the y- or vertical axis, and the D variable on the x- or the horizontal axis (the choice is arbitrary; Figure 17.7a). In order to graph the equation

2F + 1D = 144

we can find the "pure" solutions by setting each of the variables to zero, in turn. Thus, setting F to 0 we have

2*0 + D = 144

    D = 144

We graph the point D = 144, F = 0 on our coordinate system (convention has it that the horizontal axis is named first in describing a point by a pair of values; Figure 17.7b).

Setting D = 0 in the same equation, we have

2F + 0 = 144

   2F = 144

    F = 72

                    D  F
Graphing the point (0, 72) we have Figure 17.7c. We now simply draw a straight line between these two points (Figure 17.7d). The area beneath this line is the area of valid values for F and D. When combined (added) in the relation 2F + D the result will be a value less than 144. The values on the line itself will total to 144 when combined in the relation 2F + D. hence all points on the line and below are solutions to the inequality 2F + 1D ⩽ 144 (Figure 17.7e).

The value (1,1) will work

2*1 + 1 ⩽ 144

   3 ⩽ 144

as will F = 54, D = 36 (which is on the line)

2*54 + 36 ⩽ 144

   144 ⩽ 144

However, this is not the only constraint on our system. We still need to draw the line for the second equation

F + D = 120

 D   F
(0, 120)

and

 D   F
(120, 0)

so that the graph becomes as shown in Figure 17.8a. It is the area on or under *both* equations that is the "feasible" area (Figure 17.8b). Let us redraw the graph with only the feasible region indicated (Figure 17.8c). Any point on or below this line is feasible. However, not all points are "optimal." For example, if we choose D = 1, F = 1 as a solution (Figure 17.9a), we will make only $20 ($12 on the fashionable, $8 on the durable). We could

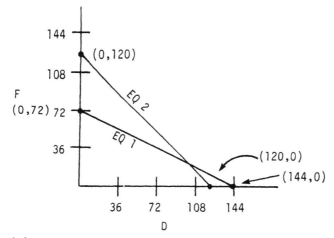

(a)

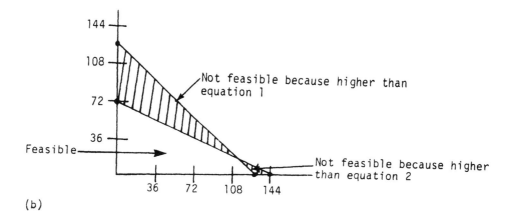

(b)

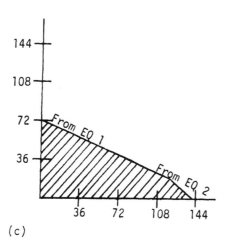

(c)

FIGURE 17.8

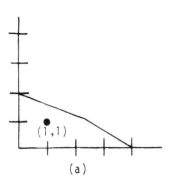

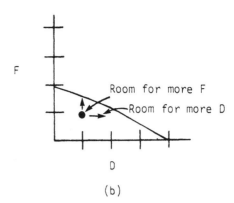

(a)                                              (b)

FIGURE 17.9

make more by choosing F = 3, D = 2 (also feasible), which results in a profit of $52 ($12 * 3 + $8 * 2). The optimal solution will be in the highest region of feasibility, on the boundary of the feasible region. Any point beneath the boundary can be improved by making more units of one or the other item (or both: Figure 17.9b). However, the boundary is a long region, consisting of many points. In order to find the optimal *single point*, we must consider the profit equation.

### The Profit Equation

The profit equation indicates the contribution of the two items we manufacture to the total profit. The fashionable denims contribute $12 each

    12F

while the durable denims contribute $8 each

    8D

The sum of these two values is total profit P

    12F + 8D = P

The profit itself can vary, so we do not place an exact value into the equation, simply indicating the profit by P.

To graph this equation, however, we must give some value to P, so we will choose one arbitrarily. If we sold only one of each of the two commodities, we would have a profit of $20, so let us begin with

    12F + 8D = $20

In order to plot this equation on our graph, we need at least two points.
                              D   F
One of these is the point (1 , 1), which would really produce the profit of $20 (Figure 17.10a). No other "real" point would provide a profit of $20 in our particular example (since other points would require fractional values, and we don't sell fractions of denim pants, or negative values, and we don't create a negative number of denims). However, we are interested only in the line itself, and its slope, not in a particular "realistic" point at this

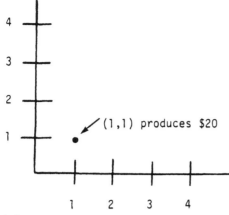

(a)

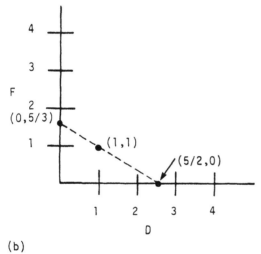

(b)

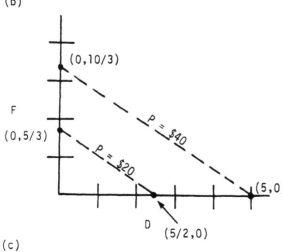

(c)

FIGURE 17.10

time, so we choose the second point arbitrarily. Any point that satisfies the relationship

    12F + 8D = 20

will do, so let us choose F = 0, in which case, D will be 2 1/2

    12*0 + 8D = 20

        8D = 20

        $D = 2\frac{1}{2}$

and plot this point, as well as the line through the pair of points (Figure 17.10b). This line is the profit equation. As indicated here, with the point (1,1) on the line, it indicates a profit of $20. For a profit of $40, we would again set up the profit equation

    12F + 8D = $40

and solve for two points. A realistic point is not necessary in order to plot the line, so we arbitrarily solve for (D,0) and (0,F)

    12*0 + 8D = 40

        8D = 40

        D = 5

    12F + 8*0 = 40

        12F = 40

        $F = 3\frac{1}{3}$

and plot these two points, as well as the line between them (Figure 17.10c).

As the reader can see, the line for a profit of $40 is parallel to, but more to the "northwest" (further from the origin) than the profit line for $20. This is a general principle. Lesser profits will be parallel lines closer to the origin. Greater profits will be parallel lines further from the origin.

On the line for a profit of $40, two "realistic" points exist

    D = 5     F = 0      Profit = $8*5 = $40

    D = 2     F = 2      Profit = $12*2 + $8*2 = $40

A particular profit line may have a single realistic point [as (1,1) in P = $20], no realistic points (e.g., for a profit of $7, which can't be attained by any combination of denims in our example), or more than one realistic point [as above with (5,0) and (2,2)]. We are interested in the slope of the profit equation more than a given single point at this time.


## The Slope of the Profit Equation

The slope of the profit equation indicates the "relative contribution" to profit of each commodity we produce. Thus, for our example, each pair of fashionable denims produces $12, each pair of durables $8, so that the ratio of their relative contributions to profit is 12/8, 3/2, or 1 1/2. Fashionable denims contribute 1 1/2 times as much to profit as durable denims.

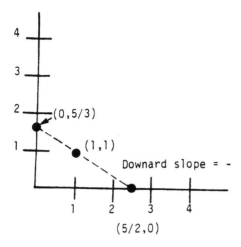

FIGURE 17.11

Alternatively, durable denims contribute 2/3 as much to profit as fashionable ones. It is this ratio of D to F (2/3) that will prove most useful in our example. The equation

$$12F + 8D = P$$

can be written in "slope-intercept" form by dividing through by the coefficient of F

$$\frac{12F}{12} + \frac{8D}{12} = \frac{P}{12}$$

so that

$$F + \frac{8}{12}D = \frac{P}{12}$$

and

$$F = -\frac{8}{12}D + \frac{P}{12}$$

The number -8/12 is the slope of the profit equation. (The slope is the ratio of unit changes on the vertical axis F to the amount of change on the horizontal axis D, or vice versa.)

The slope can be interpreted as follows: the negative sign indicates that the equation slopes downward (Figure 17.11). The fraction 8/12 or 2/3 indicates the steepness of the decline. It is the trade-off ratio between fashionable and durable denims. For every two pairs of fashionable denims we do *not* produce, we must increase our production of durable denims by three units to offset the decrease in profits

Decrease of 2 pairs of fashionable denims = -(2*$12) = $-24

Increase of 3 pairs of durable denims = (+3) * ($8) = $24

Alternatively, a decrease in production of durables of three units ($-24) can be offset by an increase of fashionables by only two units ($24). The fact that as one type of denim has its production increased, the other must have its production decreased, is what we mean by a trade-off, and is the reason for the slope of the equation being negative. As the amount of one item produced is increased, the amount of the other must be decreased, if we are operating at full capacity.

### Moving the Profit Line Out

All points on a *given* profit line represent the same amount of profit (Figure 17.12a). However, all profit lines to the northwest represent increased profits, so that our "objective" is to move a profit line as far to the northwest as possible (Figure 17.12b). In fact, we would keep moving to the northwest indefinitely, except for the *constraints*. The constraint equations indicate that points to the northwest of the boundary line are not possible (Figure 17.12c), hence we must move the profit equation as far northwest

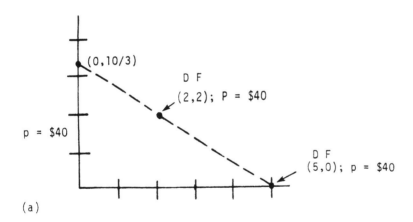

(a)

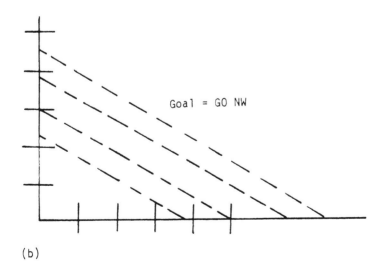

(b)

FIGURE 17.12

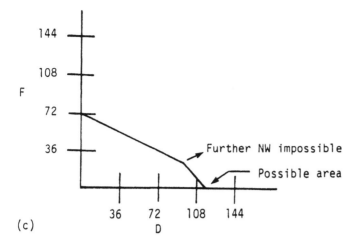

(c)

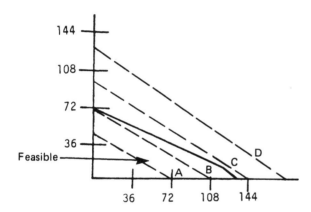

(d)

FIGURE 17.12   (continued)

as the constraint equations permit. To do so, we superimpose the profit equation on the constraint equation (Figure 17.12d). We have shown four profit equations (A,B,C,D) in Figure 17.12d, which are interpreted as follows

> A: feasilble, but profit can be increased by manufacturing more of D and more of F.
> B: feasible, and could be achieved by making only fashionable denims, since the point (D=0, F=72) intersects the profit line B. However, greater profit is possible since part of the feasible region still lies to the northwest of this line.
> C: the optimal solution; profit line intersects the feasible region at its most northwest point.
> D: not feasible, requires more resources than we have.

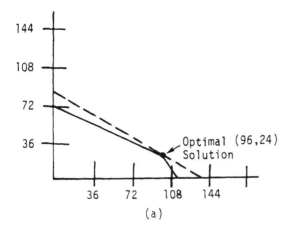

(a)

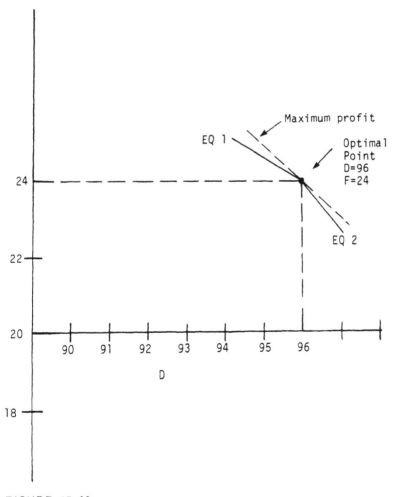

FIGURE 17.13

Since the optimal solution, point C, (Figure 17.13a) has values for both D and F, it will be a mixed solution. In order to read the solution off the graph, we blow up the area of concern (Figure 17.13b), so the D=96, F=24, and total profit is $1,056 (24*12 + 96*8), as before.

In practice, linear programming problems are solved algebraically, one method being the "simplex method." However, the graphical method is used to facilitate and intuitive understanding of the process. In summary, the process is

1.  Draw the constraint equations to create the area of feasibility (the area "within" both equations).
2.  Draw the profit equation.
3.  Move the profit equation nw, until it touches the furthest point of the feasible region.
4.  This point, the farthest nw point of the feasible region that touches (intersects) the profit equation, is the optimal "production mix."


Corner Points

The graphical method indicates something that might not be apparent otherwise. The area of feasibility (Figure 17.14a), has four "corner" points,

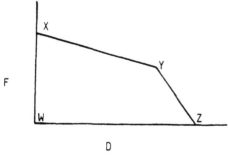

(a)

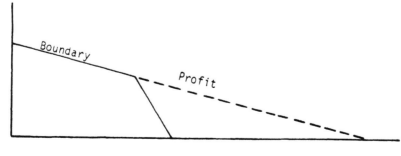

(b)

FIGURE 17.14

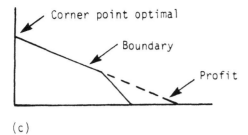

(c)

FIGURE 17.14 (continued)

here indicated by W, X, Y, and Z. A solution to the problem will occur on one of these corner points. In terms of our example, they represent the four possibilities we examined in the algebraic method

W: no production solution: D = 0, F = 0, Profit = $0
X: pure F solution: D = 0, F = 72; Profit = $864
Y: mixed solution: D = 96, F = 24; Profit = $1,056
Z: pure D solution: D = 120, F = 0; Profit = $960

wherein point Y was the optimal solution.

In the case in which the profit line coincides with a boundary line (Figure 17.14b), *all* points on that portion of the boundary line are "optimal." However, this set of points includes the corner point (Figure 17.14c), so that our rule of "one of the corner points is an optimal solution" still holds. Thus, we need examine only the corner points, calculating a profit for each, then comparing the profits to obtain a solution. It is this systematic examination of corner points that the simplex method facilitates.

## A Pure Solution

In our original problem, suppose that fashionable denims sold at a profit of $20, durables at $2. This would change the slope of the profit line (Figures 17.15a and b). Because the fashionable denims provide a much higher rate of return ($20) than the durable denims ($2), we are unwilling to "give up" making a fashionable pair of denims unless this can be offset by a considerable increase (10) in the manufacture of durable denims. The "long stretch" of the line along the x-axis indicates that the profit equation has shifted "against durables." (A very steep line would indicate a shift against fashionables.) Our area of constraint is as shown in Figure 17.15c. In this area the profit line for (8,12) hit its optimum point at the corner point representing the intersection of the two constraint lines (Figure 17.15d). However, the new profit line will hit its highest point at the corner point on the F-axis (Figure 17.15e). This is due to the superior profit of F over D, and can be seen if we calculate the new profits

1. No production: 0,0; profit still zero
2. Pure F: D = 0, F = 72, profit $1,440 ($20*72)
3. Pure D: D = 120, F = 0, profit $240 ($2*120)
4. Mixed F,D: F = 24, D = 96, profit $672 ($20*24+$2*96)

in which case the $1,440 gained by producing only fashionable denims is optimal.

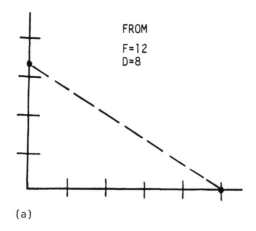

(a)

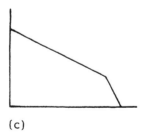

(b)

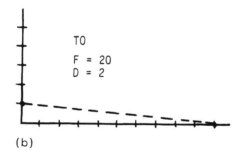

(c)

FIGURE 17.15

## Slack

If we do produce the 72 pairs of fashionable denims, we consume all of the resources in machine 1

$$\frac{2 \text{ hr}}{\text{pair}} * 72 \text{ pairs} = 144 \text{ hr}$$

However, we do not consume all the hours on machine 2

$$\frac{1 \text{ hr}}{\text{pair}} * 72 \text{ pairs} = 72 \text{ hr}$$

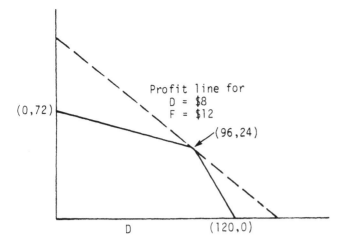

(d)

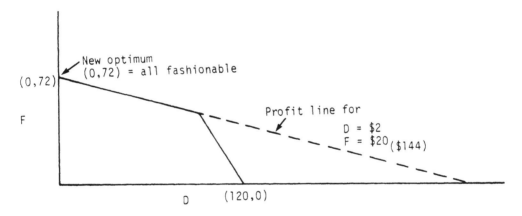

(e)

FIGURE 17.15 (continued)

and 120 hr are available. The difference between the available 120 hr and the 72 hr actually used on machine 2 (120 − 72 = 48) is the "slack." This resource could be used for other purposes (e.g., renting or leasing time on the machine), or we could attempt to speed up production on machine 1, so that the fashionable denims would require less time on machine 1, say 1 1/2 hr, in which case we could produce 96 pairs a week

$$\frac{3}{2F} = 144$$

$$3F = 288$$

$$F = 96$$

In this case the slack on machine 2 would be reduced to 24 hr

$$120 - 96 = 24 \text{ hr}$$

which could still be rented or leased to a third party.

When we convert the linear inequalities to equations, the potential slack in each equation should be indicated by introducing a "slack variable"

$$2F + D + S_1 = 144$$

$$F + D + S_2 = 120$$

In our particular problem, it simply turned out that the slack variable happened to be zero in both equations in the optimal case. However, this is not the general case; the slack variable was omitted in the interest of simplicity.

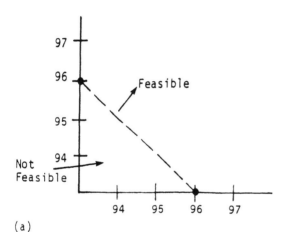

(a)

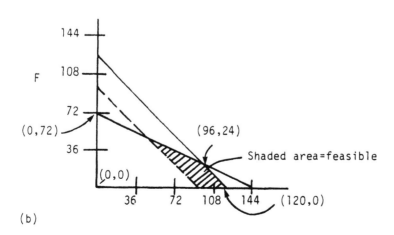

(b)

FIGURE 17.16

## Greater Than

Constraint equations can be written with the symbol "greater than" as well as less than. For example, suppose that we express a commitment (to a buyer) to produce at least 8 dozen pairs of denims (96 pairs) a week. The buyer doesn't care whether these are fashionable or durable denims, as long as the total is 8 dozen pairs. We now have the constraint equation

$$F + D \geqslant 96$$

If we remember the previously feasible solutions

|      | D    | F  | Profit   |
|------|------|----|----------|
| 1.   | 0    | 0  | $0       |
| 2.   | 0    | 72 | $864     |
| 3.   | 120, | 0  | $960     |
| 4.   | 96,  | 24 | $1,056   |

only decisions 3 and 4 are now feasible, with 4 still being optimal. Choices 1 and 2 will not produce 96 pairs of denims (producing 0 and 72 pairs, respectively).

The graphing of

$$F + D \geqslant 96$$

proceeds as before, by graphing $F + D = 96$ (Figure 17.16a). However, the new area of feasibility is northwest of the line, rather than beneath it, as the arrow indicates. This indicates that our solutions must exceed (be greater than) or at least be equal to the 96 pairs we have promised to the buyer. Fewer than 96 pairs is not feasible.

If we impose this new constraint on our previous graph (Figure 17.16b) the shaded area is the new area of feasibility, indicating that the solutions
D  F                               D  F       D  F
(0,0) and (0, 72) are no longer feasible, although (120, 0) and (96, 24) are still feasible. The feasible area has to be beneath the solid lines, the constraint equations with respect to machine resources. We cannot produce more denims than our resources allow, but the production quota must be above the dotted line, the minimum number of denims we promised the buyers; we cannot produce less than we promised. There is an "upper boundary," the boundary of machine capacity, and a "lower boundary," the boundary of fulfilling our commitments.

## Impossible Solutions

It is not the case that every set of equations will form a soluble set. The simplest example of this is to consider the following equations:

$$F + D \geqslant 12$$

$$3F + 2D \leqslant 6$$

which we rewrite as

$$D + F \geqslant 12$$

$$2D + 3F \leqslant 6$$

to indicate that D is playing the role of X, and F of Y

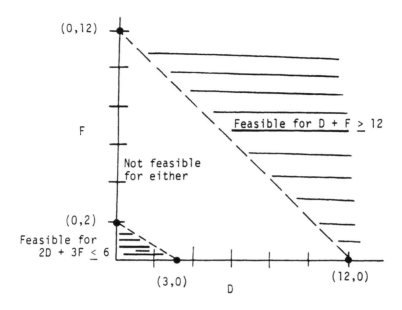

FIGURE 17.17

$$X + Y \geqslant 12$$

$$2X + 3Y \leqslant 6$$

in the conventional form of writing equations.

The first equation means we must produce at least a dozen pairs of denims a week, and the second equation indicates that we need one machine, which is available for a total of 6 hr (with F taking 3 hr per pair, and D taking 2 hr per pair). These two equations graph as shown in Figure 17.17, which indicates that the two equations have no feasible area in common. We must either reduce our commitment to produce a dozen pairs of denims a week, or purchase more machine time on machine 1. However, it is impossible to meet our current commitments with our current resources.

### Three Products: Three Variables

If we have more than two products (e.g., large pots, medium-size pots, and small pots), using two machines (machine 1, a metal punch, and machine 2, a molder), we simply increase the number of variables in our equations. There will still be only two primary constraint equations (as many equations as machines), as well as the nonnegativity constraints and the profit equation. Thus, if we have the constraints shown in Figure 17.18a, and the requirements shown in Figure 17.18b, the primary constraint equations become those shown in Figure 17.18c.

To graph these equations, we now need the three dimensions shown in Figure 17.19a. The number of dimensions in a problem is equal to the number of variables (unknowns). However, the three unknowns (L,M,S) are no longer specified by the two equations. Inequality 1 can be satisfied by

*Machine Availability*

Machine 1 — available 100 hours

Machine 2 — available 150 hours

(a)

*Product Requirements*

Large pots (L)   — 1 hour on machine 1
                      2 hours on machine 2

Medium pots (M) — 1/2 hour on machine 1
                      2 hours on machine 2

Small pots (S)   — 2 hours on machine 1
                      3 hours on machine 2
                      (they are intricate little pots)

(b)

*Machine 1*

$L + 1/2M + 2S \leq 100$

*Machine 2*

$2L + 2M + 3S \leq 150$

(c)

**FIGURE 17.18**

                      L  M  S    L  M  S   L  M  S
an entire plane of points [such as (0, 0, 50), (100, 0, 0), (0, 200, 0);
Figure 17.19b]. (NOTE: It takes three points to determine the plane.)
The second equation is also satisfied by a plane of points, e.g.,
  L  M   S    L  M  S    L  M   S
(0, 0, 50), (75, 0, 0), (0, 75, 0). The points with two variables equal
to zero are the "pure" solutions. Two planes (that are not parallel) intersect in a line (Figure 17.19c), so that one point is not uniquely defined (a
line has an infinity of points). This infinite number of points represents
an infinite number of "mixed" solutions. A third equation would generate
a third plane, in which case the three planes would intersect in a point.
This is what is meant by saying three independent equations are necessary
to solve for three unknowns. In three and four dimensions, using the
algebraic method is easier than using graphical displays.
    The main point here is that the addition of another product adds to
the number of variables in an equation, but not to the number of equations.

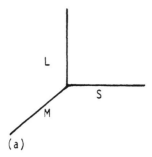

(a)

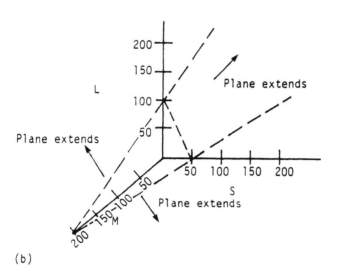

(b)

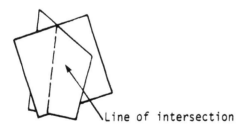

(c)

FIGURE 17.19

## Three Machines: Three Equations

If we had another machine (e.g., machine 1, the cutter, machine 2, the sewer, and machine 3, the presser), with our original two products (fashionable [F] and durable [D] denims), the number of variables in each equation remains the same (two, F and D). However, we will now have three equations, one for each machine. In order to develop the equations, we need to know the constraints on each. The constraints shown here are developed independently of those shown earlier. The machine availability and product requirements are shown in Table 17.7. The equations now become

$$\text{Machine 1: } 1/2F + 1D \leqslant 100$$
$$\text{Machine 2: } 2F + 1/2D \leqslant 150$$
$$\text{Machine 3: } 1F + 2D \leqslant 125$$

Contrary to the foregoing example, three equations in two unknowns can be solved. As before, we would test

1. 0,0
2. 0,F
3. D,0
4. The mixed solutions

However, there may be more than a single corner point to test for the mixed solution. Since each pair of equations intersects in a corner point, each pair must be tested, and this resultant point checked against the third equation for feasibility. The pure points would be found as before, setting one of the variables to zero in each of the three equations, solving for the remaining variable, and choosing the *least* of the results from each equation. The point here is not to solve the equations; rather, we are interested in the fact that the addition of another machine produces another constraint equation.

## TABLE 17.7

*Machine Availability*

Machine 1: 100 hr/week
Machine 2: 150 hr/week
Machine 3: 125 hr/week

*Product Requirements*

Fashionable (F)
  Machine 1: 1/2 hr/pair
  Machine 2: 2 hr/pair
  Machine 3: 1 hr/pair

Durable (D)
  Machine 1: 1 hr/pair
  Machine 2: 1/2 hr/pair
  Machine 3: 2 hr/pair

The increase in variables (from more products) and equations (from more machines) can extend indefinitely. However, both the graphing and the algebraic solution of the problems becomes correspondingly more complex.

## Minimization of Costs

Besides the maximization of profits (within constraints), we can also attempt to minimize costs (within constraints). In the minimization problems, the constraints are usually such that we must produce a minimum quantity of some "product mix," and we would like to do so at the least cost. A good example was produced by the authors of *The Man-Made World* (Polytechnic Institute of Brooklyn, 1971), by looking at food as the essential product to be produced, and a minimal daily quota of protein, vitamins, and carbohydrates as the constraints (the thresholds to be exceeded). The following example has been derived from their example. We will consider only vitamins.

Suppose there are three essential vitamins: A, B, and C. Suppose also that there are only two available foods: Supercereal and Vitajuice. The constraints in this problem are really requirements—the requirements of getting enough vitamins. Suppose that we need the quantities of vitamins shown in Table 17.8a. Suppose that these vitamins are provided by our two foods in the amounts shown in Table 17.8b. Suppose, also, that Supercereal sells for $3 a serving, and Vitajuice sells for $2 a serving.

The products in this problem are Supercereal (S) and Vitajuice (V), which can be taken alone or in combination to produce our daily quota of vitamins. The constraint equations are

Vitamin A: $2S + 3V \geqslant 18$

Vitamin B: $4S + 2V \geqslant 16$

Vitamin C: $2S + 6V \geqslant 24$

where the "greater than" symbol indicates that we must exceed the minimum daily quota.

The profit equation becomes a *cost* equation, since we are spending money to buy food rather than selling a product at a profit. In our example, the cost equation is

$3S + 2V = C$

since Supercereal sells for $3 a serving, Vitajuice for $2 a serving. Our objective is to minimize our costs.

TABLE 17.8a

| Vitamin | Minimal Daily Quota |
|---------|---------------------|
| A | 18 units |
| B | 16 units |
| C | 24 units |

TABLE 17.8b

| Food | Vitamin | Units Provided |
|---|---|---|
| Supercereal | A | 2 |
| | B | 4 |
| | C | 2 |
| Vitajuice | A | 3 |
| | B | 2 |
| | C | 6 |

### Solving the System of Equations

The three equations

$$A) \quad 2S + 3V \geqslant 18$$

$$B) \quad 4S + 2V \geqslant 16$$

$$C) \quad 2S + 6V \geqslant 24$$

graph as shown in Figure 17.20a, in which the feasible area is that on the line and to the northwest of the line created by constraints A, B, and C. The portion of the boundary contributed by each constraint is shown in Figure 17.20b. The origin (V = 0, S = 0) is no longer a feasible region.

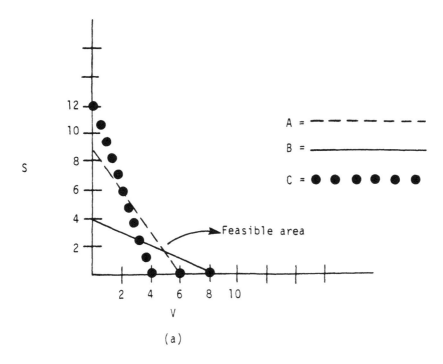

(a)

FIGURE 17.20

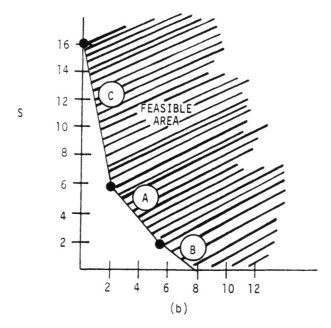

(b)

FIGURE 17.20 (continued)

Although it would provide the minimal cost of $0, it will not provide a viable life plan in terms of vitamin supply. Our attention must be centered on the points along the boundary of the feasible area, since these points will provide our minimum quota of vitamins, and one of them will do so at minimal cost.

*Vitamin A*

$$2S + 3V \geq 18$$
$$2S = 18$$
$$S = 9$$

*Vitamin B*

$$4S + 2V \geq 16$$
$$4S = 16$$
$$S = 4$$

*Vitamin C*

$$2S + 6V \geq 24$$
$$2S = 24$$
$$S = 12$$

(a)

*Vitamin A*

$$2S + 3V \geq 18$$
$$3V = 18$$
$$V = 6$$

*Vitamin B*

$$4S + 2V \geq 16$$
$$2V = 16$$
$$V = 8$$

*Vitamin C*

$$2S + 6V \geq 24$$
$$6V = 24$$
$$V = 4$$

(b)

FIGURE 17.21

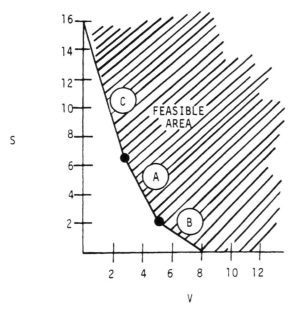

FIGURE 17.22

The pure solution for Supercereal would be found by determining the amount needed in the case of each vitamin (Figure 17.21a). Since we must obtain the minimal quota of each vitamin, and since 12 servings of Super-cereal are necessary to get the minimum required vitamin C, we must select the *largest* of these three numbers, or 12 servings of Supercereal. At $3 a serving, this is a cost of $36.

We proceed in the same fashion to find the pure solution for Vitajuice (Figure 17.21b), which indicates that we would need eight servings. At $2 a serving, this is $16, which is less than the $36 for Supercereal, so we would prefer to drink Vitajuice than to eat Supercereal from simply a cost point of view.

We now consider the mixed solutions. A mixed solution to our problem will occur at the "corner points" created by the intersection of any two of the constraint equations. The graph (Figure 17.22) indicates that the intersections of interest are those between equations C and A and equations A and B (the intersection of B and C occurs in the nonfeasible area). Let us solve for each of these points in turn.

The intersection of C and A is found by solving these equations simultaneously

$A: 2S + 3V = 18$

$C: 2S + 6V = 24$

Subtracting C from A, we have

$$2S + 3V = 18$$
$$-2S - 6V = -24$$
$$\overline{\qquad\qquad}$$
$$-3V = -6$$
$$V = 2$$

Substituting the value V = 2 into the equation for A (equation 1), we find
S

$$2S + 3*2 = 18$$

$$2S + 6 = 18$$

$$2S = 12$$

$$S = 6$$

Thus, we would have to consume two servings of Vitajuice and six of Supercereal to satisfy these requirements.

We test these values in equation B

$$4S + 2V \geqslant 16$$

$$4*6 + 2*2 \geqslant 16$$

$$24 + 4 \geqslant 16$$

$$28 \geqslant 16$$

and they do satisfy equation B. (This is also evident in the graph, since equation B falls beneath both equation A and equation C at this point, indicating that it can be satisfied by a lesser amount of both foods than will satisfy A or C at this point of the graph.)

The cost for two servings of Vitajuice is $4, while six servings of Supercereal cost $18, so that our total cost at this point would be $22. This is higher than the cost of $16 incurred by drinking only Vitajuice, so that the pure solution of Vitajuice alone is still preferred. (Although a more variety-minded consumer might consider the extra $6 worth it in order to choose from two foods. Our consumer is minimizing costs, not maximizing pleasure; if we were maximizing pleasure, we would have to consider such things as the relative preferences for each type of food in terms of taste.)

The final mixed solution can be found by solving A and B simultaneously

$$A: 2S + 3V = 18$$

$$B: 4S + 2V = 16$$

Multiplying equation A by 2, then subtracting, we have

$$4S + 6V = 36$$

$$-4S - 2V = -16$$

$$\overline{\phantom{-4S - 2V = }}$$

$$4V = 20$$

$$V = 5$$

and substituting V = 5 into equation A, we find

$$2S + 3*5 = 18$$

$$2S + 15 = 18$$

$$2S = 3$$

$$S = 3/2$$

Since we cannot buy a half-serving of Supercereal, we must increase this to two servings (one would not provide the minimum). Our cost would be

$10 for Vitajuice (5*$2) and $6 for Supercereal (2*$3), or a total of $16. We would be indifferent between this solution and pure Vitajuice (also $16) in terms of cost. The solution

$$V = 5$$
$$S = 2$$

will also satify equation C

$$2S + 6V \geqslant 24$$
$$2*2 + 6*5 = 4 + 30 = 34$$
$$34 \geqslant 24$$

so that we will have enough of all three necessary vitamins.

The Graphic Solution

The graphic solution could also have been used in this problem. We would first solve for S and V in the cost equation

$$3S + 2V = C$$
$$3S + 2V = 6$$

For V = 0,  3S = 6
$$S = 2 \qquad (0,2)$$

For S = 0,  2V = 6
$$V = 3 \qquad (3,0)$$

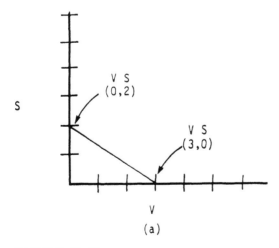

V

(a)

FIGURE 17.23

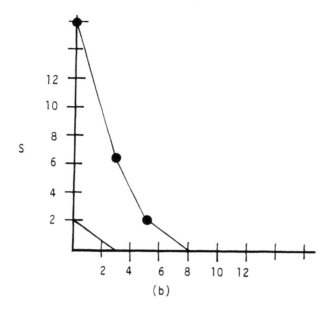

(b)

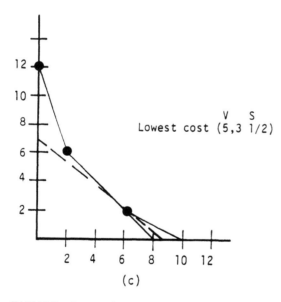

(c)

FIGURE 17.23   (continued)

and plot these points and the line they determine, the cost line of Figure 17.23a. Imposing this cost line on our graph of constraints (Figure 17.23b), we would move the line to the northwest until the *lowest* point(s) on the boundary is (are) reached. This is the minimum cost (Figure 17.23c). However, it is difficult to read the exact value (5, 3/2) off the graph. The algenraic method gives these values exactly.

As indicated above, we sometimes calculate optimal values (5, 3/2) that cannot be obtained in reality. However, we can use these figures to create an integer value that can be tested, as we did in converting 3/2 servings of Supercereal to 2 servings.

## Actions Under Certainty

The models presented in this chapter might be referred to as models of action under certainty. There is a great deal of literature on making choices under uncertainty. The uncertainty involved is that of a desired outcome being the "end result" of our action and that of another.

The linear programming model is the "cleanest" example of the three in terms of "actions under certainty." It is assumed that the demand for our product is so great that whatever number of items we produce will be consumed. We have total control over the outcomes of our actions in terms of number of each item produced, i.e., job mix; hence we can bring about any outcome in the feasible region that we wish, say implementing, i.e., choosing, the "mix" of 96 durable denims and 24 fashionable ones.

Given the assumptions

• Demand is sufficient to consume all goods produced.
• We have total control over products made.

there is no uncertainty in the "connection" between the action (choice) we implement and the outcome (in both numbers of items produced and, given the profit equation, profit).

There is some uncertainty in the forecasting model, but it is uncertainty in regard to the accuracy of the estimate of demand, not in the efficacy of our actions. If demand is estimated accurately, the number of items ordered or produced will be consumed and again we have control over this number.

The queuing model has uncertainty built into the probabilities

• Probability distribution of a person arriving in a given time period
• Probability distribution of service times

However, the model is able to "ignore" or make "irrelevant" these uncertainties in computing average queue size. It uses the average arrival rate and average service rate to compute a "stable value," the average queue size.

It cannot, however, ignore the probabilities inherent in the actual queue size, i.e., the distribution of queue sizes. Nor can it ignore the probabilities in calculating how bad things can get (e.g., queue exceeds nine persons). These calculations all have a probability attached to the outcome. Such models are called stochastic models, and the use of the probability distributions refers to uncertainty due to unknown factors. The uncertainty reflects our lack of control of the "outcome" queue size = 9, but this lack of control is attributed only to "chance."

Problems that are considered to be "decisions" (choices) made under uncertainty usually refer to situations in which our action alone is not sufficient to bring about an outcome, but in which the coproducer is known. The outcome is the "joint result" of two agents, ourselves and another agent (person or organization) or known forces of nature. We treat these situations under the topic of decision-making, in Chapter 19.

## Summary

In this chapter, we have considered some mathematical techniques of manipulating data

- Forecasting
- Queuing theory
- Linear programming

In each case, the purpose of manipulating data has been in response to a question for which we did not have an answer. In the case of forecasting, the question related to predicting next year's demands for a given product. However, the data showed only past demand. The techniques of forecasting were used to transform this data about the past into "data about the future."

In queuing theory, the question is how long can I expect the waiting lines to be at my place of business. We had no data on the length of the lines, but we did have data on arrival patterns at our place of business, as well as on the service times with which we dispatch arrivals. Queuing theory enabled us to translate these times into lengths of line, and some simple arithmetic enabled us to translate the length of line into dollar amounts.

Finally, the study of linear programming involved the attempt to answer the question "What is the maximum profit I can make (or minimum cost), and how do I make it?" We had no direct answer to this question, but we did have data on profits for each product, as well as machine times available and necessary to manufacture each product. Manipulation again enabled us to turn the data we did have into the answer we needed.

## Related Readings

Bierman, Harold Jr., Bonini, Charles P., and Hausman, Warren H. *Quantitative Analysis for Business Decisions*, 4th ed. Illinois: Richard D. Irwin, Inc., 1973.

Dorn, William S. and Greenberg, Herbert J., *Mathematics and Computing with FORTRAN Programming*, New York: John Wiley & Sons, Inc., 1967.

Gustavson, Frances G. and Gear, C. William, *Applications and Algorithms in Business*, Chicago: Science Research Associates, Inc., 1978.

Hanes, Bernard, *Mathematics for Management Science*, Columbus: Charles E. Merrill Books, Inc., 1962.

Harris, Roy D. and Maggard, Michael J., *Computer Models in Operations Management*, 2nd ed. New York: Harper & Row, 1977.

Kemeny, John G., Schleifer, Arthur, Snell, J. Laurie, and Thompson, Gerald L., *Finite Mathematics with Business Applications*. Englewood Cliffs, NJ: Prentice-Hall, Inc., 1964 (C 1962).

Kemeny, John G., Snell, J. Laurie, and Thompson, Gerald L., *Introduction to Finite Mathematics*, 3rd ed. Englewood Cliffs, NJ: Prentice-Hall, Inc., 1974.

Kertz, George J., *The Nature and Application of Mathematics*, Santa Monica, CA: Goodyear Publishing Company, Inc., 1979.

Martin, James, *Systems Analysis for Data Transmission*, Englewood Cliffs, NJ: Prentice-Hall, Inc., 1972.

Pappas, James L. and Brigham, Eugene F., *Managerial Economics*, 3rd ed. Hinsdale, IL: The Dryden Press, 1979.

Polytechnic Institute of Brooklyn, *The Man-Made World*. New York: McGraw-Hill Book Company, 1971.

Sedgewick, Robert, *Algorithms*, Reading, MA: Addison-Wesley Publishing Company, 1983.

Singh, Jagjit, *Great Ideas of Operations Research*, revised and enlarged ed. New York: Dover Publications, Inc., 1972.

Turban, Efraim and Meredith, Jack R., *Fundamentals of Management Science*, revised ed. Texas: Business Publications, Inc., 1981.

Wheelwright, Steven C. and Makridakis, Spyros, *Forecasting Methods for Management*, 2nd ed. New York: John Wiley & Sons, 1977.

# 18
# Text Processing

Objectives

The concept of data processing has long been associated with computation. It is only recently that the concept of text processing has taken on an equal prominence. This single chapter cannot do justice to the area but is included to indicate the rightful place of this form of data processing. Both physical examples (sorting, text formatting) and "intelligent" applications, i.e., the extraction of meaning from text by a machine are treated.

Upon completion of this chapter the reader should be able to

1. Use a sort package at his or her installation
2. Distinguish between ascending the descending sorts
3. Discuss how one might go about selecting the field to sort on, as well as the direction of the sort
4. Use a text editor (line or screen) to create a document, such as a letter or a computer program
5. Distinguish between insert mode (append mode) and edit mode
6. Use a text formatter to format the document
7. Distinguish between the functions of a text editor and a text formatter
8. Indicate why automated indexing is considered attractive as well as indicate some of its disadvantages
9. Define or describe the terms *stop list*, *stemming*, and *KWIC* and *KWOC indexes*, and indicate the purposes of the upper and lower threshold in selecting the index terms.

Processing data with mathematical and statistical techniques has been a fairly standard method of manipulating data. Also common, but less directly addressed, has been the processing of text. With the advent of word processing machines, text editors, text formatters, and other automated means of processing text, the concept has become more prominent. In discussing text processing, there are two levels of interest

- The physical processing of text
- The extraction of meaning from text

```
327550918        FROEHLICH    TERRY
728328069        SMITH        JOSEPH
416812942        WILLIAMS     MARY
582700193        EVANS        DOUG
```

(a)

```
.R SORT
*SORTED.FIL=SAMPLE.FIL/KEY:1:9/RECORDSIZE:25
```

(b)

```
327550918FROEHLICH      TERRY
416812942WILLIAMS       MARY
582700193EVANS          DOUG
728328069SMITH          JOSEPH
```

(c)

```
.TYPE NAMES.SRT
582700193EVANS          DOUG
327550918FROEHLICH      TERRY
728328069SMITH          JOSEPH
416812942WILLIAMS       MARY
```

(d)

```
.TYPE DOWN.FIL
416812942WILLIAMS    MARY
728328069SMITH       JOSEPH
327550918FROEHLICH   TERRY
582700193EVANS       DOUG
```

(e)

FIGURE 18.1

## Physical Processing of Text

One of the simplest methods of processing data is by physically rearranging it to "sort" the data. For example, in building an indexed sequential file, the data must be ordered by the key value. If the keys are social security numbers, we would sort the data records on these values. The sort could be done by writing a computer program of our own, or by using a package provided as a utility on a computer system. For example, given the data shown in Figure 18.1a, we might issue a command sequence such as that shown in Figure 18.1b to sort the records. The command

R SORT

requests that the SORT package be run. The next command indicates the name of file to be sorted (SAMPLE.FIL) and the name of the resulting file (SORTED.FIL). On this system (DECSYSTEM-10) the order of naming the files is

OUTPUT.FIL=INPUT.FIL

as in conventional assignment statements

C = A+B

but the conventions will vary from system to system. The phrase

/KEY:1:9

indicates the start of the key field (1) and its length (9), where the key is the field to be "sorted on." Finally, the phrase

/RECORDSIZE:25

indicates the maximum record length. These phrases are "switches" or "parameters"; they indicate information that the sort package needs to complete its job.

Since we sorted on the field social security number, the resultant file will be that shown in Figure 18.1c. We could have sorted on the last name by issuing the command

*NAMES.SRT=SAMPLE.FIL/KEY:10:10/RECORDSIZE:25

where the key field is now described as starting in column 10, and being 10 characters long. The resulting file would be that shown in Figure 18.1d.

Both of the above sorts resulted in the data being in ascending order. This is the "default" on this package. However, if the user wishes descending order, he or she can indicate this in the key switch

.R SORT
*DOWN.FIL=SAMPLE.FIL/KEY:10:10:DESCENDING/RECORDSIZE:25

where the resulting file will have the last names (key begins in column 10) in descending order (Figure 18.1e).

Finally, the above examples showed the resulting file as being separate. It may be the case that we wish the resulting file to be the same file as the input file. We indicate this by using the same name on both sides of the equal sign

| BEFORE | | AFTER | |
|---|---|---|---|
| .TYPE SAMPLE.FIL | | .TYPE SAMPLE.FIL | |
| 327550918FROEHLICH | TERRY | 728328069SMITH | JOSEPH |
| 728328069SMITH | JOSEPH | 582700193EVANS | DOUG |
| 416812942WILLIAMS | MARY | 416812942WILLIAMS | MARY |
| 582700193EVANS | DOUG | 327550918FROEHLICH | TERRY |

FIGURE 18.2

```
.R SORT
*SAMPLE.FIL=SAMPLE.FIL/KEY:1:9:DESCENDING/RECORDSIZE:25
```

In this case we wind up with one file instead of two (Figure 18.2). The resultant file has the social security numbers in descending order

(KEY:1:9:DESCENDING)

### Helping the Decisionmaker

One of the purposes of sorting the data (aside from creating index files) might be to aid the decisionmaker in understanding it. For example, a decisionmaker who ranks restaurants on taste might like to see them sorted by their rating on this field (Figure 18.3a), while a decisionmaker who emphasizes cost would like to see the sort on that field (Figure 18.3b).

Issuing reports can also be aided by flexibility in sorting the data. For example, a listing of phone numbers for students might best be sorted "ascending on last name." A class ranking would be sorted "descending on QPA" (Figure 18.3c).

| Restaurant | Star rating on taste | Cost |
|---|---|---|
| Joe's | 4 | High |
| Mary's | 4 | Low |
| ABC Diner | 3 | Medium |
| Bill's | 1 | Low |

(a)

| Restaurant | Star rating on taste | Cost | |
|---|---|---|---|
| Mary's | 4 | Low | Numerical values |
| Bill's | 1 | Low | would be necessary |
| ABC Diner | 3 | Medium | here to sort |
| Joe's | 4 | High | correctly |

(b)

| QPA | Name |
|---|---|
| 4.0 | Sherman |
| 3.9 | Franklin |
| 3.7 | Butterworth |
| . | |
| . | |
| . | |

(c)

FIGURE 18.3

One question that might arise in this discussion is "Where did the original file [SAMPLE.FIL] come from?" That is, how did we get the data into the computer in the first place. This leads us into another application of text processing, the use of an editor.

## Editors

An editor is a computer program that enables us to create files by "inserting" text, to change text (e.g., correct misspellings), and to delete text. The editor we will look at is a "line editor" called UPDATE. It is called a line editor because it looks at text as a series of lines, in the same fashion that we type lines on a typewriter. Other editors, such as screen editors, worry not about "lines" but "positions on a screen." We will discuss them briefly after looking at the line editor, UPDATE.

## Creating a File

In order to use the editor, we request it much like we did SORT

    .R UPDATE

When the system returns control to our program, we create a file by simply typing the text. For example, to create the file SAMPLE.FIL, the entire interaction was as shown in Figure 18.4a. The command

    .R UPDATE

```
.R UPDATE

FILE:
 > 327550918FROEHLICH      TERRY
 > 728328069SMITH          JOSEPH
 > 416812942WILLIAMS       MARY
 > 582700193EVANS          DOUG
 > $END
Catalog name:SAMPLE.FIL
1 blocks written on USRA:SAMPLE.FIL [134023,151171]

EXIT
```

(a)

```
        .TYPE SAMPLE.FIL
        327550918FROEHLICH      TERRY
        728328069SMITH          JOSEPH
        416812942WILLIAMS       MARY
        582700193EVANS          DOUG
```

(b)

FIGURE 18.4

requests the editor called UPDATE. The UPDATE editor replies with a request for the name of the file to be updated

FILE:

If the file already existed (and we wish to make changes to it), we would give its name. Here, it does not yet exist, so we simply hit the carriage return to indicate we are creating a "new file." The UPDATE editor then replies with a prompt

>

and we can type what we wish. In this case we typed the four data records. After each record, we hit the carriage return, so that the next record goes on the next line. In this mode, inserting the data, the editor is being used like a typewriter.

The command

$END

causes update to end the session. The dollar sign indicates that this is a command, not text to be inserted. Other editors distinguish between commands and text to be inserted by having two modes: edit mode in order to edit existing text, and insert mode to insert new text. In UPDATE, all commands are preceded by the dollar sign, which is considered a "special" character. The specialness only occurs if the dollar sign is the first character typed, so that something like

RATE:$2.39

would be taken as text. Upon receiving the $END command, UPDATE asks us for the file name

CATALOG NAME:

to which the author typed SAMPLE.FIL. UPDATE then indicates that it wrote the file out to the disk and "exited." At this point, we could type the file to see how it looks (or print it on a line printer if it is very large; Figure 18.4b).

## Making Changes to the Text

Suppose that something in our file is misspelled. For example, say we typed JSEPH for Joseph Smith's first name. We can correct this problem by issuing the command

$CHANGE/JSEPH/JOSEPH/

where the change command indicates that we want to change some text; the thing to be changed (here the spelling mistake) is given next; and the new text follows, with delimiters between the various portions of the command

$CHANGE/JSEPH/JOSEPH/
|
Text in file        New text
(to be replaced)

The change command looks for the first pattern (JSEPH) in the text, a process called "pattern matching," then substitutes the second string for the one matched. If the pattern to be matched (text supposed to be in the file) is not matched, an error message will be issued.

## Finding the Line

On a line editor, a command such as $CHANGE must be executed on the "current line." In order to do this, there is usually a command to "move" us to that line. In UPDATE, this is $TO, so that to CHANGE JSEPH to JOSEPH, we would write

    $TO2

since JSEPH SMITH is the second line, then issue the CHANGE command. The entire interaction would be as shown in Figure 18.5, where we responded SAMPLE.FIL to the request for the file name, since we wished to edit an existing file. UPDATE responded by typing out the first line of the file

    327550918FROEHLICH    TERRY

and prompted us

    >

at which point we issued the command $TO2

    > $TO2
    728328069SMITH      JSEPH

and UPDATE printed out the second line to show that it had carried out our request. We then issued the command to change the data, with UPDATE again echoing the result of the command

    $CHANGE/JSEPH/JOSEPH/

and we ended the session ($END).

The "thing" moved by $TO is called the line pointer or the cursor. The term *cursor* is actually broader in meaning than *line pointer* (indicating any character position on a screen of data), but is often used in its place when talking about "moving the line pointer" or "moving the cursor."

```
.R UPDATE

File:SAMPLE.FIL
327550918FROEHLICH    TERRY
> $TO2
728328069SMITH      JSEPH
> $CHANGE/JSEPH/JOSEPH/
728328069SMITH      JOSEPH
> $END
1 blocks written on USRA:SAMPLE.FIL  134023,151171

EXIT
```

FIGURE 18.5

An Error

An example of trying to change something that is not there is the following:

.R UPDATE

File:SAMPLE.FIL
327550918FROEHLICH   TERRY
> $CHANGE/X/XYZ/
?>

Where there is no X in the record for Froehlich, so that UPDATE responds with a question mark (what?). In this version of UPDATE, the editor also rings a bell when errors occur, in case the person is reading paper input of output when the error occurs. The use of audial signals is necessary when the display cannot be visually monitored (e.g., fire alarms in a building; not everyone is watching the alarm, so rather than have a sign light up, we turn on a siren).

What Gets Changed?

In changing JSEPH to JOSEPH, there could be no confusion about what we wanted to change. There was only one occurrence of JSEPH in the line. But suppose we wish to change Williams's social security number from

416812942

to

416812945

i.e., we want to change the last 2 to a 5. If we issue the command

$CHANGE/2/5/

the result will be

416815942

where the wrong 2 gets changed. UPDATE finds the first pattern that matches, so that we must make sure to indicate the "bad data" uniquely. For example, to change the final 2 to a 5 in 416812942, we could say

$CHANGE/42/45/

since there is only one occurrence of the sequence 42.
    The CHANGE command can also be used to delete characters, e.g.

$CHANGE/U//

would change

POUT TO POT

by deleting the U. The "deletion" of the pattern is indicated by hitting the last slash (delimeter) immediately after the second slash (nothing in between ⟶ change pattern to "nothing").
    Variations of the $TO command are $TO-2 or $TO+3, where we indicate two lines previous to this one (-2) or three lines "further down" (+3) and $TO/JSEPH/, which tells UPDATE to search for the pattern JSEPH wherever it is, a procedure called "text searching."

## Deleting Lines

Suppose that someone leaves our company or school, and we wish to delete their record from the file. The command to do so is $DELETE. For example, if we wished to delete the record for Mary Williams (line 3) we would issue the command $TO3, then the command $DELETE

```
$TO3
416812942WILLIAMS      MARY
$DELETE
582700193EVANS         DOUG
```

The delete command removes the line for Williams, and UPDATE indicates that it has been deleted by printing the next line

```
582700193EVANS      DOUG
```

as the new current line. All the lines from the one after the one deleted "on down" move up a notch.

## Inserting New Lines

Suppose we hire somebody, say Larry Williams, and wish to enter his data into the file. Suppose also that we are using our original file (with Mary Williams in it), and we wish to enter the data for Larry Williams immediately after the data for Mary Williams. The sequence of commands is to go to the line with Mary Williams

```
$TO3
```

then simply type in the new line (no $ sign; Figure 18.6a). The file now looks like Figure 18.6b with Larry after Mary.

```
.UPDATE SAMPLE.FIL  ←----shorthand way to get UPDATE
327550918FROEHLICH   TERRY
> $TO3
416812942WILLIAMS    MARY←-cursor on line 3
> 512679008WILLIAMS LARRY←-type in new line or lines
> $END
1 block written on USRA:SAMPLE.FIL  134023,151171

EXIT
```

(a)

```
.TYPE SAMPLE.FIL
327550918FROEHLICH    TERRY
728328069SMITH        JOSEPH
416812942WILLIAMS     MARY
512679008WILLIAMS     LARRY
582700193EVANS        DOUG
```

(b)

FIGURE 18.6

```
.UPDATE SAMPLE.FIL
327550918FROEHLICH    TERRY ←-- at line 1
> $BEFORE ←-put new line "before" this one
> 714528907ROMANO    MARIJEAN
> $END
1 block written on USRA:SAMPLE.FIL [134023,151171]
EXIT
```

(a)

```
.TYPE SAMPLE.FIL
714528907ROMANO    MARIJEAN
327550918FROEHLICH TERRY
728328069SMITH     JOSEPH
416812942WILLIAMS  MARY
512679008WILLIAMS  LARRY
582700193EVANS     DOUG
```
(b)

FIGURE 18.7

In UPDATE insertion is always performed after the current line. As many lines may be entered as one wishes. In order to enter text before the first line (where entering after will not work), a special command, $BEFORE, is used to override the default of inserting "after" (Figure 18.7a), so that Marijean is now the first line (Figure 18.7b).

$TO$

Since new lines are often appended to text "at the end of the file," e.g., as we write more sections in a term paper, most editors have an easy way

```
.UPDATE SAMPLE.FIL
327550918FROEHLICH    TERRY
> $TO$    ←--------------- to end of file
582700193EVANS        DOUG
> 980441601WEIDEN     BARRY←--insert record
> $END
1 block written on USRA:SAMPLE.FILE [134023,151171]
EXIT
```

(a)

```
.TYPE SAMPLE.FIL
327550918FROEHLICH TERRY
728328069SMITH     JOSEPH
416812942WILLIAMS  MARY
512679008WILLIAMS  LARRY
582700193EVANS     DOUG
980441601WEIDEN    BARRY
```
(b)

FIGURE 18.8

```
.UPDATE SAMPLE.FIL
714528907ROMANO        MARIJEAN
> $CH/MARIJEAN/MARI/ <------- $CH=$CHANGE
714528907ROMANO        MARI
> $END
1 block written on USRA:SAMPLE.FILE [134023,151171]
EXIT
```

FIGURE 18.9

to get the end of the file. In UPDATE this is $TO$, which places us on the last line of the file (Figure 18.8a). Barry is indeed inserted after the former last line (Figure 18.8b).

## Abbreviating Commands

UPDATE also allows us a shorthand way to write commands, abbreviating them to two characters (Figure 18.9), which saves typing time. This is known as "minimal character recognition." In UPDATE, we need a minimum of two characters to recognize a command. This is because of commands like

$TO
$TYPE

$TYPE can be used to type a line or range of lines, e.g.

$TYPE 10

types 10 lines. The point is that one character is not enough to distinguish TO from TYPE, so $T cannot be used as an abbreviation. In UPDATE, all commands can be distinguished by the first two characters, so that $TY is "enough" to recognize the command.

## Screen Editors

UPDATE is a line editor and is "paper" oriented. We are looking at the text as a typed "piece of paper." Screen editors look at screens of text in a more geometric fashion. They have a cursor that is positioned by pressing arrow keys (up arrow, down arrow, left arrow, right arrow) and changes are made by typing new text, deleting text, or changing text after moving the cursor in this way. The cursor does not point to a whole line, but to a character on that line. Special "function keys" are used to insert, delete, or change text.

## Other Commands and Other Editors

Many other commands exist for UPDATE, e.g., $WHERE will tell you what line you are on, in case you "get lost" while moving around the file. We have given the primary actions and commands here: inserting lines (not a command), changing them, deleting them, typing them out, and moving the line pointer. All editors will have similar commands. For example, on the editor called "ed," provided with the UNIX operating system used at the author's installation on a DEC PDP-11/780 (or VAX), some of the commonly used commands are

    p: print
    w: write
    q: quit
    d: delete
    s: substitute (like change)
    2: (for move to line 2)

where one character is enough to recognize the command.

## Text Formatters

Editors are used to type in text, change misspellings, delete lines, move lines around, etc. However, the text of the material must be typed exactly as we want it to appear. This is usually sufficient for typing in computer programs, data files, and short messages (although programs now exist to indent computer programs for readability); it is not always sufficient for larger bodies of text, e.g., creating a book.

Text formatters can be used to allow us to type in text "without formatting" (e.g., without centering a heading or indenting paragraph); one gives commands to the formatter to do the necessary rearranging. The formatter we will illustrate here is called RUNOFF. Some of the special commands in RUNOFF allow the user to set the number of lines per page, to set the left and right margins, to choose single spacing or double spacing, and to issue other commands concerned with the "physical" layout of a document. Other commands tell RUNOFF to center a line, begin a new paragraph or chapter, and other indications of the "logical" layout of the document. RUNOFF itself will number pages and chapters, and will create indexes of terms "marked" for inclusion in the index.

## Using RUNOFF

In order to use a text formatter such as RUNOFF, we must first create a file in an editor. This file will consist of

- The text we want printed
- Commands to the formatter, telling it how to print the text

For example, to create a title for our report, we would use the following:

    .C
    THIS IS THE TITLE

where .C is a command to RUNOFF and the phrase "This is the title" is the text we want printed. In the command

    .C

the period signals RUNOFF that this is a command line. The C is the command; it tells RUNOFF that we want the text following "centered" on the page. The author created the input file with the editor UPDATE (Figure 18.10a). The file has been named INPUT.TXT because it will be the input

```
.UPDATE INPUT.TXT
[Creating new file]
> .C
> THIS IS THE TITLE
> $END
 1 block written on USRA:INPUT.TXT [134023,151171]
  EXIT
```

(a)

```
.R RUNOFF

*OUTPUT.TXT=INPUT.TXT
INPUT   1 Page
*^Z
```

(b)

FIGURE 18.10

to RUNOFF. However, the name has no intrinsic meaning, i.e., we could call it "Harry" and still use it as input to RUNOFF.

After creating the input text file, we summon RUNOFF by the command

.R RUNOFF

then give it the name of the input text file and the output text file

*OUTPUT.TXT=INPUT.TXT

where the input text file is on the right, the output on the left, as in an assignment statement. The * is RUNOFF's prompt. If everything is successful, RUNOFF will respond with another prompt (*), at which point we may either give another command or exit RUNOFF. On this system the exit from RUNOFF is control-Z($Z), a "special character" recognized by RUNOFF as "the end." Note that the use of two keys (control and Z) simultaneously results in a single character, not two. The entire interaction with RUNOFF is shown in Figure 18.10b.

Upon exiting RUNOFF we would look at our output file (OUTPUT.TXT) to see if the formatting was done correctly (we could have given it an incorrect sequence of commands, or typed the text incorrectly). We do this by simply typing out the contents of the file OUTPUT.TXT

.TYPE OUTPUT.TXT


                        THIS IS THE TITLE

The reader can see that the title has been typed "off to the right." It has been centered on the page, even though the original text was left-justified in the input text file

.C
THIS IS THE TITLE

The centering is the effect of the command *C*. (Note: The page size on the terminal was wider than that of the book, so that the output will not always look exactly centered. It was.)

## Uppercase and Lowercase

In the above example the title was printed in uppercase letters. In a typewritten manuscript we would normally have used both upper- and lowercase letters. Some terminals are capable of printing both sets of characters, some are not. In doing text processing one would normally want both upper- and lowercase, so that a proper choice of terminals is necessary. On the terminal used in preparing these examples, the "default" is uppercase, but one can obtain both upper- and lowercase by typing the command

    .TTY LC

which sets the terminal to lowercase. Now when one types a letter it will be typed as lowercase except when the shift key is used to indicate uppercase, just like a typewriter.

    Using upper- and lowercase, the title example would be entered in UPDATE as shown in Figure 18.11a. The command to RUNOFF is the same (Figure 18.11b). In fact, in the following examples, we will not show the command to RUNOFF, just showing input.txt and output.txt, but implicitly assuming that the command to RUNOFF has intervened.

    The output.txt will now show the title as having both upper- and lowercase letters

    .type output.txt

This is the Title

```
 .TTY LC ←--Set terminal to lower case

 .update input.txt ←--Update recognizes upper or lower case
 Creating new file
 .c ←-------- RUNOFF also recognizes upper or lower case
 This is the Title ←---Title has both UC,LC
 $end
1 block written on USRB:INPUT.TXT [134023,151171]
EXIT
```

(a)

```
 .r runoff

 *output.txt=input.txt
 INPUT   1 page
 *^Z
```

(b)

FIGURE 18.11

### Printing the Final Output

We will examine some of the other features of RUNOFF, but before doing so, a word is in order about the final printing of the output text. The final product of RUNOFF is usually a letter, a term paper, a book, or some other document that is meant to look like it was typed by a human. Hence, the quality of the output type font is a critical issue. Many terminals and printers have a type font that is suitable for computer listings and computer runs, but is not suitable as "quality printing." Hence, the user of a text formatter must be careful in the selection of a printing device that does have a suitably "dignified" typeset. This is often at a greater expense than a comparable low-quality printer, but the extra expense is necessary to obtain realistic output.

### Paragraphs and Margins

RUNOFF enables the user to indicate that text should be indented with the command ".P", where the input text is left-justified (Figure 18.12a), and the "paragraph command" causes the indentation (Figure 18.12b). The lines of the input text are also adjusted to fit into the constraints of the left and right margins. While the input file (input.txt) has the text in relatively long lines, the output text has fitted these to the default line width of 60 characters. The right and left justification properties can be seen more clearly by setting the left and right margins (commands lm and rm; Figure 18.13a), where lm 5 says set the left margin at column 5 and rm 25 says set the right margin at 25 [the entire line is 21 characters long: (25 − 5 + 1)]. The output looks like that shown in Figure 18.13b, with the words being adjusted to the left and right margins and extra blanks inserted as necessary, much as one sees in newspaper articles.

```
.type input.txt
.P
This example is being done to illustrate the capability of RUNOFF to
format lines to right and left margins, as well as to create paragraph
indendation.
```

(a)

```
.type output.txt

    This example is being done to illustrate the capability of RUNOFF to
format lines to right and left margins, as well as to create paragraph
indentation.
```

(b)

FIGURE 18.12

```
.type input.txt
.lm 5
.rm 25
.P
```

This example is being done to illustrate the capability of RUNOFF to format lines to right and left margins, as well as to create paragraph indentation.

(a)

```
.type output.txt
```

      This example is being done to illustrate the capability of RUNOFF to format lines to right and left margins, as well as to create paragraph indentations.

(b)

**FIGURE 18.13**

## Creating Lists

RUNOFF can be used to create numbered lists, using the commands "ls" (start list), "le" (list entry), and "els" (end list; Figure 18.14a). The ls command says we are beginning a list. The le command says the next line

```
.type input.txt
.ls
.le
eggs
.le
bacon
.le
bread
.le
milk
.els
```

(a)

```
.type output.txt
```

```
1.  eggs
2.  bacon
3.  bread
4.  milk
```

(b)

```
.type input.txt
.ls
.le
eggs
.le      ◀ - - - new entry
pickles ◀
.le
bacon
.le
bread
.le
molk
.els
```

(c)

**FIGURE 18.14**

Care of the numbering:

```
.type output.txt
```

1.  eggs

2.  pickles ◄ - - - ⟶ pickles number 2, everything else adjusted

3.  bacon

4.  bread

5.  milk

(d)

**FIGURE 18.14** (continued)

contains a list item (list entry) and the "els" turns off the list facility. The output is a numbered list of items (Figure 18.14b). The reader might think it easier to type in the numbered items, and, if the list were never modified, this would be true. However, if a new item is added to the list in RUNOFF, we simply add an entry preceded by the command "le" (Figure 18.14c), and RUNOFF takes care of the numbering (Figure 18.14d), whereas a typed manuscript would have to be retyped.

It is in changing manuscripts that text formatters prove useful. If we add a line of text to a printed page, we must either "cut, paste, and photocopy" or retype the page. In using a text formatter, we add the text to the editor file, rerun RUNOFF, and RUNOFF "retypes" the manuscript for us, adjusting pages, margins, and numbering as necessary. This facilitates the modification of existing documents (which may or may not be a good thing).

## Typing Sentences

The fact that a text formatter adjusts the text to fit the margins leads to different techniques of entering text. We can enter text a sentence at a time (Figure 18.15a), which facilitates the addition of new sentences (insert between two lines), the deletion of sentences (find line and delete it), as well as the movement of sentences. RUNOFF will format them for us in the final text (Figure 18.15b). (Note that if we had typed the original text in the same form as the output text, deleting the second sentence would be a more difficult job than in the text containing one sentence per line.)

```
.type input.txt
.P
This is the first sentence.
The second sentence comes next.
```

(a)

**FIGURE 18.15**

```
.type output.txt
```

This is the first sentence.   The second sentence comes next.

**(b)**

```
.type input.txt
```

This is the first sentence.
.br ← – – – – – [ "break" line here ]
The second sentence comes next.

**(c)**

```
.type output.txt
```

This is the first sentence.
The second sentence comes next.

**(d)**

**FIGURE 18.15**   (continued)

 

There may, however, be cases in which we want the output text to show the second sentence on the second line, rather than "moving it up." The "break" command (.BR) allows us to "break off" or "end" the current line at will (Figure 18.15c), so that the output text has the text "The second sentence comes next" on a separate line (Figure 18.15d). Of course, the indentation of the first sentence (caused by the command .p) is our option. By eliminating the paragraph command, it would have been left-justified.   What our needs are will be application-dependent.

 

```
.type input.txt
.ch Introduction
This is a chapter on data processing.
.pg
We are simulating a book.
.ch Two
With chapters and pages.
.pg
This sentence should be on page 2 of Chapter Two.
```

(a)

**FIGURE 18.16**

CHAPTER 1

INTRODUCTION

This is a chapter on data processing.

INTRODUCTION                                                              Page 1-2

We are simulating a book.

CHAPTER 2

TWO

With chapters and pages.

TWO                                                                       Page 2-2

This sentence should be on page 2 of Chapter Two.

(b)

**FIGURE 18.16**   (continued)

## Chapters and Pages

As indicated above, text formatters are often used to prepare textbooks, hence, there are facilities for naming chapters (.ch), starting new pages (.pg), and numbering pages (done automatically by RUNOFF). The input file shown in Figure 18.16a thus results in the output text shown in Figure 18.16b. In any real textbook, presumably the content of each chapter would be more extensive, but the idea is the same.

RUNOFF also facilitates the creation of an index to the book. The user is allowed to choose a symbol with which to mark words that should appear in the index, then include this symbol in the text (Figure 18.17a). RUNOFF

```
.type input.txt
.flags index *     ←-asterisk=indexed word
This is about *RUNOFF.  ←-RUNOFF should appear in the index
.pg
And how *RUNOFF can create an *index.  Index will appear in the index
```

(a)

**FIGURE 18.17**

```
.type input.txt
.flags index*
This is about *RUNOFF.
.pg
And how *RUNOFF can create an *index.
.pg
.do index
```

(b)

```
.type output.txt
```

This is about RUNOFF. `←--- on page 1, not explicitly numbered`

Page 2

And how RUNOFF can create an index. `←--on page 2`

Page 3

```
Index . . . . . . . . . . . . . . . 2  ⎫
Runoff . . . . . . . . . . . . . 2  ⎬   The Index
Runoff . . . . . . . . . . . . . 1  ⎭
```

(c)

FIGURE 18.17 (continued)

will maintain a table of the words that should appear in the index and the pages on which they occurred. Then, in response to the command

*DO INDEX

it will print out the index to the book.

The entire input file for the example is shown in Figure 18.17b, and the output is shown in Figure 18.17c.

## Spacing

The final commands we'll look at involve spacing. We have already seen the use of .BR to cause a line to "break." We can also indicate spacing with the command

.bn

where $b$ stands for blank lines and $n$ indicates how many lines we wish to be blank. Hence, the command

.b1

will give a single blank line and

.b2

```
                                           .type output.txt
.type input.txt
Line One.                                  Line One.
.br                                        Line Two.
Line Two.
.b1                                        Line Three.
Line Three.
.b3                                        Line Four.
Line Four.

(a)                                        (b)
```

FIGURE 18.18

will give two blank lines. The commands shown in Figure 18.18a give the output text shown in Figure 18.18b.

### Getting the Period Right

One source of mistakes in using a text formatter like RUNOFF is the improper use of the symbol to indicate commands (for us, the period). If it is omitted the command will be interpreted as part of the text and will subsequently have to be corrected or deleted. If the period is included where it should not be, an error message will be generated, since the text will not usually be a legal command. For example, in preparing the list of grocery items, the author inadvertantly included the period on the line with pickles (Figure 18.19), and received the reprimand

?RNFILC Illegal command: ".P'I'C'K'L'E'S"

```
•type input.txt
.ls
.le
eggs
.le
.pickles
.le
bacon
.le
bread
.le
milk
.els
```

FIGURE 18.19

.c ←——center the next line of text
Mary George ←——line of text

.c
1485 Maywood
.c
Pittsburgh, PA 15260
.b1←—— leave 1 blank line
.c
February 19, 1982
.b5←—— leave 5 blank lines
Radio Station WQED
.br←—— begin a new line
5500 Fifth Avenue
.br←—— begin a new line
Pittsburgh, PA 15219
.b2←—— leave 2 blank lines
Dear Sir/Madam:
.p←——leave one blank line, then begin a paragraph, indenting 5 spaces ⎫ Type
Last month I contributed $50.00 to WQED during the winter fund-raising ⎬ some
campaign.  I was told that the following gifts would be sent to me: ⎭ text
.ls←—— begin a list after leaving 1 blank line
.le←—— begin first list element
A subscription to ↑ &Pittsburgh Magazine/%    under line text
.le←—— begin next list element
A WQED tote bag
.le←—— begin next list element
A WQED t-shirt.
.els←—— end list, leaving 1 blank line afterwards
So far I have received only the t-shirt.  Will you } type some text
check on the other gifts?
.p←—— begin a new paragraph
Thank you for your help.
.b2←—— leave 2 blank lines
Sincerely,
.b2←—— leave 2 blank lines
Mary George


FIGURE 18.20


## A Complete Example

The following example indicates how RUNOFF can be used to prepare a
letter. The example was prepared by Susan Wiedenbeck, a teaching fellow
at the University of Pittsburgh at the time. The input text is shown in
Figure 18.20, and the result is shown in Figure 18.21.


## Extracting Meaning

Another method of manipulating text concentrates not on the physical manipulation of the text, but on the extraction of meaning. An example is the

```
.type letter.out
```

                              Mary George
                             1485 Maywood
                          Pittsburgh, PA 15260

                          February 19, 1982

Radio Station WQED
5500 Fifth Avenue
Pittsburgh, PA 15219

Dear Sir/Madam:

    Last month I contributed $50.00 to WQED during the winter fund-
raising campaign.  I was told that the following gifts would be sent to
me:

   1.  A subscription to Pittsburgh Magazine

   2.  A WQED tote bag

   3.  A WQED t-shirt.

So far I have received only the t-shirt.  Will you check on the other
gifts?

    Thank you for your help.

Sincerely,

Mary George

**FIGURE 18.21**

automatic production of indexes, one of the simplest being the production
of a key-word-in-context, or KWIC, index. Another is statistical indexing.
We will examine each of these in turn.

### Indexing

In any index, we wish to produce a list of words that indicate the major
"content" topics of a particular document and a location of where these
topics may be found. In a book, the index comprises a list of words and
the pages on which the ideas represented by these words may be found.
Thus, we might find a list similar to that given in Figure 18.22a. This would
indicate that  material on the binary code could be found on p. 250 of the
text, material on the Hamming code on p. 265, etc.
    In another context, we might want to index the content of several
documents, say journal articles, rather than just the contents of a single
book or article. In order to index such a document, a human indexer

---

Codes

---

| | |
|---|---|
| ASCII | p. 262 |
| Binary | p. 250 |
| Decimal | p. 248 |
| EBCDIC | p. 263 |
| Hamming | p. 265 |
| Hexadecimal | p. 259 |
| Huffman | p. 272 |
| Morse | p. 270 |
| Octal | p. 253 |

---

(a)


Data Base Management Systems, 037
DBMS, 037
Hierarchical, 037
Network, 037

(b)


Data Base Management Systems, 037,072
DBMS, 037, 072
Hierarchical, 037
Network, 037
Relational, 072

(c)


FIGURE 18.22


would have to read the document, choose certain "key words" that are representative of the document, then include these words in a list, with the document number next to the word. Thus, if a particular journal article discussed the concepts of data base management systems (DBMS), particularly in regard to hierarchical and network structures, we might index the document as shown in Figure 18.22b, where 037 is a number assigned to the document as a unique identifying code or "key." If more than one journal article treated some of these same concepts, their document numbers would also be attached to the words that described their content. Thus, if document 072 treated DBMS, but only in regard to a relational structure, the index would be as shown in Figure 18.22c.

This process would be repeated until all the documents were read, their meaning extracted, and key words assigned. The final list of key words would be alphabetized and distributed as the index to that month's literature. Of course, the arrival of next month's journals would reinitiate the activity.

Indexing documents can be a highly labor-intensive activity; it requires indexers with a high degree of knowledge in the field, and consumes a great deal of time from receipt of the documents to publication of the index. Furthermore, there are problems of consistency in indexing; since the volume of literature usually requires a team of indexers, rather than a single indexer, there is a problem of consistency across indexers. What one indexer might consider important, another may pass over. While several techniques have been developed to "standardize" indexing (Kent, 1971), the problem still remains, albeit in a diminished form. Even with a single indexer, there is a problem of consistency over time. What strikes the indexer's attention in an article in 1969 may not provoke the same response in 1973.

In order to confront these problems

1. Highly labor-intensive activity, with labor costs always rising
2. Relatively large time delay between publication of document and inclusion of its contents in the index
3. Consistency of indexing

publishers of indexes have turned to methods of automating the indexing process. One of these is the production of the KWIC index.


## A KWIC Index

The acronym KWIC stands for key-word-in-context. The most common form of the KWIC index was disseminated by IBM. However, the format of the index in the original KWIC version somewhat obscures the concept of a key-word-in-context index, hence, an abbreviated form of the KWIC index is presented here.

The primary assumption of the KWIC index is that the title of an article is a good indicator of its content. In order to implement the KWIC index, the titles of all articles to be indexed are converted to machine-readable form, e.g., by keying them onto disk storage in a computer system. Once these titles are keyed in, a computer program is used to manipulate the words in each title, producing an index that consists entirely of these words. The method of manipulating the words in the title is to rotate the words so that each word appears first exactly one time, as a "key word," the remaining words of the title forming the context for this key word.

For example, if the title of an article were

"Data Base Management Systems"

the first key word would be *data,* with *base management systems* forming the context for this key word

Data, Base Management Systems
  |            |
Key word     Context

The title would then be rotated so that the entry is

Base, Management Systems Data
  |            |
Key word     Context

Two more rotations would give the following entries:

Management, Systems Data Base

and

Systems, Data Base Management

| Document number | Document title |
|---|---|
| 014 | Data Base Management Systems |
| 027 | Automated Data Management |
| 142 | Data Base Concepts |

(a)

Data, Base Management Systems,  014
Base, Management Systems Data,  014
Management, Systems Data Base,  014
Systems, Data Base Management,  014

(b)

Automated, Data Management,  027
Data, Management Automated,  027
Management, Automated Data,  027

(c)

Data, Base Concepts,  142
Base, Concepts Data,  142
Concepts, Data Base,  142

(d)

Automated, Data Management, 027
Base, Concepts Data, 142
Base, Management Systems Data, 014
Concepts, Data Base, 142
Data, Base Concepts, 142
Data, Base Management Systems, 014
Data, Management Automated, 027
Management, Automated Data, 027
Management, Systems Data Base, 014
Systems, Data Base Management, 014

(e)

FIGURE 18.23

To indicate how the KWIC index would work with more than one title, suppose that we have the documents given in Figure 18.23a, each with its unique number. Rotation of the first article produces Figure 18.23b. Rotation of the second article produces Figure 18.23c, and rotation of the third produces Figure 18.23d. This list would then be sorted, and the sorted list would constitute the index (Figure 18.23e).

Evaluating the KWIC Index

As can be seen from the example, certain entries, such as

Data, Base Management Systems

or

Management, Systems Data Base

or

Systems, Data Base Management

are likely to be more useful than other entries, such as

Base, Management Systems Data

or

Concepts, Data Base

since a user interested in DBMSs, the management of data, or the analysis and design of systems would be more likely to search under the terms

Data
Management
Systems

than under the terms

Concept
Base

However, the point is that a highly intellectual task of "extracting meaning from a document" has been reduced to a clerical task of keying in titles and running a set of computer programs.

One might ask how the computer recognizes a word. The response is that it recognizes a word in the same manner that a human recognizes a word in written text: by the occurrence of the blank. Whatever came before the blank was the word. The role of the blank can easily be seen if we consider the following:

BE FIT
BEFIT

where two different meanings are obtained, although the two sets of letters differ only in that one has the blank. In practice, certain terms, such as *data base*, might be considered a single word. This would require the use of a dictionary of such multiword terms.

String manipulation techniques (where the entire sentence or title is considered the "string" of characters) are used to isolate the words of the sentence. These can then be stored in an array and rotated to form the variations of the title. Then when all titles are done, another computer program can be used to sort on the key words.

The substitution of computer technology for human effort substitutes a commodity with declining costs (the current costs of hardware) for a technology (human labor) with increasing costs (few workers ask for yearly decreases in salary), although it also introduces the costs of producing computer software, a rising cost. Studies of the usefulness of such indexes indicate that while they are not ideal, they are satisfactory.

## The KWOC Index

One of the difficulties with the KWIC index is that it results in numerous entries (Figure 18.24a). This list could be reduced if we eliminated the context, which makes so many of the entries unique. Indexes composed of key words without the context are called KWOC indexes (key-word-out-of-context; Figure 18.24b). If we add the postings for each document, we have the list shown in Figure 18.24c, which is one of the common forms of indexing in information retrieval systems, the inverted file.

Automated, Data Management, 027
Base, Concepts Data, 142
Base, Management Systems Data, 014
Concepts, Data Base, 142
Data, Base Concepts, 142
Data, Base Management Systems, 014
Data, Management Automated, 027
Management, Automated Data, 027
Management, Systems Data Base, 014
Systems, Data Base Management, 014

(a)

Automated, 027
Base, 014, 142
Concepts, 142
Data, 014, 027, 142
Management, 014, 027
Systems, 014

(b)

| Postings | Keyword | Document numbers |
|---|---|---|
| 01 | Automated | 027 |
| 02 | Base | 014,142 |
| 01 | Concepts | 142 |
| 03 | Data | 014,027,142 |
| 02 | Management | 014,027 |
| 01 | Systems | 014 |

(c)

FIGURE 18.24

```
      01    Automated    027
----→ 02    Base         014,142
      01    Concepts     142
----→ 03    Data         014,027,142
      02    Management   014,027
      01    Systems      014
```

(a)

```
      02    Base         014,    142
      03    Data         014,027,142
                          ↑       ↑
```

(b)

```
      014   Data Base Management Systems
      142   Data Base Concepts
```

(c)

FIGURE 18.25


As can be seen from the list of isolated words, the KWOC index has lost the relationship of one word to other words in the document. Thus, in looking simply at the entry for *data*

    03  DATA  014,027,142

we have no indication that this term was connected to "Base Management Systems" in document 014

    014  Data Base Management Systems

or to "Base Concepts" in document 142

    142  Data Base Concepts

This connection must now be supplied by the user of the index.

One of the most common means of supplying these relationships is by searching with Boolean operators. Thus, a user interested in DBMSs might enter the query

    DATA

    and

    BASE

The system would then search for both key words (Figure 18.25a), compare the lists for key numbers that the two terms have in common (for AND; Figure 18.25b), then search the list of documents for the full titles (abstracts, etc.), and reward the user of the system with the output given in Figure 18.25c. This user would not see the title "Automated Data Management," since the word *base*, a part of the search query, did not occur in the title. This is an example of a system "missing" a relevant title. However, alternate search terms, such as *data* and *management*, or a broader search, such as the single aspect search for *data*, would retrieve the document. Of course, a broader search is also likely to turn up more "noise," or documents that are only peripherally related to our interests. As indicated earlier, the technique of good searching seeks to balance the retrieval of most relevant documents (recall) with the elimination of irrelevant documents (noise), so that the search is precise yet comprehensive.

## A Stop List

While some systems index every word in the text they are handling, it is obvious that not every word in every title is useful for indexing. Thus, we might have the title

A Study of DBMS: The Relational Approach

We do not want to search on the terms *A, of,* or *the.* Some systems include such words in a "stop list," which is consulted before a word is entered into the index.

Typical candidates for a stop list would be articles (e.g., a, an, the), prepositions (e.g., of, in), and conjunctions (e.g., and, or). Linguists refer to such terms as "function words," in contrast to "content words," such as *baseball, sun, derby, sandwich, computer,* etc. Function words are part of the "glue" that holds a sentence together. Content words add meaning to the form. Hence, the sentence

The boy hit the ball.

has the functional operator *the* to indicate that the subject and object are "definite" objects, a particular boy and a particular ball, while the words *boy,* and *ball* indicate what these definite objects are. The same form

The ___ ____ the _____.

could be used to convey another meaning, e.g.

The **girl** tackled the halfback.

in which we are still talking about two definite objects, a particular girl and a particular halfback, but the meaning of the sentence has changed.

Function words affect meanings as well. For example, the sentence

A boy hit the ball.

indicates "some indefinite" boy, in contrast to the definiteness implied by "the boy." However, the meaning involved is not as useful to searches as the meaning of content words.

Value words, such as *good, bad, useful,* and *useless,* are also candidates for the stop list. An article that states that "a relational data base is a good design" is no doubt about data bases, the design of data bases, and the relational approach to data base design. However, the adjective "good" is the author's opinion, and may not be the opinion of other authors or of the readers of the article. Since such value judgments may vary widely, and usually do not change the "content" of the article, they might be included in the stop list. In some applications, however, such as data bases of movie ratings or restaurant ratings, the evaluation would be part of the data of interest.

Finally, words that are considered "too common" to distinguish the content of one article from the content of another might be included in the stop list. Hence, in a data base of articles on education, the term *education*

TABLE 18.1
_____

Stop List
_____

a
an
bad
education
good
in
of
on
the
_____

might be eliminated as a valid index term, since all articles are presumably on education. Conversely, words like *teaching, teacher,* and *learning* would be included, since they make a distinction that does matter. This is the same principle that prevents a prudent person from entering a physics library and asking for a book on physics. The output is too voluminous and nondiscriminating.

Thus, a portion of a stop list for an education data base might include the terms listed in Table 18.1. Any term in the title that is also found in the stop list is *not* indexed, i.e., it is "stopped."

## Word Stems

The terms *teaching, teacher,* and *teach* bring up one other concern of an automated indexing system: the use of word stems. It is often the case that several variations of terms exist for the same concept. These may include variations in suffixes, such as the singular *computer* versus the plural *computers,* or prefixes, such as *prepartum* and *postpartum.* The handling of suffixes is illustrated here. One form, the "stem," is used to represent all variations of that stem. Thus, the stem

Teach -

would be used for the forms

Teach
Teacher
Teaching

In the simplest case of simply checking characters, the form "taught" would not be included in the list for "teach-," although more complex forms of analysis are possible.

The use of word stems can compress the index, as the three entries

| | |
|---|---|
| Teach | 012, 025 |
| Teacher | 012, 031, 048 |
| Teaching | 025, 048, 072 |

would now appear as a single entry

Teach -    012, 025, 031, 048, 072

It can also be useful in counting the number of occurrences of a given word in a given portion of text, a task that is useful in statistical indexing.

## Statistical Indexing

The KWIC and KWOC indexes were formed on the basis of the title of the article alone. More meaning about the content of the article might be extracted if the full text or an abstract of the text is examined (see Marcus et al., 1971, and Saracevic, 1969; also reported in Lancaster and Fayen, 1973). This is the method used in statistical indexing. Either the full text of an article, an abstract of the article, or select sentences from the article (e.g., the first paragraph and/or the last paragraph) are examined and the words extracted. These words are first tested against a stop list, to eliminate the terms not used for indexing, then reformatted into word stems. For example, in the passage

A teacher using the mastery learning method would expect the majority of students to master the material. If such learning did not occur, an examination might be made of both teaching methods and learning skills.

Such words as *a, using,* and *the* would be eliminated, and the words *teacher* and *teaching* would both appear as *teach-*. The remaining words and word stems would then be sorted and counted (by a computer program). This would result in a list such as that shown in Table 18.2. These counts would then be used to select index terms. Note that in the above list, the terms *mastery* and *master* appear as two different entries. The rule used here looked for such suffixes as *ing* and *er*. A different rule for forming word stems, e.g., taking the first six letters of any work, might have them appear as a single entry

Master-2

The determination of such rules for "stemming" is not an easy task, and will vary from system to system. However, we are interested here in the method of using the count of the words to choose the index terms.

## TABLE 18.2

Learn—2
Master—1
Mastery—1
Material—1
Method—1
Skill—1
Student—1
Teach—2

In using word counts, two thresholds are usually set for discrimination between useful index terms and nonuseful ones: the lower threshold and the upper threshold. Useful index terms occur with a frequency "within the thresholds," nonuseful terms occur with a frequency "outside the thresholds." These terms may occur too infrequently (beneath the lower threshold) or too frequently (above the upper threshold). If the term counts occur outside the boundaries set by the two thresholds, they are excluded from the index. Terms with counts within the threshold boundaries are included in the index.

The exact values of the upper and lower thresholds are usually set experimentally, for a given body of literature. Thus, the thresholds for novels might be different from the thresholds for textbooks. Within these general areas, the thresholds for murder mysteries might be different from the thresholds for comedies; the thresholds for physics texts might be different from the thresholds of history texts. Thus, a study of the literature and a little "trial and error" to see the results of various threshold settings is in order. This is true of the selection of words for the stop list and rules for "stemming" as well. In order to illustrate the point, let us assume that the thresholds have been set at 2 and 5, so that valid index terms occur 2 to 5 times (inclusively), while terms that occur once (beneath the lower threshold) or 6 or more times (above the upper threshold) are excluded. In the above hypothetical example, the words *teach*, *method*, and *learn* would be included in the index for the text, while all other terms would be excluded as occurring "too rarely," or less frequently than is demanded by the lower threshold of 2 (since all other terms occurred only one time). If the terms *master* and *mastery* were counted as the same term, we would have: *mastery*, as well as *learn* indicating that the article is about mastery learning.

### Rationale for the Thresholds

The rationale for the two thresholds is as follows:

Lower threshold: excludes "passing references"
Upper threshold: excludes terms that are "too common"

In regard to the lower threshold, a "passing reference" is the use of a term in a peripheral manner that has nothing to do with the main content of the article. Thus, in an article about baseball, we might find the following:

The crowd was already forming when we arrived at the ballpark. Both teams had taken the field as we settled into our seats for an afternoon of baseball....

After the game, we stopped at a restaurant to eat, then returned home to find that a fuse had blown out and caused the refrigerator to have nothing but warm "iced" tea.

The contention is that this hypothetical article is not about restaurants, fuses, refrigerators, or iced tea. It is the use of a lower threshold, some minimum number of times that a term must be mentioned in order to be taken as meaningful, that should eliminate such passing references. The expectation is that a term having to do with the major theme of the article will occur more than one time. While this may not be true in all styles of writing (e.g., journalists and novelists may seek to use synonyms rather than repeat a term), it is the usual case in didactic and scientific literature. Again, the method of analyzing words will vary from one type of literature to the next.

The upper threshold excludes terms that are "too common." The analogy would be to words like *education* in a data base of educational literature. If the word occurs too frequently it is thought to be nondiscriminatory, a word that will occur in all articles, hence distinguishing none.

## An Example

In teaching the introductory course in information science, one of the texts we have used has been *Information Systems: Theory and Practice*, by Burch, Strater, and Grudnitski. The following passage (p. 172) is well suited to illustrate statistical indexing or indexing by counting:

> Codes provide an abbreviated structure for classifying items in order to record, communicate, process, and/or retrieve data. Codes are designed to provide unique identification of the data to be coded.

Applying a stop list of such words as *an*, *for*, and *in*, the count of terms in the passage is that shown in Table 18.3. Using the thresholds of 2 to 5 occrrences, we have

Code-3

and

Data-2

as terms for the index. The title of the section (section 8.3) is "Coding Considerations," so that a simple count of terms has "extracted the meaning" from the passage. Of course, the system will not work infallibly; often irrelevant terms will be selected, and relevant ones missed, but, with a

## TABLE 18.3

| Code | 3(codes, codes, coded) |
|---|---|
| Abbreviate | 1 |
| Structure | 1 |
| Classify | 1 |
| Record | 1 |
| Communicate | 1 |
| Process | 1 |
| Retrieve | 1 |
| Data | 2 (data, data) |
| Decision | 1 |
| Indentif- | 1 |

TABLE 18.4

good degree of satisfaction, we have again substituted an automatic procedure (counting) for what is considered to be a uniquely human task (extracting meaning from a passage).

An example of the use of the upper threshold is produced if we consider various sections on coding. Using the same chapter, we have the sections shown in Table 18.4. In each of these sections, the word *code* itself would occur too often, exceeding an upper threshold of 5. For example, in section 8.3, the word code appears over 75 times. This would indicate that the word code is *not* a good discriminator between the various types of coding methods. However, if we take about 5 to 15 occurrences as right, terms that do occur with the "right amount of frequency" (in section 8.4) are

| | |
|---|---|
| Sequential | 7 |
| Block | 10 |
| Facet | 6 |
| Mnemonic | 7 |

each of which is a type of code. Presumably, these would be our index terms. One term that would not appear is the term *color*, as in color code, since it was used more than 15 times. Thus, not all the codes would be represented.

In the first example, we examined only the introductory two sentences of a section ("Codes provide....to be coded). In the second instance, we examined the entire text of a section in order to obtain our counts. The amount of text that we examine will depend on the precision with which we wish to index, the type of literature involved, the sophistication of the users of the system, etc.; however, in all cases, the procedures are the same

1. Isolate the words.
2. Sort the words.
3. Count the words.

which are much simpler tasks than "read the material" and "think about the material." We have also intimated that the text was keyed into computer-accessible storage (say a disk). However, as methods of reading text optically by machine, or of producing machine-readable text as a by-product of the publishing process, become more common, even this clerical task of keying the data (often a mammoth task) may be eliminated or reduced in volume.

## Summary

The methods of manipulating data presented here

1. Numerical techniques
2. Text processing techniques

are quite general. Within each general category, there are numerous individual techniques. Thus, forecasting, queuing theory, and linear programming; the computation of the mean and standard deviation in earlier sections; the creation of KWIC and KWOC indexes; and statistical indexing have been presented as "representative" of a vast body of techniques. The intent has been to illustrate the fact that while the data we have available may not be in the form required for our purposes, it can often be manipulated into that form. Thus, data that did not originally answer our questions in explicit form can be made to answer those questions given a little ingenuity and effort.

## Related Readings

Burch, Strater, and Grudnitski, *Information Systems: Theory and Practice*, 2nd ed., New York: John Wiley & Sons, 1979.

Heaps, H. S., *Information Retrieval: Computational and Theoretical Aspects*. New York: Academic Press, 1978.

Kent, Allen, *Information Analysis and Retrieval*, New York: John Wiley & Sons, 1971.

Lancaster, B. F. and Fayen, E. G., *Information Retrieval On-Line*, Los Angeles: Melville Publishing Company, 1973.

Marcus, R. S., Benenfeld, A. R., and Kugel, P., "The User Interface for the Intrex Retrieval System," in *Interactive Bibliographic Search: The User/Computer Interface*, D. E. Walker, ed. Montvale, NJ: AFIPS Press, 1971, pp. 159–201.

Meadow, Charles T., *Man-Machine Communication*, New York: John Wiley & Sons, 1970.

Salton, Gerard and McGill, Michael J., *Introduction to Modern Information Retrieval*, New York: McGraw-Hill, 1983.

Saracevic, T., "Comparative Effects of Titles, Abstracts and Full Texts on Relevance Judgments," *Proceedings of American Society of Information Science*, Vol. 6, 1969, pp. 293–299.

# X
# Decision-Making and Problem-Solving

This last section introduces two topics that are widely discussed in studies of information and information-related activities. The first, decision-making, is widely discussed in the business literature and is one of the uses of information cited in phrases that define information as data for decision-making. We take a view of information as data (and a model or a set of models) for taking action, i.e., data that enables effective action. This interpretation allows data to be considered valuable or useful even in situations in which uncertainty as to choice or outcome of action does not exist, e.g., reading a menu in a restaurant, or applying the proper velocity to launch an object into flight.

Decision-making is seen as a subset of action/outcome situations or scenarios, those in which more than one action is available. These instances of decision-making situations can be subdivided into those in which the choice of the action is equivalent to the choice of the outcome, the action being sufficient to produce the outcome (choice under certainty of outcome or sufficiency of action); and those in which the actions are not sufficient to produce the outcomes, the outcome being produced by an agent in conjunction with a state of nature (state of the environment, context in which the action is taken) or by more than one agent. The latter situations, "joint agents" yielding "joint outcomes," are referred to as decisions under uncertainty and are the primary focus of Chapter 19 in this section.

The first of these situations, an agent and a state of nature, is studied under the rubric of the expected value matrix of actions, states of nature, and outcomes with attendant payoffs. The primary analysis is in terms of the expected value of the situation requiring a decision without "further information" (expected value with no information; EVNI) and the value of the situation when the state of nature can be predicted with certainty (expected value of perfect information; EVPI). The difference between these two values (EVPI and EVNI) is the value of the perfect prediction, i.e., the value of the information provided by the predictor. In tying this to the earlier chapters, such a predictor might be a regression equation developed in the data collection and analysis stage, although such equations are usually not perfect, and thus have a value somewhere between zero (no information) and perfect information.

Types of decisionmakers, such as maximax and maximin, are examined, but in a rudimentary fashion.

After studying decisions "against nature" we look at decisions "against human opponents," or game theory. Finally, while the analysis of expected value has been done in monetary terms, the use of utility measures instead of dollar values is introduced. An analogous analysis, calculating an "unexpected utility," can be performed if one know the utilities (not an easy problem to solve).

Chapter 20 fits theoretically at the start and finish of the text. Problems in action-oriented situations are equivalent to blocked actions. The cause of the blockage, i.e., the problem "type" is either a physical inability to act or an inability to act caused by lack of knowledge. The latter is an information problem. The lack of knowledge is caused by either the lack of a model for the situation or the lack of knowledge of data values for a model believed to be appropriate. In either case, this information need generates the search for information with which we began the text.

If the search for information is successful, the action may then be implemented. If the search provides not a data value, but a list of one or more actions toward an end, i.e., a model, the actions may involve a choice, i.e., if two or more are listed. Hence, decision-making is seen as a consequence of problem-solving activity, one in which the solution involves a set of two or more actions toward the goal. Implementation is a consequence of decision-making activity, the "making real" of the choice, and leads into the area of control or "effective action," i.e., implementing actions in a manner that achieves the outcome when that is possible, and one that "maximizes" the likelihood of the outcome when full control is not possible.

The discussion of decision-making includes the topic of action/outcome matrices and their interpretation, a representation common in the business literature. The discussion of proglem-solving includes discussions of "problem spaces" and problem-solving techniques, say the use of generate and test and the traversal of search trees, that are popular in literature of psychology, cognitive science, and artificial intelligence.

In discussing problem-solving techniques, a distinction is made between heuristic (rule-of-thumb) techniques and algorithmic (procedural, guaranteed) techniques. Algorithmic techniques are distinguished according to "algorithms of search," which guarantee that all objects are considered in a generate-and-test approach, and "algorithms of transfomation," in which a sequence of operations is guaranteed to produce the solution when applied (and the method is not generate and test). These latter "transformation algorithms" are equivalent to the techniques employed under the name of data manipulation, and are probably better referred to as tasks than problems.

"True problems," those in which a solution is not known, are subdivided into "object identification" problems, wherein one seeks an object with certain attributes, but does not know how to find it; and "transformation" problems, wherein one seeks a sequence of actions to transform some "initial state" into a "goal state."

Both types of problems can be represented by search trees. The trees crystallize the task (problem) of appropriate strategy selection, e.g., depth-first search versus breadth-first search. Finally, trees that represent the pitting of the agent against a passive environment are contrasted with those involving an "opponent" who also "makes moves" (takes actions).

With the section on problem-solving we close the book where we began, since the solution to a problem (knowledge problem) involves the search for information.

# *19*
# Decision-Making

## Objectives

Upon completing this chapter the reader should be able to

1. Contrast decisions made under certainty (actions sufficient to produce outcomes) and uncertainty (coproduction)
2. Calculate the expected value of a situation requiring a decision, given a decision matrix (the EVNI)
3. Calculate the expected value of a matrix, given perfect information (EVPI)
4. Calculate the value of information (EVPI-EVNI)
5. Distinguish among the decision-making types maximax, maximin, maximum likelihood, and Bayesian (EMV)
6. Explain the difference between expected value situations involving events of nature and game theory
7. Explain the interaction of choices and payoffs, as well as the manner in which choices are anticipated
8. Explain the trade-off between information and control
9. Explain the use of decision tables and flow charts to depict branching situations
10. Distinguish between monetary value and utility
11. Explain the concepts of total utility and marginal utility
12. Explain the assumption of transitivity of preferences, and give a rationale for such an assumption

One of the common uses of information is to facilitate the process of decision-making. In making a decision, we are faced with a number of alternatives, and our task is to choose the alternative that is most desirable to reach our goal. An example of the decision-making process was given in Chapter 1: choosing a restaurant at which to have lunch.

## A Review

The reader will recall that we had arrived in a strange town, not knowing where to have lunch. By asking some people for data (report-by-others), we obtained a list of restaurants

TABLE 19.1a

| Restaurant | Good Taste? | Criteria | |
|---|---|---|---|
| | | Low Cost? | Nearby? |
| 1. Joe's Diner | Yes | Yes | No |
| 2. Mary's Place* | Yes | Yes | Yes |
| 3. Eat-A-Burger | No | Yes | Yes |
| 4. Swank-U-Pay | No | No | No |
| 5. Plain Home Cooking | Yes | No | Yes |

* = choice

TABLE 19.1b

| Restaurant | Good Taste? | Criteria | |
|---|---|---|---|
| | | Low Cost? | Nearby? |
| 1. Joe's Diner | Fair | Good | Poor |
| 2. Mary's Place | Fair | Good | Fair |
| 3. Eat-A-Burger | Poor | Good | Good |
| 4. Swank-U-Pay | Fair | Poor | Fair |
| 5. Plain Home Cooking | Good | Fair | Good |

TABLE 19.1c

| Restaurant | Good Taste? | Criteria | | Total |
|---|---|---|---|---|
| | | Low Cost? | Nearby? | |
| 1. Joe's Diner | 6 | 9 | 2 | 17 |
| 2. Mary's Place | 6 | 8 | 7 | 21 |
| 3. Eat-A-Burger | 3 | 10 | 9 | 22 |
| 4. Swank-U-Pay | 4 | 1 | 4 | 9 |
| 5. Plain Home Cooking* | 10 | 4 | 9 | 23 |

Joe's Diner
Swank-U-Pay
Mary's Place
Plain Home Cooking
Eat-A-Burger

with various attributes for each (e.g., its distance from the bus station, the taste of the food, the cost of the food, etc.). We abstracted from a list

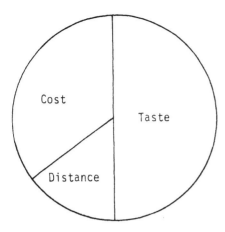

FIGURE 19.1

of "all possible" attributes, e.g., color of the facade, internal decor, height of the building, fashionability of the restaurant, to the set of criteria of interest

- Taste of food
- Cost of food
- Nearness of the restaurant

We then rated (or obtained ratings) on each restaurant in order to compare them against each other. The initial ratings were qualitative (Table 19.1a), and this "qualitativeness" made comparisons difficult. For example, in the three level rating (Table 19.1b), it was difficult to judge whether or not "two fairs" were equal to "one good." We decided to switch to a quantitative scale for the ratings (Table 19.1c), in which a comparison among restaurants was made by simply adding the values on each criterion for each restaurant. As the diagram shows, Plain Home Cooking, with a score of 23, was our choice.

Even the quantitative scale proved lacking in that the criteria were "equally weighted" when simply summed. Yet, in our mind, the criteria were "not all equal," hence, we weighted the criteria

| Taste | .5 |
| Cost | .3 |
| Distance | .2 |

where the sum total of the weights is 1.0, but the relative proportions indicate the relative importance of each criterion (Figure 19.1), in which case the overall rating for each restaurant was computed as an expected value in which the "raw" ratings (Table 19.2a), are multiplied by the "weight" (Table 19.2b) before being summed (final total on Joe's Diner = 6.1). The table for this particular decisionmaker became that shown in Table 19.2c, which indicates Plain Home Cooking is still the restaurant of choice.

Of course, a different decisionmaker might assign the weights differently

TABLE 19.2a

| Restaurant | Criteria | | |
|---|---|---|---|
| | Good Taste? (.5) | Low Cost? (.3) | Nearby? (.2) |
| 1. Joe's Diner | 6 | 9 | 2 |
| 2. Mary's Place | 6 | 8 | 7 |
| 3. Eat-A-Burger | 3 | 10 | 9 |
| 4. Swank-U-Pay | 4 | 1 | 4 |
| 5. Plain Home Cooking | 10 | 4 | 9 |

TABLE 19.2b

| Restaurant | | Good Taste? | Low Cost? | Nearby? | Total |
|---|---|---|---|---|---|
| Joe's Diner | Weights | .5 | .3 | .2 | 1.0 |
| | Values | 6.0 | 9.0 | 2.0 | |
| | Weighted value | 3.0 | 2.7 | .4 | 6.1 |

TABLE 19.2c

| Restaurant | Criteria | | | |
|---|---|---|---|---|
| | Good Taste? (.5) | Low Cost? (.3) | Nearby? (.2) | Total |
| 1. Joe's Diner | 3 | 2.7 | .4 | 6.1 |
| 2. Mary's Place | 3 | 2.4 | 1.4 | 6.8 |
| 3. Eat-A-Burger | 1.5 | 3.0 | 1.8 | 6.3 |
| 4. Swank-U-Pay | 2 | .3 | 0.8 | 3.1 |
| 5. Plain Home Cooking | 5 | 1.2 | 1.8 | 8.0 |

TABLE 19.2d

| Restaurant | Criteria | | | |
|---|---|---|---|---|
| | Good Taste? (.1) | Low Cost? (.8) | Nearby? (.1) | Total |
| 1. Joe's Diner | .6 | 7.2 | .2 | 8.0 |
| 2. Mary's Place | .6 | 6.4 | .7 | 7.7 |
| 3. Eat-A-Burger | .3 | 8.0 | .9 | 9.2 |
| 4. Swank-U-Pay | .4 | .8 | .4 | 1.6 |
| 5. Plain Home Cooking | 1.0 | 3.2 | .9 | 5.1 |

```
Taste     .1
Cost      .8
Nearby    .1
```

(reflecting, e.g., the poverty of a student), with the decision matrix becoming that shown in Table 19.2d. Now Eat-A-Burger is the overwhelming favorite, due to its economical fare.

We thus saw that some of the critical elements of the decision-making process were

- The list of alternatives
- The list of criteria by which to compare the alternatives
- The method by which criteria are weighted
- The method by which the ratings are summarized into a single overall rating
- The characteristics of the decisionmaker(s)

In this chapter we expand on these topics.

## Decision-Making Under Certainty

The lunch example is an instance of decision-making under certainty. If one implements the action of choosing a restaurant, one is relatively certain of achieving the outcome "obtain food."

However, there is a difference between this situation and the case of linear programming. In the production of denims the ultimate outcome was to make money. This outcome was "gradated," i.e., there were levels of money to be made. Hence, we examined no secondary attributes; we simply set the input variables to obtain the highest level of the single output variable.

In the case of the restaurant, the primary output variable "getting lunch" or "obtaining food" is being treated as a binary valued variable, hence an action is either capable of producing the outcome (yes or 1) or not capable of producing the outcome (no or 0). Given the choices and their respective efficacies

| Choices | Effective Toward Goal? |
|---|---|
| Go to Mary's Place | Yes |
| Go to Joe's Diner | Yes |
| Go to XYZ Cleaners | No |
| Stay put | No |

we see that the latter two choices are eliminated due to ineffectiveness toward the goal.

However, in terms of effectiveness, the first two choices are indistinguishable

```
Mary's    1
Joe's     1
```

Hence, we must examine auxiliary attributes of the goal or the implemented action

Quality of food (attribute of goal)
Cost of food (attribute of goal)
Distance to restaurant (attribute, i.e., cost, of implementing action)

in order to make the choice.

## Coproduction

We now turn to a consideration of a different type of decision situation, one in which our actions alone are not sufficient to produce the desired outcome. The successful attainment of the goal (in this case money) depends on two or more "input agents," either two people or two organizations (both being decisionmakers) or a human agent (the single decisionmaker) and "nature," with the relevant "forces of nature" being identified.

## An Example

As an example of decision-making in the coproduction situation we consider the decision by a fraternity to hold a picnic or a bingo game on each Saturday of the school year. The decision hinges on a single criterion, the profit we make from holding a picnic versus the profit we make from holding a bingo game. However, in making this decision, we see that the outcome of the decision does not depend entirely on us; it also depends on the number of people who will choose to attend the picnic versus the number of people who will decide to attend the bingo game. In order to estimate this number we would normally take a market survey. However, in our example we wish to emphasize one other point: the decision of people to attend a picnic or a bingo game is often based on the weather, and the behavior of the weather is beyond our control.

We refer to the choices

• Hold a picnic
• Hold a bingo game

as the alternatives or actions available to us. We have control over these. The behavior of the weather, here restricted to two states

• Rain
• No rain

is referred to as "events." These events are not within our control.

The interplay of our actions and the events of the weather result in certain outcomes. For two possible actions and two possible events we have four possible outcomes

• Hold picnic, rain
• Hold picnic, no rain
• Hold bingo, rain
• Hold bingo, no rain

associated with each outcome will be a "payoff," the amount of money we make. Let us say that we have estimated these payoffs as

Events

|  | Rain | No Rain |
|---|---|---|
| Hold Picnic | -3 | +10 |
| Hold Bingo | +7 | -1 |

Actions

FIGURE 19.2

- Hold picnic, rain ⟶ -3
- Hold picnic, no rain ⟶ +10
- Hold bingo, rain ⟶ +7
- Hold bingo, no rain ⟶ -1

The rationale for these payoffs is that if we hold a picnic and it rains, fewer people come. We have expended certain funds for hotdogs, buns, mustard, soda, etc., and we do not recoup the funds. Hence, the payoff for "hold picnic, rain" is negative (-3). We lost money and the amount we lost is $3 (this could be 3 million, 3,000, etc.; we are using the numbers as "representative" values rather than as real estimates).

If we hold a picnic and it does not rain, we get a good turnout, and we make money (+10). On the other hand, if we hold a bingo game and it rains, we make money (+7), since everyone wants to stay inside. And if we hold a bingo game and it does not rain, we lose money (-1), since everyone wants to go outside.

The decision situation can be summarized in the matrix of Figure 19.2, in which the actions are listed along the left-hand side of the matrix (labeling the rows) and the "events of nature" are listed across the top (labeling the columns). These events of nature could also be actions of competitors, say other fraternities, that might also be holding baseball games, casino nights, etc., which, in a free market, are presumably also out of our control. The main idea is that our actions (choices) interact with the choices of others or with chance events, so that the outcome of our decision does not hinge on our decision alone.

The outcomes of the decision-event combination are listed in the cell that is the intersection of that row value and that column value. Hence we have row 1, column 1 as representing "hold picnic, rain" with the associated payoff of -3. On the same row we have "hold picnic, no rain" with the associated payoff of +10. The second row represents the choice to hold a bingo game, and this choice is associated with "rain" (column 1) and a payoff of +7, or "no rain" (column 2) and the associated payoff of -1.

## Analysis of the Matrix

The matrix we have presented here does not present a clear choice; there is no one action that can be called "best." If we decide to hold a picnic, we can make money or lose it

|  | Interest rates go up to 15% | Interest rates go down to 5% |
|---|---|---|
| Invest money ($1000) in savings account | $150 | $50 |
| Put money under bed | 0 | 0 |

FIGURE 19.3

|  | Rain | No Rain |
|---|---|---|
| Hold picnic | -3 | +10 |

Likewise for holding a bingo game

|  | Rain | No Rain |
|---|---|---|
| Hold bingo | +7 | -1 |

and the conditions under which we make a profit or suffer a loss are exact-ly reversed for each case. Hence, we have a dilemma or trade-off between the two decisions.

Not all decision situations present a dilemma. We could have the deci-sion matrix shown in Figure 19.3, in which case the choice "invest money in savings account" clearly "dominates" the choice "put money under the bed." However, the decisions that are of interest will always involve trade-offs that make the decision interesting. These trade-offs involve the "risks" we take (losing -3 if it rains and we hold a picnic, or losing -1 if we hold a bingo game and it does not rain).

Of course, the timing of the decision is also crucial. We must decide what to do before Saturday, i.e., before we know the actual behavior of the weather. Decision-making "in hindsight" is always easier (we *should have* held a picnic), but rarely possible.

## Various Dimensions

The 2*2 matrices presented here are used for simplicity. However, it is possible to have more rows (as many as we have alternatives, i.e., pos-sible actions as choices) and more columns (as many events of nature or actions of competitors as we wish to consider relevant). In fact, the way in which we structure the matrix can affect the complexity and the effec-

Fraternity II Actions

| | Hold Sports Fair (Day) | Hold Casino (Evening) | Hold Party (Evening) |
|---|---|---|---|
| Hold Picnic (Day) | +5 | +10 | +6 |
| Hold Bingo (Day) | -2 | +7 | +4 |
| Hold Dance (Evening) | +7 | +5 | +7 |
| Show Movie (Evening) | +15 | -3 | +5 |

Fraternity I Action (label on left for the rows)

FIGURE 19.4

tiveness of the decision-making process. A four-by-three matrix, consider-ing the interplay of two fraternities, might be that shown in Figure 19.4. The payoffs shown are those for fraternity 1. Fraternity 2 would have a matrix of its own, and the values need not be the same. (Some situations, say a bet between two people, would have symmetrical payoffs, since if one wins $5, the other must lose $5. However, this is not the general case, since fraternity 2 may incur different costs, have different market projec-tions, etc.)

The reader will note that in the above matrix, the decision to hold a bingo game (by fraternity 1) is "useless" in that decision 1 "hold a picnic" dominates it (Figure 19.5a), since the value of the picnic is always higher than the value of the bingo game. If faced with these two choices, we should always choose the picnic. Hence, we can drop the "bingo choice" from the diagram (Figure 19.5b). Dropping the choice of bingo simplifies the decision we (the officers of fraternity 1) have to make, which is one of the benefits of structuring the decision process.

Fraternity 2

| | Sports | Casino | Party |
|---|---|---|---|
| Picnic | +5 | +10 | +6 |
| Bingo | -2 | +7 | +4 |

(a)

FIGURE 19.5

Fraternity 2

|  | | Sports | Casino | Party |
|---|---|---|---|---|
| Fraternity 1 | Picnic | +5 | +10 | +6 |
| | Dance | +7 | +5 | +7 |
| | Movie | +15 | -3 | +5 |

(b)

FIGURE 19.5 (continued)

The remaining choices will have trade-offs: we could show a movie (in the evening). Then, if a sports fair is held during the day, everyone will be tired in the evening and look for a sit-down activity (movie, +15). Of course, if they hold a casino night, no one ever comes to our movie (-3) so that "we don't know." There is a risk involved. Even the choice between holding a picnic when they hold casino night (+10) versus "having a dance" against casino night (+5) involves a risk. We do not lose if we are "wrong," but our payoff (+5) against what we could have made (+10) is less and represents a "loss of opportunity." Making decisions is not an easy process. For simplicity of the analysis, we will restrict our considerations to the 2*2 matrix. The method is easily extended to n*m matrices.

## Types of Decisionmakers

Several types of decisionmakers (DMs) have been identified. They are given such labels as "conservative" and "risk taking." The distinctions are based on the manner in which they examine the payoffs of the matrix, as well as the manner in which they treat the probabilities. One distinction is that made between DMs who take the probabilities into account and those who ignore them.

## Ignoring the Probabilities: Maximax and Maximin

Two DM "types" take no heed of the relative probabilities of the events "rain" and "no rain"; they concentrate only on the payoffs for each outcome. One concentrates on maximizing the maximum payoff and is called "maximax." In considering the decision matrix, the maximax DM concentrates on the largest entry in each row (Figure 19.6a); he or she compares these maximum payoffs and chooses the action with the maximum maximum payoff. Hence, a maximax DM will choose to hold a picnic, since its payoff (10) is the maximum of all the maximum payoffs (10 and 7, respectively). Since "maximax" concentrates only on the positive, this type of DM is sometimes referred to as an optimistic DM. He or she feels "the best thing

(a)

(b)

FIGURE 19.6

will happen no matter what I do, so let me concentrate on the good things in the payoff matrix" (or at least the DM acts as if that is how he or she feels).

The maximin is the "conservative" DM. He or she concentrates on the worst that can happen and tries to hedge against these indesirable outcomes. In our 2*2 matrix, the value of interest would be the two losses (Figure 19.6b). In deciding between these two "minimum" outcomes in each row, the DM chooses to maximize the minimum value (maximin), hence, he or she would hold the bingo game, since the loss of $1 is better than the loss of $3. The maximin philosophy would be appropriate in cases in which we cannot incur a large loss (we have no capital) so that protecting ourself against loss is more crucial than "making a killing." Someone with a lot of capital to absorb a loss might concentrate on making capital, hence acting like maximax. Thus, the terms *venturesome* and *conservative* might be appropriate, rather than *optimist* and *pessimist*, although the reader will see both sets of descriptive adjectives for maximax and maximin.

## Considering the Probabilities

Many DMs say "I can't make a decision unless I know the probabilities of the events of nature [or actions of our competitor]. Please tell me how likely it is to rain."

By consulting a farmer's almanac on the weather, the DM might find that in this particular season of the year, the relative frequency of rain has been .2, so that we have the likelihood

| | |
|---|---|
| Rain | .2 |
| No rain | .8 |

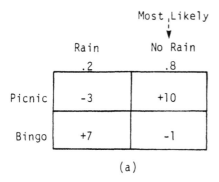

Most Likely

| | Rain<br>.2 | No Rain<br>.8 |
|---|---|---|
| Picnic | -3 | +10 |
| Bingo | +7 | -1 |

(a)

No Rain ◄---- Act as if .8 is certain

| | .8 |
|---|---|
| Picnic | +10 |
| Bingo | -1 |

(b)

FIGURE 19.7

We will base our prediction of the future on past behavior of the weather. (We are currently abstracting from weather reports about this particular Saturday.)

A DM who considers the probabilities *only* would choose to hold a picnic, since the likelihood of rain is much less than the likelihood of no rain (Figure 19.7a). The only column of interest to the "probabilitistic" DM is the column of most likelihood. He or she acts as if this column were certain (Figure 19.7b). The DM thus chooses the largest value in the column (+10) and chooses the action associated with that value (hold picnic). The maximax or maximin DM considers the row values first, selecting the largest or least value in each row, respectively, then compares these selected values across the rows. The probabilistic or "maximum likelihood" DM chooses a column first, then compares the row values in this column alone.

| | Rain | No Rain | Average |
|---|---|---|---|
| Picnic | -3 | +10 | +3.5 |
| Bingo | +7 | -1 | +3.0 |

FIGURE 19.8

## Calculating Values

Some DMs do not consider the payoffs in isolation, but in comparison to each other. For example, in considering the row values, they may take an average of each row (Figure 19.8), and the average for "hold picnic" wins out. Finally, a very popular type of DM in the theory of decision-making, if not in real life, uses the expected value to make a decision.

## The Expected Monetary Value

The DM who uses expected value considers both the payoffs and the probabilities to be important. Faced with the matrix shown in Figure 19.9a, he or she computes an expected value (EV) for each row (Figure 19.9b). Since the EV for a picnic is greater than the EV for bingo, the "EMV'er" would choose to hold a picnic. The name "EMV'er" comes from the term *expected monetary value,* since we are considering the expected value of a monetary outcome. Expected value calculations could also be applied to nonmonetary situations (see Raiffa, 1970).

The formula for EV is

$$EV = P_1 V_1 + P_2 V_2$$

for our two valued rows, where P stands for probability and V for value (payoff). Thus, we multiply the probability times the payoff for each entry, then sum the results. In the general case the formula becomes

$$EV = P_1 V_1 + P_2 V_2 + \ldots P_n V_n$$

|        | Rain<br>.2 | No Rain<br>.8 |
|--------|------|---------|
| Picnic | -3   | +10     |
| Bingo  | +7   | -1      |

(a)

$$EV_{picnic} = .2(-3) + .8(10)$$
$$= (-0.6) + 8 = 7.4$$

$$EV_{bingo} = .2(7) + .8(-1)$$
$$= 1.4 + (-0.8) = 0.6$$

(b)

FIGURE 19.9

where we sum n terms, and the summation is sometimes indicated with a sigma

$$EV = \sum_{i=1}^{n} P_i V_i$$

so that we are "summing n terms," using the subscript i to count them off (1,2,3...n).

Good treatments of EV as well as the other types of decisionmakers, and of the value of information are found Bierman, Bonini, and Hausman (1973), Lave and March (1975), and in Raiffa's more technical, but thorough and insightful, work.

## The Expected Value: A Weighted Average

In the EV calculations we made no mention of the question of whether our decision was a one-time decision or a repeated decision (i.e., Are we holding one picnic or many?). Raiffa argues that the calculation is appropriate in either case. However, it is helpful to point out that the expected value is an average, in fact a "weighted average." We will never make $7.40 holding a picnic. We will either make $10 (if it does not rain) or lose $3 (if it does rain). However, if we hold several picnics over several Saturdays, our average payoff would be $7.40. Hence, some argue that the expected value calculations are more apropos to decisions involving repeated events. Others hold that the methodology is appropriate to even a single event, since the optimum event for the long range will be optimum for the single event as well. The author tends toward the latter view; however, regardless of the viewpoint held, the consideration of the EV leads to discussions of interest, such as the EV of information, that make it a fruitful area of study.

## Repeated Decisions, One Choice

If we face a decision for a single occasion we can act as if it were a repeated decision, i.e., simply choose the largest EV. The question arises as to what to do when truly faced with several decision points, i.e., several occasions on which we have to make the same decision. Do we vary our action? The answer is no. The EV of one of the choices will be greater (or equal to) that of all other choices. The action should be selected on each occasion, even though this behavior *guarantees* that we will be wrong sometimes. The EVs are such that the payoffs when we are right will so exceed the losses when we are wrong that we will be acting optimally in the long run. Note that we might even be wrong more often than we are right, yet still be monetarily better off in the long run. This is one principle applied by people who play lotteries, although the odds of winning are so slight that many people never do get to be right that one time.

Once we have computed the EV we act as if there were only a single action. Our minds are made up.

## Prescriptive Versus Descriptive Decision-Making

Even the staunchest supporters of EV would not claim that all DMs actually do make decisions in this way. What they do argue is that a "rational" DM "should" make decisions by using the EV (or some other calculation). The distinction is between descriptive models of behavior, which describe how people actually do act, versus prescriptive models, which indicate how they should act "if they know what's good for them." Actual DMs may work on hunches, throw dice, etc. Descriptive models (such as a survey of the decision-making methods used) would describe these behaviors. Many economic models, such as the use of EV in decision-making, use prescriptive rather than descriptive models. A good example of prescriptive models in activities other than decision-making is the maxim "do unto others as you would have them do unto you," which is often prescribed although not always present if actual behavior is described.

## The Expected Value of Information

While the model of the decision situation we have set forth contains considerable information

- The list of choices (actions)
- The list of events
- The payoffs for each outcome (action-event pair)
- The probabilities of each event

it is often referred to as the "expected value with no information" or EVNI (see Bierman, Bonini, and Hausman). The point is that the information in the table is about the probability of the events (rain, no rain) in the form of "average rainfall." It says nothing about this Saturday. What we want to consider now is the value of information about "this Saturday."

## A Perfect Predictor

In order to study the value of information, we postulate the existence of a "perfect predictor," someone who can tell us the state of the weather on the particular Saturday on which we plan to hold our picnic or bingo game, and, in the case of repeated occasions, the state of the weather for each Saturday during the term or year.

If we had such a perfect predictor, and the prediction were available in time for us to use the information in making our decision, we would never make a mistake. We would always do the right thing

- If prediction is rain, hold bingo game
- If prediction is no rain, hold picnic

The payoff matrix would reduce to the positive (or maximum) values (Figure 19.10). We would now vary our action according to the prediction, and we would always be correct. Over the long run we would still have an "average payoff." However, the average should now be higher than it was before

$$EVPI = .2(+7) + .8(+10)$$

Rain    No Rain

.2       .8

| | Rain | No Rain |
|---|---|---|
| Picnic | | +10 |
| Bingo | +7 | |

FIGURE 19.10

where EVPI stands for "expected value with perfect information." The calculation .2(+7) indicates that 20% of the time we will choose to hold a bingo game (since the event "rain" and the prediction "rain" will both occur 20% of the time; remember a perfect prediction will "follow" reality, and in reality we have an average of 20% "rain"). On the other 80% of the Saturdays, we will hold a successful picnic

.8(+10)

so that the EVPI is

$$\text{EVPI} = .2(+7) + .8(+10)$$
$$= 1.4 + 8$$
$$= \$9.40$$

which is considerably higher than either of the "single action" EVPIs

Picnic: $7.40
Bingo: $0.60

In the case of no information about this coming Saturday (EVNI), we have selected the action "hold a picnic" so that the expected value of the decision is $7.40 (the bingo game would be forgotten). This is the value of the decision situation without the perfect predictor

$$\text{EVNI} = \$7.40$$

With the predictor our value is

$$\text{EVPI} = \$9.40$$

and the value of the difference

$$\text{EVPI} - \text{EVNI} = \$9.40 - \$7.40 = \$2.00$$

is the value of the information provided by the perfect predictor. Hence, we would be willing to pay up to $2 for the perfect prediction, or $2 each for repeated predictions. If the predictor charges more than $2 for each prediction we would decline, since it is "not worth it." The price of $2 is the break-even point, at which we could "take or leave" the prediction.

## Game Theory

The theory of two agents whose actions combine to coproduce the outcome is studied in "game theory" (Von Neumann and Morgenstern, 1964; Rapoport, 1973). The case most applicable to business situations is that of competitors.

The essence of a game is depicted in a matrix, similar to that of the action-event matrix, with the exception that we replace "events" by the actions of another "agent," a purposeful system. We refer to the purposeful systems or agents as "player 1" and "player 2," or "player A" and "player B," although the games played may be "nonplayful," as in the case of war or highly competitive marketing of products.

## An Example

A typical matrix is that given in Figure 19.11 (the idea for union/corporation players was adapted from Bierman, Bonini, and Hausman, 1973), in which a union is bargaining for its annual wage increase. Some increase is inevitable; hence all the payoffs are positive. However, the union wishes to maximize the increase, while the corporation seeks to minimize it. In order to maximize or minimize the outcome, each "player" selects from his or her strategies. Player A (the union), wishing to maximize the payoffs, looks for the biggest payoff in each row, hence, he or she would compare the payoffs shown in Figure 19.12a, and have a tendency to choose Strategy 2 in order to maximize the payoff at 16. However, if the corporation also knows the payoff table, it will know that player A (the union) will be "greedy" and choose strategy 2. Taking advantage of this knowledge, the corporation will choose strategy 3 (Figure 19.12b), so that the joint outcome will be +10 (Figure 19.12c). If the union looks "far enough ahead," it will realize that the choice of the corporation will be strategy 3 (anticipating the union choice of strategy 2) and choose strategy 1 instead (Figure 19.12d), achieving an outcome of 12. The corporation is interested in the minimum value in each row (Figure 19.13). It chooses the column in which the minimum value for the row occurs. In this particular example, both row minima occur in the column labeled S3 (Figure 19.14).

In this example the corporation is "locked in," since S3 is always better for the corporation than S4. The corporation will always choose S3. The union, knowing this, should choose S1. A more interesting payoff matrix is that shown in Figure 19.15a, in which the union prefers S2 (to get 15), the corporation S4 (to get 7), but, the corporation, anticipating that the union will choose S2 (to get 15) can choose S3, making the actual

Corporation Strategies

| A ⟍ B | Strategy 3 | Strategy 4 |
|---|---|---|
| **Union Strategies** Strategy 1 | +12 | +15 |
| Strategy 2 | +10 | +16 |

FIGURE 19.11

| Player A | | | Maximum of Row |
|---|---|---|---|
| Strategy 1 | 12 | 15 | 15 |
| Strategy 2 | 10 | 16 | 16 |

(a)

| Union | Corporation Chooses ↓ Strategy 3 | Strategy 4 |
|---|---|---|
| Strategy 1 | 12 | 15 |
| Strategy 2 | 10 | 16 |

(b)

| | | Corporation Choice ↓ | |
|---|---|---|---|
| | | S3 | S4 |
| | S1 | 12 | 15 |
| Union Choice | S2 | 10 | 16 |
| Outcome = 10 | | | |

(c)

| | | Corporation Choice | |
|---|---|---|---|
| | | S3 | S4 |
| Union Choice | S1 | 12 | 15 |
| | S2 | 10 | 16 |

(d)

FIGURE 19.12

Corporation

| S3 | S4 | Minimum of Row |
|----|----|----------------|
| 12 | 15 | 12 |
| 10 | 16 | 10 |

FIGURE 19.13

payoff 8 (Figure 19.15b). The union, anticipating the corporation's anticipation could choose S1, making the payoff 10 (Figure 19.15c), and the
corporation, anticipating the union's anticipation of its anticipation can
choose S2, making the outcome 7 (Figure 19.15d). Finally, the union (anticipating the anticipation of the corporation of the union's anticipation of
the corporation's anticipation) chooses S2, making the payoff 15, (Figure
19.15e) which indicates why we would like to know what the other person
is going to do!

The mathematics of game theory (developed initially by Von Neumann
and Morgenstern, 1964; and expounded in Rapoport, 1973) studies various
game situations and their anticipated outcomes. We are primarily interested
in the aspect of uncertainty in regard to the other person's choice and
how this uncertainty affects our own decision-making ability.

## Information and Control

There are two ways in which the union (or the corporation) can get better
"control" of the outcome. One is through "collusion"; a bribe or other means
of agreement can be made with a corporate officer for him or her to choose
strategy 4. Another is through information; e.g., an informant can be paid,
or telephone lines tapped, in order to find out the corporation's choice before the bargaining session.

| S3 | S4 |
|----|----|
| 12 | 15 |
| 10 | 16 |
| ↑ | |

less
"loss" to
corporation in
either case

FIGURE 19.14

Corporation

|  |  | S3 | S4 |
|--|--|----|----|
| | S1 | 10 | 7 |
| union | | | |
| | S2 | 8 | 15 |

(a)

Corporation

|  |  | S3 | S4 |
|--|--|----|----|
| | | ↓ | |
| | S1 | 10 | 7 |
| union | | | |
| → | S2 | 8 | 15 |

(b)

Corporation

↓

|  |  | S3 | S4 |
|--|--|----|----|
| → | S1 | 10 | 7 |
| union | | | |
| | S2 | 8 | 15 |

(c)

Corporation

|  |  | S3 | S4 |
|--|--|----|----|
| | | | ↓ |
| → | S1 | 10 | 7 |
| union | | | |
| | S2 | 8 | 15 |

(d)

Corporation

|  |  | S3 | S4 |
|--|--|----|----|
| | | | ↓ |
| | S1 | 10 | 7 |
| union | | | |
| → | S2 | 8 | 15 |

(e)

FIGURE 19.15

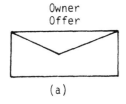
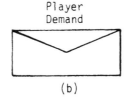

Owner
Offer

Player
Demand

(a)

(b)

FIGURE 19.16

An interesting example of game theory occurred in the collective bargaining that is customary in some professional sports. The essence of the situation is that the athlete and the owners of the team, locked in unresolvable negotiations, appeal to a third party, the arbiter, to decide the final outcome of the player's salary. Both the athlete and the owner must submit sealed statements of the salaries they wish to accept and offer. Neither knows the amount of the other's bid (Figure 19.16a and b).

The arbitrator examines both figures and chooses the one he or she feels to be more justified. Both parties must abide by the ruling. In at least one case, the player was awarded the victory in the arbitration process, only to find that his bid was lower than the owner's

| Owner's Offer | Athlete's Demand |
|---|---|
| $400,000 | $300,000 |

so that he received less money than if he had talked to the owner directly!

**Some Tools: The Decision Table**

Various means of automating the "decision" process have been developed. Situations that involve simple branching, such as the decision to go or stop at a light (Figure 19.17), can be represented by decision tables.

The branch is a "conditional branch," dependent on the state of the environment. That is, given one state of the environment (light green), we

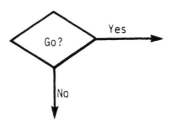

FIGURE 19.17

"go" (take the yes branch); if the light is red, we do not go (take the no path). The decision rule states these relationships between states of the environment and actions to be taken. Considering only the color of the traffic light, the condition/action pairs are

| Condition of Light | Action to Be Taken |
| --- | --- |
| Green | Go |
| Red | Stop |

The decision rules are situation/action rules (SA rules). Given a situation or context, here the state of the environment, we take a given action (see Newell and Simon, 1972). They can be stated in if-then form

If light = green then go

If light = red then stop

although they are often stated in a matrix form that we will consider shortly.

In constructing decision tables, the conditions must be exhaustive and mutually exclusive. The exhaustiveness ensures that we can always take action; the exclusivity ensures that we take only a single action.

If we expand the table to include information about obstacles in the path, we have four possible conditions (Table 19.3). The number of conditions will depend on the number of variables (here two: light color and path clear) and the values each can take on (here two each, green/red and yes/no). The computation is to multiply the number of values on each variable

| values variable 1 | | values variable 2 | | Total number of conditions |
| --- | --- | --- | --- | --- |
| 2 | * | 2 | = | 4 |

If we add a yellow light, the number of possible conditions increases to six

| Number of color values | | Path clear values | · | Total conditions |
| --- | --- | --- | --- | --- |
| 3 | * | 2 | = | 6 |

TABLE 19.3

| Light Color | Path Clear? | Action |
| --- | --- | --- |
| Green | Yes | Go |
| Green | No | Stop |
| Red | Yes | Stop |
| Red | No | Stop |

TABLE 19.4

|  | Possible Responses to Questions | | | |
|---|---|---|---|---|
| *Conditions* | | | | |
| Light green? | Y | Y | N | N |
| Path clear? | Y | N | Y | N |
| *Actions* | | | | |
| Go | X | | | |
| Wait | | X | X | X |

Not all the conditions will result in different actions, e.g., three of the conditions in the 2*2 matrix result in stopping, one in going.

## Vertical Representation

Decision rules are often listed in vertical form, the conditions listed above the actions, with the questions framed in a manner that allows for a yes-no answer (Table 19.4). The "possible responses" are the actions to take in each situation. Each question is listed with a yes/no column for each yes/no on the other question (Figure 19.18). The X in the column indicates which action should be taken if that situation is the case. Reading vertically we see that column 2 represents the situation "light green (Y) but path blocked (N on clear)," in which case the X tells us to stop.

## Simplifying Decision Tables

The decision table can be simplified by combining columns for which the response to the second question is irrelevant. For example, if the light is red, we cannot go "no matter what the condition of the path." Hence, we can combine the two columns for a no answer to "light green?" (Table

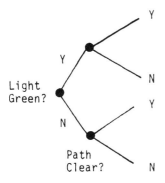

FIGURE 19.18

TABLE 19.5

|  | Possible Situations |  |  |
|---|---|---|---|
| *Conditions* |  |  |  |
| Light green? | Y | Y | N |
| Path clear? | Y | N | — |
| *Actions* |  |  |  |
| Go | X |  |  |
| Wait |  | X | X |

19.5). The dashed line indicates that the second question is unnecessary if the response to the first question is no.

## How to Recognize a Situation That Can Be Simplified

The way in which one recognizes a situation that can be simplified is to see if the second question makes a difference, i.e., if it changes the action taken. For a green light, we have the situations given in Figure 19.19a, in which the X "shifts," depending on the response to the second question.

For the red light we have the situations indicated in Figure 19.19b, in which the action is the same even though the response to the second question varies. The response to the second question has no effect on the outcome for this case, hence we can combine the two columns and place a dash in the area for the response to the second question.

An alternative to simplifying on color would have been to simplify on path clear. If the path is blocked, the color of the light is irrelevant. The reader should draw the decision table implementing the simplification by path blocked.

| Light green? | Y | Y |
|---|---|---|
| Path clear? | Y | N |
| Go | X |  |
| Wait |  | X |

(a)

| Light green? | N | N |
|---|---|---|
| Path clear? | Y | N |
| Go |  |  |
| Wait | X | X |

(b)

FIGURE 19.19

## Automated Decision-Making = Control

The use of decision matrices "automates" the decision-making process. In fact, there is really no decision to make, simply a variance in action based on a variance in the environment, which is why we include it as a method of control rather than as a method of decision-making.

The assumptions underlying the use of the decision table are

- We know the full set of inputs to our system (and can recognize them)
- We have a single action or sequence of actions to be performed for each set of inputs to our system (each condition of the environment or situation)

The "outcome" of the action is usually not represented in the decision table. For example, the action go or stop is presumably done for a two-part goal: (1) to get somewhere and (2) to get there safely. It is assumed that the action can bring about the outcome with certainty, so that our only job is to implement the correct action.

The expected value matrix *with perfect information* (Figure 19.20a) could be implemented as a decision table

If prediction = no rain, hold picnic (outcome = +10)

If prediction = rain, hold bingo game (outcome = +7)

and guarantees the outcome in each case. The table without perfect information (Figure 19.20b) could be implemented as a decision table, but the outcomes are not guaranteed. If it were implemented as a decision table, the rules would be something like the following.

If it "looks like" rain, then hold bingo, where uncertainty would be built into the rule. In practice decision tables are used in situations in

|         | Rain | No Rain |
|---------|------|---------|
| Picnic  |      | +10     |
| Bingo   | +7   |         |

(a)

|         | Rain | No Rain |
|---------|------|---------|
| Picnic  | -3   | +10     |
| Bingo   | +7   | -1      |

(b)

FIGURE 19.20

which the input to the system is known in advance or can be controlled, or in situations in which the decision is made *after* the input is known. If we could decide on holding a picnic or a bingo game at the last minute, i.e., on the day itself, the second matrix (the matrix with incertainty about the weather) could also be implemented as a decision table.

## Training

One advantage of using decision tables is that they can condense a small amount of information into a readily understandable format relatively easily. Thus, they can be used to train new employees, to serve as simple reminders of policy, etc. The decision table (Table 19.6) might be presented to a new employee of a loan firm, supplemented by a quick explanation. The employee should act as follows:

1. Take one of the following two possible actions for loan requests of $10,000 or more, depending on the value of the credit rating:
   a. Good credit ⟶ manager.
   b. Bad credit ⟶ do not bother the manager.
2. Similarly, act as follows on loans of in-between value ($1,000–$9,999):
   a. Good credit ⟶ teller grants loan.
   b. Bad credit ⟶ refer to manager for assessment.
3. For loans under $1,000, grant the loan regardless of the credit rating. Presumably this is a rule implemented by the bank through social consciousness, allowing people with bad credit ratings to rebuild their reputations.

Of course, the written rules would also suffice.

TABLE 19.6

|  | Possible Situations | | | | |
|---|---|---|---|---|---|
| *Conditions* | | | | | |
| Loan Amount | | | | | |
| $10,000 or more? | Y | Y | | | |
| $1,000–$9,999 | | | Y | Y | |
| Under $1,000 | | | | | Y |
| Credit Rating | | | | | |
| Credit good? | Y | N | Y | N | — |
| *Actions* | | | | | |
| Grant loan | | | X | | X |
| Refuse loan | | X | | | |
| Refer to manager | X | | | X | |

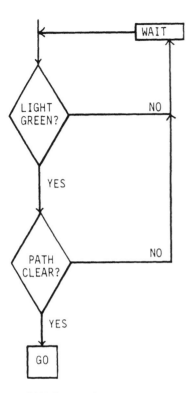

FIGURE 19.21

## Flowcharts

The decision table and the verbal descriptions of the decision table are equivalent, and the use of one or the other will depend on our own preferences (or those of the manager).

An alternative to decision tables is the use of flowcharts, such as the one shown in Figure 19.21, in which the diamond shape represents a branch point. If the light is not green, we wait, then "test again." If the light is green, we check the path. Only in the event of two yes answers will we get through to "go." The flowchart indicates that we must repeatedly test the color of the light (and the blockage of the path), something that was not as clearly represented in the decision tables.

## Multivalued Branches

The single diamond asks a single question that results in a binary (yes, no) answer. By using more than one diamond we can handle a more complex situation. For example, a program to assign grades might have the branch points given in Figure 19.22.

A flowchart for the loan company is given in Figure 19.23, in which we have asked the question about credit first. By rearranging the order

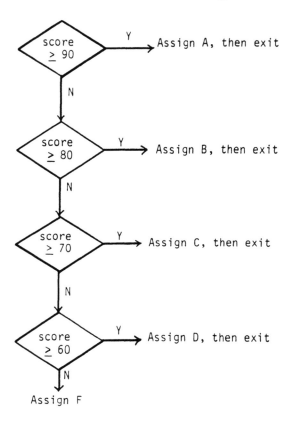

FIGURE 19.22

in which we ask the questions, the flowchart or decision table can often be simplified, facilitating comprehension and usually conserving space.

### Switching Situations

In considering the control exemplified in a decision table, we see that our action is a direct result of the input (Figure 19.24a). In fact, *we* are acting as the passive machine. The input acts as a switch controlling our output action. Of course, the assumption is that our knowledge of the environment enables us to select actions appropriately, so that what appears to be passive behavior is really the correct application of complete control. We "switch" among various courses of action according to which is most appropriate for the situation at hand (Figure 19.24b), so that the actions of a person completely in control appear to an outside observer to be similar to the passivity involved in a deterministic machine.

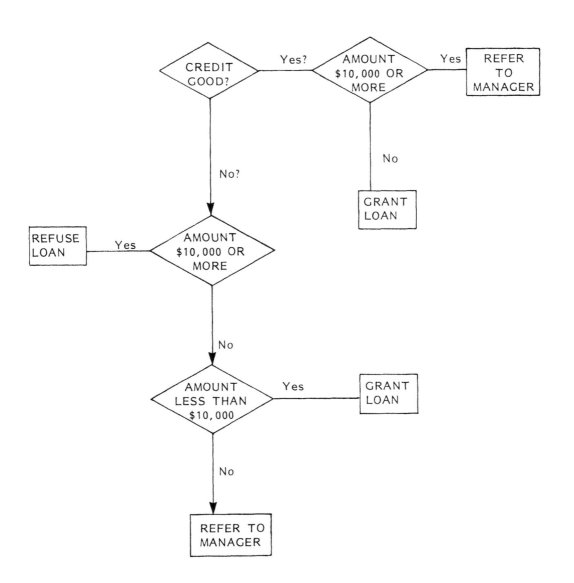

FIGURE 19.23

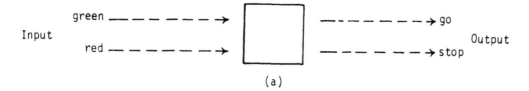

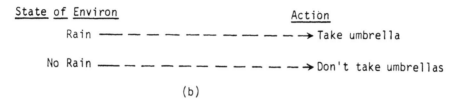

(b)

FIGURE 19.24


The Effectiveness of Our Actions

The effectiveness of our actions in achieving a particular goal is directly
related to the range of choices we have. For example, if our goal is to
travel from Chicago to Paris, we may have several means of transportation


Walk or Run
Take Cab
Take Bus
Take Train
Drive Own Car
Swim
Take Boat
Take Plane

(a)


Subgoal: get to O'Hare Airport
  Condition: live close
  Action: walk
  Condition: live too far to walk
          don't own car
  Action: take bus or take taxi

Subgoal: get from O'Hare to Paris Airport
  Condition: have funds to buy ticket
  Action: find airline that goes to Paris
        buy ticket

(b)

FIGURE 19.25

(Figure 19.25a). Some of these actions will be appropriate in the face of certain environments and goals. The overall goal of the journey is to arrive in Paris, but we may subdivide the trip into parts, each with a subgoal, so that some of the situations facing us may be those given in Figure 19.25b.

If our panoply of actions is not sufficient, we may be "blocked" by certain environmental conditions. For example, supposing that we have neither "take a boat" nor "take a plane" as options, the actions

Walk
Take taxi
Take bus
Take train
Swim

would all be sufficient to get us to the East Coast, even if we have to swim across a stream or two on the way. However, the presence of the Atlantic Ocean would represent an obstacle not easily overcome by normal taxis or swimmers

Condition: Atlantic Ocean
Action: None of the current alternatives possible

which would lead us into problem-solving techniques, possibly leading to the invention of the airplane. Hence, problem-solving techniques, i.e., techniques of learning about our environment, such as scientific research or asking somebody who already knows, are searches for the actions that can be appropriately applied in specific situations.

## Nondeterministic Situations

We have considered situations in which the outcome is certain once the action is implemented

Press accelerator $\longrightarrow$ go
    with probability = 1.0

Refuse loan $\longrightarrow$ customer gets no money
        with probability = 1.0

Assign grade of B $\longrightarrow$ student receives B on
        report card with probability = 1.0

The action is sufficient to produce the outcome.

As indicated in earlier sections, e.g., the study of the decision matrix for picnic/bingo, the outcomes are not always a function of implementing the action. Sometimes the desired outcome may not occur. In the first example, the outcomes were monetary payoffs that depended on the state of the environment. In the example of union/corporation bargaining, the outcome depends on the choice of another human being. In both these examples, our action is not sufficient to produce the outcome; the conjunction of our action and the event of nature or the other agent's action "coproduce" the outcome.

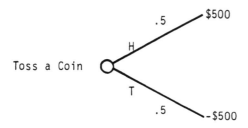

FIGURE 19.26

## Utility Theory

One of the considerations in decision theory is the fact that a dollar is not always a dollar; i.e., our evaluation of a decision situation involving money will vary depending on how much money we have. For example, if we are faced with the chance situation shown in Figure 19.26, in which the EV is zero

$$EV = .5(500) + .5(-500)$$
$$= 250 - 250 = 0$$

we may choose to participate, we may not. For example, if we are a millionaire, having the capital to absorb the loss, we may find the gamble "fun." On the other hand, if we have a small fixed income, say $800 a month, where a loss of $500 might keep us from eating for a few days, the loss of $500 might be prohibitive. In fact, we might weight the outcomes +$500 and -$500 differently, so that a gain of $500 is considered to be "nice," a loss of $500 "disastrous." For example, on a scale of 1 to 10, we might have

| Outcome | Preference |
| --- | --- |
| +500 | +4 |
| -500 | -6 |

The preference values (+4, -6) are on a different scale from the monetary ones. In the literature on decision theory, such a scale is referred to as the "utility value" of an outcome, and the units are expressed in "utils." Of course, it is still assumed that 4 utils of happiness are better than 3 utils of happiness. It is just that a util has a different scale than a dollar.

## Comparing Apples and Oranges

Once the scale is shifted to utils, we can now compare preferences among items that are not monetary in nature. For example, if we have the following preferences:

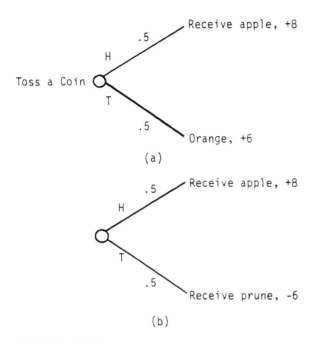

FIGURE 19.27

Apple:   8 utils
Orange:  6 utils

the decision tree for the toss of a coin in which the payoffs are an apple or an orange is that given in Figure 19.27a. The expected utility of the tree is

$$(.5)(8) + (.5)(6) = 4 + 3 = 7$$

and we would certainly play, since either outcome is desirable. Of course, if we do not like prunes

|        | Utils |
|--------|-------|
| Prunes |  -6   |

the tree shown in Figure 19.27b has a lesser EV: +1. If the game were free, the theory of EVs would say we should play (value = +1), although a "risk avoider" might choose to skip the game altogether. In this case we might say that the risk avoider is being inconsistent, either in setting the util values or in refusing to play, but that is another matter.

Trade-Offs

Very often we have a fixed amount of money to spend on "good things." For example, we may wish to buy some apples or oranges or a mixture of

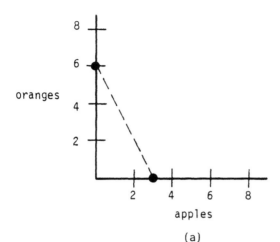

(a)

| apples | utils |
|---|---|
| 1 | 8 |
| 2 | 15 |
| 3 | 21 |
| 4 | 24 |
| 5 | 26 |
| 6 | 27 |

(b)

| oranges | utils |
|---|---|
| 1 | 6 |
| 2 | 12 |
| 3 | 17 |
| 4 | 21 |
| 5 | 24 |
| 6 | 26 |
| 7 | 27 |

(c)

FIGURE 19.28

both. Let us say that we have 60¢ and the respective prices of apples and oranges are

Apples:  20¢
Oranges:  10¢

We can choose to buy three apples or six oranges or some mixture of the two (say two apples, two oranges). Our budget can be represented by the dotted line shown in Figure 19.28a, in which the endpoints are "pure oranges" (0,6) or "pure apples" (3,0), and the points along the line represent such combinations as two apples, two oranges (2,2) or one apple, four oranges (point 1,4).

In order to decide what type of purchase to make, we must compare our relative preferences for apples and oranges. Say our utility values are those given in Figures 19.28b and c. If we go with a pure solution only, we can see that we obtain

|  | Total utils |
|---|---|
| 3 apples | 21 |
| 6 oranges | 26 |

TABLE 19.7

|  | Utils | Change in utils |
|---|---|---|
| 1 apple | 8 | +8 |
| 2 apples | 15 | +7 |
| 3 apples | 21 | +6 |
| 4 apples | 24 | +3 |
| 5 apples | 26 | +2 |
| 6 apples | 27 | +1 |

so that we might buy all oranges. However, we might find a combination preferable. For example, the combination

|  | Utils |
|---|---|
| 2 apples | 15 |
| 2 oranges | 12 |
|  | — |
|  | 27 |

gives us a higher total utility (27 utils) than either pure solution (21 for all apples, 26 for all oranges).

The reason for this is the declining "worth" of apples or oranges as we get more. For example, in considering the apples (Table 19.7), the first apple brings 8 utils (0 to 8), but the second brings only 7 utils (8 to 15 in total utility). The change in total utils is referred as the marginal utility value (here, of apples). The marginal utility of an item usually decreases as we obtain more of it. Hence, in going from five apples to six, we gain only 1 util. (Of course six apples, with cost 6*.20 = $1.20, are outside our budget line.) Thus, it is often preferable to "mix" goods rather than have all of one kind (even if that good is money, since we do need fresh air, friends, etc.).

Some mixtures, e.g.

2 apples (15), 2 oranges (12) = total 27

are equivalent to others

3 apples (21), 1 orange (6) = total 27

so that we are "indifferent" between the two bundles. Of course, one bundle (two apples, two oranges, cost = 60¢) is within our budget line, the other (three apples, one orange, cost =70¢) is not. We cannot have three apples, one orange.

The study of utility values, budget lines, and indifference curves leads into the concepts of demand curves, supply curves, and a good bit of economics. A very clear, very enjoyable presentation is given in Lave and March (1975). Here we have simply attempted to whet your appetite.

Transitivity

We mentioned earlier that a particular decisionmaker might be inconsistent in his or her preference structure. Raiffa (1970) gives a perfect example. The preferences are

> John prefers house A to house B
> John prefers house B to house C
> John prefers house C to house A

so that we have the relationships

> $A > B$
>
> $B > C$
>
> $C > A$

which is not a transitive ordering of choices. Transitivity would have

> $A > B$ and $B > C$ yield $A > C$

which is just the opposite of our decisionmaker's third preference.

The desirability of transitivity in the choice structure can be seen in considering monetary outcomes

> A: $100
> B: $50
> C: $25

where someone would prefer A to B and B to C, hence A to C. It would not make sense to prefer C ($25) to A ($100), although the wife of at least one lottery player in the state of Pennsylvania preferred the status quo (0 winnings in the lottery) to their "lucky" outcome (an instant millionaire), since she knew the winnings would change their life-style.

One might question how the comparisons about houses could become nontransitive. Raiffa gives the criteria for judgment as: cost, space, and convenience. The ratings on each of the houses are those given in Table 19.8, in which, presumably, the decisionmaker in question preferred

- A good cost over space
- Spaciousness over convenience

but

- Convenience over cost

We can see that if he or she were forced to weight the criteria this could not happen. For example, we might have the weights

TABLE 19.8

|   | Cost | Space | Convenience |
|---|------|-------|-------------|
| A | Best | Worst | Middle |
| B | Middle | Best | Worst |
| C | Worst | Middle | Best |

W(cost) = .5

W(space) = .3

W(convenience) = .2

which agree with the assessments

Cost > space

Space > convenience

but having assigned the numbers, we cannot get .2 (convenience) to be greater than .5 (cost) in importance. Hence, the inconsistency of the judgments would become evident in the weighting.

Raiffa presents an even more convincing argument. The scenario is as follows:

> Suppose that Mr. Jones has an A house or is given one. Since the DM prefers C over A, he or she should pay $X to exchange an A house for a C house.

> Then, preferring B over C, he should now be willing to pay $Y to exchange the C house for a B.

> Finally, preferring A over B, he should be willing to pay $Z to exchange a B house for an A.

He has now paid $(X+Y+Z) to obtain the A house that he had in the beginning! The exchange could go on forever

> Now take A + $X and exchange for another C ...

The infiniteness of the nontransitive exchanges, as well as the fact that we obtain what we already had, show the "inconsistency" of nontransitive choices. Yet, people have them!

In EV calculations, the nontransitive choice structure is disallowed, which indicates again the prescriptive rather than descriptive nature of the theory.

## Related Readings

Bierman, Harold, Jr., Bonini, Charles P., and Hausman, Warren H., *Quantitative Analysis for Business Decisions*, 4th ed., Illinois: Richard D. Irwin, Inc., 1973.

Davis, Gordon B., *Management Information Systems: Conceptual Foundations, Structure, and Development*, New York: McGraw-Hill, 1974.

Festinger, Leon, *A Theory of Cognitive Dissonance*, Stanford, CA: Stanford University Press, 1957.

Fishbein, Martin and Ajzen, Icek, *Belief, Attitude, Intention and Behavior: An Introduction to Theory and Research*, Reading, MA: Addison-Wesley Publishing Company, 1975.

Heinze, David Charles, *Statistical Decision Analysis for Management*, Columbus: Grid, Inc., 1973.

Kemeny, John G., Snell, J. Laurie, and Thompson, Gerald L., *Introduction to Finite Mathematics*, 3rd ed., Englewood Cliffs, NJ: Prentice-Hall, 1974.

Lave, Charles A. and March, James G., *An Introduction to Models in the Social Sciences*, New York: Harper & Row, 1975.

Newell, Allen and Simon, Herbert A., *Human Problem Solving*, Englewood Cliffs, NJ: Prentice-Hall, 1972.

Raiffa, Howard, *Decision Analysis: Introductory Lectures on Choices under Uncertainty*, Reading, MA: Addison-Wesley, 1970 (c1968).

Raiffa, Howard and Schlaifer, Robert, *Applied Statistical Decision Theory*, Cambridge, MA: M.I.T. Press, 1961.

Rapoport, Anatol, *Two-Person Game Theory: The Essential Ideas*, Ann Arbor, MI: The University of Michigan Press, 1973 (c1966).

Turban, Efraim and Meredith, Jack R., *Fundamentals of Management Science*, rev. ed., Texas: Business Publications, Inc., 1981.

Von Neumann, John, *Collected Works*, Macmillan Publishing Company, 1963.

Von Neumann, J. and Morgenstern, O., *Theory of Games and Economic Behavior*, 3rd ed., New York: John Wiley & Sons, 1964.

# 20
# Problem-Solving

## Objectives

Upon completion of this chapter the reader should be able to

1. Explain the use of means-end schemas to describe decision situations
2. Define a goal attainment problem and distinguish such problems from goal maintenance problems
3. Distinguish between algorithmic techniques and heuristic techniques in problem-solving
4. Describe the strategies of depth-first search and breadth-first search, and the advantages/disadvantages of each
5. Explain how a computer program can be written to incorporate trial and error with "backup," as in solving the problem of running a maze
6. Distinguish between problems of passive environment and problems of an opponent who also has moves (e.g., chess or tic-tac-toe)
7. Explain the concept of look-ahead in games, and distinguish it from heuristics such as "take the center square" in tic-tac-toe
8. Explain the technique of setting subgoals, and indicate how some problem solvers are reluctant to set goals that are "to the side" or that involve "backing up"
9. Indicate how the representation of a problem can aid in its solution

The study of problem-solving is one of the more diffuse topics discussed in this text. It is broader in scope than decision-making in that the decision situation is already "laid out." A decision consists in a choice between alternatives, e.g.

- Hold picnic
- Hold bingo game

that are directed toward a given goal, e.g.

- Make a profit

and have varying efficacies toward that goal. In some cases, the actions are deemed sufficient "in and of themselves" to achieve the goal (linear programming model, lunch situation). In others, they are deemed insufficient in and of themselves to achieve the goal. Successful attainment requires a coproducer. In this case, the variance in obtaining or not obtaining the goal may be due to chance events

p(rain) = .2 and rain will affect outcome
　　　　　of picnic negatively (or help bingo)

p(no rain) = .8 and lack of rain helps success
　　　　　　of picnic (or hurts bingo)

or to the interplay of our choices with another's choices

- If we hold a picnic, and fraternity B holds a picnic, how will our profits be affected?

where our estimation of the likelihood of the other person taking a particular action may also be expressed in probabilities

p(fraternity B holding picnic) = .3

p(fraternity B holding dance) = .2

p(fraternity B having no activity on this weekend) = .5

The point, however, is that in the decision situation, the goals, the alternatives toward the goals, and the efficacy of each alternative in achieving the goal are usually well specified.

In a problem situation we may not have these items so well delineated. In fact, one of the "problems" in the problem situation may be to generate the list of alternative actions. Another may be to estimate the efficacy of each alternative action.

In considering the lunch example, the problem was to generate the list of alternative actions

Go to Mary's
Go to Joe's

The actions were all deemed sufficient, hence, the next step was a choice among these actions, followed by implementation of the choice.

It is interesting to note that the decision state is not necessary to the problem-solving/solution-implementation process. If the list of sufficient actions is a "short list" of one element

Mary's Place (only diner in town)

one "has no choice" and moves directly to the implementation stage.

In the linear programming example, the problem was to find the optimal values of the input variables. There was no doubt about the "type" of alternate actions

- Make durable denims
- Make fancy denims

the question was simply how "much" of each action to implement, i.e., at what level to set the values of F and D in the equation

$$12F + 8D = P$$

|  | Rain | Rain |
|---|---|---|
| Picnic | −3 | +10 |
| Bingo | +7 | −1 |

FIGURE 20.1

The relationship between the input and output variables is known, so that the efficacy of our actions is known.

In the picnic/bingo example, the list of actions is known

- Picnic
- Bingo

and the "conditional" efficacies of each, the payoffs (Figure 20.1), are known. What is not known is the "condition that will obtain," i.e., the state of nature (of the environment) that will exist, hence, we may have uncertainties about

- What constitutes the list of actions, any of which is deemed sufficient to achieve the goal
- The optimal value of "gradated" actions, given a known input/output relationship between the action taken and the outcome
- The state of the environment or other "coproducer" when actions are insufficient but the relevant coproducer is known

We may add the case of the efficacy of actions when they are deemed "not sufficient in themselves" but the relevant coproducers are unknown (e.g., the queuing situation), situations in which there is a probability distribution of customers coming into the bank (store, etc.), but the "causes" of their coming or not coming are too diffuse to be known precisely without undue effort on our part. Our action, how many tellers to hire, is based on probability calculations that apply to the situation.

In a word, there are many "types of problems," and the multitude of definitions found in the literature on problem-solving and decision-making reflect this diversity. We begin with a fairly standard definition of a problem, although we will see that the definition is not general enough to encompass all types of problem-solving situations.

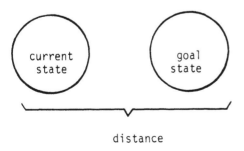

(a)

FIGURE 20.2

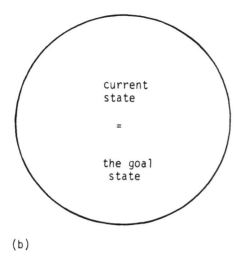

(b)

FIGURE 20.2 (continued)


Definition: Problem

A problem is seen as a discrepancy between some state we are currently in and some "desired" state (Figure 20.2a). The "problem" is to close the gap between our current state and the goal state (Figure 20.2b), so that we have "arrived." A set of actions that brings our current state into line with the goal state is a "solution" to the problem.


An Example

A simple example of a problem is that of having the goal of "being rich" when we currently are "poor"


| Current state | Goal state |
|---|---|
| Poor | Rich |


Our first task is to develop a set of alternative actions to the goal state. For example, we might have

- Work for a living
- Become a movie star
- Win the lottery
- Invent something useful
- Mug people

The next step is to assess each of the alternatives on such criteria as

- Probability of success (effectiveness of the action)
- Our own ability to implement the action (technical and/or operational feasibility)

- The social or legal feasibility of the action

For example, the choice to work for a living is usually within our control. While we must find a willing employer, if we are flexible enough in our career choices, we can usually choose this option with the near certitude of having the *means* implemented. Of course, the effectiveness of the means in achieving the goal may be in doubt. The author has implemented this means for several years without becoming rich (which was not the goal in entering into research and teaching).

Other attributes are particularly effective in achieving a given goal, e.g., winning the lottery. However, the likelihood of our being able to implement the action is in doubt, i.e., if we win the lottery, we will certainly be rich, but "choosing to win" is not within our power (although choosing to play is). In fact, it is probably better to consider the means to be "playing the lottery" since this is an action available to us, rather than winning the lottery, which is not within our control.

Other actions, such as mugging, are within our technical control, but are socially, and, in the case of mugging, legally unacceptable, hence, they too are excluded.

These considerations about the appropriateness of the possible actions are referred to as "feasibility studies." There are several types of feasibility

- Technical feasibility: Can the action be carried out with the current technology?
- Operational feasibility: Can I, or the personnel of my organization, carry out the action with my (their) current knowledge?
- Economic feasibility: Is the action cost beneficial?
- Legal feasibility: Is the action within the law?

An example of an alternative that is currently technically feasible, but was not feasible a century ago, is flying to Europe from the United States to attend a business meeting or conference tomorrow. Another would be the volume of computations available with a computer (e.g., in weather forecasting) that were simply not feasible by hand.

Operational feasibility considers the skills of oneself or of one's organizational personnel in relation to implementing a given action. For example, it is not feasible to plan a computer implementation of an auditing system if we have no personnel with computer expertise. This obstacle can be overcome with training or hiring new personnel, at an added expense in terms of both dollars and time.

An example of economic nonfeasibility is the use of a home computer in 1950 or 1960. A computer cost several hundred thousand or several million dollars at that time, an amount that was beyond the budgets of most families. However, with the advent of transistors and large-scale integrated circuits, the cost of computers dropped to hundreds of dollars or several thousand dollars, so that possession of a home computer by an individual or a family is now economically feasible.

An example of social nonfeasibility was the pollution of air, water, etc. even before the advent of laws prohibiting such pollution, or the smoking of cigarettes or cigars in elevators. Actions that cause harm to others are considered socially nonfeasible.

Finally, the law often institutionalizes concepts of social nonfeasibility by explicitly prohibiting certain actions (forbidding the emission of pollutants) or explicitly requiring corrective actions (e.g., requiring emission control devices on factories or cars).

In listing the possible alternatives to our goal, we may initially start with a fairly long and wide-ranging list. In fact, the list may be obtained by a technique such as "brainstorming," in which the problem solvers are encouraged to contribute any "solutions" that they can conceive. We would then prune the list by examining the various feasibilities, and retain only those actions that we are capable of implementing (they are technically, operationally, and economically feasible) and are acceptable to others (they are socially and legally feasible). Of course, the implementation of socially acceptable alternatives is a "choice," in that we can ignore the feelings of others. The legal implications of an action cannot be ignored, at least not without the risk of incurring the specified consequences.

## A Means-End Schema

The concept of a list of alternatives (means to a goal) and the goal (or goals) to which they lead has been formalized by many researchers (see Ackoff and Emery, 1972, Mitroff et al., 1978, and Turban and Meredith, 1981) in the concept of a means-end schema. The schema is in the form shown in Figure 20.3a, in which the symbols are interpreted as

$c_i$ = the courses of action, here numbered 1 through n (i = 1 to n)

$O_j$ = the possible outcomes, here numbered 1 through m (j = 1 to m)

$E_{ij}$ = the effectiveness of action i to achieve outcome j

The set of outcomes indicates that we may have more than one possible goal rather than a single overriding one, or that a given action may have several possible outcomes. A single goal would be represented by the vector shown in Figure 20.3b; that it is a special case of multiple outcomes with m = 1 is shown in Figure 20.3c, in which we retain the double subscript, the row values varying from 1 to n, the column value static at 1.

(a)

FIGURE 20.3

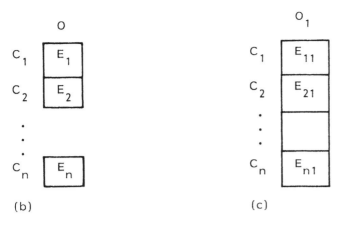

FIGURE 20.3 (continued)

In the case of the single goal, we need not order the outcomes. In the case of multiple outcomes, we might order the outcomes by their respective desirability or value

$$V(O_1) > V(O_2) > V(O_3) \ldots > V(O_m)$$

Of course, the value of the outcome will not be the sole deciding factor in choosing a particular action, since the effectiveness of a particular course of action in achieving that goal will have an effect on the "expected value" of the means-end (action-outcome) pair. In the language of business analysis, ordering outcomes would be considered to be setting objectives or "planning." The planning might be long range or short range, strategic, or tactical.

In fact, the courses of action could also be assigned a value, reflecting some innate desirability of one over another. For example, we might need to travel from Chicago to New York (outcome = arrival in New York) and have two means, both equally effective in achieving the final goal

- Fly
- Take train

and select "take train," not for its effectiveness but because "we like to travel by train." Of course, there are costs associated with each course of action, as well as other constraints, e.g., time to execute, level of exertion, so that the means-end schema of simply outcomes ($O_j$), courses of action ($C_i$), and efficiencies ($E_{ij}$) is a major simplification of the problem situation, although it can provide some general insights that are useful in the study of problem-solving.

## Varying the Matrix

In order to lend some structure to the study of problem-solving, we will look at various forms of the means-end schema. We begin with a single outcome and several courses of action, considering the implication of setting the efficacies at various levels. Given the matrix shown in Figure 20.4a,

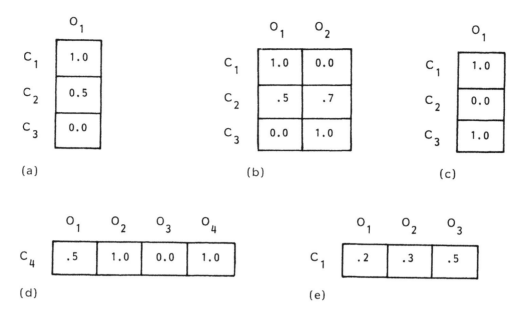

FIGURE 20.4

we see that $C_1$ can achieve the given outcome with a probability of 1.0, i.e., with certitude. We would say that $C_1$ is "sufficient" to achieve the outcome $O_1$. We see that $C_3$ cannot produce the desired outcome. In fact, with a single-column matrix, we would normally not include such a course of action in the list, with a multi-outcome situation (Figure 20.4b), we would include $C_3$ as a course of action despite its E-value of zero on outcome 1, since it is a viable alternative for outcome 2. Only courses of action with zeroes across an entire row would be eliminated.

As the reader can see, the efficacy values do not sum to one in either the row or the columns in this representation. This is because a given outcome can be achieved by more than one course of action (Figure 20.4c), and a given course of action can be effective in achieving more than one outcome (Figure 20.4d). The efficacy values are the probability of a given course of action achieving a given outcome, and have a range from 0.0 to 1.0 in each cell. Other schemes, e.g., making the row values sum to one, are also possible. We would restrict the matrix to courses of action that result in one and only one outcome from the set of outcomes upon execution of a particular action. There also might be more than one potential outcome (Figure 20.4e). However, in a single implementation of action C, only one of the potential outcomes is instantiated. In this case the probability values across the row would sum to one. Presumably the variance in the probabilities is due to the interaction of our action with those of others and any relevant events of nature. It is important to note that the various restrictions on the probability distributions (summing to one or not) reflect different representations of the problem.

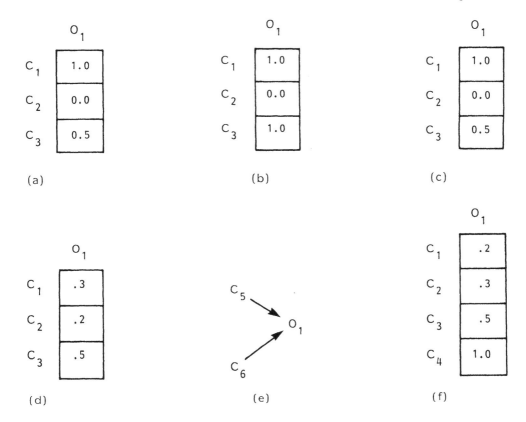

FIGURE 20.5

## Necessity and Sufficiency

By varying the efficiency values in a given column, we can represent the concepts of sufficiency and necessity. For example, if we have any course of action in a column with $E = 1.0$ (Figure 20.5a), that action is "sufficient" to accomplish the goal. If there are at least two courses of action in a given column with $E = 1.0$ (Figure 20.5b), each action is sufficient in and of itself in achieving that goal, and we have a "choice" situation.

If only a single action has $E = 1.0$ (Figure 20.5c), that action is both necessary and sufficient; it can do the job (sufficient, $E = 1.0$) and it is the only action that can do the job with "certitude" (necessary).

The case of no action having an E-value of 1.0 (Figure 20.5d), causes some interesting questions. It indicates that no single course of action is sufficient to reach the goal. However, it may be the case that two courses of action working in concert may produce the goal (Figure 20.5e), so they would be said to "coproduce" the goal. In the means-end schema, the two coproducers might be combined into a single C (Figure 20.5f), so that the coproduction is not evident. Different representations of a concept emphasize different aspects of the situation.

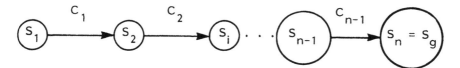

FIGURE 20.6

### Transition Diagrams

A concept that is not readily evident in the means-end schema is the idea of a "sequence of actions"

$$C_1 - C_2 - C_3 \longrightarrow O_1$$

in which we apply one operation after another (e.g., subtract 3 from both sides of an equation, then divide both sides by 2). A representation that explicitly considers sequences of actions is the transition-state diagram, in which we begin with the initial state, then apply "operators" to that state to move into an intermediate state, apply operators to the intermediate state to change it to another intermediate state, etc., until the final transition brings us into the goal state (Figure 20.6), in which $S_n$ equals the goal state ($S_g$).

The solution to a problem in this case is a sequence of operators (courses of action) that lead us from the initial state to the goal state. The transition-state diagram is frequently used in cognitive studies of individual human problem-solving behavior (Newell and Simon, 1972) and in computerized models of problem-solving (see Graham, 1979, for a good overview).

### Examining the Rows

While consideration of the possible column values for E led to a consideration of casuality and coproduction of outcomes, consideration of the row values leads to a consideration of values and choices among goals. If we have a single goal

$O_1$ only

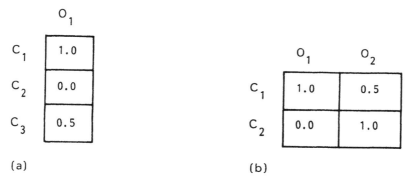

(a)                                        (b)

FIGURE 20.7

$$V(O_1) = .8 \qquad V(O_2) = .2$$

| | | |
|---|---|---|
| $C_1$ | 1.0 | 0.0 |
| $C_2$ | .9 | .1 |
| $C_3$ | 0.5 | 0.5 |

(a)

$EV(C_1) = .8(1.0) + .2(0.0) = .8 + 0 = .8$

$EV(C_2) = .8(.9) + .2(.1) = .72 + .02 = .74$

$EV(C_3) = .8(0.5) + .2(0.5) = .4 + .1 = .5$

(b)

$$V(O_1) = .8 \qquad V(O_2) = .2$$

| | | |
|---|---|---|
| $C_1$ | 1.0 | 0.0 |
| $C_2$ | 0.5 | 1.0 |
| $C_3$ | 1.0 | 1.0 |

(c)

FIGURE 20.8

the problem becomes one of generating a list of possible producers of the outcome, and estimating the efficacy of each in achieving that outcome (Figure 20.7a). The choice is among courses of action only.

If we consider several outcomes (Figure 20.7b), we see that we have a choice among goals

Choose $O_1$ and apply $C_1$
Choose $O_2$ and apply $C_2$

both of which will certainly achieve the chosen goal. Hence, we have to select a goal, setting values for the outcomes, e.g.

$V(O_1) = 25$ utils

$V(O_2) = 50$ utils

in which case we choose $O_2$ and apply action $C_2$.

The means-end schema is often used to compute expected values of the courses of action across all outcomes, with the outcomes having a value expressed in proportions or "weights" (Figure 20.8a and 20.8b). In this case the row values of the courses of action, their efficacies, sum to one. They reflect the probability that action $C_i$ will achieve outcome $O_j$.

In the representation with the cell values being independently set (Figure 20.8c), one could also compute an expected value across rows

$$EV(C_3) = 1.0(.8) + 1.0(.2) = .8 + .2 = 1.00$$

but the interpretation of such a calculation becomes cloudy. It is also unnecessary in certain cases in that the sufficiency of the action toward a given goal makes the choice of that action equivalent to the choice of the goal. Given the evaluations

$$V(O_1) = .8$$

$$V(O_2) = .2$$

the rational decisionmaker would choose outcome one, and implement the appropriate action, here $C_1$ or $C_3$.

The choice of the appropriate action may include a consideration of the "secondary outcomes." For example, given the fact that $C_1$ never brings about outcome $O_2$ (efficacy = 0.0), and that $C_3$ always brings it about (efficacy = 1.0), one who prefers

$O_1$ *and* $O_2$

to

$O_1$ *not* $O_2$

would choose course of action $C_3$. One who prefers

$O_1$ not $O_2$

would choose action $C_1$. This is the type of analysis present in the lunch example.

An alternative to computing expected values would be a strategy similar to maximax

- Find the largest $V(O_j)$
- Choose C with highest E-value in this column

However, in cases that do not guarantee the outcome (column with no C having E = 1.0), we cannot guarantee that this strategy will produce the outcome.

Another alternative might be to find all columns with at least one C-value equal to 1, then choose the outcome from this subset. This will guarantee the production of the outcome.

The means-end schemas are discussed under both headings, decision-making and problem-solving, in the literature. In terms of the analysis presented here they are examples of decision situations. They are useful in the discussion of problem-solving in that they indicate what the result of problem-solving activity is meant to be: a statement of the connection between the actions of an agent and the outcomes produced by that agent.

The means-end schema epitomizes the form of goal attainment problems. The outcomes are the goals. The courses of action summarize the sequence of actions to be implemented in order to achieve the goal.

| | $O_1$ | $O_2$ | $O_3$ |
|---|---|---|---|
| $C_1$ | 1.0 | | |
| $C_2$ | | 1.0 | |
| $C_3$ | | | 1.0 |

(a)

| | $O_1$ |
|---|---|
| $C_1$ | 1.0 |
| $C_2$ | 0.0 |
| $C_3$ | 1.0 |

(b)

FIGURE 20.9

In the situation of perfect control, we wish to have a matrix of the forms shown in Figure 20.9a or 20.9b. The first situation represents a choice among outcomes, "goal-setting" or "planning in the strategic sense." The goal is *not* a given. In fact, the choice among alternative actions is a choice of a goal.

The second situation represents that of a *given* goal, i.e., the outcome $O_1$ has been chosen. The "problem" in this case (antecedent to the matrix) is to generate the resulting list of sufficient actions. If the list generated is of length two or more, the decision situation is to choose among actions to the same goal, $O_1$.

Much of the literature on problem-solving in cognitive psychology and artificial intelligence considers cases of given goals. They seek at least one sequence of actions that will lead to that goal, i.e., one instance of a sufficient $C_i$. We turn to these considerations next.

The Study of Problem-Solving Behavior

We began the discussion of problem-solving with a discussion of real-world problems (e.g., get rich, make a profit), since these are the types of problems individuals or organizations face. However, in many studies of human problem-solving behavior, the problems are not real-world, since these prove to be too complex to be tractable. Hence, artificial problems, such as the following, are often used to stimulate the problem-solving behavior

You have three jugs, A, B, and C with capacities of 20, 5, and 7 qt, respectively. You may fill the jugs with water or empty them as often as you wish. They initially start out empty. Measure out exactly 8 quarts of water.

Solution: fill A, pour some of A into B (5 qt), pour some of A into C (7 qt), empty B and C; A now contains 8 qt (see Anderson, 1975, Hayes, 1981, or Wicklegren, 1974).

Other tasks that are used are games, such as tic-tac-toe, checkers, or chess; mathematical problems, such as word problems (John is twice as old as Mary...); logic or geometrical theorems; or problems specially constructed by the investigators. The focus of the research is not on the problem, but on the problem-solving behavior, the techniques used in problem-solving.

## An Example: Donald and Gerald

One of the most famous of the problem situations studied is the cryptarithmetic problem

```
    Donald        D = 5
  + Gerald
  ─────────
    Robert
```

in which the problem solver is to use the given information (D = 5 and the facts that Donald plus Gerald equals Robert and that each letter in the problem represents a digit) in order to obtain a solution to the problem, i.e., to make the appropriate assignments of the digits 0 through 9 to the letters $D$, $G$, $R$, $O$, $E$, $N$, $B$, $A$, $L$, and $T$. This type of problem was studied by Bartlett (1958), then received more recent emphasis in the studies of Newell and Simon (1972).

## Protocol Analysis

The interest of the researcher is in the thought process of the problem solver. In order to study this thought process, the problem solver is in-

```
    Donald              D=5
  + Gerald
    ───────
    Robert
```

Let's see, D=5 ...
so D + D = 10, I'll have zero in the
sum, and carry a 1

```
        1
    Donald
  + Gerald
    Rober∅ = T
```

so T = ∅, that's D = 5, T = ∅, so I've got two of the letters...

The result of the second column from the right must be odd since L + L + 1 is 2L + 1, 2L being even, so that 2L + 1 is odd.

Also, the result of the third column from the right must be even, since this is 2A...

FIGURE 20.10

D + G has no carry out, and D is 5
so G must be less than 5,
that is, 4,3,2, or 1
(it can't be zero since T=∅)

(a)

```
1       1
5 0 N A 4 5
3 E 9 A 4 5        ∅ = zero
9 0 B E 9 ∅        0 = letter "oh"
```

(b)

```
  Donald ──────   5 2 6 4 8 5       (NOTE: The previous stage had
+ Gerald         1 9 7 4 8 5        incorrect assignments, e.g., the
  Robert         7 2 3 9 7 0        2 4's, and the leftmost 3, so
                                    some backing up and trying again
                                    was involved.)
```

(c)

```
T = ∅
G = 1
O = 2
B = 3
A = 4
D = 5
N = 6
R = 7
L = 8
E = 9
```

(d)

FIGURE 20.11

structed to "think aloud" and a record is kept of his or her "progress." The physical record of the thought process is called a protocol, and the study of the protocol is called protocol analysis.

In order to give the flavor of a protocol analysis, the author recorded some of his thoughts in solving the problem (Figure 20.10). Some of the thoughts are correct, e.g., 2L + 1 must be odd. Others, such as the fact that the result of the column

```
  A
+ A
 ──
  E
```

must be even are not necessarily correct. There could have been a carry into this column, making the result odd (just as 2L + 1). The author simply forgot about this possibility at the time.

By trying various avenues of thought (Figure 20.11a), and moving through intermediate stages such as are shown in Figure 20.11b, the problem solver can arrive at the solution (Figure 20.11c), in which the assignments are as shown in Figure 20.11d. However, the interesting thing is not the solution but the protocol analysis and the principles of problem-solving behavior that are revealed as indicated earlier.

## Candidates and Operations

As the protocol indicates, the problem solver is involved in two types of activities

- Generating candidate solutions, i.e., values for the various letters
- Testing these candidates by performing certain manipulations, e.g., adding the resulting digits in order to see if the result is mathematically correct

Such behavior is summarized as "generate and test." The idea in this problem is to find objects that have "suitable characteristics," namely arithmetic values that make the addition of Donald's and Gerald's values equal to the result obtained by substituting Robert's values in the sum. The problem of generate and test is analogous to the retrieval of information from a data base with inverted organization: find someone or something with characteristics A and B.

Another type of problem-solving behavior is illustrated by the solution of an algebraic equation

$$2X + 3 = 15$$

Candidates are not "generated." Rather, certain manipulations are performed in order to zero in on the one candidate (or two or three in higher order equations) that fulfills the stated relationships. The problem parallels the Donald and Gerald problem in that a given relationship is stated as a constraint on the solution. However, the "generate" in the generation of candidates is eliminated. In fact, for one who knows the method of solution, the exercise is better described as a task since it is not "problematic." It does, however, show the characteristic of "steps taken to reach a goal," i.e., the transformation of an initial "given" state into a final "goal" state, and hence fits the definition of a problem given above.

## Problem Situations and Solution

Newell and Simon (1972) define a problem as a situation in which a person wants something (wants to achieve a goal state) and does not know immediately what series of actions he or she can perform to get it. They indicate that the goal or desired object may be tangible (an apple to eat) or intangible (the proof of a theorem in geometry); specific (I want *that* apple) or general (I want anything that will appease my hunger). The actions taken to achieve the goal may be physical (walking to the apple and picking it up) or mental (such as the manipulations involved in solving the problem Donald

+ Gerald = Robert). However, they concentrate their attention on mental problems, with the operations involved being the manipulation of symbols (letters and digits) rather than objects.

Problem situations involve

1. A representation of the terminal or goal state
2. An initial state (and its representation)
3. A set of operators and the conditions under which they can be applied

The solution itself is a sequence of actions that leads from the initial state to the terminal state. There may be more than one sequence of actions that will achieve the ultimate transition to the goal state. For example, in solving the equation $2X + 3 = 15$, we can subtract 3 from both sides

$$2X + 3 - 3 = 15 - 3$$
$$2X = 12$$

then divided by 2

$$\frac{2X}{2} = \frac{12}{2}$$
$$X = 6$$

or we can divide by 2 initially

$$X + \frac{3}{2} = \frac{15}{2}$$

then subtract 3/2 from both sides

$$X = \frac{15}{2} - \frac{3}{2} = \frac{12}{2} = 6$$

The task of the problem solver is to find or generate a suitable sequence of actions. Several methods of finding such a sequence are discussed, e.g.

- Recall of solution, i.e., one has seen and solved the problem before, and recalls this solution.
- Trial and error, in which one generates potential solutions, then tests them by applying them and checking the results for appropriateness.
- Heuristic search, in which one uses certain "rules of thumb," e.g., "start with the easiest part of the problem" to guide our search. It was such an heuristic search that led the author to solve for T in D + D = T first.

The solution of the equation illustrates the use of recall if one knows the procedure. The following discussion will illustrate the methods of trial and error and heuristic search. Heuristic search is really a restricted form of trial and error (generate and test) in which certain candidates are tried first because they seem "more likely" to be the right candidate.

In discussing problem-solving behavior, a distinction is made between heuristic search and algorithmic techniques. The heuristic searches are rules of thumb; the algorithms are guaranteed rules. In solving for T the author used both an heuristic and an alogorithm (5 + 5 = 10).

## Heuristics Versus Algorithms

Heuristics, or rules of thumb, are contrasted with algorithmic solutions to problems. An algorithmic solution to a problem is one that "guarantees" a solution. An example of an algorithmic or "guaranteed" solution of a problem is the solution of the equation

$$2X + 3 = 15$$

By subtracting 3 from each side of the equation to yield

$$2X = 12$$

then dividing through both sides by 2

$$X = 6$$

we obtain a solution. The operations are guaranteed in that if we apply them faithfully and correctly, we will arrive at the solution to the problem.

An heuristic approach winnows down the number of "paths" we take in looking for a solution, but it does not guarantee a solution. For example, an heuristic in solving problems might be "try a solution known to work in analogous situations." If the analogy "fits," the solution may transfer. If the analogy is not as accurate as one thought, the transferred solution may not work. An example from human affairs might be the rule of thumb

"To get a good grade, become friendly with the teacher."

This course of action may have worked in the past, say with Mr. Brown the geometry teacher, where I learned little geometry (having attained 49% on the final) but obtained an *A* due to a friendship nourished by our mutual interest in recipes.

Applying the rule of thumb to Mrs. Appleby in advanced algebra, we find that our friendship was irrelevant to the grade

40% was awarded an *F*.

and, in fact, the explanation offered when she was queried about the grade was that it was for "my own good," something of particular concern to her due to our friendship based on a mutual interest in sports.

An heuristic approach to the problem of solving the equation $2X + 3 = 15$, say on an examination, would be to copy our neighbor's answer. The heuristic would be "my neighbor usually knows the right answer." Unless my neighbor always knows the right answer, the latter solution is not guaranteed.

## Feasibility of Algorithms

It may be the case that an algorithmic solution exists for a particular problem, but that it is not practicable (not technicologically or operationally feasible). An example of such a problem is finding the correct combination to a safe with a lock consisting of 10 dials, each of which may be set to 1 of 12 digits (Figure 20.12a). If the lock had only a single dial (Figure 20.12b), we could successively try all 12 digits and would be guaranteed the solution in 12 tries. On the average it would take 6 tries to find the correct combination, and, if we were lucky, we would find it on the first try (our method is a sequential search of the "problem space," the num-

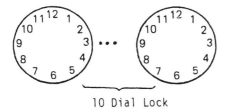

(a)

(b)

(c)

FIGURE 20.12

bers from which the single-digit combination was selected.) A lock with 2 dials (Figure 20.12c), would take 144 tries to find the 2-digit combination in the worst case; but again, we would be guaranteed to find the solution.

Why then is the 12-digit combination a problem? Simply because of the number of possible combinations. The general formula for the number of possibilities is

$$D^N$$

where D stands for the number of digits on a single dial, and N stands for the number of dials. Hence, for a single dial with 12 digits, we have

$$12^1 = 12 \text{ possibilities}$$

With two dials, we have

$$12^2 = 144 \text{ possibilities}$$

and with 12 dials we have

$$12^{12} = 61,917,364,224 \text{ or } 62 \text{ billion possibilities}$$

As Hayes (1981) has calculated, for a 10 digit dial ($10**10$), if we tried 1 combination every second, working 24 hr a day, we would spend 317 years of sleepless nights in the worst case. Of course, on the average it would take only $158\frac{1}{2}$ years, and in the best case, we might find it on the first try! (But don't bet on the first try; the odds against it are 9,999,999,999 to 1 for 10 digits, 10 dials.) Thus, the solution "try each number" in turn is simply not practicable if there are too many dials, too many characters per dial, or both (consider a combination lock with 10 dials of digits and letters, w.e., 36 possible characters per dial). We might be forced to try an heuristic, e.g., ask the wife or husband of the owner of the safe and hope she or he tells us. Of course, the hueristic is not guaranteed to succeed, so that we may never solve our problem. The algorithm is guaranteed, but is not practicable.

## A Distinction in Algorithms

The contrast between the solution of the linear equation and the solution of the safe combination illustrates that there are two types of algorithmic activities

- Algorithms to generate all possible candidates, i.e., to ensure that we try every possibility (safe problem)
- Algorithms that dictate a sequence of steps guranteed to find a single candidate solution (the equation)

While both activities are algorithmic in that they guarantee a solution, they are algorithmic in different ways: the first method (generating candidates), emphasizing the "search" for a solution, the second (performing transformations), emphasizing the "production" of the solution. Since most "true problems" (i.e., those involving unknown solutions) will involve search techniques, these will be emphasized in this chapter. The execution of a known set of transformations is more appropriately relegated to the material on data processing.

## Back to the T

In solving for the value of T, the heuristic used seemed to be something like "go with what is known first," hence the focus on the value of D. The algorithm involved was the arithmetic rule

$$5 + 5 = 10$$

and the method of recording a 10 as a 0 in the total for column 1 (rightmost column), and a carry of the 1 into column 2. These operations were used as tests in this context, and as a means to a goal. That is, the computation is performed to see if the generated candidate fits the constraints of the solution space.

## Describing the Problem

As indicated earlier, the representation of the problem involves a statement of the initial state, the goal state, and the set of operators that can be applied to transform one state or set of states into another. The definition of the operations involves the definition of the appropriate input values (the domain of operation or input operands) and the result (output) of applying a given operator to a given set of inputs.

## Representing the Operations

The rules concerning the operations might be represented as "relations," i.e., a set of ordered elements

(5, 3, +, 8)

(5, 3, *, 15)

in which the first two elements of the "ordered group" represents the input to the binary operators, the third element is the operator itself, and the fourth is the output.

If one wishes to emphasize the "transformation" aspect of the rules, one might use the representation

(5, 3, +) $\longrightarrow$ 8

(5, 3, *) $\longrightarrow$ 15

or

+(5, 3) $\longrightarrow$ 8

*(5, 3) $\longrightarrow$ 15

in which the input and output are separated by a transformation arrow.

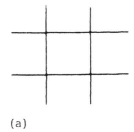

(a)

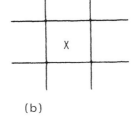

(b)

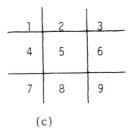

(c)

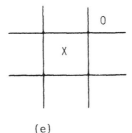

cells 1-2:   empty
cell 3:      0
cell 4:      empty
cell 5:      X
cells 6-9:   empty

(d)

(e)

FIGURE 20.13

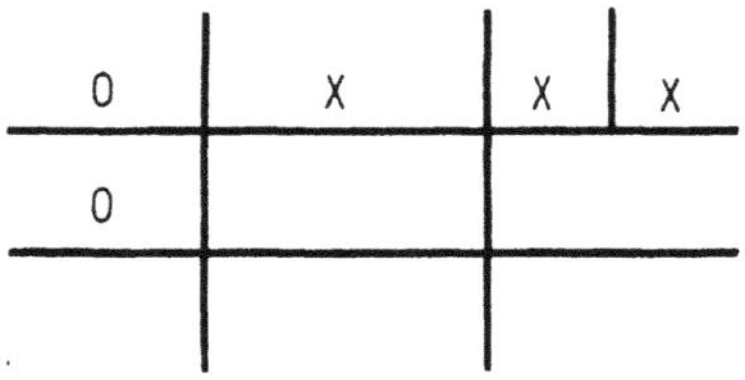

FIGURE 20.14

## Representing the States

As the above discussion indicates, we also need to represent the states of the "problem space," i.e., we need to represent the current state

$X = 5$

$Y = 3$

or

(5, 3)

and the "next" or "output" states: $Z = X + Y$, i.e., 8. In the examples of the arithmetic operations, the descriptions are not symmetrical; there are more input variables (two) than output variables (one). In other situations, such as the representations of input states and output states are symmetrical. For example, the state of a tic-tac-toe game prior to the first move is represented as shown in Figure 20.13a. After X's move, we might have Figure 20.13b. The number of elements to be described remains static at nine. The only change is in the values assigned to each cell

- Empty
- X
- O

The cells may be numbered to facilitate representation (Figure 20.13c), so that the first state was

Cells 1 through 9 equal "empty."

The second was

Cells 1 through 4: empty
Cell 5: X
Cells 6 through 9: empty

After O's move we might have the description given in Figure 20.13d, representing the "game state" given in Figure 20.13e.

The set of variables that can be used to describe a state and the value these variables can take is called the "state space." All solutions to the problem must stay within this space both "on the way" to a solution and in the statement of the final state.

In the tic-tac-toe problem space there are nine variables, the nine cells, and three values that each cell can take on (null, X, O). Any solutions outside this space, e.g., using 10 cells to obtain 3 in a row (Figure 20.14), are deemed "illegal." In terms of real-world problems they are "not feasible."

The conjunction of the state space and the operations that can be used within this space constitute the "problem space."

## Relevant Variables

The constraints on the variables to be considered and the legal values of these values correspond to real-world constraints about "what really matters," i.e., the relevant variables in a situation, and the nature of these variables—the values they can take on.

In the situation of controlling the lights in one's living room, the relevant variables are the state of the lights (output variable), the state of the switches (flipped up or down) and the connections between a given light and a given switch (e.g., swtich A goes to light A, switch B to light B).

In solving the problem of "lighting light A," we note whether or not it is already lit (the goal state may be the current state, i.e., "already attained"). If not, we locate the appropriate switch and flip it.

Solutions such as "light a bonfire," or "puff a magic wand" are deemed outside the solution space, the one being "personally infeasible," i.e., not desirable due to side effects, the other being "technically infeasible," i.e., impossible with today's technology.

## Constraints on the Operations

The operations (actions) executed "on states" are similarly constrained in regard to

- Types of operations
- Number of operations applied
- Order in which operations are applied

In regard to tic-tac-toe, the operations are either

- Place an X in a cell
- Place an O in a cell

depending on "who the player is." These constraints are directly related to the values that the variables can take on.

The constraints as to number and types of moves are not constrained due to the values that the variables can take on, but by the "rules of the game."

(X had 1st move or "moves," i.e., X made three moves)

FIGURE 20.15

In regard to tic-tac-toe, no one may make more than five moves, and no one may take more than one move at a time. Hence, solutions of the type shown in Figure 20.15 are "not feasible."

In terms of real-world "games" these constraints represent either

- Convention, e.g., no one may vote more than once in any election, as desirable as this action may seem to political candidates
- The nature of the situation, e.g., one cannot defer the choice of picnic or bingo until Saturday (when the state of the weather will be certain) due to the need to advertise prior to the event (behavioral constraint, i.e., people do not go to events they do not know about)

or

- One cannot fly to Paris "free of charge" by using one's arms and legs or by "wishing to be there" (constraints of the physical world we live in, i.e., constraints of nature)

With this brief digression into the correspondence between laboratory problem-solving situations and real-world situations, we return to the discussion of human problem-solving.

## Human Problem-Solving

There are two types of problems discussed in the literature on problem-solving.

1. One is of the variety: Find an object that has the characteristics "x and y and z."
2. Another is to find a sequence of operations that will transform object A into object B with characteristics such and such.

An example of the first type of problem is the request

- Find a chemical mixture X that when taken internally or administered by vaccine will prevent the contraction of polio.

Other examples are

- Find a palatable red wine that is not high priced.
- Find an employee who has both accounting and data processing experience.
- Find a suitable two bedroom apartment renting for $300 a month or less.

Examples of the second type of problem statement are the following:

- Find a sequence of activities that will enable me to have a strong body (e.g., three visits to the Nautilus center, one visit to each machine per visit, per week).
- Find a sequence of moves that will enable me to beat the current world champion chess player in a game of chess.

While the second set of questions can be reduced to the first, i.e., the sequence of moves can be looked at as an object, it is beneficial to keep the distinction in mind. One is a search for an object having certain attributes, the other for a set of actions that will produce an outcome.

The latter list, the sequence of actions or "moves," also shows a distinction between moves made in a relatively static environment (applying paints to a canvas) and moves made in a changing environment (making moves based on the moves of an opponent), or, in considering the more general case, maintaining one's "position" in the face of a changing world (e.g., steering an automobile along a road that curves).

## Object Identification Problems

The first type of problem, "object identification" or "object recognition," can be attacked in various ways. One is recall of the solution; if we know the answer from previous experience, we "recall the answer" and state it. Hence, a doctor recalling his or her previous advice for the cure of the common cold ("take two aspirin and call me in a few days") may reissue the advice. This method of human problem-solving is analogous to the use of data bases.

As stated above, the problem is an "inverted" one, the statement of attributes that should have specified values, the solution being the "id" returned for the object or objects fulfilling the solution.

The complementary type of problem would be the statement of the name, requesting the attributes, e.g., the statement of John's name, requesting the attribute of his height

"What is John's height?"

This latter question is better understood as an example of the generate and test method of solving the original "inverted question."

## Generate and Test

As we indicated above, one method of solving problems of the sort

Find X | X has attributes such-and-such

is "pure recall." This is, however, a solution that does not present itself in all cases. Hence, we must have alternate means of approaching such questions. One is the generate and test method of solution. If the objects that "might present a solution" are well defined, we can "look at each," and see if one or more has the appropriate attributes. In the case of John's height, the initial question might have been

"Who are good basketball players, i.e., candidates for our team?"

The qualities sought are such attributes as

- Is tall
- Can run well
- Is quick
- Has athletic ability
- Has basketball ability
  .
  .
  .

some of which overlap. In attempting to respond to the basketball question (the inverted question) we "generate people" and check their attributes for a fit, a form of pattern-matching. In terms of data base design, we are performing a sequential scan of the data base. The first method, the method of recall, is analogous to the implementation of inverted files, i.e., files that were initially created to facilitate such "direct recall" of objects having attributes of the sort "looked for."

Direct recall can be provided for in data base design if the questions can be anticipated. If they cannot, the generate and test method will be necessary. If the objects that are the "potential set" (i.e., the set from which an answer can be drawn; the suject or domain of the question, Belnap and Steel, 1976) are in the data base, the generation is easy, a sequential scan of these objects. If the objects are not contained in the data base they must be generated in some other manner.

## Alternative Methods of Generate and Test

The question of finding the combination to the safe can be used to indicate alternative methods of generation of numbers. If one does not have a list of "potential numbers," i.e., all those from

0,000,000,000

to

9,999,999,999

for a 10-digit dial, one can generate them as one goes along.

The generation may be systematic or may not. If the generation is nonsystematic, one might just try numbers at will

1,342,067,042

then

9,807,153,041

possibly using "some favorite numbers" (a heuristic, but not one that will necessarily produce all potential answers). The nonsystematic generation has the undesirable properties of

● Not necessarily generating all possible candidates
● Generating some candidates twice

Hence, one is led to some form of systematic search, e.g., starting with the number 0,000,000,000, then successively adding 1 until one reaches 9,999,999,999. This will guarantee that all numbers are generated and that the combination is found (if a combination exists; the dials could be a ploy, covering a key lock that is used by lifting a fake cover).

It is interesting to note that the problem solver in Donald and Gerald has a small list of possible numbers, 0 through 9, that can be kept at hand, in a list, and crossed off—a small data base. The "safe" problem has a list that is just as well defined, but so large that it is unlikely to be found in a handy data base.

## Manipulating the Problem Representation

Another form of solving "object-related" problems is the manipulation (transformation) of the description of the problem itself. The statement of an equation is such a problem. The original statement

$$2X + 3 = 15$$

is a description that gives the relationship of the sought-for commodity (X) in terms of its relationship to other commodities, primarily the value 15, i.e., it is three less than 15 if it is doubled first. By manipulating the description (subtracting 3, dividing by 2) we can obtain the name of the entity having these relationships, 6. A similar problem statement might be to find the person who is Judy's boss and loves Rosalind, namely Allen.

The two types of descriptors

- Attributes of object
- Relationship of object to other objects

can be mixed, e.g., find Y so that

1.  $Y = \sqrt{9}$   (relationship to 9)
2.  Y is positive   (attribute of Y)

yielding +3 as the only result.


## One Answer or Many

One thing that affects the length of search is the question of "one answer" or "many." The response to this question may or may not be known ahead of time. Algebraic theory ensures that equations of the type

$$2X + 3 = 15$$

have a single "answer," and that some descriptions have an inherent quality of oneness

Find the tallest boy in school to be captain of the basketball team.

Others, such as

Find a vaccine to fight polio.

may have one or many answers, or none. It may be that the poser of the question is able to limit the number of responses sought

- Find *one* vaccine that works
- Find *five* tall people

If such a limit can be imposed (or is inherent in the problem), one can "stop searching" early. If not, a sequential scan of all candidates is necessary.


## Heuristic Search

If one seeks "all answers" and the number for all cannot be specified, one must perform a full sequential scan. However, if a numerical limit can be placed on the number of answers "possible" or "desirable," one can stop early, and heuristics may be useful in aiding the "early finish." For example, in searching for "one tall person" to fix a lightbulb in the ceiling (the tallest person not being necessary) one might begin by considering the males (usually taller than females) and, among the males, the seniors (usually taller than freshmen).

The heuristics are "rules of thumb" about who is tall. The use of transformation rules, such as those employed in the equations are "algorithmic" in that they guarantee a solution. Both these cases are instances of reducing the search space. The generation of all candidates, by adding 1 to 0 through 9,999,999,999, or by a sequential scan of a set of objects (data base), does not reduce the search space.

We might call the use of heuristics or algorithms that reduce the search space "truncated search" or "controlled generate and test." This will distinguish these methods from those of "full generate and test."

## Search Trees

If the objects to be tested are well defined, and in a single set, the search tree describing the activity of searching is a linear list

| | |
|---|---|
| 0000000000 | No |
| ↓ | |
| 0000000001 | No |
| ↓ | |
| 0000000002 | No |
| . | |
| . | |
| . | |
| 0900817543 | No |
| . | |
| . | |
| . | |
| 9105600213 | Yes |

However, most "trees" in the literature involve branches (Figure 20.16). One might ask how the branches arise.

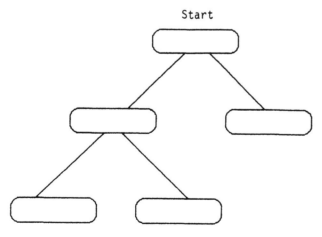

Start

FIGURE 20.16

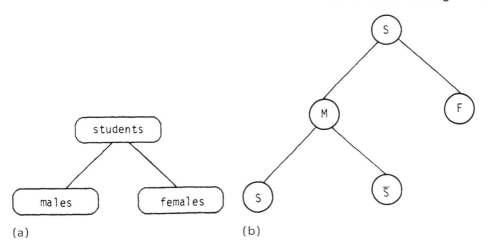

(a)

(b)

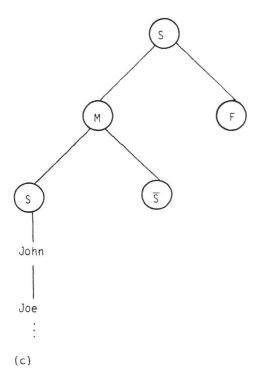

(c)

FIGURE 20.17

## Subdividing the Space

One method of creating branches is to "subdivide" the search space. This was the strategy used in looking for a "tall person." We first dichotomized between the males and the females (Figure 20.17a), then subdivided males into lowerclassmen and seniors (Figure 20.17b). We then sequentially went through the senior males until we found a "hit" (Figure 20.17c). The method of subdivision is a strategy in itself, one related to "which objects should be considered." The choice of a path is also a strategy, one of "where to begin searching."

The latter question, where to begin, and how far to go in that direction before giving up, has been studied under the terminology of breadth-first versus depth-first searching.

### Breadth First and Depth First

In examining a tree structure such as that shown in Figure 20.18a, it is easy to see that a traversal of the path from A to F will be fruitless, but that we won't know the fruitlessness of the search for a long time (examination of five nodes). Upon finding that the path from A to F is fruitless, we would "back up" to A then try G, then H, and find the goal, at which point we might say we should have tried G sooner.

On the other hand, if we face the tree shown in Figure 20.18b, a "sideways search" would lead us through the nodes

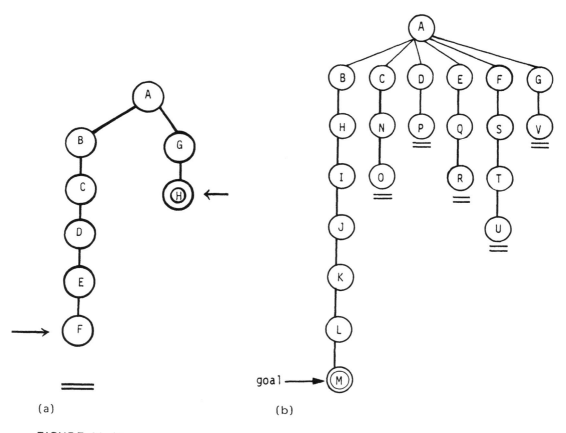

(a)                    (b)

FIGURE 20.18

```
                  A
   B    C    D    E    F    G
   H    N    P    Q    S    V
                  ‾         ‾
   I         O         R    T
             ‾         ‾
   J                   U
                       ‾
```

before we finally settle down on the path

```
   J
   K
   L
   M ←——— victory
```

in which case we would say that we should have "followed through" on B, going all the way down the tree, before trying out the other spurious candidates.

The first type of search is called "depth first," since we go down the tree as deeply as we can on any given branch before giving up. The second type of search is called "breadth first," because we try all the possibilities at a given level (broadening the number of paths examined), "advancing on all fronts at once." The characteristics of depth-first and breadth-first searches are contradictory in nature, and, if we don't know where the goal is, which is usually the case in real-world problems, we don't (can't) know which is best!

Depth-first search is particularly useful if

- There are relatively few promising paths (paths that are estimated as "might lead to a solution") among many possible paths

and

- We have some ability to judge which of the paths are most likely to be "solution paths"

It is also useful if the depth of the tree is not great, since we can eliminate branches without much cost (in time, effort of exploration, and money). The difficulty with depth-first searches really occurs with long lists, since

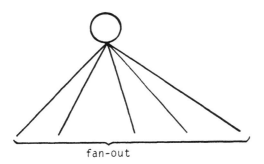

fan-out

(a)

FIGURE 20.19

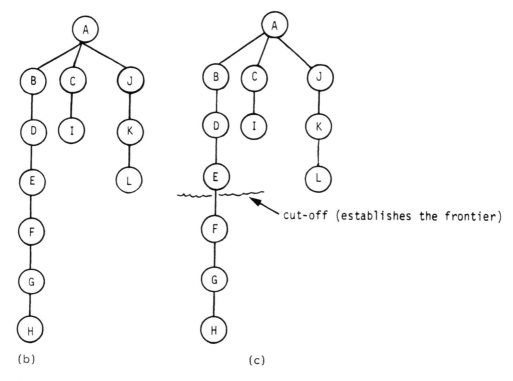

(b)                                    (c)

FIGURE 20.19   (continued)

they are essentially sequential searches of a single branch. Thus, some estimate of the number of nodes in the "sequence of nodes" leading to a solution is desirable. Of course, in real-world problems this is not always possible; and even in games, such as chess, the tree may be 40 or more moves deep, so that traversing a single branch to the "bottom" is usually not feasible. (The tree for games will be slightly different than that presented here.)

Breadth-first search is desirable if

• There are several "promising" paths or several ways to achieve a solution

and if

• Some of these paths to a solution are estimated to be relatively short

Again, in real-world problems and in complex games, the "fan-out" at each node (Figure 20.19a) explodes quite rapidly, so that at a level of three nodes deep, we may be examining several hundred nodes, prohibiting an exhaustive "left-to-right" search.

## Cutoff Points

In order to blend the concept of searching in depth with the ability to try a wide variety of solutions, a rule of thumb such as "don't search ahead more than four levels" may be implemented. Such a rule places an artificial frontier in the tree, beyond which we do not explore. For example, with a cutoff of four levels (three transitions), using the tree shown in Figure 20.19b, the problem solver would halt the exploration of the leftmost branch after examining E (Figure 20.19c). If the method of search is to return to the root (rather than just to the parent, which is another possibility), the search would proceed as

   A   B    D    E,   backup

            C    I,    and if I is not a solution, then

       J    K   L;   if L is not a solution, we would now go back to:

  F   G   H

to complete the search.

The fruitfulness of the "depth threshold" depends on both the left-to-right placement and the depth of the goal, as well as on the cutoff value of the threshold. For example, if F were a solution in the above diagram (assume G and H are not there), the threshold of four levels hindered the search. We searched through nine nodes before finding the goal at F

   A   B    D    E

            C    I

       J    K   L

            F

where a depth of five levels would have succeeded on the first try of the leftmost path

   A   B    D    E    F

instead of meandering through C, I, J, K, and L.

On the other hand, if node I were the solution, the search

   A   B    D    E

   C    I

is much faster than one going to the full depth of the leftmost branch

   A   B    D    E    F   G   H

   C    I

Hence, there are trade-offs involved; the decision as to breadth first, depth first, cutoffs, etc. is not easy.

## Real-World Problems

Real-world problems exhibit the same difficulties with the strategies of depth-first and breadth-first searches as game problems. In finding an economic fuel, should we explore one alternative, say the conversion of sugar into fuel, thoroughly, leaving all other paths unexplored? Or should we explore several alternatives, say conversion of sugar, exploration of the Antarctic Sea, fuel-hunting voyages into outer space, solar energy, and nuclear energy simultaneously? In exploring a given path, say the conversion of sugar, how far should we explore; until we spend $10 million? $10 billion? Until we have consumed 5 million work hours? 5 billion?

If there were no constraints on our money or energy, these would not be problems. However, in light of limited resources and several candidate "consumers" of the resource (e.g., nuclear fission studies, space capsule building), decisions must be made about depth first, breadth first, and the deepness of the search. In fact, in real-world problems, decisions must be made about who the problem solver might be. Should we grant $1 million to MIT to study solar energy or to UCLA? Or $500,000 each (breadth first in support of the researcher)? Is one research team more likely to succeed than another? Does it have a better track record or more technical expertise in the area? Is there a minimum level of funding necessary to do the research (prohibiting, say, the division of the $1 million between the two schools)?

The choice of solution paths may be made on the basis of likelihood judgments by "experts" (the scientists say alchemy looks best), on the basis of past experience (MIT solved our last problem), or even by popular election (the outcome of the referendum decreed that government spending would be directed at solar energy).

Even the nature of the "problems" to be considered may be a public issue. For example, is it necessary to solve the problem of finding a weapon whose force will be instantaneously deadly over an entire planet to prevent interplanetary war or should we put our efforts into finding methods of achieving interplanetary good will? (Or both?)


## The Difficulty with Pure Search

The difficulty with "pure search" as a solution-finding method is evident from the tree discussion: the length of search can be quite long. Even in a single-path tree, if there are many elements (candidates) the search can be long. If there are multiple paths the problem is simply exacerbated.

The technique of unaided generate and test is a method of "pure search," generating candidates sequentially. The use of heuristics attempts to direct the choice by a method that will shorten the search, e.g., if it is anticipated that the length of paths is small (e.g., there are "fewer seniors"), search that path (category) first.

An algorithmic solution of the type that manipulates the problem statement, e.g., the solution of an equation, searches a guaranteed path. However, it differs from the generate and test type of problems in that we do not generate "candidate numbers"; we take known steps to the single solution. It is more like running a maze than searching for certain characteristics.

The solution of recall is an algorithm "remembered" or a "list remembered." The algorithm remembered applies to the case of the equation in which a known sequence of actions can be applied to the current state (problem statement) in order to achieve the goal state (statement of form $X = 6$). The "list" is appropriate to the problem of identifying objects with a certain attribute, and is equivalent to creating a subcategory (subset) of the original data base.

### Transforming Trial and Error to
### Recall/Algorithmic Solution

The example of running a maze indicates how one might proceed from trial and error to either recall of a solution or to an algorithmic procedure for arriving at a solution. The maze, being heterogeneous in form, is an example of recall more than algorithmic solution. However, the exact sequence remembered is an algorithm in the sense of a guaranteed solution. It is a "weak algorithm" in that it applies to this specific maze, rather than to "all mazes." The algorithm "try all possible paths" is "general" but is essentially trial and error, i.e., generate and test. Complete generation, i.e., an algorithm of "candidates tried," guarantees that each candidate will be tried, but is lengthy in execution.

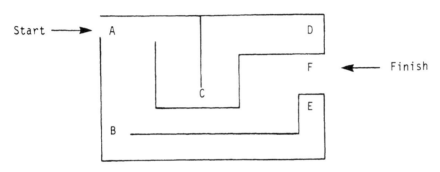

(a)

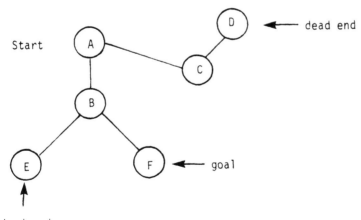

(b)

FIGURE 20.20

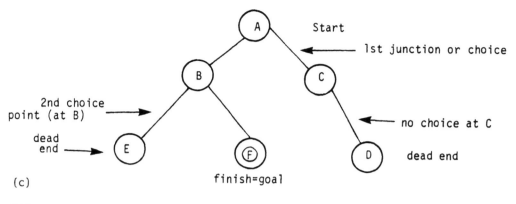

(c)

FIGURE 20.20   (continued)

## Running a Maze

The problem of running a maze can be represented by a tree structure (see Graham, 1979; Raphael, 1976). Given a maze of the form shown in Figure 20.20a, in which A is the start and F the finish, we can construct the state space shown in Figure 20.20b. Drawn a little more carefully, we see that the "possible paths" are a tree structure (Figure 20.20c). A mouse traversing this tree might first try B, then E, then back up to B, then try F and get the cheese. If it then commits the path to memory: A-B-F, the process of trial and error, with its wasteful backing up, is no longer necessary. Recall has replaced trial and error.

## The Use of Theory

The case of solving an equation differs from the case of the maze in that rules have been developed to apply to all instances of "certain form"

$$ax + b = n$$

i.e.

- Subtract b (or add)
- Divide by a (or multiply)

so that we take "the right path" for all instances without trial and error.
    In the case of the maze, the particular solution (the remembered one) fits only that maze. It is unerring but not generalizable. The general solution, try all paths, is "exhaustive search," hence, it is useful to distinguish between

- Algorithms that guarantee the generation of all candidates, and are thus exhaustive search procedures.
- Algorithms that generate a sequence of steps that are not exhaustive search, in fact "guarantee" a minimal or close to minimal number of steps in the "search process." These latter algorithms are probably better described as "nonsearch solutions."

## Using a Computer to Solve Problems

Much of today's research into problem-solving techniques is done by computer. It is interesting to see how a computer can be programmed to solve the maze problem. The solution is one of trial and error, and as in the case of the mouse, the problem is one of trying all paths without trying any twice. While a human or mouse might "mark" the paths tried by writing on the wall or by placing pieces of cheese at the entrance to blocked paths, the computer is not as physically adept. The programmer must develop other methods of representing the problem (other than "looking down corridors") and of remembering paths.

Using the maze described above, there were three end points (terminal nodes) in the tree structure: E, F, and D, with E and D being "dead ends," F being the goal. Arrival at the goal terminates the search. Arrival at E or D requires backing up. Hence, a subject (mouse, computer program) might choose the sequence

A-B-E-B'-F

in which there is only one "backup," to B, then selection of the current path. (The prime indicates a node visited while backing up.) Another problem solver (human, mouse, or otherwise) might choose to "start over" when blocked at E, choosing to go all the way back to the root and choose a child other than B at that level, in which case, he or she will be blocked again

A-B-E-B'-A'-C-D.   (C-D blocked)

We have marked B' and A' to indicate that the problem solver is simply backtracking at this point, going through B on the way to A, not selecting B for its own sake, and going to A simply to obtain a new child (path). Of course at this point, he or she would have to back up again. If he or she is still using the technique of backing up to the root and choosing another child, he or she must choose B again

A-B-E-B'-A'-C-D-C'-A'-<u>B</u>

where B' and C' both represent backtracking, but the underlined B at the end of the string indicates a new choice of B as a viable path. If the problem solver does not have a good memory, he or she may take the route B-E again

A-B-E-B'-A'-C-D-C'-A'-B-E

and be blocked again. In fact, a particularly nongifted problem solver could traverse the path

A-B-E-B'-A'-C-D-C'-A'-B-E-B'-A'-C-D-C'-A'...

forever.

In problems of the maze sort, in which we are traversing the same static paths in order to find our way out of the maze, it is particularly important to remember where we have been. In physical paths we might place marks on the wall. In a computer program we might add a field to an array of information about each node, indicating that the path had been traveled before. For example, the above maze could be represented in the two-dimensional array (matrix; Figure 20.21a) in which the *1*'s represent a

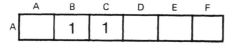

(a)

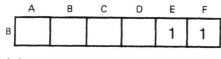

(b)

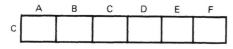

(c)

(d)

FIGURE 20.21

connection from the node on the left to the node at the top of the column. The nodes on the left are parents. The columns represent the children of the respective parents. Hence, the matrix says

    A goes to B
    A goes to C
    B goes to E
    B goes to F
    C goes to D
    D doesn't go anyplace
    E doesn't go anyplace
    F is the goal

A computer program could be generated to start at A and "look for paths" by looking for *1*'s in A's row (Figure 20.21b). If a "left-to-right" algorithm

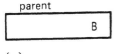

(a)

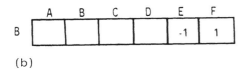

(b)

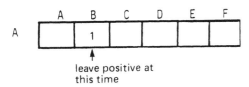

leave positive at
this time

(c)

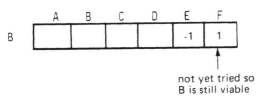

not yet tried so
B is still viable

(d)

FIGURE 20.22

is used, the program would initially try B, going to that row (Figure
20.21c). Again, using a left-to-right philosophy, it would try E and be
blocked (Figure 20.21d). It then must return to its parent, the previously
tested row, or all the way to start. In fact, to return to the parent, it
must have saved the information about who the parent was, say in a location called "previous node" or "parent node" or simply "parent" (Figure
20.22a). Since there may be a series of parents, this "previous" variable
could be implemented as a stack of previous nodes, the path being re-
traced in reverse order to the original traversals. However, the point here
is that when it returns to B, it can mark the path E as a negative one
(Figure 20.22b), indicating that it had been down that path before and it
was a dead end. We would not mark B as negative in the A row (Figure
20.22c), since B still has untried possibilities (Figure 20.22d). We would
only mark out a row when all of its possibilities were exhausted. Hence,
if we traverse C, we would first try the path C-D (Figure 20.23a), at
which point we would mark D as -1 in the C row (Figure 20.23b), and if
we examine the rest of the C row, we see that all its possibilities have

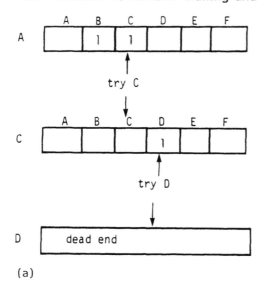

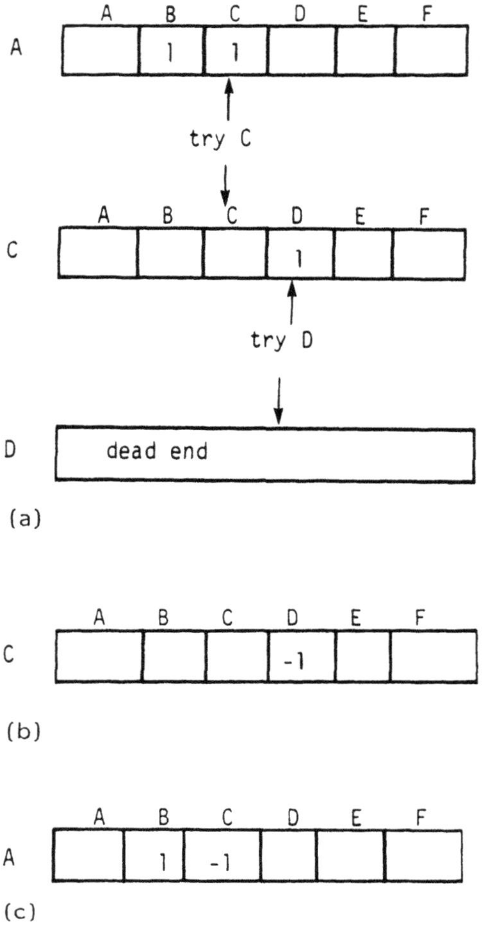

try C

try D

D    dead end

(a)

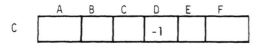

(b)

(c)

FIGURE 20.23

|   | A | B | C | D | E | F |
|---|---|---|---|---|---|---|
| A |   | 1 | -1 |   |   |   |
| B |   |   |   |   | -1 | 1 |
| C |   |   |   | -1 |   |   |
| D |   |   |   |   |   |   |
| E |   |   |   |   |   |   |
| F | goal |   |   |   |   |   |

FIGURE 20.24

been exhausted, at which point we can mark the C entry in the A row (Figure 20.23c) as being a dead end. In fact, now the matrix representation of the array is as shown in Figure 20.24, which leaves us only one choice

A ⟶ B ⟶ F

the goal! Our computer program has "learned" by marking the paths and found the goal.

### Remembering the Parents: A Stack

In the previous problem we discussed the need to remember the parent of a node; i.e., when processing the row at E, we had to remember that we came from B (Figure 20.25a). The perceptive reader might have noticed that if we want to go back to A, we also must know that the parent of B is A (Figure 20.25b), but we have a dilemma, since the single location "previous node" cannot hold two values. An assignment of B to the previous node would destroy a previous assignment of A to the previous node (Figure 20.25c).

With a single location we can never remember more than a single parent, hence, we need more than one location. A data structure particularly suited

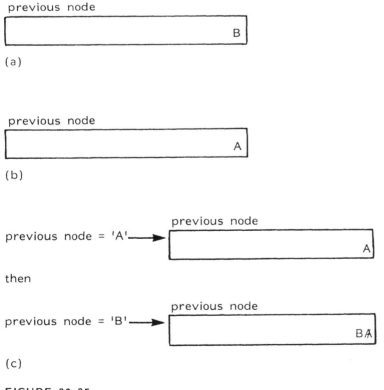

FIGURE 20.25

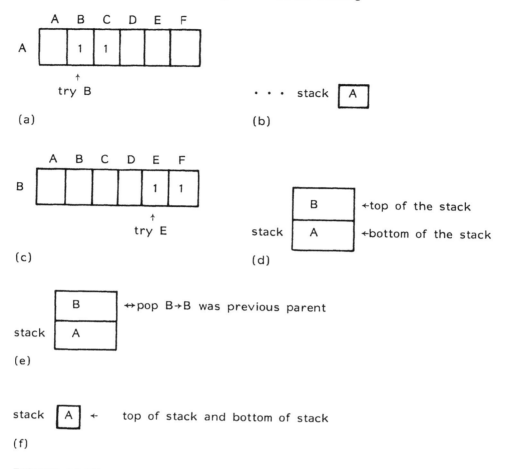

FIGURE 20.26

to handling multiple entries is a stack. A stack is simply a series of locations (say an array) in which items are "pushed onto the stack" when we
want to store them, and "popped off" when we want to retrieve them. The
items are "pushed on" so that they go one on top of the other, then popped off in *reverse order*, much as the plates in a cafeteria or pancakes on
a plate. Because of the reverse removal, the stack is sometimes referred
to as a last-in-first-out or LIFO data structure. (Queues or lines, as in a
grocery store, are first-in-first-out or FIFO.) For our example, we would
use the stack to remember the parents.

Upon choosing to go to B from A (Figure 20.26a), we push A onto the
stack (Figure 20.26b). Then, upon choosing to go to E from B (Figure
20.26c), we push B onto the stack (Figure 20.26d). Then upon finding E
to be a dead end, we "pop back up" to B (Figure 20.26e), so that the
stack is now as shown in Figure 20.26f, and we are processing B. If we
choose to continue processing B, we will try F (Figure 20.27a), first push-
ing B back onto the stack (Figure 20.27b). Of course, this line of thought
will lead to the goal. However, for our purposes, suppose that after mark-

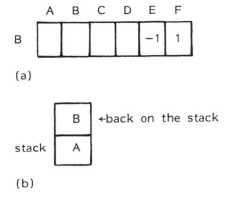

(a)

B ←back on the stack

stack A

(b)

FIGURE 20.27

ing E as a "dead end" (Figure 20.28a), we decide to go back up the tree (instead of trying F). We simply pop the stack again (remember that B was previously popped so that the stack only contains A in this example; Figure 20.28b), and we are back at A (Figure 20.28c). Note that at the root level the stack is empty (Figure 20.29a). Also, the stack must be large enough to accommodate n-1 nodes if there are n levels in a tree. Hence, our tree, with three levels (Figure 20.29b), needs a stack that can hold two parents (Figures 20.29c or 20.29d). A tree with 10 levels would need a stack with room for 9 parents or "ancestors," etc.

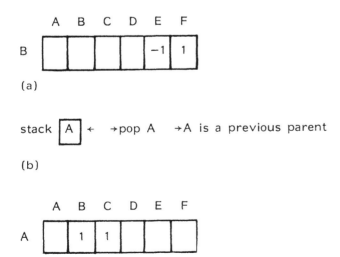

(a)

stack A ← →pop A →A is a previous parent

(b)

(c)

FIGURE 20.28

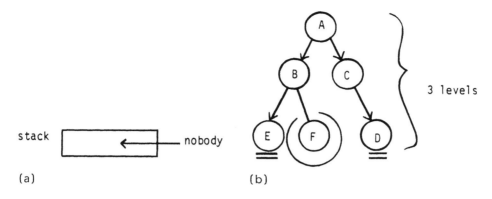

(a)

(b)

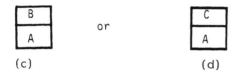

(c)            (d)

FIGURE 20.29

## Games Involving Opponents

The cases of running mazes, solving equations, developing new theorems in logic and the like, involve a problem solver pitted against a somewhat passive world. This is not the case in games of chess or tic-tac-toe, nor the games of the business world. We examined the case of competitive opponents in studying game theory, however, the game presented there was one of simultaneous choice, then outcome

Choice 1

→    outcome

Choice 2

Games such as chess and tic-tac-toe represent games in which the players alternate moves. Examples in the real world might be setting prices in a gas station or grocery store (or other moves)

- I lower the price of gas from $2 to $1.
- You lower from $1.99 to $0.99.
- I lower to 98¢.
- You lower to 97¢.
- I see futility in this "price war," and begin giving away coupons that can be redeemed for car washes.
- You begin serving coffee.
  .
  .
  .

The business game depicted has "no end" unless one of the parties goes out of business, or they "agree to coexist." Games such as chess and tic-tac-toe usually do end, possibly in a draw.

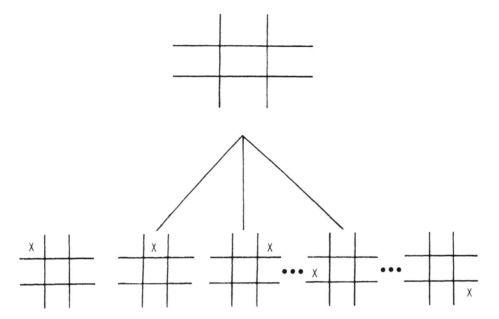

FIGURE 20.30

## Game Trees

The trees drawn to represent games are similar to the search trees. However, each level of the tree represents one player's move, with the "turns" alternating. For example, in considering the game of tic-tac-toe, assuming that the state space tree shows "our point of view" (rather than our opponents; both are equivalent, but one must actually be selected for the representation), the initial state is represented by the empty "board." If we have the first move, and we are X, we have nine possible transitions from the empty board (Figure 20.30), and we must choose one of the nine possible "next states" as an intermediate state on the way to the goal of having three X's in a row (Figure 20.31). Once we have made one move (selected an intermediate state and placed our X in an appropriate cell), our opponent is faced with eight possibilities. Say we have chosen the middle square (Figure 20.32a), our opponent now has eight choices (Figure 20.32b); once we have made our choice, the opponent has only eight possible moves. However, since we can choose any one of nine initial "next

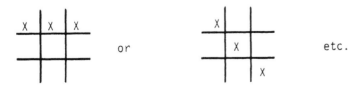

FIGURE 20.31

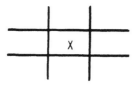

(a)

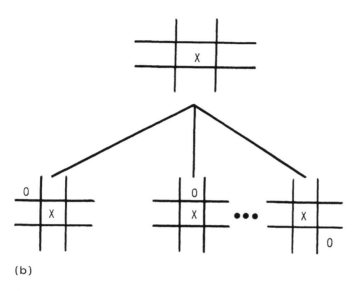

(b)

FIGURE 20.32

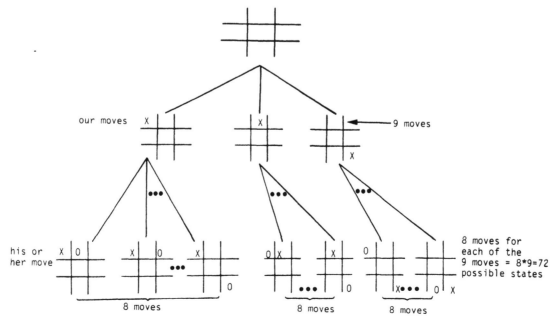

FIGURE 20.33

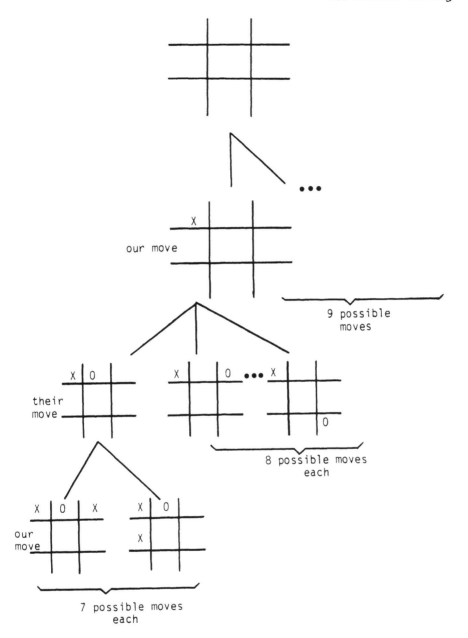

FIGURE 20.34

states" on our first move, and for each of these next states our opponent
has eight possible moves, there are 72 "possible" states in the state space
at this time (Figure 20.33).

At the next stage we have 7 possible moves for each of the 72 possible
configurations generated so far (Figure 20.34), so that at a depth of three
levels (3 moves) we would have $9 \cdot 8 \cdot 7 = 504$ possibilities. If all branches
extended to the bottom of the state space tree, we would have 9! (9 fac-

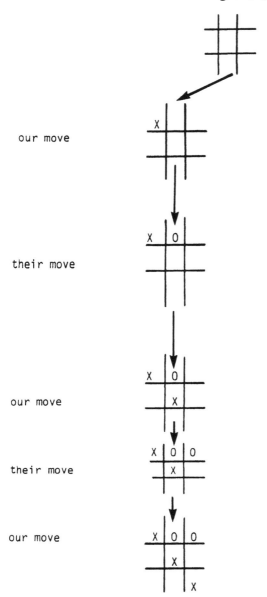

our move

their move

our move

their move

our move

FIGURE 20.35

torial or 9·8·7·6·5...1) possible configurations. The actual total is some-what less, since certain configurations terminate the tree prematurely. For example, if we have a particularly slow or beneficient opponent, the solu-tion path shown in Figure 20.35 is a possibility; the tree has only six levels (five moves) on this particular path.

If the object of the game is to "win" (as opposed to preventing the op-ponent's winning, where draws would be a win), a solution path for us is any of the eight ways in which we can get three X's in a row (Figure

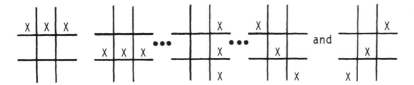

FIGURE 20.36

20.36; three winning patterns for rows, three for columns, two for diagonals).

If we compare the total number of possible paths (approximately 9! or 362,880) to the 8 solution paths, we see that winning even as trivial a game as tic-tac-toe is not a small accomplishment. Our opponent also has 8 paths in which he or she can win, so that only a total of 16 paths out of 362,880 possible paths will produce a winner.

The problem space tree can be used to describe the entire problem space by listing all possible paths) or the moves actually taken in a given game. Of course, the description of all possible moves is not practical in a large tree. However, the tree of actual moves is relatively small, having one branch of 6 to 10 levels (5 to 9 moves). Similarly, in describing the problem-solving behavior of an individual, e.g., the "moves" made in solving the Donald + Gerald problem, we can represent the subject's behavior as a tree. The tree will represent the paths actually taken in attempting a solution, and may involve a bit of backtracking as certain paths prove to be nonfruitful. In this case, even the tree of actual moves taken gets quite large.

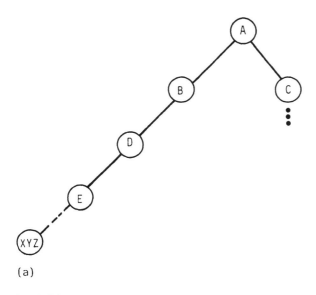

(a)

FIGURE 20.37

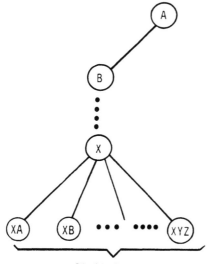

30,40,50 choices at a given level

(b)

FIGURE 20.37 (continued)

## Big Trees

Trees for a game such as chess can get quite "deep" in the sense of having many levels (Figure 20.37a), and at a given level, they can get quite broad (Figure 20.37b). It becomes impossible (or technologically infeasible) to

- Represent the entire tree at one time
- Test all possible moves before actually choosing one course of action

In order to handle the problems of size, several techniques have been developed.

## Look-Ahead

Instead of representing the entire tree at one time, a computer program or a human problem solver generates only the moves possible from a particular place in the tree. Hence, if the tic-tac-toe board (an easier example than chess) is currently in the state shown in Figure 20.38a, and it is our move, we have to examine only two possibilities (Figure 20.38b). Possibility B will lead to a victory for B and a loss for us and possibility A will lead to a draw. The choice is clear. (On paper it is clear; a computer program would have to look ahead one more time to see O's moves.)

In some situations it may be desirable to look ahead more than a single move. For example, if we have the board shown in Figure 20.39a, and it is our turn (again we are X), there are five possible moves for us at this level (Figure 20.39b). Moves B, D, and E do not advance us very far, since they do not give us two X's in a row. They would thus be eliminated at this stage of the look-ahead process. However, both A and C give us

(a)

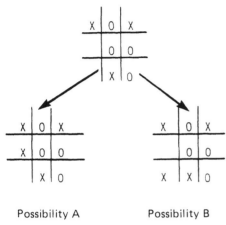

Possibility A          Possibility B

(b)

FIGURE 20.38

two X's in a row (i.e., two in three consecutive spaces, either row, column or diagonal; Figure 20.39c). The term *row* is ambiguous in that it is used in common parlance as "consecutive" and in computer jargon to name the horizontal entries, so that they are both "usable candidates" for our next move. In fact, if we are swayed by visual cues, such as "a group of X's clustered together," we might well choose A. (Informal observation of the author playing tic-tac-toe with his son, 7 years old at the time, indicates that some younger players do this, at least at the start of their tic-tac-toe and checker-playing careers.) However, a moment's reflection

(a)

FIGURE 20.39

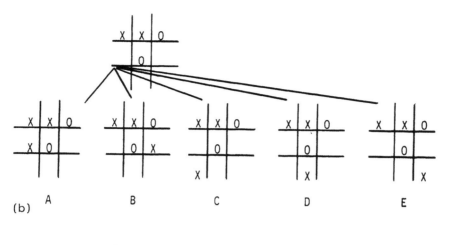

(b)

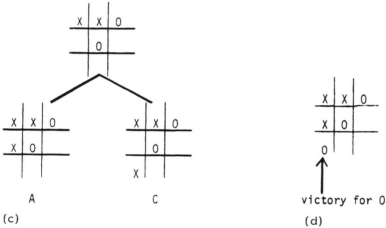

(c)

victory for O

(d)

**FIGURE 20.39** (continued)

on the possibilities for player O at the next level of the tree indicates that choice A can lead to the result shown in Figure 20.39d, which is certainly not desirable.

Choice C leads to no such victory for player O (at least not on the next move; Figure 20.40a), where the question marks indicate player O's four possible moves. Hence, given this situation, X should choose C, and looking ahead has paid off, at least temporarily.

Player O, examining his or her choices at this point (Figure 20.40b), may realize that choice B, highlighted in Figure 20.40c, will ensure getting three zeroes in a row on his or her next move. If player O is swayed by this possibility, he or she will choose B (Figure 20.40d), and X will choose to win (Figure 20.40e), in which case player O does not get a chance to exercise that next move, which is what he or she gets for not looking ahead one more time.

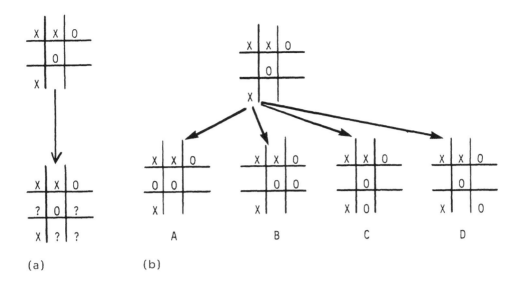

(a)

(b)

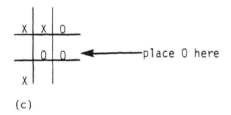

place 0 here

(c)

Aha! victory on my <u>next</u> <u>move</u>

(d)

(e)

**FIGURE 20.40**

### Pruning the Tree

In the discussion of search trees, we saw the need to "prune" the tree to eliminate certain nodes and search paths from our consideration. One meth-od used to prune the search tree is the use of heuristics, or rules of thumb, to guide the search. This method is applicable to game trees as well. For example, in tic-tac-toe, a common heuristic is

• Take the center square.

Hence, faced with any such board configuration as those shown in Figure 20.41a or 20.41b, the X=player will simply note whether or not the center

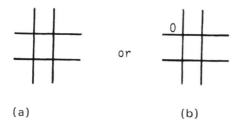

(a)                              (b)

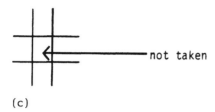

(c)

FIGURE 20.41

square is taken (Figure 20.41c), and if not, will take it, considering only a single transition at that level. Examples of heuristics in chess might be

- When possible, attack.
- Keep the bishop, which moves diagonally, away from the edge of the board.

### Distinction Between Heuristics and Look-Ahead

The use of heuristics, such as "take the center square" if available, do not involve look-ahead. They are concerned with the current board configuration. Look-ahead generates future possible configurations, evaluates each, then chooses the path that moves toward the most promising (valuable) "next position."

### Real-World Heursitics and Algorithms

The variety of heuristics and algorithms used in real life is as varied as the situations one faces. Maxims are one example of heuristics

- A bird in the hand is worth two in the bush.

which is interpreted as "sieze the current opportunity," a rule of thumb similar to "seize the center square." Of course, the maxims often give contrary or apparently contrary indications

- A stitch in time saves nine.
- Haste makes waste.

the first advising action at the first indication of need, the second cautioning against premature action.

People often implement their personal rules of thumb. For example, in a competitive situation, such as going to the grocery store (e.g., competition for grocery baskets, space in the aisle, attention of clerks, parking spots), some implement the rule

- Go early in the morning (or late in the evening).

to avoid the crowds, i.e., sidestep the competition. Others use more aggressive policies

- Cut into line.

which may or may not be successful.

Examples of algorithmic generation of candidates might be a job search

- Look at every job listing in the paper.

or the selection of classes

- Consider every class, its subject matter, teacher, times offered, place offered.

in order to find an optimal schedule.

Because such exhaustive searches are usually too lengthy to be carried out in the necessary time frame, one often "shortens" the search by relaxing the constraints on an acceptable answer. Instead of finding the optimal class schedule, which is akin to finding the "tallest student," an exhaustive search, one sets such criteria as

- Find a schedule that has
  a. No classes before 9 A.M.
  b. At least three classes I like
  c. At least two classes in my major
  d. At least three relatively easy classes
  e. No classes back to back that cross campus

and accept the first answer that satisfies these constraints. Newell and Simon (1972) refer to this as "satisficing behavior," finding a satisfactory rather than an optimal solution.

Finally, examples of algorithmic sequences of actions in the face of a passive environment include making a phone call (drop in dime, dial number, etc.) or tending a garden (sow seeds, water regularly, talk to plants, etc.).

Game situations are illustrated by such standard situations as ordering food in a restaurant, in which customers, hosts or hostesses, waiters or waitresses, and the like, have "set roles." These are "cooperative games." Both parties are presumably cojoining in producing a mutually desired outcome. The rules (protocols) of action simplify the labor of interacting.

Competitive situations are represneted by business competitors, team sports, and the like. The strategies employed are usually heuristic, although some are "well defined" enough to have predictable responses: if the competitor slashes prices, we slash our prices, offer premiums (gifts), or give better service.

Some of these situations are well defined enough to deserve a name other than "problems," e.g., tasks. Hence, the "problem" of ordering food in a restaurant is more a task or "ritual" than a "true problem." Others, such as locating the restaurant, say in a strange town, may be "truly problematic," where *problematic* is taken to mean either

   • Does not know an object filling the requirements

or

   • Does not know the sequence of actions leading to the goal

## Individual Problems Versus Problems to Society

One distinction that is useful to make in discussing problem situations is the distinction between problems to the individual and problems to society. A particular individual may not know the solution to an object identification problem (e.g., the location of a suitable apartment) or to an action sequence problem (e.g., the method of solving simultaneous equations), but this is not to say that some other individual does not know the solution (object or sequence of actions). Hence, one can ask someone (report-by-others or self-report) or look in the literature (use of archives). Alternatively, one can attempt to solve the problem oneself, by experimenting with various objects and/or sequences of actions (observation).

## Difference Reduction

Newell and Simon (1972) identified a type of problem-solving behavior that is akin to the sequence of transformations applied to linear equations. This method is called difference reduction, the essence of which is to compare the current state (representation of the problem)

$$2x + 3 = 15$$

with the goal state

$$x = ?$$

and to "remove" some of the differences between the two by applying appropriate operators (transformation rules). Hence, we applied the rule: eliminate the constant

$$
\begin{array}{r}
2x + 3 = 15 \\
-3 \quad -3 \\
\hline
2x = 12
\end{array}
$$

to obtain a representation "closer" to the goal

$$2x = 12$$

$$x = ?$$

The lone difference between the two representations is now the coefficient in the problem statement

$$2x = 12$$
$$\uparrow$$
difference

which we remove by division

$$\frac{2x}{2} = \frac{12}{2}$$

obtaining the goal state

$x = 6$

The use of difference reduction sets "subgoals," a goal closer to but not identical to the final goal. What "closer" means is another question.

## Subgoals

In reducing the difference between the problem statement

$2x + 3 = 15$

and the goal statement

$x = ?$

the difference reduction procedure produced subgoals that were obviously "closer" to the final goal. This is not always the case.

For example, given the diagram shown in Figure 20.42a in which the line represents a physical barrier between the start position and the goal, it is obvious that a "straight line solution" will not work. What is necessary

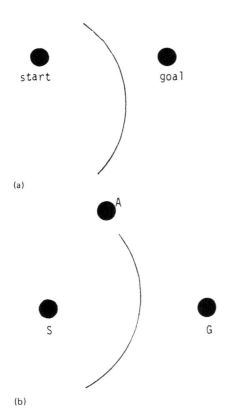

(a)

(b)

FIGURE 20.42

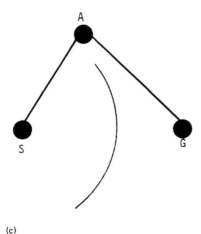

(c)

FIGURE 20.42   (continued)

is the creation of a subgoal A that will get us "around the barrier" (Figure 20.42b). We can now "go to A," then go from A to the final goal, G (Figure 20.42c).

An example of setting subgoals in everyday life might be the planning of a cross-country trip. Supposing that we wish to take the scenic route and not follow Route 66, we can either sit down and plan the entire itinerary, or we can just plan our "next stop." For example, if we are starting in Washington, D.C., we might plan a day's trip to Pittsburgh; then, having spent a day in Pittsburgh we might plan to go to Chicago, from Chicago to St. Louis, from St. Louis to Tulsa, etc., finally winding up on Hollywood Boulevard in Los Angeles.

At each stage of the trip, the immediate subgoal is the next destination. In the case of the cross-country trip these goals are roughly on a "straight" line to the final goal (Figure 20.43). This is not the case in the S-A-G example above. In that example, we must "turn away" from the goal in order to reach it. There is some research (and self-reflection) showing that it is often difficult to turn away from the "straight path" even though this path may be futile. "Turning away" or "backing up" seems to be psychologically undesirable to some people. Thus, faced with a computer

FIGURE 20.43

program that does not work we may apply "patches," none of which ever seem to solve the problem, rather than back up and design a new algorithm.

Hayes (1981) gives a good description of both this reluctance and a method by which concentrating on the subgoal as a goal, not a diversion, can be used to reduce the tension in "turning away" (see especially Chapter 2).

## Working Backwards

Another technique that is useful in problem-solving is working backwards. For example, faced with the tree shown in Figure 20.44, in which Y is the goal, a problem solver who must work forward has five possible paths to explore (five roads leading out of X). However, a problem solver who can see the goal (Y) and work backward from there, has only a single path to maneuver

$$X \quad - \quad M \quad - \quad R \quad - \quad Z \quad - \quad Y$$

In our cross-country driving problem, working backwards would result in our "starting with Hollywood Boulevard," then finding the city we wanted to be in immediately before Los Angeles, say Tuscon, and working our way back to Washington, D.C.

The methods of creating subgoals and of working backwards are often employed in mathematical proofs. For example, given the task of proving that A = C, and knowing that C = B, we could set up the subgoal of proving that A = B, hence formulating the proof in the stages

A = C   1.   goal

C = B   2.   known

A = B   3.   subgoal

and, if successful, we would then write the proof straightforwardly

A = B

B = C

A = C

While it is not treated in the literature of problem-solving, a technique used in management science called dynamic programming is a method of problem-solving by working backwards (see Bierman, Bonini, and Hausman, 1973).

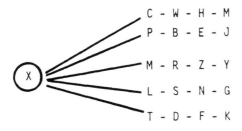

FIGURE 20.44   (Hayes, Chapter One)

(a)

(b)

FIGURE 20.45

## The Representation of the Problem

Many representations of a problem are possible, and some lend themselves to its solution more readily than others. In fact, some representations can lead to inaccurate inferences about the problem and a complete failure to solve it.

One of the most famous examples of the "power of representation" is the nine-dot problem (see virtually any book on problem solving, e.g., Newell and Simon, 1972; Hayes, 1981; Wickelgren, 1974; Anderson, 1975; and Weinberg, 1975). The essence of the problem is that the problem solver must draw four straight lines that go through all nine dots (Figure 20.45a) without lifting the pencil from the paper. Most problem solvers see an additional constraint of "the lines cannot go outside the square," which is *not* in the statement of the problem. Operating with this constraint in mind (in their internal representation of the problem), they attempt solutions such as the one shown in Figure 20.45b, which, of course, fail.

With a representation of the problem that allows the pencil to go outside the square, a solution can be readily attained (Figure 20.46a). The reader who wishes to remember the solution (the author never can) might wish to remember the "arrow-shaped" nature of the solution, remembering that the corners of the base of the arrowhead are outside the square and in line with the "topmost pair" of dots and that one starts at the uppermost right-corner dot (Figure 20.46b).

The notion that the representation of a problem can simplify the solution has been a topic treated in such diverse fields as the use of data structures in computer programming, the construction of displays in graphics, the formulation of scientific models, and the modeling of business problems.

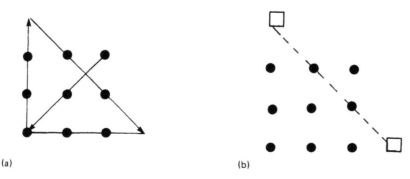

(a)

(b)

FICURE 20.46

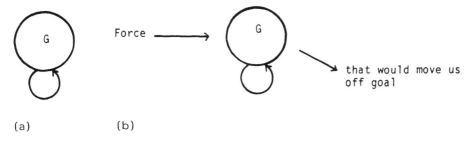

(a)          (b)

FIGURE 20.47

## Goal State Attainment and Maintenance

Most of the literature on problem-solving deals with goal state attainment. Another area of interest is goal state maintenance. The assumption is that we are already in the desired state, but that interactions with the environment, be it nature or another agent, can cause us to "be moved" from the goal state. The interaction is usually one in which we are passive with regard to the undesirable action, e.g., walking along the street, dry, happy, and singing when a cloudburst occurs; or driving to work and colliding with another car at an intersection. While the latter example seems to indicate that we are an active coparticipant, the accidental nature of the collision indicates that the goal of our behavior (and that of the other driver) was independent of the outcome "collision." We were engaged in the activity of driving to work (goal attainment), implementing the means by attempting to stay on the road (goal maintenance) while moving ahead. The event "collision" was not a goal or subgoal of our activity. The collision is an accidental result of two independent actions.

The diagram of goal state preservation would have us maintain or remain in a state (Figure 20.47a) in the face of forces opposing that stability (Figure 20.47b). Many biological processes, such as the maintenance of body temperature, are goal preservation (or desired state preservation) situations. In fact, the process of living, i.e., staying alive, is one of state maintenance. The problem of living a full life will usually involve goal attainment objectives. Goal state maintenance is studied in cybernetics.

## Postscript

We close the section on problem-solving with a reminder that problem-solving is where we began. One of the functions of knowledge is to facilitate effective action. Problems arise when that action is blocked, whether that blockage is due to the inability to implement a goal attainment sequence of actions or the inability to ward off "outside forces."

Problems can be categorized as physical or knowledge related. In physical problems we cannot implement the solution due to some physical inability, e.g., we cannot compute by hand in microseconds. These problems are not the province of information science, at least not "per se." They may trigger a search for a suitable agent or tool to use in the implementation task, e.g., a computer.

Information problems arise when the inability to act is due to a lack of knowledge. This lack of knowledge may be

- The lack of an appropriate model
- The lack of knowledge about the values of variables in a model that is appropriate and known

The first triggers an extensive search, through analogy or experimentation allied to theory, to produce an appropriate model. The latter generates a more tractable procedure (usually), the estimation of desirable values.

In some cases, the model may be specified as to the type of object (value) necessary, and we have an object identification search. In other cases the model sought may be a sequence of actions to get us "from here to there."

The blockage of action due to lack of knowledge creates an "information need," and that need triggers a search for data. The use of a model guides the data search. Seen in this light we can define information as

- The data necessary to take action

where data is interpreted in the broad sense of

- A model
- Data values

An information system is a system that produces such models and/or data values for a particular situation.

## Related Readings

Ackoff, Russell L. and Emery, Fred E., *On Purposeful Systems*, Chicago: Aldine-Atherton, Inc., 1972.

Anderson, Barry F., *Cognitive Psychology*, New York: Academic Press, 1975.

Bakan, David, *On Method: Toward a Reconstruction of Psychological Investigation*, San Francisco: Jossey-Bass, 1967.

Bartlett, Sir Frederic, *Thinking: An Experimental and Social Study*, New York: Basic Books, Inc., 1958.

Belnap, Noel D. Jr. and Steel, Thomas B. Jr., *The Logic of Questions and Answers*, London: Yale University Press, 1976.

Bierman, Harold Jr., Bonini, Charles P., and Hausman, Warren H., *Quantitative Analysis for Business Decision*, 4th ed. Illinois: Richard D. Irwin, Inc., 1973.

Churchman, C. West, *The Design of Inquiring Systems*, New York: Basic Books, Inc., 1971.

Churchman, C. West, *The Systems Approach*, New York: Delacort Press, 1968.

Graham, Neill, *Artificial Intelligence*, Blue Ridge Summit, PA: TAB Books, Inc., 1979.

Hayes, John R., *The Complete Problem Solver*, Philadelphia: the Franklin Institute, 1981.

Kuhn, Thomas S., "The Structure of Scientific Revolutions," in *International Encyclopedia of Unitied Science*, vol. 2, no. 2, Chicago: The University of Chicago Press, 1970.

Mitroff, Ian, Williams, James, and Flynn, Roger R., "On the Strength of Belief Systems," in *International Journal of General Systems*, Vol. 4, no. 3, pp. 189–199, 1978.

Mitroff, I. I. et al., "On Managing Science in the Systems Age: Two Schemes for the Study of Science as a Whole Systems Phenomenon," in *Interfaces*, vol. 4, no. 3, 1974.

Newell, Allen and Simon, Herbert A., *Human Problem Solving*, Englewood Cliffs, NJ: Prentice-Hall, 1972.

Norman, Lindsay, *Human Information Processing*, 2nd ed., New York: Academic Press, 1977.

Polya, G., *How to Solve It*, 2nd ed., Princeton, NJ: Princeton University Press, 1957.

Raphael, Bertram, *The Thinking Computer, Mind Inside Matter*, San Francisco: W. H. Freeman and Company, 1976.

Rich, Elaine, *Artificial Intelligence*, New York: McGraw-Hill Book Co., 1983.

Simon, Herbert A., *Models of Thought*, New Haven, CT: Yale University Press, 1979.

Solso, Robert L., *Cognitive Psychology*, New York: Harcourt Brace Jovanovich, Inc., 1979.

Turban, Efraim and Meredith, Jack R., *Fundamental of Management Science*, rev. ed., Plano, Texas: Business Publications, Inc., 1981.

Weinberg, Gerald M., *An Introduction to General Systems Thinking*, New York: John Wiley & Sons, 1975.

Wickelgren, Wayne A., *How to Solve Problems*, San Francisco: W. H. Freeman and Company, 1974.

Winston, Patrick Henry, *Artificial Intelligence*, Reading, MA: Addison-Wesley Publishing Company, 1977.

# Author Index

# Subject Index

Milton Keynes UK
Ingram Content Group UK Ltd.
UKHW051859071024
449327UK00025B/2018